APIs at Work

APIs
at Work

Second Edition

**Bruce Vining,
Doug Pence, and Ron Hawkins**

MC PRESS
MC Press Online, LLC
Boise, Idaho 83703

APIs at Work
Bruce Vining, Doug Pence, and Ron Hawkins

Second Edition

First Printing—July 2007
Print on Demand since July 2020

MC Press offers excellent discounts on this book when ordered in quantity for bulk purchases or special sales, which may include custom covers and content particular to your business, training goals, marketing focus, and branding interest.

For information regarding permissions or special orders, please contact:

MC Press Online, LLC
3695 W Quail Heights Court
Boise, Idaho 83703 USA

For information regarding sales and/or customer service, please contact:
Tel: 208-629-7275 Ext 500
eMail: service@mcpressnline.com

ISBN: 1-58347-069-7

For my parents

Betty and Clayton Vining

Acknowledgments

If you benefit from this book, your thanks should be directed to Merrikay Lee of MC Press. She identified the need and allowed me to participate in this project. Thanks also must go to Marianne Krcma for her wonderful editing of the manuscript.

I would also like to thank my coworkers at IBM—in particular Beth Hagemeister and Terry Hennessy of the i5/OS cryptographic development team along with Chris Gloe and Tim Mullenbach of the i5/OS TCP/IP development team for their willingness to review the chapters related to their development areas. It is an honor to work with such talented and dedicated individuals.

It is not really possible to extend enough gratitude to my immediate family. Your sacrifices are many and I am very appreciative. I really had no idea what I was getting into!

Contents

1

API Fundamentals

All APIs use a set of standards that define how system programs communicate with application programs. While every API communicates different information, they all communicate that information using the same set of standards. Notice that *standards* is plural. Different types of APIs use different ways to pass data. Some use one long variable to pass data back to your program, while others use a user space to do it. (If you are not familiar with this terminology, don't worry. You'll learn the terms as you progress through the book.) You will soon see that once you understand the different formats used, you are well on your way to using any API in the system.

Begin with the Basics

Application Programming Interfaces (APIs) are simply formal definitions of how you, as a developer, can communicate with the system. You may not be aware of it, but when you code an RPG OPEN statement or use a built-in such as %SCAN, you are, in a sense, using an API. OPEN and %SCAN are formal functions defined by the RPG language to insulate you from knowing how a given file is being opened by the system or what technology might be in use when scanning a character string. (Many, many different technologies might be used!) Likewise, Control Language (CL) represents a set of APIs. You can code a Retrieve Job Attributes (RTVJOBA) command and be confident that the

1

command will work reliably today and tomorrow, independent of what changes i5/OS might make in how a job is managed by the system.

In this book, you will learn about a set of APIs known as *system APIs*. System APIs let you get at system information or objects that you normally cannot access through more generic interfaces such as CL commands or the RPG language. You can, however, call these APIs from CL and RPG programs and then process the information returned by the APIs using the strengths of the CL and RPG languages. For the remainder of this book, when we refer to APIs, we will be referring to these system APIs.

Like RPG and CL, API standards allow for future enhancements. Even if IBM changes a particular API in the future, that API will still be compatible with older versions, so you can upgrade to new releases of i5/OS without having to change your use of APIs. Of course, you won't be able to take advantage of the new enhancements to the API unless you modify your code, but your existing code will still function just as it did when you wrote it.

Another benefit of APIs is speed. Some CL commands retrieve information about the system into a special kind of file called an *outfile*. You can then process this outfile to get at the information you want. While this method works and is easy to use, it is rather slow because the system has to build the file and then write records to it for your application to read later. For example, if you specify OUTPUT(*OUTFILE) OUTFILE(SOMENAME) with the Display Object Description command (DSPOBJD), you can then read the file SOMENAME to get at the information about the object. A much faster way to access this same information is via the Retrieve Object Description API, QUSROBJD. When you call QUSROBJD, it returns the same information as in the outfile (if not more), but as a parameter. Because it doesn't have to build and process the file, this method is much faster than using the command.

APIs can perform many different kinds of functions. For example, the Command Line API, QUSCMDLN, brings up a screen that lets you enter commands to the system. Others, like QCMDEXC and QCAPCMD, let you execute commands directly from within application programs. (See chapter 4 for examples of these handy APIs.) There are APIs to handle messages, process spool files, and work with virtually any object on the system.

Where to Get Information about APIs from IBM

The best source for information about APIs (with the exception of this fine publication, of course) is the IBM Information Center. To access it, point your browser to this site:

http://publib.boulder.ibm.com/iseries

From here, select the release of i5/OS™ you are interested in. In the Information Center, you will find APIs under the "Programming" topic. In the API topic, you can search for APIs by keyword (using the API Finder) or by category. At first, using the Finder will most likely be easiest for you. As you become more familiar with APIs, you will most likely want to browse the available APIs by category, instead.

When writing applications using APIs, you will want to use the IBM Information Center appropriate for your installed release of i5/OS. This book is written based on the API capabilities provided with V5R4 of i5/OS. IBM has enhanced existing APIs, and introduced new ones, with every release of the operating system since V1R3. You certainly will not want to miss out on the latest API capabilities.

Information Already on Your System

If you have a library called QSYSINC, you already have a wealth of information about APIs on your system. Every system comes with this library, but you have to install it. This library contains source members that could save you a great deal of time while using APIs. The QSYSINC library is installed with option 13 (System Openness Includes) of i5/OS.

The examples in this book assume that the QSYSINC library is installed. If that's not the case, ask your system administrator to install option 13 of i5/OS using either the Work with Licensed Programs menu (GO LICPGM) and option 10, or the RSTLICPGM command.

There are over 20 source files in the QSYSINC library. Most of these files are for using APIs in different languages such as C, COBOL, and RPG. The main file for ILE RPG is QRPGLESRC. Each member in the file contains data structure definitions for i5/OS provided APIs. For program (*PGM) APIs, the name of the API and the name of the member correspond. For service program (*SRVPGM) APIs, the name of the *SRVPGM and the name of the member correspond. There are also some generic members that cross multiple APIs, such as the QUSGEN member, which contains common structures for the user-space APIs.

Try to use these definitions every time you use an API. This provides consistency from program to program. It also reduces problems with erroneous definitions of the data structures. It does not completely eliminate the potential for problems with the definition, though, because some fields are defined as varying in length, where you supply the length of the field. These fields are usually dependent on how much data you want the API to return. Still, using the supplied definitions will save you lots of time overall.

One drawback to using the members in this library is its size. The structures are so well documented (when was the last time you heard *that* about an IBM manual?) that a simple structure can balloon into hundreds of lines of code. It's not uncommon for a 200-line program to expand to 1,000 lines with all of the text describing each field in each structure. Comments are not pulled into the compiled object, though, so this is not a significant problem.

The sheer volume of documentation with each API caused us a problem in writing this book. While we feel the correct way to use the API is to pull in the complete definition of the structures from QSYSINC, we could not show this with each sample program. If we did, this book would quickly have become encyclopedic. To keep the book to a manageable size, therefore, we haven't included all of the source documentation.

About the Examples

The examples in this book are written using the free-form syntax of ILE RPG. The APIs we discuss can, however, be used by non–free-form ILE RPG, in addition to languages such as CL, COBOL, Java, C, and RPG III (admittedly with some limitations related to features such as pointers not being supported by the language).

Appendix B contains the examples in the chapters re-done to use APIs from fixed-form ILE RPG, and appendix C has examples using ILE COBOL. So, Figures B2.2 and C2.2 correspond to Figure 2.2 in chapter 2. Refer to the text associated with Figure 2.2 to fully understand the code example in Figure B2.2 or C2.2.

Most of the example programs are named based on their figure names in this book. So, a reference to program FIG12_3 is a reference to the program compiled from the source shown in Figure 12.3. We recommend that you use the same convention when naming your source members. The example RPG programs are generally created with the Create Bound RPG Program command, CRTBNDRPG, with no additional parameters specified beyond PGM. That is, to create the example in Figure 2.2, you would use CRTBNDRPG

FIG2_2. In a few cases, we create a module using the Create RPG Module command, CRTRPGMOD, followed by the Create Service Program command, CRTSRVPGM. These exceptions are clearly pointed out in the book.

Our examples also tend to make heavy use of the Display Message (DSPLY) operation code. This is not to suggest that you should use DSPLY in production code or simply present an end user with the DSPLY of an error situation. We chose to use DSPLY so that the examples could provide displayable output to you, while not cluttering the example programs with how to load subfiles or work with simple display-file record formats. The intent of this book, after all, is how to use APIs, not how to use i5/OS workstation support. Having said that, some examples do use display files (*DSPFs) where it seemed more natural to provide a full set of information with a *DSPF record.

In addition, the example programs make extensive use of the lowercase letters *a* to *z*. If you are working in a Japanese environment using CCSID 5026, we strongly recommend that you change to a CCSID environment such as 5035 or 1399 when compiling and running the example programs.

At the end of each chapter, we also have a "Check Your Knowledge" section. This is an opportunity for you to write a program confirming your understanding of the chapter. The tasks in this section generally involve using APIs different from, but similar to, those used in our examples. Appendix D provides possible solutions to the tasks. As with the example programs, solutions for fixed-form RPG and ILE COBOL can be found in appendixes B and C, respectively.

The code that is available on the Web contains the complete source code for the examples used in this book. Appendix A provides a cross-reference for these examples and instructions on how to load this source onto your system. We recommend that you actually re-type the source code for the examples. Most of them are quite small, in terms of lines of code, and entering them yourself will give you a much better understanding of how they work than just reading them. You get much more of an opportunity to wonder, "Now why are they doing this?"

Pass the Data, Please…

To use a callable API, you simply code an appropriate call statement. Most APIs pass information back and forth by parameters. It's important to understand how these parameters work. Table 1.1 provides an example of how parameters are documented in the Information Center.

Table 1.1: Parameters for the Retrieve Output Queue Information API (QSPROUTQ)			
Parameter	Description	Type	Size
1	Receiver Variable	Output	Char(*)
2	Length of Receiver Variable	Input	Binary(4)
3	Format Name	Input	Char(8)
4	Qualified Output Queue Name	Input	Char(20)
5	Error Code	I/O	Char(*)

Since APIs can be called by developers using various languages, such as RPG, CL, COBOL, and C, the Information Center normally documents API parameters in a language-neutral fashion. Rather than providing a RPG-specific prototype, for example, the API parameters are described using the parameter order, a short name for the parameter, the usage type of the parameter, and the size of the parameter.

When you call APIs, you usually pass parameters just as you would if you were calling another application program. The appropriate terminology to use when describing this technique is *passing parameters by reference*. When one RPG program calls another, you generally pass parameters by reference. Your program doesn't actually pass the data from program to program, even though you specify a data field as a parameter. Instead, a pointer to that data is passed. This is why a change to the data by the called program is automatically seen in the calling program, even if the called program ends abnormally. The change to the data occurs immediately, and both programs have pointers that point to the same data.

In APIs documented as in Table 1.1, parameters are passed by reference. The order of the parameters is indicated by the parameter number (1, 2, etc.). A brief description, such as "Receiver Variable," is also provided. (The description will be very brief until you get used to APIs!) Additional information on the content of each parameter is provided later in the API documentation.

API parameters come in three types:

- *Input*—Your program is supplying information to the API.

- *Output*—The API is returning information to your program.

- *Input/Output* (*I/O*)—You are both providing information and getting information returned to you.

The vast majority of API parameters are either input or output.

Size represents the size of the parameter passed to the API. A size such as Char(8), which is used for the third parameter in Table 1.1 (Format Name), tells you that this parameter is eight bytes long. Similarly, the fourth parameter, Qualified Output Queue Name, is Char(20), or 20 bytes long. Often, you will find a parameter with a size of Char(*), as seen in Table 1.1 for the first parameter (Receiver Variable). This indicates that the parameter is of variable length, and the actual length will be specified some-where else in the call to the API. (In case you're wondering, for this example, the length would be specified in the second parameter, Length of Receiver Variable.) You will also find many APIs using a size of Binary(4). This indicates that the API is expecting a four-byte binary (or integer) value. Less frequently, you might find Binary(2) and Binary(8), which correspond to two-byte and eight-byte binary parameters, respectively. It is important that you always pass a parameter of at least the size indicated by the API documentation. Declaring or defining a parameter larger than is documented is OK, but declaring a parameter that is smaller can result in some bizarre errors. This point will be covered in more detail later.

With the above information, the QSPROUTQ API described in Table 1.1 can be prototyped as shown in Figure 1.1. (Don't worry about the ErrCde definition—we'll get to that shortly.) If you are interested in more information concerning this API (which is not really necessary at this point), you can find it in the Information Center under "Programming," "APIs," "APIs by Category," "Print," and "General Print APIs." Or, since you know the API's name, you can find it in the Information Center under "Programming," "APIs," "API Finder," and "Find by Name," using QSPROUTQ.

```
DName++++++++++ETDsFrom+++To/L+++IDc.Keywords++++++++++++++++++++++++++++
dRtvOutq          pr                    extpgm('QSPROUTQ')
d Receiver                      1       options(*varsize)
d LenReceiver                   10i 0   const
d Format                        8       const
d OutQName                      20      const
d ErrCde                                likeds(QUSEC)
```

Figure 1.1: Prototype for QSPROUTQ.

By convention, we prototype Char(*) variable-length parameters with options(*varsize) and a length of one when referencing an output parameter, and a length of 65,535 when working with input parameters. The Receiver parameter, for instance, is defined as a one-byte variable-length parameter in Figure 1.1.

Some APIs support a different method of passing data. This method is referred to as *passing parameters by value*. Passing by value actually passes the data between the programs. RPG IV, for example, supports this method with the keyword VALUE. So, if the API you are using has been categorized as pass-by-value, be sure to use the VALUE keyword. This method is generally applicable to Unix-type and C-language run-time APIs, which are documented using a different style, as shown in Figure 1.2.

```
int open(const char *path, int oflag, ...);
```

Figure 1.2: Parameters for the Open API.

With this type of API, the parameter descriptions are read differently, although in a manner that will be very familiar to developers who have worked with C. The parameters are defined within parentheses after the API name. Various types of data might be used when defining a parameter. An *int* represents a four-byte integer value, like Binary(4) does for QSPROUTQ. *Short* indicates a two-byte integer, *long long* an eight-byte integer value, an asterisk represents a pointer, and *char* represents a character variable. With this type of API, char (character) data is generally of a variable length, like Char(*) in QSPROUTQ, but you often do not explicitly tell the API how long the variable is. Instead, the end of the character string is typically indicated by a null byte, where null is defined as *x'00'*. Fortunately, ILE RPG can handle this type of character definition in many cases by using the OPTIONS(*STRING) keyword on the prototypes. If you don't see an explicit parameter defining the length of an input character parameter, you should use the OPTIONS(*STRING) keyword. The names *Path* and *Oflag* are brief descriptions of the parameters. They are further described later in the API documentation, along with whether a parameter is input, output, or I/O.

In Figure 1.2, the two defined parameters are Path and Oflag. The parameter descriptions are read right to left from the parameter name. The Path parameter is defined as a pointer (the asterisk) to a character string (char) that will not be changed by the API (*const*, for constant). The Oflag parameter is defined as a four-byte integer (int).

You may encounter several different modifiers. The const used in Figure 1.2 indicates that the parameter will be treated as a constant. Other modifiers include *signed* and *unsigned*. The signed modifier indicates that an integer value is signed (RPG type 10i 0), while unsigned indicates, well, unsigned (10u 0). The default is signed, so Oflag would be defined in RPG as 10i 0.

The int specification prior to the API name (Open) indicates that this API returns an integer when the API is called. Note that this is not a parameter passed to the API, but rather a return value that should be included in your prototype. You might also encounter APIs that have the single word *void* prior to the API name. This indicates that the API does not have a return value. This should not be confused with *void* * prior to the API name, which indicates that the API returns a pointer (the asterisk, reading right to left) to some unspecified data (typically a structure) that is further defined in the API documentation.

One item to keep in mind when working with parameters passed by value is that you can prototype a pointer parameter in two ways. If a parameter is defined as *char* *, *void* *, *int* *, etc., you can prototype it as either a pointer passed by value or as the pointed-to data type passed by reference. This is because the ILE RPG compiler will automatically pass a pointer to the data when the VALUE keyword is not specified. If this doesn't make a lot of sense to you right now, don't worry. In chapter 14, you'll look at APIs that use this prototyping flexibility. The ellipses (...) at the end of the API description indicate that additional, optional parameters can be used. We won't get into them right now, but they are also discussed in chapter 14. The RPG prototype for Open is shown in Figure 1.3. Though not necessary at this point, you can get further information on this API by going to the IBM Information Center.

```
DName++++++++++++ETDsFrom+++To/L+++IDc.Keywords+++++++++++++++++++++++++++++
dOpen              pr           10i 0  extproc('open')
d Path                            *    value options(*string)
d Oflag                         10i 0  value
```

Figure 1.3: Prototype for the Open API.

Some parameters of APIs are required, while others are optional. If a parameter is optional, all parameters after it are also optional. Optional parameters are found in groups, as shown in Table 1.2, and all parameters within a group must be used. Conversely, if you leave out one optional parameter, all subsequent parameters must be left out as well. Put another way, if you want to use optional parameter group 2, you must also use optional parameter group 1.

Table 1.2: Parameters for the Retrieve Object Description API (QUSROBJD)			
Parameter	Description	Type	Size
1	Receiver Variable	Output	Char(*)
2	Length of Receiver Variable	Input	Binary(4)
3	Format Name	Input	Char(8)
4	Object and Library Name	Input	Char(20)
5	Object Type	Input	Char(10)
Optional Parameter Group 1			
6	Error Code	I/O	Char(*)
Optional Parameter Group 2			
7	Auxiliary Storage Pool (ASP) Control	Input	Char(*)

The Retrieve Object Description API would be prototyped as in Figure 1.4.

```
DName+++++++++++ETDsFrom+++To/L+++IDc.Keywords++++++++++++++++++++++++++++
dRtvObjD         pr                  extpgm('QUSROBJD')
d Receiver                    1      options(*varsize)
d LenReceiver                10i 0   const
d Format                      8      const
d ObjName                    20      const
d ObjType                    10      const
d ErrCde                             likeds(QUSEC) options(*nopass)
d ASP                         1      const options(*varsize :*nopass)
```

Figure 1.4: Prototype for QUSROBJD.

Some API parameters are defined as being omissible, indicating that you can omit passing any specific value for the parameter when you call the API. Omitting parameters is different than not passing an optional parameter, in that parameters that follow an omitted parameter can still be used. To omit an omissible parameter, you pass a null pointer, indicating that you are not providing any actual value. This is usually accomplished by using the keyword OPTIONS(*OMIT) on the API prototype for the omissible parameter and using the *OMIT keyword for the parameter when actually calling the API.

You will see more about these parameter concepts later in this book.

Data Types

When APIs deal with numeric values, they predominantly use binary numbers. A few nuances previously noted when dealing with parameters are worth repeating, to help you avoid very common errors for users new to APIs. The IBM manuals call for a binary field as either Binary(2), Binary(4), or Binary(8). If you aren't familiar with binary numbers, you would probably define these with a length of two, four, and eight (respectively), and with a type of *B*. This makes complete sense to an RPG programmer. Nevertheless, in the world of APIs, it's completely wrong!

A Binary(4) field is a four-byte binary field, but defining the field as in Figure 1.5 indicates that you are declaring a field that can contain up to four *digits* of information. Four digits in binary format only need a two-byte field to be allocated, and while the API is expecting four bytes of data, you are only providing two bytes. The API will then look at your two-byte value, plus whatever happens to be in memory as the next two bytes (and who knows what that might be), and come up with a totally unintended value. As mentioned previously, *never* allocate less storage than the API is expecting.

```
DName+++++++++++ETDsFrom+++To/L+++IDc.Keywords++++++++++++++++++++++++++++++
dSomeNumber             s              4B 0
```

Figure 1.5: The wrong way to define a Binary(4).

Binary fields can be defined as either type *B* (binary) or *I* (integer). The preferred approach when defining API binary fields is to use the integer format, though either will work. Figure 1.6 gives examples of how to define numeric fields.

A pointer is another data type commonly used to process information returned by APIs. Unlike most other data types, a pointer doesn't really describe an element of data. Instead, as its name implies, it points to a location that contains the data you want. As you'll see a little later in this chapter, pointers are very useful when working with user spaces.

All RPG IV pointers are, by definition, 16-byte fields. They can be defined with a type code of * (asterisk). Notice we say they *can* be defined that way. In fact, they don't have to be defined at all! If you use a field in such a way that it can only be a pointer, the RPG compiler will define it for you. In Figure 1.6, look at the definition specification for the data structure named *DataDS*. It has a keyword BASED(FieldPtr). The basing variable, FieldPtr, is not defined anywhere in the source code, but the compiler knows that it is a pointer and will define it as such.

```
DName+++++++++++ETDsFrom+++To/L+++IDc.Keywords++++++++++++++++++++++++++++++
dReceiver               ds           320

   * Binary(2) fields
d TwoBytesBin            1           2b 0
d TwoBytesInt            3           4i 0
d TwoBytesB                          4b 0
d TwoBytesI                          5i 0

   * Unsigned Binary(2) fields
d TwoUBytesInt           9          10u 0
d TwoUBytesI                         5u 0

   * Binary(4) fields
d FourBytesBin          13          16b 0
d FourBytesInt          17          20i 0
d FourBtyesB                         9b 0
d FourBytesI                        10i 0

   * Unsigned Binary(4) fields
d FourUBytesInt         29          32u 0
d FourUBytesI                       10u 0

   * Binary(8) fields
d EightBytesInt         37          44i 0
d EightBytesI                       20i 0

   * Unsigned Binary(8) fields
d EightUBytesInt        53          60u 0
d EightUBytesI                      20u 0

   * Pointer field
d Pointer                            *

   * Based data structure
dDataDS                 ds                   based(FieldPtr)
```

Figure 1.6: The right way to define common API data types.

Data Values

When APIs deal with data values, they predominately expect to use your input values
as-is. In particular, and to contrast with Control Language (CL) commands, APIs that
accept object names as input values do not generally provide features such as automatic
uppercasing. As one of the goals of APIs is to provide speed, it is more efficient for the
API caller to provide uppercase values once, as opposed to having the API convert
parameter values into uppercase every time it's called.

Along the same lines, an API generally returns data in the format most efficient for the API. Date and time information, for example, is often returned in a fixed format of year, month, day, hours, minutes, and seconds, or in an internal format known as a *Time of Day timestamp*. The API caller can then reformat this time-related data to whatever format best suits the application's needs (such as YMD or Julian) using APIs that are introduced in chapter 8. It would not be very efficient for the API to guess the format the API caller wants, nor would it be efficient for an API that might return ten different time values to reformat all ten when the API caller is really only interested in using one or two.

Telling an API What to Return

One of the primary reasons to use APIs is to retrieve and return information to your programs. The Retrieve Object Description (QUSROBJD) API for example, can be used to return almost anything you would want to know about an object. As you will see, however, APIs are not always restricted to just one use. Sometimes, APIs can be used several different ways, depending on exactly what information you are trying to retrieve.

Simple logic would dictate that the more information an API has to gather about an object, the longer the API would take to run. APIs are fast, but machine cycles are cumulative. In a time when advances in hardware have far exceeded advances in software, programmers have a tendency to forget that. The more efficient our code is, the better our system will run. This is the case no matter how fast hardware becomes.

Generally, informational APIs provide you with a couple of methods for filtering your request for information. The most common way to filter API information is through the use of a *format-name parameter.* A format-name parameter accepts a record format name that describes the format of the returned information. API record format names are predetermined and available in the documentation for the API. You select the record format name that will return the data you are interested in and name it on a parameter when you call the API. The record format determines the data you get back.

Usually, API record format names end in a sequence number. The Retrieve Object Description (QUSROBJD) API, for example, accepts four record format names. Table 1.3 reflects how the manual describes them. As you have probably already guessed, the smaller the sequence numbers, the faster the response. This is not always true, but it is a good rule of thumb.

Table 1.3: Record Formats for the Retrieve Object Description API (QUSROBJD)	
Format	Description
OBJD0100	Basic information (fastest)
OBJD0200	Information similar to that displayed by the programming development manager (PDM)
OBJD0300	Service information
OBJD0400	Full information (slowest)

Keyed Interface

Another method of controlling what information an API returns is through the use of keys. Each piece of information the API deals with (called a *key*) is assigned a value by the API. You tell the API what piece (or pieces) of information you require by specifying an array of key values.

Keys allow you to filter the information you want the API to return. For instance, suppose you had a program that needed to know the name of the output queue associated with a job. You could use the List Jobs API (QUSLJOB) to get this piece of information. QUSLJOB can return lots of information about a job, but if you specify key 1501, it returns only the qualified name of the output queue (in addition to some essentials, such as the job name). An example of using a keyed interface with the List Jobs API is provided in chapter 13.

You usually pass the key(s) as a parameter, which happens to be a variable-length record. The parameter may also contain the number of keys (array elements) being passed, or the number of keys may be defined as a separate parameter. Each API documents which style you should use to specify the number of keys.

Returning Data

Generally, APIs use two methods to return data, depending on the amount of data being passed. The first method is used when a limited amount of information is to be retrieved from an API: the information is retrieved directly into a receiver variable defined as a parameter on the call to the API.

APIs that return a lot of information, such as list APIs, use the second method. The List Database Fields API (QUSLFLD), for example, returns a multiple occurring data structure with each occurrence providing information about each field in the file. As you can imagine, if you have a file with many fields, this API can return a lot of data. Because of this data issue, list APIs return their information into a *user space*. A user space can be up to 16MB in size. As you will see later, there is also an open-list type of API, which combines receiver variables and lists of large amounts of data.

All retrieval methods basically return the same type of data. In other words, they return a series of one or more data structures. Each structure generally contains some information directly related to the object or function you are working with, as well as control-related information giving you access to other data structures that contain additional information. You process the information by accessing the first data structure, processing the data you are interested in, using the control-related information to access the next structure, and continuing through all structures until you have processed all of the data needed by your application. While this might seem a little confusing at first, it will begin to make sense after you work through a few examples.

Receiver Variables

Receiver variables represent storage, typically a data structure, that you define in your program. For example, you might define a receiver variable, MyReceiver, as shown in Figure 1.7, to represent the first 29 bytes of data that can be returned by an API. The API might retrieve a lot more data than you are interested in (some return thousands of bytes!), so the API will have a way for you to say how large MyReceiver is. This is often a separate parameter called the *Length of Receiver Variable*. It is very important that you specify a correct Length of Receiver Variable. If you allocate 29 bytes, as in this example, but tell the API the length is 100 bytes, it might write on top of other data in your program. This nasty turn of events can cause very unexpected results! You can make this type of mistake even without APIs if you are passing parameters across your own application programs, and your programs do not have the same parameter definitions. Chapter 2 discusses retrieve APIs in detail.

```
DName++++++++++ETDsFrom+++To/L+++IDc.Keywords+++++++++++++++++++++++++++++
dMyReceiver        ds
d DataIWant                    10
d MoreData                     15
d EvenMore                     10i 0
```

Figure 1.7: A sample receiver variable.

APIs and User Spaces

APIs that can potentially return a lot of data usually employ a user space. A user space is an object (type *USRSPC) that you can use to hold data. As mentioned earlier, a user space can hold up to 16MB. Furthermore, a user space can increase itself, much like a database file increases as you add records to it. Therefore, you don't have to define it as 16MB to begin with—you create the user space at some size that seems reasonable to your needs. If the API returns more data than will fit, it will attempt to increase the size of the user space to the size it needs. We say "attempt" as the system will still enforce checks such as the authority to the user space object and the storage limit of the current user profile.

Before continuing the discussion of user spaces, we want to point out that the next five example programs use a common user space in the QTEMP library. Make sure you have the time to complete all five examples within the same job. It shouldn't take long, but don't stop in the middle!

Table 1.4: Parameters for the Create User Space API (QUSCRTUS)			
Parameter	**Description**	**Type**	**Size**
1	Qualified User Space Name	Input	Char(20)
2	Extended Attribute	Input	Char(10)
3	Initial Size	Input	Binary(4)
4	Initial Value	Input	Char(1)
5	Public Authority	Input	Char(10)
6	Text Description	Input	Char(50)
Optional Parameter Group 1			
7	Replace	Input	Char(10)
8	Error Code	I/O	Char(*)
Optional Parameter Group 2			
9	Domain	Input	Char(10)
Optional Parameter Group 3			
10	Transfer Size Request	Input	Binary(4)
11	Optimum Space Alignment	Input	Char(1)

You create a user space by calling an API. (You aren't surprised, are you?) The API you call is the Create User Space API, QUSCRTUS. Table 1.4 shows the parameters for the QUSCRTUS API. Figure 1.8 shows the code needed to create a user space. This API doesn't return any data; it simply performs the function of creating a user space. The code shown in Figure 1.8 creates a user space named SPACENAME in the library QTEMP. You can find full documentation on the parameters for the Create User Space API in the Information Center, by using the API Finder and searching on the name QUSCRTUS.

The first parameter, Qualified User Space Name, is the name of the user space you want to create. This parameter is defined as a 20-byte character field. The first ten bytes are for the user space name, and the next ten bytes are for the name of the library in which the user space should be created. The special value *CURLIB can be used for the library portion of this parameter.

In general, any API parameter name that starts with *Qualified* will be defined as a Char(20), with the first ten bytes being the object name and the second ten bytes being the library name. Other "Qualified" APIs might support more special values than Qualified User Space Name (for example, the special value *LIBL is often supported), or they might not support any special values, but they will share this common convention of how they are specified. Another general note: APIs tend to *not* uppercase object names. When using object names as input parameters to an API, remember to use all uppercase letters.

The second parameter, Extended Attribute, provides an attribute to associate with your user space. This attribute is used in the same way as the extended attributes PF (physical file), LF (logical file), and DSPF (display file) can be used for *FILE objects. This parameter is defined as a ten-byte character field. You can use ten blanks if you don't care about setting an extended attribute, or you can select an appropriate value such as OBJLIST (object list) or MY_SPACE.

The third parameter, Initial Size, is the initial size allocation you want to make for the user space you are creating. The parameter is defined as a Binary(4) field. The value can be from one to 16,776,704 bytes.

The fourth parameter, Initial Value, is the value you want each byte of the allocated user space to be initially set to. This is a one-byte character value. For best performance, use a null byte (x'00').

The fifth parameter, Public Authority, is the authority to the user space that you want users to have if they don't have any private authorities. This works much like the PUBAUT parameter of many create commands. It supports special values such as *ALL, *CHANGE, and *EXCLUDE.

The sixth parameter, Text Description, is simply the description you would like to associate with the user space object.

The seventh parameter, Replace, indicates whether you want to replace any user space that already exists with the same name and library as you used for the first parameter. This optional parameter is defined as a ten-byte character field, and you can specify either *NO or *YES. The API documentation states that *NO is the default.

The eighth parameter, Error Code, refers to an error-code structure that is used with many of the system APIs. You'll learn about this common structure later in this chapter and again in chapter 2.

The ninth parameter, Domain, controls the domain of the user space. This optional parameter is defined as a ten-byte character field with the special values *DEFAULT (let the system decide), *SYSTEM, and *USER. If this parameter is not used, its value is *DEFAULT.

The tenth parameter, Transfer Size Request, allows you to provide guidance to the system on how much data should be read from auxiliary storage to main storage when accessing the user space. The default is to allow the system to decide.

The eleventh parameter, Optimum Space Alignment, allows you to have the system allocate the user space in such a way as to maximize performance at the expense of supporting a slightly smaller space size (16,773,120 bytes as compared to 16,776,704 bytes). In V5R4, the default is to not use optimum alignment, although IBM has stated that this default might change in a future release.

Figure 1.8 shows a prototype based on the API documentation and the call to the Create User Space API. With the call, we are creating a user space named SPACENAME into the QTEMP library. The user space is being created with an extended attribute of MY_TEST, an initial size of 4,096 bytes that are initialized to x'00', a public authority of *CHANGE, and a text description of "A test user space." If a user space named SPACENAME already exists in QTEMP, we are replacing it.

```
DName+++++++++++ETDsFrom+++To/L+++IDc.Keywords+++++++++++++++++++++++++++
dCrtSpc            pr                    extpgm('QUSCRTUS')
d SpcName                       20       const
d SpcAttr                       10       const
d SpcSiz                        10i 0    const
d SpcVal                         1       const
d SpcAut                        10       const
d SpcTxt                        50       const
d SpcRpl                        10       const options(*nopass)
d ErrCde                                 likeds(ErrCde) options(*nopass)
d SpcDmn                        10       const options(*nopass)
d SpcTfrSiz                     10i 0    const options(*nopass)
d SpcSpcAln                      1       const options(*nopass)

dErrCde            ds
d BytPrv                        10i 0 inz(0)

dSpcName           ds
d SName                         10       inz('SPACENAME')
d SLib                          10       inz('QTEMP')

CLON01Factor1++++++++Opcode&ExtFactor2++++++++Result++++++++Len++D+HiLoEq
/free

   // Create the user space
   CrtSpc( SpcName :'MY_TEST' :4096 :x'00' :'*CHANGE'
           :'A test user space' :'*YES' :ErrCde);

   *inlr = *on;
   Return;

/end-free
```

Figure 1.8: Use the Create User Space (*QUSCRTUS*) API to create a user space.

You can verify that the user space was created and initialized to all x'00' values by using the Display File command:

```
DSPF STMF('/QSYS.LIB/QTEMP.LIB/SPACENAME.USRSPC')
```

Then, select F10, Display Hex.

Two Methods to Access Data from a User Space

If you have worked with i5/OS, you know this rule: There is always more than one way to get the job done. With user spaces, this means you can access data using two different methods. Each method has its strengths and weaknesses, which deserve some exploration.

First, consider the "slow" method, which involves the use of the Retrieve User Space API (QUSRTVUS). You give this API the name, starting position, and length of data to retrieve, and it gets that information and puts it in a variable for you. Since IBM introduced pointer support into RPGLE, this method is generally considered passé. The reason, of course, is speed. Every time you want to extract data from a user space, you have to call the API, and every call involves some overhead.

A faster method of retrieving data from a user space involves using the Retrieve User Space Pointer API (QUSPTRUS) and pointers. You simply "feed" this API the name of the user space, and it returns a pointer to your program, representing the beginning of the user space. You add "offsets" to this pointer to get at different positions in the user space. Walking through an entire list of fields in a file only requires one call to QUSPTRUS, versus one call for each data structure using QUSRTVUS.

In case the term is unfamiliar to you, an *offset* is simply the number of positions away from a central reference point. Offsets will be returned to you when you call APIs. (Don't be intimidated by some of the concepts and terminology at this stage. These concepts will be much easier to understand once you see actual code examples.)

Be aware that as you use the Retrieve User Space API (QUSRTVUS), all of the offset values returned in various data structures are relative to position 0 (zero) of the user space. You must add one to the value to get the correct position from a RPG point of view, as the first byte of a variable is position 1 rather than 0. If you are using pointer math, however, the offsets are correct, and you don't need to add one.

QUSPTRUS should usually be the obvious choice of methods to access data in a user space. However, you should be aware of the following:

- If your security level is 40 or greater, you cannot use this API on a user space that exists in the system domain. Prior to V2R3, user spaces could be created only in the system domain. After that release, you can specify either the system domain or the user domain when you create the user space.

- QUSPTRUS does not update the object-usage information. You can access the user space, and the last-used date will not be updated. If this is important, use QUSRTVUS or the Change User Space API (QUSCHGUS), which do update the object-usage information.

That being said, the preferred method of accessing a user space is still retrieving a pointer to it and using "pointer math" to access it. Most of the time, when you create a user space, you should put it in library QTEMP, which is a temporary place to store the information unique to each i5/OS session. When used this way, none of the limitations of QUSPTRUS apply. Table 1.5 shows the parameters for the Retrieve Pointer to User Space API (QUSPTRUS). Figure 1.9.A shows the code to call QUSPTRUS to retrieve a pointer to the user space created in Figure 1.8. Table 1.6 reflects the parameters for the Retrieve User Space API (QUSRTVUS). Figure 1.10 shows the code to call the QUSRTVUS API.

Table 1.5: The QUSPTRUS Parameters			
Parameter	Description	Type	Size
1	Qualified User Space Name	Input	Char(20)
2	Return Pointer	Output	Ptr(SPP)
Optional Parameter Group 1			
3	Error Code	I/O	Char(*)

The first parameter, Qualified User Space Name, is the name of the user space that you want to access. This parameter is defined as a 20-byte character field. The first ten bytes are for the user space name and the next ten bytes are for the name of the library where the user space is located. The special values *LIBL and *CURLIB can be used for the library portion of this parameter.

The second parameter, Return Pointer, is a variable that will contain a pointer to the user space when the API completes. This pointer can then be used by the application program to directly access the user space as if that space were a variable defined within the application. If you're not very familiar with pointers, don't be too concerned—you are going to see many pointer examples in the coming pages!

The third parameter, Error Code, refers to an error-code structure that is used with many of the system APIs. We'll be looking at this common error-code structure later in this chapter, and again in chapter 2.

Figure 1.9.A shows the prototype we developed based on the API documentation and the call to the Retrieve Pointer to User Space API. With the call, we are setting the pointer variable UsrSpcPtr to a value that addresses the first byte of the SPACENAME user space in the QTEMP library. Because you might not be familiar with pointers and BASED variables, Figure 1.9.A also demonstrates how this pointer might be used. After setting the UsrSpcPtr pointer, the program sets the variable PgmVar to the value "Hello from program F1_9_A" Because the variable PgmVar is BASED on the pointer UsrSpcPtr (which addresses the first byte of the SPACENAME user space), we are actually updating the contents of the SPACENAME user space in QTEMP! To verify this, you can use the command DSPF STMF('/QSYS.LIB/QTEMP.LIB/SPACENAME.USRSPC').

```
DName++++++++++ETDsFrom+++To/L+++IDc.Keywords++++++++++++++++++++++++++++
dRtvSpcPtr          pr                    extpgm('QUSPTRUS')
d SpcName                         20      const
d UsrSpcPtr                        *
d ErrCde                                  likeds(ErrCde) options(*nopass)

dErrCde             ds
d BytPrv                          10i 0 inz(0)

dSpcName            ds
d SName                           10      inz('SPACENAME')
d SLib                            10      inz('QTEMP')

dUsrSpcPtr          s              *
dPgmVar             s             50      based(UsrSpcPtr)

CLON01Factor1+++++++Opcode&ExtFactor2+++++++Result+++++++++Len++D+HiLoEq
 /free

    // Get a pointer to the user space
    RtvSpcPtr( SpcName :UsrSpcPtr :ErrCde);

    // Update the user space
    PgmVar = 'Hello from program F1_9_A';

    Return;

 /end-free
```

Figure 1.9.A: Use the Retrieve Pointer to User Space API (QUSPTRUS) to get a pointer to a user space.

Figure 1.9.B further demonstrates how we can use the pointer returned from the Retrieve Pointer to User Space API to access data within the user space. Like Figure 1.9.A,

Figure 1.9.B shows the prototype we developed based on the API documentation and the call to the Retrieve Pointer to User Space API. With the call, we are setting the pointer variable UsrSpcPtr to a value that addresses the first byte of the SPACENAME user space in the QTEMP library. After setting the UsrSpcPtr pointer, the program DSPLYs the variable PgmVar and the value "Hello from program F1_9_A" is shown.

```
DName+++++++++++ETDsFrom+++To/L+++IDc.Keywords++++++++++++++++++++++++++++
dRtvSpcPtr         pr                 extpgm('QUSPTRUS')
d SpcName                     20      const
d UsrSpcPtr                    *
d ErrCde                               likeds(ErrCde) options(*nopass)

dErrCde            ds
d BytPrv                      10i 0 inz(0)

dSpcName           ds
d SName                       10      inz('SPACENAME')
d SLib                        10      inz('QTEMP')

dUsrSpcPtr         s           *
dPgmVar            s          50      based(UsrSpcPtr)
dWait              s           1
CLON01Factor1+++++++Opcode&ExtFactor2+++++++Result++++++++Len++D+HiLoEq
/free

    // Get a pointer to the user space
    RtvSpcPtr( SpcName :UsrSpcPtr :ErrCde);

    // Retrieve data from the user space
    dsply PgmVar;

    // Change our position in the user space and retrieve different data
    UsrSpcPtr += 6;
    dsply PgmVar ' 'Wait;

    Return;

/end-free
```

Figure 1.9.B: Use the Retrieve Pointer to User Space API (QUSPTRUS) to get a pointer to a user space.

In Figure 1.9.B, as in Figure 1.9.A, the variable PgmVar is BASED on the pointer UsrSpcPtr, so we are actually displaying the first 50 bytes of the SPACENAME user space in QTEMP. The program then adds six to the pointer UsrSpcPtr and again DSPLYs the variable PgmVar. This time, the value "from program F1_9_A" is shown. By incrementing the pointer by six bytes, we have changed the data that is accessed with the BASED PgmVar variable.

The examples in chapter 3 use this type of pointer and BASED structure to great advantage when working with the contents of user spaces.

An alternative method to access data within a user space is the Retrieve User Space API, QUSRTVUS. The parameters for QUSRTVUS are shown in Table 1.6.

Table 1.6: The QUSRTVUS Parameters			
Parameter	Description	Type	Size
1	Qualified User Space Name	Input	Char(20)
2	Starting Position	Input	Binary(4)
3	Length of Data	Input	Binary(4)
4	Receiver Variable	Output	Char(*)
Optional Parameter Group 1			
5	Error Code	In/Out	Char(*)

The first parameter, Qualified User Space Name, is the name of the user space that you want to access. This parameter is defined as a 20-byte character field. The first ten bytes are for the user space name and the next ten bytes are for the name of the library where the user space is located. The special values *LIBL and *CURLIB can be used for the library portion of this parameter.

The second parameter, Starting Position, identifies the first byte of the user space that you want to retrieve. The parameter is defined as a 4-byte integer field. A value of 1 indicates that you want to start retrieving data at the first byte position of the user space, a value of 1,000 indicates you want to start retrieving data at the thousandth byte position of the user space, etc.

The third parameter, Length of Data, identifies how many bytes of data you want to retrieve from the user space, starting from the value specified for the Starting Position parameter.

The fourth parameter, Receiver Variable, identifies what variable in your application program is to receive the data from the user space. It is important that this variable be at least as large as the length specified in the Length of Data parameter.

The fifth parameter, Error Code, refers to an error code structure that is used with many of the system APIs.

Figure 1.10 shows the prototype we developed based on the API documentation and the call to the Retrieve User Space API. With the call, we are setting the program variable PgmVar to the value of the first 50 bytes of data stored in the user space SPACENAME in the QTEMP library. In this case, though, the system is actually *moving* the data from the user space to the program variable. If we now wanted to access positions 51 to 100 of the user space, we would need to call the Retrieve User Space API again, as we only retrieved the first 50 bytes on the initial call.

```
DName+++++++++++ETDsFrom+++To/L+++IDc.Keywords+++++++++++++++++++++++++++
dRtvSpcDta        pr                      extpgm('QUSRTVUS')
d SpcName                      20         const
d SpcPos                       10i 0      const
d SpcLng                       10i 0      const
d SpcDta                       1          options(*varsize)
d ErrCde                                  likeds(ErrCde) options(*nopass)

dErrCde           ds
d BytPrv                       10i 0      inz(0)

dSpcName          ds
d SName                        10         inz('SPACENAME')
d SLib                         10         inz('QTEMP')

dPgmVar           s            50
CLON01Factor1+++++++Opcode&ExtExtended-factor2++++++++++++++++++++++++++++
 /free

    // Retrieve the first 50 bytes of the user space
    RtvSpcDta( SpcName :1 :%size(PgmVar) :PgmVar :ErrCde);

    // Display the data
    dsply PgmVar;

    Return;

 /end-free
```

Figure 1.10: Use the Retrieve User Space (QUSRTVUS) API to retrieve data from a user space.

Contrast this with the pointer returned from the Retrieve Pointer to User Space API. There, we could simply add 50 to the pointer value, and the BASED PgmVar would represent positions 51 to 100 of the user space!

Automatically Extendable User Spaces

Much like a database file, a user space has the capability to increase the amount of storage it uses. When a user space is written to by a list API, the API will temporarily allow it to grow to the size needed to accommodate the returned data. The user space, however, will not grow beyond 16MB or the storage limit of your user profile.

To have a user space automatically extend itself independent of using it with a list API, use the Change User Space Attribute API (QUSCUSAT). Table 1.7 shows the parameters for QUSCUSAT.

Table 1.7: The QUSCUSAT Parameters			
Parameter	Description	Type	Size
1	Returned Library Name	Output	Char(10)
2	Qualified User Space Name	Input	Char(20)
3	Attributes to Change	Input	Char(*)
4	Error Code	I/O	Char(*)

The first parameter, Returned Library Name, is an output of the API. This parameter returns to the caller the name of the library containing the user space that was changed. This can be useful when the Qualified User Space Name parameter used a special value such as *LIBL for the library portion of the name.

The second parameter, Qualified User Space Name, is the name of the user space that you want to change. This parameter is defined as a 20-byte character field. The first ten bytes are for the user space name, and the next ten bytes are for the name of the library where the user space is located. The special values *LIBL and *CURLIB can be used for the library portion of this parameter.

The third parameter, Attributes to Change, defines what changes you want to make to the user space. This parameter is defined as a structure where the first field is a 4-byte integer representing the number of user-space attributes you will change. This field is then followed by that number of variable-length records. These records are defined as shown in Table 1.8.

Table 1.8: Variable-Length Records for the QUSCUSAT API		
Field	Description	Size
1	Key	Binary(4)
2	Length of Data	Binary(4)
3	Data	Char(*)

The first field of the variable-length record, Key, identifies which attribute is to be changed. Each attribute has a key value associated with it. The supported key values are shown in Table 1.9.

Table 1.9: Attribute Keys		
Key	Description	Size
1	Space Size	Binary(4)
2	Initial Value	Char(1)
3	Automatic Extendibility	Char(1)
4	Transfer Size Request	Binary(4)

A key value of 1, Space Size, allows you to set the size of the user space. If the user space is currently smaller than the size you specify, the system will extend the user space. If the user space is currently larger than the size you specify, the system will truncate the user space.

A key value of 2, Initial Value, allows you to set the initial value to be used for each new byte if and when the user space is extended in the future.

A key value of 3, Automatic Extendibility, allows you to define the user space as being extendible or not. A value of zero indicates that the user space is not extendible. A value of one indicates that the user space is extendible.

A key value of 4, Transfer Size Request, allows you to give a preference for how many pages of data should be read to and from auxiliary storage when working with user space data.

The second field of each variable-length record, Length of Data, indicates how many bytes of data you are supplying for the attribute being changed. In Table 1.9, the "Size" column indicates how many bytes of data are associated with each specific key. For instance, key 3, Automatic Extendibility, is documented as expecting one byte of data. This would be either zero (no extendibility) or one (extendible). Key 1, Space Size, on the other hand, expects a 4-byte binary value indicating the desired size for the user space.

The third field of each variable-length record, Data, is simply the data associated with the key value.

The fourth parameter for the API, Error Code, refers to an error-code structure that is used with many of the system APIs.

Figure 1.11 shows how to use the Change User Space Attributes API to make a user space automatically extend. With the call to the Change User Space Attributes API, we are setting the user space SPACENAME in library QTEMP to be automatically extendable. The ChgAttrDS data structure is initialized to indicate that we are changing one attribute (NbrAttrs), that the attribute key value is 3 (KeyValue), that the length of the data we are providing is one byte (DataSize), and that the value to be used is 1 (DataValue).

```
DName+++++++++++ETDsFrom+++To/L+++IDc.Keywords+++++++++++++++++++++++++++
dChgSpcAtr        pr                    extpgm('QUSCUSAT')
d SpcLib                          10
d SpcName                         20    const
d ChgAttrDS                             const likeds(ChgAttrDS)
d ErrCde                                likeds(ErrCde)

dChgAttrDS        ds
d NbrAttrs                        10i 0 inz(1)
d KeyValue                        10i 0 inz(3)
d DataSize                        10i 0 inz(1)
d DataValue                       1     inz('1')

dErrCde           ds
d BytPrv                          10i 0 inz(0)

dSpcName          ds
d SName                           10    inz('SPACENAME')
d SLib                            10    inz('QTEMP')
dSpcLib           s               10
```

Figure 1.11: Use the Change User Space Attribute (QUSCUSAT) API to change the attributes of a user space (part 1 of 2).

```
CLON01Factor1+++++++Opcode&ExtFactor2+++++++Result++++++++Len++D+HiLoEq
/free

    // Set the user space to be automatically extendible
    ChgSpcAtr( SpcLib :SpcName :ChgAttrDS :ErrCde);
    Return;

/end-free
```

Figure 1.11: Use the Change User Space Attribute (QUSCUSAT) API to change the attributes of a user space (part 2 of 2).

Note that these automatic extensions are not exclusively for writing new data to a user space. If you have a user space that is currently 10,000 bytes in size and try to read the millionth byte, the system will immediately grow the user space to a million bytes (and possibly a bit more), and then return to you that millionth byte.

For more information about user spaces, see chapter 3.

A Handy User-Space Procedure

APIs are often used in programs. Three APIs, in particular, are often employed when working with a user space:

- Create User Space, QUSCRTUS
- Retrieve User Space Pointer, QUSPTRUS
- Change User Space Attribute, QUSCUSAT

Repetitive code is bad because it introduces room for errors and creates maintenance headaches. Rather than including the code necessary to call these APIs into every program that needs a user space, we have created a procedure that does this for you. If you put this procedure in a service program, working with a user space becomes easy. You simply call the procedure and pass it a qualified name for the user space, and it returns a pointer to that space. Figure 1.12 shows this procedure.

```
h nomain

DName+++++++++++ETDsFrom+++To/L+++IDc.Keywords+++++++++++++++++++++++++++++
dCrtUsrSpc            pr              *       extproc('CrtUsrSpc')
d SpcName                            20       const

PName+++++++++++..T..................Keywords+++++++++++++++++++++++++++++
pCrtUsrSpc            b                       export

DName+++++++++++ETDsFrom+++To/L+++IDc.Keywords+++++++++++++++++++++++++++++
dCrtUsrSpc            pi              *
d SpcName                            20       const

dCrtSpc               pr                      extpgm('QUSCRTUS')
d SpcName                            20       const
d SpcAttr                            10       const
d SpcSiz                             10i 0    const
d SpcVal                              1       const
d SpcAut                             10       const
d SpcTxt                             50       const
d SpcRpl                             10       const options(*nopass)
d ErrCde                                      likeds(ErrCde) options(*nopass)
d SpcDmn                             10       const options(*nopass)
d SpcTfrSiz                          10i 0    const options(*nopass)
d SpcSpcAln                           1       const options(*nopass)

dRtvSpcPtr            pr                      extpgm('QUSPTRUS')
d SpcName                            20       const
d UsrSpcPtr                           *
d ErrCde                                      likeds(ErrCde) options(*nopass)

dChgSpcAtr            pr                      extpgm('QUSCUSAT')
d SpcLib                             10
d SpcName                            20       const
d ChgAttrDS                                   const likeds(ChgAttrDS)
d ErrCde                                      likeds(ErrCde)

dChgAttrDS            ds
d NbrAttrs                           10i 0    inz(1)
d KeyValue                           10i 0    inz(3)
d DataSize                           10i 0    inz(1)
d DataValue                           1       inz('1')

dErrCde               ds
d BytPrv                             10i 0    inz(0)
```

Figure 1.12: This CrtUsrSpc procedure is handy for working with a user space (part 1 of 2).

```
dUsrSpcPtr          s                *
dSpcLib             s               10

CLON01Factor1+++++++Opcode&ExtFactor2+++++++Result++++++++Len++D+HiLoEq
 /free

    // Create the user space
    CrtSpc( SpcName :' ' :1 :x'00' :'*CHANGE' :' ' :'*YES' :ErrCde);

    // Get a pointer to the user space
    RtvSpcPtr( SpcName :UsrSpcPtr :ErrCde);

    // Change the user space to be automatically extendable
    ChgSpcAtr( SpcLib :SpcName :ChgAttrDS :ErrCde);

    Return UsrSpcPtr;
 /end-free

PName+++++++++++..T.................Keywords++++++++++++++++++++++++++++
pCrtUsrSpc          e
```

Figure 1.12: This CrtUsrSpc procedure is handy for working with a user space (part 2 of 2).

In Figure 1.13, the CrtUsrSpc procedure has been used to create a user space named SPACENAME in the QTEMP temporary library. The attributes for this newly created user space have been modified so SPACENAME is "self-extending." In the end, the pointer variable SpcPtr will contain the pointer to the newly created user space.

You will be building several useful tools as you progress through the book, so let's integrate the CrtUsrSpc procedure into a *SRVPGM named FIG1_12 and create a binding directory APILIB that can be referenced in later examples:

```
CRTRPGMOD MODULE(FIG1_12)

CRTSRVPGM SRVPGM(FIG1_12) MODULE(FIG1_12) EXPORT(*ALL)

CRTBNDDIR BNDDIR(APILIB)

ADDBNDDIRE BNDDIR(APILIB) OBJ(FIG1_12)
```

You then compile the source in Figure 1.13 using BNDDIR(APILIB).

You have now created your own API! CrtUsrSpc is a general application-programming interface that can be used by any authorized developer within your organization. So, not only have you learned how to use system-provided APIs, you have also learned how

```
h dftactgrp(*no) bnddir('APILIB')
DName+++++++++++ETDsFrom+++To/L+++IDc.Keywords+++++++++++++++++++++++++++
dCrtUsrSpc              pr             *     extproc('CrtUsrSpc')
d SpcName                             20     const

dSpcPtr                 s              *

dSpcName                ds
d SName                               10     inz('SPACENAME')
d SLib                                10     inz('QTEMP')

CLONO1Factor1+++++++Opcode&ExtExtended-factor2+++++++++++++++++++++++++++
 /free

   SpcPtr = CrtUsrSpc(SpcName);
   Return;

 /end-free
```

Figure 1.13: CrtUsrSpc is a useful service function for other programs.

to supplement the system APIs with APIs of you own. Your API accepts one input parameter, a qualified user space name, and returns to the caller a pointer to the created user space.

Exits

In addition to calling APIs yourself to retrieve or get a list of information, you can also have i5/OS call your programs through *exit points*. Exit points are simply steps within i5/OS processing where you can indicate that you want a program to be called, or that you want the system to notify you of some event. For example, you can tell i5/OS to call one of your programs when a user profile (*USRPRF) is created or deleted, when a user uses the System Request key, or when a remote client tries to log onto the FTP or TELNET server. Other exit points allow you to specify a data queue (*DTAQ) where i5/OS can send messages to notify one of your programs that some event has taken place. An example of this type of exit is when a job starts or ends.

The use of various exit points is shown throughout this book:

- Chapter 4, "Command Processing APIs," demonstrates how to have a user program called when a command runs.

- Chapter 7, "Database File APIs," demonstrates how to have a user program called when a record is added to a file.

- Chapter 10, "Message APIs," demonstrates how to have a user program called when a message is sent.

- Chapter 12, "Security APIs," demonstrates how to have a user program called when a user profile is changed.

Exit points provide a very powerful tool with which you can better manage your system.

Continuation Handles

Some APIs can return large amounts of data, more than can fit into the variable or user space you have defined to receive it. Some APIs have a special technique called *continuation handles* built into them to handle this.

A continuation handle is a field in the receiver variable or user space that the API uses internally to keep track of the data it couldn't return to you. If you pass a continuation handle to an API, it knows that this is a continuation of a previous call.

When using a continuation handle, keep all other parameters as they were the first time you called the API. The API will return the rest of the data that couldn't fit, or it will return as much as it can, and again set the continuation field to indicate that it has still more. Like many of the concepts discussed in this chapter, this technique sounds more complicated than it really is. For an example of using continuation handles, see the List Save File API, QSRLSAVF, in chapter 16.

Domains

A domain is a characteristic of an object that controls the capability of programs to access the object. There are two types of domains: *user* or *system*. If you are operating at security level 40 or higher, access to objects in the system domain is restricted to commands and approved APIs only. So, for user spaces in the system domain, you cannot use the Retrieve User Space Pointer API (QUSPTRUS) to retrieve data; instead, you must use the Retrieve User Space API (QUSRTVUS).

Most objects are created into the system domain. You can control which libraries are allowed to contain user domain objects. This control is provided via the Allow User

Domain system value, QALWUSRDMN. This system value ships with the value *ALL, but you can change it to a list of libraries. If security is an issue in your environment (and it should be, if your system is open to the Internet), consult the proper authorities to determine if this system value needs to be modified.

In the user domain, APIs such as Retrieve User Space Pointer (QUSPTRUS) can use user spaces regardless of security level.

Offsets and Displacements

Many APIs use fields referred to as *offsets* and *displacements* when working with data that is variable in terms of the amount of data being returned. These terms, by convention, have very special meanings.

An offset represents the number of bytes from the beginning of the returned data. For a retrieve API, this is the number of bytes from the start of the receiver variable. If you are using pointers to work with the API data, you simply add the offset value to a pointer addressing the start of the receiver. If you are using positional notation (for example, the SUBST operation code or the %SUBST built-in function), you add a one to the offset and substring from the start of the receiver. If you are working with a list API, simply replace "receiver" in the preceding discussion with "user space," and you've got the concept!

A *displacement* represents the number of bytes from the beginning of the current data structure. This is typically used when the API returns a list of similar entries and also some variable-length data associated with each entry. For example, the List Fields API (QUSLFLD) returns a list of each field in a database record format. This information is returned as a list of structures, where each instance of the structure defines fixed-length elements such as the field name, field data type, the length of the field, and so on. This API can also return variable-length information, such as the default value for a field. Rather than reserving space in each structure for the maximum size of a default value, the API uses a displacement to the default value and a length of the default value. As this is a displacement, you will, if using pointers, add the provided displacement value to a pointer addressing the start of the current field structure. Compare this to offset, where you add the provided offset value to the start of the receiver/user space.

If this seems a bit confusing, don't worry. You will see many examples in future chapters that use offsets and displacements. The concept is actually very simple once you get the knack of it.

Error Handling

Most APIs accept an error-handling data structure, although UNIX-type APIs, and high-level, language-independent, ILE CEE-type APIs do not. If you include this structure when you call the API and an error occurs, you can have the system not generate CPF error messages for the world to see (and have your application program end). Instead, the API can fill in fields in this data structure describing the error that occurred. Your program can then take appropriate actions based on the error.

While the error parameter might be optional on some APIs, you should not consider it optional in your work. If you don't code to handle errors and an error does occur, i5/OS has been known to throw up some pretty cryptic error messages—just to confound the user.

Figure 1.14 shows the code necessary for the error-handling data structure. A key piece is the BytPrv field (Bytes Provided). If this field is set to zero, you are telling the API to send error messages to your program. In earlier examples in this chapter, BytPrv of ErrCde was set to zero so that any errors would be sent back to you as exception or escape messages. If BytPrv is set to eight or greater, you are telling the API to not send messages (i.e., there is no entry in your joblog), but rather return the error information in the error-handling data structure. After calling the API (in this case, the Retrieve Object Description API, QUSOBJD) with a BytPrv of 116 (the allocated %SIZE of ErrCde), you test the Bytes Available (BytAvl) field for zeros. If an error occurs, the API fills this field with the number of bytes it could have returned in the error data structure describing the error. It also fills the MsgID field with the message ID, and the ErrMsgDta field with the replacement data associated with the error message (&1, &2, etc.). If no error occurred, the BytAvl field would be zero. The error-code Bytes Provided field is essentially a big switch. If it is set to zero, you want escape messages sent to your application program. If it is set to eight or greater, you do not want escape messages.

When first developing an application using APIs, it is common to set BytPrv to zero, so that you directly receive any errors to your joblog. Once you have worked out any errors within your application, you typically set BytPrv to an appropriate value of eight or greater, so that errors do not appear in the joblog.

Figure 1.14 retrieves the object description of the user space SPACENAME in the QTEMP library created in previous examples. We haven't really discussed this API yet, but don't worry about that. The intent here is to introduce you to error handling, not any specific API. In this case, no error will occur because the user space does exist (assuming you've been trying out the examples). Try changing the user space name (SName) to another

```
DName++++++++++++ETDsFrom+++To/L+++IDc.Keywords+++++++++++++++++++++++++++++
dRtvObjD              pr                       extpgm('QUSROBJD')
d Receiver                        1            options(*varsize)
d LenReceiver                    10i 0         const
d Format                          8            const
d ObjName                        20            const
d ObjType                        10            const
d ErrCde                                       likeds(ErrCde) options(*nopass)
d ASP                         65535            const options(*varsize :*nopass)

dErrCde               ds
d BytPrv                         10i 0
d BytAvl                         10i 0
d MsgID                           7
d NotUsed                         1
d ErrMsgDta                     100

dReceiver             ds        256

dSpcName              ds
d SName                          10        inz('SPACENAME')
d SLib                           10        inz('QTEMP')

CLON01Factor1+++++++Opcode&ExtFactor2+++++++Result++++++++Len++D+HiLoEq
 /free

   BytPrv = %size(ErrCde);
   RtvObjD( Receiver  :%size(Receiver) :'OBJD0100' :SpcName
           :'*USRSPC' :ErrCde);
   if (BytAvl <> 0);
      // Error occurred and should be handled
   else;
      // Everything is OK so far and we continue on
   endif;
   return;

 /end-free
```

Figure 1.14: You can use the "optional" error data structure with an API.

name that doesn't exist, and in debug mode, enter **eval ErrCde** after calling the API to see what is returned. Try changing BytPrv to zero to see what happens when the user space doesn't exist. You can't hurt anything, and playing around with various values for BytPrv can be very educational.

Table 1.9 reflects the elements for the "optional" error-code parameter that is used with many APIs.

Table 1.9: "Optional" Error-Code Parameter Fields			
Offset Dec	**Description**	**Attribute**	**Size**
0	Bytes Provided, the number of bytes you have defined for this structure. This should be the total size of the error data structure.	Input	Binary(4)
4	Bytes Available, the number of bytes that could be returned by the error. If zero, no error occurred. If greater than zero, an error did occur.	Output	Binary(4)
8	Message ID, the seven-character message ID. This field is not reset if no error occurs, so a message ID from prior errors could be present. This is why you need to check Bytes Available first.	Output	Char(7)
15	Reserved.	Output	Char(1)
16	Message Data, the message replacement data. Like Message ID, it is not cleared if no error occurs, so text from prior errors could be present.	Output	Char(*)

If you're not sure you understand all of this, don't worry. Chapter 2 covers it with some real examples.

Common Errors to Avoid

APIs can be complicated to code even when things go exactly right the first time. They can be a nightmare to debug when things don't go exactly right. We cannot guarantee you will code bug-free every time you use an API if you adhere to the following guidelines, but we can guarantee that you will have a far better experience.

Size Is Critical

It is essential to define a receiver variable with the correct length. Be *absolutely* certain that the receiver variable is not smaller than the length you specify to the API.

In Figure 1.15, the receiver variable is defined with a length of 38 bytes (the size of the defined fields) to represent the fields that we are interested in retrieving from the API. When the Retrieve Object Description API (QUSROBJD) is called, the parameter LenReceiver is incorrectly coded to tell the API that the length of the receiver variable is 90. This is not good! It could adversely affect variables that have nothing to do with the API itself. In this example, if the API can return 90 bytes, it will return 90 bytes, and the extra 52 bytes will overflow into fields that are defined elsewhere in your program. These might be your defined variables or internal variables that the RPG compiler is using! After incorrectly calling this API, your program will behave unpredictably.

```
DName+++++++++++ETDsFrom+++To/L+++IDc.Keywords++++++++++++++++++++++++++++
dRtvObjD           pr                      extpgm('QUSROBJD')
d Receiver                       1         options(*varsize)
d LenReceiver                    10i 0     const
d Format                         8         const
d ObjName                        20        const
d ObjType                        10        const
d ErrCde                                   likeds(ErrCde) options(*nopass)
d ASP                            65535     const options(*varsize :*nopass)

dErrCde            ds
d BytPrv                         10i 0
d BytAvl                         10i 0
d MsgID                          7
d NotUsed                        1
d ErrMsgDta                      100

dReceiver          ds
d APIBytRtn                      10i 0
d APIBytAvl                      10i 0
d ObjName                        10
d ObjLibrary                     10
d ObjType                        10

dSpcName           ds
d SName                          10        inz('SPACENAME')
d SLib                           10        inz('QTEMP')

CLON01Factor1+++++++Opcode&ExtFactor2+++++++Result++++++++Len++D+HiLoEq
 /free

   BytPrv = %size(ErrCde);
   RtvObjD( Receiver  :90 :'OBJD0100' :SpcName :'*USRSC' :ErrCde);
   if (BytAvl <> 0);
      // Error occurred and should be handled
   else;
      // Everything is OK so far and we continue on
   endif;
   return;

 /end-free
```

Figure 1.15: This example shows the common error of defining receiver variables incorrectly.

This type of mistake can also happen with the error-code data structure. Figure 1.15 sets BytPrv of ErrCde to 116. Suppose you inadvertently set the size to a larger value, such as 256. If an error were to occur on the call to QUSROBJD, and if the resulting error had replacement data for the error message, then the API would feel free to return up to 240 bytes of replacement data (256 minus 16). This data would also overflow to other variables in your program. You would have a real mess!

With ILE RPG, it is reasonably easy to avoid some of these problems by using the %SIZE built-in that the language provides. With earlier levels of RPG, this is more your responsibility.

Whenever you see bizarre behavior in your program after calling an API (or any program, for that matter), always check to make sure you have all of your length fields set correctly. In particular, check any Length of Receiver Variable parameters and the Bytes Provided field of the error-code structure.

Don't Make Errors with Your Error-Handling

Many times when initially writing an application that will be using APIs, we set the Bytes Provided field of the error-code structure (QUSBPRV) to zero. This tells the API to send exception messages to the program calling the API when an error occurs. Having the program end with an escape, or exception, message is an easy way for us to detect errors when first starting out. Because of this, you will see many of the example programs starting out with QUSBPRV = 0;.

In a production environment, however, having the end user see a CPF escape message is not in anyone's best interest. Use the error-handling data structure whenever it is available with a Bytes Provided field value of at least 16 bytes. Obviously, when you use it, check it for results. Don't just code your application program so the API won't blow up with an error message when an error occurs. To do so would be like specifying a "record not found" indicator, or an "E" extender, on an RPG CHAIN operation and then not checking to see if the record was found. Bad things can happen in this situation. The proper way to check if errors occurred is to check the Bytes Available field (QUSBAVL) for zeros after each API call. If the number of bytes available is not zero, an error occurred with the execution of that API. Make sure your program is coded to take the appropriate action if an error condition occur.

Another common error is to check the error data structure's message ID or message data fields, instead of the number of bytes available. It would be only natural to assume that an error occurred if these fields were not blank. However, these fields are not reset each time the API runs, while the Number of Bytes Available field is. If you check the message ID field, have an error, correct the error, and run the API again, it might look like you still have an error condition, even when you don't.

Use QSYSINC

The include files provided with the QSYSINC library accurately define the layout of structures used with APIs. Building your own versions of these include files can only introduce errors. The example programs in this book make use of the QSYSINC-provided definitions.

Don't Assume

APIs are designed so that your application program should run for many years and releases. The intent of APIs is to allow access to the system without requiring your application programs to change unless you decide to enhance them due to a changing business environment. For this to succeed, you must not make assumptions about the system data you are working with.

It is important that you code your APIs with an eye on the future. IBM will not make incompatible changes in the format of the data the API is returning, but IBM might change the content of the data in some future release. That is, a field that today might return a value of *YES or *NO might, in the future, also return a value of *CALC (to calculate the value at run time), so *don't assume* that if the returned field is not equal to *YES that it must be *NO. Explicitly check for *NO.

New features are continually being added to the operating system, which can cause the use of new values. With this in mind, avoid using global ELSE statements when comparing data elements returned from APIs. Make sure that you code your application for the explicit value with which you are working. An example of this type of change being made, in the area of returned values, is the List Objects that Adopt Owner Authority API, QSYLOBJP. Prior to V2R3, the only object types the QSYLOBJP API might return were *PGM and *SQLPKG. Therefore, an application using QSYLOBJP might have been coded as shown in Figure 1.16, in which an object that is not a program is assumed to be a SQL package.

```
/free
  if (QSYOBJT12 = '*PGM');
     // then do some processing unique to program objects

  else;
     // do some processing unique to SQL packages

  endif;
/end-free
```

Figure 1.16: This is innocent-looking code, but it is dangerous due to the ELSE assumption.

V2R3 introduced ILE service programs that could also adopt the owner's authority. Applications written as shown in Figure 1.16 were now handling *SRVPGMs as if they were *SQLPKGs! This could lead to some unexpected results, depending on what the application program was doing. A much better coding style would be that shown in Figure 1.17.

```
/free
     select;

     when QSYOBJT12 = '*PGM';
          // then do some processing unique to program objects

     when QSYOBJT12 = '*SQLPKG';
          // then do some processing unique to SQL packages
     other;
          // send an error message logging the fact that unexpected
          // data has been encountered.  We would recommend that the
          // message indicate the API used and the value which was
          // unexpected

     endsl;
/end-free
```

Figure 1.17: This code avoids assumptions with ELSE statements.

While working with an API, you might notice that it always seems to return data in a particular order. Unless the API documentation clearly states that this is the order of returned data, *do not assume* that the current order will be maintained forever. APIs tend to return data in whatever sequence is currently the fastest or most effective. This order can, and does, change over time. If your application program needs the data in a particular order or sequence, the program should provide for that ordering. As you will see in chapter 16, sort APIs can be used in this situation.

Many APIs return variable-length data. There is an offset or displacement to where the data can be found, and then a separate "length of" field to tell your application program how long the data is. You might notice that an API always seems to return the same offset or displacement value. *Do not assume* that this will always be true, and that your application program can "hard-code" the location of this variable-length data.

If an API returns an offset or displacement value, use it, rather than assuming the location of the data. If an API returns a "length of" field, use it, rather than assuming some particular length. If an API returns a count of the number of entries, use it, rather than trying to derive some value based on your knowledge of the environment. If an API returns an indication of the status of the current data, use it, rather than assuming everything is okay.

Fundamentally, when working with APIs, always look to see what your application program is providing and what the API is returning to your application. Then, make sure you are using the available information. Anytime you find yourself having to "guess" how to process API-related data, step back a moment, and review all of the control-related information the API provides you. Many of the examples in this book are intended to help you understand how to use this control-related information.

Find an Error?

Any technical book of this size is bound to have errors inadvertently introduced into it. While every attempt has been made to provide correct information, you might find errors in the text or the example programs. Technical errors can be sent to the authors at *brucevining@brucevining.com*. These reported errors may be posted, at the authors' discretion, on the Web site *www.brucevining.com*. In no case, however, will the authors be obligated to respond to, or publish on their Web site, any errors that might be reported.

Summary

Every release of the operating system provides more APIs. They are the best way to get information out of the i5/OS that would otherwise not be readily available. Whenever one of your applications needs to see or do something out of the ordinary, there is probably an API designed to do it. Whether you simply want to list all jobs currently running in a subsystem or communicate with a Microsoft Windows program, you can use APIs to do it.

APIs do their jobs quickly and efficiently. Plus, they're upgradeable. IBM can and will enhance APIs as the i5/OS operating system continues to evolve. If you use the proper coding techniques demonstrated in this chapter, your applications should be more functional, without being more difficult to maintain.

Check Your Knowledge

If you wanted to review the documentation for an API, where would you look? If you were interested in retrieving a list of objects saved in a save file, what options do you have in finding an API that might assist you? Try to complete this task. Do not worry about how to use the API. When you complete chapter 3, you should be comfortable with how to do that. For now, just try to find the appropriate API.

See appendix D for possible solutions.

2

Retrieve APIs

In chapter 1, there is a very brief overview of retrieve APIs and receiver variables. Let's now examine this type of API in more detail.

Static Receiver Variables

For example purposes, suppose you are interested in finding out how many jobs are currently in the QBATCH job queue. Perhaps you want to proactively monitor the job queue and notify the system operator if it is developing too large a backlog. You go to the Information Center at *http://publib.boulder.ibm.com/iseries* and select "Programming," followed by "APIs," and then "API Finder." You can then use the "Find by Name" option to locate APIs related to job queues. Type in **job queue** and click **Go**. You will get a list of APIs that includes the words *job queue* in their descriptive names. This is the Retrieve APIs chapter, so select the Retrieve Job Queue Information API (QSPRJOBQ).

This chapter uses QSPRJOBQ to illustrate one of the methods of retrieving data; it's not a tutorial on the API. The goal here is not to describe this API in detail, but to introduce one style of API that is used by many APIs.

As you can see in Table 2.1, QSPRJOBQ takes five parameters. The first three are standard across retrieve APIs, and once mastered, they will open the door to many APIs beyond Retrieve Job Queue Information.

Table 2.1: Parameters for the Retrieve Job Queue Information API (QSPRJOBQ)			
Parameter	Description	Type	Size
1	Receiver Variable	Output	Char(*)
2	Length of Receiver Variable	Input	Binary(4)
3	Format Name	Input	Char(8)
4	Qualified Job Queue Name	Input	Char(20)
5	Error Code	In/Out	Char(*)

The first parameter, Receiver Variable, is an output parameter of varying length (Char (*)). This is the parameter that the API uses to return data to your program.

The second parameter, Length of Receiver Variable, is an input parameter of a four-byte binary value. This is the parameter you use to tell the API how large the receiver variable is.

The third parameter, Format Name, is an input parameter of eight bytes. This is the parameter you use to tell the API what type of data you want the API to return in the receiver variable. Some APIs only have one format, and some have many for you to select from. This particular API has two formats: JOBQ0100 for basic information, and JOBQ0200 for more detailed information.

The fourth parameter, Qualified Job Queue Name, is an input parameter of 20 bytes. This parameter varies greatly across retrieve APIs. In QSPRJOBQ, this is the parameter you use to tell the API what job queue you are interested in. In another API, such as Retrieve Member Description (QUSRMBRD), you would supply a qualified file name (*FILE) rather than a job queue name. In any case, it's a qualified name, which means the API wants both the object name and the library in which to find the object. From chapter 1, you might recall that the first 10 bytes of a qualified object name are the object name, and the second 10 bytes are the library name. The API documentation for QSPRJOBQ indicates that the special values *LIBL and *CURLIB can be used for the library name.

You'll find the fifth parameter, Error Code, on many APIs, and not just retrieve ones. This parameter was briefly discussed in chapter 1, but we'll go into much more detail later in this chapter.

Now let's get back to the task at hand: finding out how many jobs are currently on the QBATCH job queue. When you read through the Retrieve Job Queue Information documentation, you find the format of JOBQ0100 as shown in Table 2.2. There in the middle, at decimal offset 48, is Number of Jobs. Now let's get it!

Table 2.2: The "Number of Jobs" Field in the Format of JOBQ0100			
Offset Dec	**Field**	**Attribute**	**Size**
0	Bytes Returned	Binary	4
4	Bytes Available	Binary	4
8	Job Queue Name	Char	10
18	Job Queue Library Name	Char	10
28	Operator Controlled	Char	10
38	Authority to Check	Char	10
48	*Number of Jobs*	*Binary*	*4*
52	Job Queue Status	Char	10
62	Subsystem Name	Char	10
72	Text Description	Char	50
132	Sequence Number	Binary	4
136	Maximum Active	Binary	4
140	Current Active	Binary	4

As you saw in chapter 1, the QSYSINC library contains source members describing the structures (formats) used by many of the APIs. Since we are working with the *PGM API QSPRJOBQ, we will look for a source member named QSPRJOBQ in QSYSINC/QRPGLESRC. Part of this source member is shown in Figure 2.1. As you can see, the JOBQ0100 format is, indeed, provided with field QSPNBRJ for Number of Jobs.

```
DName++++++++++ETDsFrom+++To/L+++IDc.Keywords++++++++++++++++++++++++++++
D********************************************************************
D*Type Definition for the JOBQ0100 format.
D********************************************************************
DQSPQ010000         DS
D*                                                Qsp JOBQ0100
D QSPBRTN00                1       4B 0
D*                                                Bytes Returned
D QSPBAVL00                5       8B 0
D*                                                Bytes Available
D QSPJQN                   9      18
D*                                                Job Queue Name
D QSPJQLN                 19      28
D*                                                Job Queue Lib Name
D QSPOC01                 29      38
D*                                                Operator Controlled
D QSPAC                   39      48
D*                                                Authority Check
D QSPNBRJ                 49      52B 0
D*                                                Number Jobs
D QSPJQS                  53      62
D*                                                Job Queue Status
D QSPSN                   63      72
D*                                                Subsystem Name
D QSPTD                   73     122
D*                                                Text Description
D QSPSLN                 123     132
D*                                                Subsystem Lib Name
D QSPSNBR01              133     136B 0
D*                                                Sequence Number
D QSPMA00                137     140B 0
D*                                                Maximum Active
D QSPCA00                141     144B 0
D*                                                Current Active
```

Figure 2.1: Some of what is found in QSYSINC/QRPGLESRC member QSPRJOBA.

With this knowledge, let's write our first program, shown in Figure 2.2.A. We start by including two source members from QSYSINC: QSPRJOBQ because it provides the definitions for format JOBQ0100, and QUSEC because it provides the definitions for the standard API error-code parameter. We then provide a function prototype for QSPRJOBQ, a definition for the qualified job queue name (JobQ, which is initialized to QBATCH in the current jobs library list), and a wait field (to cause the program to wait for input after displaying the number of jobs on the job queue).

```
DName++++++++++ETDsFrom+++To/L+++IDc.Keywords++++++++++++++++++++++++++
d/copy qsysinc/qrpglesrc,qsprjobq
d/copy qsysinc/qrpglesrc,qusec

dRtvJobQ              pr                        extpgm('QSPRJOBQ')
d Receiver                           1          options(*varsize)
d LengthRcv                         10i 0       const
d Format                             8          const
d JobQ                              20          const
d QUSEC                                         likeds(QUSEC)

dJobQ                 ds
d JobQName                          10          inz('QBATCH')
d JobQLib                           10          inz('*LIBL')

dwait                 s             1

CLON01Factor1+++++++Opcode&ExtFactor2+++++++Result++++++++Len++D+HiLoEq
 /free
    QUSBPRV = 0;
    RtvJobQ(QSPQ010000 :%size(QSPQ010000) :'JOBQ0100' :JobQ :QUSEC);
    dsply QSPNBRJ ' ' wait;
    *inlr = *on;
    return;

 /end-free
```

Figure 2.2.A: Using a static receiver variable with QSPRJOBQ.

For the calculation specifications, let's analyze each statement individually:

- QUSBRPV = 0;—The program sets the Bytes Provided field of the QUSEC error-code structure to zero. This tells the API that if any errors are found, it should send back escape messages and end the program, as the program is not monitoring for errors. If, for instance, a QBATCH job queue is not found in your current library list, the program will be sent the error "CPF3307 – Job queue QBATCH in *LIBL not found." Try a job queue name of NOT_HERE for JobQName to see what happens (assuming that you do have a QBATCH but not a NOT_HERE job queue, that is).

- RTVJOBQ(QSPQ010000 :%SIZE(QSPQ010000) :'JOBQ0100' :JOBQ :QUSEC);–The program calls the QSPRJOBQ API, passing five parameters. They are the receiver variable QSPQ010000 from the QSPRJOBQ source member, the size of QSPQ010000, the format name JOBQ0100, the qualified name of the job queue, and the error-code structure QUSEC.

- DSPLY QSPNBRJ '' WAIT ;–The program displays the value of QSPNBRJ and waits for you to press the Enter key. When Enter is pressed, *INLR = *ON; ends the program.

That's it. You have successfully used a retrieve API and displayed an output from it!

Simply DSPLYing the number of jobs on the job queue is a good start, but what if you had multiple QBATCH job queues in your library list? How does the user know which one was returned by the API? Figure 2.2.B expands on our first example by also DSPLYing the name and library of the job queue. This is done by using the name and library that is returned by format JOBQ0100. These fields are feedback from the API, clarifying what object was used. In the case of the library name, QSPJQLN, this is the library in which the job queue was found. This feedback is useful when using special values such as *LIBL for the JobQLib variable when calling the QSPRJOBQ API. In the case of the job queue name, QSPJQN, this is simply the same value as the one we used for variable JobQName. We suspect, though, that if IBM ever came out with an Override Job Queue command, (which, quite frankly, we doubt), QSPJQN would probably contain the actual job queue name that the override pointed to.

```
DName+++++++++++ETDsFrom+++To/L+++IDc.Keywords+++++++++++++++++++++++++++
d/copy qsysinc/qrpglesrc,qsprjobq
d/copy qsysinc/qrpglesrc,qusec

dRtvJobQ            pr                     extpgm('QSPRJOBQ')
d Receiver                        1        options(*varsize)
d LengthRcv                      10i 0     const
d Format                          8        const
d JobQ                           20        const
d QUSEC                                    likeds(QUSEC)

dJobQ               ds
d JobQName                       10        inz('QBATCH')
d JobQLib                        10        inz('*LIBL')

dWait               s             1

CLON01Factor1+++++++Opcode&ExtFactor2+++++++Result++++++++Len++D+HiLoEq
 /free
  QUSBPRV = 0;

  RtvJobQ( QSPQ010000 :%size(QSPQ010000) :'JOBQ0100' :JobQ :QUSEC);
  dsply ('JobQ ' + %trim(QSPJQLN) + '/' + %trim(QSPJQN) + ' has ' +
         %char(QSPNBRJ) + ' jobs.') ' ' wait;

  *inlr = *on;
  return;
 /end-free
```

Figure 2.2.B: Using a static receiver variable with QSPRJOBQ and displaying the job queue name.

Let's take this example a step further. Rather than always using QBATCH and the current job's library list, let's define two optional parameters for our program. The first parameter is the job queue name, and the second parameter is the library to be used. Figure 2.2.C shows this new program.

```
DName++++++++++ETDsFrom+++To/L+++IDc.Keywords+++++++++++++++++++++++++++++
d/copy qsysinc/qrpglesrc,qsprjobq
d/copy qsysinc/qrpglesrc,qusec

dFig2_2_C         pr                    extpgm('FIG2_2_C')
d JobQParm                      10      const
d JobQLibParm                   10      const

dFig2_2_C         pi
d JobQParm                      10      const
d JobQLibParm                   10      const

dRtvJobQ          pr                    extpgm('QSPRJOBQ')
d Receiver                       1      options(*varsize)
d LengthRcv                    10i 0    const
d Format                         8      const
d JobQ                          20      const
d QUSEC                                 likeds(QUSEC)

dJobQ             ds
d JobQName                      10      inz('QBATCH')
d JobQLib                       10      inz('*LIBL')

dWait             s              1

CLON01Factor1+++++++Opcode&ExtFactor2+++++++Result++++++++Len++D+HiLoEq
/free
  if (%parms > 0);
     JobQName = JobQParm;
  endif;
  if (%parms > 1);
     JobQLib = JobQLibParm;
  endif;

  QUSBPRV = 0;

  RtvJobQ( QSPQ010000 :%size(QSPQ010000) :'JOBQ0100' :JobQ :QUSEC);
  dsply ('JobQ ' + %trim(QSPJQLN) + '/' + %trim(QSPJQN) + ' has ' +
        %char(QSPNBRJ) + ' jobs.') ' ' wait;

  *inlr = *on;
  return;
/end-free
```

Figure 2.2.C: Using a static receiver variable with QSPRJOBQ and optional parameters.

Program FIG2_2_C checks to see if the job-queue parameter was used. If so, the JobQName variable is updated. If the parameter was not passed, the program defaults to QBATCH. Then, it checks whether a library name was passed to the program and performs the same type of processing. From there on, the program logic remains the same.

We've been able to successfully develop three (admittedly simple) applications, all using the same call to the Retrieve Job Queue Information API.

More on Error-Handling

Now let's go back to the QUSBPRV = 0; statement. Quite often, you will want your program to continue running even if an error is found by the API. For instance, you might want to handle an incorrect job queue name by prompting the user for the correct job queue name. How could you change the sample program in Figure 2.2.C so that an incorrect job queue name wouldn't cause the program to end? The answer is simple: set QUSBPRV to a nonzero value. QUSBPRV tells the API how many bytes the program has allocated for error-related information. A value of zero indicates that no storage is available, so the API sends an escape message. A value of eight or more informs the API that the API caller wants error information returned to the program with no escape message sent. (Values of one through seven, inclusive, are invalid.) The actual value you specify controls how much information is returned in the case of an error. This is similar to how the Length of Receiver variable controls how much information is returned to a receiver variable.

Figure 2.3 shows the structure QUSEC in member QUSEC. As you can see, four fields are defined:

- QUSBPRV, Bytes Provided
- QUSBAVL, Bytes Available
- QUSEI, Exception ID
- QUSERVED, Reserved

QUSBAVL is returned when the API encounters an error and QUSBPRV is eight or greater. (A value of eight indicates that the program has allocated eight bytes: four for QUSBPRV and four for QUSBAVL.) If QUSBAVL is zero, then no error has been found; if it is non-zero, then the value represents how many bytes of error information could have been returned. QUSEI is returned when the API encounters an error and QUSBPRV is 15 or greater (four bytes for QUSBPRV, four bytes for QUSBAVL, and seven bytes for QUSEI).

QUSEI contains the error message ID (CPF3307, for example). QUSERVED is simply a one-byte reserved field.

```
DName++++++++++++ETDsFrom+++To/L+++IDc.Keywords++++++++++++++++++++++++++++
DQUSEC               DS
D*                                                    Qus EC
D QUSBPRV              1      4B 0
D*                                                    Bytes Provided
D QUSBAVL              5      8B 0
D*                                                    Bytes Available
D QUSEI                9      15
D*                                                    Exception Id
D QUSERVED            16      16
D*                                                    Reserved
D*QUSED01             17      17
D*
D*                                           Varying length
```

Figure 2.3: The *QUSEC* error-code structure.

Let's change the sample program so errors are not returned as escape messages, but rather as USEC data. To do this, change this line:

```
QUSBPRV = 0;
```

to this:

```
QUSBPRV = %size(QUSEC);
```

This indicates to the API that 16 bytes are allocated for error information.

Since i5/OS will no longer send an error message, the program also needs to be changed to check for errors. This change is shown in Figure 2.4.

```
DName++++++++++++ETDsFrom+++To/L+++IDc.Keywords++++++++++++++++++++++++++++
d/copy qsysinc/qrpglesrc,qsprjobq
d/copy qsysinc/qrpglesrc,qusec

dFig2_4              pr                   extpgm('FIG2_4')
d JobQParm                   10          const
d JobQLibParm                10          const
```

Figure 2.4: Using the error-code structure to return error-related information (part 1 of 2).

```
dFig2_4               pi
d JobQParm                        10      const
d JobQLibParm                     10      const

dRtvJobQ              pr                  extpgm('QSPRJOBQ')
d Receiver                         1      options(*varsize)
d LengthRcv                      10i 0    const
d Format                          8       const
d JobQ                            20      const
d QUSEC                                   likeds(QUSEC)

dJobQ                 ds
d JobQName                        10      inz('QBATCH')
d JobQLib                         10      inz('*LIBL')

dWait                 s            1

CLON01Factor1+++++++Opcode&ExtFactor2+++++++Result++++++++Len++D+HiLoEq
/free
  if (%parms > 0);
      JobQName = JobQParm;
  endif;
  if (%parms > 1);
      JobQLib = JobQLibParm;
  endif;

  QUSBPRV = %size(QUSEC);

  RtvJobQ( QSPQ010000 :%size(QSPQ010000) :'JOBQ0100' :JobQ :QUSEC);

  if (QUSBAVL > 0);
     dsply ('Error ' + QUSEI + ' found') ' ' wait;
  else;

     dsply ('JobQ ' + %trim(QSPJQLN) + '/' + %trim(QSPJQN) + ' has ' +
            %char(QSPNBRJ) + ' jobs.') ' ' wait;
  endif;

  *inlr = *on;
  return;
/end-free
```

Figure 2.4: Using the error-code structure to return error-related information (part 2 of 2).

After calling the API, the program is now checking QUSBAVL for a value greater than zero. (Negative values are never returned.) If it finds such a value, it displays the message ID (QUSEI). Otherwise, the program displays the number of jobs found (QSPNBRJ). Try a job queue name of NOT_HERE to see what happens.

If you allocate still more storage for the error code structure than the 16 bytes shown, and set QUSBPRV to this larger value, the program will also start receiving any replacement data (&1, &2, etc.) associated with the error message returned in the structure. In the case of CPF3307, by using DSPMSGD RANGE(CPF3307) and using option 2 to display the field data, you can see that the first 10 bytes of returned replacement data would be the job queue name (&1), and the next 10 bytes would be the library name (&2).

In Figure 2.3, notice that there is also a commented field QUSED01 with a comment of "Varying length." This is used in the QSYSINC members to indicate that you need to determine what size (if any) you would like to allocate for this additional data. If you did want to access the replacement data for an error message returned in QUSEC, you could code your program as in Figure 2.5.

```
DName+++++++++++ETDsFrom+++To/L+++IDc.Keywords+++++++++++++++++++++++++++
d/copy qsysinc/qrpglesrc,qsprjobq
d/copy qsysinc/qrpglesrc,qusec

dFig2_5           pr                    extpgm('FIG2_5')
d JobQParm                      10      const
d JobQLibParm                   10      const

dFig2_5           pi
d JobQParm                      10      const
d JobQLibParm                   10      const

dRtvJobQ          pr                    extpgm('QSPRJOBQ')
d Receiver                       1      options(*varsize)
d LengthRcv                    10i 0    const
d Format                         8      const
d JobQ                          20      const
d ErrCde                                likeds(ErrCde)

dErrCde           ds                    qualified
d EC                                    likeds(QUSEC)
d ErrorDta                     100

dJobQ             ds
d JobQName                      10      inz('QBATCH')
d JobQLib                       10      inz('*LIBL')

dWait             s              1
```

Figure 2.5: Using the error-code structure with message-replacement data (part 1 of 2).

```
CLON01Factor1+++++++Opcode&ExtFactor2+++++++Result++++++++++Len++D+HiLoEq
/free
  if (%parms > 0);
    JobQName = JobQParm;
  endif;
  if (%parms > 1);
    JobQLib = JobQLibParm;
  endif;


  ErrCde.EC.QUSBPRV = %size(ErrCde);

  RtvJobQ( QSPQ010000 :%size(QSPQ010000) :'JOBQ0100' :JobQ :ErrCde);

  if (ErrCde.EC.QUSBAVL > 0);
    if (ErrCde.EC.QUSEI = 'CPF3307');
      dsply ('Error ' + ErrCde.EC.QUSEI + ' on JobQ ' +
             %trim(%subst(ErrCde.ErrorDta :11 :10)) + '/' +
             %trim(%subst(ErrCde.ErrorDta :1 :10))) ' ' Wait;
    else;
      dsply ('Error ' + ErrCde.EC.QUSEI + ' found') ' ' wait;
    endif;

  else;

    dsply ('JobQ ' + %trim(QSPJQLN) + '/' + %trim(QSPJQN) + ' has ' +
           %char(QSPNBRJ) + ' jobs.') ' ' wait;
  endif;

  *inlr = *on;
  return;
/end-free
```

Figure 2.5: Using the error-code structure with message-replacement data (part 2 of 2).

This program adds a new data structure, ErrCde, which has subfields defined like those in QUSEC with the LIKEDS(QUSEC). It also adds a new field, ErrorDta, which can contain up to 100 bytes of replacement data. The program has also been changed to pass this new ErrCde rather than QUSEC and to check if CPF3307 has been returned. If so, the program displays a message containing the error message ID and the job queue name. If an error other than CPF3307 is returned, the program simply displays the error message ID as having been returned.

This is a trivial example of how to access the replacement data associated with an error message, but it does demonstrate how the application program can make decisions based on the error message and replacement data. In some cases, this information might be used to automate error recovery rather than simply displaying a message.

Dynamic Receiver Variables

One of the problems with returning data into a receiver variable is that you don't always know the size of the data that will be returned to you. Even if you think you know, IBM might, in the future, enhance the API to return more data than it was originally coded for. For many APIs, this is not a problem because you are only interested in specific fields at fixed locations (like QSPNBRJ in the previous example). In that case, your program would not be affected if IBM adds more fields to the receiver variable in a future release. Your API call will continue to work just fine.

But what if the API is returning both fixed information and a variable amount of information? The Retrieve Controller Description API (QDCRCTLD), for instance, not only returns fixed information such as controller name and controller category (local workstation controller, tape, etc.), but it also returns a list of the devices attached to the controller. Assuming you're interested in the device names, how do you know if you need space for 10 devices or 50 devices? You could just define the biggest data structure possible and hope for the best, but there is a better way.

Most of the data returned by the retrieve APIs begins with two binary fields: the number of bytes returned and the number of bytes available. The bytes-returned field contains the total number of bytes actually returned with the call to the API. The bytes-available field returns the total number of bytes that the API *could* return. For the purposes of this discussion, these fields can be referred to as *spatial requirement fields*.

You can use these spatial requirement fields to ensure that your receiver variable is always defined large enough to contain all the data being returned by the API. If you are going to use receiver variables where the amount of data returned can vary over time, you will be calling the API twice. Calling the API the first time allows you to find out how many bytes the API could return if sufficient storage was provided. You then allocate that much storage to a receiver variable and call it again with the variable that is now the correct size. As you can imagine, performing the API call twice hampers speed and performance, but it ensures that your program will continue to run even though your system environment changes drastically.

Figure 2.6 shows an example of how to use dynamically sized receiver variables. This sample program uses the Retrieve Controller Description API (QDCRCTLD) to get the list of devices attached to a controller. The API parameters and relevant formats are provided in Tables 2.3, 2.4, and 2.5, along with the pertinent parts of the QSYSINC QDCRCTLD source member in Figure 2.7, so that you can map the RPG field names to the API documentation. This program illustrates one of the methods of retrieving data; it's not a tutorial on the Retrieve Controller Description API (QDCRCTLD), so this example does not describe the API in detail.

```
DName+++++++++++ETDsFrom+++To/L+++IDc.Keywords++++++++++++++++++++++++++++++
d/copy qsysinc/qrpglesrc,qusec
d/copy qsysinc/qrpglesrc,qdcrctld

dRtvCtlD          pr                      extpgm('QDCRCTLD')
d Receiver                       1        options(*varsize)
d LengthRcv                     10i 0     const
d Format                         8        const
d CtlName                       10        const
d QUSEC                                   likeds(QUSEC)

dReceiver         ds                      likeds(QDCD020000)
d                                         based(ReceivePtr)
dDevice           ds                      likeds(QDCLAD00)
d                                         based(DevPtr)

dReceiverSize     s              10i 0 inz(8)
dCtlD             s              10     inz('CTL01')
dwait             s               1
dcount            s              10i 0


CLON01Factor1+++++++Opcode&ExtFactor2+++++++Result++++++++Len++D+HiLoEq
 /free
   QUSBPRV = 0;
   ReceivePtr = %alloc(ReceiverSize);
   RtvCtlD(Receiver :ReceiverSize :'CTLD0200' :CtlD :QUSEC);
   dow (Receiver.QDCBAVL01 > ReceiverSize);
       ReceiverSize = Receiver.QDCBAVL01;
       ReceivePtr = %realloc(ReceivePtr :ReceiverSize);
       RtvCtlD(Receiver :ReceiverSize :'CTLD0200' :CtlD :QUSEC);
   enddo;
   if (Receiver.QDCNBRAD00 > 0);
      DevPtr = ReceivePtr + Receiver.QDCOAD;
      for count = 1 to Receiver.QDCNBRAD00;
         dsply Device.QDCADN;
         DevPtr = DevPtr + Receiver.QDCLAD;
      endfor;
   endif;
   dsply 'End of devices' ' ' wait;
   dealloc ReceivePtr;
   *inlr = *on;
 /end-free
```

Figure 2.6: Using a dynamic receiver variable with QDCRCTLD.

Table 2.3: Parameters for the Retrieve Controller Description API (QDCRCTLD)

Parameter	Description	Type	Size
1	Receiver Variable	Output	Char(*)
2	Length of Receiver Variable	Input	Binary(4)
3	Format Name	Input	Char(8)
4	Controller Name	Input	Char(10)
5	Error Code	In/Out	Char(*)

Table 2.4: Fields for Format CTLD0200

Offset Dec	Field	Attribute	Size
0	Bytes Returned	Binary	4
4	Bytes Available	Binary	4
8	Number of Attached Devices	Binary	4
12	Date Information Retrieved	Char	7
19	Time Information Retrieved	Char	6
25	Controller Name	Char	10
35	Controller Category	Char	10
45	Online at IPL	Char	10
55	Text Description	Char	50
105	Reserved	Char	3
108	Offset to List of Attached Devices	Binary	4
112	Entry Length for List of Attached Devices	Binary	4

Table 2.5: Fields for a device entry of format CTLD0200

Offset Dec	Field	Attribute	Size
	Attached Device Name	Char	10
	Device Category	Char	10
	Device Type	Char	10
	Device Description	Char	50

```
DName+++++++++++ETDsFrom+++To/L+++IDc.Keywords++++++++++++++++++++++++++
D*********************************************************************
D*Type Definition for the CTLD0200 format.
D*********************************************************************
DQDCD020000          DS
D*                                              Qdc CTLD0200
D*QDCD010001                      108
D*                                              CTLD0100
D  QDCBRTN01                1     4B 0
D*                                              Bytes Returned
D  QDCBAVL01                5     8B 0
D*                                              Bytes Available
D  QDCNBRAD00               9    12B 0
D*                                              Num Attached Device
D  QDCDIR01                13    19
D*                                              Date Info Retrieved
D  QDCTIR01                20    25
D*                                              Time Info Retrieved
D  QDCCN02                 26    35
D*                                              Controller Name
D  QDCCC00                 36    45
D*                                              Controller Category
D  QDCOAIPL00              46    55
D*                                              Online At IPL
D  QDCTD01                 56   105
D*                                              Text Desc
D  QDCERVED03             106   108
D*                                              Reserved
D  QDCOAD                 109   112B 0
D*                                              Offset Attached Dev
D  QDCLAD                 113   116B 0
D*                                              Length Attached Dev
DQDCLAD00             DS
D*                                              Qdc List Attached D
D  QDCADN                   1    10
D*                                              Attached Device Nam
D  QDCDC                   11    20
D*                                              Device Category
D  QDCDT                   21    30
D*                                              Device Type
D  QDCDTD                  31    80
D*                                              Device Text Desc
```

Figure 2.7: Some of what is found in QSYSINC/QRPGLESRC member QDCRCTLD.

Similar to the QSPRJOBQ example, the program in Figure 2.6 first includes the QUSEC error code and QDCRCTLD members from QSYSINC, and then provides a prototype for QDCRCTLD. You should readily recognize the parameters being prototyped, as they are the same as for QSPRJOBQ, with the exception of changing the Qualified Job Queue Name parameter to Controller Name. The program then defines the data structure Receiver using LIKEDS(QDCD020000) from the QDCRCTLD include, and has Receiver based on ReceivePtr. The program also defines the data structure Device using QDCLAD00 from the QDCRCTLD include, and has Device based on DevPtr. This is done so that the program can use the fixed definitions provided by the API header file in QSYSINC while using the based nature of the new data structures to dynamically extend the size of the Receiver variable and easily process the array of returned Device data structures that are contained within the variable-length portion of the data returned.

Since the receiver variable is BASED, there is currently no storage allocated for the data structure. So, eight bytes are allocated for Receiver using the %ALLOC built-in. The program then calls the API using Receiver, with the Length of Receiver Variable parameter set to eight bytes. This is just enough to hold the bytes returned (Receiver.QDCBAVL01) and the bytes available (Receiver.QDCBAVL01) fields of Receiver. After the first call to the API, the Receiver.QDCBAVL01 field contains the number of bytes available to be returned if a sufficiently large receiver variable were used.

Next, this example falls into a DOW loop, checking to see if the number of bytes available (Receiver.QDCBAVL01) is greater than the size of the currently allocated receiver variable. If it is greater, more space is needed to store the results of the API, and the program reallocates Receiver to this larger value. On the first test of this DOW, ReceiverSize is eight and Receiver.QDCBAVL01 will most likely be greater than 100, so the program will reallocate to the larger size, call the API again, and repeat the DOW test. When Receiver.QDCBAVL01 is no longer greater than ReceiverSize, you know that the last API call returned all possible data to the program.

At this point, the program checks to see if any devices are attached to the controller, with this code:

```
if (Receiver.QDCNBRAD00 > 0);
```

If so, it sets the pointer DevPtr to the first device entry by taking the address of Receiver (ReceivePtr) and adding the offset to the first entry (Receiver.QDCOAD). Recall from chapter 1 that an offset value represents the number of bytes from the start of the receiver that gives you the location of the desired data and that a BASED variable (or data structure in this case) is immediately mapped to the storage addressed by the base pointer. What this all means is that the DEVICE data structure is now mapped over the first device entry returned by the Retrieve Controller Description API! Wasn't that easy? Aren't pointers and based variables wonderful things?

The program then loops through all device entries displaying the device name (Device.QDCADN) and using the length of each entry (Recevier.QDCLAD) to move from one entry to the next. When all device entries have been processed, the program waits for input from you, and ends after freeing the storage previously allocated.

You might wonder why this program uses a DOW loop to potentially call QDCRCTLD several times. While it might not seem likely, it is possible that after the first API call with an eight-byte receiver, the API would return a Receiver.QDCBAVL01 value indicating the need for enough storage for a receiver to hold 12 device entries. While the program is reallocating this storage based on the current Receiver.QDCBAVL01, suppose someone else on the system creates a new thirteenth device on the controller. You call the API the second time, and while there is now sufficient storage for 12 devices, the API indicates that to get all device names, the program now needs a slightly larger receiver. The program reallocates storage for this new Receiver.QDCBAVL01, and calls the API again. This time, no one has added a fourteenth device to the controller, so the program successfully displays all 13 devices.

Was this reallocation of storage really necessary after the second API call? It depends on what you are trying to accomplish. Some might decide that a static receiver variable of 1,000 bytes is good enough for their needs. Others might decide they will call the Retrieve API once with an eight-byte receiver variable to determine the current bytes available, allocate or reallocate a larger receiver variable based on this information, and call the API a second time to get a reasonably accurate view of the information available to be returned. Still others might decide to use this DOW approach and continue calling the API and reallocating storage until they are able to get the complete view of the API information—even when it might be changing dynamically as device objects might. In any case, with APIs, you get to decide how timely you want the information to be.

One final note on program FIG2_6: This example could have been written with a small optimization, but we felt doing so might also obscure the allocation of dynamic receiver variables—the intent of this section. The optimization would be in setting the ReceiverSize variable to a value of 12 (or greater) rather than eight. Doing so would allow the QDCRCTLD API to return the number of devices, Receiver.QDCNBRAD00, with the first call to the API. If Receiver.QDCNBRAD00 is zero, there is no need to call the API again with a reallocated Receiver parameter, as there are no device names to list.

An intermediate form of optimization would be to initially set the ReceiverSize variable to %SIZE(QDCD020000) while still performing the DOW memory allocation loop before checking Receiver.QDCNBRAD00. This approach is quite likely to only result in one call to the QDCRCTLD API if there are no attached devices, but might cause an unnecessary call to the API in future releases. This additional call might happen if IBM were to add more fixed fields to format CTLD0200 and you did not recompile program FIG2_6. The program would, in this case, be allocating Receiver based on the previous release definition of format CTLD0200, while QDCRCTLD would be indicating that more data is available, with the current release, by setting Receiver.QDCBAVL01 to the new, larger, size of format CTLD0200.

Summary

In this chapter you have seen how to use two APIs, the Retrieve Job Queue Information API (QSPRJOBQ), and the Retrieve Controller Description API (QDCRCTLD). You have learned much more than just these two APIs, however. By learning how to use static receiver variables, dynamic receiver variables, the error-code structure, offsets, and BASED structures, you have acquired the knowledge to now use over one hundred other retrieve-type APIs that are provided with i5/OS! Want to retrieve the attributes of a spool file? How about the status of a job, or the locks that a job is holding? Perhaps you're interested in whether a user profile is currently enabled or disabled. All of this, and much, much more, is now open to you.

Check Your Knowledge

Write a program to display whether a user profile named SAMPLE is enabled or disabled. To get you started, the Retrieve User Information API (QSYRUSRI) returns this information. The documentation for this API can be found using the API Finder and searching for the name QSYRUSRI, or by looking at the "Security" category of APIs and then the subcategory "Security-related APIs." Looking at the documentation, you'll see that format USRI0100 returns Status information starting at decimal position 36 (or 37, if your language is base-1, as in RPG). The values returned by the API for Status can be *ENABLED or *DISABLED. Looking at member QSYRUSRI in QSYSINC/QRPGLESRC, you can see that this Status corresponds to field QSYUS01 of data structure QSYI0100. For any error situations, the program should simply DSPLY the error message ID.

Your approach to this task should be very similar to the example in Figure 2.4. For one possible solution, see Figure D.2 in appendix D.

3

List APIs

Now that you are familiar with the fundamentals of retrieve APIs, it is time to take a look at a bit more complex type of API. A *list API* returns a list of data to your programs. Because of the variety of data that can be returned, list APIs can be somewhat unpredictable in terms of the amount of data returned. The first time you call a list API, it might return one item in a list; the next time you call the API, it might return 1,000 items. It all depends on what criteria you specify for the list and the current environment of your system.

As discussed in chapter 1, the type of output from an API depends largely on the volume of data that may be returned. Because list APIs have the potential for returning a tremendous amount of data, most of them require a user space.

List APIs follow their own standard regarding the format of the data returned in the user space. Once you understand this standard, you will be able to process any list API. Like all APIs, they return data in the form of data structures, and each data structure can contain fields that help you access other data structures.

Open-list APIs are very special APIs that don't require a user space to return data. Instead, they use a receiver variable while creating a list in the background. Open-list APIs are asynchronous, in that your program doesn't have to wait for the entire list to be built. These APIs can be blazingly fast when you want to quickly access the first few records in a list. They are examined later in this chapter, after the more ubiquitous user–space-based list APIs.

General Data Structure

The main data structure, common to all list APIs that require a user space, is referred to as the *general data structure*. The general data structure is the first structure returned by any list API, and it contains three principal components, as shown in Figure 3.1: a 64-byte user area, the size of the generic header data structure, and the generic header data structure itself.

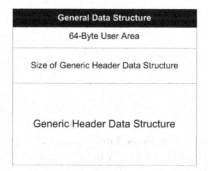

Figure 3.1: The layout of the general data structure is common to all list APIs.

Generic Header Data Structure

Depending on which API you use, there are two possible formats for the generic header data structure. Generic header format 0100 is for the original program model (OPM), while generic header format 0300 is for the Integrated Language Environment (ILE). The two formats are identical, except that the ILE version has two additional fields at the end of the generic header data structure.

Figure 3.2 shows the complete ILE version of generic header format 0300. Fields QUSEPN and QUSRSV2 differentiate the ILE format from the OPM version. The point to note here, though, is how IBM has added the ILE format to the generic header format, ensuring the backward compatibility that all AS/400 APIs share by retaining all of the previous format-0100 fields.

The new fields in the generic header format were required when ILE came along because the size of API names increased dramatically. The OPM version of the general header data structure contained a field that returned the name of the API used to put information into the user space, but this field was only 10 bytes long. In ILE, names of APIs can be up to 256 bytes. IBM could have increased the size of the field, but that would have changed the locations of all subsequent fields in the generic header. A new field could have been added to the end of the data structure, but to ensure that the new capability would not conflict with existing programs, a new structure was provided, instead. It is good to know that well-written programs will continue to run even as the system changes around them.

Generic header format 0300's code definition, shown in Figure 3.2, comes directly from the QUSGEN member of the QRPGLESRC source file in the QSYSINC library on your IBM System i. The QSYSINC library comes as a non-chargeable feature with i5/OS (option 13), but the odds are that you will need to load the feature if you have not previously used APIs.

You can use the /COPY statement to bring the IBM-supplied code definitions into your program. The /COPY statement can save you a lot of time generating programs that use a list API. The only drawback is that sometimes you end up with many field definitions that aren't pertinent to the task you are performing.

```
DName+++++++++++ETDsFrom+++To/L+++IDc.Keywords++++++++++++++++++++++++++++
D*******************************************************************
D*Type Definition for the User Space Generic Header, 300 format.
D*******************************************************************
DQUSH0300         DS
D*                                        Qus Generic Header 0300
D QUSUA00                1      64
D*                                        User Area
D QUSSGH00              65      68B 0
D*                                        Size Generic Header
D QUSSRL00              69      72
D*                                        Structure Release Level
D QUSFN00               73      80
D*                                        Format Name
D QUSAU00               81      90
D*                                        Api Used
D QUSDTC00              91     103
```

Figure 3.2: The generic header data structure comes directly from the QRPGLESRC source file in the library QSYSINC on your System i (part 1 of 2).

```
D*                                                    Date Time Created
D QUSIS00                      104    104
D*                                                    Information Status
D QUSSUS00                     105    108B 0
D*                                                    Size User Space
D QUSOIP00                     109    112B 0
D*                                                    Offset Input Parameter
D QUSSIP00                     113    116B 0
D*                                                    Size Input Parameter
D QUSOHS00                     117    120B 0
D*                                                    Offset Header Section
D QUSSHS00                     121    124B 0
D*                                                    Size Header Section
D QUSOLD00                     125    128B 0
D*                                                    Offset List Data
D QUSSLD00                     129    132B 0
D*                                                    Size List Data
D QUSNBRLE00                   133    136B 0
D*                                                    Number List Entries
D QUSSEE00                     137    140B 0
D*                                                    Size Each Entry
D QUSSIDLE00                   141    144B 0
D*                                                    CCSID List Ent
D QUSCID00                     145    146
D*                                                    Country ID
D QUSLID00                     147    149
D*                                                    Language ID
D QUSSLI00                     150    150
D*                                                    Subset List Indicator
D QUSRSV1                      151    192
D*                                                    Reserved 1
D QUSEPN                       193    448
D*                                                    Entry Point Name
D QUSRSV2                      449    576
D*                                                    Reserved 2
```

Figure 3.2: The generic header data structure comes directly from the QRPGLESRC source file in the library QSYSINC on your System i (part 2 of 2).

The main function of the generic header data structure is to provide information about the contents of the rest of the user space. Table 3.1 provides a description of each field in this structure. Obviously, you won't need to process every field, but we will later note some of the more important ones that are critical when processing a list API.

Table 3.1: Generic Header Fields		
0100 Field Name	0300 Field Name	Description
QUSUA	QUSUA00	The user area. Put anything you want in this area; you can use it as a scratch pad.
QUSSGH	QUSSGH00	The size of the generic header information that follows, not including the 64-byte user area (QUSUA).
QUSSRL	QUSSERL00	The structure's release level, which contains a code indicating one of two different generic header data-structure layouts. Code 0100 indicates a *PGM API layout. Code 0300 indicates an ILE *SRVPGM layout. Note that this refers to the type of API you called, not the type of program you are using.
QUSFN	QUSFN00	The format name.
QUSAU	QUSAU00	The name of the API used to put information into the user space. If it is an ILE-type API, this field is reserved, and the API-used information can be retrieved from QUSENP.
QUSDTC	QUSDTC00	The date and time when the user space was created, in the format *CYYMMDDhhmmss.*
QUSIS	QUSIS00	The information status, which is a code describing the accuracy of the data in the user space. The possible codes are as follows: • C—Complete and accurate. • I—Incomplete. • P—Partial but accurate.
QUSSUS	QUSSUS00	The combined size of the user area, generic header, input parameter section, and list data section in bytes.
QUSOIP	QUSOIP00	An offset to the input parameter data structure. (This data structure is discussed later in this chapter.)
QUSSIP	QUSSIP00	The size of the input parameter section that QUSOIP/QUSOIP00 points to.
QUSOHS	QUSOHS00	An offset to the header section data structure (discussed later in this chapter).
QUSSHS	QUSSHS00	The size of the header section data structure that QUSOHS/QUSOHS00 points to.
QUSOLD	QUSOLD00	An offset to the list data structure (discussed later in this chapter).

Table 3.1: Generic Header Fields (continued)		
0100 Field Name	0300 Field Name	Description
QUSSLD	QUSSLD00	The size of the list data structure that QUSOLD/QUSOLD00 points to.
QUSNBRLE	QUSNBRLE00	The number of entries in the list.
QUSSEE	QUSSEE00	The size of each fixed-length entry in the list. This will be zero for variable-length list entries, where each list entry identifies how to access the next list entry.
QUSSIDLE	QUSSIDLE00	The CCSID for character data returned in a list entry.
QUSCID	QUSCID00	The country ID.
QUSLID	QUSLID00	The language ID.
QUSSLI	QUSSLI00	The subset list indicator.
QUSERVED00	QUSRSVI	Reserved.
	QUSEPN	The API entry point name.
	QUSRSV2	Reserved.

Several offset fields in the generic header are used to access the data that interests you. As a review of chapter 1, an offset is simply the number of bytes from a central reference point that tells you where to get something (generally a field or data structure). By convention, *offset* is in reference to the beginning of the object in question. For list APIs, this would be the beginning of the user space. Whenever an API returns an offset to data and you want to access that data, *always use the provided offset*, even if it looks like the API always returns data to the same location in the user space. New releases of i5/OS may change the location of the returned data, and using the provided offset value to access the data will ensure that your application continues to run in these future releases.

Three fields represent the heart of list APIs:

- QUSOLD/QUSOLD00 — The offset to the list data
- QUSNBRLE/QUSNBRLE00 — The number of list entries
- QUSSEE/QUSSEE00 — The size of each entry

Most list APIs are called as *PGMs rather than *SRVPGM functions, so we will use the *PGM API 0100 field names for the remainder of this chapter rather than providing both names in the text. The concepts behind how to work with list APIs are the same whether the list is created by a *PGM- or *SRVPGM-based API.

The offset to list entries (QUSOLD) tells you where the first entry in the list begins. The number of entries in the list (QUSNBRLE) tells you how many entries you can process. Note that it is not considered an error for the number of list entries (QUSNBRLE) to be zero; it simply indicates an empty list based on your selection criteria. The size of each entry (QUSSEE) tells you how large each entry is, so that you can access the next entry in the list. Essentially, you get to the first entry using QUSOLD, fall into a DO or FOR loop to process QUSNBRLE entries, and step through each entry using QUSSEE. This process is shown in Figure 3.3.A.

```
h dftactgrp(*no) bnddir('APILIB')

DName++++++++++++ETDsFrom+++To/L+++IDc.Keywords+++++++++++++++++++++++++
d/copy qsysinc/qrpglesrc,qusgen

dCrtUsrSpc          pr                  *      extproc('CrtUsrSpc')
d SpcName                             20       const

dGenHdr             ds                         likeds(QUSH0100)
d                                              based(GenHdrPtr)

dSpcName            ds
d SName                               10       inz('TESTSPACE')
d SLib                                10       inz('QTEMP')

dListEntryPtr       s                   *
dCount              s                 10i 0

CLON01Factor1+++++++Opcode&ExtFactor2+++++++Result+++++++++Len++D+HiLoEq
 /free

    // Create user space and get a pointer to the start of the space
    GenHdrPtr = CrtUsrSpc( SpcName);

    // Call the List API

    // Since the generic header begins at the start of the space,
    // GenHdrPtr and the BASED GenHdr data structure now give us
    // access to the contents of the generic header
```

Figure 3.3.A: The processing of a list API makes use of information from the general data structure: accessing list entries (part 1 of 2).

```
    // Assume ListEntryPtr is a pointer used to BASE the start of
    // an individual list entry.  Set ListEntryPtr to the first entry

    ListEntryPtr =  GenHdrPtr + GenHdr.QUSOLD;

    // process all entries
    for Count = 1 to GenHdr.QUSNBRLE;
        // process the current list entry
        // and then go to next entry in list
        ListEntryPtr += GenHdr.QUSSEE;
    endfor;

    // exit when the list has been processed
    *inlr = *on;
    return;

/end-free
```

Figure 3.3.A: The processing of a list API makes use of information from the general data structure: accessing list entries (part 2 of 2).

While the FOR loop process adequately describes the heart of the program, there are a few other pieces of the generic header data structure that should be used to ensure your program works right every time.

The information status field (QUSIS) gives a small but important piece of information regarding the results of the call to the API. This small bit of information is a status code that indicates whether the API correctly returned everything you asked for. If the API performed as requested, the code will be *C* (complete). If it did not, the code will be *I* (incomplete). If the API returned the correct information, but it could not all fit in the user space, the code will be *P* (partial but accurate).

You need to test this status field after the call to the API. If it's *C*, everything is fine. Process the user space information. If the return code is *I*, send an error message and get out. If the return code is *P* (and the API makes use of continuation handles), you need to process the user space information, and then call the API again to get more of the information loaded. When you call it a second time, pass a continuation handle as a parameter. This continuation handle is retrieved from the unique header section of the API, which will be discussed shortly. Then repeat the processing loop. An example of using a continuation handle with the List Save File API, QSRLSAVF, can be found in chapter 16. If the API doesn't use continuation handles, you need to call the API and request less information, so that all results can fit into the user space. Alternatively, you could use an open-list equivalent to the list API, if one is available. Open-list APIs can return much more information than list APIs.

This check of the information status field is shown in Figure 3.3.B.

```
h dftactgrp(*no) bnddir('APILIB')

DName+++++++++++ETDsFrom+++To/L+++IDc.Keywords++++++++++++++++++++++++
d/copy qsysinc/qrpglesrc,qusgen

dCrtUsrSpc              pr              *    extproc('CrtUsrSpc')
d SpcName                              20    const

dGenHdr                 ds                   likeds(QUSH0100)
d                                            based(GenHdrPtr)

dSpcName                ds
d SName                                10    inz('TESTSPACE')
d SLib                                 10    inz('QTEMP')

dListEntryPtr           s               *
dCount                  s              10i 0

CLON01Factor1+++++++Opcode&ExtFactor2+++++++Result++++++++Len++D+HiLoEq
 /free

    // Create user space and get a pointer to the start of the space
    GenHdrPtr = CrtUsrSpc( SpcName);

    // Call the List API
    // Since the generic header begins at the start of the space,
    // GenHdrPtr and the BASED GenHdr data structure now give us
    // access to the contents of the generic header

    // Check on the status of the returned list
    if (GenHdr.QUSIS = 'C') or (GenHdr.QUSIS = 'P');

        // Assume ListEntryPtr is a pointer used to BASE the start of
        // an individual list entry.  Set ListEntryPtr to the first entry
        ListEntryPtr =  GenHdrPtr + GenHdr.QUSOLD;

        // process all entries
        for Count = 1 to GenHdr.QUSNBRLE;
            // process the current list entry
```

Figure 3.3.B: The processing of a list API makes use of information from the general data structure: checking the status (part 1 of 2).

```
            // and then go to next entry in list
            ListEntryPtr += GenHdr.QUSSEE;
        endfor;

    // List status is not Complete or Partial
    else;
        // Report an error
    endif;

    // exit when the list has been processed
    *inlr = *on;
    return;

/end-free
```

Figure 3.3.B: The processing of a list API makes use of information from the general data structure: checking the status (part 2 of 2).

Because list APIs can potentially return thousands of list entries, our example programs that use list APIs are written so that you can exit from the list processing once you have verified the results of the program. After the list has been generated, the sample programs DSPLY how many list entries were returned, along with an indication of whether the list was complete or partial. Following this, the example programs DSPLY the first list entry and wait for input from you. If you simply press Enter, the program DSPLYs the next entry in the list. If you type any character and then press Enter, the program stops processing the list and ends. This ability to exit the list processing is available to you after each list entry DSPLY.

The processing for this support is shown in Figure 3.3.C. This processing is not typical of list processing in a production environment. Generally, your applications will want to process the entire list that is returned by an API. The example programs take this approach because it can become quite tedious watching a DSPLY of 5,000 list entries when just one or two would be sufficient to make a point.

```
h dftactgrp(*no) bnddir('APILIB')

DName+++++++++++ETDsFrom+++To/L+++IDc.Keywords++++++++++++++++++++++
d/copy qsysinc/qrpglesrc,qusgen
```

Figure 3.3.C: Making the examples a bit less tedious to use (part 1 of 3).

```
dCrtUsrSpc        pr                  *     extproc('CrtUsrSpc')
d SpcName                            20     const

dGenHdr           ds                        likeds(QUSH0100)
d                                           based(GenHdrPtr)

dSpcName          ds
d SName                              10     inz('TESTSPACE')
d SLib                               10     inz('QTEMP')
dCurrentEntry     s                  20     based(ListEntryPtr)
dListEntryPtr     s                   *
dCount            s                  10i 0
dWait             s                   1

CLON01Factor1+++++++Opcode&ExtFactor2+++++++Result++++++++Len++D+HiLoEq
 /free

    // Create user space and get a pointer to the start of the space
    GenHdrPtr = CrtUsrSpc( SpcName);

    // Call the List API

    // Since the generic header begins at the start of the space,
    // GenHdrPtr and the BASED GenHdr data structure now give us
    // access to the contents of the generic header


    // Check on the status of the returned list
    if (GenHdr.QUSIS = 'C') or (GenHdr.QUSIS = 'P');

        // Show how many entries were found
        if (GenHdr.QUSIS = 'C');
            dsply ('Complete list of ' + %char(GenHdr.QUSNBRLE) +
                    ' entries.');
        endif;
        if (GenHdr.QUSIS = 'P');
            dsply ('Partial list of ' + %char(GenHdr.QUSNBRLE) +
                    ' entries.');
        endif;

    // Assume ListEntryPtr is a pointer used to BASE the start of
    // an individual list entry.  Set ListEntryPtr to the first entry
        ListEntryPtr =  GenHdrPtr + GenHdr.QUSOLD;

        // process all entries
        for Count = 1 to GenHdr.QUSNBRLE;
            // process the current list entry

            // display the current entry and wait for input
```

Figure 3.3.C: Making the examples a bit less tedious to use (part 2 of 3).

```
            // if character entered, leave the list
            dsply CurrentEntry ' ' Wait;
            if Wait <> ' ';
                leave;
            endif;

            // if no character entered, go to next entry in the list
            ListEntryPtr += GenHdr.QUSSEE;
        endfor;

    // List status is not Complete or Partial
    else;
        // Report an error
    endif;

    // exit when the list has been processed
    Wait = *blanks;
    dsply 'End of List' ' ' Wait;
    *inlr = *on;
    return;

/end-free
```

Figure 3.3.C: Making the examples a bit less tedious to use (part 3 of 3).

With the preceding figures for background, Figure 3.3.D shows a complete example of how to process the results of a list API. In this example, the List Objects API, QUSLOBJ, is being used to get a list of all objects in the current jobs *CURLIB. For now, don't be too concerned with the specifics of calling this API. You will learn more about it later in this chapter. We simply want to demonstrate here how to process the results of a list API. The program FIG3_3_D DSPLYs the type of object, the library, and the name of each object found in *CURLIB.

```
h dftactgrp(*no) bnddir('APILIB')

DName+++++++++++ETDsFrom+++To/L+++IDc.Keywords++++++++++++++++++++++++
d/copy qsysinc/qrpglesrc,qusgen
d/copy qsysinc/qrpglesrc,quslobj

dCrtUsrSpc        pr              *     extproc('CrtUsrSpc')
d SpcName                        20     const
```

Figure 3.3.D: The processing of a list API makes use of information from the general data structure, bringing it all together (part 1 of 3).

```
dListObj            pr                          extpgm('QUSLOBJ')
d SpcName                           20          const
d Format                             8          const
d ObjLibName                        20          const
d ObjTyp                            10          const

dGenHdr             ds                          likeds(QUSH0100)
d                                               based(GenHdrPtr)

dListEntry          ds                          likeds(QUSL010003)
d                                               based(ListEntryPtr)
dSpcName            ds
d SName                             10          inz('TESTSPACE')
d SLib                              10          inz('QTEMP')

dObjLibName         ds
d ObjName                           10          inz('*ALL')
d LibName                           10          inz('*CURLIB')

dListEntryPtr       s                   *
dCount              s               10i 0
dWait               s                1
CLON01Factor1+++++++Opcode&ExtFactor2+++++++Result++++++++Len++D+HiLoEq
/free

  // Create user space and get a pointer to the start of the space
  GenHdrPtr = CrtUsrSpc( SpcName);

  // Call the List API
  ListObj( SpcName :'OBJL0100' :ObjLibName :'*ALL');

  // Check on the status of the returned list
  if (GenHdr.QUSIS = 'C') or (GenHdr.QUSIS = 'P');

    // Show how many entries were found
    if (GenHdr.QUSIS = 'C');
       dsply ('Complete list of ' + %char(GenHdr.QUSNBRLE) +
             ' entries.');
    endif;
    if (GenHdr.QUSIS = 'P');
       dsply ('Partial list of ' + %char(GenHdr.QUSNBRLE) +
             ' entries.');
    endif;

    // Assume ListEntryPtr is a pointer used to BASE the start of
    // an individual list entry.  Set ListEntryPtr to the first entry

    ListEntryPtr =  GenHdrPtr + GenHdr.QUSOLD;
```

Figure 3.3.D: The processing of a list API makes use of information from the general data structure, bringing it all together (part 2 of 3).

```
     // process all entries
     for Count = 1 to GenHdr.QUSNBRLE;
         // process the current list entry

         // display the current entry and wait for input
         // if character entered, leave the list
         dsply (%trimr(ListEntry.QUSOBJTU) + ' ' +
                %trim(ListEntry.QUSOLNU) + '/' +
                %trim(ListEntry.QUSOBJNU) + ' found.') ' ' Wait;
         if Wait <> ' ';
             leave;
         endif;

         // if no character entered, go to next entry in the list
         ListEntryPtr += GenHdr.QUSSEE;
     endfor;

 // List status is not Complete or Partial
 else;
     // Report an error
 endif;

 // exit when the list has been processed
 Wait = *blanks;
 dsply 'End of List' ' ' Wait;
 *inlr = *on;
 return;

/end-free
```

Figure 3.3.D: The processing of a list API makes use of information from the general data structure, bringing it all together (part 3 of 3).

The generic header data structure is common to all list APIs that require a user space. However, every API also has its own *header section* data structure, unique to that API. Be sure not to confuse the two structures.

Header Section

The unique header section is located by using the QUSOHS/QUSOHS00 field found in the generic header section. The field definition for QUSOHS is shown in Figure 3.2 and defined in Table 3.1. The header section may contain feedback information about the input parameters to the API. If a parameter accepted special values such as *LIBL or *CURRENT, this section will return what each special value resolved to when the API ran.

For instance, one of the parameters of the List Fields API (QUSLFLD) is the qualified name of the file from which you want to retrieve information. The library portion of the qualified name accepts *LIBL, which tells the API to search the job's library list until it finds a library that contains the file. When this happens, the header section will contain the name of the library in which the API found the file.

Input Parameter Section

Another useful data structure that the generic header data structure points to is the *input parameter* section. This data structure is located via the QUSOIP offset field. This section contains the parameters that you passed to the API when you called it. This information can be useful, as a user space might be created into a shared library such as QGPL (as opposed to QTEMP) and exist for an extended period of time. If this list were to be accessed by another job in the future, this input parameter section could be used to determine the contents of the user space.

The input parameter section can also contain a copy of the continuation handle value that you passed as a parameter when you called the API.

List Data Section

The *list data* section is at the heart of every list API. It is the information you are looking for when you run the API in the first place. It is located by using the offset found in the QUSOLD field of the generic header section.

The format of the information in the list data section varies from API to API. Even within an API, the format can vary depending on the amount and type of information you request. You control the format of this data with a format name parameter of the API.

The number of entries in the list is contained in the QUSNBRLE field in the generic header data structure. The size of each entry is usually contained in the QUSSEE field. However, some of the more complicated list APIs might return lists where each entry is of a different size. In these cases, the QUSNBRLE field will be zero, and the length of the entry can be found in a field within each list entry of the returned data. An example of processing a list containing variable-length entries is shown later in this chapter, in Figure 3.12.

This all sounds complicated, and it is, but looking at some examples will help you better understand the concepts. Therefore, it's time to introduce an application program. The first version of this program involves a user space accessed via pointers. The second version uses the Retrieve User Space API (QUSRTVUS) to get the list information from the user space. (You might recall that these two approaches were briefly discussed in chapter 1.) The differences in the two techniques will become readily apparent as you review these examples.

Program to Find Files with Deleted Records

Every well-written application must be designed to clean up after itself. The odds are that files used within any application will eventually contain some deleted records. Even though they are no longer used by the application, deleted records take up disk space. Therefore, they should be purged from the file. This is generally done using the Reorganize Physical File command (RGZPFM), but "reorganizing" a file can take some time, depending on the number of records in the file. Realistically, you wouldn't want to reorganize every file in the library; you only want to reorganize files containing a given percentage of deleted records.

Figure 3.4 shows a program that looks at all physical files in a particular library and provides a DSPLY listing of files that exceed a certain percentage of deleted records. The percentage is variable, passed into the program as a parameter. As you will see later in this book, this program could also automatically reorganize the files for you by calling an API to run CL commands like RGZPFM. For now, the emphasis is on how to use a list API, not how to build a complete application. Chapter 4, which deals with command-processing APIs, will supplement this example by using the RGZPFM command from an application program.

The program in Figure 3.4 uses five different APIs to accomplish its purpose. Understanding and using this many APIs in a single program is not as hard as it might seem at first. Three of the APIs (QUSCRTUS, QUSCUSAT, and QUSPTRUS) are covered in chapter 1; they simply create and return a pointer to an extendable user space that the List Objects API (QUSLOBJ) can use. These three APIs are all contained in the CrtUsrSpc procedure created in chapter 1. (See the section "A Handy User-Space Procedure" in that chapter for more details.) The two APIs we will look at in more detail in this chapter are List Objects (QUSLOBJ) and Retrieve Member Description (QUSRMBRD). The data structure definitions for these APIs are copied from member QUSLOBJ of QSYSINC/ QRPGLESRC for the List Objects API and from member QUSRMBRD of QSYSINC/ QRPGLESRC for the Retrieve Member Description API.

The program is prototyped to accept two parameters. The first is the name of the library to be searched for files, and the second is the percentage of records within a file that need to be deleted before the program should notify you. The program starts with some general housecleaning, by setting the API error-code structure to 16, so that exceptions are not sent back to the user. The program then calls the CrtUsrSpc procedure to create the user space and retrieve a pointer to it.

At this point, we're ready to get our first list. The program calls the List Objects API (QUSLOBJ) asking for the information related to format OBJL0200, which populates the user space with a list of all files in the requested library. Table 3.2 lists all of the parameter details of this API. Figure 3.5 lists the fields that are returned with format OBJL0200 of QUSLOBJ. The documentation for this API can be found in the Information Center under "Programming," "APIs," "APIs by category," "Object," and "Object-related APIs."

```
h dftactgrp(*no) bnddir('APILIB')

DName+++++++++++ETDsFrom+++To/L+++IDc.Keywords+++++++++++++++++++++++
dFig3_4           pr                extpgm('FIG3_4')
d LibName                    10     const
d DltPct                     15  5  const

dFig3_4           pi
d LibName                    10     const
d DltPct                     15  5  const

d/copy qsysinc/qrpglesrc,qusgen
d/copy qsysinc/qrpglesrc,quslobj
d/copy qsysinc/qrpglesrc,qusrmbrd
d/copy qsysinc/qrpglesrc,qusec

dCrtUsrSpc        pr              * extproc('CrtUsrSpc')
d SpcName                    20     const

dListObj          pr                extpgm('QUSLOBJ')
d SpcName                    20     const
d Format                      8     const
d ObjLibName                 20     const
d ObjTyp                     10     const
d QUSEC                             likeds(QUSEC) options(*nopass)
d AutCtl                   65535    const options(*nopass :*varsize)
d SltCtl                   65535    const options(*nopass :*varsize)
d ASPCtl                   65535    const options(*nopass :*varsize)
```

Figure 3.4: List files with deleted records using the QUSPTRUS API (part 1 of 4).

```
dRtvMbrD              pr                    extpgm('QUSRMBRD')
d Receiver                          1       options(*varsize)
d LengthRcv                         10 i 0  const
d Format                            8       const
d QualFileName                      20      const
d MbrName                           10      const
d OvrPrc                            1       const
d QUSEC                                     likeds(QUSEC) options(*nopass)
d FndPrc                            1       const options(*nopass)

d* list API generic header
dGenHdr               ds                    likeds(QUSH0100)
d                                           based(GenHdrPtr)

d* List Object API (QUSLOBJ) format OBJL0200
dListEntry            ds                    likeds(QUSL020002)
d                                           based(LstPtr)

dSpcName              ds
d SName                             10      inz('OBJLIST')
d SLib                              10      inz('QTEMP')

dObjLibName           ds
d                                   10      inz('*ALL')
d ObjLib                            10

dQualFileName         ds
d FileName                          10
d FileLibName                       10

dCount                s             10 i 0
dWait                 s             1

CLON01Factor1+++++++Opcode&ExtFactor2+++++++Result++++++++Len++D+HiLoEq
 /free

    // set ErrCde bytes provided to 16 to avoid exceptions
    QUSBPRV = %size(QUSEC);

    // create the user space for the list of files
    GenHdrPtr = CrtUsrSpc(SpcName);

    // get the list of files
    ObjLib = LibName;
    ListObj( SpcName :'OBJL0200' : ObjLibName :'*FILE' :QUSEC);

    // check if API call failed
    if (QUSBAVL > 0);
        dsply ('List Objects failed with ' + QUSEI) ' ' wait;
```

Figure 3.4: List files with deleted records using the *QUSPTRUS* API (part 2 of 4).

```
      *inlr = *on;
      return;
endif;

// check to see if the list is complete
if (GenHdr.QUSIS = 'C') or (GenHdr.QUSIS = 'P');
    if (GenHdr.QUSIS = 'C');
        dsply ('Complete list of ' + %char(GenHdr.QUSNBRLE) +
                ' entries.');
    endif;
    if (GenHdr.QUSIS = 'P');
        dsply ('Partial list of ' + %char(GenHdr.QUSNBRLE) +
                ' entries.');
    endif;

    // get to the first list entry and process the list
    LstPtr = GenHdrPtr + GenHdr.QUSOLD;
    for Count = 1 to GenHdr.QUSNBRLE;

        // check to see if information was available
        if (ListEntry.QUSIS01 <> ' ');
            dsply ('Error with ' + %trimr(ListEntry.QUSOBJTU00) +
                    ' ' + ListEntry.QUSOBJNU00);

        else;
            // check to see if this is a physical file
            if (ListEntry.QUSEOA = 'PF');
            // retrieve member description for number deleted rcds
            FileName = ListEntry.QUSOBJNU00;
            FileLibName = ListEntry.QUSOLNU00;
            RtvMbrD( QUSM0200 :%size(QUSM0200) :'MBRD0200'
                    :QualFileName :'*FIRST' :'0' :QUSEC);
            // check for API failure
            if (QUSBAVL > 0);
                // check if no member
                if (QUSEI = 'CPF3C26'); // no error, just skip
                else;
                    dsply (%trimr(ListEntry.QUSOBJNU00) +
                            ' failed with ' + QUSEI);
                endif;
            else;
                // check for records and percentage deleted while
                // avoiding divide by 0
                if ((QUSNCRU > 0) or (QUSNDRU > 0));
                if ((QUSNDRU/(QUSNDRU+QUSNCRU) * 100) > DltPct);
                    dsply ('File ' + %trimr(FileName) + ' has ' +
                            %char(QUSNDRU) + ' deleted records');
                endif;
```

Figure 3.4: List files with deleted records using the QUSPTRUS API (part 3 of 4).

```
              endif;
            endif;
          endif;
        endif;
        LstPtr = LstPtr + GenHdr.QUSSEE;
      endfor;
    else;
    dsply 'List Object API did not return valid data';
    endif;
    dsply 'End of List' ' ' Wait;
    *inlr = *on;
    Return;

/end-free
```

Figure 3.4: List files with deleted records using the QUSPTRUS API (part 4 of 4).

Table 3.2: Parameter Description of the List Objects API (QUSLOBJ)				
Parameter	Description		Type	Size
1	The user space name/library. The first 10 bytes are the name, and the second 10 are the library. The library-name special values of *LIBL and *CURLIB are supported.		Input	Char(20)
2	The list format name, as follows:		Input	Char(8)
	Format Name	Description		
	OBJL0100	Object name.		
	OBJL0200	Text and extended attribute.		
	OBJL0300	Basic object information.		
	OBJL0400	Creation information.		
	OBJL0500	Save and restore information.		
	OBJL0600	Usage information.		
	OBJL0700	All object information.		
3	The object and library name of objects to list. The first 10 bytes are the object name, and the second 10 bytes are the library name. The object can be a name, a generic name, or one of the special values *ALL, *ALLUSR, and *IBM. The library can be a name or one of the special values *ALL, *ALLUSR, *CURLIB, *LIBL, or *USRLIBL.		Input	Char(20)

Table 3.2: Parameter Description of the List Objects API (QUSLOBJ) (continued)			
Parameter	Description	Type	Size
4	The type of object to list. The API accepts a valid type or the special value *ALL.	Input	Char(10)
Optional Parameter Group 1			
5	The standard error data structure.	I/O	Char(*)
Optional Parameter Group 2			
6	The authority control.	Input	Char(*)
7	The selection control.	Input	Char(*)
Optional Parameter Group 3			
8	The Auxiliary Storage Pool (ASP) control.	Input	Char(*)

```
DName++++++++++ETDsFrom+++To/L+++IDc.Keywords+++++++++++++++++++++++++++
D*********************************************************************
D*Type Definition for the OBJL0200 format.
D*********************************************************************
DQUSL020002       DS
D*                                          Qus OBJL0200
D QUSOBJNU00          1     10
D*                                          Object Name Used
D QUSOLNU00          11     20
D*                                          Object Lib Name Used
D QUSOBJTU00         21     30
D*                                          Object Type Used
D QUSIS01            31     31
D*                                          Information Status
D QUSEOA             32     41
D*                                          Extended Obj Attr
D QUSTD06            42     91
D*                                          Text Description
D QUSUDA             92    101
D*                                          User Defined Attr
D QUSERVED22        102    108
D*                                          Reserved
```

Figure 3.5: The contents of the List Objects API (QUSLOBJ) format OBJL0200.

The key pieces of information we are interested in, within format OBJL0200, are fields QUSOBJNU00 (the name of the object), QUSOLNU00 (the library where the object is located), QUSISO1 (the status of the information returned for the object), and QUSEOA (the extended attribute associated with the object).

The information status field, QUSISO1, indicates whether or not the QUSLOBJ API could return the object-related information. If this field is set to a blank, then all information for the object was returned. Information on other possible status values can be found in the Information Center.

The extended attribute field, QUSEOA, tells us what specific type of object we are working with. For instance, a *FILE object might have extended attributes such as PF for physical file, LF for logical file, and DSPF for display file.

Table 3.3 lists all of the parameters of the Retrieve Member Description API (QUSRMBRD), and Figure 3.6 lists the contents of format MBRD0200. This format gives you the number of records in the file, in field QUSNCRU. The number of deleted records is returned in field QUSNDRU. With this, the program can calculate the percentage of deleted records and DSPLY the file only if it is greater than the parameter value passed in the second parameter. For complete documentation on QUSRMBRD, see the Information Center under "Programming," "APIs," "APIs by category," "Database and File," and "File APIs."

Table 3.3: Retrieve Member Description, QUSRMBRD			
Parameter	Description	Type	Size
1	The receiver variable.	Output	Char(*)
2	The length of the receiver variable provided in parameter 1.	Input	Binary(4)
3	The format name, as follows:	Input	Char(8)
	<table><tr><td>Name</td><td>Description</td></tr><tr><td>MBRD0100</td><td>The member name and basic source information.</td></tr><tr><td>MBRD0200</td><td>The member name with expanded information.</td></tr><tr><td>MBRD0300</td><td>The member name with full information.</td></tr><tr><td>MBRD0400</td><td>Data space index information for a physical file member.</td></tr><tr><td>MBRD0500</td><td>Data space materialized query table information for a physical file member.</td></tr></table>		

Table 3.3: Retrieve Member Description, QUSRMBRD (continued)

Parameter	Description	Type	Size
4	The file and library name. The first 10 bytes are the name, and the second 10 are the library. Library name special values of *LIBL and *CURLIB are supported.	Input	Char(20)
5	The member name within the file. The special values *FIRST and *LAST are supported.	Input	Char(10)
6	Override, which determines whether to process overrides to find the file to retrieve information from. Zero means no; one means yes.	Input	Char(1)
Optional Parameter Group 1			
7	The error code data structure.	I/O	Char(*)
Optional Parameter Group 2			
8	Find member processing, which specifies how to search for a member. The default, zero, means find the file and then the member. One means find the member name directly. This is a faster method if the member name is known but the library is specified as *LIBL.	Input	Char(1)

```
DName++++++++++ETDsFrom+++To/L+++IDc.Keywords+++++++++++++++++++++++++++
D*********************************************************************
D*Record structure for QUSRMBRD MBRD0200 format
D*********************************************************************
DQUSM0200         DS                             Qdb Mbrd0200
D*
D QUSBRTN03              1      4B 0
D*                                              Bytes Returned
D QUSBAVL04              5      8B 0
D*                                              Bytes Available
D QUSDFILN00             9     18
D*                                              Db File Name
D QUSDFILL00            19     28
D*                                              Db File Lib
D QUSMN03               29     38
D*                                              Member Name
D QUSFILA01             39     48
D*                                              File Attr
D QUSST01               49     58
```

Figure 3.6: The contents of the Retrieve Member Description API (QUSRMBRD) format MBRD0200 (part 1 of 3).

```
D*                                                Src Type
D QUSCD03                    59      71
D*                                                Crt Date
D QUSSCD                     72      84
D*                                                Src Change Date
D QUSTD04                    85     134
D*                                                Text Desc
D QUSSFIL01                 135     135
D*                                                Src File
D QUSEFIL                   136     136
D*                                                Ext File
D QUSLFIL                   137     137
D*                                                Log File
D QUSOS                     138     138
D*                                                Odp Share
D QUSERVED12                139     140
D*                                                Reserved
D QUSNBRCR                  141     144B 0
D*                                                Num Cur Rec
D QUSNBRDR                  145     148B 0
D*                                                Num Dlt Rec
D QUSDSS                    149     152B 0
D*                                                Dat Spc Size
D QUSAPS                    153     156B 0
D*                                                Acc Pth Size
D QUSNBRDM                  157     160B 0
D*                                                Num Dat Mbr
D QUSCD04                   161     173
D*                                                Change Date
D QUSSD                     174     186
D*                                                Save Date
D QUSRD                     187     199
D*                                                Rest Date
D QUSED                     200     212
D*                                                Exp Date
D QUSNDU                    213     216B 0
D*                                                Nbr Days Used
D QUSDLU                    217     223
D*                                                Date Lst Used
D QUSURD                    224     230
D*                                                Use Reset Date
D QUSRSV101                 231     232
D*                                                Reserved1
D QUSDSSM                   233     236B 0
D*                                                Data Spc Sz Mlt
```

Figure 3.6: The contents of the Retrieve Member Description API (QUSRMBRD) format MBRD0200 (part 2 of 3).

```
D QUSAPSM                   237    240B 0
D*                                                Acc Pth Sz Mlt
D QUSMTC                    241    244B 0
D*                                                Member Text Ccsid
D QUSOAI                    245    248B 0
D*                                                Offset Add Info
D QUSLAI                    249    252B 0
D*                                                Length Add Info
D QUSNCRU                   253    256U 0
D*                                                Num Cur Rec U
D QUSNDRU                   257    260U 0
D*                                                Num Dlt Rec U
D QUSRSV203                 261    266
D*                                                Reserved2
```

Figure 3.6: The contents of the Retrieve Member Description API (QUSRMBRD) format MBRD0200 (part 3 of 3).

Let's look at the processing of FIG3_4 in detail. When FIG3_4 uses the CrtUsrSpc procedure, a pointer to the start of the created user space is returned. This pointer value is assigned to the pointer variable GenHdrPtr. This pointer is used to BASE the GenHdr data structure, which is defined LIKEDS the generic header (QUSH0100) common to all list APIs. The pointer addresses the start of the user space that was used when calling QUSLOBJ, and the generic header is located at the start of the user space, so the program already has direct access to the data in the generic header! Before using this information, though, the program needs to see if any error was found on the call to the QUSLOBJ API. To do this, it checks the Bytes Available field (QUSBAVL) of the Error Code parameter used when calling QUSLOBJ. If QUSBAVL is not zero, the program DSPLYs an error message that provides the error message ID (QUSEI), and then ends. If no error was found on the API call, it checks the Information Status field (QUSIS) of the generic header to see if there were any errors in returning information from the API.

If the API returned all files (QUSIS = 'C') or a partial list of files (QUSIS = 'P'), then the program can use the offset to the List Data field (QUSOLD) in the general data structure to get to the first entry in the list. It does this by adding QUSOLD to GenHdrPtr to get a pointer value for LstPtr. LstPtr is used to BASE the ListEntry data structure, which is defined LIKEDS format OBJL0200 (QUSL020002) of the QUSLOBJ API. The program now has direct access to the first list entry (in this case, the first file found in the specified library) through the data structure ListEntry.

QUSNBRLE (the number of entries returned) is used as the basis for the FOR loop that processes each OBJL0200 entry in the list. However, you don't want to reorganize every file in the library; you only want to reorganize files that have a particular percentage of deleted records. The List Object API doesn't return the number of deleted records and the number of current records, but the Retrieve Member Description API (QUSRMBRD) does.

As ListEntry is positioned over the first returned entry, the program examines the status of the file information returned. If a problem was found in returning the file information (QUSISO1 is not blank), the program will DSPLY that an error was found, and go on to the next list entry. Exactly how it moves to the next list entry will be covered shortly. If an error was not found, it checks to see if this is a physical file. This is done by examining the Extended Object Attribute field (QUSEOA) for a value of "PF." (Though we didn't mention it earlier, we used format OBJL0200 when calling QUSLOBJ because this format is the fastest to access while still returning the extended object attribute.) If the file is a physical file, the program calls the Retrieve Member Description API (QUSRMBRD) to get more information about the file. Note that we are making a simplifying assumption in calling QUSRMBRD—namely, that there is only one member in each file. In a production environment, you would most likely want to find all members that exist in the file, and call QUSRMBRD for each member. How would you do this? As you might expect, the answer is to use an API—in this case, the List Database File Members API (QUSLMBR). In chapter 7 (which deals with database APIs), you will see QUSLMBR used to supplement the current example.

As the program did after calling QUSLOBJ, the first thing it needs to do is determine if an error was found in the call to QUSRMBRD. It checks to see if QUSBAVL has a value greater than zero, and if so, it does some additional error-handling. From looking at the documentation in the Information Center on QUSRMBRD, you can see (at the bottom of the documentation) that several errors might be returned. One is CPF3C26, no members found in the file. The program checks for this particular error message ID (QUSEI), and if that is the problem, it simply moves to the next file, as the file clearly doesn't need to be reorganized if it has no members!. If any other error message is returned, the program DSPLYs the name of the file and the error that was returned, and again moves to the next list entry, or file. If no error is found, the program determines the percentage of deleted records in the file. If it is greater than the specified percentage, the program DSPLYs the name of the file, the number of deleted records in the file, and again moves to the next file.

Now we're ready to talk about just how the program moves on to the next file. The answer is quite simple. The generic header includes the size of each entry (QUSSEE), which is simply added to the current value of LstPtr. This causes the ListEntry data structure (which is BASED on LstPtr) to now automatically address the next file. The program simply returns to the start of the FOR loop. When all of the entries have been processed (the program has gone through the FOR loop QUSNBRLE times), the program DSPLYs the "End of List" message, and ends.

Comparing Methods to Access the List Information

Let's take another look at the function provided in Figure 3.4, this time using the Retrieve User Space API (QUSRTVUS) to retrieve the list information. Figure 3.7 shows the differences between the two techniques. Several changes were made to the program to use QUSRTVUS.

First, the program in Figure 3.7 adds a prototype for QUSRTVUS and removes the data structure definitions for GenHdr and ListEntry. As shown in Figure 3.4, these data structures were defined based on the pointer fields GenHdrPtr and LstPtr, respectively. Because the user space isn't accessed via a pointer in this example, the BASED definitions have been removed, and the program will work directly with the structures as defined in the QSYSINC header files. This program also defines a new field, LstOfs (List Offset), to represent the position (offset) into the user space.

Another change to note: the call to the CrtUsrSpc procedure no longer defines a variable to receive the returned pointer to the user space (though the prototype still does). Because getting a pointer to the user space doesn't matter in this example, this call has been changed to no longer reference the returned pointer.

The next change is the biggest. After the call to the List Objects API (QUSLOBJ) comes the code to access the user space. The use of pointers allows the program in Figure 3.4 to immediately access the generic header of the user space. The new version of the program in Figure 3.7 needs to add a call to the Retrieve User Space API (QUSRTVUS) with the generic header data structure (QUSH0100) as the parameter in which to return data.

With the generic header data structure loaded, the program can access the fields of the data structure in the same manner as in Figure 3.4—in this case, to determine the value of QUSIS. More changes are needed, though, to access the list entries. As shown in Figure 3.4, the pointer method simply adds the offset to the pointer field like this to get direct access to the list entry:

```
LstPtr = GenHdrPtr + GenHdr.QUSOLD;
```

The program in Figure 3.7 needs the following to accomplish the same function:

```
LstOfs = QUSOLD + 1;

RtvUsrSpc(SpcName :LstOfs :%size(QUSL020002) :QUSL020002 :QUSEC);
```

A one is added to QUSOLD because QUSRTVUS is position-based rather than offset-based. The call to QUSRTVUS is needed to access the data in the entry. Note that this call is not necessary when using pointers, and this call to QUSRTVUS is actually *moving* data from the user space to the program-defined data structure QUSL020002 (defined due to the /COPY of QUSLOBJ). This movement of data is not needed when using pointers. Between the additional calls and resulting movement of data, you can expect that using pointers is a more efficient way of working with list APIs.

The Retrieve User Space API (QUSRTVUS) is located within the FOR loop and is executed once each time through the loop. The starting position is incremented at the end of each loop by adding the size of the List Entry field (QUSSEE) to the last starting position. With the pointer method, the pointer field LstPtr is incremented by adding the QUSSEE field to it each time through.

It should be readily apparent that using pointers to access list information is actually easier than using the Retrieve User Space API (QUSRTVUS). It's also much faster because you don't have to repeatedly call the API and move the data from the user space to your variables. We highly recommend using the pointer method whenever you can. Refer to chapter 1 for a discussion on the reasons and limitations for using each method.

```
h dftactgrp(*no) bnddir('APILIB')

DName++++++++++ETDsFrom+++To/L+++IDc.Keywords+++++++++++++++++++++++++++
dFig3_7           pr                    extpgm('FIG3_7')
d LibName                       10      const
d DltPct                        15   5 const

dFig3_7           pi
d LibName                       10      const
d DltPct                        15   5 const

d/copy qsysinc/qrpglesrc,qusgen
d/copy qsysinc/qrpglesrc,quslobj
d/copy qsysinc/qrpglesrc,qusrmbrd
d/copy qsysinc/qrpglesrc,qusec
```

Figure 3.7: Use *QUSRTVUS* rather than pointers to user spaces (part 1 of 4).

```
dCrtUsrSpc          pr              *      extproc('CrtUsrSpc')
d SpcName                          20      const

dListObj            pr                     extpgm('QUSLOBJ')
d SpcName                          20      const
d Format                            8      const
d ObjLibName                       20      const
d ObjTyp                           10      const
d QUSEC                                    likeds(QUSEC) options(*nopass)
d AutCtl                        65535      const options(*nopass :*varsize)
d SltCtl                        65535      const options(*nopass :*varsize)
d ASPCtl                        65535      const options(*nopass :*varsize)

dRtvMbrD            pr                     extpgm('QUSRMBRD')
d Receiver                          1      options(*varsize)
d LengthRcv                       10i 0    const
d Format                            8      const
d QualFileName                     20      const
d MbrName                          10      const
d OvrPrc                            1      const
d QUSEC                                    likeds(QUSEC) options(*nopass)
d FndPrc                            1      const options(*nopass)

dRtvUsrSpc          pr                     extpgm('QUSRTVUS')
d SpcName                          20      const
d StartPos                        10i 0    const
d Length                          10i 0    const
d SpcData                           1      options(*varsize)
d QUSEC                                    likeds(QUSEC) options(*nopass)

dSpcName            ds
d SName                            10      inz('OBJLIST')
d SLib                            10      inz('QTEMP')

dObjLibName         ds
d                                 10      inz('*ALL')
d ObjLib                          10

dQualFileName       ds
d FileName                        10
d FileLibName                     10

dCount              s             10i 0
dWait               s              1
dLstOfs             s             10i 0
CL0N01Factor1+++++++Opcode&ExtFactor2+++++++Result+++++++Len++D+HiLoEq
  /free
```

Figure 3.7: Use QUSRTVUS rather than pointers to user spaces (part 2 of 4).

```
// set ErrCde bytes provided to 16 to avoid exceptions
QUSBPRV = %size(QUSEC);

// create the user space for the list of files
CrtUsrSpc(SpcName);

// get the list of files
ObjLib = LibName;
ListObj( SpcName :'OBJL0200' : ObjLibName :'*FILE' :QUSEC);

// check if API call failed
if (QUSBAVL > 0);
    dsply ('List Objects failed with ' + QUSEI) ' ' wait;
    *inlr = *on;
    return;
endif;

// get the generic header
RtvUsrSpc(SpcName :1 :%size(QUSH0100) :QUSH0100 :QUSEC);

// check if API call failed
if (QUSBAVL > 0);
    dsply ('Unable to retrieve user space: ' + QUSEI) ' ' wait;
    *inlr = *on;
    return;
endif;

// check to see if the list is complete
if (QUSIS = 'C') or (QUSIS = 'P');
    if (QUSIS = 'C');
        dsply ('Complete list of ' + %char(QUSNBRLE) + ' entries.');
    endif;
    if (QUSIS = 'P');
        dsply ('Partial list of ' + %char(QUSNBRLE) + ' entries.');
    endif;

    // set LstOfs to where the first entry can be found
    LstOfs = QUSOLD + 1;

    for Count = 1 to QUSNBRLE;

      RtvUsrSpc(SpcName :LstOfs :%size(QUSL020002) :QUSL020002
        :QUSEC);

        // check if API call failed
        if (QUSBAVL > 0);
            dsply ('Unable to retrieve user space: ' + QUSEI) ' ' wait;
            *inlr = *on;
```

Figure 3.7: Use QUSRTVUS rather than pointers to user spaces (part 3 of 4).

```
                return;
            endif;

            // check to see if information was available
            if (QUSISO1 <> ' ');
                dsply ('Error with ' + %trimr(QUSOBJTUO0) +
                        ' ' + QUSOBJNUO0);

            else;
                // check to see if this is a physical file
                if (QUSEOA = 'PF');
                    // retrieve member description for number deleted rcds
                    FileName = QUSOBJNUO0;
                    FileLibName = QUSOLNUO0;
                    RtvMbrD( QUSMO200 :%size(QUSMO200) :'MBRD0200'
                            :QualFileName :'*FIRST' :'0' :QUSEC);
                    // check for API failure
                    if (QUSBAVL > 0);
                        // check if no member
                        if (QUSEI = 'CPF3C26'); // no error, just skip
                        else;
                            dsply (%trimr(QUSOBJNUO0) +
                                    ' failed with ' + QUSEI);
                        endif;
                    else;
                        // check for records and percentage deleted while
                        // avoiding divide by 0
                        if ((QUSNCRU > 0) or (QUSNDRU > 0));
                        if ((QUSNDRU/(QUSNDRU+QUSNCRU) * 100) > DltPct);
                            dsply ('File ' + %trimr(FileName) + ' has ' +
                                    %char(QUSNDRU) + ' deleted records');
                        endif;
                        endif;
                    endif;
                endif;
            endif;
            LstOfs = LstOfs + QUSSEE;
        endfor;
    else;
    dsply 'List Object API did not return valid data';
    endif;
    dsply 'End of List' ' ' Wait;
    *inlr = *on;
    Return;

/end-free
```

Figure 3.7: Use QUSRTVUS rather than pointers to user spaces (part 4 of 4).

Open-List APIs

The open-list API, as mentioned earlier, doesn't require a user space. Even though an open-list API can return a lot of information, it returns this information into a *receiver variable*. The reason for this technique is that open-list APIs return a "partial" list, where you select which portion of the list you currently want to process. While your program is processing this partial list that the API returned, the API goes out to get more information for you to process. This sequence is referred to as *asynchronous processing*.

Open-list APIs were created with one goal in mind: speed in getting back to you. An open-list API will return as many records as you request as soon as it can. While your program is acting on this partial list, the API will continue to finish the list in the background, using other jobs. The program operator doesn't have to wait while the complete list is being created, which is especially helpful in interactive programming. Because both your program and the API are working on different parts of the same task, response time is improved. It's a variation of the old adage, "two heads are better than one."

Prior to V5R3, using open-list APIs required that you have the Host Servers option of OS/400 installed (option 12). When dealing with open-list APIs on releases prior to V5R3, you also need to be aware that they reside in library QGY. For these older releases, you will have to take some action to ensure that your application program can find this library. Do this either by adding it to your library list or by hard-coding the call (an option we would not recommend, as the open-list APIs did move to the QSYS library in V5R3).

V5R3 also introduced much greater capacity for open-list APIs. Previously, open-list APIs could build a list of up to 16MB in the background. Starting with V5R3, many open-list APIs were enhanced to support returning a list that could be gigabytes in size. As with most changes in APIs, this change was done transparently to the API caller.

The open-list APIs return only the number of records, or list entries, requested into a receiver variable, along with a request handle that can be used to access the next set of records. The Get List Entry API (QGYGTLE) uses the request handle to fill the receiver variable, whenever it is called, with the next set of records. Therefore, you call the open-list API once, and then you call the Get List Entry API (QGYGTLE) as many times as needed to get the rest of the records—one block of records at a time.

The open-list APIs return a control data structure that contains information about the list. The structure contains control information similar to what is found in the generic header of list APIs—information such as how many records were returned, the length of each record returned, and whether or not the list is complete. This information allows you to process the list in the receiver variable. Figure 3.8 shows this control structure as it is provided in the QGY member of QSYSINC/QRPGLESRC. Table 3.4 shows some further definitions for the control structure fields.

```
DName+++++++++++ETDsFrom+++To/L+++IDc.Keywords+++++++++++++++++++++++++++++
D*************************************************************************
D*List information structure
D*************************************************************************
DQGYLI              DS
D*                                              Qgy List Info
D QGYTR07           1       4 B  0
D*                                              Total Records
D QGYRRTN02         5       8 B  0
D*                                              Records Returned
D QGYRH07           9      12
D*                                              Request Handle
D QGYRL07          13      16 B  0
D*                                              Record Length
D QGYIC07          17      17
D*                                              Info Complete
D*QGYDT13                  13
D*                                              Date Time
D QGYLSI01         31      31
D*                                              List Status Indicator
D QGYERVED56       32      32
D*                                              Reserved
D QGYRTNIL01       33      36 B  0
D*                                              Returned Info Length
D QGYFBR01         37      40 B  0
D*                                              First Buffer Record
D QGYRSV214        41      80
D*                                              Reserved2
```

Figure 3.8: This code shows the open-list control data structure format.

Table 3.4: Fields in the Open-List Control Field Data Structure	
Field	**Description**
QGYTR07	The total number of records in the list.
QGYRRTN02	The number of records returned to the receiver variable on this call.
QGYRH07	The request handle to be used to access subsequent blocks of records into the receiver variable. Used with the QGYGTLE API, it is valid until the Close List API (QGYCLST) is called.

Table 3.4: Fields in the Open-List Control Field Data Structure (continued)	
Field	**Description**
QGYRL07	The length of each record returned. If the record is of variable length, this value is zero, and the actual length of each record is contained within each record.
QGYIC07	A code that indicates if the request for data has been fulfilled, as follows:

Code	Description
C	Complete and accurate. All requested records were returned.
I	Incomplete. Something went wrong; bad data.
P	Partial. The receiver variable is full, but you requested more records than would fit.

QGYDT13	The date and time when the list was created, in *CYYMMDDHHMMSS* format.
QGYLSI01	A code indicating the status of the building of the list, as follows:

Code	Description
0	The building of the list is pending.
1	The list is being built.
2	The building of the list is completed.
3	An error occurred during the building of the list. The next call to QGYGTLE will signal an error.
4	The list is primed and ready, but hasn't started building yet.

QGYERVED56	A field reserved for alignment purposes.
QGYRTNIL01	The number of bytes returned to the variable field.
QGYFBR01	The number of the first record returned in the receiver variable.
QGYRSV214	A field reserved for alignment purposes.

When using open-list APIs, remember to always call the Close List API (QGYCLST) when you are done processing the list. This is key; otherwise, the list will continue to exist until your job ends. If you call many open-list APIs as part of your job, you will find that your job is consuming more and more storage unless you use QGYCLST.

Using an Open List to Find Files with Deleted Records

Figure 3.9 shows a version of the now-familiar program from Figure 3.4 based on the Open List of Objects API (QGYOLOBJ).

```
h dftactgrp(*no)

DName+++++++++++ETDsFrom+++To/L+++IDc.Keywords+++++++++++++++++++++++++++
dFig3_9            pr                    extpgm('FIG3_9')
d LibName                      10        const
d DltPct                       15  5     const

dFig3_9            pi
d LibName                      10        const
d DltPct                       15  5     const

d/copy qsysinc/qrpglesrc,qgyolobj
d/copy qsysinc/qrpglesrc,qgy
d/copy qsysinc/qrpglesrc,qusrmbrd
d/copy qsysinc/qrpglesrc,qusec

dOpnListObj        pr                    extpgm('QGYOLOBJ')
d RcvVar                        1        options(*varsize)
d LenRcvVar                    10i 0     const
d ListInfo                     80
d NbrRcdRqs                    10i 0     const
d SortInfo                               const likeds(QGYOSI)
d QualObjNam                   20        const
d ObjType                      10        const
d AuthCtl                                const likeds(QGYOAC)
d SelCtl                                 const likeds(SelCtl)
d NbrKeys                      10i 0     const
d KeysToRtn                              const likeds(KeysToRtn)
d QUSEC                                  likeds(QUSEC)
d JobID                     65535        const options(*nopass :*varsize)
d JobIDFmt                      8        const options(*nopass)
d ASPCtl                    65535        const options(*nopass :*varsize)

dGetNextEnt        pr                    extpgm('QGYGTLE')
d RcvVar                        1        options(*varsize)
d LenRcvVar                    10i 0     const
d RqsHandle                     4        const
d ListInfo                     80
d NbrRcdRqs                    10i 0     const
d StrRcd                       10i 0     const
d QUSEC                                  likeds(QUSEC)
```

Figure 3.9: An RPG program using the Open List of Objects API (QGYOLOBJ) (part 1 of 4).

```
dCloseList            pr                      extpgm('QGYCLST')
d RqsHandle                        4          const
d QUSEC                                       likeds(QUSEC)

dRtvMbrD              pr                      extpgm('QUSRMBRD')
d Receiver                         1          options(*varsize)
d LengthRcv                       10i 0       const
d Format                           8          const
d QualFileName                    20          const
d MbrName                         10          const
d OvrPrc                           1          const
d QUSEC                                       likeds(QUSEC) options(*nopass)
d FndPrc                           1          const options(*nopass)

dKeysToRtn            ds
d Keys                            10i 0 dim(10)

dRcvVar               ds        4096

dRcvVarEntry          ds                      based(RcvVarEntPtr)
d                                             qualified
d Hdr                                         likeds(QGYORV01)
d KeyHdr                                      likeds(QGYOKD)
d KeyData                         10

dSelCtl               ds                      qualified
d Ctl                                         likeds(QGYOSC)
d Status                           1

dObjLibName           ds
d                                 10          inz('*ALL')
d ObjLib                          10

dQualFileName         ds
d FileName                        10
d FileLibName                     10

dCount                s           10i 0
dWait                 s            1

CLON01Factor1+++++++Opcode&ExtFactor2+++++++Result++++++++Len++D+HiLoEq
 /free

  // set ErrCde bytes provided to 16 to avoid exceptions
  QUSBPRV = %size(QUSEC);
```

Figure 3.9: An RPG program using the Open List of Objects API (QGYOLOBJ) (part 2 of 4).

```
// get ready to call the QGYOLOBJ API
QGYNBRK = 0;                   // no need to sort API output
QGYOAC = *loval;      // initialize input structure
QGYFL04 = %size(QGYOAC);   // no authority controls needed
SelCtl.Ctl = *loval;          // initialize selection structure
SelCtl.Ctl.QGYFL05 = %size(SelCtl); // room for on one status value
SelCtl.Ctl.QGYSOOS = 0;       // select
SelCtl.Ctl.QGYSOO1 = 20;      // displacement to status
SelCtl.Ctl.QGYNBRS = 1;       // number of supplied statuses
SelCtl.Status = ' ';          // return entries with no errors
Keys(1) = 202;                // return extended object attribute

// get the list of files
ObjLib = LibName;
OpnListObj( RcvVar :%size(RcvVar) :QGYLI :50 :QGYOSI :ObjLibName
          :'*FILE' :QGYOAC :SelCtl :1 :KeysToRtn :QUSEC);

// check if API call failed
if (QUSBAVL > 0);
   dsply ('Open List Objects failed with ' + QUSEI) ' ' Wait;
   *inlr = *on;
   return;
endif;

dow (QGYIC07 = 'C') or (QGYIC07 = 'P'); // information returned?
   RcvVarEntPtr = %addr(RcvVar);

   for Count = 1 to QGYRRTN02;

       // check to see if this is a physical file
       if (RcvVarEntry.KeyData = 'PF');

           // retrieve member description for number deleted rcds
           FileName = RcvVarEntry.Hdr.QGYON00;
           FileLibName = RcvVarEntry.Hdr.QGYOL03;
           RtvMbrD( QUSM0200 :%size(QUSM0200) :'MBRD0200'
                   :QualFileName :'*FIRST' :'0' :QUSEC);
           // check for API failure
           if (QUSBAVL > 0);
               // check if no member
               if (QUSEI = 'CPF3C26'); // no error, just skip
               else;
                   dsply (%trimr(RcvVarEntry.Hdr.QGYON00) +
                           ' failed with ' + QUSEI);
               endif;
           else;
```

Figure 3.9: An RPG program using the Open List of Objects API (QGYOLOBJ) (part 3 of 4).

101

```
                        // check for records and percentage deleted while
                        // avoiding divide by 0
                        if ((QUSNCRU > 0) or (QUSNDRU > 0));
                        if ((QUSNDRU/(QUSNDRU+QUSNCRU) * 100) > DltPct);
                            dsply ('File ' + %trimr(FileName) + ' has ' +
                                        %char(QUSNDRU) + ' deleted records');
                        endif;
                        endif;
                    endif;
                endif;
                RcvVarEntPtr = RcvVarEntPtr + QGYRL07;
            endfor;

    if ((QGYFBR01 + QGYRRTN02) < QGYTR07) or
        (QGYLSI01 <> '2');
        GetNextEnt( RcvVar :%size(RcvVar) :QGYRH07 :QGYLI :50
                    :QGYFBR01 + QGYRRTN02  :QUSEC);
            if (QUSBAVL > 0);
                dsply ('Failure ' + QUSEI + ' on next set of records');
                leave;
            endif;
    else;
    leave;
    endif;
    enddo;
    dsply 'End of List' ' ' Wait;
    CloseList( QGYRH07 :QUSEC);  // close the open list handle
    *inlr = *on;
    Return;

/end-free
```

Figure 3.9: An RPG program using the Open List of Objects API (QGYOLOBJ) (part 4 of 4).

You will notice that Figure 3.9 makes quite a few changes. First, it replaces the prototypes related to the List Objects API (QUSLOBJ) and user spaces with prototypes for the Open List of Objects API (QGYOLOBJ), the Get List Entries API (QGYGTLE), and the Close List API (QGYCLST). The parameters for these APIs are documented in Tables 3.5, 3.6, and 3.7, respectively. Full documentation for the QGYOLOBJ API can be found in the Information Center, under "Programming," "APIs," "APIs by category," "Object," and "Object-related APIs." Full documentation for the QGYGTLE and QGYCLST APIs can be found in the Information Center under "Programming," "APIs," "APIs by category," and "Process Open List."

Table 3.5: Parameters for the Open List of Objects API (QGYOLOBJ)			
Parameter	**Description**	**Type**	**Size**
1	The receiver variable.	Output	Char(*)
2	The length of the receiver variable in parameter 1.	Input	Binary(4)
3	The list information.	Output	Char(80)
4	The number of records to return.	Input	Binary(4)
5	The sort information.	Input	Char(*)
6	The qualified object name.	Input	Char(20)
7	The object type.	Input	Char(10)
8	Authority control.	Input	Char(*)
9	Selection control.	Input	Char(*)
10	The number of keyed fields to return.	Input	Binary(4)
11	The key of fields to return.	Input	Array(*) of Binary(4)
12	The standard error-code structure.	I/O	Char(*)
Optional Parameter Group 1			
13	Job identification information.	Input	Char(*)
14	The format of job identification information.	Input	Char(8)
Optional Parameter Group 2			
15	Auxiliary storage pool (ASP) control.	Input	Char(*)

Many of the parameters for QGYOLOBJ should look familiar to you. The first parameter is the receiver variable, where the API will return information to you. The second parameter is used to specify the length, or size, of the first parameter. The third parameter is the standard list-information parameter reviewed in Figure 3.8 and Table 3.4.

Other parameters, however, are quite new. The fourth parameter, which holds the number of records to return, can be used to indicate how many records you want returned in the receiver variable without having to wait for the entire list to be created. In the case of the List Objects API, you had to wait for the entire list to be built before the API returned to your program, and you had no ability to control that.

The fifth parameter allows you to specify how you want the returned list entries to be sequenced or sorted. The current example doesn't use this capability, but it could be used, for instance, to return all the file names in alphabetical order. One point to keep in mind: in general, if you have the open-list API sort the returned entries, then the API must build the entire list first.

The sixth and seventh parameters are the qualified object name and the object type you want the list to be built on. These are equivalent to the third and fourth parameters of the List Objects API (QUSLOBJ).

The eighth parameter allows you to specify what type of authority-checking you want the API to use. For instance, you have the capability to tell the API to ignore any adopted authorities associated with the program calling the API.

The ninth parameter allows you to specify selection or omission criteria for the list of returned objects. For instance, you could omit any objects that the user does not have authority to, or only list objects that are damaged.

The tenth and eleventh parameters work together. Back in chapter 1, you were introduced briefly to keyed interfaces. The Open List of Objects API uses keys to identify exactly what pieces of information you want. In Figure 3.5, you can see that the List Objects API with format OBJL0200 is returning more information than you really need. You need the extended object attribute to make sure you're working with a physical file, but this format is also returning the object descriptive text and user-defined attribute, neither of which is used in the program. In looking at the Open List of Objects API, you can see that there is a key (202) defined as being just the extended object attribute. The tenth and eleventh parameters indicate to the API how many keys (pieces of data) you want and the key values, respectively.

Table 3.6: Parameters for the Get List Entries API (QGYGTLE)			
Parameter	Description	Type	Size
1	The receiver variable.	Output	Char(*)
2	The length of the variable receiver in parameter 1.	Input	Binary(4)
3	The request handle retrieved from the call to the open-list API. It is used to access the list created by that call.	Input	Char(4)
4	The open-list control data structure. (See Table 3.4 for details.)	Output	Char(80)

Table 3.6: Parameters for the Get List Entries API (QGYGTLE) (continued)			
Parameter	Description	Type	Size
5	The number of records to retrieve into the receiver variable, starting with the record indicated in parameter 6 (the starting-record parameter). This parameter must be zero or greater. If it is zero, only the open-list control data structure is returned.	Input	Binary(4)
6	The starting record; the number of the first record that will be put in the receiver variable. There are two special values: <table><tr><td>Value</td><td>Description</td></tr><tr><td>0</td><td>Only the open-list control data structure is returned. The number of records to return must also be zero.</td></tr><tr><td>-1</td><td>The whole list should be built before the list information is returned to the caller.</td></tr></table>	Input	Binary(4)
7	The standard error-code data structure.	I/O	Char(*)

Many of the parameters for the Get List Entries API should look familiar by now. The two parameters you haven't seen before are the third (the request handle) and the sixth (the starting record).

The request handle is simply a value returned in the List Information parameter of open-list APIs. This value is used with other API calls to identify which open list you are currently working with. You can have many lists open at the same time.

The starting record value can be used to indicate which record in the list you want returned first in the receiver variable. If you look at the API documentation in the Information Center, you will also find that special values such as zero and negative one can be used. This number is typically set to the number of the next record to be processed in the list, by adding the first entry number of the current receiver variable to the number of entries in the current receiver variable. Basically, it is a counter for the number of records you have retrieved (plus one). You can, however, set this to any value you want, so that you could skip over entries or go back and reprocess entries in the list. In this example, we are simply moving sequentially through the list.

Table 3.7: Parameters for the Close List API (QGYCLST)			
Parameter	Description	Type	Size
1	The request handle to the list that is to be closed. The handle was generated by one of the open-list APIs.	Input	Char(4)
2	The standard error-code data structure.	I/O	Char(*)

For the Close List API, the only two parameters are the request handle and the standard API error-code structure.

Combining Fixed-Size QSYSINC Structures with Variable-Length Fields

In Figure 3.9, you can see that most of the data structures we will be using are copied from QRPGLESRC in library QSYSINC. We use the provided structures within our own structures so that we can provide additional storage for variable-length fields. In QSYSINC, IBM provides the definitions for fixed-length fields and structures, but we need to determine how much storage to associate with variable-length information. Figure 3.10 shows two user-defined structures that combine IBM-supplied definitions and our own definitions.

```
DName+++++++++++ETDsFrom+++To/L+++IDc.Keywords+++++++++++++++++++++++++++++
dRcvVarEntry      ds                      based(RcvVarEntPtr)
d                                         qualified
d Hdr                                     likeds(QGYORV01)
d KeyHdr                                  likeds(QGYOKD)
d KeyData                    10

dSelCtl           ds                      qualified
d Ctl                                     likeds(QGYOSC)
d Status                      1
```

Figure 3.10: Combining IBM definitions with our own.

Let's look at how the RcvVarEntry data structure is defined. First, we elect to use this as a BASED structure, using the RcvVarEntPtr as a pointer to each occurrence of the structure. As you hopefully found in chapters 1 and 2, using pointers and BASED structures is easy and efficient once you get the hang of it. We also specify QUALIFIED, as we are embedding additional structure definitions within RcvVarEntry. According to the API documentation for the receiver variable of QGYOLOBJ, the receiver starts with a fixed-size structure containing the object name, library, type, etc. Looking at the QGYOLOBJ member of QSYSINC/QRPGLESRC, you can see that this is the QGYORV01 structure provided by IBM. Rather than typing in our own definition, we use LIKEDS to declare Hdr as being defined like QGYORV01. Returning to the API documentation, following this object information is another structure that provides control information for returned fields. This is information such as the length of the field information returned, and the key for the field information returned. We will be using a key to return information (specifically key 202 for the extended object attribute), so we need to include these definitions. They are provided by IBM with the data structure QGYOKD. IBM, however, does not provide any definition within QGYOKD for the size of the data we want returned. This makes sense, as IBM doesn't know in advance what keys we might request! Again returning to the API documentation, the data associated with key 202 is a Char(10). With this in mind, we define our own field KeyData as a 10-byte field following the definition of KeyHdr with LIKEDS(QGYOKD).

In a similar manner, the data structure SelCtl is defined using the IBM-supplied definition QGYOSC. Since only you know how many status fields you intend to use, the definition of Status as a one-byte field is left to you. In a different application, you might very well want Status to be an array of X one-byte elements, to represent multiple status values.

Initializing Input Structures

One of the first things the program does after setting an appropriate bytes provided (QUSBPRV) for the standard error code structure is to prime various input parameters to QGYOLOBJ. The general approach when using input structures to an API is to first initialize the structure to *LOVAL (or x'00'). This is because many input reserved fields must be set to *LOVAL, and we don't want to actually reference those reserved fields by name because what is reserved this release might not be in the next release. When the API starts to use a reserved field for some purpose, IBM will replace the reserved name with a meaningful name and make sure that a *LOVAL found in this renamed field will enable the API to work like it would in the previous release. This initialization can be seen in Figure 3.9 with these lines of code:

```
QGYOAC = *loval
SelCtl.Ctl = *loval;
```

After setting the input structures to *LOVAL, the program sets the appropriate fields within the structures to indicate what results we want from the API. In the case of the Selection Control format (SelCtl), we want to have QGYOLOBJ only return those objects with a status of blank (meaning no errors were found in accessing the object). As we only need to specify one status value, the length of SelCtl (SelCtl.Ctl.QGYFL05) is set to 21 bytes, the displacement to the status value (SelCtl.Ctl.QGYSO01) is set to 20 (recall that displacement and offset values start at zero, not one), and the number of the status values (SelCtl.Ctl.QGYNBRS) is set to one. We also indicate that we want the data associated with key 202 (the extended object attribute) to be returned by the API.

The program then calls the API and immediately checks to see if any error was found on the call operation. If no error was found, it checks to see if information was successfully retrieved from QGYOLOBJ by checking if the Information Complete indicator of the List Information structure (QGYIC07) is *C* for complete or *P* for partial. If it was successful, it processes the returned data.

The program has been coded as a loop to process the records found in the return variable. The FOR loop is conditioned by the number of records returned (QGYRRTN02), with processing similar to that in Figure 3.4. It checks to see if the file is a physical file by examining RcvVarEntry.KeyData . If so, it calls QUSRMBRD to determine how many deleted records are in the file. When the program has finished processing the current file, it moves on to the next one by adding the size of each entry (QGYRL07) to the basing pointer, RcvVarEntPtr.

When the program has completed the processing of the current receiver variable (that is, it's processed QGYRRTN02 entries), it checks to see if more entries might be available in the list. It does this by checking to see if either more entries exist in the list or if the list is not complete:

```
if ((QGYFBR01 + QGYRRTN02) < QGYTR07) or QGYLSI01 <> '2';
```

Remember that an open-list API can be adding more records to the total list while you're processing the entries currently available in the receiver variable. If the list is complete, has the program processed all of the entries? It determines this by checking whether the starting entry in the receiver variable (QGYFBR01) plus the number of entries in the receiver variable (QGYRRTN02) is less than the number of entries in the total list (QGYTR07). If so, it calls the Get List Entry API (QGYGTLE) to get more entries. If the list is not complete, additional records might now be available, and we call again the QGYGTLE API to get more entries.

108

The QGYGTLE API is used to retrieve another set of records from the list already opened using the Open List of Objects API (QGYOLOBJ). The same format for the receiver variable is used in both APIs to make it easier to process the information.

Processing Lists with Variable-Length Entries

So far, we have only looked at list APIs that return entries of the same size or length. Some list APIs, however, return entries of different lengths. The List Module Information API (QBNLMODI), for instance, with format MODL0300, returns list entries containing the names of procedures found within a *MODULE object. As procedure names can range from one byte to several hundred bytes, it would be very inefficient to simply reserve space in every entry for the largest possible procedure name. Instead, the QBNLMODI API uses an "offset and length" approach to returning each procedure name. Due to the various procedure-name lengths, each list entry may be of a different length, so QBNLMODI also defines a field in each list entry that indicates the length of the entry. This length information can then be used to access the next length entry. QBNLMODI also sets the generic header field QUSSEE, size of each entry, to zero, indicating that fixed-length entries are not being used.

As with the other list APIs shown in this chapter, the intent is not to go into great detail on QBNLMODI's specifics. Rather, the intent is to demonstrate how to work with it. For that reason, only a brief description of the parameters for QBNLMODI are shown in Table 3.8. The fields contained with format MODL0300 are in Figure 3.11, and an example program processing the MODL0300 variable-length records of QBNLMODI is in Figure 3.12. Full documentation for the QBNLMODI API can be found in the Information Center under "Programming," "APIs," "APIs by category," and "Program and CL Command."

Table 3.8: Parameters for the List Module Information API (QBNLMODI)			
Parameter	Description	Type	Size
1	The qualified user space name.	Input	Char(20)
2	The format name.	Input	Char(8)
3	The qualified module name.	Input	Char(20)
4	The standard error-code structure.	I/O	Char(*)

You should be able to recognize the intent of each of these parameters. The only one that requires additional information is the format name.

The QBNLMODI API supports five formats:

- MODL0100—Module export information

- MODL0200—Module import information

- MODL0300—Module procedure information

- MODL0400—Referenced system objects information

- MODL0500—Module copyright information

For the sample program, we use format MODL0300, as shown in Figure 3.11.

```
DName+++++++++++ETDsFrom+++To/L+++IDc.Keywords++++++++++++++++++++++++++++
D*********************************************************************
D*Type definition for the MODL0300
D*********************************************************************
DQBNL030001        DS
D*                                          Qbn LMODI MODL0300
D QBNES01              1      4 B 0
D*                                          Entry Size
D QBNMN04              5     14
D*                                          Module Name
D QBNMLIBN01          15     24
D*                                          Module Library Name
D QBNPT               25     25
D*                                          Procedure Type
D QBNERVED04          26     28
D*                                          Reserved
D QBNPNO00            29     32 B 0
D*                                          Procedure Name Offs
D QBNPNL00            33     36 B 0
D*                                          Procedure Name Leng
D QBNPAO              37     46
D*                                          Procedure ArgOpt
```

Figure 3.11: The QSYSINC-provided definition for format MODL0300 of QBNLMODI.

The QSYSINC-provided data structure QBNL030001 for format MODL0300 includes four fields of interest to us: QBNES01, the size of the current list entry that is used to access the next list entry; QBNMN04, the module name; QBNPNO00, the offset to the procedure name; and QBNPNL00, the length of the procedure name.

With this information, FIG3_12 DSPLYs the name of the module and up to the first 20 bytes of the procedure name. In looking at the source shown in Figure 3.12, you should quickly notice that the only real change from earlier list API processing examples is that instead of adding QUSSEE to LISTENTRYPTR, we are now adding LISTENTRY.QBNES01. Obviously, moving from fixed-length list entries to variable-length list entries isn't too difficult!

```
h dftactgrp(*no) bnddir('APILIB')

DName++++++++++ETDsFrom+++To/L+++IDc.Keywords++++++++++++++++++++++++++
d/copy qsysinc/qrpglesrc,qusgen
d/copy qsysinc/qrpglesrc,qbnlmodi
d/copy qsysinc/qrpglesrc,qusec

dCrtUsrSpc          pr                 *    extproc('CrtUsrSpc')
d SpcName                             20    const

dListMod            pr                      extpgm('QBNLMODI')
d SpcName                             20    const
d Format                               8    const
d ModLibName                         20    const
d QUSEC                                     likeds(QUSEC)

dGenHdr             ds                      likeds(QUSH0100)
d                                           based(GenHdrPtr)

dListEntry          ds                      likeds(QBNL030001)
d                                           based(ListEntryPtr)

dSpcName            ds
d SName                               10    inz('TESTSPACE')
d SLib                                10    inz('QTEMP')

dObjLibName         ds
d ObjName                             10    inz('*ALL')
d LibName                             10    inz('*CURLIB')

dProcedure          s                  20   based(ProcPtr)
dCount              s                10 i 0
dWait               s                  1
```

Figure 3.12: Processing list API output with variable-length entries (part 1 of 3).

```
CLONO1Factor1+++++++Opcode&ExtFactor2+++++++Result++++++++Len++D+HiLoEq
/free

    // Create user space and get a pointer to the start of the space
    GenHdrPtr = CrtUsrSpc( SpcName);

    // Call the List API
    ListMod( SpcName :'MODL0300' :ObjLibName :QUSEC);

    // Check on the status of the returned list
    if (GenHdr.QUSIS = 'C') or (GenHdr.QUSIS = 'P');

        // Show how many entries were found
        if (GenHdr.QUSIS = 'C');
            dsply ('Complete list of ' + %char(GenHdr.QUSNBRLE) +
                    ' entries.');
        endif;
        if (GenHdr.QUSIS = 'P');
            dsply ('Partial list of ' + %char(GenHdr.QUSNBRLE) +
                    ' entries.');
        endif;

        // Set ListEntryPtr to the first entry
        ListEntryPtr =  GenHdrPtr + GenHdr.QUSOLD;

        // process all entries
        for Count = 1 to GenHdr.QUSNBRLE;
            // process the current list entry

            // display the current entry and wait for input
            // if character entered, leave the list
            ProcPtr = GenHdrPtr + ListEntry.QBNPNO00;
            if ListEntry.QBNPNL00 < 20;
                dsply ('Module ' + %trimr(ListEntry.QBNMN04) +
                        ' contains ' +
                        %subst(Procedure :1 :ListEntry.QBNPNL00)) ' '
            Wait;
            else;
                dsply ('Module ' + %trimr(ListEntry.QBNMN04) +
                        ' contains ' +
                        Procedure) ' ' Wait;
            endif;

            if Wait <> ' ';
                leave;
            endif;
```

Figure 3.12: Processing list API output with variable-length entries (part 2 of 3).

```
        // if no character entered, go to next entry in the list
        ListEntryPtr += ListEntry.QBNES01;
    endfor;

// List status is not Complete or Partial
else;
    // Report an error
endif;

// exit when the list has been processed
Wait = *blanks;
dsply 'End of List' ' ' Wait;
*inlr = *on;
return;

/end-free
```

Figure 3.12: Processing list API output with variable-length entries (part 3 of 3).

Summary

The list APIs are powerful tools. They return a lot of information relatively quickly by way of user spaces. While each list API is unique, they all follow the same set of standards. Now that you know the standards, you should be able to process any of the list APIs.

Open-list APIs can be even faster than standard list APIs. Open-list APIs process asynchronously, so that you can get some of the records returned to process while the rest of the list is being built in the background. They also follow a set of standards, so once you master one, you can easily move on to others.

Both list and open-list APIs follow very similar approaches when it comes to how you process the list of entries.

Check Your Knowledge

Write a program to display the active subsystems on your system. To get you started, the List Active Subsystems API (QWCLASBS) returns this information. The documentation for this API can be found using the API Finder and searching for the name QWCLASBS, or by looking at the Work Management category of APIs. Looking at the documentation, you will see that only one format is supported, and the name of the format is SBSL0100. This format returns the subsystem name starting at decimal position zero (or one, if your language is base-1 as in RPG) and the subsystem library at decimal position 10. Looking at member QWCLASBS in QSYSINC/QRPGLESRC, you can see that the subsystem name and subsystem library fields correspond to fields QWCSDN and QWCSDLN of data structure QWCLO100, respectively.

For any error situations, the program should simply DSPLY the error message. To create the user space, use the CrtUsrSpc procedure from chapter 1. The user space should be named SBSLIST and created into QTEMP.

Your approach to this task should be very similar to Figure 3.4. For one possible solution, see Figure D.3 in appendix D.

4

Command-Processing APIs

T his chapter covers some of the callable APIs used to work with commands from within your application programs. It includes several very useful examples to show you how to use the QCMDEXC API to run commands and the QCMDCHK API to check a command string for validity from within your program. Consolidating these two APIs, the QCAPCMD API delivers maximum flexibility to your application by allowing you to edit a command string for validity, prompt the command string, return command parameters, and run the command. Also included is a discussion of the Command Analyzer Retrieve Exit program, which allows a user program to run whenever a particular command is used on the system. As you will see, the command-processing APIs enhance the usability and flexibility of your existing applications and give you many more options when writing new applications.

The documentation for these APIs can be found in the Information Center under the API category "Program and CL Command."

Defining the QCMDEXC API

QCMDEXC, the Execute Command API, just might be the most common and well-known API of them all. It has been around since the beginning and has become a longstanding friend to i5/OS programmers everywhere. The beauty of QCMDEXC is its simplicity and power. It was designed with a single purpose: to let you process i5/OS commands from within your high-level-language programs.

Almost anything you would ever want to do with a single command can be done using QCMDEXC without ever leaving your program. For instance, you can submit jobs, manipulate library lists, override printer parameters, perform Open Query File on your database files, and execute a myriad of other functions, all from within your application program.

The pages ahead provide these examples for using QCMDEXC to get flexibility from within your programs:

- Run a simple command like Work with Spooled Files (WRKSPLF).

- Run the Reorganize Physical File Member (RGZPFM) command.

- Run the Open Query File (OPNQRYF) command to sequence a file into the order you want before listing it.

- Override printer parameters to send the printed output to a specific printer and change the number of copies.

- Submit a job.

As mentioned earlier, QCMDEXC is both versatile and easy to use. Generally, all you need to do is call QCMDEXC and pass it two parameters: the command you want to run and the length of the command. Table 4.1 lists the definitions of these parameters.

Table 4.1: Parameters for the Execute Command API (QCMDEXC)			
Parameter	Description	Type	Size
1	Command String	Input	Char()
2	Length of Command String	Input	Packed(15 5)
Optional Parameter Group 1			
3	IGC Process Control	Input	Char(3)

The first parameter, Command String, is the command you want to run. If the command contains embedded blanks, the string must be enclosed within apostrophes. The second parameter, Length of Command String, is the length of the command specified in the first parameter, from one to 32,702 bytes. The third parameter, IGC Process Control, indicates whether ideographic data (also known as double-byte or DBCS data) is contained within the command string. The only value supported is *IGC*.

The example in Figure 4.1 shows how to embed the Work with Spool Files command (WRKSPLF) into an application program. You can see how simple it is.

```
DName+++++++++++ETDsFrom+++To/L+++IDc.Keywords+++++++++++++++++++++++++++++++++
dCmdExc          pr                    extpgm('QCMDEXC')
d Command                      65535    const options(*varsize)
d CmdLength                    15 5     const
d IGC                          3        const options(*nopass)

dCommand         s             100      inz('WRKSPLF')

CLON01Factor1+++++++Opcode&ExtFactor2+++++++Result++++++++Len++D+HiLoEq+
 /free
   CmdExc( Command :%len(%trimr(Command)));
   *inlr = *on;
   return;
 /end-free
```

Figure 4.1: Use QCMDEXC to run WRKSPLF from within an RPG program.

One drawback of the QCMDEXC API, however, is the lack of an error-code parameter to easily recover from errors found in the command. Fortunately, another API, Process Commands (QCAPCMD), can do everything QCMDEXC can, plus quite a bit more. This API will be discussed later in this chapter.

Using QCMDEXC to Run RGZPFM

In Figure 3.4 of chapter 3, you saw a program to DSPLY the list of files containing a percentage of deleted records above a certain level. Now, let's modify that example so the program automatically reorganizes the files rather than simply listing them. This changed program is shown in Figure 4.2.

```
h dftactgrp(*no) bnddir('APILIB')

DName+++++++++++ETDsFrom+++To/L+++IDc.Keywords++++++++++++++++++++++++++++
dFig4_2           pr                    extpgm('FIG4_2')
d LibName                       10      const
d DltPct                        15  5 const

dFig4_2           pi
d LibName                       10      const
d DltPct                        15  5 const

d/copy qsysinc/qrpglesrc,qusgen
d/copy qsysinc/qrpglesrc,quslobj
d/copy qsysinc/qrpglesrc,qusrmbrd
d/copy qsysinc/qrpglesrc,qusec

dCrtUsrSpc        pr                 *
d SpcName                       20      const

dListObj          pr                    extpgm('QUSLOBJ')
d SpcName                       20      const
d Format                         8      const
d ObjLibName                    20      const
d ObjTyp                        10      const
d QUSEC                                 likeds(QUSEC) options(*nopass)
d AutCtl                     65535      const options(*nopass :*varsize)
d SltCtl                     65535      const options(*nopass :*varsize)
d ASPCtl                     65535      const options(*nopass :*varsize)

dRtvMbrD          pr                    extpgm('QUSRMBRD')
d Receiver                       1      options(*varsize)
d LengthRcv                    10i 0 const
d Format                         8      const
d QualFileName                 20      const
d MbrName                      10      const
d OvrPrc                        1      const
d QUSEC                                 likeds(QUSEC) options(*nopass)
d FndPrc                        1      const options(*nopass)

dCmdExc           pr                    extpgm('QCMDEXC')
d Command                    65535      const options(*varsize)
d CmdLength                    15  5 const
d IGC                          3      const options(*nopass)

d* list API generic header
dGenHdr           ds                    likeds(QUSH0100)
d                                       based(GenHdrPtr)
d* List Object API (QUSLOBJ) format OBJL0200
```

Figure 4.2: Use *QCMDEXC* to run *RGZPFM* from within an RPG program (part 1 of 3).

```
dListEntry         ds                      likeds(QUSL020002)
d                                          based(LstPtr)

dSpcName           ds
d SName                       10           inz('OBJLIST')
d SLib                        10           inz('QTEMP')

dObjLibName        ds
d                             10           inz('*ALL')
d ObjLib                      10

dQualFileName      ds
d FileName                    10
d FileLibName                 10

dCount             s          10i 0
dWait              s          1
dCommand           s          100
dMbrName           s          10           inz('*FIRST')

CLON01Factor1+++++++Opcode&ExtFactor2+++++++Result++++++++Len++D+HiLoEq+
 /free

   // set ErrCde bytes provided to 16 to avoid exceptions
   QUSBPRV = %size(QUSEC);

   // create the user space for the list of files
   GenHdrPtr = CrtUsrSpc(SpcName);

   // get the list of files
   ObjLib = LibName;
   ListObj( SpcName :'OBJL0200' : ObjLibName :'*FILE' :QUSEC);

   // check if API call failed
   if (QUSBAVL > 0);
      dsply ('List Objects failed with ' + QUSEI) ' ' Wait;
      *inlr = *on;
      return;
   endif;

   // check to see if the list is complete
   if (GenHdr.QUSIS = 'C') or (GenHdr.QUSIS = 'P');

      // get to the first list entry and process the list
      LstPtr = GenHdrPtr + GenHdr.QUSOLD;
      for Count = 1 to GenHdr.QUSNBRLE;
         // check to see if information was available
```

Figure 4.2: Use *QCMDEXC* to run *RGZPFM* from within an RPG program (part 2 of 3).

119

```
            if (ListEntry.QUSISO1 <> ' ');
                dsply ('Error with ' + %trimr(ListEntry.QUSOBJTU00) +
                       ' ' + ListEntry.QUSOBJNU00);

            else;
                // check to see if this is a physical file
                if (ListEntry.QUSEOA = 'PF');
                    // retrieve member description for number deleted rcds
                    FileName = ListEntry.QUSOBJNU00;
                    FileLibName = ListEntry.QUSOLNU00;
                    RtvMbrD( QUSM0200 :%size(QUSM0200) :'MBRD0200'
                            :QualFileName :'*FIRST' :'0' :QUSEC);
                    // check for API failure
                    if (QUSBAVL > 0);
                        // check if no member
                        if (QUSEI = 'CPF3C26'); // no error, just skip
                        else;
                            dsply (%trimr(ListEntry.QUSOBJNU00) +
                                   ' failed with ' + QUSEI);
                        endif;
                    else;
                        // check for records and percentage deleted while
                        // avoiding divide by 0
                        if ((QUSNCRU > 0) or (QUSNDRU > 0));
                        if ((QUSNDRU/(QUSNDRU+QUSNCRU) * 100) > DltPct);
                            Command = ('RGZPFM FILE(' + %trimr(FileLibName) +
                                       '/' + %trimr(FileName) + ') MBR(' +
                                       %trimr(MbrName) + ')');
                            CmdExc( Command :%len(%trimr(Command)));
                            dsply ('Reorganized file ' + FileName);
                        endif;
                        endif;
                    endif;
                endif;
            endif;
            LstPtr = LstPtr + GenHdr.QUSSEE;
        endfor;
    else;
    dsply 'List Object API did not return valid data';
    endif;
    dsply 'End of List' ' ' Wait;
    *inlr = *on;
    Return;

/end-free
```

Figure 4.2: Use *QCMDEXC* to run *RGZPFM* from within an RPG program (part 3 of 3).

This program includes these changes from the one in Figure 3.4:

- A prototype for the QCMDEXC API is added.

- A new field, MbrName, is added and initialized to *FIRST. This is not really necessary, as the RGZPFM command defaults to MBR(*FIRST). However, it was done to demonstrate how you can specify a variable MbrName if you want to—for instance, when working with any member in a file, as we will be doing later in this book, in Figure 7.5.

- The QCMDEXC API is called to execute RGZPFM when the percentage of deleted records exceeds the specified threshold and sends a message to inform the user that the file was reorganized. The RPG built-in %TRIMR is used in determining the size of the command string to avoid trailing blanks.

This should demonstrate how easy it is to embed a command within an application program.

Using QCMDEXC to Run OPNQRYF

Most report programs have a variety of sequence and sort options provided to the end user. If you could sequence and select your data dynamically, you could add a great deal of flexibility to your programs, thus reducing the amount of maintenance performed.

The sample program in Figure 4.3 allows you to do just that. This simple list program prints the customer file in customer-name or customer-number order. The DDS for the CUSTOMER file is shown in Figure 4.4.A, and a program to load a few records is provided in Figure 4.4.B.

At this time, create the library SOMELIB and then create and load the SOMELIB/CUSTOMER physical file. In later chapters, you'll be creating more objects into this library (and using the CUSTOMER file), so don't delete the library (or the CUSTOMER file) when you're done with the current example. Also, remember to add SOMELIB to your jobs library list.

The FIG4_3 program lists the customer records in various sequences by executing the Open Query File command (OPNQRYF) from within the application program. When the program is called, a parameter is passed that determines the sequence in which the records are printed. If the value *1* is passed to the program, the list prints in customer-name order. If the value *2* is passed, the list prints in customer-number order. Any other value causes an error message to be DSPLYed.

Take a look at the code in Figure 4.3. In particular, note the USROPN (User Controlled Open) keyword specified on the File Description Specification for the CUSTOMER file. This tells the system that the open and close of the CUSTOMER database file is user-controlled; in other words, it is controlled from within the program.

The program must not open the file during program initialization because then you could not perform the necessary file overrides or create an alternate path for the data. The override for OPNQRYF will not be effective once the file has been opened. Therefore, before opening the file, you must perform the overrides on it. The Override Data Base File command (OVRDBF) tells the system that you want this program and the OPNQRYF command to share the same data path to the CUSTOMER database file.

```
FFilename++IPEASF.....L.....A.Device+.Keywords++++++++++++++++++++++++++
fCustomer  if   e              disk     usropn
fQsysprt   o    f   132        printer  oflind(*inof)


DName+++++++++++ETDsFrom+++To/L+++IDc.Keywords++++++++++++++++++++++++++
dFig4_3            pr                   extpgm('FIG4_3')
d Sequence                        1     const

dFig4_3            pi
d Sequence                        1     const

dCmdExc            pr                   extpgm('QCMDEXC')
d Command                     65535     const options(*varsize)
d CmdLength                      15  5  const
d IGC                             3     const options(*nopass)

dCommand           s            100
dWait              s              1


CLON01Factor1+++++++Opcode&ExtFactor2+++++++Result++++++++Len++D+HiLoEq
 /free
   // override the Customer file to specify a shared Open Data Path
   Command = 'OVRDBF FILE(CUSTOMER) SHARE(*YES)';
   CmdExc( Command :%len(%trimr(Command)));

   // use OPNQRYF to sequence the records base on the Sequence parameter
   select;
     when (Sequence = '1'); // customer name order
       Command = 'OPNQRYF CUSTOMER ALWCPYDTA(*OPTIMIZE) KEYFLD(CUSTNAME)';
     when (Sequence = '2'); // customer number order
       Command = 'OPNQRYF CUSTOMER ALWCPYDTA(*OPTIMIZE) KEYFLD(CUSTNBR)';
```

Figure 4.3: This program uses QCMDEXC to run OPNQRYF from within an RPG program. (part 1 of 2).

```
  other;
    dsply 'Invalid value for sequence' ' ' Wait;
    *inlr = *on;
    return;
  endsl;
  CmdExc( Command :%len(%trimr(Command)));

  // open the file and start the report
  open Customer;
  except Heading;
  // read and write the records
  read CusRec;
  dou %eof(Customer);
      except Detail;
      read CusRec;
  enddo;

  // close the file
  Command = 'CLOF OPNID(CUSTOMER)';
  CmdExc( Command :%len(%trimr(Command)));
  *inlr = *on;
  return;

 /end-free

OFilename++DF..N01N02N03Excnam++++B++A++Sb+Sa+.....................
oqsysprt  e              Heading         2 02
o         or    of
o                                        72 'Customer List'
o         e              Heading         1
o         or    of
o                                        15 'Customer Number'
o                                        45 'Customer Name'
o         ef             Detail          1
o                        CustNbr         15
o                        CustName        65
```

Figure 4.3: This program uses QCMDEXC to run OPNQRYF from within an RPG program. (part 2 of 2).

```
AAN01N02N03T.Name++++++RLen++TDpBLinPosFunctions++++++++++++++++++++++++
          R CUSREC
            CUSTNBR        10
            CUSTNAME       40
          K CUSTNBR
```

Figure 4.4.A: The DDS for the CUSTOMER file.

```
FFilename++IPEASF.....L.....A.Device+.Keywords+++++++++++++++++++++++++++
fCustomer  o    e              disk

CLON01Factor1+++++++Opcode&ExtFactor2+++++++Result++++++++Len++D+HiLoEq
 /free
  CUSTNBR = '0000000001';
  CUSTNAME = 'ABC Company';
  write CUSREC;
  CUSTNBR = '0000000002';
  CUSTNAME = 'XYZ Company';
  write CUSREC;
  CUSTNBR = '0000000003';
  CUSTNAME = 'DEF Inc.';
  write CUSREC;
  CUSTNBR = '0000000004';
  CUSTNAME = 'IMPASSIONED Marketing';
  write CUSREC;
  *inlr = *on;
  return;
 /end-free
```

Figure 4.4.B: The FIG4_4_B RPG program loads four records into the CUSTOMER file defined in Figure 4.4.A.

The program uses QCMDEXC to perform the Override Data Base File command for the CUSTOMER database file, and then again to perform the Open Query File operation to sequence the data. A SELECT WHEN is used to determine the appropriate KEYFLD parameter of OPNQRYF based on the parameter value passed to the program FIG4_3. Once the OPNQRYF command has been performed, the CUSTOMER file can be opened for use within the program.

The QCMDEXC API is called three times in the example in Figure 4.3. First, it is used to run the OVRDBF command, so the system knows to share the open data path between the OPNQRYF command and the program. Second, QCMDEXC is used to perform the OPNQRYF command, where the data is sequenced. Third, QCMDEXC is used to close the CUSTOMER file once the program is finished with the list. Failure to close the file could cause some interesting and unintended results in subsequent programs that used the CUSTOMER database file if the program was being called within the same job and the shared open was still in effect.

Using QCMDEXC to Override Printer Parameters

Directing report output to desired printers and output queues is standard fare for an application programmer. If you have not used QCMDEXC for the task, however, you'll want to check out the example in Figure 4.5, which uses the QCMDEXC API to change printers and the number of copies printed from within a print program. Parameter 1 is the number of copies to print, and parameter 2 is the printer device to which the output should be directed.

```
FFilename++IPEASF.....L.....A.Device+.Keywords++++++++++++++++++++++++++
fCustomer  if   e              disk
fQsysprt   o    f  132         printer oflind(*inof) usropn


DName+++++++++++++ETDsFrom+++To/L+++IDc.Keywords++++++++++++++++++++++++++
dFig4_5           pr                    extpgm('FIG4_5')
d NbrCopies                     2       const
d Printer                      10       const

dFig4_5           pi
d NbrCopies                     2       const
d Printer                      10       const

dCmdExc           pr                    extpgm('QCMDEXC')
d Command                   65535       const options(*varsize)
d CmdLength                 15 5        const
d IGC                           3       const options(*nopass)

dCommand          s            100

CLON01Factor1+++++++Opcode&ExtFactor2+++++++Result++++++++Len++D+HiLoEq
/free
   // check if any overrides specified
   if %parms > 0;
      Command = 'OVRPRTF FILE(QSYSPRT) COPIES(' + NbrCopies + ')';
      if %parms > 1;
         Command = %trimr(Command) +
                   ' DEV(' + %trim(Printer) + ') OUTQ(*DEV)';
      endif;
      CmdExc( Command :%len(%trimr(Command)));
   endif;

   // open Qsysprt and write to it
   open Qsysprt;
   except Heading;
```

Figure 4.5: This program uses QCMDEXC to override printer attributes (part 1 of 2).

```
     // read and write the records
     read CusRec;
     dou %eof(Customer);
         except Detail;
         read CusRec;
     enddo;

     // close the file
     close Qsysprt;
     *inlr = *on;
     return;
     /end-free


OFilename++DF..N01N02N03Excnam++++B++A++Sb+Sa+.......................
oqsysprt   e               Heading       2 02
o          or    of
o                                        72 'Customer List'
o          e               Heading       1
o          or    of
o                                        15 'Customer Number'
o                                        45 'Customer Name'
o          ef              Detail        1
o                          CustNbr       15
o                          CustName      65
```

Figure 4.5: This program uses *QCMDEXC* to override printer attributes (part 2 of 2).

As in the previous example, the file being overridden must remain closed while the file overrides are performed. Notice the USROPN keyword specified on the File Description Specification of the printer file (QSYSPRT). It tells the system this file is user-controlled. You code the open and close of QSYSPRT yourself once you have performed the desired file overrides.

The %PARMS built-in function tells the program whether or not parameters are passed to it. If the program in Figure 4.5 is called with parameter 1 specified (the %PARMS value is greater than zero), then the first parameter is used to specify the number of copies. If the second parameter is also specified (the %PARMS value is greater than one), then the second parameter is used to specify the printer device for the report. If no parameters are passed to the program, the override is not performed. Once any necessary override to the printer file has been performed, the printer file is opened, and the rest of the simple list program is completed.

Using QCMDEXC to Submit a Job to a Job Queue

Have you ever wondered why there is no Submit Job opcode (SBMJOB) that allows you to submit jobs from within your RPG program? We have, too. Fortunately, you can use QCMDEXC to do this. You prompt for a printer ID and number of copies, validate the values entered, and then submit a program to the job queue.

The program you'll submit is the customer list from the previous example (Figure 4.5). The display file coded in Figure 4.6 presents the prompt screen shown in Figure 4.7.

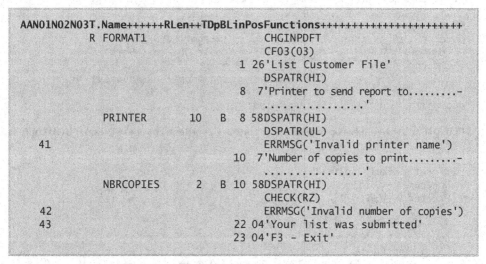

```
AAN01N02N03T.Name++++++RLen++TDpBLinPosFunctions++++++++++++++++++++++++++
            R FORMAT1                    CHGINPDFT
                                         CF03(03)
                                     1 26'List Customer File'
                                         DSPATR(HI)
                                     8  7'Printer to send report to.........-
                                         .................'
              PRINTER      10   B    8 58DSPATR(HI)
                                         DSPATR(UL)
     41                                  ERRMSG('Invalid printer name')
                                    10  7'Number of copies to print.........-
                                         .................'
              NBRCOPIES     2   B   10 58DSPATR(HI)
                                         CHECK(RZ)
     42                                  ERRMSG('Invalid number of copies')
     43                             22 04'Your list was submitted'
                                    23 04'F3 - Exit'
```

Figure 4.6: This DDS produces the Customer-List Prompt Screen display file.

Figure 4.7: The Customer-List Prompt Screen allows users to enter the printer ID and number of copies.

127

The program is shown in Figure 4.8. It first establishes the default values for the NbrCopies field (the number of copies) and the Printer field (the desired printer). It then presents a prompt screen. The program has been coded to continue presenting the prompt screen until F3 is pressed. If the entries keyed pass the edits, the values are used to build a SBMJOB command. The QCMDEXC API is then executed to submit the job to the job queue, and a confirmation message is sent to the screen.

```
FFilename++IPEASF.....L.....A.Device+.Keywords+++++++++++++++++++++++++++
Ffig4_6     cf  e             workstn


DName++++++++++++ETDsFrom+++To/L+++IDc.Keywords++++++++++++++++++++++++++++
dCmdExc              pr                 extpgm('QCMDEXC')
d Command                     65535     const options(*varsize)
d CmdLength                      15   5 const
d IGC                             3     const options(*nopass)

dCommand             s          100


CLON01Factor1+++++++Opcode&ExtFactor2+++++++Result++++++++Len++D+HiLoEq
 /free

    // set default values
    NbrCopies = '01';
    Printer = 'QPRINT';

    // loop until F3 is used to exit
    dou (*in03 = *on);
        exfmt Format1;
        *in43 = *off;  // clear successful submission message
        if (*in03 = *on);
            leave;
        endif;
        if Printer = *blanks;
            *in41 = *on;
            iter;
        endif;
        if ((NbrCopies < '01') or (NbrCopies > '99'));
            *in42 = *on;
            iter;
        endif;
        // seems to be OK so submit the job
        Command = 'SBMJOB CMD(CALL PGM(FIG4_5) PARM(''' + NbrCopies +
                '''  ''' + %trimr(Printer) + '''))';
        CmdExc( Command :%len(%trimr(Command)));
```

Figure 4.8: This program is an example of using the QCMDEXC command to submit jobs from within an RPG program (part 1 of 2).

```
       *in43 = *on;
  enddo;
  *inlr = *on;
  return;

/end-free
```

Figure 4.8: This program is an example of using the QCMDEXC command to submit jobs from within an RPG program (part 2 of 2).

Using the System Function Instead of Calling QCMDEXC

One of the highly productive features of the Integrated Language Environment (ILE) in i5/OS is the ability to access the run-time functions of one language from another language. The C language, for instance, provides many APIs that can be accessed by RPG, COBOL, and CL developers. One example is C's system function. This function provides the same high-level capability as the QCMDEXC API—executing a CL command—but you don't have to pass the size of the command. Just pass the command you want executed (as a parameter), and the function will figure out the length of the command based on the C language convention that character strings end with a null (x'00') character.

Figure 4.9 shows an example of the code necessary to execute the system function. The call to the function is prototyped and accessed using the EXTPROC keyword. It accepts only one parameter: the command to be executed. As noted, the length of the command does not have to be passed to this function. Both keywords VALUE and OPTIONS(*STRING) should be used on the command parameter. C functions expect strings to be null-terminated, and the OPTIONS(*STRING) keyword handles this requirement for you. The prototype for system also shows that an integer is returned by the API. The API documentation says that this returned integer will be a zero if no error was found in executing the command, a one if an error was found, and a negative one if no command string was supplied.

If the command failed, the API sets the global variable _EXCP_MSGID to the error message ID returned by the command processor. To access this, we define the field CPFMsgID. Defining the field with IMPORT('_EXCP_MSGID') causes the field to be loaded with the contents of the global variable _EXCP_MSGID.

The logic of the program is very simple, as it is only intended to demonstrate how to code using the system function. The program accepts a command as a parameter and passes that command to the system function. If any errors are encountered, it will display the CPF message number. If not, the command is executed without any further interaction with the caller.

There are a few important points to note when working with C library functions. First, you should compile the program using the QC2LE binding directory. This binding directory exports the service programs making up the C-language API environment. Second, remember that procedure names are case-sensitive. This is true of any procedure/function, but it seems to catch non-C developers the most when working with C APIs, as the API names tend to be all lowercase. Third, and perhaps more important, remember that using the C library functions will in many ways introduce you to a new environment that is very different from the i5/OS environment you work in with RPG or COBOL. Rather than receiving CPF error messages, you will often work with a return value from the API which provides a general indication of success and failure. In the case of the system API, you do have access to one CPF error message with _EXCP_MSGID, but with most C APIs, you will be working with a C message variable known as *errno*. We will discuss this variable in more depth later in this book.

```
h dftactgrp(*no) bnddir('QC2LE')

DName+++++++++++ETDsFrom+++To/L+++IDc.Keywords++++++++++++++++++++++++++++
dFig4_9           pr                        extpgm('FIG4_9')
d Command                         30        const

dFig4_9           pi
d Command                         30        const

dSystem           pr             10i 0 extproc('system')
d Command                          *    value options(*string)

dCPFMsgID         s               7        import('_EXCP_MSGID')
dWait             s               1


CLON01Factor1+++++++Opcode&ExtFactor2+++++++Result++++++++Len++D+HiLoEq
 /free

   if (System(Command)) = 1;  // system API failed
      dsply CPFMsgID ' ' Wait;
   endif;

   *inlr = *on;
   return;

 /end-free
```

Figure 4.9: This program example uses C's system function to execute commands.

The QCMDCHK API

The Check Command Syntax API (QCMDCHK) lets you edit and prompt a command from within your program. This API is reasonably simple; it only requires that you pass the command you want to run and the length of the command string. The API edit checks the command, and when prompted, it returns the prompted values to your program. Figure 4.10 shows the use of this API to prompt the WRKACTJOB command. If the user were to specify additional parameters for the command while being prompted, these additional parameters would be returned to program FIG4_10.

```
DName+++++++++++ETDsFrom+++To/L+++IDc.Keywords++++++++++++++++++++++++++++
dCmdChk            pr                     extpgm('QCMDCHK')
d Command                         1       options(*varsize)
d CmdLength                      15 5 const
d IGC                             3       const options(*nopass)

dCommand           s            100       inz('?WRKACTJOB')

CLON01Factor1++++++Opcode&ExtFactor2++++++Result++++++++Len++D+HiLoEq
 /free
   CmdChk( Command :%size(Command));
   *inlr = *on;
   return;
 /end-free
```

Figure 4.10: This program example uses the QCMDCHK API to prompt the WRKACTJOB command.

As you can see in Table 4.2, the QCMDCHK parameters are virtually the same as those for QCMDEXC.

Table 4.2: Parameters for the Check Command Syntax API (QCMDCHK)			
Parameter	Description	Type	Size
1	Command String	I/O	Char(*)
2	Length of Command String	Input	Packed(15 5)
Optional Parameter Group 1			
3	IGC Process Control	Input	Char(3)

The first parameter, Command String, is the command you want to syntax check. If the command contains embedded blanks, the string must be enclosed within apostrophes. The command is not run. The second parameter, Length of Command String, is the length of the command specified in the first parameter, from one to 32,702 bytes. The third parameter, IGC Process Control, indicates whether ideographic data (also known as double-byte or DBCS data) is contained within the command string. The only value supported is *IGC*.

A Complete Command-Processing API

By now, you probably feel that you have a pretty good understanding of the QCMDEXC and QCMDCHK APIs. You know that QCMDEXC can be used to execute almost any command from within your program, and that QCMDCHK can be used to prompt for and edit a command from within your program. What if you simply wanted the operator to press a function key to get a window where a command could be entered? You would probably want to edit the command for validity. You might also want to record the information that the user entered in response to that prompt.

One way to accomplish these goals would be to combine QCMDCHK and QCMDEXC, but a better way would be to use the Process Commands API (QCAPCMD). QCAPCMD lets you edit a command string for validity, allow prompting, and return the command parameters to your program. It can either process the entered command or simply verify that the command is valid, and let you pass the changed command on to i5/OS to be run.

Table 4.3 documents the parameters for QCAPCMD. They might seem complicated at first, but a practical example is provided in Figure 4.12 to help you see the flexibility of this API.

Table 4.3: Required Input Parameters for the Command-Processing API (QCAPCMD)				
Parameter	Description		Type	Size
1	Source Command String		Input	Char(*)
2	Length of Source Command String		Input	Binary(4)
3	Options Control Block		Input	Char(*)
4	Options Control Block Length		Input	Binary(4)
5	Options Control Block Format		Input	Char(8)
6	Changed Command String		Output	Char(*)
7	Length Available For Changed Command String		Input	Binary(4)
8	Length of Changed Command String Available to Return		Output	Binary(4)
9	Error Code		I/O	Char(*)

The first parameter, Source Command String, is the command string to be prompted or run. The Length of Source Command String parameter is the length of the command specified in the first parameter, from one to 32,702 bytes.

The third parameter, Options Control Block, is a structure that specifies what processing options are to be used when working with the command passed in the first parameter. The Options Control Block Length parameter sets the length of this structure, and the Options Control Block Format parameter defines its layout. The only supported format is CPOP0100. The QSYSINC-provided definition for format CPOP0100 is shown in Figure 4.11.

```
DName++++++++++ETDsFrom+++To/L+++IDc.Keywords+++++++++++++++++++++++++++
D*********************************************************************
D*Type definition for the CPOP0100
D*********************************************************************
DQCAP0100            DS
D*                                              Qca PCMD CPOP0100
D QCACMDPT            1      4B 0
D*                                              Command Process Typ
D QCABCSDH            5      5
D*                                              DBCS Data Handling
D QCAPA               6      6
D*                                              Prompter Action
D QCACMDSS            7      7
D*                                              Command String Synt
D QCAMK               8     11
D*                                              Message Key
D QCASIDCS           12     15B 0
D*                                              CCSID Command String
D QCAERVED           16     20
D*                                              Reserved
```

Figure 4.11: The QSYSINC-provided definition for format CPOP0100 of the QCAPCMD API.

The QSYSINC-provided definition for data structure QCAP0100 includes several sub-fields. The first, QCACMDPT, defines the type of command processing to be done. The supported values are zero through 10:

- 0—Run the command.

- 1—Syntax-check the command.

- 2—Run the command as with value 0, but also support S/36 environment commands and prompt for any missing parameters that are required.

- 3—Syntax-check the command with additional support consistent with value 2.

- 4—Check the command based on the rules for a CL program statement.

- 5—Check the command based on the rules for a CL batch job stream.

- 6—Check the command based on the rules for a command definition statement.

- 7—Check the command based on the rules for a binder definition statement.

- 8—Check the command based on rules similar to those used by PDM for user-defined options.

- 9—Check the command based on the rules for an ILE CL program statement.

- 10—Prompt the command string with the QIBM_QCA_CHG_COMMAND exit point enabled prior to prompting

As you can see from this list, the QCAPCMD API has a lot more flexibility built into it than you find with the preceding APIs (QCMDEXC, QCMDCHK, and system). This API can do all that the previously discussed APIs can, plus quite a bit more!

The second field, QCABCSDH, is related to double-byte processing within the command string and will not be discussed in this book.

The third field, QCAPA, controls whether prompting is to be done with the command string. The supported values are zero through three:

- 0—Never prompt the command string.

- 1—Always prompt the command string.

- 2—Prompt the command if prompt-control characters are found in the command string.

- 3—Show the help for the command.

The fourth field, QCACMDSS, specifies what syntax should be used when processing the command. A value of zero means use the i5/OS conventions of *library/object name*. A value of one means use the S/38 conventions of *object.library name*.

The fifth field, QCAMK, can be used to provide a message mark key for a request message that should be replaced by the command string.

The sixth field, QCASIDCS, allows you to specify what CCSID the command string is encoded in. The supported values are zero for job CCSID, 1200 for UTF-16, or 1208 for UTF-8.

The seventh field, QCAERVED, is a reserved field that must be set to nulls (the x'00' character).

An example of QCAPCMD in action will help to bring everything together. Remember the simple list program in Figure 4.5, where QCMDEXC is used to override the printer attributes? The sample program in Figure 4.12 submits that job to the job queue. Granted, that is really no big deal in itself, but the program prompts for the Submit Job command, which allows the operator to change job-queue parameters as desired. The command will then not only be submitted to the job queue, but the completed command (including whatever parameters were added during the prompting process) will be returned to the program so the command string could, if desired, be logged by the application program.

```
DName+++++++++++ETDsFrom+++To/L+++IDc.Keywords++++++++++++++++++++++++++
d/copy qsysinc/qrpglesrc,qcapcmd
d/copy qsysinc/qrpglesrc,qusrjobi
d/copy qsysinc/qrpglesrc,qusec

dProcessCmd       pr                      extpgm('QCAPCMD')
d SourceCmd                      65535    const options(*varsize)
d LenSrcCmd                      10i 0    const
d CtlBlk                         65535    const options(*varsize)
d LenCtlBlk                      10i 0    const
d CtlBlkFmt                          8    const
d ChgCmd                             1    options(*varsize)
d LenAvlChgCmd                   10i 0    const
d LenRtnChgCmd                   10i 0
d QUSEC                                   likeds(QUSEC)

dRtvJobI          pr                      extpgm('QUSRJOBI')
d RcvVar                             1    options(*varsize)
d LenRcvVar                      10i 0    const
d RcvVarFmt                          8    const
d JobName                           26    const
d IntJobID                          16    const
d QUSEC                                   likeds(QUSEC) options(*nopass)
d Reset                              1    const options(*nopass)
```

*Figure 4.12: This example uses **QCAPCMD** to prompt commands from within a RPG program (part 1 of 2).*

```
dCommand              s              100
dCmdLen               s              10i 0
dNbrCopies            s               2    inz('01')
dWait                 s               1

CLON01Factor1+++++++Opcode&ExtFactor2+++++++Result++++++++Len++D+HiLoEq
/free

    // set error processing to not send exceptions
    QUSBPRV = %size(QUSEC);

    // get correct printer default for current job
    RtvJobI( QUSI030000 :%size(QUSI030000) :'JOBI0300' :'*' :' ' :QUSEC);

    if (QUSBAVL > 0); // check for error on API call
        dsply 'Error calling QUSRJOBI' ' ' Wait;
        *inlr = *on;
        return;
    endif;

    Command = 'SBMJOB CMD(CALL PGM(FIG4_5) PARM(''' + NbrCopies +
                  ''' ''' + %trimr(QUSPDN) + ''')) JOB(LISTCUST)';

    QCAP0100 = *loval; // initialize input structure to nulls
    QCACMDPT = 0;         // Run command
    QCABCSDH = '0';       // Ignore DBCS
    QCAPA = '1';          // Prompt command
    QCACMDSS = '0';       // User i5/OS syntax

    ProcessCmd( Command :%len(%trimr(Command)) :QCAP0100 :%size(QCAP0100)
                  :'CPOP0100' :Command :%size(Command) :CmdLen :QUSEC);

    if (QUSBAVL > 0);
        dsply 'Error submitting job' ' ' Wait;
    endif;

    *inlr = *on;
    return;

/end-free
```

Figure 4.12: This example uses **QCAPCMD** to prompt commands from within a RPG program (part 2 of 2).

Before performing the prompt for the Submit Job command, another API needs to be run to establish the default values for the operator of the program. Rather than hard-coding the printer device as we did in earlier examples, here we use a retrieve API. (This type of API was discussed in chapter 2.) The Retrieve Job Information API (QUSRJOBI) retrieves job attributes and returns them to your program. For the purposes of this program, the user's default printer ID is retrieved. That value is used as a default when the list program is submitted to the job queue. The parameters for QUSRJOBI are described in Table 4.4.

Table 4.4: Parameters for the Retrieve Job Information API (QUSRJOBI)			
Parameter	Description	Type	Size
1	Receiver Variable	Output	Char(*)
2	Length of Receiver Variable	Input	Binary(4)
3	Format Name	Input	Char(8)
4	Qualified Job Name	Input	Char(26)
5	Internal Job Identifier	Input	Char(16)
Optional Parameter Group 1			
6	Error Code	I/O	Char(*)
Optional Parameter Group 2			
7	Reset Performance Statistics	Input	Char(3)

You should be reasonably acquainted with the first three parameters by now; they are on many retrieve-type APIs. For the third parameter, Format Name, the Retrieve Job Information API supports several formats:

- JOBI0100 for basic performance information

- JOBI0150 for additional performance information

- JOBI0200 for information similar to that found with the Work with Active Jobs (WRKACTJOB) command

- JOBI0300 for job queue and output queue information

- JOBI0400 for job attribute information

- JOBI0500 for message logging information

- JOBI0600 for active job information

- JOBI0700 for library list information

- JOBI0750 for extended library-list information

- JOBI0800 for active-job signal information

- JOBI0900 for active-job SQL cursor information

- JOBI1000 for elapsed performance statistics

The fourth parameter, Qualified Job Name, allows you to specify what job, by name, is to be accessed. This parameter is made up of three subfields: Job Name, User Name, and Job Number. The Job Name subfield is the first ten bytes of the qualified job name and can have either a specific name or one of two special values. The special values are '*' for the job the API is running in, or '*INT' for a job that is identified with the fifth parameter, Internal Job Identifier. The User Name subfield is the next ten bytes of the Qualified Job Name parameter. It must specify a specific user profile name, or be set to blanks if a special value was used for the job name. The Job Number subfield is the last six bytes of the Qualified Job Name parameter. It can be either a specific job number, or blanks if a special value was use for the job name.

The fifth parameter, Internal Job Identifier, is an identifier returned by other APIs such as the List Jobs API (QUSLJOB). This identifier, if known, allows the system to more quickly locate the job to be retrieved than when a qualified job name is used. We will not be taking advantage of this capability in the sample program here. The List Job API is, however, discussed in chapter 13.

The sixth parameter is the error-code structure found with many system APIs, already discussed in chapters 1 and 2. The seventh parameter, Reset Performance Statistics, is related to format JOBI1000 of the Retrieve Job Information API and will not be used in the sample program.

The QUSRJOBI API is actually very simple to use, and it returns a veritable plethora of useful job information to your program. As you can see from the list of formats supported for the third parameter, you can extract a lot of job information from library list to performance data using this API. If you take a look at the QUSRJOBI source member in source file QRPGLESRC (library QSYSINC), you will see a detailed list of what each of these formats actually provides. Figure 4.12 uses format JOBI0300, so Figure 4.13 provides the definition for this format.

We specified the JOBI0300 format when calling the QUSRJOBI API because we were interested in information about the job and output queues. Within the information returned, we used the default printer ID (QUSPDN) in putting together the Submit Job command. If you look at the definition specifications for format JOBI0300, however, you'll see that there is a lot of other information at your disposal.

```
DName++++++++++++ETDsFrom+++To/L+++IDc.Keywords++++++++++++++++++++++++++++
D********************************************************************
D*Record structure for QUSRJOBI JOBI0300 format
D********************************************************************
DQUSI030000        DS
D*                                                    Qwc JOBI0300
D QUSBR02                  1      4B 0
D*                                                    Bytes Return
D QUSBA02                  5      8B 0
D*                                                    Bytes Avail
D QUSJN04                  9     18
D*                                                    Job Name
D QUSUN04                 19     28
D*                                                    User Name
D QUSJNBR04               29     34
D*                                                    Job Number
D QUSIJID02               35     50
D*                                                    Int Job ID
D QUSJS07                 51     60
D*                                                    Job Status
D QUSJT05                 61     61
D*                                                    Job Type
D QUSJS08                 62     62
D*                                                    Job Subtype
D QUSJN05                 63     72
D*                                                    Jobq Name
D QUSJL                   73     82
D*                                                    Jobq Lib
D QUSJP                   83     84
D*                                                    Jobq Priority
D QUSON                   85     94
D*                                                    Outq Name
D QUSOL                   95    104
D*                                                    Outq Lib
D QUSOP                  105    106
D*                                                    Outq Priority
D QUSPDN                 107    116
D*                                                    Prt Dev Name
D QUSSJN                 117    126
D*                                                    Subm Job Name
D QUSSUN                 127    136
D*                                                    Subm User Name
D QUSSJNBR               137    142
D*                                                    Subm Job Num
D QUSSMN                 143    152
D*                                                    Subm Msgq Name
```

Figure 4.13: Data definitions from QSYSINC *for format* JOBI0300 *of the* QUSRJOBI *API (part 1 of 2).*

139

```
D QUSSML                    153     162
D*                                              Subm Msgq Lib
D QUSSOJ                    163     172
D*                                              Sts On Jobq
D QUSDPOJ                   173     180
D*                                              Date Put On Jobq
D QUSJD                     181     187
D*                                              Job Date
```

Figure 4.13: Data definitions from QSYSINC for format JOBI0300 of the QUSRJOBI API (part 2 of 2).

The next step in putting together the Submit Job command involves concatenating the various components of the SBMJOB and CALL commands. After that, we set the correct control values for the QCAPCMD API. One important aspect that is shown here is the initializing of the entire QCAP0100 data structure to *LOVAL (or nulls). Many APIs that use input data structures document that reserved fields need to be set to null values. In QCAP0100, there is a reserved field named QCAERVED, but you do not want to explicitly set this field within your program to *LOVAL (or x'00'). The definition for reserved fields may change over time as i5/OS adds more capabilities to the API, and in some cases the entire reserved field may disappear. By initializing the entire structure, not the specific reserved fields of the structure, you are writing your application in a way that best accommodates future changes in the APIs that you use.

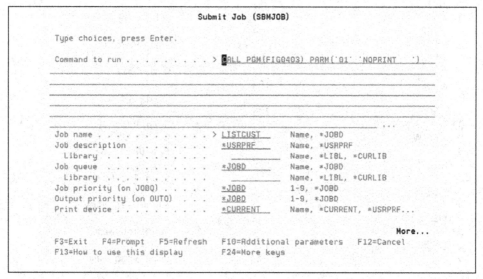

```
                          Submit Job (SBMJOB)

    Type choices, press Enter.

    Command to run . . . . . . . . . > CALL PGM(FIG0403) PARM('01' 'NOPRINT   ')
    _____
    _____
    _____
    _____
                                                                       ...
    Job name . . . . . . . . . . . > LISTCUST     Name, *JOBD
    Job description  . . . . . . .   *USRPRF      Name, *USRPRF
      Library  . . . . . . . . . .                Name, *LIBL, *CURLIB
    Job queue  . . . . . . . . . .   *JOBD        Name, *JOBD
      Library  . . . . . . . . . .                Name, *LIBL, *CURLIB
    Job priority (on JOBQ) . . . .   *JOBD        1-9, *JOBD
    Output priority (on OUTQ) . . .  *JOBD        1-9, *JOBD
    Print device . . . . . . . . .   *CURRENT     Name, *CURRENT, *USRPRF...

                                                                    More...
    F3=Exit   F4=Prompt   F5=Refresh   F10=Additional parameters   F12=Cancel
    F13=How to use this display      F24=More keys
```

Figure 4.14: This screen is the result of using QCAPCMD to prompt commands from within a RPG program.

When the program is run, you will see a screen similar to the one in Figure 4.14. Operators can use the prompting features as desired to modify the Submit Job commands, but all of the default information has been provided for them up front. Once the prompting is complete, the job will be submitted (unless it is terminated by the operator).

A nice feature of this API is that the final command submitted to the job queue (after prompting) is actually returned to the program as the sixth parameter of the API (Command, in the program). We elected not to do anything with it for this example, but this information could be written to a log file or printed on a submitted job report somewhere.

The IBM Command-Line API

If all you want to do is provide the user a command line, you can use the Command Line API (QUSCMDLN). This is among the easiest of all APIs to use. It is even easier than using QCMDEXC. All you do is call it; there are no parameters to worry about.

Figure 4.15 shows the command entry screen that is presented when you run QUSCMDLN. Commands entered on the command line can be prompted via the F4 function key. Using the F9 function key retrieves previous commands. The API provides both of these capabilities. There is no coding necessary to provide these functions other than calling the API!

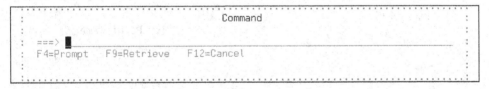

Figure 4.15: A command-entry screen results from using the Command Line API (QUSCMDLN).

The Command-Analyzer Retrieve Exit Program

Just like there are many callable APIs on the system, there are also many exit points provided with i5/OS. An *exit point* gives you the ability to have a user program, known as an *exit program*, receive control when some predefined event takes place. In the case of commands, an exit point allows you to receive information about when a specific command is to be run on the system. There is also an exit point that allows you to not only know when a command is to be run, but also to change the command before it's run! For now, we'll look at the Command-Analyzer Retrieve Exit program, but when you get more adventurous, you may want to look at the Command-Analyzer Change Exit program, also. The documentation for both programs can be found in the "Program and CL Command" category of system APIs. Exit programs are found by scrolling to the bottom of the APIs within the category.

Table 4.5 shows the parameter passed to the Command-Analyzer Retrieve Exit program, and Figure 4.16 shows the QSYSINC-provided definitions for the parameter.

Table 4.5: Parameter for the Command-Analyzer Retrieve Exit Program			
Parameter	Description	Type	Size
1	Retrieve Command Exit Information	Input	Char(*)

The only parameter, Retrieve Command Exit Information, provides information about the command that is being processed. Only one format is currently supported, RTVC0100, which is specified when you register your exit program with the system. This registration process will be shown later, in Figure 4.18. The QSYSINC-provided definition for format RTVC0100 is shown in Figure 4.16.

```
DName+++++++++++ETDsFrom+++To/L+++IDc.Keywords++++++++++++++++++++++++++++
D********************************************************************************
D*Type definition for format RTVC0100
D********************************************************************************
DECAC010000         DS
D*                                              Qca Rtv RTVC0100
D ECAEPN00                  1     20
D*                                              Exit Point Name
D ECAEPFN00                21     28
D*                                              Exit Point Format Name
D ECACMDN00                29     38
D*                                              Command Name
D ECALIBN00                39     48
D*                                              Library Name
D ECAERVED00               49     52
D*                                              Reserved
D ECAOCS0                  53     56B 0
D*                                              Original Command String
D ECAOCSL                  57     60B 0
D*                                              Original Command String
D ECARCS0                  61     64B 0
D*                                              Replacement Cmd String
```

Figure 4.16: Data definitions from QSYSINC for the Command-Analyzer Retrieve Exit program (part 1 of 2).

```
D ECARCSL              65     68B 0
D*                                      Replacement Cmd String
D ECAPCC000            69     72B 0
D*                                      Proxy Cmd Chain Offset
D ECANOPC00            73     76B 0
D*                                      Number Of Proxy Com
D*                                            @PCA
D*ECAOCMDS             77     77
D*                                      Original Command St
D*
D*ECARCMDS             78     78
D*                                      Replacement Command
D*
D*ECAPCMDC00           79     79
D*                                      Proxy Command Chain
D*
```

Figure 4.16: Data definitions from QSYSINC for the Command-Analyzer Retrieve Exit program (part 2 of 2).

Within the QSYSINC-provided ECAC010000 data structure are several fields. The first, ECAEPN00, is the name of the exit point calling the exit program. For the command-analyzer retrieve exit, this will be 'QIBM_QCA_RTV_COMMAND'. This information can be used when one exit program is registered to multiple exit points.

The second field, ECAEPFN00, is the exit-point format name. For the command analyzer retrieve exit, this will be 'RTVC0100'. As with ECAEPN00, ECAEPFN00 can be used to determine why the exit program is being called.

The third field, ECACMDN00, is the name of the command being processed. The fourth field, ECALIBN00, is the name of the library where the command returned in ECACMDN00 was located. The fifth field, ECAERVED00, is a reserved field not currently being used. The sixth field, ECAOCSO, is the offset to the original command string that was to be processed. The seventh field, ECAOCSL, is the length of the original command string located at offset ECAOCSO.

The eighth field, ECARCSO, is the offset to the replacement command string. A replacement command string, overriding the original command string, is possible if an exit program is register to the QIBM_QCA_CHG_COMMAND exit point and has changed the original command. This field will be set to zero if no change has been made by an exit program.

The ninth field, ECARCSL, is the length of the replacement command string located at offset ECARCSO (if ECARCSO is greater than zero). The tenth field, ECAPCC000, is the offset to the proxy that resulted in the command being processed. The eleventh field, ECANOPC00, is the number of entries in the proxy chain.

Using the information from Table 4.5 and Figure 4.16, we can write the program shown in Figure 4.17. This program will be called by i5/OS whenever the End Job (ENDJOB) command is used. The program will create a report showing the ENDJOB command that was run. Writing an exit program is not that much different from writing a program that calls a retrieve-type API. The only difference is that now i5/OS is calling you, rather than you calling an i5/OS API.

```
FFilename++IPEASF.....L.....A.Device+.Keywords+++++++++++++++++++++++++
fQsysprt    o    f   132        printer

DName+++++++++++ETDsFrom+++To/L+++IDc.Keywords++++++++++++++++++++++++++
d/copy qsysinc/qrpglesrc,ecartcmd

dFig4_17              pr                    extpgm('FIG4_17')
d Receiver                                 likeds(ECAC010000)

dFig4_17              pi
d Receiver                                 likeds(ECAC010000)

dCmdPtr               s                *
dCmd                  s            100     based(CmdPtr)
dCmdLine              s            100
dCount                s            10i 0

CLON01Factor1+++++++Opcode&ExtFactor2+++++++Result++++++++Len++D+HiLoEq
 /free

    if Receiver.ECARCSO <> 0;      // get replacement command string
       CmdPtr = %addr(Receiver) + Receiver.ECARCSO;
       Count = Receiver.ECARCSL;
    else;                          // no replacement, use original command
       CmdPtr = %addr(Receiver) + Receiver.ECAOCSO;
       Count = Receiver.ECAOCSL;
    endif;

    except Header;

    dow Count > 0;
```

Figure 4.17: A program to log the use of the End Job (ENDJOB) command (part 1 of 2).

```
   if Count < 100;
      CmdLine = Cmd;
      %subst(CmdLine :Count + 1 :100 - Count) = *blanks;
   else;
     CmdLine = Cmd;
     CmdPtr = CmdPtr + 100;
   endif;
   Count -= 100;
   except Detail;
   enddo;

   *inlr = *on;
   return;

 /end-free

OFilename++DF..N01N02N03Excnam++++B++A++Sb+Sa+.......................
oQsysprt    e                 Header        2 1
o                                               58 'ENDJOB Requests'
oQsysprt    e                 Detail        1
o                             CmdLine            110
```

Figure 4.17: A program to log the use of the End Job (ENDJOB) command (part 2 of 2).

The program FIG4_17 defines the one parameter passed (Receiver) using the fixed-size fields of the ECAC010000 data structure provided in QSYSINC/QRPGLESRC member ECARTCMD. The name of this member is found in the Information Center documentation. The API documentation shows that there are both fixed-size fields and variable-length fields. The variable-length fields represent the original command string, the replaced command string in case a program used the QIBM_QCA_CHG_COMMAND exit point to change the original command, and the proxy command chain if proxy commands are being used.

We don't have any idea in advance just how large these command strings and proxy chains might be (especially if IBM were to add more parameters or support for a longer proxy chain in some future release), so trying to define the maximum size of the Receiver data structure when developing the program could be a problem. Fortunately, with pointers, we don't have to worry about it! We can simply define what we do know (the fields provided in the QSYSINC member) and define the variable-length fields as stand-alone fields based on a pointer, where we will set the pointer to an appropriate value based on the fixed fields in Receiver. This is what is being done with the definitions of CmdPtr and Cmd, which we will discuss in more detail a bit later. The program also defines the two fields CmdLine and Count, which are used to control the formatting of the command when it's printed.

When program FIG4_17 is run, it first checks to see if the offset to the replacement command string (ECARCSO) is zero. If it's not, then another program using the QIBM_QCA_CHG_COMMAND exit point has replaced the command string initially processed with another command string. In this case, the program sets CmdPtr to the start of the replacement command string with this line:

```
CmdPtr = %addr(Receiver) + Receiver.ECARCSO
```

This causes Cmd to represent the first 100 bytes of the replacement command string because Cmd is defined as Based(CmdPtr). The program then sets Count to the total length of the replacement command string.

If the offset to the replacement command string (ECARCSO) is zero, then the original command is being run. The program sets CmdPtr to the start of the original command string with this line:

```
CmdPtr = %addr(Receiver) + Receiver.ECAOCSO;
```

This causes Cmd to represent the first 100 bytes of the original command string. The Count is then set to the total length of the original command string. In either case, CmdPtr now points at the command string to be processed and Count reflects the length of that command string.

FIG4_17 then prints a header line and begins to process the command that is to be run. The main processing involves breaking up the command (which in theory could be hundreds or thousands of characters long) into 100-byte lines so that we can print it. Essentially, the program checks to see if any part of the command to be printed has not already been printed (Count is greater than zero). If more printing is needed, and if the Count of bytes in the command string is greater than or equal to 100, FIG4_17 moves the current 100 bytes of Cmd to CmdLine, increments the pointer CmdPtr by 100 bytes so that Cmd now represents the next 100 bytes of the command, and decrements Count by 100. If less than 100 bytes remain to be printed, the remaining bytes of Cmd are moved to CmdLine, and the remainder of CmdLine is set to blanks. The 100 bytes of command text held in CmdLine is then printed. If no additional command text needs to be printed (Count is less than or equal to zero), the program ends.

One aspect of the FIG4_17 program still needs to be discussed. You might wonder why the command text to be printed is moved to CmdLine from Cmd. The reason has to do with the blank filling of the last printed line when the text that remains is less than 100 bytes. FIG4_17 defines Cmd as being 100 bytes, but this is really just an arbitrary definition, as we don't know in advance if the ENDJOB command text might be 50 bytes or 150 bytes. We simply picked 100 as a convenient number of bytes to print on one line of the generated report.

Cmd is also defined as being Based on CmpPtr, where the amount of storage actually allocated to the command text might be 50 bytes, or it might be 150 bytes. If it is 50 bytes and FIG4_15 simply moves *BLANKS to bytes 51 through 100, we don't know what storage is really being overwritten. This would be similar to having an RPG program pass a parameter to another program where the caller defines the parameter as 10 bytes, and the called program defines the parameter as 40 bytes. If the called program modifies the thirty-fifth byte of the parameter, strange things might happen when the called program returns! Likewise, modifying the passed parameters at locations beyond the length defined by the exit point is dangerous. In this case, if the defined length is less than 100 bytes, we cannot assume it is safe to modify up to 100 bytes. Instead, we need to copy the defined length to a local variable that we have allocated.

It isn't really necessary to move Cmd to CmdLine when the length (Count) is 100 or more because there is no need for blank-filling the printed line. In this case, we could have used another Except line, directly outputting CmdLine. We elected to copy the data to CmdLine primarily for consistency.

You should also be aware that, while the QIBM_QCA_RTV_COMMAND exit point will pass you the command to be run, there is no guarantee that the command will run successfully. For example, if a user does an ENDJOB on a job that does not exist, the exit program is called prior to the system determining that the job cannot be found. That being said, this exit point is extremely powerful in terms of being able to track command usage on the system.

To activate the FIG4_17 program in library SOMELIB, you need to register the program and associate it with the ENDJOB command. Do this with the Add Exit Program (ADDEXITPGM) command as shown in Figure 4.18, or by using the Work with Registration Information (WRKREGINF) command and adding the exit program to exit point QIBM_QCA_RTV_COMMAND.

```
ADDEXITPGM EXITPNT(QIBM_QCA_RTV_COMMAND) FORMAT(RTVC0100) PGMNBR(*LOW)
PGM(SOMELIB/FIG4_17) PGMDTA(*JOB *CALC 'ENDJOB      QSYS        ')
```

Figure 4.18: Registering FIG4_17 with the ENDJOB command.

To deactivate the exit program, use the RMVEXITPGM command as shown in Figure 4.19, or use the Work with Registration Information (WRKREGINF) command and remove the exit programs associated with exit point QIBM_QCA_RTV_COMMAND. Note that the program number (PGMNBR) for your system may be other than the *1* used in Figure 4.19 if there have been exit programs previously registered to this exit point. You should verify the program number using WRKREGINF.

```
RMVEXITPGM EXITPNT(QIBM_QCA_RTV_COMMAND) FORMAT(RTVC0100) PGMNBR(1)
```

Figure 4.19: Deregistering FIG4_17 from the ENDJOB command.

As you might expect, there are also APIs to add and remove exit programs (along with APIs for registering and deregistering exit points). We will not discuss these APIs in this book as using the command interface is sufficient. If you are interested in using these APIs, the documentation for them can be found in the Information Center under the API category "Registration Facility."

Summary

As you have seen, APIs provide some very powerful capabilities for integrating CL commands within your applications. Take the time to learn how to use the command-processing APIs. You will find that the ability to run a CL command from within an application, or receive control when a CL command is run, opens up a huge world of opportunities!

Check Your Knowledge

Assuming that you have a library named somelib, write a program to create a data queue (*DTAQ) named testq in that library. The *DTAQ should be a standard *FIFO queue with a maximum entry length of 1,000 bytes. Use the Execute Command API (QCMDEXC) and the command CRTDTAQ. The documentation for this API can be found by searching the API Finder for the name QCMDEXC, or by looking at the "Program and CL Command" category of APIs.

One possible solution to this task can be found in Figure D.4 in appendix D.

5

Object APIs

Everything on the system is an object. If you run the WRKOBJ command and use F4 with the Type parameter, you will see a listing of many different types of objects. Libraries, files, user spaces, and output queues are all objects. If you want to work with an i5/OS object programmatically, APIs are, without a doubt, your best bet. However, if all of the object APIs were included in this chapter, you would have to carry it around in a wheelbarrow. Therefore, this chapter limits the exploration of object-related APIs to just a few generic ones. Later chapters focus on APIs for specific types of objects. Chapter 6, for instance, focuses on APIs for data queues.

In chapter 3, you saw how to use the List Objects (QUSLOBJ) and Open List of Objects (QGYOLOBJ) APIs, which work with pretty much any type of object. We won't go over that material again here. This chapter starts off with Retrieve Object Description API (QUSROBJD), which allows you to access information about a specific object (as opposed to getting a list of objects). This API tells you everything you want to know about an object, and then some. Ironically, one of our favorite uses for this API involves calling it, but ignoring all of the data that it is capable of returning about the object. We call it just to see if an object exists. You'll learn about this procedure in detail.

Libraries are one of the most common objects on the system because most other types of objects reside in a library. As you are aware, a library object is really nothing more than a directory that groups objects together. You typically want to know the total size of all of the objects that reside in the library. A simple solution to this problem involves the Retrieve Library Description API (QLIRLIBD). The sample program provided in this chapter returns the summarized size of all objects within a given library.

The documentation for the APIs covered in this chapter can be found in the Information Center under the category "Object," and the subcategory "Object-related APIs."

To Exist or Not to Exist, That Is the Question

With apologies to Mr. Shakespeare, the question of whether a given object exists or not is often important when you need to edit operator entries. For example, you might present users with a screen that allows them to enter a printer name or output queue to which the program will send a report. Frequently, a user will mistype the name of the desired printer or output queue. To avoid surprising the operator with CPF-type system errors, it is better for your program to determine if the object name really exists on the system. Of course, even better would be to display a list of printers or output queues, and let users select their destinations. Why have them type in names, when APIs such as Open List of Printers (QGYRPRTL) and List Objects (QUSLOBJ) can present them with a list?

Figure 5.1 shows the code for a procedure called Exists. It uses the Retrieve Object Description API (QUSROBJD) to attempt to retrieve information about a given object. For the purposes of this example, it really doesn't matter what information it finds. We are more interested in what the API does *not* find. If the specified object is not found, the API fills the standard error data structure with an error code, informing you that the object doesn't exist.

```
h nomain
 *
 * This procedure returns a 'Y'if an object exists
 *                          a 'N'if it doesn't exist
 *

DName++++++++++++ETDsFrom+++To/L+++IDc.Keywords+++++++++++++++++++++++++
dExists              pr           1     extproc('Exists')
d ObjectName                     10     const
d ObjectType                     10     const
d ObjectLib                      10     const options(*nopass)
```

Figure 5.1: The EXISTS procedure attempts to retrieve information about a given object (part 1 of 3).

```
PName++++++++++.....T.................... Keywords++++++++++++++++++++++++
pExists                b                   export

DName+++++++++++ETDsFrom+++To/L+++IDc... Keywords+++++++++++++++++++++++++
dExists                pi          1
d ObjectName                       10      const
d ObjectType                       10      const
d ObjectLib                        10      const options(*nopass)

d/copy qsysinc/qrpglesrc,qusec
d/copy qsysinc/qrpglesrc,qusrobjd

dRObjD                 pr                  extpgm('QUSROBJD')
d Receiver                         1       options(*varsize)
d ReceiverLen                      10i  0  const
d Format                           8       const
d ObjLibName                       20      const
d ObjectType                       10      const
d QUSEC                                    likeds(QUSEC) options(*nopass)
d ASPControl                       65535   const options(*varsize :*nopass)

dObjLibName            ds
d ObjName                          10
d ObjLib                           10      inz('*LIBL')

dWait                  s           1

CLON01Factor1+++++++Opcode&ExtFactor2+++++++Result++++++++Len++D+HiLoEq
 /free
  QUSBPRV = %size(QUSEC);
  ObjName = ObjectName;
  if (%parms = 3);
     ObjLib = ObjectLib;
  endif;
  RObjD( QUSD0100   :%size(QUSD0100) :'OBJD0100' :ObjLibname
        :ObjectType :QUSEC);
  select;
    when (QUSBAVL = 0);    // object found with no error
         return 'Y';
    when ((QUSEI = 'CPF9801') or (QUSEI = 'CPF9811') or
         (QUSEI = 'CPF9812') or (QUSEI = 'CPF9814')); // not found
         return 'N';
    when ((QUSEI = 'CPF9802') or (QUSEI = 'CPF9820') or
         (QUSEI = 'CPF9821') or (QUSEI = 'CPF9822') or
         (QUSEI = 'CPF9825')); // found but not authorized
         return 'Y';
```

Figure 5.1: The EXISTS procedure attempts to retrieve information about a given object (part 2 of 3).

```
    other;
      dsply ('Unexpected error: ' + QUSEI + ' received') ' ' Wait;
      return 'N';
    endsl;

 /end-free

 PName+++++++++++..T.................Keywords+++++++++++++++++++++++++++
 pExists             e
```

Figure 5.1: The EXISTS procedure attempts to retrieve information about a given object (part 3 of 3).

The procedure in Figure 5.1 is primarily concerned with inspecting the standard error-code structure. The documentation for QUSROBJD shows that many error messages might be returned by the API. The first thing the procedure does is look to see if any error was returned (with QUSBAVL = 0;) . If no error was returned, then the object was found, and the procedure Exists returns the value Y to indicate this.

If an error was found by the API, the procedure starts looking for specific errors based on the API documentation. First, it tests for an error related to the object not being found. If any of several "not found" situations occurred (CPF9801, CPF9811, CPF9812, or CPF9814), the procedure simply returns the value N. But it's not done yet! The object might have been found, but we aren't authorized to use it. The procedure next checks for these types of errors (CPF9802, CPF9820, CPF9821, or CPF9822). If found, the procedure returns the value of Y because the object does exist; we just can't use it! For any other error, it DSPLYs that an unexpected error occurred and provides the error-message ID.

Take a closer look at QUSROBJD. This API uses seven parameters, described in Table 5.1.

The first parameter, Receiver Variable, will hold the returned data.

The second parameter, Length of Receiver Variable, is the size we have allocated for the data to be returned in the first parameter. As mentioned previously, if you pass a length value greater than the actual size allocated for the first parameter, the data returned could overflow into other fields. Wanting to make sure we do not define the length greater than the actual length of the variable we are using, we pass %SIZE(QUSD0100) for the second parameter in the example program. We are using data structure QUSD0100 as that is the IBM provided definition for format OBJD0100, the format we are calling for with the QUSROBJD API. (Strictly speaking, we could simply pass a fixed value of eight for the Length of Receiver Variable parameter. This is the minimum size that can be used and would minimize the movement of data into the program's QUSD0100 data structure, and we really don't care

Table 5.1: Retrieve Object Description API (QUSROBJD)			
Parameter	Description	Type	Size
1	Receiver Variable	Output	Char(*)
2	Length of Receiver Variable	Input	Binary(4)
3	Format Name	Input	Char(8)
4	Qualified Object Name	Input	Char(20)
5	Object Type	Input	Char(10)
Optional Parameter Group 1			
6	Error Code	I/O	Char(*)
Optional Parameter Group 2			
7	Auxiliary Storage Pool (ASP) Control	Input	Char(*)

about the information being returned. We shudder, however, at the thought of using such an approach, since we're trying to introduce good programming technique when working with system APIs, not how to code for the one-in-a-thousand exception.)

The third parameter, Format Name, describes the format of the data being returned. The QUSROBJD API supports four formats:

- OBJD0100—Basic information
- OBJD0200—Information similar to that displayed by PDM
- OBJD0300—Service information
- OBJD0400—Full information

Remember, we only really care about whether or not the object exists, not information related to the object. Therefore, the program uses format OBJD0100, as it is documented as being the fastest one to retrieve.

The fourth parameter, Qualified Object Name, is the object name and library. The special values *CURLIB and *LIB are supported for the library name. The fifth parameter, Object Type, is the object type for the object identified in the Qualified Object Name parameter.

153

The sixth parameter is the standard error structure, and the seventh parameter allows you to specify optional auxiliary storage pool information.

The FIG5_1 program defines two required and one optional parameters. The two required parameters are Object Name and Object Type. The optional third parameter is the library where the object is located. If the Library parameter is not passed, FIG5_1 defaults to *LIBL. As FIG5_1 simply passes the Library parameter on to the QUSROBJD API, the special value *CURLIB, supported by the API, is also supported by FIG5_1.

QUSROBJD is a relatively easy API to use, but don't let its simplicity fool you. It can return some high-powered information. Want to know the last time a file was saved? Want to know who created the object, and when? How about who owns it? This API can return all of this information and more.

Checking whether an object exists is a reasonably frequent activity, so let's add this to the APILIB *BNDDIR created in chapter 1. We do that with these lines:

```
CRTRPGMOD MODULE(FIG5_1)

CRTSRVPGM SRVPGM(FIG5_1) EXPORT(*ALL)

ADDBNDDIRE BNDDIR(APILIB) OBJ((FIG5_1))
```

To use Exists, create the program shown in Figure 5.2. Calling FIG5_2, you should see the message "Object found."

```
h dftactgrp(*no) bnddir('APILIB')

DName+++++++++++ETDsFrom+++To/L+++IDc.Keywords++++++++++++++++++++++++
dExists           pr              1    extproc('Exists')
d ObjectName                      10   const
d ObjectType                      10   const
d ObjectLib                       10   const options(*nopass)

dWait             s               1
```

*Figure 5.2: Use the EXISTS procedure to see if the APILIB *SRVPGM exists (part 1 of 2).*

```
CLON01Factor1+++++++Opcode&ExtFactor2+++++++Result++++++++Len++D+HiLoEq
  /free
    if (Exists( 'FIG5_1' :'*SRVPGM') = 'Y');
        dsply 'Object found' ' ' Wait;
    else;
        dsply 'Object not found' ' ' Wait;
    endif;
    *inlr = *on;
    return;
  /end-free
```

*Figure 5.2: Use the EXISTS procedure to see if the APILIB *SRVPGM exists (part 2 of 2).*

An Alternative to DSPLIBD and DSPLIB

System administrators often need to know the size of a library. IBM's Display Library Description (DSPLIBD) command shows information about the library, but not the size of all the objects in it. The Display Library (DSPLIB) command will show the size of the objects within a library when using OUTPUT(*PRINT), but processing a report within a program isn't considered a reliable way to process information, as report layouts can change with new releases or different languages (such as English and German). How can an application obtain the total size of a library?

There is an API, of course, that will give you this essential information: the Retrieve Library Description API (QLIRLIBD). This API tells you everything there is to know about a library. Sometimes, however, you might be looking for object information, like who owns the library, when it was created, and when it was last saved.

You already know that the Retrieve Object Description API (QUSROBJD) can be used to retrieve information common to all objects. A program that uses the Retrieve Library Description API and the Retrieve Object Description API will show you library information that is considerably more useful than the DSPLIBD and DSPLIB commands. The output from such a program is shown in Figure 5.3. It combines object information with specific library information to present a panel with more pertinent information.

The code for this display file is shown in Figure 5.4. The program itself is shown in Figure 5.5.

The first thing the program in Figure 5.5 does is call QUSROBJD to get information about the library. Table 5.1 shows the parameters for this API. The program uses format OBJD0400, shown in Figure 5.6, which returns all information about the object. Here are the specific fields of interest to us:

```
                        Display Library Description

     Library: RON          Ron Hawkins

     Owned by:             QPGMR
     Created by:           QPGMR

     Created date:           12/20/96
     Last Saved Date/Time:   08/10/00      56:19
     Restored Date/Time:     06/13/99 22:20:37


     Number of objects:           277
     Size of all objects:    299569152




      F3=Exit
```

Figure 5.3: This Display Library Description screen presents the number and size of objects in a library.

```
AAN01N02N03T.Name++++++RLen++TDpBLinPosFunctions+++++++++++++++++++++++
                                       CA03(03)
          R FORMAT1
                                    1 29'Display Library
Description'
                                    3  2'Library:'
              LIBRARY      10A  O   3 11
              QUSTD14      50A  O   3 24
                                    5  2'Owned by:'
              QUSOBJ007    10A  O   5 24
                                    6  2'Created by:'
              QUSCUP04     10A  O   6 24
                                    8  2'Created date:'
              CRTDATE      10A  O   8 24
                                    9  2'Last Saved Date/Time:'
              LSTSAVDAT    10A  O   9 24
              LSTSAVTIM    6Y   00  9 35 EDTWRD('  :  : 0')
                                   10  2'Restored Date/Time:'
              RSTDATE      10A  O  10 24
              RSTTIME      6Y   00 10 35 EDTWRD('  :  : 0')
                                   13  2'Number of objects:'
              TOTALOBJS    10Y  00 13 37 EDTCDE(1)
                                   14  2'Size of all objects:'
              TOTALSIZE    20Y  00 14 24 EDTCDE(1)
                                   24  2'F3=Exit'
```

Figure 5.4: The display file used by the FIG5_5 program.

```
FFilename++IPEASFRlen+LKlen+AIDevice+.Keywords++++++++++++++++++++++++
fFIG5_4    cf   e            workstn

DName+++++++++++ETDsFrom+++To/L+++IDc.Keywords++++++++++++++++++++++++
dFig5_5             pr                extpgm('FIG5_5')
d Library                     10      const

dFig5_5             pi
d Library                     10      const

d/copy qsysinc/qrpglesrc,qusrobjd
d/copy qsysinc/qrpglesrc,qlirlibd
d/copy qsysinc/qrpglesrc,qus
d/copy qsysinc/qrpglesrc,qusec

dRObjD              pr                extpgm('QUSROBJD')
d Receiver                     1      options(*varsize)
d ReceiverLen                10i 0    const
Format                         8      const
d ObjLibName                  20      const
d ObjectType                  10      const
d QUSEC                                likeds(QUSEC) options(*nopass)
d ASPControl               65535      const options(*varsize :*nopass)

dRLibD              pr                extpgm('QLIRLIBD')
d Receiver                     1      options(*varsize)
d RecieverLen                10i 0    const
d Library                     10      const
d Attributes               65535      const options(*varsize)
d QUSEC                                likeds(QUSEC)

dObjLibName         ds
d ObjName                     10
d ObjLib                      10      inz('QSYS')

dAttributes         ds
d NbrAttributes              10i 0
d Key                        10i 0    dim(10)

dReceiver           ds        256     qualified
d Hdr                                  likeds(QLIRR)

dEntry              ds                based(EntryPtr)
d                                      qualified
d EntryHdr                             likeds(QUSVR4)
```

Figure 5.5: A program that displays information related to a library (part 1 of 3).

```
d Key6LibSiz                    10i 0 overlay(Entry :13)
d Key6LibMult                   10i 0 overlay(Entry :*next)
d Key6LibSts                    1    overlay(Entry :*next)
d Key7NbrObjs                   10i 0 overlay(Entry :13)

dCount              s           10u 0
dWait               s           1

CL0N01Factor1+++++++Opcode&ExtFactor2+++++++Result++++++++Len++D+HiLoEq
 /free
  QUSBPRV = %size(QUSEC);
  ObjName = Library;

  dou (*in03 = *on);

     RObjD( QUSD0400 :%size(QUSD0400) :'OBJD0400' :ObjLibName
            :'*LIB'  :QUSEC);

     if (QUSBAVL <> 0);
        dsply ('Error ' + QUSEI + ' while retrieving library object')
              ' 'Wait;
        *inlr = *on;
        return;
     endif;

     if (QUSCDT16 <> *blanks);      // creation date
        CrtDate = %char(%date(%subst(QUSCDT16:2:6):*YMD0):*JOBRUN);
     endif;

     if (QUSORDT03 <> *blanks);     // restore date
        RstDate = %char(%date(%subst(QUSORDT03:2:6):*YMD0):*JOBRUN);
        RstTime = %dec(%subst(QUSORDT03:8:6):6:0);
     endif;

     if (QUSOSDT03 <> *blanks);     // save date
        LstSavDat = %char(%date(%subst(QUSOSDT03:2:6):*YMD0):*JOBRUN);
        LstSavTim = %dec(%subst(QUSOSDT03:8:6):6:0);
     endif;

     NbrAttributes = 2;
     Key(1) = 6;                    // library size
     Key(2) = 7;                    // number of objects in library

     RLibD( Receiver :%size(Receiver) :Library :Attributes :QUSEC);
```

Figure 5.5: A program that displays information related to a library (part 2 of 3).

```
    if (QUSBAVL <> 0);
        dsply ('Error ' + QUSEI + ' while retrieving library desc')
                ' ' Wait;
        *inlr = *on;
        return;
    endif;

    EntryPtr = %addr(Receiver) + %size(Receiver.Hdr);

    for Count = 1 to Receiver.Hdr.QLIVRRTN;
        select;
            when (Entry.EntryHdr.QUSCK = 6);
                TotalSize = Entry.Key6LibSiz * Entry.Key6LibMult;
            when (Entry.EntryHdr.QUSCK = 7);
                TotalObjs = Entry.Key7NbrObjs;
            other;
                dsply ('Unexpected key ' + %char(Entry.EntryHdr.QUSCK) +
                        ' found.') ' ' Wait;
            endsl;
            EntryPtr = EntryPtr + Entry.EntryHdr.QUSLVR00;
    endfor;

    exfmt Format1;
 enddo;

 *inlr = *on;
 return;

/end-free
```

Figure 5.5: A program that displays information related to a library (part 3 of 3).

- QUSTD14—The text description for the object.

- QUSOBJO07—The user profile of the owner of the object.

- QUSCUP04—The user profile of who created the object.

- QUSCDT16—The date and time the object was created. This is returned in *CYYMMDDHHMMSS* format.

- QUSOSDT03—The date and time the object was last saved. This is returned in *CYYMMDDHHMMSS* format.

- QUSORDT03—The date and time the object was last restored. This is returned in *CYYMMDDHHMMSS* format.

For information on the other fields returned by format OBJD0400, see the Information Center.

Format OBJD0400 gives everything you need except the total number and size of all the objects in the library. For that, the QLIRLIBD API is used. Prior to calling QLIRLIBD,

```
DName++++++++++++ETDsFrom+++To/L+++IDc.Keywords++++++++++++++++++++++++
D********************************************************************
D*Type Definition for the OBJD0400 format.
D********************************************************************
DQUSD0400              DS
D*                                        Qus OBJD0400
D QUSBRTN09            1        4B 0
D*                                        Bytes Returned
D QUSBAVL10            5        8B 0
D*                                        Bytes Available
D QUSOBJN03            9        18
D*                                        Object Name
D QUSOBJLN02          19        28
D*                                        Object Lib Name
D QUSOBJT03           29        38
D*                                        Object Type
D QUSRL04             39        48
D*                                        Return Lib
D QUSASP07            49        52B 0
D*                                        Aux Storage Pool
D QUSOBJO07           53        62
D*                                        Object Owner
D QUSOBJD07           63        64
D*                                        Object Domain
D QUSCDT16            65        77
D*                                        Create Date Time
D QUSCDT17            78        90
D*                                        Change Date Time
D QUSEOA07            91        100
D*                                        Extended Obj Attr
D QUSTD14             101       150
D*                                        Text Description
D QUSSFILN09          151       160
D*                                        Source File Name
D QUSSFLN09           161       170
D*                                        Source File Lib Name
D QUSSFMN05           171       180
D*                                        Source File Mbr Name
D QUSSFUDT04          181       193
```

Figure 5.6: Format OBJD0400 of QUSROBJD as provided in QSYSINC (part 1 of 4).

```
D*                                            Source File Update Date
D QUSOSDT03              194      206
D*                                            Object Saved Date Time
D QUSORDT03              207      219
D*                                            Object Restored Date Time
D QUSCUP04              220      229
D*                                            Creator User Profile
D QUSSOBJC04            230      237
D*                                            System Object Creation
D QUSRD02               238      244
D*                                            Reset Date
D QUSSS05               245      248B 0
D*                                            Save Size
D QUSSSNBR03            249      252B 0
D*                                            Save Sequence Number
D QUSORAGE05            253      262
D*                                            Storage
D QUSSCMD03             263      272
D*                                            Save Command
D QUSSVID03             273      343
D*                                            Save Volume ID
D QUSSD05               344      353
D*                                            Save Device
D QUSSFILN10            354      363
D*                                            Save File Name
D QUSSFLN10             364      373
D*                                            Save File Lib Name
D QUSSL09               374      390
D*                                            Save Label
D QUSSL10               391      399
D*                                            System Level
D QUSPILER04            400      415
D*                                            Compiler
D QUSOBJL05             416      423
D*                                            Object Level
D QUSUC04               424      424
D*                                            User Changed
D QUSLPGM04             425      440
D*                                            Licensed Program
D QUSPTF04              441      450
D*                                            PTF
D QUSAPAR04             451      460
D*                                            APAR
D QUSLUD                461      467
D*                                            Last Used Date
D QUSUIU01              468      468
```

Figure 5.6: Format OBJD0400 of QUSROBJD as provided in QSYSINC (part 2 of 4).

```
D*                                        Usage Information Update
D QUSDUC01          469    472B 0
D*                                        Days Used Count
D QUSOBJS00         473    476B 0
D*                                        Object Size
D QUSOBJSM00        477    480B 0
D*                                        Object Size Multiplier
D QUSOBJCS04        481    481
D*                                        Object Compress Status
D QUSAC04           482    482
D*                                        Allow Change
D QUSCBPGM04        483    483
D*                                        Changed By Program
D QUSUDA05          484    493
D*                                        User Defined Attr
D QUSOASPI00        494    494
D*                                        Overflow ASP Indicator
D QUSSADT02         495    507
D*                                        Save Active Date Time
D QUSOBJAV04        508    517
D*                                        Object Audit Value
D QUSPG03           518    527
D*                                        Primary Group
D QUSJS30           528    528
D*                                        Journal Status
D QUSJN20           529    538
D*                                        Journal Name
D QUSJLIB02         539    548
D*                                        Journal Library
D QUSJI02           549    549
D*                                        Journal Images
D QUSJEO02          550    550
D*                                        Journal Entries Omitted
D QUSJSDT02         551    563
D*                                        Journal Start Date Time
D QUSDS05           564    564
D*                                        Digitally Signed
D QUSSSIU           565    568B 0
D*                                        Save Size In Units
D QUSSSM05          569    572B 0
D*                                        Save Size Multiplier
D QUSLASPN14        573    576B 0
D*                                        Lib Aux Storage Pool Num
D QUSOASPD          577    586
D*                                        Object Aux Storage Pool
D QUSLASPD          587    596
D*                                        Lib Aux Storage Pool Dev
D QUSDSST04         597    597
```

Figure 5.6: Format OBJD0400 of QUSROBJD as provided in QSYSINC (part 3 of 4).

```
D*                              Digitally Signed Sys Tru
D QUSDSM04          598   598
D*                              Digitally Signed Multipl
D QUSRSV117         599   600
D*                              Reserved1
D QUSASS03          601   604B 0
D*                              Associated Space Size
D QUSOSA03          605   605
D*                              Optimum Space Alignment
D QUSOASPG00        606   615
D*                              Object ASP Group
D QUSLASPG01        616   625
D*                              Library ASP Group
D QUSSJRFA00        626   635
D*                              Starting Jrn Rcv For App
D QUSSJRL00         636   645
D*                              Starting Jrn Rcv Lib
D QUSLASPD01        646   655
D*                              Starting Jrn Rcv Lib ASP
D QUSLASPG02        656   665
D*                              Starting Jrn Rcv Lib ASP
D QUSERVED57        666   666
D*                              Reserved
```

Figure 5.6: Format OBJD0400 of QUSROBJD as provided in QSYSINC (part 4 of 4).

though, the program reformats the relevant data from OBJD0400 to a form suitable for display. The specific fields reformatted are the creation date (QUSCDT16), the most recent restore date (QUSORDT03), and the most recent save date (QUSOSDT03).

Depending on the number of objects in the library, the QLIRLIBD API can take quite some time to run. It accepts five parameters, described in Table 5.2. The parameters are pretty standard for retrieve-type APIs. The first parameter is the name of the variable that will

Table 5.2: Retrieve Library Description API (QLIRLIBD)			
Parameter	Description	Type	Size
1	Receiver Variable	Output	Char(*)
2	Length of Receiver Variable	Input	Binary(4)
3	Library Name	Input	Char(10)
4	Attributes to Retrieve	Input	Char(*)
5	Error Code	I/O	Char(*)

hold the information being returned, and the second parameter is the length of the first one. Parameter 3 is the name of the library that the API is to retrieve information about, parameter 4 is an array of keys, and parameter 5 is the standard error data structure.

Where most retrieve APIs have a record format name that describes the format of the data being returned, this API uses a method we refer to as the *key method*. Simply put, the API assigns a key value to each piece of information that it can return to you. You give the API a list of keys, and it returns the corresponding value that each of the keys represent. In chapter 3, you also saw this use of keys in the Open List of Objects (QGYOLOBJ) API.

The documentation for the third parameter indicates this is a structure where the first field is a Binary(4) value, representing the number of keys being passed to the API. Immediately following this field is an array of Binary(4) values, where each array element represents the attribute key we want to use. Table 5.3 shows the keys that are defined and the type of data associated with each key. In the sample program, Attributes is the data structure representing the third parameter. NbrAttributes is the field within Attributes that defines the number of keys to process. Key is the array of key values. It is defined to hold ten array entries.

Table 5.3 shows that key 6 corresponds to the total size of all the objects in the library, and key 7 corresponds to the total number of all objects in the library. The program sets

Table 5.3: Key Values for the QLIRLIBD API		
Key	Description	Size
1	Type of Library	Char(1)
2	Auxiliary Storage Pool (ASP) Number	Binary(4)
3	Create Authority	Char(10)
4	Create Object Auditing	Char(10)
5	Description	Char(50)
6	Library Size Information	Char(12)
7	Number of Objects in Library	Binary(4)
8	Auxiliary Storage Pool (ASP) Device Name	Char(10)
9	Auxiliary Storage Pool (ASP) Group Name	Char(10)

Key(1) to six and Key(2) to seven. This could have been done as part of the definition specification, but later we will show how flexibly the program can be written in terms of supporting an arbitrary number of keys.

Since you specify at run time what attributes to return, there is no fixed structure defined to return the selected key information for the receiver variable of QLIRLIBD. Instead, the API returns a control structure at the start of the receiver variable, followed by an array of variable-length records. The control structure is shown in Figure 5.7. The format of the variable-length records is shown in Table 5.4, and the QSYSINC-provided definition for the variable-length records is in Figure 5.8.

```
DName+++++++++++ETDsFrom+++To/L+++IDc.Keywords+++++++++++++++++++++++
DQLIRR          DS
D*                                              Qli Rlibd Rtn
D QLIBRTN              1       4B 0
D*                                              Bytes Returned
D QLIBAVL              5       8B 0
D*                                              Bytes Available
D QLIVRRTN             9      12B 0
D*                                              Vlen Records Return
D QLIVRAVL            13      16B 0
D*                                              Vlen Records Availa
D*QLIVR               17      17
D*
D*                             Varying length
```

Figure 5.7: The QSYSINC-provided format of the control structure returned in the receiver variable.

Table 5.4: Variable-Length Records for the QLIRLIBD API		
Field	Description	Size
1	Length of returned data	Binary(4)
2	Key identifier	Binary(4)
3	Size of field	Binary(4)
4	Field value	Char(*)

Within the QSYSINC provided structure, QLIRR, are four subfield definitions. The subfield QLIVRRTN contains the number of variable-length records returned. This field will be used to control how many variable-length records are processed for the returned library information.

```
D***********************************************************
D*Type Definition for the 4 Field Variable Length Record.
D***********************************************************
DQUSVR4                 DS
D*                                          Qus Vlen Rec 4
D QUSLVR00                  1      4B 0
D*                                          Length Vlen Record
D QUSCK                     5      8B 0
D*                                          Control Key
D QUSLD                     9     12B 0
D*                                          Length Data
D*QUSDATA00                13     13
D*
D*                              Varying length
```

Figure 5.8: The QSYSINC-provided format of variable-length records returned in the receiver variable.

The QSYSINC-provided data structure QUSVR4 defines three subfields. They are QUSLVR00, the length of the current variable-length record; QUSCK, the key associated with the current variable-length record; and QUSLD, the length of the data returned for the key value returned in the field QUSCK. Because several APIs use this same definition for variable-length records, the data structure is defined in the QUS member of QSYSINC/QRPGLESRC, rather than being duplicated in several different header files. The QLIRLIBD header file refers you to the QUS header file for this definition.

The FIG5_5 program defines the data structure Entry, which represents one variable-length record of the type shown in Table 5.4. The data structure is BASED on the pointer variable EntryPtr and has several subfields. The first set of fields are defined LIKEDS(QUSVR4), and map to the first three fields described in Table 5.4. Following these fields, the data structure defines the data associated with key values 6 and 7 using OVERLAYs.

Now let's look at what the program does when calling QLIRLIBD. As we just discussed, prior to calling the API, the program sets NbrAttributes to two, Key(1) to six, and Key(2) to seven. As the API supports many more key values than these two, and the Attributes array is defined with up to ten elements; you can easily add (or remove) keys that represent data of interest.

After calling QLIRLIBD, the program sets the pointer EntryPtr to the address of the first key's returned data, and then falls into a FOR loop processing all returned keys (Receiver.Hdr.QLIVRRTN). A common mistake at this point would be to fall into a FOR loop for NbrAttributes. The mistake assumes that all requested key values will be returned. As the API provides you with a count of the number of keys actually returned, this value should be used.

In this simple example, you should not experience any problem returning both of the two requested keys, but if some future application change were to add X more keys and leave the Receiver data structure the same size, there might not be sufficient space for all of the requested data. In such a situation, you would not want to be processing data that wasn't returned! To detect this situation, the program could check to see if Receiver.Hdr.QLIVRRTN is less than NbrAttributes (or Receiver.Hdr.QLIVRAVL). If so, the program could DSPLY a message indicating that a problem has been encountered. Alternatively, the program could be written to use a dynamic receiver variable, as discussed in chapter 2, so that you always have sufficient space allocated for Receiver.

Each requested key is processed within the SELECT group. In addition, an OTHER group is coded just in case a developer adds a new key value to the Key array and forgets to add an appropriate WHEN group. The data associated with each Key occurrence is defined by way of OVERLAYs in the Entry data structure. After the SELECT group is ended, the program advances to the next Entry to be processed by adding the length of the current entry (Entry.EntryHdr.QUSLVR00) to the pointer EntryPtr. When the FOR loop completes, the program EXFMTs the FORMAT1 display record and ends.

Coding the program this way, it is reasonably straightforward to add new keys as you decide you would like more information about the library in your display panel. For instance, adding support for the create authority of the library can be accomplished in five easy steps:

1. Add a field CRTAUT to FORMAT1 of the FIG5_4 display file.

2. Set NbrAttributes to a value of three.

3. Set Key(3) to a value of three.

4. Add to the Entry data structure a definition for Key3Aut as a 10-byte character field defined as OVERLAY(Entry:13).

5. Add a WHEN group as follows:

```
when Entry.EntryHdr.QUSCK = 3; CrtAut = Entry.Key3Aut;
```

Summary

In this chapter, you have seen how to use the Retrieve Object Description API (QUSROBJD) to obtain a wide variety of information about objects on your system. You have also seen how to use QUSROBJD to test for the existence of an object.

In addition, you saw how to process a keyed interface like the one used with the Retrieve Library Description API (QLIRLIBD), in a manner that allows you to easily add new keys and avoid common errors in areas such as how to exit from a FOR loop.

Check Your Knowledge

Write a program to rename the data queue TESTQ in library SOMELIB to renamedq. If the *DTAQ RENAMEDQ already exists, replace it. This data queue is the one you created in the "Check Your Knowledge" exercise for chapter 4.

To get you started, the Rename Object API (QLIRNMO) can rename an existing object, move an object to a different library, or both. The documentation for this API can be found in the API Finder by searching for the name qlirnmo, or by looking at the "Objects" category of APIs and then the subcategory "Object-related APIs." The documentation shows that there are optional parameters to support auxiliary storage pools, but you will not use that support in this example. For any error situations, the program should simply DSPLY the error message ID.

One possible solution to this task can be found in Figure D.5 in appendix D.

6

Data-Queue APIs

The data-queue APIs are among the oldest and most used APIs on the system. Two of these APIs, Send to a Data Queue (QSNDDTAQ) and Receive Data Queue (QRCVDTAQ), actually predate the System i—they were originally introduced on the IBM System/38. The age of some of the data-queue APIs should not mislead you into thinking they should be avoided. The age of these APIs is more an indication of their importance!

Queuing Your Data

A data queue is a fast method of passing data between programs that are often running in different jobs. This data is often referred to as a *message* or a *data-queue entry*. (We use these two terms interchangeably.) You use tools on the system to put the data on the queue, and one or more jobs can take data off the data queue via the Receive Data Queue API (QRCVDTAQ) or Retrieve Data Queue Message API (QMHRDQM). You can use a variety of methods to put data on the queue, as you will see a little later. Reading data from a data queue usually involves one or more jobs that continually monitor the data queue and take data off it. The information may be retrieved either as it arrives or later.

Now for the standard question, "Data-queue APIs: What can you do with them?" This is a great question to ask of any API, but it is especially pertinent regarding data queues because for most RPG shops, the data queue is a bit of an enigma, yet is also one of the first objects that cause programmers to turn to APIs. It is one of those objects on the system that is designed to enhance program communications.

For starters, you can use a data queue to communicate between two programs in different jobs. For instance, suppose you have an order-entry program that allows the user to press a function key to print out a bill on demand. Conventional wisdom would dictate that the print function be a separate program that gets called when the function key is pressed. However, is there really a good reason to generate a report at the priority of the interactive job or to tie up the order-entry operator while generating the report when he or she could be entering the next order? A better approach in this case might be to have the print program running all the time, waiting on a data queue. When the user presses the function key, instead of calling the print program, the data-entry program puts data on the data queue using the Send Data Queue API (QSNDDTAQ). As soon as data is put on the queue, the print program running in a different job wakes up and prints the information while the order-entry operator is off entering the next order.

Let's extend this idea a bit. What if we have various order-entry clerks entering phone orders, and the function key, rather than printing a bill, actually causes the order to be processed? This processing may involve multiple steps with various degrees of complexity, depending on the size and type of order. We might have ten order-entry clerks, all entering orders that go to one common data queue (that is, there is not a separate data queue per clerk). In the background, we might have 20 batch jobs reading data from a single data queue and processing the orders, while the clerks are entering the next orders.

This approach can provide significant flexibility to our operation! If one of the clerks has just entered a complex order that might take quite a bit of time to process, we have not stopped him or her from receiving the next phone order. If we need to hire additional order-entry clerks, we can simply hire and train them, without changing the system environment. We don't have to create new data queues for the new clerks, as all orders go through a common queue. If we notice that our processing of orders is getting a bit behind (there are APIs to determine how many orders are on a data queue waiting to be processed), we can simply start up more batch jobs to process the orders until we catch up. If the order processing needs to be temporarily stopped for some reason, the order-entry clerks simply continue taking new orders, as the processing is not being done within their jobs. The new orders simply get queued up until we can resume processing in the background jobs.

Another good use for data queues involves passing data from one system to another. Using the remote data-queue feature, you can create a data queue with one end sitting on one system and the other end on another. You write to the data queue from one system and read the data off the queue from the other. This method is another example of how data queues can be used to enhance program-to-program communications. In chapter 12, you will learn how to use remote data queues to send passwords (encrypted, of course!) from one system to another, so that passwords can be synchronized across systems. Using remote data queues, we can do this without having to know how to write communications programs. And even better, your program that is reading and writing to the data queue does not know if the data queue is local or remote.

The preceding scenarios involve user-written programs that write data to the data queue. You can, however, also associate data queues with various objects on your system, and the system will write information onto the queue for you. For instance, if you attach a data queue to an output queue, the system will write information to the data queue every time a spooled file goes to Ready status. This might be useful, for example, in a server program that automatically moves spooled files among a select group of printers. It would allow you to design print servers that would balance the load across printers and improve the overall throughput of the system.

The documentation for the data-queue APIs can be found in the Information Center under the category "Object," and the subcategory "Data Queue APIs."

Using Data Queues for Job-Related Information

You know that data queues are all about communication, and that data queues can be associated with many i5/OS objects. Data queues can also be associated with exit points within i5/OS. This capability allows you to find out whenever a job is started, ended, or submitted to a job queue. In other words, it lets you monitor jobs on the system.

When would this ability be useful? Just use your imagination. How about a chance to get even with that guy on the loading docks who had the audacity to talk bad about your system *and* your favorite sports team? Want to know whenever he signs on? Want to change the run priority of his jobs to 90 each time? Better yet, *randomly* change his priority! Of course, you could also make more constructive use of this ability, like being notified every time QSECOFR signs on your system.

In any case, that's the initial example we're going to show about using data queues: how to set up the system so that any time a job is started or submitted to a job queue for later processing, the job name is written to a data queue. (We'll leave the decision as to what action to take for a particular user up to you.)

To find the documentation for the job-notification support of i5/OS we will be using, go to the Information Center. Under "Programming," select "APIs," and then "APIs by category." Within the category list you will see "Work Management." Since jobs are controlled by work management, select that category. Paging to the bottom of the category, you'll find work-management exit programs, including job notification. This exit point logs notification messages to data queues when an i5/OS job starts, ends, or is placed on a job queue.

The documentation says that a QSYSINC header file is provided with the member name EJOBNTFY. It also mentions that you can register data queue names and libraries that you want to associate with subsystems on the system. The subsystem will then send messages to these registered data queues when jobs start, end, or are placed on a job queue. The data queues need to be created with the Create Data Queue (CRTDTAQ) command, with an entry length of 144 bytes or greater, keyed, and a key length of four. The key values that can be used are as follows:

- 0001 for a job-start notification message

- 0002 for a job-end notification message

- 0004 for a job-queue notification message

Let's start by creating an appropriate data queue. Enter the command in Figure 6.1 to create the data queue FIG6_1. For the purposes of this example, the data queue must be a keyed data queue with a key length of four bytes and a minimum entry length of at least 144. (An entry length of 200 is used in this example.)

```
CRTDTAQ DTAQ(SOMELIB/FIG6_1) MAXLEN(200) SEQ(*KEYED) KEYLEN(4)
```

Figure 6.1: The command to create a data queue.

Having created the data queue, you need to tell the system that you want job-notification information put on the data queue. This technique is called using a *job-notification exit point*. So, the first thing you have to do to make it work is to register the data queue with the system exit point. You register job-notification exit points using the Add Exit

Program (ADDEXITPGM) command, as shown in Figure 6.2. Of course, you must have adequate authority to run this command.

```
ADDEXITPGM EXITPNT(QIBM_QWT_JOBNOTIFY) FORMAT(NTFY0100) PGMNBR(*LOW)
PGM(SOMELIB/FIG6_1) PGMDTA(*JOB 24 '0007*ANY          *ANY')
```

Figure 6.2: Registering an exit program/data queue with the system exit point QIBM_QWT_JOBNOTIFY.

The EXITPNT parameter identifies which exit point we are registering. The name QIBM_QWT_JOBNOTIFY is taken directly from the API documentation. Similarly, the FORMAT parameter value of NTFY0100 is provided in the documentation. PGMNBR is not used by this exit point, and we use the value *LOW, as that allows i5/OS to determine what value to use. PGM specifies the qualified name of the data queue we are registering. The parameter keyword pgm is a bit misleading, as we are not using a *PGM in this example. The exit points historically (and most often) work through calling a user program, so the command keyword is oriented toward *PGM objects. Obviously, the system is flexible enough to allow exit points to work with other object types!

The contents of the last parameter, PGMDTA, will be defined by the exit point we are registering with. In the case of QIBM_QWT_JOBNOTIFY, it allows us to further define exactly when we want this data queue to be used. The PGMDTA parameter is comprised of three elements. The first element is the CCSID associated with the program data. For QIBM_QWT_JOBNOTIFY, we can use the default value of *JOB. The next element is the length of the data being provided in the third element. The third element is used to define what type of information we want logged to the data queue. Table 6.1 shows how this third element is documented for the QIBM_QWT_JOBNOTIFY exit point.

From the API documentation, we see that 0007, used in Figure 6.2, means we want job-start, job-end, and job-queue notifications. The first *any indicates we are interested in job activity from any subsystem, and the second indicates that the subsystem can be associated with any library.

Table 6.1: Program Data Definition for the Job-Notification Exit Point		
Decimal Offset	Field	Size
0	Notification type	Char(4)
4	Subsystem description	Char(10)
14	Subsystem description library	Char(10)

From the exit point documentation, we also note that messages will not start being sent to the data queue until the subsystem is started (or restarted, in the case of an already active subsystem). If we want to start logging messages to the FIG6_1 data queue, then we need to start a subsystem on our system.

We have finally come to the point where we want to write a program to read data-queue messages. In our case, these are messages related to job starts, job ends, and job-queue activity.

Using the Receive Data Queue API (QRCVDTAQ)

The Receive Data Queue API (QRCVDTAQ) is used to read the data-queue entry. Table 6.2 has the parameters for this API.

Table 6.2: Receive Data Queue API (QRCVDTAQ)			
Parameter	Description	Type	Size
1	Data Queue Name	Input	Char(10)
2	Library Name	Input	Char(10)
3	Length of Data	Output	Packed(5,0)
4	Data	Output	Char(*)
5	Wait Time	Input	Packed(5,0)
Optional Parameter Group 1:			
6	Key Order	Input	Char(2)
7	Length of Key Data	Input	Packed(3,0)
8	Key Data	I/O	Char(*)
9	Length of Sender Information	Input	Packed(3,0)
10	Sender Information	Output	Char(*)
Optional Parameter Group 2:			
11	Remove Message	Input	Char(10)
12	Size of Data Receiver	Input	Packed(5,0)
13	Error Code	I/O	Char(*)

Despite its initial appearance, this API is not very complicated. Many of the parameters, however, do not follow the style used with most of the system APIs in this book. As mentioned at the beginning of this chapter, some of the data-queue APIs pre-date the standards currently used for the development of APIs. We will point out the major differences as we encounter them.

The first parameter, Data Queue Name, is the name of the data queue from which to read a message.

The second parameter, Library Name, is the library in which the data queue specified by the first parameter is to be found. The special values *CURLIB and *LIBL are supported. You might already notice one difference between this API and most system APIs. Generally object names are passed as one parameter, so you would normally expect to pass a parameter named "Qualified Data Queue Name." For QRCVDTAQ, however, the data queue name is passed as two separate parameters.

The third parameter, Length of Data, returns the length of the data associated with the message received from the data queue. An important word of warning is warranted here: It is very easy to be fooled by this parameter, especially when you become well acquainted with API standards for retrieving information.

On most APIs, the Length of Data parameter is an input value, where you specify how large your receiver variable is. (If necessary, refer to chapter 2 to review this standard.) The QRCVDTAQ API pre-dates the standards followed by most i5/OS APIs, however. It uses the Length of Data parameter to tell you how much data was returned or associated with the message received. The API *assumes* that you have already allocated a sufficiently large receiver variable to accommodate the message received. As data queues can hold messages up to 64,512 bytes in size, this may or may not be a good assumption! If you only use the first five parameters when calling this API and the returned value for parameter 3 is greater than the allocated size of parameter 4, you can be sure the API has overwritten storage associated with your program. You might now start experiencing the bizarre behaviors warned about in chapter 1 in the section "Size Is Critical."

Additional parameters have been added to this API to provide it with more consistency when working with other i5/OS APIs. Specifically, optional parameter 12 provides the support more typically found with retrieve/receive APIs—an input parameter where you tell the API how large your receiver parameter is. Optional parameter 13 supports the standard error-code structure found in most APIs. When using the QRCVDTAQ API, you should always use optional parameter group 2. It takes a little bit more coding, but it might save you a lot of grief debugging a problem sometime down the road. If you use the twelfth parameter, Size of Data Receiver, then the value returned for the third parameter, Length of Data, will represent the full size of the message received, but the data actually returned in the fourth parameter, Data, will be truncated to the size specified by the twelfth parameter.

A less critical, but still important, difference between the third parameter in this API (Length of Data) and most other APIs is the data type of this parameter. Most APIs use Binary(4) values when working with numeric data. This API uses *packed decimal*, which affects the prototype for this parameter. This is not a large impact to applications using the data-queue APIs, but it is a difference that can be easily overlooked when glancing at the API documentation.

The fourth parameter, Data, is the variable that will receive the data-queue message. If the twelfth parameter, Size of Data Receiver, is not passed on the API call, the API will return the full data-queue message regardless of the size you have allocated for this parameter. If the Size of Data Receiver parameter *is* passed, the API will truncate the message to the specified size of the data receiver.

The fifth parameter, Wait Time, allows you to specify how long you want the API to wait to receive data on the data queue. If there is no data on the queue, do you want it to wait until data is put on? If so, specify a negative one for this parameter. This special value will cause your program to wait, without consuming any processing cycles, until a message is put on the data queue. At this point, the API will return control to your program with the data-queue entry in parameter 4 and the size of the entry in parameter 3. On the other hand, if you specify zero, the API will not wait at all if there are no messages/entries on the data queue. It will simply return to you with parameter 3 set to a value of zero. Alternatively, you can put the number of seconds you want to wait for a message. If a message is put on the data queue before the number of seconds, you will receive the data-queue entry, and parameter 3 will have a value greater than zero. If no message is put on the data queue within the specified number of seconds, control will be returned back to your program, and parameter 3 will have a value of zero. Note that parameter 5 is defined as packed decimal.

In many cases, the next five parameters are not necessary for a given application, but they are passed on the API call because we want to use optional parameter group 2, as discussed above. As you learned in chapter 1, if you want to use a given optional parameter group, you must also use all preceding optional parameter groups. Having said this, though, our example program does use optional parameter group 1. The sixth, seventh, and eighth parameters support keyed data queues. That is the type of queue you must use to track a job's starting and ending, as you might recall from Figure 6.1.

The sixth parameter, Key Order, specifies the type of comparison being done on the key. You can specify the following values:

- GT—Greater than
- LT—Less than
- NE—Not equal
- EQ—Equal
- GE—Greater than or equal
- LE—Less than or equal

The seventh parameter, Length of Key Data, is the length of the data-queue message key you are comparing. Note that this parameter is defined as packed decimal.

The eighth parameter, Key Data, is defined as an input and output parameter. When calling the API, you provide the actual comparison data you want used in order to find a particular message. The example program uses a key of hex'00's (*LOVAL), a key length of four, and a key order of GE. This combination essentially says we want any message that happens to be on the data queue. The eighth parameter is also defined as an output parameter. When the API returns to your application program, this parameter will be set to the actual key value found for the received message. This returned value can be quite handy when working with key orders such as GT, LT, or NE.

The ninth parameter, Length of Sender Information, is the length you have allocated for the tenth parameter. A value of zero is supported in case you do not care what job sent the message you just received. Note that this parameter is defined as packed decimal.

The tenth parameter, Sender Information, provides information about the sender of the data-queue message. This information includes the full job name and the current user profile for the job when the message was sent. Note that this information is only available if the SENDERID parameter of the CRTDTAQ command was set to *YES.

The eleventh parameter, Remove Message, allows you to control whether or not the message that you retrieve from the data queue is removed from the data queue or retained so that it can be read again. In general, you only want to process a particular entry once, so you would remove the entry from the data queue. This is the default behavior.

The twelfth parameter, Size of Data Receiver, is where you can provide the size of your fourth parameter (where the received data-queue message is returned). You should always specify this parameter to avoid problems down the road with the overwriting of program variables. When your program is reading data, and you have the ability to specify the maximum amount of data your program is prepared to handle, always take advantage of that capability. This parameter is that capability. It avoids future problems where the system might try to give your program more data than it was written to handle. Note that this parameter is defined as packed decimal.

The thirteenth parameter is the standard error-code structure that you have already seen many times.

Despite outward appearances, this API is relatively simple. As a matter of fact, so is the program that uses it. You simply set up a loop to continually call the Receive Data Queue API (QRCVDTAQ) until the key read from the queue is STOP. The exit point will not send this STOP value; instead, we will have a user program send this message key to cause the example program to end when we want to shut it down. The API will wait on the call to QRCVDTAQ until there is some data to get. It will then bring that data into the variable Receiver, where you can parse it to get the user of the job. Sending STOP to the data queue terminates the program at the end of the day. Another program, shown in Figure 6.5, uses the Send Data Queue API (QSNDDTAQ) to send this STOP message.

Note that sending and receiving the STOP message key does not stop the subsystem from sending additional messages to the data queue. Only ending the subsystem will do that. The STOP message key simply causes our example program to end. Additional job activity in the subsystem will continue to cause messages to be queued in the data queue for later processing when our example program is restarted. To stop the queuing of job-related messages, we need to deregister the FIG6_1 data queue from the QIBM_QWT_JOBNOTIFY exit point. This deregistration process is discussed later in this chapter. The program to monitor for job activity is shown in Figure 6.3.

```
DName++++++++++ETDsFrom+++To/L+++IDc.Keywords++++++++++++++++++++++
d/copy qsysinc/qrpglesrc,qrcvdtaq
d/copy qsysinc/qrpglesrc,ejobntfy
d/copy qsysinc/qrpglesrc,qusec

dRcvDtaQ              pr                extpgm('QRCVDTAQ')
d DtaQName                     10       const
d DtaQLib                      10       const
d ReceiverLenRtn               5 0
d Receiver                     1        options(*varsize)
d WaitTime                     5 0      const
d KeyOrder                     2        const options(*nopass)
d KeyLen                       3 0      const options(*nopass)
d KeyValue                     1        options(*varsize :*nopass)
d SndrInfoLen                  3 0      const options(*nopass)
d SndrInfo                     1        options(*varsize :*nopass)
d RmvMsg                       10       const options(*nopass)
d ReceiverLen                  5 0      const options(*nopass)
d QUSEC                                 likeds(QUSEC) options(*nopass)

dReceiver             ds       200      qualified
d StrEnd                                likeds(EJOQJSEN)
d                                       overlay(Receiver :1)
d JobQ                                  likeds(EJOQJQN)
d                                       overlay(Receiver :1)

dReceiverLenRtn       s        5 0
dKeyValue             s        4
dWait                 s        1

CLON01Factor1+++++++Opcode&ExtFactor2+++++++Result++++++++Len++D+HiLoEq
 /free

   QUSBPRV = %size(QUSEC);

   //process until 'STOP' is received from program FIG6_4
   dow (KeyValue <> 'STOP');

       KeyValue = *loval;

       RcvDtaQ( 'FIG6_1' :'SOMELIB' :ReceiverLenRtn :Receiver :-1
                :'GE'     :4        :KeyValue        :0          :QRCQSI
                :'*YES'   :%size(Receiver) :QUSEC);
```

Figure 6.3: The job-monitoring program uses the QRCVDTAQ API (part 1 of 2).

```
    if (QUSBAVL > 0);
        dsply ('Unexpected error ' + QUSEI + ' accessing data queue')
                ' ' Wait;
        leave;
    endif;

    select;
    when (KeyValue = 'STOP');
        leave;
    when (KeyValue = '0001');
        if (ReceiverLenRtn >= %size(Receiver.StrEnd) and
            (Receiver.StrEnd.EJOMI = '*JOBNOTIFY'));
            if (%subst(Receiver.StrEnd.EJOQJN :11 :10) = 'BIGAL');
            // do whatever you want to Big Al
            dsply 'Changed Big Al job' ' ' Wait;
            endif;
        else;
            dsply ('Key 0001 message ' + Receiver.StrEnd.EJOMI +
                    ' received.') ' ' Wait;
            leave;
        endif;
    when (KeyValue = '0002');
    when (KeyValue = '0004');
        if (ReceiverLenRtn >= %size(Receiver.JobQ) and
            (Receiver.JobQ.EJOMI00 = '*JOBNOTIFY'));
            if (%subst(Receiver.JobQ.EJOQJN00 :11 :10) = 'BIGAL');
            // do whatever you want to submitted job of Big Al
            dsply 'Changed submitted job' ' ' Wait;
            endif;
        else;
            dsply ('Key 0004 message ' + Receiver.JobQ.EJOMI00 +
                    ' received.') ' ' Wait;
            leave;
        endif;
    other;
        dsply 'Unexpected key during processing' ' ' Wait;
    ends1;
  enddo;

  *inlr = *on;
  return;

/end-free
```

Figure 6.3: The job-monitoring program uses the QRCVDTAQ API (part 2 of 2).

The program in Figure 6.3 processes all job-notification messages from the FIG6_1 data queue. (Figure 6.4 shows the QSYSINC-supplied definitions that are being used.)

If the KeyValue is 0001 (start) or 0004 (job queue), the program further examines the received message. First, FIG6_3 verifies that the message is of the minimum expected length and is associated with the QIBM_QWT_JOBNOTIFY exit point. If it isn't, the program DSPLYs appropriate error text and exits. Note that it is not necessarily an error if the message received is larger than the message expected. This could happen if IBM were, in a future release, to add additional information to the job-notification data queue message. In this situation, FIG6_3 is "protected" from the larger message, because the twelfth parameter, Size of Data Receiver, limits the amount of data received to the size of the defined receiver variable (the fourth parameter, Data).

If a supported message was received, FIG6_3 looks at the qualified job name (Receiver.StrEnd.EJOQJN or Receiver.JobQ.EJOQJN00, respectively) to determine if the user profile name (at positions 11 through 20 of these fields) is equal to BIGAL. When the user profile of the qualified job name is BIGAL, the program does additional processing. (The additional processing is not shown, but think of it as being to set the job's run priority to 90 based on our earlier scenario.) It then DSPLYs a message to show that the job has been changed. If you have read chapter 4, you should easily be able to add the appropriate CHGJOB command to FIG6_3 to accomplish this! The program also checks to see if any unexpected KeyValue values are received. If so, it DSPLYs "Unexpected key during processing."

```
DName++++++++++++ETDsFrom+++To/L+++IDc.Keywords+++++++++++++++++++++++++
D*********************************************************************
D*Type Definition for the Job Start and Job End Notification
D*Messages
D*********************************************************************
DEJOQJSEN            DS
D*                                                Qwt Job Start End Notify
D EJOMI                     1     10
D*                                                Message Identifier
D EJOMF                    11     12
D*                                                Message Format
D EJOIJI                   13     28
D*                                                Internal Job Identifier
D EJOQJN                   29     54
D*                                                Qualified Job Name
D EJOERVED                 55     74
D*                                                Reserved
```

Figure 6.4: Definitions from EJOBNTFY in QSYSINC/QRPGLESRC (part 1 of 2).

```
D**************************************************************
D*Type Definition for the Job Queue Notification Messages
D**************************************************************
DEJOQJQN              DS
D*                                    Qwt Job Queue Notify
D EJOMIOO             1       10
D*                                    Message Identifier
D EJOMFOO             11      12
D*                                    Message Format
D EJOIJIOO            13      28
D*                                    Internal Job Identifier
D EJOQJNOO            29      54
D*                                    Qualified Job Name
D EJOQJQNOO           55      74
D*                                    Qualified Job Queue Name
```

Figure 6.4: Definitions from EJOBNTFY in QSYSINC/QRPGLESRC (part 2 of 2).

We have now laid all the necessary groundwork, and if you have been working through the example, you are ready to submit the program shown in Figure 6.3. However, you might want to first review and create the program in Figure 6.5. This is the program that "STOPs" FIG6_3. Before calling program FIG6_3, consider submitting it to a job queue, as the program is going to wait forever on the data queue (because parameter 5 is set to negative one). If called interactively, your terminal might be tied up for a long time so having a second interactive session available is advisable. If submitting FIG6_3, you should also submit it to a queue where other jobs are not going to stack up behind it.

For testing purposes, you might want to run FIG6_3 interactively, so you can easily see the displayed messages (or look for the messages in QSYSOPR, since batch job DSPLY operations go to QSYSOPR). In a production environment, you will, of course, want to remove the DSPLY operations. For testing, simply create a user profile named BIGAL, start a subsystem with some workstation entries (after registering your data queue as shown in Figure 6.2), sign onto the system as BIGAL, and use TFRJOB to transfer your BIGAL job to the new subsystem. You should see messages being sent for KeyValue 0004 and then 0001. Use TFRJOB to transfer a job signed on with a user profile other than BIGAL. You shouldn't see any message related to this non-BIGAL job DSPLYed (although job-notification messages are being sent to the FIG6_1 data queue). When you're done testing, call the program shown in Figure 6.5 (FIG6_5) to stop the FIG6_3 program, end the test subsystem, and remove the data queue FIG6_1 from the job-notification exit point.

You can remove the FIG6_1 data queue from the job-notification exit point by using the Work with Registration Information (WRKREGINF) command, scrolling down to the entry for QIBM_QWM_JOBNOTIFY (the exit point we registered the data queue to in Figure 6.2), taking option 8 to work with exit programs, and then using option 4 to remove the data queue. There is also the Remove Exit Program (RMVEXITPGM) command, which could be used to remove the data queue, but we want to make you aware of WRKREGINF so that you can see many of the exit points that are available to you. Job notification is only one of many doors that are opening to you as you become familiar with APIs!

Using the Send Data Queue API (QSNDDTAQ)

Now that you have the monitoring program running in the background, you'll need a way to end it. The answer is the program in Figure 6.5. This program uses the Send Data Queue API (QSNDDTAQ) to write an entry with a key value of STOP. The monitoring program in Figure 6.3 is coded to end itself when it reads an entry with this key. Table 6.3 shows the parameters for QSNDDTAQ.

```
DName++++++++++++ETDsFrom+++To/L+++IDc.Keywords+++++++++++++++++++++++
dSndDtaQ          pr                    extpgm('QSNDDTAQ')
d DtaQName                     10       const
d DtaQLib                      10       const
d DataLen                       5 0     const
d Data                      65535       const options(*varsize)
d KeyLen                        3 0     const options(*nopass)
d KeyValue                  65535       const options(*varsize :*nopass)
d Asynch                       10       const options(*nopass)
d JrnEntry                     10       const options(*nopass)


CLON01Factor1+++++++Opcode&ExtFactor2+++++++Result++++++++Len++D+HiLoEq
 /free

   // end the FIG6_3 program by sending a KeyValue of 'STOP'
   SndDtaQ( 'FIG6_1' :'SOMELIB' :1 :' ' :4 :'STOP');
   *inlr = *on;
   return;

 /end-free
```

Figure 6.5: Use the QSNDDTAQ API to end the monitoring program.

Table 6.3: Send Data Queue API (QSNDDTAQ)			
Parameter	Description	Type	Size
1	Data Queue Name	Input	Char(10)
2	Library Name	Input	Char(10)
3	Length of Data	Input	Packed(5,0)
4	Data	Input	Char(*)
Optional Parameter Group 1:			
5	Length of Key Data	Input	Packed(3,0)
6	Key Data	Input	Char(*)
Optional Parameter Group 2:			
7	Asynchronous Request	Input	Char(10)
Optional Parameter Group 3			
8	Data Is from a Journal Entry	Input	Char(10)

The first six parameters for this API are essentially the same as for the QRCVDTAQ API, so we won't go over them again. The seventh parameter, Asynchronous Request, is related to how messages should be processed when a distributed data-management queue is being used. Distributed data-management data queues provide the support to be able to send a message to a data queue that resides on a different system. We will be working with distributed data-management data queues in chapter 12, which deals with security APIs. This parameter is not used by the example program here.

The eighth parameter, Data Is from a Journal Entry, relates to the recovering of messages in a data queue from a journal. This parameter is also not used by the example program.

Using the Retrieve Data Queue Description API (QMHQRDQD)

When working with data queues, you might want to determine how many messages are currently on the queue. This type of information can be used to monitor whether or not queue processing is getting behind in terms of workload. If you detect that the data queue is becoming backlogged, you might want to start up more server or reader jobs.

There is, as you should expect, an API to tell you how many messages are on a data queue, along with quite a bit more information about the queue. The API is named Retrieve Data Queue Description (QMHQRDQD). The API's parameters are described in Table 6.4, the QSYSINC QMHQRDQD QRPGLESRC member is provided in Figure 6.6, and a program that displays the number of messages in the FIG6_1 data queue is in Figure 6.7. As this is a standard retrieve-type API, we won't go into any detail on how the program is coded. You should be quite familiar with this type of API by now. (Review chapter 2 if you need a refresher.)

Table 6.4: Retrieve Data Queue Description API (QMHQRDQD)			
Parameter	Description	Type	Size
1	Receiver Variable	Output	Char(*)
2	Length of Receiver Variable	Input	Binary(4)
3	Format Name	Input	Char(8)
4	Qualified Data Queue Name	Input	Char(20)

You should be comfortable with all four of the parameters supported by the QMHQRDQD API. They are all quite standard. For the third parameter, Format Name, the API supports two formats. Format RDQD0100 is for retrieving information related to local data queues, and is shown in Figure 6.6. Format RDQD0200 is for retrieving information related to distributed data-management data queues. Format RDQD0200 returns information such as the remote data-queue name and the remote location. This format is not used by the example program here.

```
DName++++++++++++ETDsFrom+++To/L+++IDc.Keywords++++++++++++++++++++++
D*******************************************************************
D*Type Definition for the RDQD0100 format.
D*******************************************************************
DQMHD0100         DS
D*                                            Qmh Qrdqd RDQD0100
D QMHBR                  1      4B 0
D*                                            Bytes Return
D QMHBAVL                5      8B 0
D*                                            Bytes Available
D QMHML                  9     12B 0
D*                                            Message Length
```

Figure 6.6: Definitions from QMHQRDQD in QSYSINC/QRPGLESRC (part 1 of 2).

```
D QMHKL                      13     16B 0
D*                                              Key Length
D QMHUENCE                    17     17
D*                                              Sequence
D QMHISI                      18     18
D*                                              Include Sender Id
D QMHFI                       19     19
D*                                              Force Indicators
D QMHTEXT                     20     69
D*                                              Text
D QMHTYPE01                   70     70
D*                                              Type
D QMHAR                       71     71
D*                                              Automatic Reclaim
D QMHERVED09                  72     72
D*                                              Reserved
D QMHNBRM                     73     76B 0
D*                                              Number Messages
D QMHMNBRM                    77     80B 0
D*                                              Max Number Messages
D QMHDQN                      81     90
D*                                              Data Queue Name
D QMHDQLIB                    91    100
D*                                              Data Queue Library
D QMHMNEA                    101    104B 0
D*                                              Max Number Entries Allo
D QMHINBRE                   105    108B 0
D*                                              Initial Number Entries
D QMHMNES                    109    112B 0
D*                                              Max Number Entries Spec
```

Figure 6.6: Definitions from QMHQRDQD in QSYSINC/QRPGLESRC (part 2 of 2).

Within the QSYSINC-provided data structure, QMHD0100, there are several subfields. The one we are interested in for the sample program is QMHNBRM, the number of messages currently on the data queue. Definitions for all the fields returned can be found in the Information Center.

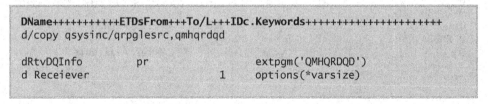

```
DName++++++++++++ETDsFrom+++To/L+++IDc.Keywords++++++++++++++++++++++
d/copy qsysinc/qrpglesrc,qmhqrdqd

dRtvDQInfo         pr                     extpgm('QMHQRDQD')
d Receiever                       1       options(*varsize)
```

Figure 6.7: Use the QMHQRDQD API to retrieve data-queue descriptive information (part 1 of 2).

```
d ReceiverLen                   10i 0  const
d Format                         8     const
d QualDQName                    20     const

dQualDQName        ds
d DQName                        10     inz('FIG6_1')
d DQLibrary                     10     inz('SOMELIB')

dWait              s             1

CLON01Factor1+++++++Opcode&ExtFactor2+++++++Result+++++++Len++D+HiLoEq
 /free

   RtvDQInfo( QMHD0100 :%size(QMHD0100) :'RDQD0100' :QualDQName);
   dsply ('Number of messages is: ' + %char(QMHNBRM)) ' ' Wait;
   *inlr = *on;
   return;

 /end-free
```

Figure 6.7: Use the QMHQRDQD API to retrieve data-queue descriptive information (part 2 of 2).

Summary

In this chapter, you have seen how data queues can provide quick solutions to many programming problems, and that they can eliminate a lot of system overhead when used with a properly designed system. Several other data-queue APIs exist that were not covered in this chapter, but you have learned the fundamentals of sending and receiving messages through data queues, along with retrieving information about a data queue. This is generally sufficient for at least 95 percent of typical application development.

Check Your Knowledge

Figure 6.5 contains the program FIG6_5, which sends a blank message of one byte and a key value of STOP to the FIG6_1 data queue in the library SOMELIB. We now want to expand on that example by sending some additional data. The new data to be sent is a 30-byte text field explaining why the STOP command was sent, followed by a timestamp of when STOP was sent. The data should be formatted as shown in Figure 6.8. The Reason will be "Big Al told me to," and the StopTime will be the current system timestamp, which can be accessed using the %TIMESTAMP built-in.

```
DName++++++++++ETDsFrom+++To/L+++IDc.Keywords++++++++++++++++++++++
dMsgData          ds
d Reason                        30
d StopTime                       z
```

Figure 6.8: The layout of the data to be sent.

Your approach to this task should be very similar to the example in Figure 6.5. For one possible solution, see Figure D.6.A in appendix D.

Next, modify the FIG6_3 program so when the message key STOP is received, the program DSPLYs the Reason followed by the StopTime. For one possible solution, see Figure D.6.B in appendix D. The solution provided, in addition to DSPLYing the two fields, also checks to make sure the STOP message is long enough to contain the Reason and StopTime fields. It does this by checking the returned value ReceiverLenRtn.

While the MsgData structure is not overly complex, this task should demonstrate to you how easily you can send data from an application in one job to another application program running in a different job. Just think of MsgData as representing order information to be picked in the warehouse, or on-demand report-generation parameters. You can probably envision many scenarios within your organization where this capability can be of use.

7

Database File APIs

One of the best decisions IBM ever made was to provide the System i with a fully integrated database, DB2 for i5/OS. Gone are the days of having to describe the file buffer layouts in every program you write. Externally described files are used to externalize and standardize database definitions. This eliminates work and errors. Each file can now contain a complete, definitive description of the data within it. Above and beyond the field definitions you use when writing your high-level-language programs, the description of the file can be accessed using the file APIs.

The discussion of file APIs in this chapter opens with an API that you don't call; rather, DB2 for i5/OS calls your program. The API is known as a *trigger*. Your trigger program can be called by the system when an access is made to a record within a specific file. This capability to have your trigger program called when a record is read, updated, added, or deleted enables you to extend applications without having to modify the original program working with the file. These extensions could range from simply logging of who is updating a particular field to propagating database changes in one file to other related files and applications that the original updating program is not even aware of.

Following a discussion of triggers, this chapter discusses an API that might not be used all that often, but does tie in very nicely with the example in chapter 3 of finding files with deleted records. Namely, the List Database File Members API (QUSLMBR) enables you to determine how many deleted records exist in each member of a file. The example in chapter 3 made the simplifying assumption that there was only one member in any given file. This chapter removes that assumption.

After that, you'll look at the List Fields API (QUSLFLD), which allows you to determine what fields are in a file. To complete this chapter, you'll learn more about a file than you probably ever wanted to know with the Retrieve Database File Description API (QDBRTVFD).

The documentation for the APIs covered in this chapter can be found in the Information Center under the category "Database and File," and the subcategory "File APIs."

Triggers

Triggers are one type of exit program that i5/OS supports. Triggers allow you to define a set of actions that are to be run automatically when a change or read operation is performed on a specified database file. You specify the actions to be performed by writing a program in a language such as RPG, COBOL, C, or CL. The change operation can be a WRITE, an UPDATE, or a DELETE in a high-level language application or utility, such as interactive SQL or the Data File Utility. Likewise, the read operation can be a READ in an application program or utility.

An exit program can be thought of as a retrieve API in reverse. Similar to retrieve APIs, your program typically receives information from the system in structures passed as discrete parameters. These structures follow the same general guidelines found in retrieve APIs, as discussed in chapter 2. The main distinction is that now i5/OS is calling your program rather than you calling the i5/OS retrieve API.

The parameters for a trigger program are shown in Table 7.1, and the QSYSINC-provided ILE RPG definition for a trigger buffer is in Figure 7.1.

The trigger program is called with two parameters. The Trigger Buffer parameter provides information to the trigger program about the file and record being processed. The Length of Trigger Buffer parameter tells you how large the Trigger Buffer parameter is. The detailed layout of the Trigger Buffer parameter is found in Figure 7.1.

The QSYSINC include defines the data structure QDBTB, which provides quite a bit of information about the file, record, and operation. The first field, QDBFILN02, is the name

Table 7.1: Database Trigger Parameters

Parameter	Description	Type	Size
1	Trigger Buffer	Input	Char(*)
2	Length of Trigger Buffer	Input	Binary(4)

```
DName+++++++++++ETDsFrom+++To/L+++IDc.Keywords++++++++++++++++++++++++
DQDBTB              DS
D*                                              Qdb Trigger Buffer
D QDBFILN02              1       10
D*                                              File Name
D QDBLIBN02             11       20
D*                                              Library Name
D QDBMN00              21       30
D*                                              Member Name
D QDBTE                31       31
D*                                              Trigger Event
D QDBTT                32       32
D*                                              Trigger Time
D QDBCLL               33       33
D*                                              Commit Lock Level
D QDBRSV104            34       36
D*                                              Reserved 1
D QDBDAC               37       40B 0
D*                                              Data Area Ccsid
D QDBCR                41       44B 0
D*                                              Current Rrn
D QDBRSV204            45       48
D*                                              Reserved 2
D QDBORO               49       52B 0
D*                                              Old Record Offset
D QDBORL               53       56B 0
D*                                              Old Record Len
D QDBORNBM             57       60B 0
D*                                              Old Record Null Byte Map
D QDBRNBML             61       64B 0
D*                                              Old Record Null Map Size
D QDBNRO               65       68B 0
D*                                              New Record Offset
D QDBNRL               69       72B 0
D*                                              New Record Len
D QDBNRNBM             73       76B 0
D*                                              New Record Null Byte Map
D QDBRNBML00           77       80B 0
D*                                              New Record Null Map Size
```

Figure 7.1: Definitions from TRGBFR in QSYSINC/QRPGLESRC.

of the file. The second field, QDBLIBNO2, is the library name where the file is located. The third field, QDBMN00, is the member within the file. And QDBCR is the relative record number of the record that caused the trigger program to be called. The contents of the record being processed are provided in the trigger buffer.

The fourth field of QDBTB, QDBTE, indicates the type of processing that is being done. Values that might be passed to the trigger program are one for insert or writing of a record, two for deleting a record, three for updating a record, and four for reading a record. In the case of updates (QDBTE = '3'), you actually get the contents of the original record along with the new record within the trigger buffer! Additional information on each of these fields can be found in the Information Center.

Because the record length can vary from file to file, the contents of the record being processed are not at a fixed location within the first parameter, or of a fixed size. The record contents are accessed using offsets and lengths. In the case of the initial, or original, record image, you would use the old record offset (QDBORO) and the old record length (QDBORL) to access the record contents. The program in Figure 7.2 processes insert/write operations to the CUSTOMER file created back in Figure 4.4.A of chapter 4.

The program FIG7_2 first defines the two parameters passed to the program, TriggerBuffer and BufferLength. The TriggerBuffer, parameter is defined as being

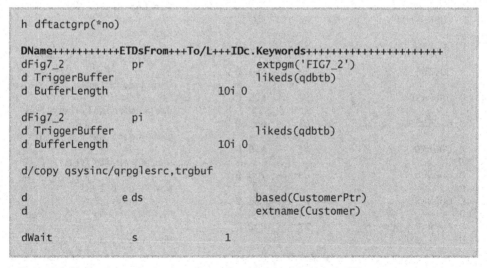

```
h dftactgrp(*no)

DName+++++++++++ETDsFrom+++To/L+++IDc.Keywords+++++++++++++++++++++++
dFig7_2           pr                    extpgm('FIG7_2')
d TriggerBuffer                         likeds(qdbtb)
d BufferLength                 10i 0

dFig7_2           pi
d TriggerBuffer                         likeds(qdbtb)
d BufferLength                 10i 0

d/copy qsysinc/qrpglesrc,trgbuf

d                 e ds                  based(CustomerPtr)
d                                       extname(Customer)

dWait             s            1
```

Figure 7.2: Display the customer name for newly added records (part 1 of 2).

```
CL0N01Factor1++++++Opcode&ExtFactor2+++++++Result++++++++Len++D+HiLoEq
 /free
   if TriggerBuffer.QDBTE <> '1'
      or TriggerBuffer.QDBFILN02 <> 'CUSTOMER    ';
      dsply ('Program called for file ' + TriggerBuffer.QDBFILN02 +
              ' code ' + TriggerBuffer.QDBTE) ' ' Wait;
   else;
      CustomerPtr = %addr(TriggerBuffer) + TriggerBuffer.QDBNRO;
      dsply ('You have added the customer name ' +
              %subst(CUSTNAME :1 :12)) ' ' Wait;
   endif;

   *inlr = *on;
   return;
 /end-free
```

Figure 7.2: Display the customer name for newly added records (part 2 of 2).

LIKEDS(QDBTB). QDBTB is the name of the data structure in Figure 7.1 and is copied into the program from QSYSINC member TRGBUF of file QRPGLESRC. FIG7_2 also declares a data structure BASED on the pointer CustomerPtr and defined to have the same subfield definitions as the external CUSTOMER file. When called, program FIG7_2 checks to see if this is not an insert or write operation (QDBTE <> '1') and if the file is not CUSTOMER (QDBFILN02 <> 'CUSTOMER'). If either are true, an informational message is DSPLYed. If the call is for writing a new record to the CUSTOMER file, FIG7_2 accesses the new record contents by taking the address of the first parameter and adding to this the provided offset to the new record image (QDBNRO). The pointer CustomerPtr is set to this calculated value and, as the CustomerPtr BASED data structure is defined the same as the CUSTOMER record extname(Customer), all of the fields of the record are now available just as if FIG7_2 had read the record from the database file!

You're ready now to test the FIG7_2 program, but you need to associate it with the CUSTOMER file. You do this with the Add Physical File Trigger (ADDPFTRG) command:

```
ADDPFTRG FILE(CUSTOMER) TRGTIME(*AFTER) TRGEVENT(*INSERT) PGM(FIG7_2)
```

To test FIG7_2, call the same program used back in Figure 4.4.B to initially load the CUSTOMER file. FIG7_2 now DSPLYs the name of the newly added customer. You should see four DSPLYs corresponding to the four records added to the CUSTOMER file.

Triggers represent a very powerful exit capability within the database that you will want to explore further. Besides the ability to track record changes, you can also change the contents of the record before the record is actually written to the database! You can do all of this without the application program that's initially writing the record being aware that the trigger even exists.

Get a List of File Members

The List Database File Members API (QUSLMBR) is no different in style than the list APIs discussed in chapter 3. For this reason, there will not be any lengthy discussion of how to process the list. If you need a refresher, review chapter 3.

The parameters for QUSLMBR are shown in Table 7.2. The QSYSINC-provided ILE RPG definition for format MBRL0100, Member Names, is in Figure 7.3. Figure 7.4 shows a program which simply DSPLYs the member names found in the source file QRPGLESRC. Figure 7.5 then incorporates the use of QUSLMBR in the sample program FIG4_2, which reorganizes any file members that contain deleted records beyond a certain percentage.

Table 7.2: List Database File Members, QUSLMBR			
Parameter	Description	Type	Size
1	Qualified User Space Name	Input	Char(20)
2	Format Name	Input	Char(8)
3	Qualified Database File Name	Input	Char(20)
4	Member Name	Input	Char(10)
5	Override Processing	Input	Char(1)
Optional Parameter Group 1			
6	Standard Error Code	I/O	Char(*)

Most of the parameters in Table 7.2 should be quite familiar to you by now. The two that might need discussion are the second, Format Name, and the fifth, Override Processing.

The QUSLMBR API supports five formats:

- MBRL0100—Member name
- MBRL0200—Member name and source information

- MBRL0310—Member name and basic description

- MBRL0320—Member name and extended description

- MBRL0330—Member name and full description

The example program will be using MBRL0100, which returns only the member names. (The Information Center provides documentation on the other formats.)

The fifth parameter, Override Processing, allows you to control whether or not file overrides are in effect. A value of zero indicates that no override processing is to be done by the API. A value of one indicates that overrides are to be in effect when calling the API.

```
DName++++++++++ETDsFrom+++To/L+++IDc.Keywords+++++++++++++++++++++++++
D****************************************************************
D*Type Definition for the MBRL0100 format of the userspace in the
D*QUSLMBR API.
D****************************************************************
DQUSL010000        DS
D*                                              Qdb Ldbm MBRL0100
D QUSMN00                  1     10
D*                                              Member Name
```

Figure 7.3: Definitions from QUSLMBR in QSYSINC/QRPGLESRC.

Within the QSYSINC-provided data structure QUSL010000 there is one field, QUSMN00. QUSMN00 is the name of a member within the file specified by the third parameter of the QUSLMBR API, Qualified Database File Name.

```
h dftactgrp(*no) bnddir('APILIB')

DName++++++++++ETDsFrom+++To/L+++IDc.Keywords+++++++++++++++++++++++++
d/copy qsysinc/qrpglesrc,qusgen
d/copy qsysinc/qrpglesrc,quslmbr
d/copy qsysinc/qrpglesrc,qusec

dListMbr            pr                    extpgm('QUSLMBR')
d MbrSpcName                      20      const
d MbrFormat                        8      const
d DBName                          20      const
d MbrName                         10      const
d Override                         1      const
```

Figure 7.4: Use the QUSLMBR API to list all members in *CURLIB/QRPGLESRC (part 1 of 3).

```
d QUSEC                                likeds(QUSEC) options(*nopass)

dCrtUsrSpc          pr         *       extproc('CrtUsrSpc')
d SpcName                      20      const

dMbrGenHdr          ds                 likeds(QUSH0100)
d                                      based(MbrGenHdrPtr)

dMbrEntry           ds                 likeds(QUSL010000)
d                                      based(MbrPtr)

dMbrSpcName         ds
d MbrSpc                       10      inz('MBRLIST')
d MbrSpcLib                    10      inz('QTEMP')

dDBName             ds
d DBFName                      10      inz('QRPGLESRC')
d DBFLib                       10      inz('*CURLIB')

dMbrCount           s          10i 0
dWait               s          1

CL0N01Factor1+++++++Opcode&ExtFactor2+++++++Result++++++++Len++D+HiLoEq
/free

    // set error code bytes provided to 16 to prevent exceptions
    QUSBPRV = %size(QUSEC);

    // create the user space for the list of members
    MbrGenHdrPtr = CrtUsrSpc(MbrSpcName);

    // get the list of members
    ListMbr( MbrSpcName :'MBRL0100' :DBName :'*ALL' :'0' :QUSEC);
    // check if API call failed
    if (QUSBAVL <> 0);
       dsply ('List Members failed with ' + QUSEI) ' ' Wait;
    else;

        // check to see if valid data was returned
        if (MbrGenHdr.QUSIS = 'C') or (MbrGenHdr.QUSIS = 'P');
           if (MbrGenHdr.QUSIS = 'C');
              dsply ('Complete list of ' + %char(MbrGenHdr.QUSNBRLE) +
                     ' entries returned.');
           endif;
```

Figure 7.4: Use the QUSLMBR API to list all members in *CURLIB/QRPGLESRC (part 2 of 3).

```
              if (MbrGenHdr.QUSIS = 'P');
                  dsply ('Partial list of ' + %char(MbrGenHdr.QUSNBRLE) +
                         ' entries returned.');
              endif;

              // get the first member entry and process the list
              MbrPtr = MbrGenHdrPtr + MbrGenHdr.QUSOLD;

              // process all returned member names
              for MbrCount = 1 to MbrGenHdr.QUSNBRLE;

                  dsply MbrEntry.QUSMN00 ' ' Wait;
                  if (Wait <> *blanks);
                     leave;
                  endif;

                   // get the next member entry
                   MbrPtr += MbrGenHdr.QUSSEE;
              endfor;

              // indicate that the member list is finished
              Wait = *blanks;
              dsply 'End of member list' ' ' Wait;

          else;
              dsply 'Invalid data returned by API' ' ' Wait;
          endif;
       endif;

       *inlr = *on;
       return;

     /end-free
```

Figure 7.4: Use the QUSLMBR API to list all members in *CURLIB/QRPGLESRC (part 3 of 3).

```
h dftactgrp(*no) bnddir('APILIB')

DName+++++++++++ETDsFrom+++To/L+++IDc.Keywords++++++++++++++++++++++++
dFig7_5           pr                    extpgm('FIG7_5')
d LibName                    10    const
d DltPct                     15   5 const

dFig7_5           pi
d LibName                    10    const
d DltPct                     15   5 const
```

Figure 7.5: Use the QUSLMBR API to reorganize any members having more than X percent of deleted records (part 1 of 5).

```
d/copy qsysinc/qrpglesrc,qusgen
d/copy qsysinc/qrpglesrc,quslobj
d/copy qsysinc/qrpglesrc,quslmbr
d/copy qsysinc/qrpglesrc,qusrmbrd
d/copy qsysinc/qrpglesrc,qusec

dCrtUsrSpc        pr                *    extproc('CrtUsrSpc')
d SpcName                      20        const

dListObj          pr                     extpgm('QUSLOBJ')
d SpcName                      20        const
d Format                        8        const
d ObjLibName                   20        const
d ObjTyp                       10        const
d QUSEC                                  likeds(QUSEC) options(*nopass)
d AutCtl                    65535        const options(*nopass :*varsize)
d SltCtl                    65535        const options(*nopass :*varsize)
d ASPCtl                    65535        const options(*nopass :*varsize)

dListMbr          pr                     extpgm('QUSLMBR')
d MbrSpcName                   20        const
d MbrFormat                     8        const
d DBName                       20        const
d MbrName                      10        const
d Override                      1        const
d QUSEC                                  likeds(QUSEC) options(*nopass)

dRtvMbrD          pr                     extpgm('QUSRMBRD')
d Receiver                      1        options(*varsize)
d LengthRcv                   10i 0      const
d Format                        8        const
d QualFileName                 20        const
d MbrName                      10        const
d OvrPrc                        1        const
d QUSEC                                  likeds(QUSEC) options(*nopass)
d FndPrc                        1        const options(*nopass)

dCmdExc           pr                     extpgm('QCMDEXC')
d Command                   65535        const options(*varsize)
d CmdLength                    15  5     const
d IGC                           3        const options(*nopass)
```

Figure 7.5: Use the *QUSLMBR API* to reorganize any members having more than X percent of deleted records (part 2 of 5).

```
d* List Object API generic header

 dGenHdr          ds                      likeds(QUSH0100)
d                                         based(GenHdrPtr)

d* List Object API (QUSLOBJ) format OBJL0200
dListEntry       ds                      likeds(QUSL020002)
d                                         based(LstPtr)

dMbrGenHdr       ds                      likeds(QUSH0100)
d                                         based(MbrGenHdrPtr)

dMbrEntry        ds                      likeds(QUSL010000)
d                                         based(MbrPtr)

dSpcName         ds
d SName                          10      inz('OBJLIST')
d SLib                           10      inz('QTEMP')

dMbrSpcName      ds
d MbrSpc                         10      inz('MBRLIST')
d MbrSpcLib                      10      inz('QTEMP')

dObjLibName      ds
d                               10      inz('*ALL')
d ObjLib                        10

dQualFileName    ds
d FileName                      10
d FileLibName                   10

dCount           s             10i 0
dMbrCount        s             10i 0
dWait            s             1
dCommand         s             100

CLON01Factor1+++++++Opcode&ExtFactor2+++++++Result++++++++Len++D+HiLoEq
 /free

   // set ErrCde bytes provided to 16 to avoid exceptions
   QUSBPRV = %size(QUSEC);

   // create the user spaces for the list of files and list of members
   GenHdrPtr = CrtUsrSpc(SpcName);
   MbrGenHdrPtr = CrtUsrSpc(MbrSpcName);
```

Figure 7.5: Use the QUSLMBR API to reorganize any members having more than X percent of deleted records (part 3 of 5).

```
// get the list of files
ObjLib = LibName;
ListObj( SpcName :'OBJL0200' : ObjLibName :'*FILE' :QUSEC);

// check if API call failed
if (QUSBAVL > 0);
    dsply ('List Objects failed with ' + QUSEI) ' ' Wait;
    *inlr = *on;
    return;
endif;

// check to see if the object list is complete
if (GenHdr.QUSIS = 'C') or (GenHdr.QUSTS = 'P');

    // get to the first list entry and process the list
    LstPtr = GenHdrPtr + GenHdr.QUSOLD;
    for Count = 1 to GenHdr.QUSNBRLE;

        // check to see if information was available
        if (ListEntry.QUSIS01 <> ' ');
            dsply ('Error with ' + %trimr(ListEntry.QUSOBJTU00) +
                      ' ' + ListEntry.QUSOBJNU00);

        else;
            // check to see if this is a physical file
            if (ListEntry.QUSEOA = 'PF');
                FileName = ListEntry.QUSOBJNU00;
                FileLibName = ListEntry.QUSOLNU00;

                // get the list of members
                ListMbr( MbrSpcName :'MBRL0100' :QualFileName :'*ALL'
                      :'0' :QUSEC);

                // check if API call failed
                if (QUSBAVL <> 0);
                  dsply ('List Members of ' + FileName + ' failed - '
                        + QUSEI);
                else;

                    // check to see if valid data was returned
                    if (MbrGenHdr.QUSIS = 'C')or(MbrGenHdr.QUSIS = 'P');

                    // get the first member entry and process the list
                    MbrPtr = MbrGenHdrPtr + MbrGenHdr.QUSOLD;
```

Figure 7.5: Use the QUSLMBR API to reorganize any members having more than X percent of deleted records (part 4 of 5).

```
                    // process all returned member names
                    for MbrCount = 1 to MbrGenHdr.QUSNBRLE;

                        // retrieve member description for nbr deleted rcds
                        RtvMbrD( QUSM0200 :%size(QUSM0200) :'MBRD0200'
                                :QualFileName :MbrEntry.QUSMN00 :'0' :QUSEC);
                        // check for API failure
                        if (QUSBAVL > 0);
                            // check if no member
                            if (QUSEI = 'CPF3C26'); // no error, just skip
                            else;
                                dsply (%trimr(ListEntry.QUSOBJNU00) +
                                        ' failed with ' + QUSEI);
                            endif; // general error with retrieving mbr desc
                        else;
                            // check for records and percentage deleted while
                            // avoiding divide by 0
                            if ((QUSNCRU > 0) or (QUSNDRU > 0));
                                if ((QUSNDRU/(QUSNDRU+QUSNCRU) * 100) > DltPct);
                                    Command = ('RGZPFM FILE(' +
                                            %trimr(FileLibName) +
                                            '/' + %trimr(FileName) + ') MBR(' +
                                            %trimr(MbrEntry.QUSMN00) + ')');
                                    CmdExc( Command :%len(%trimr(Command)));
                                    dsply ('Reorganized file ' + %trimr(FileName)
                                            + ' mbr ' + MbrEntry.QUSMN00);
                                endif;  // exceeds threshold
                            endif;      // 0 records found
                        endif; // check error on retrieve member description

                        MbrPtr += MbrGenHdr.QUSSEE;
                        endfor;         // get next member
                    else;
                        dsply ('QUSLMBR invalid data for ' + FileName);
                    endif; // check for valid data in member list
                endif;       // check error on list members
            endif;           // check for physical file
        endif;               // check for object information available
        LstPtr += GenHdr.QUSSEE;
        endfor;              // get next object
    else;
        dsply 'List Object API did not return valid data';
    endif;

    dsply 'End of List' ' ' Wait;
    *inlr = *on;
    Return;

/end-free
```

*Figure 7.5: Use the **QUSLMBR API** to reorganize any members having more than X percent of deleted records (part 5 of 5).*

Because program FIG7_5 uses two user spaces, one for the List Objects API and the other for the List Database Members API, we have to make sure we maintain separate lists and variables associated with each list. The FIG7_5 program uses the data structure SpcName to hold the name of the user space used for the List Objects API, and the data structure MbrSpcName for the List Database Members API. As both APIs are list-based, both will have the generic header that is common to all list APIs. For this reason, we also declare data structures GenHdr and MbrGenHdr. Both data structures are defined as LIKEDS(QUSH0100) because they have the same format, but they are qualified by GenHdr and MbrGenHdr, respectively, so that list information such as the number of list entries, the offset to the first list entry, and the size of each list entry can be managed independently. Along the same lines, FIG7_5 also defines both Count and MbrCount. These are used in the FOR loops to control how many entries are processed within each list. We sure don't want to confuse the number of members with the number of objects!

Another point is worth making with the FIG7_5 program. You might notice that we only create one user space for the List Database Members API, but we might call this API as many times as there are physical files in the library. List APIs always replace any data that might be in the user space if the API needs to write data to that location. So, when the program calls QUSLMBR for file A, it gets a list of members in file A. If it then calls QUSLMBR for file B and specifies the same user space, the API might write over any data that already exists in the user space. That data will be replaced with member data associated with file B. If file A had 10 members and file B had only one member, then the data about file A members 2 through 10 might still physically be stored in the user space, but you won't have any reliable way to get to it, as the generic header for the user space will have been rewritten by the second API call. You can only get the offset, size, and number of member entries associated with file B.

Because list APIs simply write over the contents of a user space, there are a few considerations to keep in mind. First, for performance reasons, you do not have to delete and then re-create user spaces to call a list API multiple times with the same named user space. Just create the user space once and call the API as many times as needed, processing the results after each call. Also, do not try to reference BASED data in a user space after calling a list API to replace data in the user space. Your BASED variables(s) will still be pointing to the user space, but they will be using the data values associated with the most recent call. Finally, if you need to keep track of data from one list to another, either use different user spaces or store the necessary data in variables you define within your application.

If your program involves five list APIs, using the output of one as the input to the next (as FIG7_5 does with two list APIs), you will need five user spaces, five views of the respective generic headers, and essentially five sets of variables for operations such as looping controls.

Get a List of Fields in a File

Figure 7.4 shows a simple program that lists the members within a file. As list APIs all follow a set of standards, you might expect that this program could be used as a model for other list APIs. This is, indeed, the case! Figure 7.6 shows how to use the List Fields API (QUSLFLD) to DSPLY a list of field names from the CUSTOMER file created in Figure 4.4.A.

```
h dftactgrp(*no) bnddir('APILIB')

DName+++++++++++ETDsFrom+++To/L+++IDc.Keywords++++++++++++++++++++++
d/copy qsysinc/qrpglesrc,qusgen
d/copy qsysinc/qrpglesrc,quslfld
d/copy qsysinc/qrpglesrc,qusec

dListFld          pr                    extpgm('QUSLFLD')
d SpcName                     20        const
d Format                       8        const
d DBName                      20        const
d RcdFmtName                  10        const
d Override                     1        const
d QUSEC                                 likeds(QUSEC) options(*nopass)

dCrtUsrSpc        pr              *     extproc('CrtUsrSpc')
d SpcName                      20       const

dGenHdr           ds                    likeds(QUSH0100)
d                                       based(GenHdrPtr)

dFldEntry         ds                    likeds(QUSL0100)
d                                       based(FldPtr)

dSpcName          ds
d SName                       10        inz('LSTFLD')
d Slib                        10        inz('QTEMP')
```

Figure 7.6: Use the QUSLFLD API to list all fields in *LIBL/CUSTOMER (part 1 of 3).

```
dDBName           ds
d DBFName                      10    inz('CUSTOMER')
d DBFLib                       10    inz('*LIBL')

dFldCount         s           10i 0
dWait             s            1

CLON01Factor1+++++++Opcode&ExtFactor2+++++++Result++++++++Len++D+HiLoEq
/free

  // set error code bytes provided to 16 to prevent exceptions
  QUSBPRV = %size(QUSEC);

  // create the user space for the list of fields
  GenHdrPtr = CrtUsrSpc(SpcName);

  // get the list of fields
  ListFld( SpcName :'FLDL0100' :DBName :'CUSREC' :'0' :QUSEC);

  // check if API call failed
  if (QUSBAVL <> 0);
     dsply ('List Fields failed with ' + QUSEI) ' ' Wait;
  else;
   // check to see if valid data was returned
   if (GenHdr.QUSIS = 'C') or (GenHdr.QUSIS = 'P');
      if (GenHdr.QUSIS = 'C');
         dsply ('Complete list of ' + %char(GenHdr.QUSNBRLE) +
                ' entries returned.');
      endif;
      if (GenHdr.QUSIS = 'P');
         dsply ('Partial list of ' + %char(GenHdr.QUSNBRLE) +
                ' entries returned.');
      endif;

        // get the first field entry and process the list
        FldPtr = GenHdrPtr + GenHdr.QUSOLD;

        // process all returned field names
        for FldCount = 1 to GenHdr.QUSNBRLE;

           dsply FldEntry.QUSFN02 ' ' Wait;
           if (Wait <> *Blanks);
              leave;
           endif;
```

Figure 7.6: Use the QUSLFLD API to list all fields in *LIBL/CUSTOMER (part 2 of 3).

```
            // get the next field entry
            FldPtr += GenHdr.QUSSEE;
        endfor;

        // indicate that the field list is finished
        dsply 'End of field list' ' ' Wait;
    else;
        dsply 'Invalid data returned by API' ' ' Wait;
    endif;
endif;

*inlr = *on;
return;

/end-free
```

*Figure 7.6: Use the **QUSLFLD API** to list all fields in ***LIBL/CUSTOMER** (part 3 of 3).*

In comparing Figures 7.4 and 7.6, you will see that most of the modification involved changing the comments from "member" to "field"! The changes basically involved the following:

- Replace the /copy of QSYSINC member QUSLMBR with QUSLFLD.

- Replace the prototype of QUSLMBR with a prototype of QUSLFLD.

- Replace the definition of MbrEnty with FldEntry.

- Replace the call to QUSLMBR with a call to QUSLFLD.

- Make minor field-name changes to make the program more self-documenting.

- Replace the field name QUSMN00, Member Name, with the field name QUSFN02, Field Name, returned by QUSLFLD.

The actual processing of the list contents remains the same. You should find this to be true of any of the list APIs that return fixed-size list entries. It might have taken you a while the first time you coded an F-spec in RPG to open a full procedural, externally described, keyed file for update. Once you knew how, however, you could open most any file. The same is true with list APIs: learn one and you've got it!

So you can see what FIG7_6 is doing, Table 7.3 provides the parameter descriptions for QUSLFLD, and Figure 7.7 provides the relevant QSYSINC definition for format FLDL0100. Note that this API takes a qualified file name (as opposed to a qualified *database* file

205

name for QUSLMBR) for the third parameter. This API not only works with database files (like QUSLMBR does), but also display files, printer files, etc. You will also notice in reviewing Figure 7.7 that a large amount of information is available to you about the fields in a file. We only used the field names in the example program, but you can just as easily get to all the other information that the system provides to you.

Table 7.3: List Fields, QUSLFLD			
Parameter	Description	Type	Size
1	Qualified User Space Name	Input	Char(20)
2	Format Name	Input	Char(8)
3	Qualified File Name	Input	Char(20)
4	Record Format Name	Input	Char(10)
5	Override Processing	Input	Char(1)
Optional Parameter Group 1			
6	Standard Error Code	I/O	Char(*)

The second parameter, Format Name, can be one of three values:

- FLDL0100—Basic field information
- FLDL0200—Basic field information and default value
- FLDL0300—Basic field information, default value, and alternative field name

Program FIG7_6 uses format FLDL0100.

The fifth parameter, Override Processing, is defined the same as in Table 7.2 and the List Members API.

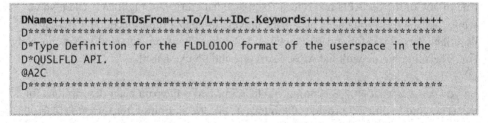

```
DName+++++++++++ETDsFrom+++To/L+++IDc.Keywords+++++++++++++++++++++++++
D*******************************************************************
D*Type Definition for the FLDL0100 format of the userspace in the
D*QUSLFLD API.
@A2C
D*******************************************************************
```

Figure 7.7: Definitions from QUSLFLD in QSYSINC/QRPGLESRC (part 1 of 4).

```
DQUSL0100       DS
D*                                      Qdb Lfld FLDL0100
D QUSFN02              1    10
D*                                      Field Name
D QUSDT               11    11
D*                                      Data Type
D QUSU                12    12
D*                                      Use
D QUSOBP             13    16B 0
D*                                      Output Buffer Position
D QUSIBP             17    20B 0
D*                                      Input Buffer Position
D QUSFLB             21    24B 0
D*                                      Field Length Bytes
D QUSIGITS           25    28B 0
D*                                      Digits
D QUSDP              29    32B 0
D*                                      Decimal Positions
D QUSFTD             33    82
D*                                      Field Text Description
D QUSEC00            83    84
D*                                      Edit Code
D QUSEWL             85    88B 0
D*                                      Edit Word Length
D QUSEW              89   152
D*                                      Edit Word
D QUSCH1            153   172
D*                                      Column Heading1
D QUSCH2            173   192
D*                                      Column Heading2
D QUSCH3            193   212
D*                                      Column Heading3
D QUSIFN            213   222
D*                                      Internal Field Name
D QUSAFN            223   252
D*                                      Alternate Field Name
D QUSLAF            253   256B 0
D*                                      Length Alternate Field
D QUSDBCSC          257   260B 0
D*                                      Number DBCS Characters
D QUSNVA            261   261
D*                                      Null Values Allowed
D QUSVFI            262   262
D*                                      Variable Field Indicato
D QUSDTF            263   266
D*                                      Date Time Format
```

Figure 7.7: Definitions from QUSLFLD in QSYSINC/QRPGLESRC (part 2 of 4).

```
D QUSDTS                267    267
D*                                           Date Time Separator
D QUSVLFI               268    268
D*                                           Variable Length Field I
D QUSCCSID00            269    272B 0
D*                                           Field Description CCSID
D QUSCCSID01            273    276B 0
D*                                           Field Data CCSID
D QUSCCSID02            277    280B 0
D*                                           Field Column Heading CC
D QUSCCSID03            281    284B 0
D*                                           Field Edit Words CCSID
D QUSCS2DL              285    288B 0
D*                                           UCS2 Displayed Length
D QUSFDES               289    292B 0
D*                                           Field Data Encoding Sch
D QUSMLOL               293    296B 0
D*                                           Maximum Large Object Le
D QUSLOPL               297    300B 0
D*                                           Large Object Pad Length
D QUSUDTNL              301    304B 0
D*                                           UDT Name Length
D QUSUDTN               305    432
D*                                           UDT Name
D QUSUDTLN              433    442
D*                                           UDT Library Name
D QUSDC03               443    443
D*                                           Datalink Control
D QUSDI03               444    444
D*                                           Datalink Integrity
D QUSDRP                445    445
D*                                           Datalink Read Permissio
D QUSDWP                446    446
D*                                           Datalink Write Permissi
D QUSDR                 447    447
D*                                           Datalink Recovery
D QUSDUC02              448    448
D*                                           Datalink Unlink Control
D QUSRNBR               449    452B 0
D*                                           Row Number
D QUSCNBR               453    456B 0
D*                                           Column Number
D QUSOWIDC              457    457
D*                                           ROWID Column
D QUSIC                 458    458
D*                                           Identity Column
```

Figure 7.7: Definitions from QUSLFLD in QSYSINC/QRPGLESRC (part 3 of 4).

```
D QUSTEDBY              459   459
D*                                        GENERATED BY
D QUSICC                460   460
D*                                        IC Cycle
D QUSICOSW              461   476P 0
D*                                        IC Orig Start With
D QUSICCSW              477   492P 0
D*                                        IC Curr Start With
D QUSICIB               493   496B 0
D*                                        IC Increment By
D QUSVALUE              497   512P 0
D*                                        IC MINVALUE
D QUSVALUE00            513   528P 0
D*                                        IC MAXVALUE
D QUSCACHE              529   532U 0
D*                                        IC CACHE
D QUSORDER              533   533
D*                                        IC ORDER
D QUSERVED47            534   544
D*                                        Reserved
```

Figure 7.7: Definitions from QUSLFLD in QSYSINC/QRPGLESRC (part 4 of 4).

Retrieve File Description

Have you ever run IBM's Display File Description (DSPFD) command? You probably use it all the time. What programmer doesn't? We *used* to use it all the time, too.

After all, IBM's Display File Description (DSPFD) command tells you everything there is to know about a file. Want to know the number of members, triggers, and constraints? It's in there. Want to know the type and size of the access path? It's in there. Is the file journaled? How about the name of the journal, the type of images being recorded, and the last date and time journaling was started? All of this and much more can be found with that single command. There are pages and pages of information displayed whenever you run that command. Of course, you can filter the information by selecting different options for the TYPE parameter, but there doesn't seem to be one single view that gives us exactly what we're looking for 90% of the time. We have to page through panel after panel of extraneous information just to get what we are looking for.

Admittedly, the problem is really our own. We want to see a combination of record information, object information, and file information all on one single screen. What we're looking for is some basic information. How many records are in the file, or how many fields? When the file was last created or saved? Who created the file? We want to get to the basic information about a file easily. Okay, we're lazy. We don't want to have to scroll through page after page to get this information; we want it all on one screen!

Rather than just whine about it (which is generally our most common course of action), we decided to do something. Of course, we turned to APIs for the solution, and soon we found the Retrieve File Description API (QDBRTVFD). With this API in our arsenal, we could write a program that would display the information that we felt was most pertinent on a single screen.

In Figure 7.8, you can see the result of our efforts. This display combines the most pertinent object information (object owner, creator, and creation date) with the most important file information, all on a single panel.

```
                         Display File Description

Physical File  . . . .   FAMLY        Family Master File
  Library . . . . . . .   DM2FILES
                                       File Type. . . . . . .   PF
Level check. . . . . .   No            Member name. . . . . .   FAMLY
Records in file. . . .   000000657     Number of members. . .   01
Deleted records in file. 000000000
File size. . . . . . .   000331776     Record Format. . . . .   FAMREC
Owned by . . . . . . .   QPGMR         Number of Formats. . .   01
Created by . . . . . .   RON           Record length. . . . .   000403
Created. . . .  06/24/98 10:02 AM      Number of fields . . .   0055
Saved. . . . .  04/21/00 05:41 PM      Initial member size. .   *NOMAX
Source file. . . . . .   SOURCE        Currently journaled. .   No
  Library . . . . . . .   C50LIB       Current or last journal. CPUJRN
                                         Library . . . . . . .   E50FILES

    Key Field        Size   Text
    01  FMNUM      000009 P Family Number




                                                               Bottom
   F3=Exit
```

Figure 7.8: Use QDBRTVFD to create your own version of DSPFD.

Figure 7.9 shows the DDS to create the display file. As you can see from the figure, this program uses a simple, straightforward subfile. We made the display a subfile because we also wanted to show the key fields in the file. A description of every field in the file is contained within the file description.

```
AAN01N02N03T.Name++++++RLen++TDpBLinPosFunctions++++++++++++++++++++++
                                           CF03(03)
           R SFLRCD                         SFL
             SFKEY           3      18  4
             SFFLD          10    0 18  8
             SFFSIZ          6   00 18  19EDTWRD('    ,    ')
             SFTYPE          1    0 18  27
             SFTEXT         38    0 18  29
           R SFLCTL                         SFLCTL(SFLRCD)
                                            SFLSIZ(12)
                                            SFLPAG(4)
                                            SFLDSPCTL
                                            OVERLAY
      21                                     SFLDSP
      25                                     SFLCLR
                                         1 28'Display File Description'
                                         3  2'File . .  . . . . . . .'
             OUTFILENAM     10    0  3 28
             FILDSC         40    0  3 40
                                         4  2'Library  . . . . . . .'
             OUTLIBNAME     10    0  4 28
                                         5 43'File Type . . . . . .'
             OUTTYPE         5    0  5 70
                                         6  2'Records in file  . . .'
             NBRRCD         11   00  6 28EDTWRD('   ,    ,    , 0 ')
                                         6 43'Member name . . . . .'
             OUTMEMBER      10    0  6 70
                                         7  2'Deleted records in file '
             NBRDLT         11   00  7 28EDTWRD('   ,    ,    , 0 ')
                                         7 43'Number of members  . . .'
             NBRMBR          5   00  7 70EDTWRD('  , 0 ')
                                         8  2'File size . . . . . . .'
             FILSIZ         11   00  8 28EDTWRD('   ,    ,    , 0 ')
                                         9  2'Level check . . . . . .'
             LVLCHK          3    0  9 28
                                         9 43'Record format . . . . .'
             OUTFORMAT      10    0  9 70
                                        10  2'Owned by . . . . . . . .'
             OWNER          10    0 10 28
                                        10 43'Number of formats  . . .'
             NBROFFMTS       2   00 10 76EDTWRD('0 ')
                                        11  2'Created by . . . . . . .'
             CRTBY          10    0 11 28
                                        11 43'Record length  . . . . .'
```

Figure 7.9: The DDS shows coding for the Display File Description (part 1 of 2).

```
                    OUTRECLEN       5  OO 11 72EDTWRD('  , 0 ')
                                       12  2'Created  . . .'
                    CRTDAT          8   O 12 19
                    CRTTIM          8   O 12 28
                                       12 43'Number of fields . . . . .'
                    NBRFIELDS       4  OO 12 74EDTWRD(' , 0 ')
                                       13  2'Saved  . . . .'
                    LSTSVD          8   O 13 19
                    SVDTIM          8   O 13 28
                                       13 43'Initial member size  . .'
                    MBRSIZ         10   O 13 70
                                       14  2'Source file  . . . . . .'
                    SRCFIL         10   O 14 28
                                       14 43'Currently journaled  . .'
                    JRNLD           3   O 14 70
                                       15  3'Library . . . . . . . .'
                    SRCLIB         10   O 15 28
                                       15 43'Current or last journal '
                    JRNNAM         10   O 15 70
                                       16 44'Library . . . . . . . .'
                    JRNLIB         10   O 16 70
                                       17  4'Key'
                                       17  8'Field'
                                       17 22'Size'
                                       17 29'Text'
         R FMT1
                                       23  4'F3=Exit'
```

Figure 7.9: The DDS shows coding for the Display File Description (part 2 of 2).

The focus of this book, of course, is APIs. Take a look at the RPG program in Figure 7.10. It uses three different APIs to gather the information we elected to put on one screen. Don't be too concerned right now with the details of how the program works. We'll be going through that shortly.

```
FFilename++IPEASF.....L.....A.Device+.Keywords+++++++++++++++++++++++++
fFIG7_9    cf   e               workstn sfile(sflrcd:RelRecNbr)

DName++++++++++ETDsFrom+++To/L+++IDc.Keywords+++++++++++++++++++++++++++
dFig7_10        pr                      extpgm('FIG7_10')
d FileLib                    20         const
d MemberName                 10         const
d EntryFmt                   10         const
```

Figure 7.10: Use QDBRTVFD as a better display-file description (part 1 of 9).

212

```
dFig7_10              pi
d FileLib                       20    const
d MemberName                    10    const
d EntryFmt                      10    const

d/copy qsysinc/qrpglesrc,qusrobjd
d/copy qsysinc/qrpglesrc,qdbrtvfd
d/copy qsysinc/qrpglesrc,qusrmbrd
d/copy qsysinc/qrpglesrc,qusec

dRtvObjD              pr                extpgm('QUSROBJD')
d Receiver                       1    options(*varsize)
d LenReceiver                  10i 0  const
d Format                         8    const
d QualObjName                   20    const
d ObjType                       10    const
d QUSEC                                likeds(QUSEC) options(*nopass)
d ASP                        65535    const options(*varsize :*nopass)

dRtvFD                pr                extpgm('QDBRTVFD')
d Receiver                       1    options(*varsize)
d LenReceiver                  10i 0  const
d QualFileName                  20
d Format                         8    const
d QualFileName                  20    const
d RcdFmtName                    10    const
d OvrPrc                         1    const
d System                       10    const
d FmtType                      10    const
d QUSEC                                likeds(QUSEC)

dRtvMbrD              pr                extpgm('QUSRMBRD')
d Receiver                       1    options(*varsize)
d LengthRcv                    10i 0  const
d Format                         8    const
d QualFileName                  20    const
d MbrName                       10    const
d OvrPrc                         1    const
d QUSEC                                likeds(QUSEC) options(*nopass)
d FndPrc                         1    const options(*nopass)

dRtvMbrD              pr                extpgm('QUSRMBRD')
dHeader               ds                likeds(QDBQ25)
d                                       based(RtvFDPtr)
```

Figure 7.10: Use QDBRTVFD *as a better display-file description (part 2 of 9).*

```
dJrnHdr          ds                        likeds(QDBQ40)
d                                          based(JrnPtr)

dFileHdr         ds                        likeds(QDBQ36)
d                                          based(FilePtr)

dKeyHdr          ds                        likeds(QDBQ39)
d                                          based(KeyPtr)

dPFHdr           ds                        likeds(QDBQ26)
d                                          based(PFPtr)

dFldHdr          ds                        likeds(QDBQ41)
d                                          based(FldHdrPtr)

dFldInfo         ds                        likeds(QDBQ42)
d                                          based(FldInfoPtr)

dFldTxt          ds                        likeds(QDBQ43)
d                                          based(FldTxtPtr)

dFileLibIn       ds
d FileName                          10
d LibName                           10

dSFLSiz          c                         12

dRelRecNbr       s                  4 0
dRtnNamLib       s                 20
dI               s                10i 0
dJ               s                 3i 0
dK               s                10i 0
dMaxKeys         s                10i 0
dWait            s                  1

CL0N01Factor1+++++++Opcode&ExtFactor2+++++++Result++++++++Len++D+HiLoEq
 /free

   QUSBPRV = %size(QUSEC);      // set error code size
   FileLibIn = FileLib;         // make local copy of qualified file

   // retrieve object description to verify that the object exists
   // and to determine the current owner of the object

   RtvObjd( QUSD0300 :%size(QUSD0300) :'OBJD0300' :FileLibIn :'*FILE'
            :QUSEC);
```

Figure 7.10: Use *QDBRTVFD* as a better display-file description (part 3 of 9).

```
if (QUSBAVL > 0);
    dsply ('Error ' + QUSEI + ' retrieving object description')
            ' ' Wait;
    *inlr = *on;
    return;
endif;

// determine if this is a physical or logical file

if (QUSEOA06 <> 'PF') and (QUSEOA06 <> 'LF');
    dsply (%trimr(%subst(FileLib:11:10)) + '/' +
           %trimr(%subst(FileLib:1:10)) + ' is not correct file type')
            ' ' Wait;
    *inlr = *on;
    return;
endif;

LibName = QUSRL03;                  // Use returned lib name in future

// load object level information to subfile control record

OutFileNam = QUSOBJNO2;            // File name
OutLibName = QUSRL03;             // Library name
Owner = QUSOBJO06;                // Owner
CrtBy = QUSCUPO3;                 // Created by
SrcFil = QUSSFILNO7;             // Source file
SrcLib = QUSSFLNO7;              // Source libarary
OutType = QUSEOA06;              // Extended attribute of file

// Format creation date and time to job format
CrtDat = %char(%date(%subst(QUSCDT14   :1 :7)    :*CYMD0) :*jobrun);
CrtTim = %char(%time(%subst(QUSCDT14   :8 :6)    :*HMS0)  :*jobrun);

// Format last saved date and time to job format
if (QUSOSDT02 <> *blanks);          // Never saved?
    LstSvd = %char(%date(%subst(QUSOSDT02 :1 :7)   :*CYMD0) :*jobrun);
    SvdTim = %char(%time(%subst(QUSOSDT02 :8 :6)   :*HMS0)  :*jobrun);
endif;

// get general File Description Information
// first find out how much storage is needed for format FILD0100

RtvFD( QDBQ25 :8 :RtnNamLib :'FILD0100' :FileLibIn
    :' ' :'0' :'*LCL' :'*EXT' :QUSEC);
if (QUSBAVL > 0);
    dsply ('Error ' + QUSEI + ' retrieving file description 1')
            ' ' Wait;
    *inlr = *on;
    return;
endif;
```

Figure 7.10: Use *QDBRTVFD* as a better display-file description (part 4 of 9).

```
// allocate the storage and call the API again with the based
// receiver variable

RtvFDPtr = %alloc(QDBFYAVL);
RtvFD( Header :QDBFYAVL :RtnNamLib :'FILD0100' :FileLibIn
       :' ' :'0' :'*LCL' :'*EXT' :QUSEC);
if (QUSBAVL > 0);
   dsply ('Error ' + QUSEI + ' retrieving file description 2')
         ' ' Wait;
   *inlr = *on;
   return;
endif;


// load file level information to subfile control record

NbrMbr = Header.QDBHMNUM;                    // Number of members
NbrOfFmts = Header.QDBMTNUM;                 // Number of formats
NbrFields = Header.QDBXFNUM;                 // Number of fields
OutRecLen = Header.QDBFMXRL;                 // Max record length

// Determine LVLCHK value
if (%bitand(%subst(Header.QDBBITS27 :2 :1) :x'80') = x'80');
   LvlChk = 'Yes';
   else;
   LvlChk = 'No ';
endif;


// Determine journaling status
if (Header.QDBFJORN = 0);
   Jrnld = 'No';
else;
   JrnPtr = RtvFDPtr + Header.QDBFJORN;
   JrnNam = JrnHdr.QDBFOJRN;
   JrnLib = JrnHdr.QDBFOLIB;
   if (JrnHdr.QDBFJACT = '1');
       Jrnld = 'Yes';
   else;
       Jrnld = 'No';
   endif;
endif;


// Get initial member allocation size
PFPtr = RtvFDPtr + Header.QDBPFOF;
if (PFHdr.QDBPRNUM = 0);
   MbrSiz = '*NOMAX';
else;
```

*Figure 7.10: Use **QDBRTVFD** as a better display-file description (part 5 of 9).*

```
        if (PFHdr.QDBPRNUM >= 1000000);
            MbrSiz = '> 1M';
        else;
            MbrSiz = %editw(PFHdr.QDBPRNUM :'          , 0 ');
        endif;
    endif;

    // Get format and key field information

    RelRecNbr = 1;
    FilePtr = RtvFDPtr + Header.QDBFOS;          // File scope array
    for I = 1 to Header.QDBLBNUM;                // Number of based members
        if (FileHdr.QDBFT01 = EntryFmt) or       // Correct record format?
    (EntryFmt = '*FIRST');                       // Use first rcd format?
        OutFormat = FileHdr.QDBFT01;             // Set format name
        if (%bitand(%subst(Header.QDBBITS27 :1 :1) // keyed access?
            :x'02') = x'02');                    // Yes
            KeyPtr = RtvFDPtr + FileHdr.QDBFKSOF; // Get Key info

            // get general Field Description Information
            // find out how much storage is needed for FILD0200
            RtvFD( QDBQ41 :8 :RtnNamLib :'FILD0200' :FileLibIn
                  :OutFormat :'0' :'*LCL' :'*EXT' :QUSEC);
            if (QUSBAVL > 0);
                dsply ('Error '+QUSEI+' retrieving field description 1')
                ' ' Wait;
                *inlr = *on;
                return;
            endif;

            // allocate the storage needed
            FldHdrPtr = %alloc(QDBBYAVA00);
            RtvFD( FldHdr :QDBBYAVA00 :RtnNamLib :'FILD0200'
                  :FileLibIn :OutFormat :'0' :'*LCL' :'*EXT' :QUSEC);
            if (QUSBAVL > 0);
                dsply ('Error '+QUSEI+' retrieving field description 2')
                    ' ' Wait;
                *inlr = *on;
                return;
            endif;

            FldInfoPtr = FldHdrPtr + %size(FldHdr); // Field array
            if SFLSiz < Header.QDBFKNUM00;
                MaxKeys = SFLSiz;
            else;
                MaxKeys = Header.QDBFKNUM00;
            endif;
```

Figure 7.10: Use QDBRTVFD as a better display-file description (part 6 of 9).

```
        for J = 1 to MaxKeys;              // Number of keys
          SfKey = %char(J);                // Key number
          if (KeyHdr.QDBFKFLD = *blanks);
            SfFld = '*NONE';
              SfType = *blanks;
              SfFSiz = 0;
              SfText = *blanks;
              write SflRcd;
              RelRecNbr += 1;              // Subfile record
          else;
              SfFld = KeyHdr.QDBFKFLD;        // Key field name
              for K = 1 to FldHdr.QDBLDNUM; // Number of fields
                if (FldInfo.QDBFFLDC = KeyHdr.QDBFKFLD);
                  select;
                    when FldInfo.QDBFFTYP = x'0000';
                          SfType = 'B';
                          SfFSiz = FldInfo.QDBFFLDD;
                    when FldInfo.QDBFFTYP = x'0001';
                          SfType = 'F';
                          SfFSiz = FldInfo.QDBFFLDB;
                    when FldInfo.QDBFFTYP = x'0002';
                          SfType = 'S';
                          SfFSiz = FldInfo.QDBFFLDD;
                    when FldInfo.QDBFFTYP = x'0003';
                          SfType = 'P';
                          SfFSiz = FldInfo.QDBFFLDD;
                    when FldInfo.QDBFFTYP = x'0004';
                          SfType = 'A';
                          SfFSiz = FldInfo.QDBFFLDB;
                    when FldInfo.QDBFFTYP = x'0005';
                          SfType = 'G';
                          SfFSiz = FldInfo.QDBFFLDB;
                    when FldInfo.QDBFFTYP = x'000B';
                          SfType = 'D';
                          SfFSiz = FldInfo.QDBFFLDB;
                    when FldInfo.QDBFFTYP = x'000C';
                          SfType = 'T';
                          SfFSiz = FldInfo.QDBFFLDB;
                    when FldInfo.QDBFFTYP = x'000D';
                          SfType = 'Z';
                          SfFSiz = FldInfo.QDBFFLDB;
                  other;
```

Figure 7.10: Use *QDBRTVFD* as a better display-file description (part 7 of 9).

```
                            SfType = ' ';
                      endsl;
                      if (FldInfo.QDBFTXTD <> 0);
                          FldTxtPtr = FldInfoPtr + FldInfo.QDBFTXTD;
                          SfText = FldTxt.QDBFFTXT;
                      else;
                          SfText = *blanks;
                      endif;
                      write SflRcd;
                      RelRecNbr += 1;                  // Subfile record
                      FldInfoPtr = FldHdrPtr + %size(FldHdr);//reset fld
                      leave;
                      endif;
                      FldInfoPtr = FldInfoPtr + FldInfo.QDBFDEFL;
                    endfor;
                endif;
                KeyPtr = KeyPtr + %size(KeyHdr);  // Get next key fld
           endfor;
           leave;
         else;
           SfFld = 'No keys';
           write SflRcd;
           RelRecNbr += 1;                          // Subfile record
         endif;
      else;
         FilePtr = FilePtr + %size(FileHdr);  // Goto next format
      endif;
   endfor;

if (RelRecNbr > 1);                          // Subfile rcds written?
   *in21 = *on;                              // Yes, write subfile
endif;


// Get member data
RtvMbrD( QUSM0200 :%size(QUSM0200) :'MBRD0200' :FileLibIn
        :MemberName :'0' :QUSEC :'0');
if (QUSBAVL > 0);
   dsply ('Error ' + QUSEI + ' retrieving member information')
         ' ' Wait;
   *inlr = *on;
   return;
endif;
OutMember = QUSMN03;                                // Member name
FilSiz = (QUSDSS * QUSDSSM) + (QUSAPS * QUSAPSM);  // Total Size
NbrRcd = QUSNBRCR;                                 // Number records
NbrDlt = QUSNBRDR;                                 // Number deleted records
```

*Figure 7.10: Use **QDBRTVFD** as a better display-file description (part 8 of 9).*

219

```
    write Fmt1;
    exfmt SflCtl;
    *inlr = *on;
    return;

     /end-free
```

Figure 7.10: Use QDBRTVFD as a better display-file description (part 9 of 9).

The program FIG7_10 accepts the three parameters FileLib, MemberName, and EntryFmt as shown in Figure 7.11. FileLib is defined as a 20-byte field, where the first 10 bytes are the file name and the last 10 bytes are the library name. MemberName is defined as a 10-byte field for the file member name, and EntryFmt is a 10-byte field for the record format name. Although it might not be obvious just looking at FIG7_10, special values such as *LIBL and *CURLIB are supported for the library portion of the FileLib parameter. You'll see why in just a bit.

```
DName++++++++++ETDsFrom+++To/L+++IDc.Keywords++++++++++++++++++++++++++
dFig7_10          pr                    extpgm('FIG7_10')
d FileLib                      20       const
d MemberName                   10       const
d EntryFmt                     10       const

dFig7_10          pi
d FileLib                      20       const
d MemberName                   10       const
d EntryFmt                     10       const
```

Figure 7.11: The function prototype for our version of retrieving file information.

After doing a bit of housecleaning—namely, setting the error-code bytes provided in field QUSBPRV to 16 and making a local copy of the FileLib parameter value—FIG7_10 calls the Retrieve Object Description API (QUSROBJD), as shown in Figure 7.12. This API is actually providing several functions. First, the API will return errors such as "File not found," in which case FIG7_10 DSPLYs that an error was encountered and then terminates. Second, the API supports special values such as *LIBL and *CURLIB as inputs for the object name. So, if the caller of FIG7_10 chooses to use either of these special values, we can simply pass them on to the API for it to handle. The API then returns the actual library name used as part of the returned structure. Finally, of course, the API will return the information we need, such as the object's owner, who created it, and what source was used in creating it.

```
QUSBPRV = %size(QUSEC);        // set error code size
FileLibIn = FileLib;           // make local copy of qualified file

// retrieve object description to verify that the object exists
// and to determine the current owner of the object

RtvObjd( QUSD0300 :%size(QUSD0300) :'OBJD0300' :FileLibIn :'*FILE'
       :QUSEC);
```

Figure 7.12: Housecleaning and calling QUSROBJD.

The parameters for the Retrieve Object Description API are given in Table 7.4. This API was briefly discussed in chapter 5, and since it's a simple retrieve API, we won't cover it in any great detail here. If you have questions about how to use this type of API, review chapter 2.

Table 7.4: Retrieve Object Description, QUSROBJD			
Parameter	Description	Type	Size
1	Receiver Variable	Output	Char(*)
2	Length of Receiver Variable	Input	Binary(4)
3	Format Name	Input	Char(8)
4	Qualified Object Name	Input	Char(20)
5	Object Type	Input	Char(10)
Optional Parameter Group 1			
6	Error Code	In/Out	Char(*)
Optional Parameter Group 2			
7	Auxiliary Storage Pool (ASP) Control	Input	Char(*)

The Retrieve Object Description API supports four different formats, providing various types of information about the object. We chose the OBJD0300 format, as we want some of the information found in that format. (The Information Center provides documentation on all of the supported formats and the detailed definitions of what is available.) The QSYSINC-provided include for format OBJD0300 of member QUSROBJD in QRPGLESRC is shown in Figure 7.13. In chapter 5, you can find examples using formats OBJD0100 (Figure 5.1) and OBJD0400 (Figure 5.5).

```
DName+++++++++++ETDsFrom+++To/L+++IDc.Keywords++++++++++++++++++++++++
D*******************************************************************
D*Type Definition for the OBJD0300 format.
D*******************************************************************
DQUSD0300          DS
D*                                                   Qus OBJD0300
D QUSBRTN08               1      4B 0
D*                                                   Bytes Returned
D QUSBAVL09               5      8B 0
D*                                                   Bytes Available
D QUSOBJN02               9     18
D*                                                   Object Name
D QUSOBJLN01             19     28
D*                                                   Object Lib Name
D QUSOBJT02              29     38
D*                                                   Object Type
D QUSRL03                39     48
D*                                                   Return Lib
D QUSASP06               49     52B 0
D*                                                   Aux Storage Pool
D QUSOBJO06              53     62
D*                                                   Object Owner
D QUSOBJD06              63     64
D*                                                   Object Domain
D QUSCDT14               65     77
D*                                                   Create Date Time
D QUSCDT15               78     90
D*                                                   Change Date Time
D QUSEOA06               91    100
D*                                                   Extended Obj Attr
D QUSTD13               101    150
D*                                                   Text Description
D QUSSFILN07            151    160
D*                                                   Source File Name
D QUSSFLN07             161    170
D*                                                   Source File Lib Name
D QUSSFMN04             171    180
D*                                                   Source File Mbr Name
D QUSSFUDT03            181    193
D*                                                   Source File Update
D QUSOSDT02             194    206
D*                                                   Object Saved Date Time
D QUSORDT02             207    219
D*                                                   Object Restored DateTime
D QUSCUP03              220    229
D*                                                   Creator User Profile
```

Figure 7.13: Format *OBJD0300* of *QUSROBJD* as provided in *QSYSINC* (part 1 of 2).

```
D QUSSOBJC03           230    237
D*                                        System Object Creation
D QUSRD01              238    244
D*                                        Reset Date
D QUSSS04              245    248B 0
D*                                        Save Size
D QUSSSNBR02           249    252B 0
D*                                        Save Sequence Number
D QUSORAGE04           253    262
D*                                        Storage
D QUSSCMD02            263    272
D*                                        Save Command
D QUSSVID02            273    343
D*                                        Save Volume ID
D QUSSD04              344    353
D*                                        Save Device
D QUSSFILN08           354    363
D*                                        Save File Name
D QUSSFLN08            364    373
D*                                        Save File Lib Name
D QUSSL07              374    390
D*                                        Save Label
D QUSSL08              391    399
D*                                        System Level
D QUSPILER03           400    415
D*                                        Compiler
D QUSOBJL04            416    423
D*                                        Object Level
D QUSUC03              424    424
D*                                        User Changed
D QUSLPGM03            425    440
D*                                        Licensed Program
D QUSPTF03             441    450
D*                                        PTF
D QUSAPAR03            451    460
D*                                        APAR
```

Figure 7.13: Format OBJD0300 of QUSROBJD as provided in QSYSINC (part 2 of 2).

As shown in Figure 7.14, after calling the QUSROBJD API, FIG7_10 checks to see if an error was encountered (QUSBAVL > 0). If so, it DSPLYs the error message ID and ends the program. If no error was found, FIG7_10 determines if the object retrieved was either a physical file or a logical file (QUSEOA06 <> 'PF' or 'LF'). If it was neither, FIG7_10 DSPLYs an error message and terminates, because this program, as written, only handles these two file types.

```
if (QUSBAVL > 0);
    dsply ('Error ' + QUSEI + ' retrieving object description')
           ' ' Wait;
    *inlr = *on;
    return;
endif;
 // determine if this is a physical or logical file

 if (QUSEOA06 <> 'PF') and (QUSEOA06 <> 'LF');
    dsply (%trimr(%subst(FileLib:11:10)) + '/' +
           %trimr(%subst(FileLib:1:10)) + ' is not correct file type')
           ' ' Wait;
    *inlr = *on;
     return;
 endif;
```

Figure 7.14: Check for errors on the call to *QUSROBJD* or with the type of file found.

If no error was found and the file type is supported, Figure 7.15 shows that FIG7_10 then saves the library name where the object was found (LIBNAME = QUSRL03) and primes various fields of the subfile control record defined in Figure 7.9. The library name is saved for performance reasons. Later in the program, FIG7_10 will be calling other APIs to gather additional information about the file. While these APIs also accept special values such as *LIBL and *CURLIB, we get better performance by simply using the actual library name, now that we know it from calling QUSROBJD.

```
LibName = QUSRL03;                  // Use returned lib name in future

// load object level information to subfile control record

OutFileNam = QUSOBJN02;             // File name
OutLibName = QUSRL03;               // Library name
Owner = QUSOBJO06;                  // Owner
CrtBy = QUSCUP03;                   // Created by
SrcFil = QUSSFILN07;                // Source file
SrcLib = QUSSFLN07;                 // Source library
OutType = QUSEOA06;                 // Extended attribute of file

// Format creation date and time to job format
CrtDat = %char(%date(%subst(QUSCDT14  :1 :7)   :*CYMD0) :*jobrun);
CrtTim = %char(%time(%subst(QUSCDT14  :8 :6)   :*HMS0)  :*jobrun);

// Format last saved date and time to job format
if (QUSOSDT02 <> *blanks);          // Never saved?
    LstSvd = %char(%date(%subst(QUSOSDT02 :1 :7)   :*CYMD0) :*jobrun);
    SvdTim = %char(%time(%subst(QUSOSDT02 :8 :6)   :*HMS0)  :*jobrun);
endif;
```

Figure 7.15: Prime the subfile control record with the object data found.

It is now time to call the Retrieve Database File Description API (QDBRTVFD). The parameter descriptions for QDBRTVFD are listed in Table 7.5.

Table 7.5: Retrieve File Description, QDBRTVFD			
Parameter	Description	Type	Size
1	Receiver Variable	Output	Char(*)
2	Length of Receiver Variable	Input	Binary(4)
3	Qualified Returned File Name	Output	Char(20)
4	Format Name	Input	Char(8)
5	Qualified Database File Name	Input	Char(20)
6	Record Format Name	Input	Char(10)
7	Override Processing	Input	Char(1)
8	System	Input	Char(10)
9	Format Type	Input	Char(10)
10	Error Code	I/O	Char(*)

The QDBRTVFD API is typical of most retrieve-type APIs. While some API users refer to this API as being "graduate level" in terms of use, this is really not the case. The API can be mind-boggling in terms of the amount of data available, but it's actually very straightforward to use, so long as you're comfortable with retrieve-type APIs and you know what data you want.

The first two parameters are fairly standard. The Receiver Variable parameter holds the retrieved information, and the Length of Receiver Variable parameter holds the size of the receiver variable you have allocated in your program.

The third parameter, Qualified Returned File Name, returns to you the qualified name of the file the API accessed. If overrides are used in accessing the file, this parameter might be different from the file name specified in parameter 5 (the qualified file name you requested information about).

The fourth parameter, Format Name, describes what data you want returned in the receiver variable (parameter 1). As mentioned in chapter 1, most APIs follow a convention in which the format name with the lowest number sequence is the fastest to retrieve, and higher sequence numbers return the data found in lower sequence numbers plus additional information. For QDBRTVFD, however, this is not the case. Each format returns distinctly different types of information. In program FIG7_10, we actually call QDBRTVFD multiple times, as we need information found in different formats. We first call QDBRTVFD requesting format FILD0100 to get general file information, such as the number of members, number of fields, and maximum record length. Later, we call the API again, requesting format FILD0200 to get additional information on the fields within the file.

The fifth parameter, Qualified Database File Name, is the name and library of the file you want information about. As mentioned earlier, when calling the API, we use the name as it was returned by the Retrieve Object Description API (QUSROBJD).

The sixth parameter, Record Format Name, is the record format name for the file. The special value *FIRST is supported.

The seventh parameter, Override Processing, controls whether or not overrides should be honored by the API. This parameter is defined as discussed earlier in this chapter when the QUSLMBR and QUSLFLD APIs were reviewed.

The eighth parameter, System, controls whether you want the information retrieved from a local or remote system. The supported values are *LCL, *RMT, and *FILETYPE.

The ninth parameter, Format Type, controls how you want to handle field definitions when working with logical files that can be mapping physical file fields. Supported values are *EXT, which indicates you want the fields as they are defined in the logical file, and *INT, which indicates you want the fields as they are defined in the underlying physical files. This parameter only applies when using format FILD0200 and logical files.

The tenth parameter is the standard error-code structure. It describes how you want to handle error situations that the API might encounter.

Because this API can return a highly variable amount of data depending on the characteristics of the file, we use the technique of dynamically allocated receiver variables illustrated in Figure 2.6 of chapter 2 . In this way, we don't have to guess how large a receiver variable to allocate. We simply let the API tell us how large a receiver variable it needs in order to return all of the requested information. This dynamic allocation is shown in Figure 7.16.

```
CLON01Factor1+++++++Opcode&ExtFactor2+++++++Result++++++++Len++D+HiLoEq
// get general File Description Information
// first find out how much storage is needed for format FILD0100

RtvFD( QDBQ25 :8 :RtnNamLib :'FILD0100' :FileLibIn
      :' ' :'0' :'*LCL' :'*EXT' :QUSEC);
if (QUSBAVL > 0);
   dsply ('Error ' + QUSEI + ' retrieving file description 1')
         ' ' Wait;
   *inlr = *on;
   return;
endif;

// allocate the storage and call the API again with the based
// receiver variable

RtvFDPtr = %alloc(QDBFYAVL);
RtvFD( Header :QDBFYAVL :RtnNamLib :'FILD0100' :FileLibIn
      :' ' :'0' :'*LCL' :'*EXT' :QUSEC);
```

Figure 7.16: Dynamically allocating storage for QDBRTVFD.

As mentioned before, a huge amount of information is available from the Retrieve Database File Description API. In the case of format FILD0100, Figure 7.18 shows the base structure returned. This structure, in turn, provides access to additional structures detailing information such as join specifications, select/omit definitions, and constraint information. When you have the opportunity, you might want to examine the contents of these structures, just to get a feel for what is available. For now, all we need are the specific fields necessary to complete our FIG7_9 panel. For this, we can use the BASED structure Header, which is defined LIKEDS(QDBQ25) and provides the number of members (QDBHMNUM), formats (QDBMTNUM), and fields (QDBXFNUM); the maximum record length (QDBFMXRL), and whether the level check is specified (QDBBITS27). In the case of QDBBITS27, we need to examine a specific bit in order to determine if level-check is on or off. This is done using the %BITAND built-in function, shown in Figure 7.17. While the vast majority of APIs do not require the use of individual bits, some do. QDBRTVFD is one of them!

```
RtvFD( Header :QDBFYAVL :RtnNamLib :'FILD0100' :FileLibIn
      :' ' :'0' :'*LCL' :'*EXT' :QUSEC);
if (QUSBAVL > 0);
   dsply ('Error ' + QUSEI + ' retrieving file description 2')
         ' ' Wait;
```

Figure 7.17: Accessing information from QDBQ25 (part 1 of 2).

```
   *inlr = *on;
   return;
endif;

// load file level information to subfile control record

NbrMbr = Header.QDBHMNUM;                    // Number of members
NbrOfFmts = Header.QDBMTNUM;                 // Number of formats
NbrFields = Header.QDBXFNUM;                 // Number of fields
OutRecLen = Header.QDBFMXRL;                 // Max record length

// Determine LVLCHK value
if (%bitand(%subst(Header.QDBBITS27 :2 :1) :x'80') = x'80');
   LvlChk = 'Yes';
   else;
   LvlChk = 'No ';
endif;
```

Figure 7.17: Accessing information from QDBQ25 (part 2 of 2).

```
DName+++++++++++ETDsFrom+++To/L+++IDc.Keywords++++++++++++++++++++++++++++
D*********************************************************************
D*
D*File Definition Template (FDT) Header
D*
D*********************************************************************
D*This section is always located at the beginning of the
D*returned data.
D*********************************************************************
DQDBQ25              DS
D*                                     Header information - The
D*                                     FDT starts here
D QDBFYRET             1      4B 0
D*                                     Bytes returned - The length
D*                                     of the data returned
D QDBFYAVL             5      8B 0
D*                                     Bytes available - The number
D*                                     of bytes provided for the
D*                                     file definition template
D*                                     data
D*QDBFHFLG                    2
D  QDBBITS27           9     10
D*  QDBRSV100           2             BITS
D*  QDBFHFPL00          1             BIT
D*  QDBRSV200           1             BIT
```

Figure 7.18: The start of format FILD0100 of QDBRTVFD, as provided in QSYSINC (part 1 of 12).

```
D* QDBFHFSU00              1              BIT
D* QDBRSV300               1              BIT
D* QDBFHFKY00              1              BIT
D* QDBRSV400               1              BIT
D* QDBFHFLC00              1              BIT
D* QDBFKFS000              1              BIT
D* QDBRSV500               1              BIT
D* QDBFHSHR00              1              BIT
D* QDBRSV600               2              BITS
D* QDBFIGCD00              1              BIT
D* QDBFIGCL00              1              BIT
D*                                        Attribute Bytes
D QDBRSV7                 11      14
D*                                        Reserved.
D QDBLBNUM                15      16B 0
D*                                        Number Of Data Members
D*                                        1 = Externally described
D*                                            physical file, or program
D*                                            described physical file
D*                                            that is NOT linked to a
D*                                            Data Dictionary.
D*                                        1-32 = Number of Data
D*                                            Dictionary record
D*                                            formats for a program
D*                                            described physical
D*                                            file that is linked to
D*                                            a Data Dictionary.
D*                                        1-256=Number of based on
D*                                            physical files for
D*                                            a logical file.
D QDBLBNUM                15      16B 0

D*QDBFKDAT                         14
D  QDBFKNUM00             17      18B 0
D  QDBFKMXL00             19      20B 0
D* QDBFKFLG00              1
D  QDBBITS28              21      21
D* QDBRSV802               1              BIT
D* QDBFKFCS02              1              BIT
D* QDBRSV902               4              BITS
D* QDBFKFRC02              1              BIT
D* QDBFKFLT02              1              BIT
D  QDBFKFDM00             22      22
D  QDBRSV1000             23      30
D*                                        Keyed Sequence Access Path
```

Figure 7.18: The start of format FILD0100 of QDBRTVFD, as provided in QSYSINC (part 2 of 12).

```
D QDBFHAUT            31    40
D*                                Public Authority (AUT)
D*                                '*CHANGE    ' = Public change
D*                                            authority.
D*                                '*ALL       ' = Public all
D*                                            authority.
D*                                '*USE       ' = Public use
D*                                            authority.
D*                                '*EXCLUDE   ' = Public exclude
D*                                            authority.
D*                                'authorization-list-name'
D*                                            = Name of the
D*                                            authorization
D*                                            list whose
D*                                            authority is
D*                                            used for the
D*                                            file.
D*                                This is the original public
D*                                authority that the file was
D*                                created with, NOT the current
D*                                public authority for the file.
D QDBFHUPL            41    41
D*                                Preferred Storage Unit (UNIT)
D*                                X'00' = The storage space for
D*                                        the file and its
D*                                        members can be
D*                                        allocated on any
D*                                        available auxiliary
D*                                        storage unit (*ANY).
D*                                X'01'-X'FF' = The unit
D*                                            identifier (a
D*                                            number from 1
D*                                            to 255 assigned
D*                                            when the disk
D*                                            device is
D*                                            configured) of
D*                                            a specific
D*                                            auxiliary
D*                                            storage unit on
D*                                            the system.
D QDBFHMXM            42    43B 0
D*                                Maximum Members (MAXMBRS)
D*                                0 = No maximum is specified
D*                                    for the number of members,
D*                                    the system maximum of
D*                                    32,767 members is used
D*                                    (*NOMAX).
```

Figure 7.18: The start of format FILD0100 of QDBRTVFD, as provided in QSYSINC (part 3 of 12).

230

```
D*                                1-32,767 = The value for the
D*                                           maximum number of
D*                                           members that the
D*                                           file can have
D*                                           (maximum-members).
D QDBFWTFI        44    45B 0
D*                                Maximum File Wait Time
D*                                (WAITFILE)
D*                                -1 = The default wait time
D*                                     specified in the class
D*                                     description is used as
D*                                     the wait time for the
D*                                     file (*CLS).
D*                                0 = A program does NOT wait
D*                                    for the file, an
D*                                    immediate allocation of
D*                                    the file is required
D*                                    (*IMMED).
D*                                1-32,767 = The number of
D*                                           seconds that a
D*                                           program waits for
D*                                           the file (number-
D*                                           of-seconds).
D QDBFHFRT        46    47B 0
D*                                Records To Force A Write
D*                                (FRCRATIO)
D*                                0 = There is NO force write
D*                                    ratio, the system
D*                                    determines when the
D*                                    records are written to
D*                                    auxiliary storage (*NONE).
D*                                1-32,767 = The number of
D*                                           inserted, updated,
D*                                           or deleted records
D*                                           that are processed
D*                                           before they are
D*                                           explicitly forced
D*                                           to auxiliary
D*                                           storage (number-
D*                                           of-records-before-
D*                                           force).
D QDBHMNUM        48    49B 0
D*                                Number Of Members
D*                                0-32,767 = The current number
D*                                           of members for the
D*                                           file.
```

Figure 7.18: The start of format FILD0100 of QDBRTVFD, as provided in QSYSINC (part 4 of 12).

231

```
D QDBPSIZE               50      51B 0
D*                                   Access path page size.     @AMA
D*                                   -1 = NA, 4G Access path.
D*                                    0 = Key length page size.
D*                                   8,16,32,64,128,256,512=Ksize
D QDBRSV11               52      58
D*                                   Reserved.
D QDBFBRWT               59      60B 0
D*                                   Maximum Record Wait Time
D*                                   (WAITRCD)
D*                                   -2 = The wait time is the
D*                                        maximum allowed by the
D*                                        system, 32,767 seconds
D*                                        (*NOMAX).
D*                                   -1 = A program does NOT wait
D*                                        for the record, an
D*                                        immediate allocation of
D*                                        the record is required
D*                                        (*IMMED).
D*                                   1-32,767 = The number of
D*                                        seconds that a
D*                                        program waits for
D*                                        the record
D*                                        (number-of-
D*                                        seconds).
D*QDBQAAF00                       1
D QDBBITS29              61      61
D*  QDBRSV1200            7          BITS
D*  QDBFPGMD00            1          BIT
D*                                   Additional Attribute Flags
D QDBMTNUM               62      63B 0
D*                                   Total Number Of Record
D*                                   Formats
D*                                   1-32 = Number of record
D*                                        formats for the file.
D*QDBFHFL2                        2
D QDBBITS30              64      65
D*  QDBFJNAP00            1          BIT
D*  QDBRSV1300            1          BIT
D*  QDBFRDCP00            1          BIT
D*  QDBFWTCP00            1          BIT
D*  QDBFUPCP00            1          BIT
D*  QDBFDLCP00            1          BIT
D*  QDBRSV1400            9          BITS
D*  QDBFKFND00            1          BIT
D*                                   Additional Attribute Flags
```

Figure 7.18: The start of format FILD0100 of QDBRTVFD, as provided in QSYSINC (part 5 of 12).

```
D QDBFVRM                    66    67B 0
D*                                       Additional Attribute Flags

D*                                       First Supported
D*                                       Version Release Modification
D*                                       Level
D*                                       X'0000' = Pre-Version 2
D*                                                 Release 1
D*                                                 Modification 0 file.
D*                                       X'1500' = Version 2 Release 1
D*                                                 Modification 0,
D*                                                 V2R1M0, file.
D*                                       X'1501' = Version 2 Release 1
D*                                                 Modification 1,
D*                                                 V2R1M1, file.
D*                                       X'1600' = Version 2 Release 2
D*                                                 Modification 0,
D*                                                 V2R2M0, file.
D*                                       X'1700' = Version 2 Release 3
D*                                                 Modification 0,
D*                                                 V2R3M0, file.
D*                                       X'1F00' = Version 3 Release 1
D*                                                 Modification 0,
D*                                                 V3R1M0, file.
D*                                       X'2000' = Version 3 Release 2
D*                                                 Modification 0,
D*                                                 V3R2M0, file.
D*                                       X'2400' = Version 3 Release 6
D*                                                 Modification 0,
D*                                                 V3R6M0, file.
D*                                       X'2500' = Version 3 Release 7
D*                                                 Modification 0,
D*                                                 V3R7M0, file.
D*                                       X'2900' = Version 4 Release 1
D*                                                 Modification 0,
D*                                                 V4R1M0, file.
D*                                       X'2A00' = Version 4 Release 2
D*                                                 Modification 0,
D*                                                 V4R2M0, file.
D*                                       X'2B00' = Version 4 Release 3
D*                                                 Modification 0,
D*                                                 V4R3M0, file.
D*                                       X'2C00' = Version 4 Release 4
D*                                                 Modification 0,
D*                                                 V4R4M0, file.
D*                                       New Database support is used
```

Figure 7.18: The start of format FILD0100 of QDBRTVFD, as provided in QSYSINC (part 6 of 12).

233

```
D*                                    in the file which will
D*                                    prevent it from being saved
D*                                    and restored to a prior
D*                                    Version Release and
D*                                    Modification level.
D QDBFVRM                66     67B 0

D*QDBQAAF2                       2
D  QDBBITS31             68     69
D*   QDBFHMCS00           1          BIT
D*   QDBRSV1500           1          BIT
D*   QDBFKNLL00           1          BIT
D*   QDBFNFLD00           1          BIT
D*   QDBFVFLD00           1          BIT
D*   QDBFTFLD00           1          BIT
D*   QDBFGRPH00           1          BIT
D*   QDBFPKEY00           1          BIT
D*   QDBFUNQC00           1          BIT
D*   QDBR11800            2          BITS
D*   QDBFAPSZ00           1          BIT
D*   QDBFDISF00           1          BIT
D*   QDBR11900            3          BITS
D*                                    Additional Attribute Flags
D QDBFHCRT               70     82
D*                                    File Level Identifier
D*                                    The date of the file in
D*                                    internal standard format
D*                                    (ISF), CYYMMDDHHMMSS.
D*QDBFHTX                        52
D  QDBRSV1800            83     84
D  QDBFHTXT00            85     134
D*                                    File Text Description
D QDBRSV19              135     147
D*                                    Reserved
D*QDBFSRC                        30
D  QDBFSRCF00           148     157
D  QDBFSRCM00           158     167
D  QDBFSRCL00           168     177
D*                                    Source File Fields
D QDBFKRCV              178     178
D*                                    Access Path Recovery
D*                                    (RECOVER)
D*                                    'A' = The file has its access
D*                                         path built after the
D*                                         IPL has been completed
D*                                         (*AFTIPL).
D*                                    'N' = The access path of the
```

Figure 7.18: The start of format FILD0100 of QDBRTVFD, as provided in QSYSINC (part 7 of 12).

```
D*                                      file is NOT built
D*                                      during or after an IPL
D*                                      (*NO).  The file's
D*                                      access path is built
D*                                      when the file is next
D*                                      opened.
D*                              'S' = The file has its access
D*                                      path built during the
D*                                      IPL (*IPL).
D QDBRSV20             179    201
D*                                      Reserved.
D QDBFTCID             202    203U 0
D*                                      Coded Character Set
D*                                      Identifier, CCSID, For
D*                                      Text Description (TEXT)
D*                                      0 = There is NO text
D*                                          description for the file.
D*                                      1-65,535 = The CCSID for the
D*                                                 file's text
D*                                                 description.
D QDBFASP              204    205
D*                                      Auxiliary Storage Pool (ASP)
D*                                      X'0000' = The file is
D*                                                located on the
D*                                                system auxiliary
D*                                                storage pool.
D*                                      X'0002'-X'0010' = The user
D*                                                auxiliary storage
D*                                                pool the file is
D*                                                located on
D*                                                (asp-identifier).
D*QDBFNBIT00                   1
D   QDBBITS71          206    206
D*    QDBFHUDT00        1            BIT
D*    QDBFHLOB00        1            BIT
D*    QDBFHDTL00        1            BIT
D*    QDBFHUDF00        1            BIT
D*    QDBFHLON00        1            BIT
D*    QDBFHLOP00        1            BIT
D*    QDBFHDLL00        1            BIT
D*    QDBQLVOL00        1            BIT
D*                                    Complex Object flags.
D QDBXFNUM             207    208B 0
D*                                    Maximum Number Of Fields
D*                                    1-8000 = The number of fields
D*                                             in the file's record
D*                                             format that contains
```

Figure 7.18: The start of format FILD0100 of QDBRTVFD, as provided in QSYSINC (part 8 of 12).

```
D*                                        the largest number
D*                                        of fields.
D QDBRSV22               209    282
D*                                     Reserved.
D*QDBFIDFL00                     2
D  QDBBITS75             283    284
D*   QDBR12100            5            BITS
D*   QDBFFHIC00           1            BIT
D*   QDBFFHR00            1            BIT
D*   QDBR12200            9            BITS
D*                                     Identity/Rowid flags.
D QDBFODIC               285    288B 0
D*                                     Offset from the start of the
D*                                     FDT header, Qdbfh, to the
D*                                     IDDU/SQL Data Dictionary
D*                                     Area, Qdbfdic.
D QDBRSV23               289    302
D*                                     Reserved.
D QDBFFIGL               303    304B 0
D*                                     File Generic Key Length
D*                                     0-2000 = The length of the
D*                                              key before the first
D*                                              *NONE key field for
D*                                              the file.
D*                                     If this file has an arrival
D*                                     sequence access path, this
D*                                     field is NOT applicable.
D QDBFMXRL               305    306B 0
D*                                     Maximum Record Length
D*                                     1-32766 = The length of the
D*                                               record in the
D*                                               file's record
D*                                               format that
D*                                               contains the
D*                                               largest number of
D*                                               bytes.
D QDBRSV24               307    314
D*                                     Reserved.
D QDBFGKCT               315    316B 0
D*                                     File Generic Key Field Count
D*                                     0-120 = The count of the
D*                                             number of key fields
D*                                             before the first
D*                                             *NONE key field for
D*                                             the file.
D*                                     If this file has an arrival
D*                                     sequence access path, this
```

Figure 7.18: The start of format FILD0100 of QDBRTVFD, as provided in QSYSINC (part 9 of 12).

```
D*                               field is NOT applicable.
D QDBFOS           317   320B 0
D*                               Offset from the start of the
D*                               FDT header, Qdbfh, to the
D*                               File Scope Array, Qdbfb.
D QDBRSV25         321   328
D*                               Reserved.
D QDBFOCS          329   332B 0
D*                               Offset from the start of the
D*                               FDT header, Qdbfh, to the
D*                               Alternative Collating
D*                               Sequence Table section,
D*                               Qdbfacs.
D QDBRSV26         333   336
D*                               Reserved.
D QDBFPACT         337   338
D*                               Access Path Type
D*                               'AR' = Arrival sequence
D*                                      access path.
D*                               'KC' = Keyed sequence access
D*                                      path with duplicate
D*                                      keys allowed.
D*                                      Duplicate keys are
D*                                      accessed in first-
D*                                      changed-first-out
D*                                      (FCFO) order.
D*                               'KF' = Keyed sequence access
D*                                      path with duplicate
D*                                      keys allowed.
D*                                      Duplicate keys are
D*                                      accessed in first-
D*                                      in-first-out
D*                                      (FIFO) order.
D*                               'KL' = Keyed sequence access
D*                                      path with duplicate
D*                                      keys allowed.
D*                                      Duplicate keys are
D*                                      accessed in last-
D*                                      in-first-out
D*                                      (LIFO) order.
D*                               'KN' = Keyed sequence access
D*                                      path with duplicate
D*                                      keys allowed.
D*                                      No order is guaranteed
D*                                      when accessing
D*                                      duplicate keys.
D*                                      Duplicate keys are
```

Figure 7.18: The start of format FILD0100 of QDBRTVFD, as provided in QSYSINC (part 10 of 12).

```
D*                                      accessed in one of the
D*                                      following methods:
D*                                      (FCFO) (FIFO) (LIFO).
D*                              'KU' = Keyed sequence access
D*                                      path with NO duplicate
D*                                      keys allowed (UNIQUE).
D*                              'EV' = Encoded Vector with a
D*                                      1, 2, or 4 byte vector
D*
D QDBFPACT              337     338

D QDBFHRLS              339     344
D*                                      File Version Release
D*                                      Modification Level
D*                                      'VxRyMz' = Where x is the
D*                                                 Version, y is the
D*                                                 Release, and z is
D*                                                 the Modification
D*                                                 level
D*                                                 example V2R1M1
D*                                                 Version 2 Release
D*                                                 1 Modification 1
D QDBRSV27              345     364
D*                                      Reserved.
D QDBPFOF               365     368B 0
D*                                      Offset from the start of the
D*                                      FDT header, Qdbfh, to the
D*                                      Physical File Specific
D*                                      Attributes section, Qdbfphys.
D QDBLFOF               369     372B 0
D*                                      Offset from the start of the
D*                                      FDT header, Qdbfh, to the
D*                                      Logical File Specific
D*                                      Attributes section, Qdbflogl.
D*QDBFSSFP00                        6
D* QDBFNLSB01                       1
D    QDBBITS58          373     373
D*   QDBFSSCS02           3               BITS
D*   QDBR10302            5               BITS
D QDBFLANG01            374     376
D QDBFCNTY01            377     378
D*                                      Sort Sequence Table
D QDBPFOF               365     368B 0

D QDBFJORN              379     382B 0
D*                                      Offset from the start of the
D*                                      FDT header, Qdbfh, to the
```

Figure 7.18: The start of format FILD0100 of QDBRTVFD, as provided in QSYSINC (part 11 of 12).

```
D*                              Journal Section, Qdbfjoal.
D QDBFEVID              383     386U 0
D*                              Initial number of distinct
D*                              values an encoded vector
D*                              access path was allowed at
D*                              creation. Default will be set
D*                              to hex zeros
D QDBRSV28             387     400
D*                              Reserved.
D*****************************************************************
D*
D*The FDT header ends here.
D*
D*****************************************************************
```

Figure 7.18: The start of format FILD0100 of QDBRTVFD, as provided in QSYSINC (part 12 of 12).

We also need additional information that is not found directly in data structure QDBQ25. Within QDBQ25, we can determine if the file has been previously journaled (QDBFJORN <> 0), but not the name of the journal and the journal library if journaling is in effect. For this, we need the data found in structure QDBQ40. Fortunately, QDBQ25 does give us the offset to this journal information (QDBFJORN). The QSYSINC definition for QDBQ40 is shown in Figure 7.20.

This information is easily accessed by defining the structure JrnHdr in FIG7_10 as being LIKEDS(QDBQ40) and BASED(JrnPtr). In FIG7_10, we simply set JrnPtr by taking the address of the receiver variable and adding the offset QDBFJORN. We can then start working with the contents of the QDBQ40 data structure. In our case, this means retrieving the journal name, journal library, and current journal status.

```
// Determine journaling status
if (Header.QDBFJORN = 0);
    Jrnld = 'No';
else;
    JrnPtr = RtvFDPtr + Header.QDBFJORN;
    JrnNam = JrnHdr.QDBFOJRN;
    JrnLib = JrnHdr.QDBFOLIB;
    if (JrnHdr.QDBFJACT = '1');
        Jrnld = 'Yes';
    else;
        Jrnld = 'No';
    endif;
endif;
```

Figure 7.19: Journal-related information.

```
DName++++++++++ETDsFrom+++To/L+++IDc.Keywords++++++++++++++++++++++++++
D*********************************************************************
D*
D*Journal Section
D*
D*The journal information of this physical file.
D*
D*********************************************************************
D*This section can be located with the offset Qdbfjorn, which is
D*located in the FDT header section.
D*********************************************************************
DQDBQ40          DS
D*                                    Journal Section
D QDBFOJRN            1    10
D*                                    Journal Name
D QDBFOLIB           11    20
D*                                    Journal Library Name
D*QDBFOJPT            1
D  QDBBITS41         21    21
D*   QDBR10600         1              BIT
D*   QDBFJBIM00        1              BIT
D*   QDBFJAIM00        1              BIT
D*   QDBR10700         1              BIT
D*   QDBFJOMT00        1              BIT
D*   QDBR10800         3              BITS
D*                                    Journaling Option Flags
D QDBFJACT           22    22
D*                                    Journaling Options.
D*                                    '0' = The file is not being
D*                                          journaled.
D*                                    '1' = The file is being
D*                                          journaled.
D QDBFLJRN           23    35
D*                                    Last Journaling date
D*                                    Stamp-This is the date
D*                                    that corresponds to the most
D*                                    recent time that journaling
D*                                    was started for the file.
D*                                    The date is in
D*                                    internal standard format
D*                                    (ISF), CYYMMDDHHMMSS.
D QDBR105            36    64
D*                                    Reserved.
```

Figure 7.20: The journal section of format *FILD0100* of *QDBRTVFD*, as provided in *QSYSINC*.

```
// Get initial member allocation size
PFPtr = RtvFDPtr + Header.QDBPFOF;
if (PFHdr.QDBPRNUM = 0);
   MbrSiz = '*NOMAX';
else;
   if (PFHdr.QDBPRNUM >= 1000000);
      MbrSiz = '> 1M';
   else;
      MbrSiz = %editw(PFHdr.QDBPRNUM :'        , 0 ');
   endif;
endif;
```

Figure 7.21: Member information.

In a similar vein, Figure 7.21 shows how we access the member allocation size by defining the data structure PfHdr as being LIKEDS(QDBQ26) and BASED(PFPtr), with PFPtr being set to the address of the receiver variable plus QDBPFOF (the offset to the physical file attributes provided in QDBQ25). QDBQ26 is shown in Figure 7.22.

```
DName++++++++++++ETDsFrom+++To/L+++IDc.Keywords+++++++++++++++++++++++++++
D*********************************************************************
D*
D*Physical File Specific Attributes
D*
D*********************************************************************
D*This section can be located with the offset QDBPFOF, which is
D*located in the FDT header section.
D*********************************************************************
DQDBQ26          DS
D*                              Physical File Attributes
D QDBFPALC            1     2
D*                              Allocate/Contiguous Storage
D*                              (ALLOCATE and CONTIG)
D*                              'DN' = New members added to
D*                                   the file allow the
D*                                   system to determine
D*                                   storage space that is
D*                                   allocated for the
D*                                   member (ALLOCATE(*NO)).
D*                              'IC' = New members added to
D*                                   the file use the
D*                                   initial number of
D*                                   records (SIZE
D*                                   parameter) to
```

Figure 7.22: The physical file section of format FILD0100 of QDBRTVFD as provided in QSYSINC (part 1 of 4).

```
D*                                      determine storage
D*                                      space that is
D*                                      allocated for the
D*                                      member
D*                                      (ALLOCATE(*YES)), and
D*                                      the storage is
D*                                      attempted to be
D*                                      allocated contiguously
D*                                      (CONTIG(*YES)).
D*                               'IN' = New members added to
D*                                      the file use the
D*                                      initial number of
D*                                      records (SIZE
D*                                      parameter) to
D*                                      determine storage
D*                                      space that is
D*                                      allocated for the
D*                                      member
D*                                      (ALLOCATE(*YES)), and
D*                                      the storage is NOT
D*                                      attempted to be
D*                                      allocated contiguously
D*                                      (CONTIG(*NO)).
D QDBFCMPS             3      3
D*                                      Maximum Percentage Of Deleted
D*                                      Records Allowed (DLTPCT)
D*                                      X'00' = The number of deleted
D*                                              records in the file's
D*                                              member is NOT checked
D*                                              when the member is
D*                                              closed (*NONE).
D*                                      X'01'-X'64' = The largest
D*                                                    percentage of
D*                                                    deleted records
D*                                                    that the file's
D*                                                    member should
D*                                                    have (deleted-
D*                                                    records-
D*                                                    threshold-
D*                                                    percentage).
D QDBFS00              4      7U 0
D*                                      For SQL Partitioned Tables
D*                                      offset from the start
D*                                      of the FDT header, Qdbfh, to
D*                                      the SQL Partitioned Area.
```

Figure 7.22: The physical file section of format FILD0100 of QDBRTVFD as provided in QSYSINC (part 2 of 4).

```
D QDBRSV29              8    11
D*                           Reserved.
D QDBPRNUM              12   15B 0
D*                           Initial Number Of Records
D*                           (SIZE)
D*                           0 = The number of records
D*                               that can be inserted into
D*                               each member of the file
D*                               is NOT limited by the
D*                               user.  The maximum size
D*                               of each member is
D*                               determined by the system
D*                               (*NOMAX).
D*                           1-2,147,483,646 = The number
D*                               of records that can be
D*                               inserted before an
D*                               automatic extension
D*                               occurs (number-of-
D*                               records).
D QDBFPRI              16    17B 0
D*                           Increment Number Of Records
D*                           (SIZE)
D*                           0-32,767 = The maximum number
D*                                      of additional
D*                                      records that can
D*                                      be inserted into
D*                                      the member after
D*                                      an automatic
D*                                      extension occurs
D*                                      (increment-value).
D QDBRINUM             18    19B 0
D*                           Maximum Number Of Increments
D*                           (SIZE)
D*                           0-32,767 = The maximum number
D*                                      of increments
D*                                      that can be
D*                                      automatically
D*                                      added to the
D*                                      member (number-of-
D*                                      increments).
D QDBFORID             20    23B 0
D*                           Offset from the start of the
D*                           FDT header, Qdbfh, to the
D*                           Record ID Codes for program
D*                           described physical files,
```

Figure 7.22: The physical file section of format FILD0100 of QDBRTVFD as provided in QSYSINC (part 3 of 4).

```
D*                                 Qdbforid.
D*QDBFLAGS                          1
D QDBFORID               20    23B 0
D  QDBBITS33             24    24
 D*   QDBFRDEL00          1             BIT
 D*   QDBRSV3000          3             BITS
 D*   QDBFSQLT00          1             BIT
 D*   QDBFMQT00           1             BIT
 D*   QDBFSQPT00          1             BIT
 D*   QDBRSV3100          1             BIT
 D*                                     Flags
D QDBFOTRG               25    28B 0
 D*                                Offset from the start of the
 D*                                FDT header, Qdbfh, to the
 D*                                Trigger Description Area,
 D*                                Qdbftrg
D QDBFTRGN               29    30B 0
 D*                                Number of triggers
D QDBFOFCS               31    34B 0
 D*                                This is the offset from the
 D*                                start of the FDT header,
 D*                                Qdbfh, to the Constraint
 D*                                Definition Area,
 D*                                Qdb_Qdbf_constraint
D QDBFCSTN               35    38B 0
 D*                                Number of constraint for the
 D*                                File
D QDBFODL                39    42B 0
 D*                                Offset from the start of the
 D*                                FDT header, Qdbfh, to the
 D*                                datalinks area,
 D*                                Qdb_Qdbfdtalnk.
D QDBFM                  43    46U 0
 D*                                For SQL materialized query
 D*                                tables, offset from the start
 D*                                of the FDT header, Qdbfh, to
 D*                                the SQL Area.
D QDBRSV32               47    48
 D*                                Reserved.
```

Figure 7.22: The physical file section of format FILD0100 of QDBRTVFD as provided in QSYSINC (part 4 of 4).

Information on the format and key fields is available through QDBQ36 and QDBQ39, which are accessed with field QDBFOS of QDBQ25 to get to QDBQ36, and then field QDBFKSOF of QDBQ36 to get to QDBQ39. The contents of QDBQ36 are shown in Figure 7.23, the contents of QDBQ39 are in Figure 7.24.

244

```
DName+++++++++++ETDsFrom+++To/L+++IDc.Keywords++++++++++++++++++++++++++
D*******************************************************************
D*
D*File Scope Array
D*
D*The file scope array is present for all Database files.
D*The number of data members, Qdbflb#, contains the number of
D*file scope array entries.  Each entry contains a based on
D*physical file name, and optionally a record format name.
D*
D*Externally Described Physical Files:
D*   There is only one entry.  The entry names the physical
D*   file record format.  The file name portion of the entry
D*   is NOT used.
D*
D*Program Described Physical Files:
D*   There is one entry for each Data Dictionary record format.
D*   The entry names the Data Dictionary record format.  The
D*   file name portion of the entry is NOT used.
D*
D*Non-Join Logical Files:
D*   There is one entry for each based on physical file.  Each
D*   entry names the based on physical file and describes the
D*   logical file record format to use with the based on file.
D*
D*Join Logical Files:
D*   There is one entry for each based on physical file.  Each
D*   entry names the based on physical file.  Only the first
D*   entry describes the logical file record format to use with
D*   the join logical file.
D*
D*SQL View Logical Files:
D*   There is one entry for each based on physical file.  Each
D*   entry names the base on file which will be either an
D*   externally described physical file, or another view
D*   logical file.  Only the first entry describes the logical
D*   file record format to use with the view logical file.
D*
D*******************************************************************
D*This section can be located with the offset Qdbfos, which is
D*located in the FDT header section.
D*******************************************************************
DQDBQ36             DS
D*                                             Qdb Qdbfb
D QDBRSV48                  1     48
D*                                     Reserved.
```

Figure 7.23: The File Scope array section of format FILD0100 of QDBRTVFD, as provided in QSYSINC (part 1 of 4).

245

```
D QDBFBF                 49    58
D*                             Based On Physical File Name
D QDBFBFL                59    68
D*                             Based On Physical File's
D*                             Library Name
D QDBFT01                69    78
D*                             Record Format Name
D*                             The name of this particular
D*                             record format for the file.
D QDBRSV49               79   115
D*                             Reserved.
D QDBFBGKY              116   117 B 0
D*                             Record Format Generic Key
D*                             Field Count
D*                             0-120 = The count of the
D*                                     number of key fields
D*                                     before the first
D*                                     *NONE key field for
D*                                     the record format.
D*                             If this file has an arrival
D*                             sequence access path, this
D*                             field is NOT applicable.
D QDBRSV50              118   119
D*                             Reserved.
D QDBFBLKY             120   121 B 0
D*                             Record Format Maximum Key
D*                             Length
D*                             1-2000 = Maximum length of
D*                                      the key for the
D*                                      record format.
D*                             If this file has an arrival
D*                             sequence access path, this
D*                             field is NOT applicable.
D QDBRSV51             122   123
D*                             Reserved.
D QDBFFOGL            124   125 B 0
D*                             Record Format Generic Key
D*                             Length
D*                             0-2000 = The length of the
D*                                      key before the first
D*                                      *NONE key field for
D*                                      the record format.
D*                             If this file has an arrival
D*                             sequence access path, this
```

Figure 7.23: The File Scope array section of format FILD0100 of QDBRTVFD, as provided in QSYSINC (part 2 of 4).

```
D*                                      field is NOT applicable.
D QDBRSV52              126     128
D*                                      Reserved.
D QDBFSOON              129     130 B 0
D*                                      Number Of Select/Omit
D*                                      Statements
D*                                      1-32767 = The number of
D*                                                Select/Omit
D*                                                statements for this
D*                                                record format.
D QDBFSOOF              131     134 B 0
D*                                      Offset from the start of the
D*                                      FDT header, Qdbfh, to the
D*                                      Select/Omit Specification
D*                                      Array, Qdbfss.
D QDBFKSOF              135     138 B 0
D*                                      Offset from the start of the
D*                                      FDT header, Qdbfh, to the
D*                                      Key Specification Array,
D*                                      Qdbfk.
D QDBFKYCT              139     140 B 0
D*                                      Record Format Full Key Field
D*                                      Count
D*                                      0-120 =   The count of the
D*                                                total number of key
D*                                                fields for the record
D*                                                format.
D*                                      If this file has an arrival
D*                                      sequence access path, this
D*                                      field is NOT applicable.
D QDBFGENF              141     142 B 0
D*                                      Generic Key Field Count For
D*                                      All Record Formats With This
D*                                      Record Format Name
D*                                      0-120 =   The count of the
D*                                                number of key fields
D*                                                before the first
D*                                                *NONE key field for
D*                                                all the record
D*                                                formats with this
D*                                                record format's name.
D*                                      If this file has an arrival
D*                                      sequence access path, this
D*                                      field is NOT applicable.
```

Figure 7.23: The File Scope array section of format FILD0100 of QDBRTVFD, as provided in QSYSINC (part 3 of 4).

```
D QDBFODIS              143     146B 0
D*                                      Offset from the start of the
D*                                      FDT header, Qdbfh, to the
D*                                      Distributed File Definition
D*                                      Section Qdbf_dis, which
D*                                      contains the Partition Key
D*                                      Array, Qdbf_dis_pkeyarr.
D QDBRSV53              147     160
D*                                      Reserved.
```

Figure 7.23: The File Scope array section of format FILD0100 of QDBRTVFD, as provided in QSYSINC (part 4 of 4).

```
DName+++++++++++ETDsFrom+++To/L+++IDc.Keywords+++++++++++++++++++++++++++++
D******************************************************************
D*
D*Key Specification Array
D*
D*The key specification array entries describe the record
D*format's fields that are used in defining the access path
D*for the file.
D*
D*Non-Join Logical Files:
D*  There can be one key specification array for each file
D*  scope array entry.
D*
D*Join Logical Files:
D*  There can only be one key specification array for the
D*  join logical file.  The first scope array entry for the
D*  join logical file will contain the offset to the file's
D*  key specification array.
D*
D******************************************************************
D*This section can be located with the offset Qdbfksof, which
D*is located in the Scope array entry section.
D******************************************************************
DQDBQ39              DS
D*                                      Key Specification Array
D QDBFKFLD              1      10
D*                                      key Statement Field Name
D*                                      X'40's = The key statement
D*                                              field is a *NONE key
D*                                              field.
D QDBRSV59             11      13
D*                                      Reserved.
```

Figure 7.24: The Key Specification array section of format FILD0100 of QDBRTVFD, as provided in QSYSINC (part 1 of 2).

```
D*QDBFKSQ                        1
D  QDBBITS40         14    14
D*  QDBFKSAD00        1         BIT
D*  QDBFKSN00         2         BITS
D*  QDBRSV6000        1         BIT
D*  QDBFKSAC00        1         BIT
D*  QDBFKSZF00        1         BIT
D*  QDBFKSDF00        1         BIT
D*  QDBFKFT00         1         BIT
D*                              Key Statement Sequencing
D  QDBRSV61          15    32
D*                              Reserved.
```

Figure 7.24: The Key Specification array section of format FILD0100 of QDBRTVFD, as provided in QSYSINC (part 2 of 2).

As shown in Figure 7.25, FIG7_10 first loops through the formats in QDBQ36 to find the correct record format. The program then determines if the file is keyed with this line:

```
%bitand(%subst(Header.QDBBITS27 :1 :1)
```

If so, it accesses QDBQ39 through KeyPtr to load the FIG7_9 subfile with key field information. Because QDBQ39 does not provide the text description for the key fields, and we want that as part of the display panel, FIG7_10 calls the Retrieve Database File Description API using format FILD0200. We don't know in advance how many fields might be in the file, so we also don't know how much storage to allocate for the receiver variable when using format FILD0200. By this time you hopefully know how to handle this situation. We'll simply call QDBRTVFD using the dynamic-receiver-variable-size approach, as we did earlier with format FILD0100. Figure 7.26 shows the initial structure (QDBQ41) returned with format FILD0200.

```
// Get format and key field information

RelRecNbr = 1;
FilePtr = RtvFDPtr + Header.QDBFOS;        // File scope array
for I = 1 to Header.QDBLBNUM;              // Number of based members
    if (FileHdr.QDBFT01 = EntryFmt) or     // Correct record format?
    (EntryFmt = '*FIRST');                 // Use first rcd format?
    OutFormat = FileHdr.QDBFT01;           // Set format name
    if (%bitand(%subst(Header.QDBBITS27 :1 :1) // keyed access?
        :x'02') = x'02');                  // Yes
```

Figure 7.25: Finding the correct record format and accessing field information (part 1 of 2).

```
        KeyPtr = RtvFDPtr + FileHdr.QDBFKSOF; // Get Key info
        // get general Field Description Information
        // find out how much storage is needed for FILD0200
        RtvFD( QDBQ41 :8 :RtnNamLib :'FILD0200' :FileLibIn
              :OutFormat :'0' :'*LCL' :'*EXT' :QUSEC);
        if (QUSBAVL > 0);
            dsply ('Error '+QUSEI+' retrieving field description 1')
            ' ' Wait;
            *inlr = *on;
            return;
        endif;

        // allocate the storage needed
        FldHdrPtr = %alloc(QDBBYAVA00);
        RtvFD( FldHdr :QDBBYAVA00 :RtnNamLib :'FILD0200'
              :FileLibIn :OutFormat :'0' :'*LCL' :'*EXT' :QUSEC);
        if (QUSBAVL > 0);
            dsply ('Error '+QUSEI+' retrieving field description 2')
                    ' ' Wait;
            *inlr = *on;
            return;
        endif;
```

Figure 7.25: Finding the correct record format and accessing field information (part 2 of 2).

```
DName+++++++++++ETDsFrom+++To/L+++IDc.Keywords++++++++++++++++++++++++++++
D*********************************************************************
D* Record Structure for QDBRTVFD FILD0200 format
D*********************************************************************
D*********************************************************************
D*
D*            FMTD HEADER
D*
D*********************************************************************
D*This section is always located at the beginning of the
D*returned data.
D*********************************************************************
DQDBQ41               DS
D*                                    Header information
D*                                    The FMTD starts here.
D QDBBYRTN00            1         4B 0
D*                                    Bytes Returned
D*                                    The length, in bytes, of the
D*                                    data returned.
D QDBBYAVA00            5         8B 0
```

Figure 7.26: The header of format FILD0200 of QDBRTVFD, as provided in QSYSINC (part 1 of 5).

```
D*                              Bytes Available
D*                              The total length, in bytes,
D*                              of the format.
D QDBRSV62            9    32
D*                              Reserved
D*                              Record status flags
D*QDBFFMTF                 1
D   QDBBITS42          33   33
D* QDBFRITY00          1           BIT
D* QDBFRILT00          1           BIT
D* QDBFRITX00          1           BIT
D* QDBFRMEP00          1           BIT
D* QDBFRDRV00          1           BIT
D* QDBDFRNI00          1           BIT
D* QDBFRDFI00          1           BIT
D* QDBFCAT000          1           BIT
D*                              Record format DBCS flags
D QDBFXLT0            34   37B 0
D*                              Offset from start of FMTD
D*                              header to the translate table
D*                              specifications (Qddfxl).
D*                              (DB)  CREATE: Y    EXTRACT: Y
D*                              (DF)               EXTRACT: N
D*                              (QQ)  QUERY:  Y
D QDBFRCA0            38   41B 0
D*                              OFFSET to the SELECTION
D*                              specifications for CASE
D*                              operators in this record
D*                              format(Qddfcsl). This is only
D*                              valid for query formats
D*                              (DB)  CREATE: N EXTRACT: N
D*                              (DF)               EXTRACT: N
D*                              (QQ) QUERY:  Y
D QDBFDIC0            42   45B 0
D*                              Offset from start of FMTD
D*                              header to the IDDU/SQL
D*                              dictionary format
D*                              information (Qddfdic).
D*                              (DB) CREATE : Y      EXTRACT: Y
D*                              (DF)               EXTRACT: N
D*                              (QQ)  QUERY:  Y
D QDBFRCID            46   47U 0
D*                              Common Coded Character Set
D*                              Identifier.
D*                              Note:  Before using this
D*                              field, you should check
```

Figure 7.26: The header of format FILD0200 of QDBRTVFD, as provided in QSYSINC (part 2 of 5).

```
D*                                    Qddfrsid, if it is zero, then
D*                                    NOT all character fields in
D*                                    the format use the same coded
D*                                    character set identifier
D*                                    (CCSID), and this field is
D*                                    not valid.
D*                                    65535 = The format contains
D*                                            no character fields.
D*                                    nnnnn = All character fields
D*                                            in the format use
D*                                            this coded character
D*                                            set identifier
D*                                            (CCSID).
D*                                    (QQ)  QUERY:  Y
D QDBFSRCD00            48      49U 0
D*                                    Source File Coded Character
D*                                    Set Identifier.
D*                                    nnnnn = The coded character
D*                                            set identifier
D*                                            (CCSID) specified for
D*                                            the character portion
D*                                            of the source file
D*                                            which contained the
D*                                            DDS used to create
D*                                            the format.  (CCSID).
D*                                    (DB)  CREATE: R    EXTRACT: Y
D*                                    (DF)               EXTRACT: Y
D*                                    (QQ)  QUERY:  Y
D QDBFRTCD              50      51U 0
D*                                    Format Text Coded Character
D*                                    Set Identifier.
D*                                    nnnnn = The coded character
D*                                            set identifier
D*                                            (CCSID) for the text
D*                                            description (TEXT) of
D*                                            the format.
D*                                    (DB)  CREATE: R    EXTRACT: Y
D*                                    (DF)               EXTRACT: Y
D*                                    (QQ)  QUERY:  Y
D QDBFRLCD              52      53U 0
D*                                    Long Comment Coded Character
D*                                    Set Identifier.
D*                                    nnnnn = The coded character
D*                                            set identifier
D*                                            (CCSID) for the
D QDBBYAVA00             5       8B 0
```

Figure 7.26: The header of format FILD0200 of QDBRTVFD, as provided in QSYSINC (part 3 of 5).

```
D*                                        information about the
D*                                        content and purpose
D*                                        of the format.
D*                              (DB)  CREATE: R    EXTRACT: Y
D*                              (DF)               EXTRACT: Y
D*                              (QQ)  QUERY:  Y
D QDBRSV64            54    60
D*                                   Reserved
D*QDBTFLGS00                1
D   QDBBITS65          61    61
D*   QDBR11305         1               BIT
D*   QDBFUCSD00        1               BIT
D*   QDBFDLNK00        1               BIT
D*   QDBFDUDT00        1               BIT
D*   QDBFDLOB00        1               BIT
D*   QDBFUTFD00        1               BIT
D*   QDBR11400         2               BITS
D*                                   Format flags
D*QDBDFLGS                  1
D   QDBBITS43          62    62
D*   QDBRSV6500        1               BIT

D*   QDBFRVAR00        1               BIT
D*   QDBFRGPH00        1               BIT
D*   QDBFRDTT00        1               BIT
D*   QDBFRNUL00        1               BIT
D*   QDBFRSID00        1               BIT
D*   QDBFESID00        1               BIT
D*   QDBRSV6600        1               BIT
D*                                   Flags
D QDBRSV67            63    66
D*                                   Reserved
D QDBFRLEN            67    70B 0
D*                                   Record Length
D*                                   The sum of the lengths of all
D*                                   fields the format contains,
D*                                   excluding neither fields.
D*                              (DB)  CREATE: R    EXTRACT: Y
D*                              (DF)               EXTRACT: Y
D*                              (QQ)  QUERY:  R
D QDBFNAME            71    80
D*                                   Record Format Name
D*                                   The name associated with the
D*                                   format.
D*                              (DB)  CREATE: R    EXTRACT: Y
D*                              (DF)               EXTRACT: Y
```

Figure 7.26: The header of format FILD0200 of QDBRTVFD, as provided in QSYSINC (part 4 of 5).

253

```
D*                                (QQ)   QUERY:  R
D QDBDFSEQ                81     93
D*                                Level Identifier
D*                                The modification level
D*                                identifier of the format. It
D*                                is used to verify the format
D*                                has not been changed since
D*                                compile time, if LVLCHK(*YES)
D*                                is requested.
D*                                (DB)   CREATE: N     EXTRACT: Y
D*                                (DF)                 EXTRACT: Y
D*                                (QQ)   QUERY:  N
D QDBFTEXT               94    143
D*                                Text Description (TEXT)
D*                                The text description of the
D*                                format.
D*                                (DB)   CREATE: Y     EXTRACT: Y
D*                                (DF)                 EXTRACT: Y
D*                                (QQ)   QUERY:  Y
D QDBLDNUM              144    145B 0
D*                                Number of Fields
D*                                The number of fields in the
D*                                format.  There is one field
D*                                header for each field.
D*                                (DB)   CREATE: R     EXTRACT: Y
D*                                (DF)                 EXTRACT: Y
D*                                (QQ)   QUERY:  R
D QDBQIO                146    149B 0
D*                                    Offset from start of Format
D*                                header to the Identity column
D*                                information (Qdb_Qddfidcl).
D*                                (DB)   CREATE: R   EXTRACT: Y
D*                                (DF)                 EXTRACT: Y
D*                                (QQ)   QUERY:  N
D QDBRSV68              150    256
D*                                Reserved
D*QDBFFLDX              257    257
D*
D*                                Start of Field Definitions
D*                                (varying length)
```

Figure 7.26: The header of format FILD0200 of QDBRTVFD, as provided in QSYSINC (part 5 of 5).

At the end of QDBQ41, there is an array of field descriptions. Each occurrence of an array entry is defined by structure QDBQ42. The first array entry is accessed by adding the size of QDBQ41 to the address of the FILD0200 receiver variable, as follows:

```
FldInfoPtr = FldHdrPtr + %size(FldHdr)
```

The number of array entries (the number of fields, in other words) is provided with QDBLDNUM of QDBQ41. QDBQ42 contains a substantial amount of information on each field. This information includes data type (QDBFFTYP), size (QDBFFLDD or QDBFFLDB, depending on the data type), and an offset (QDBFTXTD) to the text description associated with the field. The layout of QDBQ42 is shown in Figure 7.27. The field text description itself is provided in structure QDBQ43 and shown in Figure 7.28.

```
DName+++++++++++ETDsFrom+++To/L+++IDc.Keywords+++++++++++++++++++++++++++
D*******************************************************************
D*
D*         FIELD HEADER
D*
D*******************************************************************
D*This section is located immediately after the FMTD header
D*******************************************************************
DQDBQ42          DS
D*                                  Field Definition
D*                                  The definition for a field in
D*                                  format.  There is a linked
D*                                  list of these field
D*                                  definitions, one for each
D*                                  field.  The number of fields
D*                                  is stored in the variable
D*                                  Qddffldnum.
D QDBFDEFL              1       4B 0
D*                                  Length of Field
D*                                  The length of the entire
D*                                  field structure, including
D*                                  all sub-sections.
D*                                  (DB)  CREATE: R   EXTRACT: Y
D*                                  (DF)               EXTRACT: Y
D*                                  (QQ)  QUERY:  R
D QDBFFLDI              5      34
D*                                  Internal Field Name
D*                                  The name of the field in the
D*                                  logical format, if this is a
```

Figure 7.27: The field header of format FILD0200 of QDBRTVFD, as provided in QSYSINC (part 1 of 14).

```
D*                                  logical format.  If this is a
D*                          .       physical format, this name is
D*                                  a duplicate of Qddfflde.
D*                                  (DB)  CREATE: R   EXTRACT: Y
D*                                  (DF)              EXTRACT: Y
D*                                  (QQ)  QUERY:  R
D QDBFFLDE           35      64
D*                                  External Field Name
D*                                  The name of the field in the
D*                                  physical format, if this is a
D*                                  physical format.  If this is
D*                                  a logical format, this name
D*                                  is the name of the field in
D*                                  a physical format, on which
D*                                  this field is based.
D*                                  (DB)   CREATE: R    EXTRACT: Y
D*                                  (DF)               EXTRACT: Y
D*                                  (QQ)   QUERY:  R
D QDBFFTYP           65      66
D*                                  Data Type
D*                                  The data type of the field.
D*                                  X'0000' = BINARY . . . . . .
D*                                  X'0001' = FLOAT  . . . . . .
D*                                  X'0002' = ZONED DECIMAL . .
D*                                  X'0003' = PACKED DECIMAL . .
D*                                  X'0004' = CHARACTER   . . . .
D*                                  X'8004' = VAR CHARACTER  . .
D*                                  X'0005' = GRAPHIC    . . . .
D*                                  X'0006' = DBCS-CAPABLE . . .
D*                                  X'8005' = VAR GRAPHIC  . . .
D*                                  X'8006' = VAR DBCS-CAPABLE .
D*                                  X'000B' = DATE . . . . . . .
D*                                  X'000C' = TIME . . . . . . .
D*                                  X'000D' = TIMESTAMP   . . . .
D*                                  X'4004' = BLOB/CLOB  . . . .
D*                                  X'4005' = DBCLOB . . . . . .
D*                                  X'4006' = CLOB-OPEN  . . . .
D*                                  X'8044' = DATALINK-CHAR  . .
D*                                  X'8046' = DATALINK-OPEN  . .
D*                                  X'FFFF' = NULL . . . . . . .
D*                                          NULL is only valid
D*                                          for data base query
D*                                          formats. If NULL is
D*                                          specified, query
D*                                          will determine the
D*                                          type and attributes
```

Figure 7.27: The field header of format FILD0200 of QDBRTVFD, as provided in QSYSINC (part 2 of 14).

256

```
D*                                            of the field from
D*                                            the based on fields
D*                                            if Qddffvar is off.
D*                                            If Qddffvar is on
D*                                            then the attributes
D*                                            are set from the
D*                                            variable's operand.
D*                                    (DB)    CREATE: R    EXTRACT: Y
D*                                    (DF)                 EXTRACT: Y
D*                                    (QQ)    QUERY:  R
D QDBFFIOB           67     67
D*                                   Usage
D*                                   X'01' = Input-Only
D*                                           The field can be used
D*                                           for input operations
D*                                           only.
D*                                   X'02' = Output Only
D*                                           The field can be used
D*                                           for output operations
D*                                           only.
D*                                   X'03' = Both
D*                                           The field can be used
D*                                           for both input and
D*                                           output operations.
D*                                   X'04' = Neither
D*                                           The field can be used
D*                                           for neither input nor
D*                                           output operations.
D*                                   X'FF' = Unknown
D*                                           The usage is set
D*                                           appropriately during
D*                                           query processing.
D*                                           This value is only
D*                                           valid for query.
D*                                   (DB)    CREATE: R    EXTRACT: Y
D*                                   (DF)                 EXTRACT: Y
D*                                   (QQ)    QUERY:  R
D QDBFFOBO           68     71B 0
D*                                   Output Buffer Offset
D*                                   The offset from the start of
D*                                   the output buffer, indicating
D*                                   the position of this field
D*                                   within the buffer.
D*                                   (DB)    CREATE: R    EXTRACT: Y
D*                                   (DF)                 EXTRACT: Y
D*                                   (QQ)    QUERY:  N
```

Figure 7.27: The field header of format FILD0200 of QDBRTVFD, as provided in QSYSINC (part 3 of 14).

```
D QDBFFIBO               72      75B 0
D*                                   Input Buffer Offset
D*                                   The offset from the start of
D*                                   the input buffer, indicating
D*                                   the position of this field
D*                                   within the buffer.
D*                                   (DB)  CREATE: R    EXTRACT: Y
D*                                   (DF)               EXTRACT: Y
D*                                   (QQ)  QUERY:  N
D QDBFFLDB               76      77B 0
D*                                   Length
D*                                   The length of the field.
D*                                     For character fields, this
D*                                     is the number of
D*                                     characters.
D*                                     For float fields:
D*                                     4 = Single
D*                                     8 = Double
D*                                    - For variable length fields,
D*                                     this is the maximum length
D*                                     the field can be, plus two
D*                                     for the length.
D*                                    - For date/time/timestamp
D*                                     fields, this is the length
D*                                     of the formatted data.  So
D*                                     this may vary, depending on
D*                                     the format specified.
D*                                    - For graphic data fields,
D*                                     this is the number of
D*                                     bytes.
D*                                   (DB)  CREATE: R    EXTRACT: Y
D*                                   (DF)               EXTRACT: Y
D*                                   (QQ)  QUERY:  R, unless data
D*                                     type (Qddffldt) is X'FFFF'.
D QDBFFLDD               78      79B 0
D*                                   Number of Digits
D*                                   The number of digits in the
D*                                   field.
D*                                    - For numeric fields, this
D*                                     is the number of digits.
D*                                    - For graphic data fields,
D*                                     this is the number of DBCS
D*                                     characters the field can
D*                                     contain.
D*                                   (DB)  CREATE: R    EXTRACT: Y
D*                                   (DF)               EXTRACT: Y
```

Figure 7.27: The field header of format FILD0200 of QDBRTVFD, as provided in QSYSINC (part 4 of 14).

```
D*                              (QQ)  QUERY:  R, unless data
D*                              type (Qddffldt) is x'FFFF'.
D QDBFFLDP           80    81B 0
D*                              Decimal Positions
D*                              The number of decimal
D*                              positions to the right of the
D*                              decimal point.
D*                              (DB)  CREATE: R    EXTRACT: Y
D*                              (DF)               EXTRACT: Y
D*                              (QQ)  QUERY:  R, unless data
D*                              type (Qddffldt) is x'FFFF'.
D QDBFFKBS          82    82
D*                              Keyboard Shift (REFSHIFT)
D*                              The keyboard shift attribute
D*                              of the field.
D*                              'X' = Alphabetic only
DName++++++++++++ETDsFrom+++To/L+++IDc.Keywords++++++++++++++++++++++++++++
D*                              'A' = Alphameric shift
D*                              'N' = Numeric shift
D*                              'S' = Signed numeric
D*                              'Y' = Numeric only
D*                              'D' = Digits only
D*                              'M' = Numeric only character
D*                              'W' = Katakana
D*                              'H' = Hexadecimal
D*                              'I' = Inhibit keyboard entry
D*                              'J' = DBCS only
D*                              'E' = DBCS either
D*                              'O' = DBCS open
D*                              'B' = Binary character
D*                              X'00' = No shift specified
D*                              (DB)  CREATE: Y    EXTRACT: Y
D*                              (DF)               EXTRACT: Y
D*                              (QQ)  QUERY:  R, unless data
D*                              type (Qddffldt) is x'FFFF'.
D*QDBQ100                 1
D  QDBBITS44         83    83
D*  QDBFFIAT00        1            BIT
D*  QDBFFITX00        1            BIT
D*  QDBFFICH00        1            BIT
D*  QDBFFIVC00        1            BIT
D*  QDBFFRND00        1            BIT
D*  QDBFFCID00        1            BIT
D*  QDBRSV6900        2            BITS
D*                              Field Status Byte 1
D QDBFJREF           84    85B 0
```

Figure 7.27: The field header of format FILD0200 of QDBRTVFD, as provided in QSYSINC (part 5 of 14).

```
D*                              Join Reference (JREF)
D*                              (Logical files only)
D*                              For fields whose names are
D*                              specified in more than one
D*                              physical file, this value
D*                              identifies which physical
D*                              file contains the field.
D*                              0 = The fields previously
D*                                   defined in this format
D*                                   will be searched for the
D*                                   external name.  If the
D*                                   field is not found, the
D*                                   based on file formats
D*                                   will be searched.  If the
D*                                   field name is found in
D*                                   more than one file
D*                                   format, an error is
D*                                   signalled.  This value is
D*                                   only allowed on a query
D*                                   format.
D*                              n =  The external field name
D*                                   is to be found in the
D*                                   file format referenced
D*                                   by using this value as a
D*                                   join reference index into
D*                                   the file list.
D*                              (DB)  CREATE: R    EXTRACT: Y
D*                              (DF)                        N
D*                              (QQ)  QUERY:  R
D*QDBQ203                  1
D   QDBBITS45      86     86
D*   QDBFFNUL00     1              BIT
D*   QDBFFDFT00     1              BIT
D*   QDBFFVAR00     1              BIT
D*   QDBRSV7000     5              BITS
D*                              Field Status Byte 2
D*QDBQ204                  1
D   QDBBITS46      87     87
D*   QDBFCORR00     1              BIT
D*   QDBFFRRN00     1              BIT
D*   QDBRSV7100     5              BITS
D*   QDBFFMEP00     1              BIT
D*                              Flags
D   QDBFVARX       88     89B 0
D*                              Variable Field Index
D*                              Index into the list of all
```

Figure 7.27: The field header of format FILD0200 of QDBRTVFD, as provided in QSYSINC (part 6 of 14).

```
D*                              variable field values for the
D*                              query.
D*                              (QQ)  QUERY:  Y
D QDBRSV72       90    91
D*                              Reserved
D QDBFLALC       92    93B 0
D*                              Allocated Length
D*                              The number of bytes allocated
D*                              for the field in the fixed
D*                              portion of the file.
D*                              or...
D*                              Date/Time/Timestamp Length
D*                              The number of bytes the
D*                              based-on field for the date/
D*                              time/timestamp occupies.
D*                              (QQ)  QUERY:  R, unless field
D*                              type (Qddffldt) is x'FFFF'
D QDBFDTTF       94    94
D*                              Date Format (DATFMT)
D*                              The format of the date field.
D*                              Note:  Before using this
D*                                     field, you should
D*                                     check Qddfftyp, if it
D*                                     is not '000B'X,
D*                                     '000C'X or '000D'X,
D*                                     then this field is not
D*                                     valid.
D*                              'FE'X = The date format
D*                                      associated with the
D*                                      job is used.
D*                              'FF'X = The date format
D*                                      associated with the
D*                                      QDT is used.
D*                              '01'X = *USA (IBM USA
D*                                      Standard) format is
D*                                      used.
D*                                      e.g. mm/dd/yyyy
D*                              '03'X = *ISO (International
D*                                      Standards
D*                                      Organization) format
D*                                      is used.
D*                                      e.g. yyyy-mm-dd
D*                              '05'X = *EUR (IBM European
D*                                      Standard) format is
D*                                      used.
D*                                      e.g. dd.mm.yyyy
```

Figure 7.27: The field header of format FILD0200 of QDBRTVFD, as provided in QSYSINC (part 7 of 14).

261

```
D*                              '07'X = *JIS Japanese
D*                                       Industrial Standard
D*                                       Christian Era) format
D*                                       is used.
D*                                       e.g. yyyy-mm-dd
D*                              '17'X = *MDY (Month/Day/Year)
D*                                       format is used.
D*                                       e.g. mm/dd/yy
D*                              '18'X = *DMY (Day/Month/Year)
D*                                       format is used.
D*                                       e.g. dd/mm/yy
D*                              '19'X = *YMD (Year/Month/Day)
D*                                       format is used.
D*                                       e.g. yy/mm/dd
D*                              '1A'X = *JUL (Julian) format
D*                                       is used.
D*                                       e.g. yy/ddd
D*                              or...
D*                              Time Format (TIMFMT)
D*                              The format of the time field.
D*                              'FE'X = The time format
D*                                       associated with the
D*                                       job is used.
D*                              'FF'X = The time format
D*                                       associated with the
D*                                       QDT is used.
D*                              '01'X = *USA (IBM USA
D*                                       Standard) format is
D*                                       used.
D*                                       e.g. hh:mm AM or
D*                                       hh:mm PM
D*                              '03'X = *ISO (International
D*                                       Standards
D*                                       Organization) format
D*                                       is used.
D*                                       e.g. hh.mm.ss
D*                              '05'X = *EUR (IBM European
D*                                       Standard) format is
D*                                       used.
D*                                       e.g. hh.mm.ss
D*                              '07'X = *JIS Japanese
D*                                       Industrial Standard
D*                                       Christian Era) format
D*                                       is used.
D*                                       e.g. hh:mm:ss
```

Figure 7.27: The field header of format FILD0200 of QDBRTVFD, as provided in QSYSINC (part 8 of 14).

```
D*                              '09'X = The SAA timestamp is
D*                                      used.
D*                              '1B'X = *HMS (Hour/Minute/
D*                                      Second) format is
D*                                      used.
D*                                      e.g. hh:mm:ss
D*                              (QQ)   QUERY:   Y
D QDBFDTTS            95     95
D*                              Date Separator (DATSEP)
D*                              The separator character to be
D*                              used with a date field.
D*                              or...
D*                              Time Separator (TIMSEP)
D*                              The separator character to be
D*                              used with a time field.
D*                              Note:  Before using this
D*                                     field, you should
D*                                     check Qddfftyp, if it
D*                                     is not '000B'X,
D*                                     '000C'X or '000D'X,
D*                                     then this field is not
D*                                     valid.
D*                              '00'X = The default separator
D*                                      associated with the
D*                                      job is to be used.
D*                              'EE'X = The implied separator
D*                                      is to be used.
D*                              '/'   = The slash separator
D*                                      is to be used.
D*                              '-'   = The dash separator
D*                                      is to be used.
D*                              '.'   = The period separator
D*                                      is to be used.
D*                              ','   = The comma separator
D*                                      is to be used.
D*                              ' '   = The blank separator
D*                                      is to be used.
D*                              ':'   = The colon separator
D*                                      is to be used.
D*                              (QQ)   QUERY:   Y
D QDBFCSID            96     97 U 0
D*                              Common Coded Character Set
D*                              Identifier (CCSID)
D*                              00000 = The CCSID associated
D*                                      with the job is to be
D*                                      used for data
D*                                      translation.
```

Figure 7.27: The field header of format FILD0200 of QDBRTVFD, as provided in QSYSINC (part 9 of 14).

```
D*                              65535 = No data translation
D*                                      is to be done.
D*                              nnnnn = This coded character
D*                                      set identifier
D*                                      (CCSID) is to be used
D*                                      for data translation.
D*                              (QQ)    QUERY:  Y
D QDBFTSID          98     99 U 0
D*                              Text Description Common Coded
D*                              Character Set Identifier
D*                              00000 = The CCSID associated
D*                                      with the job is to be
D*                                      used for translating
D*                                      the text description.
D*                              65535 = The text description
D*                                      is not to be
D*                                      translated.
D*                              nnnnn = This coded character
D*                                      set identifier
D*                                      (CCSID) is to be used
D*                                      for translating the
D*                                      text description.
D*                              (QQ)    QUERY:  Y
D QDBFHSID         100    101 U 0
D*                              Column Heading Common Coded
D*                              Character Set Identifier
D*                              00000 = The CCSID associated
D*                                      with the job is to be
D*                                      used for translating
D*                                      the column headings.
D*                              65535 = The column headings
D*                                      are not to be
D*                                      translated.
D*                              nnnnn = This coded character
D*                                      set identifier
D*                                      (CCSID) is to be used
D*                                      for translating the
D*                                      column headings.
D*                              (QQ)    QUERY:  Y
D QDBFLSID         102    103 U 0
D*                              Long Comment Common Coded
D*                              Character Set Identifier
D*                              00000 = The CCSID associated
D*                                      with the job is to be
D*                                      used for translating
D*                                      the long comment.
```

Figure 7.27: The field header of format FILD0200 of QDBRTVFD, as provided in QSYSINC (part 10 of 14).

```
D*                                  65535 = The long comment is
D*                                          not to be translated.
D*                                  nnnnn = This coded character
D*                                          set identifier
D*                                          (CCSID) is to be used
D*                                          for translating the
D*                                          long comment.
D*                                  (QQ)    QUERY:  Y
D QDBFLDUR              104    104
D*                                  Labeled Duration
D*                                  The type of labeled duration
D*                                  this field defines.
D*                                  '00'X = The field is not a
D*                                          labeled duration.
D*                                  '0D'X = Year/Years.
D*                                  '0E'X = Month/Months.
D*                                  '0F'X = Day/Days.
D*                                  '10'X = Hour/Hours.
D*                                  '11'X = Minute/Minutes.
D*                                  '12'X = Second/Seconds.
D*                                  '13'X = Microsecond/
D*                                          Microseconds.
D*                                  (QQ)    QUERY:  Y
D*QDBFFLGS00             1
D   QDBBITS79           105    105
D*    QDBQD07             1           BIT
D*    QDBQJ02             1           BIT
D*    QDBQD08             1           BIT
D*    QDBQJ03             1           BIT
D*    QDBQD09             1           BIT
D*    QDBQD10             1           BIT
D*    QDBQJ04             1           BIT
D*    QDBQSAA00           1           BIT
D*                                  Flags.
D QDBFWSID              106    107 U 0
D*                                  Edit Word Common Coded
D*                                  Character Set Identifier
D*                                  00000 = The CCSID associated
D*                                          with the job is to be
D*                                          used for translating
D*                                          the edit word.
D*                                  65535 = The edit word is not
D*                                          to be translated.
D*                                  nnnnn = This coded character
D*                                          set identifier
D*                                          (CCSID) is to be used
D*                                          for translating the
D*                                          edot word.
D*                                  (QQ)    QUERY:  Y
```

Figure 7.27: The field header of format FILD0200 of QDBRTVFD, as provided in QSYSINC (part 11 of 14).

```
D QDBRSV6100                108    108
D*                                        Reserved
D QDBRSV6200                109    109
D*                                        Reserved
D QDBRSV6300                110    111 U 0
D*                                        Reserved.
D*QDBLAGCO00                         1
D   QDBBITS73               112    112
D*    QDBRSV6401              3              BITS
D*    QDBDFUCS00              1              BIT
D*    QDBDFUDT00              1              BIT
D*    QDBQIC00                1              BIT
D*    QDBQRC00                1              BIT
D*    QDBDFUTF00              1              BIT
D*                                        Complex Object flags.
D*QDBQ209                             5
D   QDBFDSPL00              113    114 U 0
D   QDBBITS81               115    115
D*    QDBFUCSP00              1              BIT
D*    QDBFUCSM00              1              BIT
D*    QDBFUCSL00              1              BIT
D*    QDBR13000               5              BITS
D   QDBNCODE00              116    117
D*                                        UCS-2 field values.        @AMA
D QDBRSV74                 118    180
D*                                        Reserved                   @AMA
D QDBFCPLX                 181    184 B 0
D*                                        Offset from start of Field
D*                                        header to the Complex Object
D*                                        field information
D*                                        (Qdb_Qddffcpli).
D*                                        (DB)  CREATE: R   EXTRACT: Y
D*                                        (DF)               EXTRACT: Y
D*                                        (QQ)  QUERY:  N
D QDBBMAXL                 185    188 B 0
D*                                        Maximum length of the LOB.
D*                                        (DB)  CREATE: R   EXTRACT: Y
D*                                        (DF)               EXTRACT: Y
D*                                        (QQ)  QUERY:  N
D QDBBPADL                 189    190 U 0
D*                                        Pad length of the LOB.
D*                                        (DB)  CREATE: R   EXTRACT: Y
D*                                        (DF)               EXTRACT: Y
D*                                        (QQ)  QUERY:  N
D QDBFDICD                 191    194 B 0
D*                                        Offset from start of Field
D*                                        header to IDDU/SQL dictionary
D*                                        field information (Qddfdicf)
D*                                        (QQ)  QUERY:  Y
```

Figure 7.27: The field header of format FILD0200 of QDBRTVFD, as provided in QSYSINC (part 12 of 14).

```
D QDBFDFTD              195     198 B 0
D*                                  Offset from start of Field
D*                                  header to default value
D*                                  description (Qddfdft)
D*                                  (QQ)  QUERY:  Y
D QDBFDERD              199     202 B 0
D*                                  Offset from start of Field
D*                                  header to derived field
D*                                  description (or to the
D*                                  concatenated field description
D*                                  if its file is externally
D*                                  described) (Qddfderv)
D*                                  (QQ)  QUERY:  Y
D QDBRSV75             203     208
D*                                  Reserved
D QDBFTXTD             209     212 B 0
D*                                  Offset from start of Field
D*                                  header to field text
D*                                  description (Qddfftxt)
D*                                  (QQ)  QUERY:  N
D QDBR102              213     214
D*                                  Reserved
D QDBFREFD             215     218 B 0
D*                                  Offset from start of Field
D*                                  header to field reference
D*                                  information (Qddfrefi)
D*                                  (QQ)  QUERY:  N
D QDBFEDTL             219     220 B 0
D*                                  Length of the edit code /
D*                                  edit word information for the
D*                                  field
D*                                  (QQ)  QUERY:  N
D QDBFEDTD             221     224 B 0
D*                                  Offset from start of Field
D*                                  header to the edit code /
D*                                  edit word information
D*                                  (Qddfedcw)
D*                                  (QQ)  QUERY:  N
D QDBRSV76             225     226
D*                                  Reserved
D QDBDFCHD             227     230 B 0
D*                                  Offset from start of Field
D*                                  header to the column heading
D*                                  information (Qddfcolh)
D*                                  (QQ)  QUERY:  N
D QDBFVCKL             231     232 B 0
D*                                  Length of the validity
D*                                  checking data present for the
D*                                  field.
```

Figure 7.27: The field header of format FILD0200 of QDBRTVFD, as provided in QSYSINC (part 13 of 14).

267

```
D*                                  (QQ)  QUERY:  N
D QDBFVCKD              233    236 B 0
D*                                  Offset from start of Field
D*                                  header to the validity
D*                                  checking data (Qddfvchk)
D*                                  (QQ)  QUERY:  N
D QDBFXALS              237    240 B 0
D*                                  Offset from start of Field
DName+++++++++++ETDsFrom+++To/L+++IDc.Keywords++++++++++++++++++++++++++
D*                                  header to alias name entry
D*                                  (QQ)  QUERY:  N
D QDBFFPND              241    244 B 0
D*                                  Offset from start of Field
D*                                  header to the the field
D*                                  prompted numeric editing
D*                                  information (Qddfdfne)
D*                                  (QQ)  QUERY:  N
D QDBRSV77              245    252
D*                                  Reserved
D*QDBDFVPX              253    253
D*
D*                                  START OF THE VARIABLE PORTION
D*                                  OF THE FIELD DESCRIPTION
D*                                  (varying length)
```

Figure 7.27: The field header of format FILD0200 of QDBRTVFD, as provided in QSYSINC (part 14 of 14).

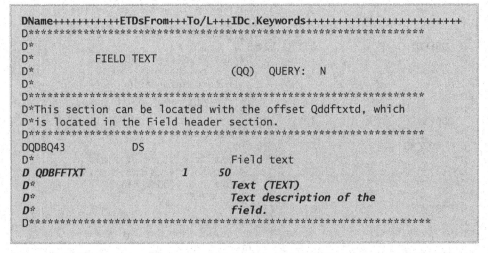

```
DName+++++++++++ETDsFrom+++To/L+++IDc.Keywords++++++++++++++++++++++++++
D*********************************************************************
D*
D*        FIELD TEXT
D*                                  (QQ)  QUERY:  N
D*
D*********************************************************************
D*This section can be located with the offset Qddftxtd, which
D*is located in the Field header section.
D*********************************************************************
DQDBQ43                DS
D*                                  Field text
D QDBFFTXT               1     50
D*                                  Text (TEXT)
D*                                  Text description of the
D*                                  field.
D*********************************************************************
```

Figure 7.28: Field text information of format FILD0200 of QDBRTVFD, as provided in QSYSINC.

In figure 7.29, FIG7_10 first checks to see if the number of key fields is greater than the size of the subfile page (12). Note that this hard-coding of 12 subfile records can be avoided. We could have used the Retrieve Display File Description API, QDFRTVFD, to determine the subfile size at run-time, but the QDFRTVFD API is similar to the QDBRTVFD API in terms of having pages and pages of structure definitions. To avoid many pages of definitions, we elected to simply hard-code the subfile size in this case. If the number of keys defined for the file is greater than 12, then the key-field processing is limited to only include the first 12 keys.

To load the subfile, FIG7_10 reads each key field in KeyHdr (QDBQ39), and then loops through FldInfo (QDBQ42) looking for an entry with the same key field name. When found, the program sets the appropriate data type, size, and field description fields of the subfile record and writes the record. Field FldInfo.QDBFDEFL provides the length of each occurrence of QDBQ42 and is used to step through all of the returned fields. FIG7_10 continues this pattern until all key fields have been processed.

```
FldInfoPtr = FldHdrPtr + %size(FldHdr); // Field array
if SFLSiz < Header.QDBFKNUM00;
    MaxKeys = SFLSiz;
else;
    MaxKeys = Header.QDBFKNUM00;
endif;

for J = 1 to MaxKeys;              // Number of keys
    SfKey = %char(J);              // Key number
    if (KeyHdr.QDBFKFLD = *blanks);
        SfFld = '*NONE';
        SfType = *blanks;
        SfFSiz = 0;
        SfText = *blanks;
        write SflRcd;
        RelRecNbr += 1;            // Subfile record
    else;
        SfFld = KeyHdr.QDBFKFLD;        // Key field name
        for K = 1 to FldHdr.QDBLDNUM; // Number of fields
        if (FldInfo.QDBFFLDE = KeyHdr.QDBFKFLD);
            select;
            when FldInfo.QDBFFTYP = x'0000';
                SfType = 'B';
                SfFSiz = FldInfo.QDBFFLDD;
            when FldInfo.QDBFFTYP = x'0001';
                SfType = 'F';
                SfFSiz = FldInfo.QDBFFLDB;
            when FldInfo.QDBFFTYP = x'0002';
                SfType = 'S';
```

Figure 7.29: Load the key field subfile (part 1 of 2).

```
                          SfFSiz = FldInfo.QDBFFLDD;
               when FldInfo.QDBFFTYP = x'0003';
                          SfType = 'P';
                          SfFSiz = FldInfo.QDBFFLDD;
               when FldInfo.QDBFFTYP = x'0004';
                          SfType = 'A';
                          SfFSiz = FldInfo.QDBFFLDB;
               when FldInfo.QDBFFTYP = x'0005';
                          SfType = 'G';
                          SfFSiz = FldInfo.QDBFFLDB;
               when FldInfo.QDBFFTYP = x'000B';
                          SfType = 'D';
                          SfFSiz = FldInfo.QDBFFLDB;
               when FldInfo.QDBFFTYP = x'000C';
                          SfType = 'T';
                          SfFSiz = FldInfo.QDBFFLDB;
               when FldInfo.QDBFFTYP = x'000D';
                          SfType = 'Z';
                          SfFSiz = FldInfo.QDBFFLDB;
                   other;
                          SfType = ' ';
                   endsl;
                   if (FldInfo.QDBFTXTD <> 0);
                       FldTxtPtr = FldInfoPtr + FldInfo.QDBFTXTD;
                       SfText = FldTxt.QDBFFTXT;
                   else;
                       SfText = *blanks;
                   endif;
                   write SflRcd;
                   RelRecNbr += 1;              // Subfile record
                   FldInfoPtr = FldHdrPtr + %size(FldHdr);//reset fld
                   leave;
                endif;
                FldInfoPtr = FldInfoPtr + FldInfo.QDBFDEFL;
                endfor;
             endif;
             KeyPtr = KeyPtr + %size(KeyHdr);// Get next key fld
          endfor;
          leave;
       else;
          SfFld = 'No keys';
          write SflRcd;
          RelRecNbr += 1;                       // Subfile record
       endif;
    else;
       FilePtr = FilePtr + %size(FileHdr);// Goto next format
    endif;
 endfor;

if (RelRecNbr > 1);                            // Subfile rcds written?
   *in21 = *on;                                // Yes, write subfile
endif;
```

Figure 7.29: Load the key field subfile (part 2 of 2).

The only thing left now is for the program to get the member information, to show the current number of records and the number of deleted records. To do that, the Retrieve Member Description API (QUSRMBRD) is used as shown in Figure 7.30. This API was discussed in chapter 3 and is a standard retrieve-type API, there's no need to go into any detail on its usage in FIG7_10. For reference purposes, the API parameters and MBRD0200 format are shown in Table 7.6 and Figure 7.31, respectively.

```
// Get member data
RtvMbrD( QUSM0200 :%size(QUSM0200) :'MBRD0200' :FileLibIn
        :MemberName :'0' :QUSEC :'0');
if (QUSBAVL > 0);
    dsply ('Error ' + QUSEI + ' retrieving member information')
           ' ' Wait;
    *inlr = *on;
    return;
endif;

OutMember = QUSMN03;                       // Member name
FilSiz = (QUSDSS * QUSDSSM) + (QUSAPS * QUSAPSM);  // Total Size
NbrRcd = QUSNBRCR;                         // Number records
NbrDlt = QUSNBRDR;                         // Number deleted records

write Fmt1;
exfmt SflCtl;
*inlr = *on;
return;
```

Figure 7.30: Using **QUSRMBRD** *to access member information.*

Table 7.6: Retrieve Member Description, QUSRMBRD			
Parameter	**Description**	**Type**	**Size**
1	Receiver Variable	Output	Char(*)
2	Length of Receiver Variable	Input	Binary(4)
3	Format Name	Input	Char(8)
4	Qualified Object Name	Input	Char(20)
5	Database Member Name	Input	Char(10)
6	Override Processing	Input	Char(1)
Optional Parameter Group 1			
7	Error code	I/O	Char(*)

```
DName++++++++++ETDsFrom+++To/L+++IDc.Keywords++++++++++++++++++++++++++
D*********************************************************************
D*Record structure for QUSRMBRD MBRD0200 format
D*********************************************************************
DQUSM0200         DS
D*                                            Qdb Mbrd0200
D QUSBRTN03              1      4B 0
D*                                            Bytes Returned
D QUSBAVL04              5      8B 0
D*                                            Bytes Available
D QUSDFILN00             9     18
D*                                            Db File Name
D QUSDFILL00            19     28
D*                                            Db File Lib
D QUSMN03               29     38
D*                                            Member Name
D QUSFILA01             39     48
D*                                            File Attr
D QUSST01               49     58
D*                                            Src Type
D QUSCD03               59     71
D*                                            Crt Date
D QUSSCD                72     84
D*                                            Src Change Date
D QUSTD04               85    134
D*                                            Text Desc
D QUSSFIL01            135    135
D*                                            Src File
D QUSEFIL              136    136
D*                                            Ext File
D QUSLFIL              137    137
D*                                            Log File
D QUSOS                138    138
D*                                            Odp Share
D QUSERVED12           139    140
D*                                            Reserved
D QUSNBRCR             141    144B 0
D*                                            Num Cur Rec
D QUSNBRDR             145    148B 0
D*                                            Num Dlt Rec
D QUSDSS               149    152B 0
D*                                            Dat Spc Size
D QUSAPS               153    156B 0
D*                                            Acc Pth Size
D QUSNBRDM             157    160B 0
D*                                            Num Dat Mbr
```

Figure 7.31: Format *MBRD0200* of *QUSRMBRD*, as provided in *QSYSINC* (part 1 of 2).

```
D QUSCD04                161    173
D*                                           Change Date
D QUSSD                  174    186
D*                                           Save Date
D QUSRD                  187    199
D*                                           Rest Date
D QUSED                  200    212
D*                                           Exp Date
D QUSNDU                 213    216B 0
D*                                           Nbr Days Used
D QUSDLU                 217    223
D*                                           Date Lst Used
D QUSURD                 224    230
D*                                           Use Reset Date
D QUSRSV101              231    232
D*                                           Reserved1
D QUSDSSM                233    236B 0
D*                                           Data Spc Sz Mlt
D QUSAPSM                237    240B 0
D*                                           Acc Pth Sz Mlt
D QUSMTC                 241    244B 0
D*                                           Member Text Ccsid
D QUSOAI                 245    248B 0
D*                                           Offset Add Info
D QUSLAI                 249    252B 0
D*                                           Length Add Info
D QUSNCRU                253    256U 0
D*                                           Num Cur Rec U
D QUSNDRU                257    260U 0
D*                                           Num Dlt Rec U
D QUSRSV203              261    266
D*                                           Reserved2
```

Figure 7.31: Format MBRD0200 of QUSRMBRD, as provided in QSYSINC (part 2 of 2).

Summary

This chapter just skims the surface of file APIs. By whetting your appetite, we hope to encourage you to look into some of the other file-level APIs. You can write a lot of tools using these types of APIs.

You have seen in this chapter how you can use file APIs to improve on IBM commands. We used APIs here to write a better Display File Field (DSPFFD) command, by limiting the information shown about each field to one single subfile record.

Check Your Knowledge

Write a program to display if the CUSTOMER file, created in chapter 4, has an override in effect using the TOFILE parameter of the Override with Data Base File command, OVRDBF. Do this without opening the CUSTOMER file and using the open feedback information data structure.

To get you started, review the documentation for the Retrieve File Override Information API, QDMRTVFO. In the API Finder, search for the name *QDMRTVFO*, or look in the "Database and File" category of APIs, and then in the subcategory "File APIs."

One possible solution to this task can be found in Figure D.7 of appendix D.

8

Date and Time APIs

This chapter covers some of the callable APIs used to work with dates and times from within your application programs. First, you'll learn about the Convert Time and Date Format API (QWCCVTDT), which allows you to convert date and time values from and to a variety of formats. Next, you'll look at the Adjust Time API (QWCADJTM), which allows you to make small changes to the system time. Finally, you'll examine a family of ILE functions, known as the Common Execution Environment or CEE APIs, which provide several capabilities. These functions include easy addition and subtraction of days relative to a given date and very flexible user-controlled formatting.

Documentation for the Convert Date and Time Format API and the Adjust Time API can be found in the Information Center using the Finder function or in the API category "Date and Time." The CEE date and time APIs can be found using the Finder function, or in the API category "ILE CEE," subcategory "Date and Time APIs."

Using the Convert Date and Time Format API (QWCCVTDT)

Business applications often work with date and time values, as it's frequently necessary to change a given value to a particular format, such as *MMDDYYYY*, in order to present the information to a user or another application. QWCCVTDT, the Convert Date and Time

Format API, is very useful for this purpose. This section provides examples of several ways to use QWCCVTDT to get different formats for a given date or time value. These examples include the following:

- Convert a date and time where the date portion is in *YYYYMMDD* format to a *MMDDYYYY* format, where *YYYY* is a four-digit year, *MM* is the month, and *DD* the day of month.

- Convert a date and time from the format often used internally by i5/OS to a format such as *YYYYMMDD*. This internal format, often referred to as *DTS or *system timestamp*, is often returned by other system APIs.

- Convert a date and time value from one time zone to another.

QWCCVTDT is a very versatile and easy-to-use API, although it might appear daunting at first, due to the number of parameters it supports. Generally, all you need to do is call QWCCVTDT and pass it five parameters. Table 8.1 lists the definitions of these parameters.

Table 8.1: Parameters for the Convert Date and Time Format API (QWCCVTDT)			
Parameter	Description	Type	Size
1	Input Format	Input	Char(10)
2	Input Variable	Input	Char(*)
3	Output Format	Input	Char(10)
4	Output Variable	Output	Char(*)
5	Error Code	I/O	Char(*)
Optional Parameter Group 1			
6	Input Time Zone	Input	Char(10)
7	Output Time Zone	Input	Char(10)
8	Time Zone Information	Output	Char(*)
9	Length of Time Zone Information	Input	Binary(4)
10	Precision Indicator	Input	Char(1)
Optional Parameter Group 2			
11	Input Time Indicator	Input	Char(1)

In the first parameter, Input Format, you tell QWCCVTDT the format of the date and time variable you are supplying in the second parameter, Input Variable. There is a wide range of supported formats:

- *CURRENT—You don't supply an input value for the second parameter (Input Variable), the date and time to be converted. The system simply uses the current date and time.

- *DTS—The second parameter, Input Variable, contains a system timestamp. This type of variable is discussed later in this chapter.

- *JOB—The second parameter's date information is formatted according to the job attribute DATFMT.

- *SYSVAL—The second parameter's date information is formatted according to the system value QDATFMT.

- *YMD—The second parameter's date information is formatted as *YYMMDD*, where *YY* is a two-digit year, *MM* is a two-digit month, and *DD* is a two-digit day of the month.

- *YYMD—The second parameter's date information is formatted as *YYYYMMDD*.

- *MDY—The second parameter's date information is formatted as *MMDDYY*.

- *MDYY—The second parameter's date information is formatted as *MMDDYYYY*.

- *DMY—The second parameter's date information is formatted as *DDMMYY*.

- *DMYY—The second parameter's date information is formatted as *DDMMYYYY*.

- *JUL—The second parameter's date information is formatted as *YYDDD*, where *DDD* is a three-digit day of the year.

- *LONGJUL—The second parameter's date information is formatted as *YYYYDDD*.

The second parameter, Input Variable, is the date and time information to be converted. The length of the Input Variable parameter is determined by the input format specified with the first parameter, Input Format, and the tenth parameter, Precision Indicator. The Input Variable parameter is not used if the Input Format parameter is set to *CURRENT. Otherwise, this parameter is set as follows:

- If the input format is *DTS, the input variable is an eight-byte value.

- If the input format is *YMD, *MDY, *DMY, or *JUL, the input variable is either 16 or 19 bytes, depending on the value of the tenth parameter, Precision Indicator. In either case, the first 16 bytes are formatted as *CxxxxxxHHMMSSmmm*, where *C* is a century digit with zero for years starting with 19 and one for years starting with 20, *xxxxxx* is the formatted date, and *HHMMSSmmm* is the time in hours, minutes, seconds, and milliseconds.

- If the input format is *YYMD, *MDYY, *DMYY, or *LONGJUL, the input variable is either 17 or 20 bytes, depending on the value used for the tenth parameter, precision indicator. In either case, the first 17 bytes are formatted as *xxxxxxxxHHMMSSmmm*, where *xxxxxxxx* is the formatted date and *HHMMSSmmm* is the time in hours, minutes, seconds, and milliseconds.

In the third parameter, Output Format, you specify what format you want the input variable converted to. This parameter has all the same formats available as the Input Format parameter, except the *CURRENT format. One additional format is available for the Output Format parameter: *DOS. This format can be used when the input format is either *CURRENT or *DTS.

The fourth parameter, Output Variable, is the receiver variable that will be set to the input variable value after conversion to the requested output format. Note that there is no Length of Output Variable parameter with the QWCCVTDT API. You must ensure that you have allocated sufficient storage for this parameter based on the output format you have selected. Defining too small of an output variable for the output format you asked for will lead you right into the problems discussed in the chapter 1 section "Size is Critical." As we have found out for ourselves, it is all to easy to change the output format and forget to change the size of the output variable!

The fifth parameter is the standard error-code structure found with many system APIs.

The sixth parameter, Input Time Zone, starts the first optional group for the QWCCVTDT API. This parameter specifies the time zone to be associated with the input variable. If the input format is *CURRENT, the Input Time Zone parameter is not used. Otherwise, you can specify a particular time zone object or one of the special values *SYS, *JOB, or *UTC. If this parameter is not specified, it defaults to *SYS. Similarly, the seventh parameter, Output Time Zone, controls the time zone to be associated with the output variable. You can specify a particular time zone object or one of the special values *SYS, *JOB, or *UTC. If this parameter is not specified, it defaults to *SYS.

The eighth parameter, Time Zone Information, is an output parameter that can be used to retrieve information about the output time zone object. The ninth parameter, Length of Time Zone Information, is the size of the variable in the eighth parameter.

The tenth parameter, Precision Indicator, specifies the precision of the time values used for the input and output variables. If a zero is specified, time is represented as *HHMMSSmmm*, as described in the discussion of the second parameter. If a one is specified, time is represented as *HHMMSSmmmmmm*, where *mmmmmm* is microseconds. For this reason, the earlier formats might be 16 or 17 bytes long, or 19 or 20 bytes long.

The eleventh parameter, Input Time Indicator, is used when the input variable date and time value might be repeated. This repeating of time can occur when the input time zone observes daylight saving time and the time specified is in the window of when time moves backwards. A value of zero indicates that the input variable represents a time value in standard time. A value of one indicates that the input variable represents a time value in daylight saving time.

There are quite a few parameters to this API, but fortunately, they are not that difficult to understand. The example in Figure 8.1 shows how to convert from a *YYYYMMDD* format to a *MMDDYYYY* format. You can see how simple it is.

```
DName+++++++++++ETDsFrom+++To/L+++IDc.Keywords+++++++++++++++++++++++++++++
d/copy qsysinc/qrpglesrc,qusec

dCvtDate          pr                    extpgm('QWCCVTDT')
d InputFmt                      10      const
d InputValue                 65535      const options(*varsize)
d OutputFmt                     10      const
d OutputValue                    1      options(*varsize)
d QUSEC                                 likeds(QUSEC)
d InputTZ                       10      const options(*nopass)
d OutputTZ                      10      const options(*nopass)
d TZInfo                     65535      const options(*nopass :*varsize)
d LenTZInfo                   10i 0     const options(*nopass)
d Precision                      1      const options(*nopass)
d InputTimeInd                   1      const options(*nopass)

dReceiver         s            20
dYYMDValue        s            20       inz('20061013103006000')

dWait             s             1
```

Figure 8.1: Using QWCCVTDT to convert from a YYYYMMDD formatted date to a *MDYY formatted date (part 1 of 2).

```
CL0N01Factor1+++++++Opcode&ExtFactor2+++++++Result++++++++Len++D+HiLoEq+
/free

    // set error code bytes provided to 16 to prevent exceptions
    QUSBPRV = %size(QUSEC);

    // Convert YYMDValue which holds October 13 2006 at 10:30:06 AM
    CvtDate( '*YYMD' :YYMDValue :'*MDYY' :Receiver :QUSEC);

    // check if API call failed
    if (QUSBAVL <> 0);
        dsply ('QWCCVTDT API failed with ' + QUSEI) ' ' Wait;
    else;
        dsply ('Date is: ' + %editw(%dec(%subst(Receiver :1 :14) :14 :0)
                            :' / /   &  :  : ')) ' ' Wait;
    endif;
    *inlr = *on;
    return;

/end-free
```

Figure 8.1: Using QWCCVTDT to convert from a YYYYMMDD formatted date to a *MDYY formatted date (part 2 of 2).

FIG8_1 calls QWCCVTDT with five parameters. The first parameter defines the format (*YYMD) of the input date and time value. The second parameter provides the date and time value that is input to the API for conversion. The third parameter defines the desired format (*MDYY) of the output date and time. The fourth parameter is the receiver variable, where the API will return the converted date to the application program. The fifth parameter is the standard error-code parameter found with many APIs.

Basically, FIG8_1 converts the YYMDValue variable (20061013103006000) to a *MMDDYY* format (10132006103006000). It then DSPLYs the result, edited in the form of *MM/DD/YYYY HH:MM:SS*.

Converting a System Timestamp Using the QWCCVTDT API

Many APIs return date and time information in an eight-byte value known as the system timestamp. This represents, believe it or not, the number of microseconds that have elapsed since August 23, 1928 at 12:03:06 and 314,752 microseconds, P.M. This format is quite good at storing very granular time values in a small amount of storage, but it's not very handy at presenting time to a user! As you probably expect, this is one case where QWCCVTDT comes to the rescue.

Let's go back to the List Objects API (QUSLOBJ). The example program FIG3_4 generated a list of *FILE objects using format OBJL0200. This program used OBJL0200 because we wanted to examine the file's extended object attribute to determine if the file was a physical file. What if you were writing another application to list objects and display the date and time the object was created? In Figure 8.2, you can see that this information is available with the QUSLOBJ API and format OBJL0300 with field QUSCDT00 at position 125. However, the date and time is an eight-byte character field. The Information Center's field description shows that the Creation Date and Time is defined as being in system timestamp format. How can you display it?

Figure 8.3 shows a program that DSPLYs all data queues in the SOMELIB library, along with the date and time the data queue was created. (This library was previously created in chapter 4 and the data queue SOMELIB/FIG6_1 was created in chapter 6.) To convert the system timestamp to a more friendly format, we simply identify the input time format (parameter 1) as being *DTS, the input time value (parameter 2) as being the field QUSCDT00, and then specify with parameter 3 what format we would like to work with.

```
DName+++++++++++ETDsFrom+++To/L+++IDc.Keywords+++++++++++++++++++++++++++
D*****************************************************************
D*Type Definition for the OBJL0300 format.
D*****************************************************************
DQUSL030000     DS
D*                                      Qus OBJL0300
D QUSOBJNU01          1     10
D*                                      Object Name Used
D QUSOLNU01          11     20
D*                                      Object Lib Name Used
D QUSOBJTU01         21     30
D*                                      Object Type Used
D QUSIS02            31     31
D*                                      Information Status
D QUSEOA00           32     41
D*                                      Extended Obj Attr
D QUSTD07            42     91
D*                                      Text Description
D QUSUDA00           92    101
D*                                      User Defined Attr
```

Figure 8.2: Format OBJL0300 from QSYSINC member QUSLOBJ (part 1 of 2).

```
D QUSERVED23           102    108
D*                                          Reserved
D QUSASP               109    112B 0
D*                                          Aux Storage Pool
D QUSOBJO              113    122
D*                                          Object Owner
D QUSOBJD              123    124
D*                                          Object Domain
D QUSCDT00             125    132
D*                                          Create Date Time
D QUSCDT01             133    140
D*                                          Change Date Time
D QUSORAGE             141    150
D*                                          Storage
D QUSOBJCS             151    151
D*                                          Object Compress Status
D QUSAC                152    152
D*                                          Allow Change
D QUSCBPGM             153    153
D*                                          Changed By Program
D QUSOBJAV             154    163
D*                                          Object Audit Value
D QUSDS00              164    164
D*                                          Digitally Signed
DD QUSDSST             165    165
D*                                          Digitally Signed Sys Tru
D QUSDSM               166    166
D*                                          Digitally Signed Multipl
D QUSRSV207            167    168
D*                                          Reserved2
D QUSLASPN09           169    172B 0
D*                                          Lib ASP Number
```

Figure 8.2: Format OBJL0300 from QSYSINC member QUSLOBJ (part 2 of 2).

```
h dftactgrp(*no) bnddir('APILIB')

DName+++++++++++ETDsFrom+++To/L+++IDc.Keywords+++++++++++++++++++++++++++
dFig8_3          pr                    extpgm('FIG8_3')
d LibName                       10     const

dFig8_3          pi
d LibName                       10     const
```

Figure 8.3: Using QWCCVTDT to convert a system timestamp to a *MDYY formatted date (part 1 of 4).

```
d/copy qsysinc/qrpglesrc,qusgen
d/copy qsysinc/qrpglesrc,quslobj
d/copy qsysinc/qrpglesrc,qusec

dCrtUsrSpc          pr              *    extproc('CrtUsrSpc')
d SpcName                          20    const

dListObj            pr                   extpgm('QUSLOBJ')
d SpcName                          20    const
d Format                            8    const
d ObjLibName                       20    const
d ObjTyp                           10    const
d QUSEC                                  likeds(QUSEC) options(*nopass)
d AutCtl                        65535    const options(*nopass :*varsize)
d SltCtl                        65535    const options(*nopass :*varsize)
d ASPCtl                        65535    const options(*nopass :*varsize)

dCvtDate            pr                   extpgm('QWCCVTDT')
d InputFmt                              const
d InputValue                    65535    const options(*varsize)
d OutputFmt                             const
d OutputValue                           options(*varsize)
d QUSEC                                  likeds(QUSEC)
d InputTZ                               const options(*nopass)
d OutputTZ                              const options(*nopass)
d TZInfo                        65535    const options(*nopass :*varsize)
d LenTZInfo                      10i 0   const options(*nopass)
d Precision                         1    const options(*nopass)
d InputTimeInd                      1    const options(*nopass)

d* list API generic header
dGenHdr             ds                   likeds(QUSH0100)
d                                        based(GenHdrPtr)

d* List Object API (QUSLOBJ) format OBJL0300
dListEntry          ds                   likeds(QUSL030000)
d                                        based(LstPtr)

dSpcName            ds
d SName                           10    inz('OBJLIST')
d SLib                            10    inz('QTEMP')

dObjLibName         ds
d                                  10    inz('*ALL')
d ObjLib                          10

dCount              s              10i 0
dReceiver           s              20
dWait               s               1
```

Figure 8.3: Using QWCCVTDT *to convert a system timestamp to a* *MDYY *formatted date (part 2 of 4).*

```
CLON01Factor1+++++++Opcode&ExtFactor2+++++++Result++++++++Len++D+HiLoEq+
/free

   // set ErrCde bytes provided to 16 to avoid exceptions
   QUSBPRV = %size(QUSEC);

   // create the user space for the list of data queues
   GenHdrPtr = CrtUsrSpc(SpcName);

   // get the list of data queues
   ObjLib = LibName;
   ListObj( SpcName :'OBJL0300' : ObjLibName :'*DTAQ' :QUSEC);

   // check if API call failed
   if (QUSBAVL > 0);
      dsply ('List Objects failed with ' + QUSEI) ' ' Wait;
      *inlr = *on;
      return;
   endif;
   // check to see if the list is complete
   if (GenHdr.QUSIS = 'C') or (GenHdr.QUSIS = 'P');
      if (GenHdr.QUSIS = 'C');
         dsply ('Complete list of ' + %char(GenHdr.QUSNBRLE) +
                 ' entries returned.');
      endif;
      if (GenHdr.QUSIS = 'P');
         dsply ('Partial list of ' + %char(GenHdr.QUSNBRLE) +
                 ' entries returned.');
      endif;

      // get to the first list entry and process the list
      LstPtr = GenHdrPtr + GenHdr.QUSOLD;
      for Count = 1 to GenHdr.QUSNBRLE;

         // check to see if information was available
         if (ListEntry.QUSIS02 <> ' ');
            dsply ('Error with ' + %trimr(ListEntry.QUSOBJTU01) +
                    ' ' + ListEntry.QUSOBJNU01) ' ' Wait;

         else;
         // convert creation date to MM/DD/YYYY HH:MM:SS format
            CvtDate( '*DTS' :ListEntry.QUSCDT00 :'*MDYY'
                    :Receiver :QUSEC);

         // check if API call failed
```

Figure 8.3: Using *QWCCVTDT* to convert a system timestamp to a *MDYY formatted date (part 3 of 4).

```
            if (QUSBAVL <> 0);
                dsply ('QWCCVTDT API failed with ' + QUSEI) ' ' Wait;
            else;
                dsply (%trimr(ListEntry.QUSOBJNU01) + ' created on ' +
                    %editw(%dec(%subst(Receiver :1 :14)
                        :14 :0) :' / /    &at&  :  ')) ' ' Wait;
            endif;
        endif;
        if (Wait <> *blanks);
            leave;
        endif;
        LstPtr = LstPtr + GenHdr.QUSSEE;
    endfor;
else;
    dsply 'List Object API did not return valid data';
endif;
dsply 'End of List' ' ' Wait;
*inlr = *on;
Return;

/end-free
```

*Figure 8.3: Using QWCCVTDT to convert a system timestamp to a *MDYY formatted date (part 4 of 4).*

Converting Time Values from One Time Zone to Another Using QWCCVTDT

i5/OS provides several dozen time-zone descriptions that describe how time is managed in various parts of the world. These time-zone descriptions include information such as whether daylight saving time (DST) is observed, and, if so, the rules for starting and ending it, what name(s) are associated with standard and DST time values, and the like. By using parameters 6 through 11 of the Convert Date and Time Format API (QWCCVTDT), you can have i5/OS convert time values from one time zone to another with correct adherence to DST rules. Figure 8.4 shows a program that converts the current system time to the corresponding time in a different time zone and DSPLYs the result. The time zone name is passed as a parameter to the program.

If you are not familiar with time-zone descriptions, you can use the WRKTIMZON command to see which ones are available on your system. Suppose you want to determine the current time in Eastern Australia. You can see with WRKTIMZON that one time-zone description name for Australian Eastern Standard Time is QP1000AEST. Using the current time in Eastern Australia as an example, FIG8_4 calls the Convert Date and Time Format API with the following:

```
DName++++++++++ETDsFrom+++To/L+++IDc.Keywords+++++++++++++++++++++++++++++
dFig8_4           pr                    extpgm('FIG8_4')
d TimeZone                        10    const

dFig8_4           pi
d TimeZone                        10    const

d/copy qsysinc/qrpglesrc,qwccvtdt
d/copy qsysinc/qrpglesrc,qusec

dCvtDate          pr                    extpgm('QWCCVTDT')
d InputFmt                        10    const
d InputValue                   65535    const options(*varsize)
d OutputFmt                       10    const
d OutputValue                      1    options(*varsize)
d QUSEC                                 likeds(QUSEC)
d InputTZ                         10    const options(*nopass)
d OutputTZ                        10    const options(*nopass)
d TZInfo                       65535    const options(*nopass :*varsize)
d LenTZInfo                     10i 0   const options(*nopass)
d Precision                        1    const options(*nopass)
d InputTimeInd                     1    const options(*nopass)

dReceiver         s               20
dWait             s                1

CLON01Factor1+++++++Opcode&ExtFactor2+++++++Result+++++++Len++D+HiLoEq+
/free

   // set ErrCde bytes provided to 16 to avoid exceptions
   QUSBPRV = %size(QUSEC);

   // get current time in target time zone
   CvtDate( '*CURRENT' :' '        :'*MDYY'          :Receiver :QUSEC
         :' '          :TimeZone :QWCTZI :%size(QWCTZI)
         :'1');

            // check if API call failed
            if (QUSBAVL <> 0);
               dsply ('Conversion to ' + %trimr(TimeZone) +
                     ' failed with ' + QUSEI) ' ' Wait;
            else;
               dsply (%editw(%dec(%subst(Receiver :1 :14)
                     :14 :0) :' /  /      &at& :  : &') +
                     QWCCATZN) ' ' Wait;
            endif;
   *inlr = *on;
   return;

/end-free
```

Figure 8.4: Using *QWCCVTDT* to convert time using time-zone descriptions.

- The first parameter is set to *CURRENT (the current system time).

- The second parameter is set to a literal blank. The Information Center documentation for this parameter says it is not used when *CURRENT is specified for the first parameter, but we need to pass something for it. The API doesn't care what.

- The third parameter is set to *MDYY to indicate we want the current date and time returned in a month, day, year order.

- The fourth parameter is the receiver variable for the API to return the time.

- The fifth parameter is the standard error-code data structure.

- The sixth parameter is set to a literal blank for the same reason as the second parameter was set that way.

- The seventh parameter is set to the time-zone name passed as a parameter to FIG8_4. In the example scenario, this would be QP1000AEST. Special values such as *UTC, *SYS, and *JOB are also supported by the API.

- The eighth parameter is an output parameter where the API can return information about the time zone used in parameter 7. FIG8_4 uses the data structure QWCTZI, as we are going to display the time zone's abbreviated name along with the returned time value. This parameter could be passed as a literal blank (as was done for parameters 2 and 6) if we didn't need this information. In this case, we would also need to set the ninth parameter to zero. The QWCTZI data structure is provided by the QSYSINC include-file member QWCCVTDT. Figure 8.5 shows the definition of QWCTZI.

- The ninth parameter is set to the size of the eighth parameter.

- The tenth parameter is set to one to indicate we want the time returned with a precision of microseconds. Zero can be used for milliseconds.

If your system was currently configured for Rochester, Minnesota in the United States (the system value QTIMZON is perhaps set to QN0600CST), and the current system time was 12:37:11 P.M. on June 15, 2006, then calling FIG8_4 with the value QP1000AEST should DSPLY *6/16/2006 at 03:37:11 AEST*.

```
DName++++++++++ETDsFrom+++To/L+++IDc.Keywords++++++++++++++++++++++++++++
D*************************************************************************
D*Type definition for Time Zone Information structure
D*************************************************************************
DQWCTZI           DS
D*                                                    Qwc Time Zone Info
D QWCBRTN11              1      4B 0
D*                                                    Bytes Returned
D QWCBAVL12              5      8B 0
D*                                                    Bytes Available
D QWCTZN                 9     18
D*                                                    Time Zone Name
D QWCERVED27            19     19
D*                                                    Reserved
D QWCCDSTI              20     20
D*                                                    Current DST Indicat
D QWCCUTCO              21     24B 0
D*                                                    Current UTC Offset
D QWCCFTZN              25     74
D*                                                    Current Full Time Z
D QWCCATZN              75     84
D*                                                    Current Abbr Time Z
D QWCTZMID              85     91
D*                                                    Current Time Zone M
D QWCCTZMF              92    101
D*                                                    Current Time Zone M
D QWCTZMFL             102    111
D*                                                    Current Time Zone M
```

Figure 8.5: The QSYSINC-provided Time Zone Information parameter definition.

Defined within the QSYSINC-provided data structure QWCTZI are several subfields. The first two, QWCBRTN11 and QWCBAVL12, are the standard bytes-returned and bytes-available fields found with most retrieve-type APIs. The third field, QWCTZN, is the name of the returned time-zone object. The fourth field, QWCERVED27, is a reserved field.

The fifth field, QWCCDSTI, indicates whether the time zone is currently observing daylight saving time. A value of zero is returned if the time returned in the fourth parameter is not within a DST definition. A value of one is returned if the time returned does reflect DST.

The sixth field, QWCUTCO, returns the current offset from UTC for the time returned in the fourth parameter.

The seventh field, QWCCFTZN, returns the full name of the time zone that is currently in effect for the time returned in the fourth parameter.

The eighth field, QWCCATZN, returns the abbreviated name of the time zone that is currently in effect for the time returned in the fourth parameter. This value is used by program FIG8_4 in the DSPLY of the current time.

The ninth field, QWCZMID, returns the message ID of the message that contains the full and abbreviated time-zone names for the time zone in effect for the time returned in the fourth parameter. The special value *NONE can be returned if a message ID was not used when creating the time-zone object.

The tenth field, QWCCTZMF, returns the message file name where the message ID specified in field QWCZMID is to be found.

The eleventh field, QWCTZMFL, returns the library associated with the file found in field QWCCTZMF.

Adjusting the System Time

Built into i5/OS is the ability to keep your system's clock synchronized with an external time server. This ability is known as *Simple Network Time Protocol* (*SNTP*) client support. Let's say, however, that you have not configured your system with SNTP client, that you have noticed the system time is off by five minutes, and that you want to correct this. You could correct it by using the CHGSYSVAL command and updating QTIME, but this type of update causes QTIME to immediately become the new value. A five-minute change immediately jumps the clock either forward or backward five minutes. Depending on how you have written your applications, this time shift could be very disruptive. Alternatively, you could use the Navigator function of i5/OS and have the system perform a time adjustment, where the system time is gradually changed to correct the five-minute discrepancy. This approach avoids having a jump in time values that applications might be sensitive to, but requires an operator to use the System i Navigator. As you might expect, there is a third solution: use an API.

The Adjust Time API (QWCADJTM) adjusts time by increasing or decreasing the time-of-day clock to a maximum change of plus or minus two hours per API call. The parameters are shown in Table 8.2.

You can probably guess the intent of these parameters by now, since the system APIs tend to be so consistent. However, to review, we'll go through them. The first parameter, Adjustment Variable, is a data structure used to control the time adjustment. The second

Table 8.2: Parameters for the Adjust Time API (QWCADJTM)			
Parameter	Description	Type	Size
1	Adjustment Variable	Input	Char(*)
2	Length of Adjustment Variable	Input	Binary(4)
3	Adjustment Format Name	Input	Char(8)
4	Error Code	I/O	Char(*)

parameter, Length of Adjustment Variable, is the size of the first parameter. The third parameter, Adjustment Format Name, defines the format of the data in the first parameter. There is one supported format, ADJT0100, which is shown in Table 8.3. The QSYSINC-provided definition for format ADJT0100 is shown in Figure 8.6. The fourth parameter is the standard error-code structure found with many system APIs.

Table 8.3: Fields for Format ADJT0100 of the Adjust Time API (QWCADJTM)		
Offset Decimal	Description	Size
0	Time Adjustment Amount	Binary(8) Unsigned
8	Time Adjustment Direction	Char(1)

```
DName+++++++++++ETDsFrom+++To/L+++IDc.Keywords++++++++++++++++++++++++++++
D*****************************************************************************
D*Type Definition for the ADJT0100 format for the adjustment var.
D*****************************************************************************
DQWCT0100        DS
D*                                                  Qwc ADJT0100
D QWCTAI              1       8U 0
D*                                                  Time Adjustment Interval
D QWCTAD              9       9
D*                                                  Time Adjustment Direction
```

Figure 8.6: The QSYSINC definition for QWCADJTM.

Within the QSYSINC-provided data structure QWCT0100 are two fields. The first, QWCTAI, represents the number of microseconds in which the system time is to be adjusted. The second, QWCTAD, indicates the direction of the time adjustment. A value of zero indicates that time is to be sped up by QWCTAI microseconds. A value of one indicates that time is to be slowed down by QWCTAI microseconds.

Figure 8.7 shows the source for a program that takes two parameters. The first parameter, TimeChange, is the number of minutes to adjust the system clock by. The second parameter, TimeDirection, indicates the direction of the time change. A value of *I* is used to increase the system time by TimeChange minutes. A value of *D* is used to decrease the system time by TimeChange minutes.

```
DName+++++++++++ETDsFrom+++To/L+++IDc.Keywords++++++++++++++++++++++++++++
dFig8_7           pr                    extpgm('FIG8_7')
d TimeChange                      15  5 const
d TimeDirection                    1    const

dFig8_7           pi
d TimeChange                      15  5 const
d TimeDirection                    1    const

d/copy qsysinc/qrpglesrc,qwcadjtm
d/copy qsysinc/qrpglesrc,qusec

dAdjTime          pr                    extpgm('QWCADJTM')
d QWCTO100                              const likeds(QWCTO100)
d LengthQWCTO100                  10i 0 const
d Format                           8    const
d QUSEC                                 likeds(QUSEC)

dWait             s                1

CLON01Factor1+++++++Opcode&ExtFactor2+++++++Result++++++++Len++D+HiLoEq+
/free

  // set ErrCde bytes provided to  16 to avoid exceptions
  QUSBPRV = %size(QUSEC);

  // set number of microseconds to adjust clock by.
  //     Multiply number of minutes by microseconds in a minute
  QWCTAI = (TimeChange * 60000000);

  // set direction of adjustment
  select;
     when (TimeDirection = 'I');
          QWCTAD = '0';
     when (TimeDirection = 'D');
          QWCTAD = '1';
     other;
          dsply ('Error on direction: ' + TimeDirection) ' ' Wait;
          *inlr = *on;
          return;
     endsl;
```

Figure 8.7: Using the Adjust Time API (QWCADJTM) (part 1 of 2).

```
AdjTime( QWCT0100 :%size(QWCT0100) :'ADJT0100' :QUSEC);

// check if API call failed
if (QUSBAVL > 0);
    dsply ('Time adjustment failed with ' + QUSEI) ' ' Wait;
endif;

*inlr = *on;
return;

/end-free
```

Figure 8.7: Using the Adjust Time API (QWCADJTM) (part 2 of 2).

ILE CEE Date and Time APIs

Chapter 1 mentions that there are various standards for the APIs provided in i5/OS. The Integrated Language Environment Common Execution Environment (ILE CEE) represents one of these standards. These APIs are available with other computing environments such as AIX, VM, and MVS. Since they are supported in multiple environments, they do not follow the standards that apply to i5/OS-specific APIs. These standards include such areas as naming (i5/OS-specific APIs start with a *Q*; ILE CEE APIs do not) and error handling (i5/OS-specific APIs typically use the error-code structure you have seen in previous examples: ILE CEE APIs use a feedback structure). You will find, though, that the ILE CEE APIs are quite easy to use and do provide very useful functions.

The ILE CEE APIs provide many services in areas such as math (including cosine, factorial, and square root), storage management (including allocating and freeing storage), and of course time. Within the ILE CEE time-related APIs, time is usually stored as what is known as a *Lilian date*. Lilian dates are based on the adoption of the Gregorian calendar on October 14, 1582. So, Lilian day 1 is October 15, 1582, day 2 is October 16, 1582, day 155,227 is October 13, 2007, and day 371,530 is December 31, 2599. Lilian days are defined as four-byte integer values. Likewise, time is used by the ILE CEE APIs as the number of seconds since midnight of October 14, 1582. So, Lilian second 1 is October 14, 1582 00:00:01, and second 13,411,636,200 is October 13, 2007 06:30:00. Lilian times are defined as eight-byte floating-point values. The valid range for date and time values are from October 15, 1582 to December 31, 9999.

Because dates and times are stored as simple numeric values, it is easy to do calculations. For example, to find the difference in days between two dates, you can just subtract one from the other. Similarly, adding 30 days to a date is just simple addition. The APIs also provide powerful formatting options such as returning a Lilian time value in a format such as *Saturday, Oct 13 2007 06:30:00 A.M.*

Adding 30 Days to a Date

There are many situations where you might want to determine a date in the future by adding some fixed number of days to the current date. We will look at two ILE CEE APIs that can be used to do just that. The first, Get Current Local Time (CEELOCT), returns the current local time as a Lilian date. The second, Convert Lilian Date to Character Format (CEEDATE), formats a Lilian date to a character string. Both APIs can be found in the "ILE CEE" category of system APIs, under the subcategory "Date and Time APIs." Table 8.4 shows the parameters for the Get Current Local Time API.

Table 8.4: Parameters for the Get Current Local Time API (CEELOCT)			
Parameter	Description	Type	Size
1	Output Lilian	Output	INT4
2	Output Seconds	Output	FLOAT8
3	Output Gregorian	Output	CHAR23
Omissible Parameter			
4	fc	Output	FEEDBACK

The first parameter, Output Lilian, is defined as an INT4, which is the ILE CEE convention for representing an integer or Binary(4) value. This is the Lilian day representing the current date. For instance, if today is October 13, 2007, this parameter would return the value *155,227.*

The second parameter, Output Seconds, is defined as a FLOAT8, which is the ILE CEE convention for representing an eight-byte floating-point value. This is the Lilian second representing the current date and time. If today is October 13, 2007 at 06:30:00, this parameter would return the value *13,411,636,200.*

The third parameter, Output Gregorian, is defined as a CHAR23, which is the ILE CEE convention for representing a Char(23) value. This is the current Gregorian date. If today is October 13, 2007 at 06:30:00, this parameter would return the value *20071013063000xxx000000,* representing *YYYYMMDDHHmmSSxxx000000,* where

YYYY is the four-digit year, *MM* is the two-digit month, *DD* the two-digit day, *HH* the two-digit hour, *mm* is the two-digit minute, *SS* is the two-digit second, *xxx* is the three-digit millisecond, and *000000* is a constant of six zeroes.

The fourth parameter, fc, is defined as a FEEDBACK, which is the ILE CEE convention for providing feedback, or error information, to the API caller. FEEDBACK is represented by a 12-byte data structure that we will examine in more detail later. This parameter is omissible, meaning that it can be omitted using the RPG special value *OMIT. When fc is omitted, the API caller is not directly informed of errors that might occur.

The parameters for the Convert Lilian Date to Character Format API, CEEDATE, are shown in Table 8.5. The first parameter, Input Lilian Date, is defined as an INT4. This is the Lilian day value that we want formatted to a character string.

Table 8.5: Parameters for the Convert Lilian Date to Character Format API (CEEDATE)			
Parameter	Description	Type	Size
1	Input Lilian Date	Input	INT4
2	Picture String	Input	VSTRING
3	Output Character Date	Output	VSTRING
Omissible Parameter			
4	fc	Outut	FEEDBACK

The second parameter, Picture String, is defined as a VSTRING, which is the ILE CEE convention for representing a variable-length character string. With i5/OS-specific APIs, this would typically be defined as Char(*) and have a separate parameter that defines the length of the Char(*) parameter. With CEEDATE, there is no parameter being passed to indicate the length or size of the Picture String parameter. Instead, the ILE CEE APIs rely on an ILE operational descriptor being passed when the CEE API is called. This operational descriptor then describes to the API the characteristics of the parameters. To pass operational descriptors on the API call, we need to use the RPG special value OPDESC on the API prototype. If you are using the RPG CALLB operation code rather than prototypes, you need to use the *D* extender, as in CALLB(D).

A picture string represents the desired format of the date. The Information Center provides extensive examples of picture strings; we will only cover the basics here. The picture character *Y* represents a year value, where you can have from one to four consecutive *Y*s to indicate where one to four digit year values should be placed. *MM* represents the two-digit numeric value for the month, and *MMM* or *Mmm* is the three-character value for the month, as in *JAN* or *Jan*. *Mmmmmmmmmm* is the 10-character value for the month, as in *January*. *DD* is the two-digit numeric value for the day, *Wwwwwwwww* is the 10-character value for the day of the week (as in *Monday*), *HH* is for the two-digit numeric value for the hour, *MI* is the two-digit numeric value for the minute, *SS* is the two-digit numeric value for the second, and *AP* is the two-character *AM* or *PM* indicator.

The third parameter, Output Character Date, is also defined as a VSTRING. It is used to return to the API caller the Input Lilian Date formatted as requested in the Picture String parameter. As an example, if Input Lilian Date was 155,227 and the Picture String was "Wwwwwwwwwz, Mmm DD YYYY," then this parameter would return "Saturday, Oct 13 2007."

The fourth parameter, fc, is the feedback parameter that we will look at a bit later in this chapter.

With this as an introduction to the APIs, Figure 8.8 shows a program to get the current local time, add 30 days to the current date, and then DSPLY the calculated date using the picture string "Wwwwwwwwwz, Mmm DD YYYY."

```
 h dftactgrp(*no)

DName++++++++++++ETDsFrom+++To/L+++IDc.Keywords++++++++++++++++++++++++++++++++
dGetCurTim       pr                    extproc('CEELOCT')
d LilianDay                     10i 0
d LilianSec                      8 f
d Gregorian                     23
d fc                            12     options(*omit)

dFormatDate      pr                    extproc('CEEDATE') OPDESC
d LilianDay                     10i 0 const
d Picture                    65535     const options(*varsize)
d Date                           1     options(*varsize)
d fc                            12     options(*omit)

dLilianDay       s              10i 0
dLilianSec       s               8 f
dGregorian       s              23
```

Figure 8.8: Using the ILE CEE date and time APIs (part 1 of 2).

```
dDate              s              30
dwait              s              1

CLON01Factor1+++++++Opcode&ExtFactor2+++++++Result++++++++Len++D+HiLoEq+
 /free

   GetCurTim( LilianDay :LilianSec :Gregorian :*omit);

   LilianDay += 30;                // add 30 days to the current date

   FormatDate(LilianDay :'Wwwwwwwwwz, Mmm DD YYYY' :Date :*omit);

   dsply Date ' ' wait;
   *inlr = *on;
   return;

 /end-free
```

Figure 8.8: Using the ILE CEE date and time APIs (part 2 of 2).

As you can see in Figure 8.8, there isn't much to the program! It simply calls CEELOCT to get the current date as a Lilian date (the variable LilianDay), adds 30 to LilianDay, has CEEDATE format the date, and then DSPLYs the result. The one item that might be overlooked is the use of OPDESC in the prototype for CEEDATE. If you forget this part, you will receive error message CEE0502, *Missing operational descriptor*, when you try to run your program.

ILE CEE Feedback Error Handling

As mentioned earlier, the ILE CEE APIs do not use the common error-code structure that you have seen with previous APIs. Instead, they use a feedback data structure, as defined in Table 8.6.

In Figure 8.8, we used the RPG special value *OMIT for the fc feedback parameter. This causes the ILE CEE APIs to return escape messages to the caller of the API if any errors are found. What if we want to handle the errors ourselves? In that case, we will pass the feedback data structure to the API and examine it when the API returns. This is similar to the way we can set Bytes Provided, QUSBPRV, of the QUSEC error-code structure to a non-zero value and then examine the data structure to determine what, if any, errors have occurred.

Table 8.6: The ILE CEE Feedback Structure

Offset Decimal	Description	Size
0	Message severity, where a 2 corresponds to i5/OS severity 20, 3 corresponds to 30, and 4 corresponds to 40.	Binary(2) Unsigned
2	Message number, which is a hex value representing the message ID.	Binary(2) Unsigned
3	Flags which are further defined in the ILE Concepts manual.	Char(1)
4	Facility ID, which corresponds to an i5/OS message ID prefix such as CPF, CEE, or MCH.	Char(3)
5	Additional information that, if non-zero, represents the message reference key of the error message.	Binary(4) Unsigned

Figure 8.9 shows the same program as Figure 8.8, except we are now using the fc feedback parameter along with another ILE CEE API: Get, Format, and Dispatch a Message (CEEMSG).

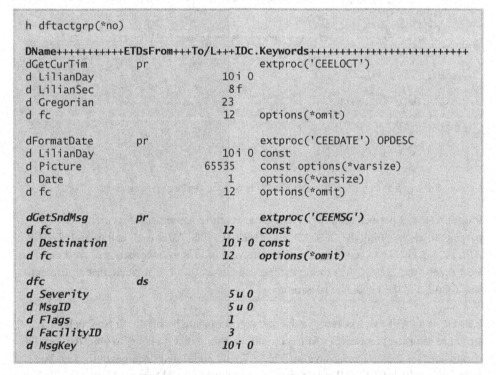

```
h dftactgrp(*no)

DName++++++++++ETDsFrom+++To/L+++IDc.Keywords+++++++++++++++++++++++++++++
dGetCurTim        pr                      extproc('CEELOCT')
d LilianDay                      10i 0
d LilianSec                       8f
d Gregorian                      23
d fc                             12      options(*omit)

dFormatDate       pr                      extproc('CEEDATE') OPDESC
d LilianDay                      10i 0 const
d Picture                     65535       const options(*varsize)
d Date                            1       options(*varsize)
d fc                             12       options(*omit)

dGetSndMsg        pr                      extproc('CEEMSG')
d fc                             12       const
d Destination                 10i 0 const
d fc                             12       options(*omit)

dfc               ds
d Severity                     5u 0
d MsgID                        5u 0
d Flags                          1
d FacilityID                     3
d MsgKey                      10i 0
```

Figure 8.9: Using the ILE CEE Date and Time APIs with the feedback parameter (part 1 of 2).

```
dLilianDay        s               10i 0
dLilianSec        s                8f
dGregorian        s               23

dDate             s               30
dwait             s                1

CLON01Factor1+++++++Opcode&ExtFactor2+++++++Result+++++++Len++D+HiLoEq+
 /free

    GetCurTim( LilianDay :LilianSec :Gregorian :fc);
    if (Severity > 0);
       GetSndMsg(fc :1 :*omit);
       dsply 'Errors found, see previous messages' ' ' wait;
       *inlr = *on;
       return;
    endif;

    LilianDay += 30;                // add 30 days to the current date

    FormatDate(LilianDay :'Wwwwwwwwwwz, Mmm DD YYYY' :Date :fc);
    if (Severity > 0);
       GetSndMsg(fc :1 :*omit);
       dsply 'Errors found, see previous messages' ' ' wait;
       *inlr = *on;
       return;
    endif;

    dsply Date ' ' wait;
    *inlr = *on;
    return;

 /end-free
```

Figure 8.9: Using the ILE CEE Date and Time APIs with the feedback parameter (part 2 of 2).

Program FIG8_9 defines the fc feedback data structure and passes it as the fourth parameter when calling the CEELOCT and CEEDATE APIs. After each call to an ILE CEE API, FIG8_9 checks to see if the Severity returned in fc is greater than zero. If it is, FIG8_9 calls the CEEMSG API to log the message, uses DSPLY to indicate that a problem was found, and then ends the program.

CEEMSG is an API that can retrieve the message associated with the fc feedback data structure returned in an earlier API call, and then send that message to your job log. The parameters for the API are shown in Table 8.7, and additional documentation can be found in the "ILE CEE" APIs category, in the subcategory "Message Services APIs."

Table 8.7: Parameters for the Get, Format, and Dispatch a Message API (CEEMSG)			
Parameter	Description	Type	Size
1	Input fc	Input	FEEDBACK
2	Destination Code	Input	INT4
Omissible Parameter			
3	fc	Output	FEEDBACK

In previous examples, when an error was encountered, we used DSPLY to return the actual message ID to the user. In a production environment, we might also do error recovery based on the actual message that was sent by the API. To do the same with the ILE CEE APIs, we need to further process the fc feedback data structure. Figure 8.10 shows one way of retrieving the actual message ID.

```
h dftactgrp(*no) bnddir('QC2LE')


DName+++++++++++ETDsFrom+++To/L+++IDc.Keywords++++++++++++++++++++++++++++
dGetCurTim        pr                    extproc('CEELOCT')
d LilianDay                     10i 0
d LilianSec                      8f
d Gregorian                     23
d fc                            12    options(*omit)

dFormatDate       pr                    extproc('CEEDATE') OPDESC
d LilianDay                     10i 0 const
d Picture                    65535     const options(*varsize)
d Date                           1     options(*varsize)
d fc                            12     options(*omit)

dHexToChar        pr                    extproc('cvthc')
d ErrorMsgID                     *     value
d MsgID                          *     value
d Size                         10i 0 value

dfc               ds
d Severity                      5u 0
d MsgID                         5u 0
d Flags                          1
d FacilityID                     3
d MsgKey                       10i 0
```

Figure 8.10: Using the ILE CEE Date and Time APIs with the feedback parameter to determine the error message ID (part 1 of 2).

```
dLilianDay          s              10i 0
dLilianSec          s               8f
dGregorian          s              23

dErrorMsgID         s               4
dDate               s              30
dwait               s               1

CLON01Factor1+++++++Opcode&ExtFactor2+++++++Result++++++++Len++D+HiLoEq+
/free

  GetCurTim( LilianDay :LilianSec :Gregorian :fc);
  if (Severity > 0);
    HexToChar(%addr(ErrorMsgID) :%addr(MsgID) :4);
    dsply ('Error ' + FacilityID + ErrorMsgID + ' found') ' ' wait;
    *inlr = *on;
    return;
  endif;
  LilianDay += 30;              // add 30 days to the current date

  FormatDate(LilianDay :'Wwwwwwwwwz, Mmm DD YYYY' :Date :fc);
  if (Severity > 0);
    HexToChar(%addr(ErrorMsgID) :%addr(MsgID) :4);
    dsply ('Error ' + FacilityID + ErrorMsgID + ' found') ' ' wait;
    *inlr = *on;
    return;
  endif;

  dsply Date ' ' wait;
  *inlr = *on;
  return;

/end-free
```

Figure 8.10: Using the ILE CEE Date and Time APIs with the feedback parameter to determine the error message ID (part 2 of 2).

In the fc data structure, two elements need to be combined to find the message ID of the error. FacilityID is a three-byte character value representing the message ID prefix, with values such as "CPF" or "CEE." MsgID is a two-byte unsigned integer value representing the number associated with the error message. For instance, if FacilityID is "CEE" and MsgID is x'2512', then the complete message ID is CEE2512. Unfortunately, MsgID is a hex value rather than a numeric value of 2512, so we can't use a built-in such as %char to obtain the character string 2512. There is an API that can convert a hex string to a character string, however. That API is Convert Hex to Character, CVTHC. The documentation for this API can be found in the Information Center under "Programming," "Languages,"

"C and C++," and then the "ILE C/C++ for System i MI Library Reference." Although the documentation is located under the C language, one of the wonderful features of i5/OS is the ability to use any given API from any of the other ILE languages—in this case, ILE RPG. The parameters for CVTHC are shown in Figure 8.11.

```
void cvthc (char *receiver, const char *source, int size);
```

Figure 8.11: Parameters for the Convert Hex to Character API (CVTHC).

The Receiver parameter is a pointer to a character parameter that returns the converted string; SOURCE is a pointer to the hex string to convert; and SIZE is the number of hex characters to be converted. Based on our review of C prototypes in chapter 1, we can provide the prototype shown in Figure 8.12.

```
DName+++++++++++ETDsFrom+++To/L+++IDc.Keywords+++++++++++++++++++++++++++++
dHexToChar        pr                 extproc('cvthc')
d ErrorMsgID                    *    value
d MsgID                         *    value
d Size                       10i 0 value
```

Figure 8.12: Function prototype for the CVTHC API.

Now, when an error is returned by the ILE CEE API (Severity is greater than zero) FIG8_9 calls the CVTHC API to convert the two-character (four-hex character) value of MsgID to the four-character field ErrorMsgID. FIG8_10 then uses DSPLY to display the actual error message encountered. The one other change made in FIG8_10 was to add a BNDDIR('QC2LE') specification to the RPG H-spec. This is currently needed because APIs specific to C run-time (that is, APIs that are found in the C language manuals) are not automatically included when compiling ILE RPG programs. All of the C run-time APIs can, however, be found by including the binding directory QC2LE in your RPG compilation process.

Summary

In this chapter, you have seen how to use several date- and time-related APIs to format dates and times and easily add and subtract dates. You have also seen how to call C run-time APIs for utility functions, such as converting a hex string to a displayable character string. With these functions now in your toolbox, you should be able to process date and time fields in ways you never imagined before!

Check Your Knowledge

Figure 8.8 shows how to get the current date using CEELOCT and format it using CEEDATE. Assume you have a character variable named *MyDate*, defined with a length of eight bytes that holds the value *20070401*, representing April 1, 2007 in a *YYYYMMDD* format. You need to format this date as *Sun, April 01 2007*.

As a starting point, the Convert Date to Lilian Format API, CEEDAYS, converts a character string to a Lilian date using a user-specified picture string. The documentation for this API can be found using the API Finder, and searching for the name *CEEDAYS*, or by looking at the "Date and Time APIs" subcategory of "ILE CEE" APIs.

One possible solution to this task can be found in Figure D.8 of appendix D.

9

Character Conversion APIs

Character data, such as names, addresses, and descriptions, most likely represents a significant amount of the data you store on the System i. Often, this character data is stored and simply retrieved for display and print purposes, but you might also need to process this character data within an application.

One possible form of processing character data is to convert stored mixed-case names ("ABC Company") to uppercase ("ABC COMPANY"), for search purposes. This is useful when you want data values such as "Company," "COMPANY," and "COmpAny" to be treated as equivalent. For this type of processing, the system provides Convert Case APIs. The Convert Case function is provided as both a program API (QLGCNVCS) and a procedure API (QlgConvertCase) within a service program. This chapter starts with an example that uses the QlgConvertCase API to monocase (convert to either all-uppercase or all-lowercase) character data.

There is a growing need for the ability to convert data from one encoding system to another. You might, for instance, currently store your character data as EBCDIC, but want to exchange the data with another system using ASCII or UTF-8. While i5/OS provides many automatic character-encoding conversions with commands such as CPYTOSTMF, CPYF with FMTOPT(*MAP), and file I/O with DB2 or the Integrated File

System, sometimes you need to have direct program control of the conversion. In this case, a set of APIs generically referred to as *iconv* are useful. Iconv is an industry-standard interface for converting character data across various encodings. There are three iconv APIs: iconv_open to define what type of conversion is being requested, iconv to actually do the conversion, and iconv_close to indicate that all of the necessary conversions have been completed. Having once defined the conversion using iconv_open, you can call iconv multiple times. This chapter covers this family of APIs.

The documentation for these APIs can be found in the Information Center under the API category "National Language Support." The case-conversion APIs are in the subcategory "National Language Support-related APIs," and the iconv-related APIs are in the subcategory "Data Conversion APIs."

Monocasing Character Data Using the Convert Case API

The Convert Case API, QlgConvertCase, allows you to easily convert data from mixed case to either all-uppercase or all-lowercase. Now, you might be wondering at this point why you would want to use an API when RPG provides built-in functions such as %xlate for uppercasing, as shown in Figure 9.1.

```
DName+++++++++++ETDsFrom+++To/L+++IDc.Keywords+++++++++++++++++++++++++
dUpper            c                 'ABCDEFGHIJKLMNOPQRSTUVWXYZ'
dLower            c                 'abcdefghijklmnopqrstuvwxyz'
dText             s              20

CLON01Factor1+++++++Opcode&ExtFactor2+++++++Result++++++++Len++D+HiLoEq
 /free
   Text = %xlate( Lower :Upper :'Beckie');
 /end-free
```

Figure 9.1: RPG uppercasing of character data.

After the %xlate built-in runs, the variable Text is set to "BECKIE," which certainly looks like an easy way to uppercase data. But what if the input string, rather than having the value "Beckie," has the value "Adélaïde." After the %xlate built-in runs, the variable Text is now "ADéLAïDE" rather than the correct "ADÉLAÏDE." The obvious solution is to add the constants é and ï to Lower, and the corresponding É and Ï to Upper (along with quite a few other Latin characters), but you will find this still isn't quite right. The reason is that the character é can only be represented in your RPG source code as one hexadecimal value. In the case of CCSID 37 (for simplicity, think of this as North American English), this would be x'51'. If your program was running in the United States, you would probably be OK. But what if your program was running in France with a CCSID of 297 (French) where the é is x'C0' and x'51' is the curly-bracket character, {? Your program would convert a string such as "{aéiou}" to "éAéIOUÈ," which is decidedly incorrect.

To solve this, you could create additional versions of the Lower and Upper constants for each Latin-1 language environment your program might run in (such as English, French, German, and Spanish). This becomes unwieldy very quickly, however. And when your program needs to run (unchanged) in an environment that doesn't use Latin-1, such as Greek or Cyrillic, it becomes extremely awkward. Is there a solution to this dilemma? Of course there is! Use the Convert Case API. This API allows you to pass in a character string and the CCSID the character string is encoded in. The API then returns the correctly cased string.

Table 9.1 shows the parameters for the Convert Case API. The first parameter, Request Control Block, defines what type of case conversion you want performed. Figure 9.2 shows the layout of the Request Control Block when using a CCSID-based conversion.

Table 9.1: The Convert Case API, OLGCVTCS or QlgConvertCase			
Parameter	Description	Type	Size
1	Request Control Block	Input	Char(*)
2	Input Data	Input	Char(*)
3	Output Data	Output	Char(*)
4	Length of Data	Input	Binary(4)
5	Error Code	In/Out	Char(*)

```
DName+++++++++++ETDsFrom+++To/L+++IDc.Keywords+++++++++++++++++++++++
D*******************************************************************
D*Structure for CCSID based request
D*******************************************************************
DQLGIDRCB00         DS
D*                                              Qlg CCSID ReqCtlBlk
D QLGTOR02                      1      4B 0
D*                                              Type of Request
D QLGIDOID00                    5      8B 0
D*                                              CCSID of Input Data
D QLGCR00                       9     12B 0
D*                                              Case Request
D QLGERVED04                   13     22
D*                                              Reserved
```

Figure 9.2: The QSYSINC QLG member when using a CCSID-based conversion.

Type of Request (QLGTOR02) can be one of several options: Type 1 indicates a CCSID-based request, type 2 is table-object based, and type 3 is user-defined. Our example uses type 1.

The CCSID of Input Data (QLGIDOID00) identifies how the character data is represented or encoded. This can be a specific CCSID, such as 37 for EBCDIC North American English, 297 for EBCDIC French, 1252 for Windows Latin-1, or 1208 for UTF-8. You can also use the special value of zero to have the API use the current job CCSID, which is generally the value you will want. If you are interested in using specific CCSID values (and there are hundreds of them), the i5/OS Information Center lists the CCSIDs supported by the system. This list can be found by looking under the "Programming" and then choosing "Globalization."

Case Request (QLGCR00) specifies the type of case conversion to be performed. The supported values are zero to convert the input data to uppercase and one to convert the input data to lowercase. Reserved (QLGERVED04) is simply reserved space in the request control block. As is usual for APIs, this reserved field must be set to x'00's.

Figure 9.3 shows how to use the QlgConvertCase API. First, the program sets the Error Code Bytes Provided field (QUSBPRV) to zero so exceptions are sent to the program. After this, the program initializes the entire request control block (QLGIDRCB00) to x'00's. As mentioned in earlier chapters, this is done so we don't reference the actual reserved field, QLGERVED04, in the program. QLGERVED04, being reserved, may be renamed or redefined in future releases as new functionality is added to the API. Therefore, we don't want to explicitly reference this field within the application program. After initializing QLGIDRCB00 to x'00's, the program sets the specific fields that control the conversion. The program sets the conversion type (QLGTOR02) to one (CCSID based), the CCSID (QLGIDOID00) to zero (the job CCSID is to be used), and the case request (QLGCR00) to zero (uppercase).

```
h dftactgrp(*no)

DName+++++++++++ETDsFrom+++To/L+++IDc.Keywords++++++++++++++++++++++
d/copy qsysinc/qrpglesrc,qlg
d/copy qsysinc/qrpglesrc,qusec

dConvertCase      pr                    extproc('QlgConvertCase')
d Request                      65535    const options(*varsize)
d InputData                    65535    const options(*varsize)
d OutputData                       1    options(*varsize)
d InputDataLen                 10i 0    const
d QUSEC                                 likeds(QUSEC)

dInputData        s            40       inz('Some mixed TeXt')
dOutputData       s            40
dWait             s             1

CLON01Factor1+++++++Opcode&ExtFactor2+++++++Result++++++++Len++D+HiLoEq
 /free
  QUSBPRV = 0;                  // use exceptions for errors
  QLGIDRCB00 = *loval;          // set input structure to x'00'
  QLGTOR02 = 1;                 // use CCSID for monocasing
  QLGIDOID00 = 0;               // use the job CCSID
  QLGCR00 = 0;                  // convert to uppercase
  ConvertCase( QLGIDRCB00 :InputData :OutputData
             :%len(%trimr(InputData)) :QUSEC);
  dsply OutputData;
  QLGCR00 = 1;                          // convert to lowercase
  ConvertCase( QLGIDRCB00 :OutputData :InputData
             :%len(%trimr(OutputData)) :QUSEC);
  dsply InputData;
  *inlr = *on;
  return;
 /end-free
```

Figure 9.3: Converting to uppercase and lowercase using a CCSID-based conversion request.

QlgConvertCase is then called with an InputData parameter of "Some mixed TeXt." The result "SOME MIXED TEXT" is DSPLYed.

To lowercase the string, the program simply sets the case request to one (lowercase) and calls QlgConvertCase again, this time reversing the Input and Output parameters. The second DSPLY shows "some mixed text."

The correct uppercasing of strings such as "Adélaïde" and "{aéiou}" can now be done automatically by simply running the program in a job having the correct job CCSID. In the United States, this would most likely be 37; in France, 297. If this program were to be run in a job CCSID of 37, but it knew that the data was really encoded in 297, then by setting QLGIDOID00 to 297 rather than zero, the program would again correctly case the input data. The same is true for other language environments, such as Greek or Cyrillic. As more businesses move into a global marketplace, APIs such as Convert Case are clearly becoming more important for programmer productivity (and for the correct handling of national language data).

Converting Character Data Using ICONV

Business applications often have to work with data in different encodings. While most i5/OS-based applications work with EBCDIC data, you might need to exchange data with other systems that prefer to work with data in ASCII, Unicode, or simply a different EBCDIC CCSID. To help address this, the system provides a family of APIs often generically referred to as *iconv*. The iconv APIs conform to an industry standard and are documented in the Information Center in a style following that standard.

The first API, iconv_open, is used to define what type of conversion you want. The parameters for iconv_open are shown in Figure 9.4. In the industry-standard iconv_open API, the descriptors (parameters) controlling the conversion (tocode and fromcode) are defined as character strings. If you wanted to convert character data from a CCSID such as 37 (EBCDIC Latin-1) to a CCSID such as 1252 (Windows Latin-1), you would specify (among other things) a From value of "IBMCCSID00037" and a To value of "IBMCCSID01252."

```
iconv_t iconv_open (char *tocode, char *fromcode)
```

Figure 9.4: The iconv_open parameters.

Since CCSID values are typically represented as numeric values within i5/OS, IBM also supplies an API unique to System i known as QtqIconvOpen. The parameters for QtqIconvOpen are shown in Figure 9.5. If you are developing applications to run only on i5/OS, QtqIconvOpen is the most natural conversion API to use. If you are developing applications intended to run on multiple platforms, use iconv_open instead. Functionally, the two APIs are identical. The only difference is in the data types used to describe the conversion. The iconv and iconv_close APIs don't need i5/OS-unique versions of the industry-defined APIs, as you will see shortly.

```
iconv_t QtqIconvOpen (QtqCode_t *tocode, QtqCode_t *fromcode)
```

Figure 9.5: QtqIconvOpen parameters.

As introduced in chapter 1, the industry-standard parameter definition shown in Figure 9.5 takes a bit of getting used to if you're not familiar with the C language. The QtqIconvOpen API is being defined as accepting two parameters (tocode and fromcode), which are pointers (as shown by the asterisk preceding the parameter name) to structures of type QtqCode_t. The API returns a return value of type iconv_t. The format of QtqCode_t, as provided in the QSYSINC library, is shown in Figure 9.6.

```
DName++++++++++++ETDsFrom+++To/L+++IDc.Keywords++++++++++++++++++++++++
DQTQCODE              DS
D*                                            QtqCode T
D QTQCCSID             1      4B 0
D*                                            CCSID
D QTQCA               5      8B 0
D*                                            cnv alternative
D QTQSA               9     12B 0
D*                                            subs alternative
D QTQSA00            13     16B 0
D*                                            shift alternative
D QTQLO              17     20B 0
D*                                            length option
D QTQMEO             21     24B 0
D*                                            mx error option
D QTQERVED02         25     32
D*                                            reserved
```

Figure 9.6: The QSYSINC QTQICONV member when using QtqIconvOpen.

The Information Center documentation for QtqIconvOpen shows that for the first parameter (tocode), the only field used within the QtqCode_t (QTQCODE in the QSYSINC RPG include) structure is QTQCCSID, the CCSID we want the data converted to. QTQCCSID is defined as an integer field (this is the data type for CCSIDs with most other i5/OS APIs). It can be a discrete value such as 37 or the special value zero to represent the current job CCSID.

For the second parameter (fromcode), there are many choices to specify how the conversion should be performed. QTQCCSID can, as with the tocode parameter, be a discrete value or the special value of zero to represent the current job CCSID.

QTQCA, the conversion alternative, allows you to control what happens when characters in the From CCSID do not exist in the To CCSID. One option, Enforced Subset, converts only characters that exactly match in both the From and To CCSIDs. All other characters are replaced with a substitution character (typically x'3F'). This option is specified by using a value of 57. A second option, Best Fit, converts characters to other similar characters if an exact match does not exist. An example would be converting an á in the From CCSID to an *a* in the To CCSID if á does not exist in the To CCSID. This option is specified by using a value of 102.

There is a third option, Default Conversion, specified by using a value of zero. This option is also referred to as *Round-Trip Conversion*, because if a character in the From CCSID does not exist in the To CCSID, the system will use a character in the To CCSID that does not exist in the From CCSID to represent the character being converted. As an example, if only the From CCSID data contains the character á and only the To CCSID contains the character ψ, the system can convert á to ψ. The ψ will not make any sense to users of the To CCSID, but that's because they don't have the original á character within their character set. If this data is subsequently converted back to the original CCSID, the system will convert ψ back to á. This ability to round-trip the data from one CCSID to another and back again, without losing the original character, gives this option its name. The Enforced Subset and Best Fit options cannot provide this round-trip capability because the data is converted to non-unique characters (either substitution characters or best-fit characters, respectively), so the original characters cannot be restored.

QTQSA, the substitution alternative, is used in conjunction with the Enforced Subset conversion alternative. It allows you to specify whether you want the number of characters substituted to be returned when actually converting the data. A value of zero means do not return the number of substitutions; a one means return the number.

QTQSA00, the shift-state alternative, is primarily related to conversions dealing with double-byte data (DBCS) and is not covered in this book.

QTQLO, the length option, controls how the iconv API is to determine the length of your input data when actually doing a conversion. A value of zero indicates that the API caller will explicitly specify the length of the data when later calling the conversion API, iconv.

A value of one indicates that the length of the data is to be determined by having the API search for a null byte (x'00') to indicate the end of data. The example program in this chapter uses option 0, but RPG users could also use option 1 by specifying options(*string) on the iconv prototype or explicitly concatenating x'00' to the end of the input data.

QTQMEO, the error option for mixed data, is related to conversion of DBCS data to single-byte data (SBCS) and is not covered in this book.

QtqIconvOpen returns a return value of type iconv_t. Iconv_t is defined as an array of 13 integer values and represents the conversion choices you passed to the API. This array is then passed unchanged as input to the iconv and iconv_close APIs. If, after calling QtqIconvOpen, the first element is set to a value of negative one, then an error was found by QtqIconvOpen. Further information on the error can be found through an industry-standard mechanism known as *errno*. The use of errno is not covered in this chapter, but you can find more information about it in chapter 14. Errno is also updated when errors occur while calling iconv and iconv_close.

Figure 9.9 shows a complete program using the QtqIconvOpen, iconv, and iconv_close APIs. Procedure SetConvert in this example program shows a call to the QtqIconvOpen API using a From CCSID of 37 (EBCDIC Latin-1), a To CCSID of 819 (ISO Latin-1), a default conversion choice of round trip, no count of substitutions being returned, and the caller explicitly specifying the length of data to convert.

The parameters for the second API in this family, iconv, are shown in Figure 9.7. This is the API that actually performs the data conversion.

```
size_t iconv (iconv_t cd, char **inbuf, size_t *inbytesleft,
                      char **outbuf, size_t *outbytesleft)
```

Figure 9.7: The iconv parameters.

The iconv API is defined as taking five parameters and returning a return value. The first parameter, iconv_t cd, is the conversion descriptor that was previously returned by QtqIconvOpen. This is passed by value and should not be modified by the application program.

The second parameter, char **inbuf, is read right to left and defined as a pointer (the last asterisk) to a pointer (the first asterisk) to the characters (the char) to be converted. When you call iconv, the secondary pointer (the first asterisk) should point to the first character to be converted. When iconv returns to the application program, this secondary pointer value will have been modified to point to the byte following the last character that was converted. As an example, if you wanted to convert the first five characters in the string "abcdefghijk," you would call iconv with a pointer to a pointer which pointed at *a*. After iconv successfully converted the five characters ("abcde"), this secondary pointer would now be pointing to *f*, not the initial *a*. By subtracting the address of the start of the variable from the returned pointer, you can then calculate how many characters were, in fact, converted.

The third parameter, size_t *inbytesleft, is defined as a pointer to a variable of type size_t. This variable represents the number of bytes to convert. When iconv returns to the application, this value, the number of bytes to convert, will have been decremented to reflect the number of bytes remaining to be converted. To follow with the example from the previous paragraph, you might have called iconv with a value of 11 to represent the 11 characters to convert, and iconv may have returned after only converting five characters. In this case, the number of bytes to convert would have been decremented to a value of 6 (the remaining number of characters). The data type size_t is defined as a four-byte unsigned integer (10u 0).

The fourth parameter, char **outbuf, is similar to the second parameter, but it points to the output buffer where the converted data is returned. It is a pointer to a pointer pointing to the first available byte in the output buffer to return data in. Like the secondary pointer for the inbuf parameter, the secondary pointer here is also modified by the iconv API. Upon return, this pointer will point to the byte following the last byte of converted output data. By subtracting the start of the variable from the returned pointer, you can calculate how many bytes of converted data were generated.

The fifth parameter, size_t *outbytesleft, is similar to the third parameter, except that this parameter represents how many bytes remain available in the output buffer to store converted data. Like the third parameter, iconv updates this value to reflect the number of available bytes remaining after having converted data on the call to iconv.

Iconv returns a size_t return value where a positive number reflects the number of substitutions performed (if, that is, you asked for this information using field QTQSA when calling the QtqIconvOpen API). A zero value indicates no error on the API call, and a value of negative one indicates that an error was found. As size_t is defined by the industry standard as being an unsigned value, and the industry standard also calls for a negative value to be returned for an error situation, this bring up an interesting situation in terms of incompatible requirements. We resolve this by using a signed integer (10i 0) as the return value in our function prototype for iconv.

When you are converting data across CCSIDs, keep in mind that the number of characters being converted does not necessarily equal the number of bytes. What takes one byte to represent a character in one CCSID may very well require two, three, or even more bytes in another CCSID. Converting "Adélaïde," for instance, from CCSID 37 to CCSID 1208 (UTF-8) will cause the number of bytes to grow from eight to 10. Earlier we mentioned that iconv might return after only converting the first five characters when we had asked for eleven characters to be converted. One reason this could happen would be if only eleven bytes of storage were available in the output buffer and the number of bytes necessary exceeded the eleven bytes. In this situation iconv would convert what it could with the available space and return an ERRNO value of 3491. As you will see in chapter 14, an ERRNO of 3491 represents E2BIG – insufficient space.

The parameters for the third API in this family, iconv_close, are shown in Figure 9.8. This is the API that is called after all conversions are finished.

```
int iconv_close (iconv_t cd)
```

Figure 9.8: The iconv_close parameters.

The iconv_close API is defined as accepting one parameter and returning a return value. The input parameter is the conversion descriptor initially returned by QtqIconvOpen and used as an input parameter to iconv. The return value is set to zero if the API completes successfully. Otherwise, it is set to negative one to indicate an error was found.

Having introduced the three APIs (QtqIconvOpen, iconv, and iconv_close) let's now take a more detailed look at the program in Figure 9.9.

```
h dftactgrp(*no)

DName+++++++++++ETDsFrom+++To/L+++IDc.Keywords+++++++++++++++++++++++
d/copy qsysinc/qrpglesrc,qtqiconv

dSetConvert       pr              10i 0
d InputCCSID                      10i 0 value
d OutputCCSID                     10i 0 value

dConvert          pr              10i 0
d Input                             * value
d Len_Input                       10i 0 value
```

Figure 9.9: Converting character data using iconv. (part 1 of 4).

```
dEndConvert        pr              10i 0 extproc('iconv_close')
d ConvDesc                               value like(cd)

dcd                ds
d cdBins                           10i 0 dim(13)

dInput_Variable1   s               50    inz('Some variable data')
dInput_Variable2   s               50    inz('More data')
dOutput_Value      s             4096
dLen_Output        s               10i 0
dRtnCde            s               10i 0
dwait              s                1

CLON01Factor1+++++++Opcode&ExtFactor2+++++++Result++++++++Len++D+HiLoEq
 /free
    // Set the input CCSID to 37 and desired output as 819
    RtnCde = SetConvert(37 :819);

    if RtnCde = 0;    // no error found
       Len_Output = Convert( %addr(Input_Variable1)
                             :%len(%trimr(Input_Variable1)));
       if Len_Output = -1;
          dsply 'Text conversion error found' '' wait;
       else;

       // Output_Value now contains the converted field with a length of
       // Len_Output bytes

       endif;

       // Convert another variable
        Len_Output = Convert( %addr(Input_Variable2)
                             :%len(%trimr(Input_Variable2)));
       if Len_Output = -1;
          dsply 'Text conversion error found' '' wait;
       else;
       endif;

       // Close the cd after all conversions are done
       RtnCde = EndConvert(cd);
    else;
       dsply 'Error setting up conversion' '' wait;
    endif;
    *inlr = *on;
    return;
 /end-free
pSetConvert        b
```

Figure 9.9: Converting character data using iconv. (part 2 of 4).

```
DName+++++++++++ETDsFrom+++To/L+++IDc.Keywords++++++++++++++++++++++
dSetConvert        pi                  10i 0
d InputCCSID                           10i 0value
d OutputCCSID                          10i 0value

dConvertOpen       pr                  52a  extproc('QtqIconvOpen')
d ToCode                                *   value
d FromCode                              *   value

dToCode            ds                       likeds(qtqcode)

dFromCode          ds                       likeds(qtqcode)

 /free
   FromCode = *loval;
   ToCode = *loval;
   FromCode.QTQCCSID = InputCCSID;
   ToCode.QTQCCSID = OutputCCSID;
   cd = ConvertOpen( %addr(ToCode) :%addr(FromCode));
   if cdBins(1) = -1;
       return -1;
   else;
       return 0;
   endif;
 /end-free
pSetConvert        e

pConvert           b

DName+++++++++++ETDsFrom+++To/L+++IDc.Keywords++++++++++++++++++++++
dConvert           pi                  10i 0
d Input_Pointer                         *   value
d Input_Length                         10i 0value

diconv             pr                  10i 0extproc('iconv')
d ConvDesc                                  value like(cd)
d InputData                             *   value
d InputDataLeft                        10u 0
d OutputData                            *   value
d OutputDataLeft                       10u 0

dOutBufPtr         s                    *
dInBytesLeft       s                   10u 0
dOutBytesLeft      s                   10u 0
```

Figure 9.9: Converting character data using iconv. (part 3 of 4).

```
/free
  // reset InBytesLeft, OutBytesLeft, and OutBufPtr each time as iconv
  // API updates these values
  InBytesLeft = Input_Length;
  OutBytesLeft = %len(Output_Value);
  OutBufPtr = %addr(Output_Value);
  RtnCde = iconv( cd :%addr(Input_Pointer) :InBytesLeft
                     :%addr(OutBufPtr) :OutBytesLeft);

  if RtnCde = -1;
     return -1;
  else;
     return (%len(Output_Value) - OutBytesLeft);
  endif;
 /end-free
pConvert                e
```

Figure 9.9: Converting character data using iconv. (part 4 of 4).

We'll start by looking at the procedures SetConvert and Convert, which mask the details of QtqIconvOpen and iconv from the application developer. These two procedures would be good candidates for implementation within a service program so that all application developers would have easy access to their functions.

SetConvert is prototyped as accepting two parameters: InputCCSID (the CCSID we want to convert from), and OutputCCSID (what we want to convert to). The SetConvert procedure initializes the tocode and fromcode parameters of QtqIconvOpen with a standard set of conversion alternatives (basically, the default zero values for the conversion alternative, substitution alternative, length option, etc.), sets the appropriate CCSID values in the tocode and fromcode parameters, and calls QtqIconvOpen. Upon return from the API, SetConvert examines the first element of the returned conversion descriptor. If an error was encountered (cdBins(1) = -1), it returns negative one to the caller of SetConvert. Otherwise, SetConvert returns zero. The conversion descriptor itself (cd) is defined as a program-wide variable.

The Convert procedure is prototyped as accepting two input parameters: Input (the data to be converted), and Len_Input (the length of the data to be converted). Convert always resets the values of InBytesLeft, OutBytesLeft, and OutBufPtr to initial values. InBytesLeft is set to the Length of Data to Convert value passed in by the caller of Convert. OutBytesLeft is set to the allocated size of Output_Value, which is a program-wide variable always used to return converted data to. OutBufPtr is set to the first byte of the Output_Value program-wide variable. Convert then calls the iconv API, storing the resulting data in the variable Output_Value. Convert tests to see if an error was encountered (RtnCde = -1). If so, it returns a value of negative one to its caller. If no error was found, Convert returns the number of bytes successfully converted, as follows:

```
%len(Output_Value) - OutBytesLeft
```

Close examination of the iconv function prototype in the Convert procedure might cause you to think we've made an error. As you saw earlier, the iconv API defines the third and fifth parameters (InBytesLeft and OutBytesLeft, respectively) as being pointers to unsigned integer values. In Convert, however, we're simply passing unsigned integer values. How can this be? As mentioned in chapter 1, a pointer passed by value that points to a variable is the same as that variable being passed by reference. This means the three definitions in Figure 9.10 are equivalent. Since the prototype can be coded in multiple ways, and we prefer, when possible, to see the actual data type (10u 0, for instance) to aid in program documentation (not to mention additional compile-time checking), we have prototyped iconv using the first style. Personally, we prefer to avoid the third style, passing a pointer by reference, because of the ambiguity in the prototype of which pointer we're referring to. This, however, is a matter of personal choice.

The one parameter we don't have a lot of flexibility in prototyping is the first, the conversion descriptor. This parameter is passed directly by value, not as a pointer to the conversion descriptor. As such, this parameter must be coded in the function prototype as being passed by VALUE.

```
DName++++++++++++ETDsFrom+++To/L+++IDc.Keywords++++++++++++++++++++++++
diconv             pr              10i 0 extproc('iconv')
d ConvDesc                               value like(cd)
d InputData                        *     value
d InputDataLeft                    10u 0
d OutputData                       *     value
d OutputDataLeft                   10u 0

   RtnCde = iconv( cd :%addr(Input_Pointer) :InBytesLeft
                   :%addr(OutBufPtr) :OutBytesLeft);

diconv             pr              10i 0 extproc('iconv')
d ConvDesc                               value like(cd)
d InputData                        *     value
```

Figure 9.10: Three equivalent ways to prototype iconv (part 1 of 2).

```
d InputDataLeft                          *   value
d OutputData                             *   value
d OutputDataLeft                         *   value

  RtnCde = iconv( cd :%addr(Input_Pointer) :%addr(InBytesLeft)
                  :%addr(OutBufPtr) :%addr(OutBytesLeft));

diconv              pr          10i 0 extproc('iconv')
d ConvDesc                            value like(cd)
d InputData                      *
d InputDataLeft                 10u 0
d OutputData                     *
d OutputDataLeft                10u 0

  RtnCde = iconv( cd :Input_Pointer :InBytesLeft
                  :OutBufPtr :OutBytesLeft);
```

Figure 9.10: Three equivalent ways to prototype iconv (part 2 of 2).

The main program in Figure 9.9 starts by calling SetConvert, asking for a conversion descriptor to convert data from CCSID 37 (EBCDIC Latin-1) to CCSID 819 (ISO Latin-1, also often referred to as ASCII). This part of the program is restated in Figure 9.11.

```
CLON01Factor1+++++++Opcode&ExtFactor2+++++++Result+++++++++Len++D+HiLoEq
   // Set the input CCSID to 37 and desired output as 819
   RtnCde = SetConvert(37 :819);
```

Figure 9.11: Calling procedure SetConvert.

The program then checks to see if an error was found when creating the conversion descriptor. If not, it converts the Input_Variable1 data ("Some variable data") to CCSID 819. If an error is encountered when converting the data, the program DSPLYs the error text "Text conversion error found." Otherwise, the converted data is now in the first Len_Output bytes of variable Output_Value. If an error is encountered when creating the conversion descriptor, the program DSPLYs the error text "Error setting up conversion," as shown in Figure 9.12.

```
CLON01Factor1+++++++Opcode&ExtFactor2+++++++Result++++++++Len++D+HiLoEq
    if RtnCde = 0;      // no error found
       Len_Output = Convert( %addr(Input_Variable1)
                                  :%len(%trimr(Input_Variable1)));
       if Len_Output = -1;
           dsply 'Text conversion error found' '' wait;
       else;

       // Output_Value now contains the converted field with a length of
       // Len_Output bytes
       endif;
    else;
       dsply 'Error setting up conversion' '' wait;
    endif;
```

Figure 9.12: Converting data.

After this conversion of Input_Variable1 to Output_Value, you have entered a realm where you cannot always trust your eyes! This is because the system assumes that character data is encoded in the CCSID of your job, or the default CCSID if the CCSID is 65535. The variable Output_Value is now breaking this assumption, in that it is encoded in CCSID 819 rather than, let's assume, CCSID 37. If you were to enter a debug environment, set a breakpoint at a statement following the successful conversion ('ELSE;' of 'IF LEN_OUTPUT = -1;'), and then display the contents of OUTPUT_VALUE ('EVAL OUTPUT_VALUE'), you would get a result similar to what is shown in Figure 9.13.

```
> EVAL output_value
  OUTPUT_VALUE =
            ....5...10...15...20...25...30.
       1    'ë?_ÁÎ/ÊÑ/Â%ÁÀ/È/
      61    '
```

Figure 9.13: Displaying the Output_Value parameter in debug.

The conversion was successful, but you sure can't tell it by looking! What you need to do, when working with character data that is no longer encoded in the job CCSID, is display the character data in hex mode ('EVAL OUTPUT_VALUE:X'). Now you get results similar to what is shown in Figure 9.14. (Strictly speaking, you also have the options of using 'EVAL OUTPUT_VALUE:A' for ASCII encoded data and 'EVAL OUTPUT_VALUE:U' for UCS-2 encoded data. These, however, are really only effective when the character set of your job/device has the same character set as the CCSID of Output_Value, so we hesitate

to recommend them. In the specific case of program FIG9_9, 'EVAL OUTPUT_VALUE:A'
would be effective in Latin-1 based jobs like CCSID 37.)

```
EVAL output_value:x
   00000     536F6D65 20766172 6961626C 65206461   - ë?_Á.Î/ÊÑ/Â%Á.À/
   00010     74614040 40404040 40404040 40404040   - È/
```

Figure 9.14: Displaying the Output_Value parameter in debug with the hex option.

From here, you can verify the results by examining the displayed code points and
looking them up in the appropriate code page table. In the Information Center, look
under the "Programming" topic for "Globalization" to find these tables. In code page
819, for instance, x'53' (the first two characters shown with 'EVAL OUTPUT_VALUE:X') is
the uppercase letter *S*. This correctly represents the initial letter *S* of the variable
Input_Variable1.

In the previous output, shown in Figure 9.13, it is fairly obvious that a simple display of
the Output_Value variable won't work, as Output_Value now contains ASCII-encoded
data. You get true "garbage" displayed, as the system believes the data to be in the
EBCDIC CCSID of your job. This "don't trust your eyes" warning applies, though, to
any CCSID conversion, and can easily be overlooked when converting to another
EBCDIC CCSID. If you were to change the initial value of Input_Variable1 to
"Adélaïde" and request a conversion to CCSID 297 (EBCDIC French), then, after a
successful conversion, an eval Output_Value would show results similar to Figure 9.15.

```
EVAL output_value
OUTPUT_VALUE =
           ....5...10...15...20...25...30.
     1    'Ad{laïde
    61    '
```

Figure 9.15: Displaying the Output_Value parameter in debug with CCSID 297-encoded data.

In this case, some of the data looks right and some of the data looks wrong. You could
easily start looking for a problem in your application where none exists. The reality is
that 'EVAL OUTPUT_VALUE:X' will show that the Output_Value variable is right.

Another warning, related to CCSID processing assumptions, needs to be made
concerning our use of the %trimr built-in function in Figure 9.12. Input_Variable1 is

320

defined as being of a character data type, so %trimr is trimming trailing blanks to determine the effective length of the Input_Variable1 variable value. This works as expected when the value of Input_Variable1 is EBCDIC encoded, but can produce unexpected results when the value of Input_Variable1 is encoded using a non-EBCDIC CCSID. The reason is that the EBCDIC blank character (x'40') is a non-blank character in other encodings. In CCSID 819, for instance, x'40' is the at-sign character (@). In UTF-16, the second byte of many characters is x'40'. If the last character in Input_Variable1 happens to be the CCSID 819 @, or a UTF-16 character such as ꭰ (x'FB40'), then %trimr (when working with variables defined as character) will remove this trailing x'40' byte from the length passed to the Convert procedure.

Trying to debug this type of situation can be very difficult. So, make sure your use of the %trim related built-in functions is always done when the CCSID of the data matches the data type of your input variable. By "matches," we mean that %trimr would, for instance, be appropriate when working with UTF-16 data so long as the input variable was also defined as being UTF-16. For RPG, this would be data type C with a CCSID of 1200.The Characters to Trim parameter of built-ins such as %trimr can be used to provide some additional controls beyond simply truncating x'40's from the input string, but you need to keep the CCSID in mind!

Resuming our discussion of program FIG9_9, the program then converts another variable using the same conversion descriptor, as shown in Figure 9.16. Once the conversion descriptor has been created, you can use it as many times as needed. The program can also have multiple conversion descriptors open at the same time. Just make sure to use the right descriptor!

```
CLON01Factor1++++++++Opcode&ExtFactor2++++++++Result++++++++++Len++D+HiLoEq
// Convert another variable
    Len_Output = Convert( %addr(Input_Variable2)
                            :%len(%trimr(Input_Variable2)));
    if Len_Output = -1;
        dsply 'Text conversion error found' '' wait;
    else;
    endif;
```

Figure 9.16: Converting more data.

When all of the conversions are done, iconv_close is called to free up the resources associated with the conversion descriptor, as shown in Figure 9.17.

```
// Close the cd after all conversions are done
RtnCde = EndConvert(cd);
```

Figure 9.17: Closing the conversion environment.

And that's it. Using Figure 9.9 as a building block, you are now ready to convert data from any CCSID to any other CCSID.

Summary

There are many situations where character data needs to be converted from one form to another. In this chapter, you have seen how to use APIs to convert case and to convert from one CCSID to another. Using these APIs within your application programs, you can build robust applications that are easy to maintain and enabled for the wide world of character data.

Check Your Knowledge

Write a program that reads the CUSTOMER file created in Figure 4.4.A and displays those customer names (CUSTNAME) that contain the string "mpa" in any combination of uppercase and lowercase characters, such as "Mpa," "mPa," or "MPA." One possible solution to this task can be found in Figure D.9 of appendix D.

10

Message APIs

Messages are a way of life with i5/OS. Every time you start, hold, or cancel a job, the system issues a message. While your job is executing, the system sends messages to the job log. If the system needs human intervention, such as pressing the Start button on a printer or loading a tape on a tape drive, the system notifies the interested parties by sending a message.

Since messages are such an integral part of i5/OS, you would probably like to know when certain ones are sent on the system. For this, the system provides an exit capability through *watches*. Watches allow you to define a program that should be automatically called when a particular message is sent to the QSYSOPR system-operator message queue, the QHST history log, the job log of one or more jobs, or a regular message queue. This chapter first looks at how to write watch exit programs and then how to associate a watch exit program with messages that might be sent on the system.

Application programs often want to send messages to either another program or a user. The system provides for many types of messages to meet the various needs of developers. These messages include completion messages to indicate that a particular piece of work has finished, status messages to indicate the current status of work, diagnostic messages to provide possible error-related information, and escape messages to indicate a general failure. This chapter also looks at how to send messages from your application program using the Send Program Message API, QMHSNDPM.

Messages are frequently stored as message descriptions in a message file. The chapter concludes with a look at how the Retrieve Message API, QMHRTVM, can be used to search for messages in a message file that have a particular word in either its first- or second-level text. Many times, we've wondered if there was already a message describing a certain situation, but had no fast, easy way to determine what that message might be. With this API, that problem has been solved!

Watch Exit Programs

Watches provide the ability to have i5/OS call one or more user programs when a particular message is sent to the system operator, the history log, the job log of one or more jobs, or to a message queue. There is the Start Watch API (QSCSWCH) to begin a watch session, the End Watch API (QSCEWCH) to end a watch session, and the Watch for Event exit program capability. All three are discussed in the "Problem Management" category of System APIs under the subcategory "Monitoring."

We'll start by explaining how to write a watch exit program. Following that, you'll see how to use the Start Watch API to associate a watch exit program with messages and message queues on the system. The parameter descriptions for a watch exit program are shown in Table 10.1.

Table 10.1: Watch Exit Program Parameters			
Parameter	Description	Type	Size
1	Watch Option Setting	Input	Char(10)
2	Session ID	Input	Char(10)
3	Error Detected	Output	Char(10)
4	Event Data	Input	Char(*)

The first parameter, Watch Option Setting, tells the exit program why it was called. Watch exit programs can currently be called in two situations. One is if a watched-for message is sent on the system (*MSGID), and the other is if a watched-for Licensed Internal Code (LIC) error log entry is recorded on the system (*LICLOG). The two values supported, therefore, are *MSGID and *LICLOG. Although you can start a watch for either of these situations, we only discuss message watches in this book.

The second parameter, Session ID, is the name of the session calling the exit program. When a watch is started, a session ID can either be generated by the system or specified by the user.

The third parameter, Error Detected, is an output from the exit program back to i5/OS. If the exit program returns blanks for this parameter, no error was encountered in the exit program, and i5/OS should continue calling the exit program whenever the watched-for message is sent again. Any other value informs i5/OS that an error has been encountered within the exit program, and i5/OS will stop calling the exit program.

The fourth parameter, Event Data, is data associated with the message that was sent and that triggered the call to the watch exit program. For messages (a watch session setting of *MSGID), the format of this event data is shown in Figure 10.1.

```
DName+++++++++++ETDsFrom+++To/L+++IDc.Keywords++++++++++++++++++++++++
D*******************************************************************
D*Watch Exit Program called because a message id and any
D*associated comparison data is matched.
D*This structure is for the user exit program called by
D*STRWCH cmd or Start Watch (QSCSWCH) API
D*******************************************************************
DESCQWFM            DS
D*                                              Qsc Watch For Msg
D ESCLWI            1      4B 0
D*                                              Length Watch Information
D ESCMID00          5     11
D*                                              Message ID
D ESCERVED01       12     12
D*                                              Reserved
D ESCMQN           13     22
D*                                              Message Queue Name
D ESCMQL           23     32
D*                                              Message Queue Lib
D ESCJN            33     42
D*                                              Job Name
D ESCUN            43     52
D*                                              User Name
```

Figure 10.1: A watch message format from QSYSINC/QRPGLESRC member ESCWCHT (part 1 of 3).

```
D ESCJNBR                    53      58
D*                                             Job Number
D ESCRSV2                    59      62
D*                                             Reserved2
D ESCSPGMN                   63     318
D*                                             Sending Program Name
D ESCSPGMM                  319     328
D*                                             Sending Program Module
D ESCOSP                    329     332B 0
D*                                             Offset Sending Procedure
D ESCLOSP                   333     336B 0
D*                                             Length Of Sending Proced
D ESCRPGMN                  337     346
D*                                             Receiving Program Name
D ESCRPGMM                  347     356
D*                                             Receiving Program Module
D ESCORP                    357     360B 0
D*                                             Offset Receiving Procedu
D ESCLORP                   361     364B 0
D*                                             Length Of Receiving Proc
D ESCMS                     365     368B 0
D*                                             Msg Severity
D ESCMT                     369     378
D*                                             Msg Type
D ESCMT00                   379     386
D*                                             Msg Timestamp
D ESCMK                     387     390
D*                                             Msg Key
D ESCMFILN                  391     400
D*                                             Msg File Name
D ESCMFILL                  401     410
D*                                             Msg File Library
D ESCRSV3                   411     412
D*                                             Reserved3
D ESCOCD01                  413     416B 0
D*                                             Offset Comparison Data
D ESCLOCD01                 417     420B 0
D*                                             Length Of Comparison Dat
D ESCCA                     421     430
D*                                             Compare Against
D ESCRSV4                   431     432
D*                                             Reserved4
D ESCCCSID                  433     436B 0
D*                                             Comparison Data CCSID
D ESCOCDF                   437     440B 0
D*                                             Offset Comparison Data F
```

Figure 10.1: A watch message format from QSYSINC/QRPGLESRC member ESCWCHT (part 2 of 3).

```
D ESCORD                    441    444B 0
D*                                             Offset Replacement Data
D ESCLORD                   445    448B 0
D*                                             Length Of Replacement Da
D ESCCCSID00                449    452B 0
D*                                             Replacement Data CCSID
D*ESCSP                     453    453
D*
D*                                             variable length data @B2M
D*ESCRP                     454    454
D*
D*                                             variable length data @B2M
D*ESCCD01                   455    455
D*
D*                                             variable length data @B2M
D*ESCRD                     456    456
D*
D*                                             variable length data @B2M
```

Figure 10.1: A watch message format from QSYSINC/QRPGLESRC member ESCWCHT (part 3 of 3).

As you can see, a wealth of information about the message is available to the exit program. This includes the message ID, the qualified message queue name, the name of the job sending the message, the program sending the message, the message severity, the message key, the replacement data associated with the message occurrence, and much more. (It should be pointed out that the exit program does not run in either the job sending the message or the job receiving the message—it runs in its own job.) With this amount of information, our exit program can be used in a variety of ways. One possible application is to automate various tasks on the system.

For example, when the history log of i5/OS becomes full, the messages are written to a database file. Message CPF2456 is then sent to the QSYSOPR message queue to inform the operator that the file is full and should be saved. Figure 10.2 shows a watch exit program that can automate the saving of new QHST files to save files.

Two specific fields within the QSYSINC-provided data structure ESCCQWFM are used in the example program. The first one, ESCMID00, contains the message ID that caused the watch program to be called. The other field, ESCORD, contains an offset to the replacement data associated with the message ESCMID00.

```
h dftactgrp(*no)

DName++++++++++++ETDsFrom+++To/L+++IDc.Keywords++++++++++++++++++++++++
d/copy qsysinc/qrpglesrc,escwcht

dFig10_2          pr
d Type                          10    const
d Session                       10    const
d Error                         10
d Data                                likeds(ESCQWFM)

dFig10_2          pi
d Type                          10    const
d Session                       10    const
d Error                         10
d Data                                likeds(ESCQWFM)

dCmdExc           pr                  extpgm('QCMDEXC')
d Command                    65535    const
d CmdLength                      15   5 const
d IGC                            3    const options(*nopass)

dMsgDtaPtr        s              *
dMsgDta           ds            75    based(MsgDtaPtr)
d File                   1      10
d Lib                   11      20

dCommand          s             80
dWait             s              1

CLON01Factor1+++++++Opcode&ExtFactor2+++++++Result+++++++++Len++D+HiLoEq
 /free
  Error = *blanks;  // assume all is well until shown otherwise

  // Check to make sure this is a *MSGID watch
  if (Type = '*MSGID');

     // Check to make sure this is for CPF2456
     if (Data.ESCMID00 = 'CPF2456');

        //  Get to the message replacement data
        MsgDtaPtr = %addr(Data) + Data.ESCORD;
```

Figure 10.2: Watch for the message CPF2456—"Log version &1 in &2 closed and should be saved" (part 1 of 2).

```
      // Save the log
      Command = 'SAVOBJ OBJ(' + File + ') LIB(' + Lib +
                        ') DEV(*SAVF) SAVF (QGPL/MYSAVES)';
      CmdExc( Command :%len(%trimr(Command)));

      // Not CPF2456
      else;
          dsply ('Unexpected ' + Data.ESCMID00 + ' received.') ' ' Wait;
          Error = '*ERROR';
      endif;

  // Not a *MSGID watch
  else;
      dsply ('Wrong type ' + %trimr(Type) + ' received.') ' ' Wait;
      Error = '*ERROR';
  endif;

  *inlr = *on;
  return;
  /end-free
```

Figure 10.2: Watch for the message CPF2456—"Log version &1 in &2 closed and should be saved"
(part 2 of 2).

After initializing the Error parameter to blanks (indicating the exit program has no errors and should continue to be called by i5/OS), the program checks to see if it is being called for a message watch (Type = '*MSGID'). If not, the appropriate error text is DSPLYed and the Error parameter is set to *ERROR so that the watch exit program is not called again. If Type is *MSGID, the program checks to see if it's being called for message ID CPF2456 (Data.ESCMID00 = 'CPF2456'). If not, appropriate error text is DSPLYed and the Error parameter is again set to *ERROR.

If both checks are successful, the program accesses the message-replacement data by setting the pointer MsgDtaPtr to the address of the Data parameter and adding to this address the offset to the replacement data (Data.ESCORD). It does this because message CPF2456 returns the file name and library name of the new QHST file in the first 20 bytes of the message replacement data, and we have plans for that information. We know how this replacement data is defined by displaying the message description CPF2456 in QCPFMSG and looking at the message-replacement variable usage and definitions. The data structure MsgDta defines the two fields, File and Lib, that map to the replacement data we are interested in. As MsgDta is BASED on MsgDtaPtr, the program now has direct access to these values.

The program then constructs a SAVOBJ command string, using the watched message replacement data (fields File and Lib) to set the OBJ and LIB parameters of the SAVOBJ command. The program also specifies that the save is to save file QGPL/MYSAVES. Note that we have made a simplifying assumption here, namely, that the save file is empty or previously cleared. In a production environment, you would probably want dynamic creation of the save file and the usage of appropriately named save files.

After the SAVOBJ command string has been generated, the program uses the Execute Command API, QCMDEXC (introduced in chapter 4) to run the command. The program then exits.

Starting a Watch

Having looked at the FIG10_2 program, let's now look at the Start Watch API, QSCSWCH. It is used to associate program FIG10_2 with the sending of message CPF2456 to the system operator message queue. The parameter descriptions for QSCSWCH are listed in Table 10.2.

Table 10.2: The Start Watch API (QSCSWCH)			
Parameter	Description	Type	Size
1	Session ID	Input	Char(10)
2	Started Session ID	Output	Char(10)
3	Watch Program	Input	Char(20)
4	Watch for Message	Input	Char(*)
5	Watch for LIC Log Entry	Input	Char(*)
6	Error Code	I/O	Char(*)

The first parameter, Session ID, allows you to name the watch. This name will be displayed on commands such as Work with Watches (WRKWCH), used on APIs such as End Watch (QSCEWCH), and passed to the watch exit program at run time. A meaningful name can help both operators and developers. If you don't care to name a watch session, you can use the special value *GEN, and the system will generate a watch-session ID name for you.

The second parameter, Started Session ID, is an output from the API that is used to return the name of the started session. This is primarily used as feedback from the API when *GEN is used for the first parameter.

The third parameter, Watch Program, is the qualified name of the exit program to be called when the watched-for message is sent to a watched message queue. As with most qualified names used in API calls, the first 10 bytes is the name of the program, and the second 10 bytes is the name of the library where the program is located. This program will be called once each time the watched-for message sent. If the watched-for message is sent to multiple message queues, the exit program will be called once for each occurrence of the message being sent to each of the watched message queues.

The fourth parameter, Watch for Message, is a structure that provides information to the system on what message(s) and queue(s) are to be watched. This structure starts with a Binary(4) field indicating how many messages are to be watched for. Immediately following this field is an array of variable-length sub-structures of the type shown in Figure 10.3. These sub-structures are where you define the messages to watch for.

The fifth, Watch for LIC Log Entry, is a structure that provides information to the system on what LIC log-entry identifiers are to be watched. The fifth parameter, Error Code, is the standard API error-code structure.

```
DName++++++++++++ETDsFrom+++To/L+++IDc.Keywords++++++++++++++++++++++++
D*********************************************************************
D*Format for message information
D*********************************************************************
DQSCWFMF          DS
D*                                                  Qsc Watch For Msg Fmt
D QSCLMI                 1      4B 0
D*                                                  Length Message Informati
D QSCMID                 5     11
D*                                                  Message ID
D QSCERVED              12     12
D*                                                  Reserved
D QSCMQN02              13     22
D*                                                  Message Queue Name
D QSCMQL                23     32
D*                                                  Message Queue Lib
D QSCJN                 33     42
D*                                                  Job Name
D QSCUN                 43     52
D*                                                  User Name
D QSCJNBR               53     58
D*                                                  Job Number
```

Figure 10.3: The format from QSYSINC/QRPGLESRC member QSCSWCH for starting a watch (part 1 of 2).

```
D QSCRSV2                 59      64
D*                                           Reserved2
D QSCOCD                  65      68B 0
D*                                           Offset Comparison Data
D QSCLOCD                 69      72B 0
D*                                           Length Of Comparison Dat
D QSCCA                   73      82
D*                                           Compare Against
D*QSCCD                   83      83
D*
D*                                      variable length data
```

Figure 10.3: The format from QSYSINC/QRPGLESRC member QSCSWCH for starting a watch (part 2 of 2).

There are several fields defined within the QSYSINC-provided QSCWFMF data structure. The first, QSCLMI, is set to the size of the current occurrence of the QSCWFMF data structure. This size then provides a displacement for the API to the next occurrence of the QSCWFMF data structure. The number of occurrences, or array elements, is controlled by the initial Binary(4) field provided at the start of the fourth parameter.

The QSCWFMF data structure shown in Figure 10.3 allows you to specify what message to watch for and what message queues to monitor for the watched message. Each structure can specify one message ID (QSCMID), and you can have up to 100 of these structures per call to the Start Watch API.

You can specify what queue to monitor for each message. The Message Queue Name field (QSCMQN02) can be a message queue name or a special value. The defined special values are *SYSOPR for the QSYSOPR message queue, *JOBLOG for watching the job log of one or more jobs, and *HSTLOG for the QHST message queue.

If you use the special value *JOBLOG for the message queue, you can also specify what jobs to watch. The Job Name Field (QSCJN) can be a specific name such as PLANT0001, a generic name such as PLANT*, or one of two special values. The special values are the single asterisk (*) for the current job, and *ALL for all jobs on the system. Similar to the Job Name field, the Job User Name (QSCUN) can be a specific name such as ROBERTS, a generic name such as ROB*, or the special value *ALL. The Job Number field (QSCJNBR) likewise supports a special value of *ALL.

You can also specify message-comparison data for each message. This allows you to filter which occurrences of a message actually cause the watch exit program to be called.

You might, for instance, only want the exit program called when a particular watched message is sent by program PGM01A, or when the message replacement data for a message contains a particular value (perhaps a specific object name). You can specify this comparison data by setting the fields QSCOCD, the offset to the comparison data, and QSCLOD, the length of the supplied comparison data, to appropriate values and then providing the comparison data at offset QSCOCD.

As you can see, this structure provides a lot of control over determining when you want your exit program to receive control. Figure 10.4 shows how to use the Start Watch API, QSCSWCH, to associate program FIG10_2 with message CPF2456 being sent to the system-operator message queue QSYSOPR.

```
h dftactgrp(*no)

DName+++++++++++ETDsFrom+++To/L+++IDc.Keywords+++++++++++++++++++++++
d/copy qsysinc/qrpglesrc,qscswch
d/copy qsysinc/qrpglesrc,qusec

dStartWatch      pr                    extpgm('QSCSWCH')
d SessionID                   10       const
d StrSsnID                    10
d WatchPgm                    20       const
d Messages                 65535       const options(*varsize)
d LICs                     65535       const options(*varsize)
d QUSEC                              likeds(QUSEC)

dWatchPgm        ds
d Pgm                         10       inz('FIG10_2')
d Lib                         10       inz('*CURLIB')

dMessages        ds                    qualified
d NbrMsgs                    10i 0
d MsgFormat                          likeds(QSCWFMF)

dLICs            ds                    qualified
d NbrLICs                    10i 0

dStrSsnID        s            10
```

Figure 10.4: Start a watch for message CPF2456—"Log version &1 in &2 closed and should be saved" (part 1 of 2).

```
CLON01Factor1+++++++Opcode&ExtFactor2+++++++Result++++++++Len++D+HiLoEp
/free
  QUSBPRV = 0;

  // Watch for CPF2456 in the QSYSOPR message queue
  Messages.NbrMsgs = 1;
  Messages.MsgFormat = *loval;
  Messages.MsgFormat.QSCLMI = %size(Messages.MsgFormat);
  Messages.MsgFormat.QSCMID = 'CPF2456';
  Messages.MsgFormat.QSCMQNO2 = '*SYSOPR';
  Messages.MsgFormat.QSCJN = *blanks;
  Messages.MsgFormat.QSCUN = *blanks;
  Messages.MsgFormat.QSCJNBR = *blanks;
  Messages.MsgFormat.QSCCA = *blanks;

  // No LIC logs are being watched for
  LICs.NbrLICs = 0;

  StartWatch('QHSTSAVES' :StrSsnID :WatchPgm :Messages :LICs :QUSEC);

  *inlr = *on;
  return;
/end-free
```

Figure 10.4: Start a watch for message CPF2456—"Log version &1 in &2 closed and should be saved" (part 2 of 2).

Figure 10.4 defines a data structure, Messages, that has two sub-elements. The first is a Binary(4) field for the number of messages to be watched, NbrMsgs, and then one occurrence, MsgFormat, of the QSCWFMF structure defined in Figure 10.3.

After initializing the Error Code Bytes Provided field, QUSBPRV, to zero to indicate we want exceptions returned as messages, the program sets Messages.NbrMsgs to one and initializes the Messages.MsgFormat sub-structure. Messages.MsgFormat is first set to all null values (x'00'), as there are reserved fields within the structure. Then, specific subfields are set to their appropriate values. The length of the message information, Messages.MsgFormat.QSCLMI, is set to the size of Messages.MsgFormat, the message ID is set to CPF2456, the message queue is set to the special value *QSYSOPR, the full watched job name is set to blanks, and the Compare Against field is also set to blanks. The program then initializes the number of LIC log entries to watch, LICs.NbrLICs, to zero, as we're not interested in LIC log entries.

After this setup is complete, FIG10_4 calls the Start Watch API with a session ID name of QHSTSAVES, and ends. The watch is now active and, in this scenario, we have now automated the saving of QHST history files.

To end the watch session, use the Work with Watches command, WRKWCH WCH(*STRWCH). Select option 2, End, with the QHSTSAVES session.

Sending Program Messages

Applications often need to send messages to end users informing them of what is going on. This is especially true if the application is performing a long-running task. For this reason, i5/OS has the concept of status messages. Status messages typically show up at the bottom of the screen while a function is running, and then disappear. You will now learn how to send a status message from your application program.

Let's start by creating a message file named MSGS in the SOMELIB library. A user message file is not actually required to send messages, but using message files and message descriptions is a better way to write applications than using text embedded within an application. If you've ever been involved with an application program that needs to support translations into multiple national languages, you'll know this all too well! Using message files is the better way to write an application, so that's how we'll build this example. Figure 10.5 shows the command to create the message file and add the message description MSG0001 to the MSGS message file.

```
CRTMSGF MSGF(SOMELIB/MSGS)

ADDMSGD MSGID(MSG0001) MSGF(SOMELIB/MSGS) MSG('Job is doing some work.
Please be patient')
```

Figure 10.5: Create the message file SOMELIB/MSGS.

To send this message to the user, you use the Send Program Message API, QMHSNDPM. The parameter descriptions for this API are shown in Table 10.3. The full documentation for the API can be found in the "Message Handling" category of System APIs.

Do not be dismayed by the number of parameters and the references to call stack entries. In general, using this API is straightforward enough, but there is a lot of flexibility built into it for those who need direct control when sending messages from one program to another.

	Table 10.3: The Send Program Message API (QMHSNDPM)			
Parameter	**Description**	**Type**	**Size**
1	Message Identifier	Input	Char(7)
2	Qualified Message File Name	Input	Char(20)
3	Message Data or Immediate Text	Input	Char(*)
4	Length of Message Data or Immediate Text	Input	Binary(4)
5	Message Type	Input	Char(10)
6	Call Stack Entry	Input	Char(*) or Pointer
7	Call Stack Counter	Input	Binary(4)
8	Message Key	Output	Char(4)
9	Error Code	I/O	Char(*)
Optional Parameter Group 1			
10	Length of Call Stack Entry	Input	Binary(4)
11	Call Stack Entry Qualification	Input	Char(20)
12	Display Program Messages Screen Wait Time	Input	Binary(4)
Optional Parameter Group 2			
13	Call Stack Entry Data Type	Input	Char(10)
14	Coded Character Set Identifier	Input	Binary(4)

The first parameter, Message Identifier, identifies what message you want to send. A message ID must be provided if you are sending an escape, notify, or status message. If you are sending an impromptu message, also known as *immediate text*, you can use blanks for this parameter.

The second parameter, Qualified Message File Name, specifies what message file is to be used to locate the message identifier passed in the first parameter. As with any API qualified name, the first 10 bytes are the message file name, and the second 10 bytes are the library where the message file can be found. The special values *CURLIB and *LIBL can be used for the library portion of this parameter.

The third parameter, Message Data or Immediate Text, can contain the message replacement data to be used with a predefined message's substitution variables (if a message ID was used for the first parameter), or the immediate text that is to be sent (if the first parameter was set to blanks).

The fourth parameter, Length of Message Data or Immediate Text, is the length of the data provided in the third parameter.

The fifth parameter, Message Type, specifies what type of message is being sent. The supported types are as follows:

- *CMD—Command
- *COMP—Completion
- *DIAG—Diagnostic
- *ESCAPE—Escape
- *INFO—Informational
- *INQ—Inquiry
- *NOTIFY—Notify
- *RQS—Request
- *STATUS—Status

For a complete definition of these types (and other types not supported by this API) see the Information Center.

The sixth parameter, Call Stack Entry, provides a reference point to an active program or procedure within your job that you want to send the message to. Special values include an asterisk (*) for the current call stack entry (that is, yourself) and *EXT for the external message queue of the job. There are several other special values for this parameter, but these two will suffice for our discussion of this API.

The seventh parameter, Call Stack Counter, provides the location within your job's call stack where the message should be sent. If a value of zero is used, the message is sent to the call stack entry identified with the sixth parameter. If a value of one is used, the message is sent to Call Stack Entry 1 before the call stack entry identified with the sixth parameter. If a value of two is used, the message is sent to Call Stack Entry 2 before the call stack entry identified with the sixth parameter, and so on. If the sixth parameter is set to the special value *EXT, this parameter is ignored.

The eighth parameter, Message Key, is an output parameter. It can be used with other APIs to reference the message you are sending. The ninth parameter is the standard error-code structure found with many APIs. The remaining parameters are not used by any of the examples in this chapter, and so they are not discussed here. See the Information Center API documentation if you are interested in learning about these optional parameters.

The program to actually send the message MSG0001 created in Figure 10.5 is shown in Figure 10.6. As you can see, the program initializes the Error Code Bytes Available field, QUSBPRV, to zero, and then calls the Send Program Message API. On the call, we specify that we want message MSG0001, from the message file MSGS in SOMELIB (QualMsgF), sent as a *STATUS message to the external (*EXT) message queue associated with the job.

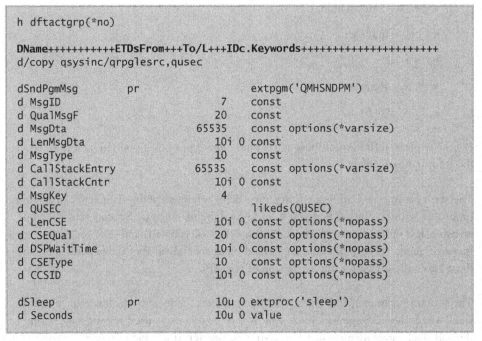

```
h dftactgrp(*no)

DName++++++++++ETDsFrom+++To/L+++IDc.Keywords+++++++++++++++++++++++
d/copy qsysinc/qrpglesrc,qusec

dSndPgmMsg          pr                     extpgm('QMHSNDPM')
d MsgID                          7         const
d QualMsgF                      20         const
d MsgDta                     65535         const options(*varsize)
d LenMsgDta                    10i 0 const
d MsgType                      10         const
d CallStackEntry            65535         const options(*varsize)
d CallStackCntr                10i 0 const
d MsgKey                        4
d QUSEC                                   likeds(QUSEC)
d LenCSE                       10i 0 const options(*nopass)
d CSEQual                      20         const options(*nopass)
d DSPWaitTime                  10i 0 const options(*nopass)
d CSEType                      10         const options(*nopass)
d CCSID                        10i 0 const options(*nopass)

dSleep              pr         10u 0 extproc('sleep')
d Seconds                      10u 0 value
```

Figure 10.6: Display a status message (part 1 of 2).

```
dQualMsgF          ds
d MsgF                        10    inz('MSGS')
d MsgL                        10    inz('SOMELIB')

dMsgKey            s           4

CLON01Factor1++++++Opcode&ExtFactor2+++++++Result++++++++Len++D+HiLoEq
 /free
   QUSBPRV = 0;
   SndPgmMsg( 'MSG0001' :QualMsgF :' ' :0 :'*STATUS' :'*EXT' :0
            :MsgKey :QUSEC);
   Sleep(10);
   *inlr = *on;
   return;
 /end-free
```

Figure 10.6: Display a status message (part 2 of 2).

If that was all the program did, you would most likely never see the message. It would be shown and removed so quickly that you would have a difficult time even knowing it was there. To make sure you can see the message, we use the sleep API to cause the program to delay 10 seconds before ending. In a production environment, the program would presumably be off doing database I/O, heavy computations, or some such. But as we didn't have anything like that to do in FIG10_6, we elected just to let the program sleep.

The sleep API documentation can be found in the Information Center in the System API category "Unix-Type APIs," and then subcategory "Signal APIs." The parameter description for sleep is shown in Figure 10.7.

```
unsigned int sleep (unsigned int seconds)
```

Figure 10.7: The sleep API.

The sleep API

The sleep API suspends a job, or more technically correct a thread, for a specified number of seconds. The job consumes no CPU while sleeping; it's just delayed for the number of seconds you specify. There are related APIs that can cause the requested sleep period to be shorter than specified. These are also described in the documentation for the "Signal APIs" subcategory. In FIG10_6, we expect to sleep for the full specified time period. You could, though, write an application where you want to sleep for X seconds, but be awakened if work becomes available for you to process before X seconds have passed.

339

The sleep API accepts one parameter, Seconds, which is defined as an unsigned integer (10u 0). The Seconds parameter specifies the number of seconds the job should be suspended. The sleep API defines a return value that is also an unsigned integer value. If the return value is zero, sleep suspended the job for the full requested period of time. If the return value is a positive value, it represents the number of seconds remaining of the requested period of time. That is, if you asked for 10 seconds but were awakened after seven seconds, the return value would be three. If the return value is negative one, an error was encountered, and ERRNO should be examined to gather additional information. (Access to ERRNO is described in chapter 14.) In program FIG10_6, we simply ignore the return value of the sleep API.

Sending Program Messages with Replacement Data

To add a bit more to FIG10_6, and to make more realistic use of a status message, let's now send a message with replacement data. The replacement data will be a variable indicating to the user an estimated time to completion. For the sake of good form, we'll also send a completion messages when the program is done. The new messages are shown in Figure 10.8.

```
ADDMSGD MSGID(MSG0002) MSGF(SOMELIB/MSGS) MSG('Job is doing some work.
Remaining time is &1 seconds.') FMT((*BIN 4))

ADDMSGD MSGID(MSG0003) MSGF(SOMELIB/MSGS) MSG('Job has completed.')
```

Figure 10.8: Create two more messages.

Message MSG0002 is defined as having one replacement variable (&1). The variable &1 is further defined as being a 4-byte binary value. Figure 10.9 shows the modified FIG10_6, which sends status messages reflecting the current state of the program and a completion message when finished.

```
h dftactgrp(*no)

DName++++++++++ETDsFrom+++To/L+++IDc.Keywords++++++++++++++++++++++++++
d/copy qsysinc/qrpglesrc,qusec

dSndPgmMsg        pr                    extpgm('QMHSNDPM')
d MsgID                        7        const
```

Figure 10.9: Display a status message with replacement data along with a completion message (part 1 of 2).

```
d QualMsgF                      20      const
d MsgDta                     65535      const options(*varsize)
d LenMsgDta                    10i 0    const
d MsgType                      10       const
d CallStackEntry            65535       const options(*varsize)
d CallStackCntr                10i 0    const
d MsgKey                        4
d QUSEC                                 likeds(QUSEC)
d LenCSE                       10i 0    const options(*nopass)
d CSEQual                      20       const options(*nopass)
d DSPWaitTime                  10i 0    const options(*nopass)
d CSEType                      10       const options(*nopass)
d CCSID                        10i 0    const options(*nopass)

dSleep            pr           10u 0    extproc('sleep')
d Seconds                      10u 0    value

dQualMsgF         ds
d MsgF                         10       inz('MSGS')
d MsgL                         10       inz('SOMELIB')

dMsgTxt           ds
d Seconds                      10i 0

dMsgKey           s             4

CLON01Factor1+++++++Opcode&ExtFactor2+++++++Result++++++++Len++D+HiLoEq
 /free
   QUSBPRV = 0;
   Seconds = 10;
   SndPgmMsg( 'MSG0002' :QualMsgF :MsgTxt :%size(MsgTxt)
             :'*STATUS' :'*EXT' :0 :MsgKey :QUSEC);
   Sleep(5);
   Seconds = 5;
   SndPgmMsg( 'MSG0002' :QualMsgF :MsgTxt :%size(MsgTxt)
             :'*STATUS' :'*EXT' :0 :MsgKey :QUSEC);
   Sleep(5);
   SndPgmMsg( 'MSG0003' :QualMsgF :' ' :0 :'*COMP' :'*EXT' :0
             :MsgKey :QUSEC);
   *inlr = *on;
   return;
 /end-free
```

Figure 10.9: Display a status message with replacement data along with a completion message (part 2 of 2).

341

FIG10_9 defines the data structure MsgTxt to hold the message replacement data for message MSG0002. This data structure has one sub-element, Seconds, which is defined as a 4-byte integer (10i 0). Seconds reflects the amount of time remaining for FIG10_9 to continue running. MsgTxt is then passed as the third parameter, along with the size of MsgTxt as the fourth parameter, on the first two calls to the Send Program Message API. The first two calls use message MSG0002 as a status message indicating the amount of time remaining until the task finishes. At the end of the program, FIG10_9 sends the completion message MSG0003.

Using Retrieve Message to Read Message Descriptions

Many applications have hundreds, if not thousands, of message descriptions stored in message files. The next sample program will show you how to read these message descriptions and process them within your application program. Specifically, the sample program will scan all messages in a specified message file, looking to see if a given word is found in either the first level or second level text of the message. If found, the program will print the message ID. Many more types of applications are possible with this technique—merging message descriptions across message files, printing all messages within a given range, etc.—but the prerequisite for any of these types of applications is the ability to read a message file. You will see that by using the Retrieve Message API (QMHRTVM), this is fairly straightforward.

Table 10.4 shows the parameters for the Retrieve Message API. Although it has quite a few parameters, the API itself is just like any other retrieve API.

The first parameter is the receiver variable where the Retrieve Message API returns data to the API caller. The second parameter is the size of the receiver variable, and the third parameter is the format you want used in returning the data.

The Retrieve Message API supports four formats. Formats RTVM0100 and RTVM0200 are primarily used when you are reading a specific message description and you know in advance the ID of the message you want. Formats RTVM0300 and RTVM0400 can be used for either keyed access by the message ID (similar to how RTVM0100 and RTVM0200 are used) or when sequentially reading through the message file. We will be sequentially reading all messages in the message file, so we will use the RTVM0300 format. This format returns all of the information necessary to the application. Format RTVM0400 also returns all of the necessary information, but it also returns additional information that we

Table 10.4: The Send Program Message API (QMHSNDPM)			
Parameter	Description	Type	Size
1	Message Information	Output	Char(*)
2	Length of Message Information	Input	Binary(4)
3	Format Name	Input	Char(8)
4	Message ID	Input	Char(7)
5	Qualified Message File Name	Input	Char(20)
6	Replacement Data	Input	Char(*)
7	Length of Replacement Data	Input	Binary(4)
8	Replace Substitution Values	Input	Char(10)
9	Return Format Control Characters	Input	Char(10)
10	Error Code	I/O	Char(*)
Optional Parameter Group 1			
11	Retrieve Option	Input	Char(10)
12	CCSID to Convert to	Input	Binary(4)
13	CCSID of Replacement Data	Input	Binary(4)

don't need. To get the best performance, select the format that provides the least amount of unnecessary information. Figure 10.10 shows the QSYSINC definition for format RTVM0300.

The fourth parameter is the message identifier for the message description we want returned. The fifth parameter is the qualified message file name.

The sixth parameter is the replacement data for the message. When retrieving the message description, you can optionally provide the replacement data for the substitution variables defined in the message. The values passed in this parameter would be used in the same way that the third parameter of the Send Program Message API was used when sending status messages in FIG10_9, and the values will be merged into the message text returned in the receiver variable. The seventh parameter is the length of the replacement data in the sixth parameter.

The eighth parameter allows you to control whether or not the substitution variables defined in the message are replaced by the replacement data provided in the sixth parameter. A *NO indicates that you want the substitution variables (the literals &1, &2, &3, etc.) returned. A *YES indicates that you want the substitution variables replaced by the replacement data provided in the sixth parameter.

The ninth parameter allows you to specify whether or not format-control characters (such as &N and &P) are returned in the message second level text. A *NO indicates you do not want the format control characters returned, a *YES indicates you do.

The tenth parameter is the standard error-code structure.

The eleventh parameter, Retrieve Option, is what allows us to sequentially read through a message file. Three special values can be used. The first, *MSGID, indicates that we want the API to return the message description associated with the message ID passed in the fourth parameter. This value is not going to help us initially in our current task, as we don't know the message IDs. The second special value, *NEXT, indicates that we want the API to return the message description associated with the next message following the message ID passed in the fourth parameter. This special value is closer to what we're looking for. All we need now is to be able to identify the first message ID within the message file, and then we can use *NEXT to read through the rest of the file. The third special value, *FIRST, retrieves the first message in the message file and ignores the fourth parameter. With this, we now have the necessary retrieval options to read all message descriptions stored in any message file!

The remaining two parameters are related to CCSID conversions of the message text and CCSID processing of the replacement data. These are important functions, but they're not something we need to be concerned with for our sample program.

```
DName++++++++++ETDsFrom+++To/L+++IDc.Keywords+++++++++++++++++++++++++
D*******************************************************************
D*Type Definition for the RTVM0300 format.
D****                                                          ***
D*NOTE: The following type definition only defines the fixed
D*   portion of the format. Any varying length field will
D*   have to be defined by the user.
D*******************************************************************
```

Figure 10.10: Format RTVM0300 from QSYSINC/QRPGLESRC member QMHRTVM (part 1 of 3).

```
DQMHM030000          DS
D*                                          Qmh Rtvm RTVM0300
D QMHBR03             1      4B 0
D*                                          Bytes Return
D QMHBAVL09           5      8B 0
D*                                          Bytes Available
D QMHMS09             9     12B 0
D*                                          Message Severity
D QMHAI00            13     16B 0
D*                                          Alert Index
D QMHAO03            17     25
D*                                          Alert Option
D QMHLI02            26     26
D*                                          Log Indicator
D QMHMID             27     33
D*                                          Message ID
D QMHERVED19         34     36
D*                                          Reserved
D QMHNRDF            37     40B 0
D*                                          Number Replace Data
D QMHSIDCS07         41     44B 0
D*                                          Text CCSID Convert
D QMHSIDCS08         45     48B 0
D*                                          Data CCSID Convert
D QMHCSIDR07         49     52B 0
D*                                          Text CCSID Returned
D QMHORT             53     56B 0
D*                                          Offset Reply Text
D QMHLRRTN00         57     60B 0
D*                                          Length Reply Return
D QMHLRAVL00         61     64B 0
D*                                          Length Reply Availa
D QMHOMRTN           65     68B 0
D*                                          Offset Message Retu
D QMHLMRTN04         69     72B 0
D*                                          Length Message Retu
D QMHLMAVL04         73     76B 0
D*                                          Length Message Avai
D QMHOHRTN           77     80B 0
D*                                          Offset Help Returne
D QMHLHRTN04         81     84B 0
D*                                          Length Help Returne
D QMHLHAVL04         85     88B 0
D*                                          Length Help Availab
D QMHOF              89     92B 0
D*                                          Offset Formats
```

Figure 10.10: Format RTVM0300 from QSYSINC/QRPGLESRC member QMHRTVM (part 2 of 3).

```
D QMHLFRTN                    93      96B 0
D*                                                  Length Formats Retu
D QMHLFAVL                    97     100B 0
D*                                                  Length Formats Avai
D QMHLFE                     101     104B 0
D*                                                  Length Format Eleme
D*QMHRSV203                  105     105
D*
D*                                          Varying length
D*QMHDR00                    106     106
D*
D*                                          Varying length
D*QMHSSAGE04                 107     107
D*
D*                                          Varying length
D*QMHMH04                    108     108
D*
D*                                          Varying length
D*QMHRDF                             18      DIM(00001)
D* QMHLSRD00                         9B 0  OVERLAY(QMHRDF:00001)
D* QMHFSODP00                        9B 0  OVERLAY(QMHRDF:00005)
D* QMHSVT00                          10     OVERLAY(QMHRDF:00009)
D*
D*
D*                                          Varying length
```

Figure 10.10: Format RTVM0300 from QSYSINC/QRPGLESRC member QMHRTVM (part 3 of 3).

Format RTVM0300 returns quite a bit of information related to a message description. We're specifically interested in the following fields:

- The message ID, to identify the message containing the searched-for word

- The first-level message text, so it can be scanned for the searched-for word

- The second-level text, so it can be scanned for the searched-for word

In scanning the fields of the QSYSINC-provided QMHM030000 data structure, we quickly find that the message ID is returned in field QMHMID. However, the first- and second-level text fields for a message do not appear to be returned at a fixed location or with a fixed length. Given the variable-length nature of these fields, this makes sense. Instead, we find that the API returns an offset to the first level text, QMHOMRTN, the length of the first level text, QMHLMRTN04, an offset to the second level text, QMHOHRTN, and the length of the second level text, QMHLHRTN04. With this, we have everything we need.

Figure 10.11 shows how this information is used to scan for a given word within the first- and second-level text. Program FIG10_11 accepts one parameter, Word. This parameter is the word that the program will scan for in the retrieved message's first- and second-level text.

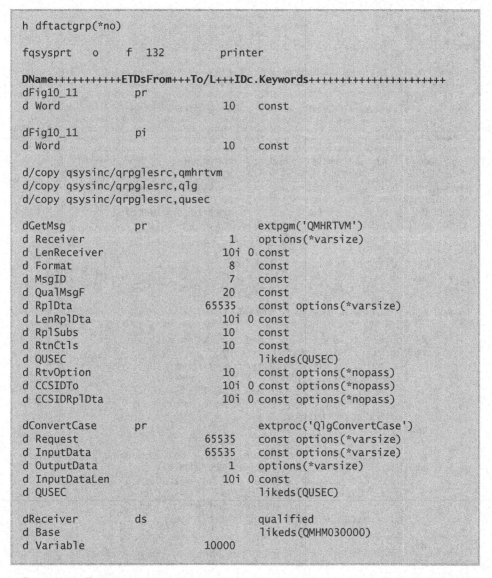

```
h dftactgrp(*no)

fqsysprt   o   f  132         printer

DName+++++++++++ETDsFrom+++To/L+++IDc.Keywords++++++++++++++++++++++
dFig10_11          pr
d Word                        10   const

dFig10_11          pi
d Word                        10   const

d/copy qsysinc/qrpglesrc,qmhrtvm
d/copy qsysinc/qrpglesrc,qlg
d/copy qsysinc/qrpglesrc,qusec

dGetMsg            pr                    extpgm('QMHRTVM')
d Receiver                      1        options(*varsize)
d LenReceiver                  10i 0 const
d Format                        8        const
d MsgID                         7        const
d QualMsgF                     20        const
d RplDta                    65535        const options(*varsize)
d LenRplDta                   10i 0 const
d RplSubs                      10        const
d RtnCtls                      10        const
d QUSEC                                  likeds(QUSEC)
d RtvOption                    10        const options(*nopass)
d CCSIDTo                      10i 0 const options(*nopass)
d CCSIDRplDta                  10i 0 const options(*nopass)

dConvertCase       pr                    extproc('QlgConvertCase')
d Request                   65535        const options(*varsize)
d InputData                 65535        const options(*varsize)
d OutputData                    1        options(*varsize)
d InputDataLen                10i 0 const
d QUSEC                                  likeds(QUSEC)

dReceiver          ds                    qualified
d Base                                   likeds(QMHM030000)
d Variable                  10000
```

Figure 10.11: Find all messages using a particular word, and print the message ID (part 1 of 3).

```
dMsgTxt           s             132    based(MsgTxtPtr)
dHlpTxt           s            3000    based(HlpTxtPtr)
dNewMsgTxt        s             132
dNewHlpTxt        s            3000
dQualMsgF         s              20    inz('QCPFMSG   QSYS        ')
dNewWord          s              10
dMsgID            s               7
dHit              s             10u 0
dwait             s               1

CLON01Factor1+++++++Opcode&ExtFactor2+++++++Result++++++++Len++D+HiLoEq
 /free
   if %parms = 0;
      dsply 'Required word parameter not passed' ' ' wait;
   else;
   QUSBPRV = 0;

   // Convert the parameter value to uppercase
   QLGIDRCB00 = *loval;            // set input structure to x'00'
   QLGTOR02 = 1;                   // use CCSID for monocasing
   QLGIDOID00 = 0;                 // use the job CCSID
   QLGCR00 = 0;                    // convert to uppercase
   ConvertCase( QLGIDRCB00 :Word :NewWord
                :%len(%trimr(Word)) :QUSEC);

   // Get the first message in QualMsgF
   GetMsg( Receiver :%size(Receiver) :'RTVM0300' :' ' :QualMsgF
           :' ' :0 :'*NO' :'*NO' :QUSEC :'*FIRST' :0 :0);

   dow (Receiver.Base.QMHMID <> *blanks);

       // Convert to uppercase the first level message text
       if (Receiver.Base.QMHLMRTN04 > 0);
          MsgTxtPtr = %addr(Receiver) + Receiver.Base.QMHOMRTN;
          ConvertCase( QLGIDRCB00 :MsgTxt :NewMsgTxt
                       :Receiver.Base.QMHLMRTN04 :QUSEC);
          Hit = %scan(%trim(NewWord) :NewMsgTxt);
          NewMsgTxt = *blanks;
       endif;

       // if not found in first level text, look at second level text
       if (Hit = 0) and Receiver.Base.QMHLHRTN04 > 0;
          HlpTxtPtr = %addr(Receiver) + Receiver.Base.QMHOHRTN;
          ConvertCase( QLGIDRCB00 :HlpTxt :NewHlpTxt
                       :Receiver.Base.QMHLHRTN04 :QUSEC);
          Hit = %scan(%trim(NewWord) :NewHlpTxt);
          NewHlpTxt = *blanks;
       endif;
```

Figure 10.11: Find all messages using a particular word, and print the message ID (part 2 of 3).

```
       if (Hit <> 0);
           MsgID = Receiver.Base.QMHMID;
           except GotOne;
           Hit = 0;
       endif;

       // Get the next message
       GetMsg( Receiver :%size(Receiver) :'RTVM0300'
               :Receiver.Base.QMHMID :QualMsgF :' ' :0 :'*NO' :'*NO'
               :QUSEC :'*NEXT' :0 :0);
    enddo;
    endif;

    *inlr = *on;
    return;
   /end-free

oqsysprt    e              GotOne
o                          MsgID                     10
```

Figure 10.11: Find all messages using a particular word, and print the message ID (part 3 of 3).

Program FIG10_11 first tests to see if the Word parameter was passed. If not, it DSPLYs appropriate error text. If a parameter was passed, the program initializes the Bytes Provided field of the error-code structure to zero to indicate that errors should be returned as exception messages to the program. The program then uses the Convert Case API, QlgConvertCase, to convert the variable Word to uppercase and store the results in variable NewWord. (The Convert Case API was discussed in chapter 9.)

The program then calls the Retrieve Message API, QMHRTVM, requesting that the *FIRST message in message file QualMsgF (QCPFMSG in QSYS) be returned in the receiver variable, using format RTVM0300. The receiver variable is defined as being LIKEDS(QMHM030000), which is the QSYSINC include for format RTVM0300, followed by 10,000 bytes for the variable data that might be returned by the API. This variable data will include the first-level text, the second-level text, the substitution variable formats, and more. Based on the current maximums for these fields, we feel that 10,000 bytes would be sufficient. (If you really wanted to be sure you had sufficient storage, you could enhance this program by using the dynamic receiver variable approach introduced in chapter 2.)

After the message has been retrieved, the program falls into a do-while (DOW) loop that is exited when the returned messaged ID, Receiver.Base.QMHMID, is all blanks. When using the special values *FIRST or *NEXT for the Retrieve Options parameter, a blank message ID field indicates that the end of the message file has been encountered.

If a message description was returned, and first-level text exists for the message (Receiver.Base.QMHLMRTN04 > 0), then the first-level text is accessed by setting the pointer MsgTxtPtr to the address of the Receiver variable (%addr(Receiver)), plus the offset to the message text value (QMHOMRTN). As MsgTxtPtr is defined as the BASED pointer for the MsgTxt field, the program now has direct access to the first-level text of the message. The first-level text, MsgTxt, is now converted to uppercase by the QlgConvertCase API. The uppercased results are stored in the work field NewMsgTxt.

FIG10_11 then scans the uppercased NewMsgTxt field for occurrences of the uppercased value stored in the NewWord field. If that value is found in NewMsgTxt, the field Hit is set to a positive value. Technically, this positive value is the first position in NewMsgTxt where the value was found, but we really don't care about the position (in this application, anyway). All we are interested in is whether the value is found or not. If Hit is zero, the value was not found in NewMsgTxt. The program sets NewMsgTxt to blanks after the %scan to make sure there are no trailing characters remaining in NewMsgTxt when a subsequent call to the Retrieve Message API has a message with shorter first-level text than the current message. If the value is not found in NewMsgTxt (Hit = 0), the same process is applied to the second-level text. If the word *is* found in either the first- or second-level text (Hit <> 0), the message ID is written to the QSYSPRT printer file.

Whether the word is found or not, the program next calls the Retrieve Message API asking for the *NEXT message description following the current message ID (Receiver.Base.QMHMID is being passed as the fourth parameter of the API call). It then continues the DOW loop. When all messages have been processed, the program ends.

Summary

This chapter provides some tools and examples for using message-handling APIs to watch for a message, send a message, and read message descriptions from a message file. However, there are many more APIs that deal with handling messages. This chapter barely scratches the surface of all that is available. Be sure to explore the message APIs on your own.

Check Your Knowledge

Earlier in this chapter, you saw how to send status and completion messages. Add two new messages to the SOMELIB/MSGS message file. The first message is message description MSG0006, with a first-level text of "I found a problem with my input." The second message is MSG0007 with a first-level text of "This problem has caused me to stop running."

Write a program that sends message MSG0006 as a diagnostic message to your program's caller. This diagnostic message should be followed by message MSG0007 as an escape message to your caller. To get you started, your program's caller is one call stack entry above your program boundary in the call stack.

One possible solution to this task can be found in Figure D.10.B of appendix D.

11

Cryptographic Services APIs

Cryptography is the science of keeping data secure. With cryptography, you can store information in a database so that even authorized users cannot understand the data without going through an application program of your design. Cryptography also allows you to communicate with others, for instance over the Internet, so that any third party viewing the data exchange is unable to understand the data. Another aspect of cryptography is in the area of *data integrity*, which is the ability to verify that the data stored or exchanged has not been modified or altered.

Cryptographic operations, once thought to be of interest only for top-secret government projects, are today of great interest to businesses of all sizes. Cryptographic operations include activities such as the encryption and decryption of data to ensure that data can only be read by the users for whom it's intended, and hashing to validate that information has not been altered since the hash was created.

i5/OS supports cryptographic operations in many areas. Field-level encryption and decryption capabilities are available with the i5/OS DB2 database when using SQL. Session-level encryption and decryption capabilities are available with Secure Sockets Layer (SSL), which can be used in conjunction with applications such as File Transfer Protocol (FTP) and the Telnet server. There is also an entire category of System APIs to give applications direct access to cryptographic operations.

You can spend a lifetime mastering cryptography. In this chapter, we do not even attempt to go over the pros and cons of various cryptographic algorithms, and we most certainly will not look at any of the theory behind these algorithms! What we will do is introduce some of the cryptographic operations that you can incorporate into your applications.

In this chapter, we first look at the encryption and decryption APIs available. We start by encrypting the data found in the records of the CUSTOMER file, created in chapter 4. We then decrypt the records to make them once again understandable.

Following that, we look at APIs related to cryptographic key management. When working with encrypted data, one of the most difficult tasks is managing the keys used to encrypt the data. Applications need access to the keys to encrypt and decrypt the data, but you don't want these keys to be accessed or modified without proper controls. Using the key-management APIs, you will see how to effectively manage cryptographic keys.

The documentation for these APIs can be found in the Information Center under the API category "Cryptographic Services."

Encrypting Data

Before we start looking at the encryption and decryption APIs, it is important to point out that you should read all of this chapter before incorporating cryptographic operations into your applications. This section is intended to introduce the APIs that are used for encryption and decryption. In order to not initially overwhelm you with a large number of APIs, these first sample programs make a very simplifying assumption about how a cryptographic key is used—namely, that the key used for encryption and decryption is actually stored, unencrypted, as a variable within the sample program. You will not want to take this approach when actually working with confidential data.

Having the key value as a variable within the program gives application programmers access to the key value. Users authorized to debug the application program with commands such as STRDBG would also have access to the key value, as would service personnel authorized to use commands such as DMPJOB. Once the key value is known, the data is no longer secure. The section "Using Key-Management APIs" later in this chapter goes over APIs that you use to avoid this exposure. Do not skip this section!

With this warning out of the way, let's look at the Encryption API, Qc3EncryptData. The parameters for Qc3EncryptData are shown in Table 11.1.

Table 11.1: The Encrypt Data API (Qc3EncryptData)			
Parameter	Description	Type	Size
1	Clear Data	Input	Char(*)
2	Length of Clear Data	Input	Binary(4)
3	Format of Clear Data	Input	Char(8)
4	Algorithm Description	Input	Char(*)
5	Format of Algorithm Description	Input	Char(8)
6	Key Description	Input	Char(*)
7	Format of Key Description	Input	Char(8)
8	Cryptographic Service Provider	Input	Char(1)
9	Cryptographic Device Name	Input	Char(10)
10	Encrypted Data	Output	Char(*)
11	Length of Area Provided for Encrypted Data	Input	Binary(4)
12	Length of Encrypted Data Returned	Output	Binary(4)
13	Error Code	I/O	Char(*)

The first parameter, Clear Data, is the data to be encrypted. This data can be of any type—Character, Binary, Packed Decimal, Zoned Decimal, Floating Point, Image—it makes no difference to the Qc3EncryptData API. In our example, we encrypt CUSTNAME from the CUSTOMER file, but in a production application, it could be a data structure, an entire record format, or some other data that is encrypted.

The second parameter, Length of Clear Data, is used in two different ways depending on the format of the clear data, which is specified by the third parameter. When using format DATA0100, this value is the length of the data provided in the first parameter (in bytes except for CFB 1-bit, where the length is given in bits). When using format DATA0200, this value is the number of array elements.

The third parameter, Format of Clear Data, defines the content of the first parameter. Two formats are supported. The first, DATA0100, indicates that the first parameter is simply the raw data to be encrypted. This is the format used in the sample programs. The other format, DATA0200, indicates that the first parameter is an array of pointers and lengths. Each pointer addresses the data to be encrypted. The associated length defines the number of bytes to encrypt at that address. This format is useful when converting large amounts of noncontiguous data in one API call.

The fourth parameter, Algorithm Description, defines what algorithm and algorithm options are to be used when encrypting the data.

The fifth parameter, Format of Algorithm Description, defines the contents of the fourth parameter. Several possible formats are available. The first, ALGD0100, indicates that an *algorithm context token* is being passed as the fourth parameter. With an algorithm context token, the algorithm description has been previously defined, and a token identifying the set of algorithm rules has been returned to the application. The second format, ALGD0200, indicates that a block cipher algorithm is to be used. Block algorithms include Data Encryption Standard (DES), Triple DES, Advanced Encryption Standard (AES), and RC2. Other supported formats are ALGD0300 for stream cipher algorithms and ALGD0400 for public key algorithms (PKA). The sample programs in this chapter use the AES block cipher algorithm and format ALGD0200.

The sixth parameter, Key Description, defines the key to be used when encrypting the data provided in the first parameter.

The seventh parameter, Format of Key Description, defines the contents of the sixth parameter. Several possible formats are available. The first format, KEYD0100, indicates that a *key context token* is being passed as the sixth parameter. With a key context token, the key specification has been previously defined, and a token identifying the set of key value parameters returned to the application. A key context is created using the Create Key Context API, Qc3CreateKeyContext, which will be discussed shortly.

The second format, KEYD0200, indicates that the parameters associated with the key value (key value, key type, etc.) are being passed in the sixth parameter. Other supported formats are KEYD0400 for passing a key store label in the sixth parameter (which will be discussed in the "Using Key-Management APIs" section), KEYD0500 for passing an RSA Data Security, Inc. Public-Key Cryptography Standard #5 (PKCS5) passphrase, KEYD0600 for passing a PKA key imbedded within an ASCII-encoded Privacy Enhanced Mail (PEM) formatted certificate, KEYD0700 for passing a certificate label from the system certificate store to identify a PKA key, KEYD0800 for passing a distinguished name for a certificate in the system certificate store to identify a PKA key, and KEYD0900 for passing an application identifier assigned to a certificate label in the system certificate store to identify a PKA key.

The eighth parameter, Cryptographic Service Provider, identifies where the cryptographic operation should be performed. The possible values are zero (any provider can be used), one (only a software-based provider can be used), or two (only a hardware-based provider can be used). The examples in this chapter all use zero, having the system select the provider.

The ninth parameter, Cryptographic Device Name, is used when the Cryptographic Service Provider parameter is set to two. It requires that hardware-based cryptographic operations be performed using a particular device. This parameter can be omitted when not applicable. It will not be used in the sample programs for this chapter.

The tenth parameter, Encrypted Data, is the receiver variable where the Qc3EncryptData API will return the encrypted data.

The eleventh parameter, Length of Data Provided for Encrypted Data, is the allocated length of the tenth parameter. For block, stream, and PKA algorithms, this value is given in bytes (bits for CFB 1-bit) and must be equal to or greater than the value passed for the second parameter, Length of Clear Data (except for PKA, where the eleventh parameter must be equal to or greater than the key size). In addition, if padding of the data is being done (as can be the case with block cipher algorithms such as AES), this size must accommodate the pad characters.

The twelfth parameter, Length of Encrypted Data Returned, is the actual length of the encrypted data returned to the application. The thirteenth parameter is the standard API error-code structure.

With that introduction to the Qc3EncryptData API, Figure 11.1 shows a program to encrypt the CUSTOMER file (created in Figures 4.4.A and 4.4.B of chapter 4).

```
h dftactgrp(*no)

FFilename++IPEASF.....L.....A.Device+.Keywords++++++++++++++++++++++++++++
fCustomer  if   e           disk
fEncrCust  o    e           disk

DName+++++++++++ETDsFrom+++To/L+++IDc.Keywords++++++++++++++++++++++++++++
d/copy qsysinc/qrpglesrc,qc3cci
d/copy qsysinc/qrpglesrc,qusec
```

Figure 11.1: Program to encrypt CUSTOMER data (part 1 of 3).

```
dCrtKeyCtx           pr                  extproc('Qc3CreateKeyContext')
d KeyString                    65535     const options(*varsize)
d LenKeyString                 10i 0     const
d KeyFormat                    1         const
d KeyType                      10i 0     const
d KeyForm                      1         const
d KeyEncrKey                   8         const options(*omit)
d KeyAlgorithm                 8         const options(*omit)
d KeyContext                   8
d QUSEC                                  likeds(QUSEC)

dGenPRN              pr                  extproc('Qc3GenPRNs')
d PRN                          1         options(*varsize)
d LenPRN                       10i 0     const
d PRNType                      1         const
d PRNParity                    1         const
d QUSEC                                  likeds(QUSEC)

dEncrypt             pr                  extproc('Qc3EncryptData')
d ClearData                    65535     const options(*varsize)
d LenClearData                 10i 0     const
d ClearDataFmt                 8         const
d AlgDesc                      65535     const options(*varsize)
d AlgDescFmt                   8         const
d KeyDesc                      65535     const options(*varsize :*omit)
d KeyDescFmt                   8         const options(*omit)
d CryptoProvider               1         const
d CryptoDevice                 10        const options(*omit)
d EncrData                     1         options(*varsize)
d LenEncrData                  10i 0     const
d RtnLenEncrData               10i 0
d QUSEC                                  likeds(QUSEC)

dDstKeyCtx           pr                  extproc('Qc3DestroyKeyContext')
d KeyContext                   8         const
d QUSEC                                  likeds(QUSEC)

dCustomerDS          ds                  likerec(CUSREC :*Input)

dEncrCustDS          ds                  likerec(ENCRREC :*Output)

dKey                 s         16        dtaara('CLEARKEY')
dLenEncrRtn          s         10i 0

CLON01Factor1+++++++Opcode&ExtFactor2+++++++Result++++++++Len++D+HiLoEq
 /free
   QUSBPRV = 0;
```

Figure 11.1: Program to encrypt CUSTOMER data (part 2 of 3).

```
// Describe the encryption algorithm to use
QC3D0200 = *loval;                    // Initialize format to x'00'
QC3BCA = 22;                          // AES
QC3BL = 16;                           // Block length of 16
QC3MODE = '1';                        // CBC
QC3PO = '1';                          // Pad to 16 byte boundary
QC3PC = *loval;                       // Pad with x'00'

// Create a key encrypting context
in Key;
CrtKeyCtx( Key :%size(Key) :'0' 22 :'0' :*OMIT :*OMIT
           :QC3KCT :QUSEC);
Key = *blanks;

// Process all records from the Customer file

read CusRec CustomerDS;
dow not %eof;

// Get an initialization vector for this customer
GenPRN( EncrCustDS.IV :%size(EncrCustDS.IV) :'0' :'0' :QUSEC);
QC3IV = EncrCustDS.IV;

// Encrypt the customer data
Encrypt ( CustomerDS.CustName :%size(CustomerDS.CustName) :'DATA0100'
          :QC3D0200 :'ALGD0200' :QC3D010000 :'KEYD0100'
          :'0' :*OMIT :EncrCustDS.EncrData :%size(EncrCustDS.EncrData)
          :LenEncrRtn :QUSEC);

// Write the encrypted customer data
EncrCustDS.CustNbr = CustomerDS.CustNbr;
write EncrRec EncrCustDS;
read CusRec CustomerDS;
enddo;

// When done, clean up
DstKeyCtx ( QC3D010000   :QUSEC);

*inlr = *on;
return;
/end-free
```

Figure 11.1: Program to encrypt CUSTOMER data (part 3 of 3).

Note that program FIG11_1 declares a new file, ENCRCUST, which will store the encrypted results. The DDS for ENCRCUST is shown in Figure 11.2. You should create this file now.

```
AANO1NO2NO3T.Name++++++RLen++TDpBLinPosFunctions++++++++++++++++++++++++
          R  ENCRREC
             CUSTNBR         10
             ENCRDATA        48H
             IV              16H
          K  CUSTNBR
```

Figure 11.2: DDS for the encrypted customer file, ENCRCUST.

The ENCRCUST file has three fields. The first, CUSTNBR, is the unencrypted customer number and is also defined as the key to ENCRCUST. CUSTNBR is left unencrypted so that application programs can continue to access customer data based on the clear (unencrypted) customer number. The second field, ENCRDATA, is the rest of the CUSTOMER record in encrypted form. Although CUSTOMER has only one non-key field, CUSTNAME, ENCRDATA could be the encrypted form of any number of fields defined within a record format. The third field, IV, is an initialization value that can be used when encrypting and decrypting the customer data. This field, and the reason we have it in the record format, is explained later, in the discussion of the parameters associated with AES.

FIG11_1 also declares the data area CLEARKEY. The command for creating CLEARKEY is shown in Figure 11.3. You should create this data area now. The CLEARKEY data area is used to store the encryption key FIG11_1 will be using. We are using a key value of 'NOT a good way'. You can choose to initialize the data area to any 16-byte value you want.

```
CRTDTAARA DTAARA(CLEARKEY) TYPE(*CHAR) LEN(16) VALUE('NOT a good way')
```

Figure 11.3: Creating the CLEARKEY data area to hold the cryptographic key.

Program FIG11_1 first initializes QUSBPRV, the Bytes Provided field of the error-code structure, to zero. This indicates that errors should be returned as escape messages. The program then defines an algorithm using format ALGD0200. The RPG definition from QSYSINC/QRPGLESRC member QC3CCI for format ALGD0200 is shown in Figure 11.4, and the code initializing this structure is shown in Figure 11.5.

```
DName++++++++++ETDsFrom+++To/L+++IDc.Keywords++++++++++++++++++++++
D*ALGD0200 algorithm description structure
DQC3D0200            DS
D*                                                    Qc3 Format ALGD0200
D QC3BCA                    1      4B 0
D*                                                    Block Cipher Alg
D QC3BL                     5      8B 0
D*                                                    Block Length
D QC3MODE                   9      9
D*                                                    Mode
D QC3PO                    10     10
D*                                                    Pad Option
D QC3PC                    11     11
D*                                                    Pad Character
D QC3ERVED                 12     12
D*                                                    Reserved
D QC3MACL                  13     16B 0
D*                                                    MAC Length
D QC3EKS                   17     20B 0
D*                                                    Effective Key Size
D QC3IV                    21     52
D*                                                    Init Vector
```

Figure 11.4: ALGD0200 format from QSYSINC/QRPGLESRC member QC3CCI.

Several fields are defined within the ALGD0200 format (the RPG QC3D0200 data structure). The first, QC3BCA, specifies what block cipher algorithm is to be used. Supported values are 20 for DES, 21 for Triple DES, 22 for AES, and 23 for RC2. As mentioned earlier, the sample programs will be using AES as the cryptographic algorithm.

The second field, QC3BL, specifies the block length to be used. For AES, the valid block values are 16, 24, or 32. These values, specified in bytes, correspond to 128-bit encryption, 192-bit encryption, and 256-bit encryption, respectively. The sample program uses a block length of 16 bytes.

The third field, QC3MODE, specifies the mode of operation. The two valid modes for AES are zero for Electronic Code Book (ECB) and one for Cipher Block Chaining (CBC). In the sample programs, CBC mode is used to avoid an exposure that exists with ECB. This exposure is discussed in more detail later in this chapter.

The fourth field, QC3PO, is the pad option to be used with block cipher algorithms such as AES. The valid values are zero for no padding, one to pad using the value specified in field QC3PC, and two for padding with the pad counter. With block ciphers such as AES, each encrypted block of data must be a multiple of the block length. This field can be used to have the Qc3EncryptData API add the appropriate number of pad characters, as opposed to having the application program do it. The sample program uses a block length (QC3BL) of 16 and the data to be encrypted (CustName) is 40 bytes in length. Therefore, using this option will cause the API to return 48 bytes of encrypted data (the next multiple of 16 greater than 40). This is why the ENCRCUST field ENCRDATA is defined as 48 bytes in Figure 11.2.

The fifth field, QC3PC, is the pad character to use if QC3PO is set to one. The sample programs use a null byte (x'00') as the pad character. The sixth field, QC3ERVED, is a reserved area and must be set to x'00'. The seventh field, QC3MACL, is the Message Authentication Code (MAC) length. This field is not used by Qc3EncryptData. The eighth field, QC3EKS, is the effective key size; for AES, it must be set to zero.

The ninth field, QC3IV, is an initialization vector, or value, that can be used when encrypting and decrypting data. To best understand this field, first consider encryption without it. If a buffer or variable to be encrypted has the clear text value of 'ABCDE', and it is encrypted under a fixed key value, the resulting encrypted value might be 'VWXYZ'. If subsequent buffers also contain the clear text value of 'ABCDE', then the resulting encrypted values will again be 'VWXYZ'. This repeated encrypted text can make crypt-analysis of the text stream easier, in terms of deriving the key under which the clear text was encrypted. An initialization vector allows you to specify a random value to be used in conjunction with the clear text when encrypting the data. The initialization vector does not need to be kept secret, but should be unique to each message. It must also be available to later decrypt the encrypted data. The sample programs use a different random number for the initialization vector, or value, used with each ENCRCUST record.

In Figure 11.5, the QC3D0200 structure is first initialized to null bytes. Then, the appropriate algorithm and algorithm choices are set. This example uses AES with CBC and a block length of 16 bytes, and has the API provide any necessary padding.

```
CLON01Factor1+++++++OpCode&ExtFactor2+++++++Result++++++++Len++D+HiLoEq
    // Describe the encryption algorithm to use
    QC3D0200 = *loval;                // Initialize format to x'00'
    QC3BCA = 22;                      // AES
    QC3BL = 16;                       // Block length of 16
    QC3MODE = '1';                    // CBC
    QC3PO = '1';                      // Pad to 16 byte boundary
    QC3PC = *loval;                   // Pad with x'00'
```

Figure 11.5: Describing an algorithm.

After defining the algorithm to be used, FIG11_1 then creates a key context, as shown in Figure 11.6. In this code, the program reads the CLEARKEY data area to access the key value to be used for encryption, creates a key context using the Qc3CreateKeyContext API, and then sets the key value to blanks.

```
CLON01Factor1+++++++Opcode&ExtFactor2+++++++Result++++++++Len++D+HiLoEq
  // Create a key encrypting context
  in Key;
  CrtKeyCtx( Key :%size(Key) :'0' :22 :'0' :*OMIT :*OMIT
            :QC3KCT :QUSEC);
  Key = *blanks;
```

Figure 11.6: Creating a key context.

The token for the key context is stored in the field QC3KCT. This field is defined in the QSYSINC-provided data structure, which is shown in Figure 11.7. After the key context has been created, the key is no longer needed, and it is set to blanks. This setting of the key value to blanks is done to minimize, though it does not eliminate, the exposure of having the key value accessible as a variable in the program while it's running.

```
DName++++++++++++ETDsFrom+++To/L+++IDc.Keywords++++++++++++++++++++++++++
D*KEYD0100 key description format structure
DQC3D010000        DS
D*                                             Qc3 Format KEYD0100
D QC3KCT                1       8
D*                                             Key Context Token
```

Figure 11.7: QSYSINC/QRPGLESRC member QC3CCI definition for KEYD0100 format.

Creating a Key Context

As mentioned earlier when introducing the Qc3EncryptData API, a key context is the ability to specify a key and associated parameters once, and then reference those specifications in subsequent cryptographic operations by use of a token. The API to create a key context is Qc3CreateKeyContext. Its parameters are shown in Table 11.2.

Table 11.2: The Create Key Context API (Qc3CreateKeyContext)			
Parameter	Description	Type	Size
1	Key String	Input	Char(*)
2	Length of Key String	Input	Binary(4)
3	Key Format	Input	Char(1)
4	Key Type	Input	Binary(4)
5	Key Form	Input	Char(1)
6	Key-Encrypting Key	Input	Char(*)
7	Key-Encrypting Algorithm	Input	Char(8)
8	Key Context Token	Output	Char(8)
9	Error Code	I/O	Char(*)

The first parameter, Key String, specifies the key to be used. The second parameter, Length of Key String, is the length of the first parameter. The third parameter, Key Format, defines the contents of the first parameter. Several possible formats are available:

- A zero indicates that the first parameter is the actual key value to be used.

- A one indicates that the first parameter is a Basic Encoding Rules (BER) string.

- A four indicates that the first parameter is a key store label identifying a key from a key store file. This format will be used later in this chapter, in the section "Using Key-Management APIs."

- A five is for a PKCS5 passphrase.

- A six is for a PEM certificate.

The fourth parameter, Key Type, defines the type of key to be generated. Several different types can be used:

- 1 for Message Digest 5 (MD5) Hash Message Authentication Code (HMAC)

- 2 for Secure Hash Algorithm 1 (SHA-1) HMAC

- 3 for SHA-256 HMAC

- 4 for SHA-384 HMAC

- 5 for SHA-512 HMAC

- 20 for DES

- 21 for Triple DES

- 22 for AES

- 23 for RC2

- 30 for RC4-compatible

- 50 for RSA public

- 51 for RSA private

The key type indicates which key formats can be used. For instance, if AES is specified for this parameter (key type 22), then the Key Format parameter must be a zero, four, or five.

The fifth parameter, Key Form, defines how the Key String parameter is to be interpreted. If the Key Form parameter is zero, the Key String parameter is not currently encrypted. If Key Form is one, Key String is currently encrypted with a key-encrypting key (further defined by parameters 6 and 7). If it's two, the Key String parameter is currently encrypted with a master key (further defined by the sixth parameter). The FIG11_1 sample program uses zero as the key form.

The sixth parameter, Key-Encrypting Key, defines the key under which the Key String parameter is encrypted. For a key form of zero, this parameter must be set to blanks or omitted. The seventh parameter, Key-Encrypting Algorithm, must also be set to blanks or omitted when using a key form of zero.

The eighth parameter, Key Context Token, is a token returned to the application program that uniquely identifies the key-selection choices described by the other parameters. This token is passed to other APIs, such as Qc3EncryptData and Qc3DecryptData, to indicate which key is in effect for the API call. This token should not be modified by the application program. Using a modified token will result in an error message and can cause a 10-second delay the first time the token is used in an API call such as Qc3EncryptData. The next attempt to use the modified token can cause a 20-second delay, with each subsequent attempt adding another 10 seconds, up to a maximum of 10 minutes per API call.

The ninth parameter is the standard error-code structure.

In Figure 11.6, the program is creating a key context where the key will conform to AES, the key is 16 bytes long, and a key value of 'NOT a good way' is being passed to the Qc3CreateKeyContext API as an unencrypted text string. The returned context token is then stored in the field QC3KCT.

Having set appropriate algorithm and key contexts, FIG11_1 now reads the first record from the CUSTOMER file and enters into a DO-WHILE loop. This loop will continue until all CUSTOMER records have been read and encrypted.

Generating a Pseudorandom Number

When a CUSTOMER record is read, and before the data is encrypted, FIG11_1 generates a pseudorandom number using the Generate Pseudorandom Numbers API, Qc3GenPRNs. A pseudorandom number is generated per record to be encrypted, and will be used to set the initialization vector previously discussed for the Qc3CreateAlgorithmContext API and the QC3IV field of the ALGD0200 format. Table 11.3 shows the parameters for the Qc3GenPRNs API, and Figure 11.8 show the call to Qc3GenPRNs.

Table 11.3: The Generate Pseudorandom Numbers API (Qc3GenPRNs)			
Parameter	Description	Type	Size
1	PRN Data	Output	Char(*)
2	Length of PRN Data	Input	Binary(4)
3	PRN Type	Input	Char(1)
4	PRN Parity	Input	Char(1)
5	Error Code	I/O	Char(*)

The first parameter, PRN Data, is the receiver variable where Qc3GenPRNs returns the generated pseudorandom number.

The second parameter, Length of PRN Data, defines the number of bytes the API is to return to the application. This value must not exceed the allocated size of the first parameter.

The third parameter, PRN Type, defines whether a real pseudorandom number or a test pseudorandom number is wanted. A zero indicates a real pseudorandom number, a one indicates a test number.

The fourth parameter, PRN Parity, defines whether or not a particular parity is requested for each byte of the generated pseudorandom number. The values are zero for no specific parity setting, one for odd parity, and two for even parity.

The fifth parameter is the standard API error-code structure.

In Figure 11.8, FIG11_1 is requesting a real pseudorandom number that is 16 bytes in length with no particular parity setting. The generated number is stored in the variable EncrCustDS.IV. This field is defined in the ENCRREC record format, which is written to the ENCRCUST file along with the encrypted CUSTOMER file data. Field QC3IV, the initialization vector/value of data structure QC3D0200 (format ALGD0200), is then also set to the generated pseudorandom number.

```
CL0N01Factor1+++++++Opcode&ExtFactor2+++++++Result++++++++Len++D+HiLoEq
   read CusRec CustomerDS;
   dow not %eof;

   // Get an initialization vector for this customer
   GenPRN( EncrCustDS.IV :%size(EncrCustDS.IV) :'0' :'0' :QUSEC);
   QC3IV = EncrCustDS.IV;
```

Figure 11.8: Using the Generate Pseudorandom Numbers API (Qc3GenPRNs).

Figure 11.9 shows the remainder of the processing for each CUSTOMER record.

```
CL0N01Factor1+++++++Opcode&ExtFactor2+++++++Result++++++++Len++D+HiLoEq
   // Encrypt the customer data
   Encrypt ( CustomerDS.CustName :%size(CustomerDS.CustName) :'DATA0100'
           :QC3D0200 :'ALGD0200' :QC3D010000 :'KEYD0100'
           :'0' :*OMIT :EncrCustDS.EncrData
           :%size(EncrCustDS.EncrData)
           :LenEncrRtn :QUSEC);

   // Write the encrypted customer data
   EncrCustDS.CustNbr = CustomerDS.CustNbr;
   write EncrRec EncrCustDS;
   read CusRec CustomerDS;
   enddo;
```

Figure 11.9: Encrypting the customer name with an initialization value.

PGM11_1 calls the Qc3EncryptData API for encryption of the customer name as it's stored in the CUSTOMER file (CustomerDS.Custname). The encrypted name, with padding to a 16-byte boundary added by the API, is written to the field EncrCustDS.EncrData. This field is defined in the ENCRREC record format, which is later written to the ENCRCUST file. The key to be used is identified by the key context QC3D010000, and the algorithm is defined in data structure QC3D0200.

Next, PGM11_1 sets EncrCustDS.CustNbr of the ENCRREC record format to the customer number field in CUSTOMER (CustomerDS.CustNbr) and writes a new record to the ENCRCUST file. The record contains the customer number (CustNbr), the encrypted data (EncrData), and the initialization value used to encrypt the data (IV). FIG11_1 then reads the next CUSTOMER record and continues in the DO-WHILE loop, generating pseudorandom numbers, encrypting the customer name, and writing out new encrypted records into ENCRCUST. When all records in CUSTOMER have been processed, FIG11_1 destroys the key context previously created, and exits. This is shown in Figure 11.10.

```
CLON01Factor1+++++++Opcode&ExtFactor2+++++++Result++++++++Len++D+HiLoEq
    // When done, clean up
    DstKeyCtx ( QC3D010000  :QUSEC);

    *inlr = *on;
    return;
```

Figure 11.10: When the program is done.

Decrypting Data

With the customer data encrypted in the ENCRCUST file, we need to be able to decrypt the data and use it within an application. The parameters for the Decrypt Data API, Qc3DecryptData, are shown in Table 11.4.

Table 11.4: The Decrypt Data API (Qc3DecryptData)			
Parameter	Description	Type	Size
1	Encrypted Data	Input	Char(*)
2	Length of Encrypted Data	Input	Binary(4)
3	Algorithm Description	Input	Char(*)
4	Format of Algorithm Description	Input	Char(8)

Parameter	Description	Type	Size
	Table 11.4: The Decrypt Data API (Qc3DecryptData) (continued)		
5	Key Description	Input	Char(*)
6	Format of Key Description	Input	Char(8)
7	Cryptographic Service Provider	Input	Char(1)
8	Cryptographic Device Name	Input	Char(10)
9	Clear Data	Output	Char(*)
10	Length of Area Provided for Clear Data	Input	Binary(4)
11	Length of Clear Data Returned	Output	Binary(4)
12	Error Code	I/O	Char(*)

Many of these parameters are similar to those used with the Encrypt Data API, Qc3EncryptData. The first parameter, Encrypted Data, is the data that is to be decrypted. The second parameter, Length of Encrypted Data, is simply the length of the data provided in the first parameter.

The third parameter, Algorithm Description, defines what algorithm and algorithm options are to be used when decrypting the data. The fourth parameter, Format of Algorithm Description, defines the contents of the third parameter. As with Qc3EncryptData, several possible formats are available. The first format, ALGD0100, indicates that an algorithm context token is being passed as the third parameter. The second format, ALGD0200, indicates that a block cipher algorithm is to be used. Other supported formats are ALGD0300 for stream cipher algorithms and ALGD0400 for public key algorithms (PKA). As FIG11_1 used AES to encrypt the data, the program decrypting the data will use format ALGD0200 and the AES algorithm.

The fifth parameter, Key Description, defines the key to be used when decrypting the data provided in the first parameter. The sixth parameter, Format of Key Description, defines the contents of the fifth parameter. Several possible formats are available:

- KEYD0100 to indicate that a key context token is being passed

- KEYD0200 for directly passing the key value and parameters

- KEYD0400 for passing a key store label

369

- KEYD0500 for passing a PKCS5 passphrase

- KEYD0600 for passing a PKA key embedded within an ASCII-encoded PEM-based certificate

- KEYD0700 for passing a certificate label from the system certificate store to identify a PKA key

- KEYD0800 for passing a distinguished name for a certificate in the system certificate store to identify a PKA key

- KEYD0900 for passing an application identifier assigned to a certificate label in the system certificate store to identify a PKA key

The seventh parameter, Cryptographic Service Provider, identifies where the cryptographic operation should be performed. The possible values are zero (any provider can be used), one (only a software-based provider can be used), or two (only a hardware-based provider can be used). The examples in this chapter all use zero, so the system can use any appropriate provider.

The eighth parameter, Cryptographic Device Name, is used when the Cryptographic Service Provider parameter is set to two. It requires that hardware-based cryptographic operations be performed using a particular device. This parameter can be omitted when not applicable.

The ninth parameter, Clear Data, is the receiver variable where the Qc3DecryptData API will return the original clear data.

The tenth parameter, Length of Data Provided for Clear Data, is the allocated length of the ninth parameter. For block, stream, and PKA algorithms, this value is given in bytes and must be equal to or greater than the value passed for parameter 2 (the length of the encrypted data in parameter 1).

The eleventh parameter, Length of Clear Data Returned, is the actual length of the clear data returned. The twelfth parameter is the standard API error-code structure.

The sample program in Figure 11.11 shows how to decrypt the data encrypted with the FIG11_1 program. Program FIG11_11 displays the clear-text customer number and decrypted customer name for each record found in the ENCRCUST file. The records are processed sequentially, using the key defined over the customer number.

```
h dftactgrp(*no)

FFilename++IPEASF.....L.....A.Device+.Keywords+++++++++++++++++++++++++++
fEncrCust  if  e        k disk

DName+++++++++++ETDsFrom+++To/L+++IDc.Keywords+++++++++++++++++++++++++++
d/copy qsysinc/qrpglesrc,qc3cci
d/copy qsysinc/qrpglesrc,qusec

dCrtKeyCtx          pr                    extproc('Qc3CreateKeyContext')
d KeyString                    65535      const options(*varsize)
d LenKeyString                 10i0       const
d KeyFormat                    1          const
d KeyType                      10i0       const
d KeyForm                      1          const
d KeyEncrKey                   8          const options(*omit)
d KeyAlgorithm                 8          const options(*omit)
d KeyContext                   8
d QUSEC                                   likeds(QUSEC)

dDecrypt            pr                    extproc('Qc3DecryptData')
d EncrData                     65535      const options(*varsize)
d LenEncrData                  10i0       const
d AlgDesc                      65535      const options(*varsize)
d AlgDescFmt                   8          const
d KeyDesc                      65535      const options(*varsize :*omit)
d KeyDescFmt                   8          const options(*omit)
d CryptoProvider               1          const
d CryptoDevice                 10         const options(*omit)
d ClearData                    1          options(*varsize)
d LenClearData                 10i0       const
d RtnLenClrData                10i0
d QUSEC                                   likeds(QUSEC)

dDstKeyCtx          pr                    extproc('Qc3DestroyKeyContext')
d KeyContext                   8          const
d QUSEC                                   likeds(QUSEC)

dEncrCustDS         ds                    likerec(ENCRREC :*Input)

dCustomerDS         e ds                  extname(Customer :CUSREC)
d                                         qualified

dKey                s          16         dtaara('CLEARKEY')
dLenClearRtn        s          10i0
```

Figure 11.11: Decrypting encrypted data (part 1 of 2).

```
CL0N01Factor1+++++++Opcode&ExtFactor2+++++++Result++++++++Len++D+HiLoEq
/free
  QUSBPRV = 0;

  // Describe the encryption algorithm to use
  QC3D0200 = *loval;                    // Initialize format to x'00'
  QC3BCA = 22;                          // AES
  QC3BL = 16;                           // Block length of 16
  QC3MODE = '1';                        // CBC
  QC3PO = '0';                          // Leave padding

  // Create a key encrypting context
  in Key;
  CrtKeyCtx( Key :%size(Key) :'0' :22 :'0' :*OMIT :*OMIT
            :QC3KCT :QUSEC);
  Key = *blanks;

  // Process all records from the EncrCust file in CustNbr sequence

  read EncrRec EncrCustDS;
  dow not %eof;

  // Set the initialization vector for this customer
  QC3IV = EncrCustDS.IV;

  // Decrypt the customer data
  Decrypt ( EncrCustDS.EncrData :%size(EncrCustDS.EncrData)
           :QC3D0200 :'ALGD0200' :QC3D010000 :'KEYD0100' :'0' :*OMIT
           :CustomerDS.CustName :%size(CustomerDS.CustName)
           :LenClearRtn :QUSEC);

  // Display the decrypted customer data
  dsply (EncrCustDS.CustNbr + ' ' + CustomerDS.Custname);

  // Get next encrypted record
  read EncrRec EncrCustDS;
  enddo;

  // When done, clean up
  DstKeyCtx ( QC3D010000   :QUSEC);

  *inlr = *on;
  return;
/end-free
```

Figure 11.11: Decrypting encrypted data (part 2 of 2).

As you can see, program FIG11_11 is very similar to the encryption program, FIG11_1. Here are the major differences:

- The CUSTOMER file F-spec has been removed.

- The ENCRCUST file is now an input file processed by key.

- The function prototype for Qc3EncryptData has been replaced with a function prototype for Qc3DecryptData.

- The definition for the CUSTOMER file fields are now accessed using the extname keyword, so that the program does not need to explicitly define the fields.

- The Qc3DecryptData API is called rather than the Qc3EncryptData API.

- The data is DSPLYed to the user rather than written to a file.

From an API point of view, the only difference is in the API being called. As the parameters for Qc3EncryptData are so similar to those used for Qc3EncryptData, we will not be looking at this particular program in any more detail.

Using Key-Management APIs

As mentioned earlier in this chapter, the programs FIG11_1 and FIG11_11 have a problem. While they are very useful for demonstrating how to use the encryption and decryption APIs, they do not provide much protection of the key values being used for encryption. The keys are just too easy to access. For this reason, i5/OS provides a set of key-management cryptographic APIs. These APIs assist you in storing and handling cryptographic keys.

i5/OS can support up to eight *master keys* that cannot be directly modified or read by any user. This includes QSECOFR! In addition, these master key values can be set by multiple users, where each user provides one part of the key, so that no single person knows the entire key. These master keys can then be used to protect additional keys, which are then used within application programs in an encrypted form, so that the actual key value is not known to the application. This is a much greater level of protection than that shown in FIG11_1 and FIG11_11—and all it takes is a few more API calls!

The program in Figure 11.12 demonstrates how to load and set a master key.

```
h dftactgrp(*no)

DName++++++++++ETDsFrom+++To/L+++IDc.Keywords+++++++++++++++++++++++++++
d/copy qsysinc/qrpglesrc,qc3cci
d/copy qsysinc/qrpglesrc,qusec

dLoadMasterKey     pr                    extproc('Qc3LoadMasterKeyPart')
d MasterKeyID                     10i 0  const
d PassPhrase                      65535  const options(*varsize)
d LenPassPhrase                   10i 0  const
d CCSIDPhrase                     10i 0  const
d QUSEC                                  likeds(QUSEC)

dSetMasterKey      pr                    extproc('Qc3SetMasterKey')
d MasterKeyID                     10i 0  const
d KVV                             20
d QUSEC                                  likeds(QUSEC)

dCrtKeyStore       pr                    extproc('Qc3CreateKeyStore')
d QualKeyStore                    20     const
d MasterKeyID                     10i 0  const
d PublicAut                       10     const
d TextDesc                        50     const
d QUSEC                                  likeds(QUSEC)

dGenKeyRcd         pr                    extproc('Qc3GenKeyRecord')
d QualKeyStore                    20     const
d RcdLabel                        32     const
d KeyType                         10i 0  const
d KeySize                         10i 0  const
d PublicKeyExp                    10i 0  const
d DisallowFnc                     10i 0  const
d CryptoProvider                  1      const
d CryptoDevice                    10  0  const options(*omit)
d QUSEC                                  likeds(QUSEC)

dPassPhrase1       s              256    inz('I love my System i')
dPassPhrase2       s              256    inz('I sure am glad I do not -
d                                        need to know how cryptography -
d                                        works in order to use it')
dKeyStoreFile      s              20     inz('ABCSTORE  SOMELIB')
dRcdKey            s              32     inz('Customer file')
dRtnLenKString     s              10i 0
DKVV               s              20     dtaara('MYKVV')
```

Figure 11.12: Setting up the key-management environment (part 1 of 2).

```
CLON01Factor1+++++++Opcode&ExtFactor2+++++++Result++++++++Len++D+HiLoEq
 /free
 QUSBPRV = 0;

 // Load one part of master key 3
 LoadMasterKey ( 3 :PassPhrase1 :%len(%trim(PassPhrase1)) :0 :QUSEC);

 // Load another part of the master key
 LoadMasterKey ( 3 :PassPhrase2 :%len(%trim(PassPhrase2)) :0 :QUSEC);

 // Set the master key and save the key verification value (KVV)
 in *lock KVV;
 SetMasterKey (3 :KVV :QUSEC);
 out KVV;

 // Create a key store using master key 3
 CrtKeyStore ( KeyStoreFile :3 :'*EXCLUDE' :'Division ABC key store';
               :QUSEC);

 // Generate a key record using AES key of 16 bytes (128 bits)
 GenKeyRcd ( KeyStoreFile :RcdKey :22 :16 :0 :0 :'0' :*OMIT :QUSEC);

 *inlr = *on;
 return;
 /end-free
```

Figure 11.12: Setting up the key-management environment (part 2 of 2).

Loading a Master Key

The eight master keys maintained by i5/OS are loaded with the Load Master Key Part API, Qc3LoadMasterKeyPart. The parameters for this API are shown in Table 11.5, and the pertinent part of program FIG11_12 is shown in Figure 11.13.

Table 11.5: The Load Master Key Part API (Qc3LoadMasterKeyPart)			
Parameter	Description	Type	Size
1	Master Key ID	Input	Binary(4)
2	Passphrase	Input	Char(*)
3	Length of Passphrase	Input	Binary(4)
4	CCSID of Passphrase	Input	Binary(4)
5	Error Code	I/O	Char(*)

The first parameter, Master Key ID, specifies which of the eight master keys you are working with. The possible values are one through eight. The sample program uses master key 3.

The second parameter, Passphrase, is simply a text string that will be used as an input into the master key. The third parameter, Length of Passphrase, is the length, in bytes, of the text string. The value can be from one through 256. The fourth parameter, CCSID of Passphrase, is the CCSID associated with the text. A special value of zero is supported to indicate the job CCSID should be used.

The fourth parameter is the standard API error-code structure.

In Figure 11.13, the program is loading two parts of master key 3. The first use of Qc3LoadMasterKeyPart is using the passphrase 'I love my System i'. The second use of the API uses the passphrase 'I sure am glad I do not have to know how cryptography works in order to use it'. In this sample program, the passphrases are being load sequentially, but in a production environment, the two calls to Qc3LoadMasterKeyPart could be in different programs running in different jobs on different days. You can load the various parts of the key when you want to. There is no limit to the number of passphrases you can use in loading a master key.

```
DName++++++++++ETDsFrom+++To/L+++IDc.Keywords+++++++++++++++++++++++++++
dPassPhrase1        s            256     inz('I love my System i')
dPassPhrase2        s            256     inz('I sure am glad I do not -
d                                         need to know how cryptography -
d                                         works in order to use it')

CLON01Factor1+++++++Opcode&ExtFactor2+++++++Result++++++++Len++D+HiLoEq
 /free
  QUSBPRV = 0;

  // Load one part of master key 3
  LoadMasterKey ( 3 :PassPhrase1 :%len(%trim(PassPhrase1)) :0 :QUSEC);

  // Load another part of the master key
  LoadMasterKey ( 3 :PassPhrase2 :%len(%trim(PassPhrase2)) :0 :QUSEC);
 /end-free
```

Figure 11.13: Loading parts of master key 3.

Setting a Master Key

Once all of the parts of the master key have been loaded, you then use the Set Master Key API, Qc3SetMasterKey. The parameters for this API are shown in Table 11.6, and the actual call is in Figure 11.14.

Table 11.6: The Set Master Key API (Qc3SetMasterKey)			
Parameter	Description	Type	Size
1	Master Key ID	Input	Binary(4)
2	Key Verification Value	Output	Char(20)
3	Error Code	I/O	Char(*)

The first parameter, Master Key ID, specifies which of the eight master keys you are working with. The possible values are one through eight. The sample program uses master key 3.

The second parameter, Key Verification Value, is an output value that can be used, at a later time, to determine if the master key has been changed. If the master key has changed, keys encrypted under it need to be re-encrypted. This aspect of key management will not be discussed in this chapter.

The third parameter is the standard API error-code structure.

In Figure 11.14, program FIG11_12 has defined a data area MYKVV, which is associated with variable KVV. FIG11_12 first reads the data area, locking it for update. It then sets master key 3 based on the previously loaded passphrases, and writes the returned key-verification value to the data area.

```
DName++++++++++++ETDsFrom+++To/L+++IDc.Keywords++++++++++++++++++++++++++++
dKVV                   s            20    dtaara('MYKVV')

CLON01Factor1++++++Opcode&ExtFactor2++++++Result++++++++Len++D+HiLoEq
 /free
   QUSBPRV = 0;

   // Set the master key and save the key verification value (KVV)
   in *lock KVV;
   SetMasterKey (3 :KVV :QUSEC);
   out KVV;
 /end-free
```

Figure 11.14: Setting master key 3.

Creating a Key Store File

Having set master key 3, the program next creates a key store file using the Create Key Store API (Qc3CreateKeyStore). The parameters for this API are shown in Table 11.7, and the pertinent portions of program FIG11_12 are in Figure 11.15.

Table 11.7: The Create Key Store API (Qc3CreateKeyStore)			
Parameter	Description	Type	Size
1	Qualified Key Store File Name	Input	Char(20)
2	Master Key ID	Input	Binary(4)
3	Public Authority	Input	Char(10)
4	Text Description	Input	Char(50)
5	Error Code	I/O	Char(*)

The first parameter, Qualified Key Store File Name, is the name of the database file to be created. As with other qualified names used for APIs, the first ten characters contain the file name, and the second ten characters contain the library name. The special value *CURLIB is supported for the library name. The sample program uses the file ABCSTORE in library SOMELIB.

The second parameter, Master Key ID, specifies which of the eight master keys you want to associate with this key store file. The possible values are one through eight; the sample program uses master key 3. A key store file is used to store cryptographic keys. When these keys are stored, they are encrypted under the master key associated with the key store file so that the clear-text form of the key cannot be directly accessed.

The third parameter, Public Authority, is the public authority you want granted to the key store file. Supported values are the typical *ALL, *CHANGE, *EXCLUDE, *LIBAUTCRT, *USE, or the name of an authorization list. The sample program uses *EXCLUDE.

The fourth parameter, Text Description, is the object description for the key store file. The fifth parameter is the standard API error-code structure.

In Figure 11.15, the program creates the key store file ABCSTORE in library SOMELIB. The key store file is associated with master key 3, has an object description of 'Division ABC key store', and has a public authority of *EXCLUDE. In addition to encrypting the

```
DName+++++++++++ETDsFrom+++To/L+++IDc.Keywords+++++++++++++++++++++++++++
dKeyStoreFile       s            20    inz('ABCSTORE  SOMELIB')

CLON01Factor1++++++Opcode&ExtFactor2++++++Result++++++++Len++D+HiLoEq
 /free
  QUSBPRV = 0;

  // Create a key store using master key 3
  CrtKeyStore ( KeyStoreFile :3 :'*EXCLUDE' :'Division ABC key store'
              :QUSEC);
 /end-free
```

Figure 11.15: Creating a key store file.

keys stored within the file, the file is also created by the system such that users cannot read, write, update, or delete records from the file. The only way to access the contents of the file is through the system-provided APIs or service commands such as Dump Object (DMPOBJ).

Generating a Key Record

Having created a key store file, the program next calls the Generate Key Record API (Qc3GenKeyRecord) to generate a random key and store the generated key in the key store file. The parameters for this API are shown in Table 11.8, and the pertinent portions of FIG11_12 are in Figure 11.16.

Table 11.8: The Generate Key Record API (Qc3GenKeyRecord)			
Parameter	Description	Type	Size
1	Qualified Key Store File Name	Input	Char(20)
2	Record Label	Input	Char(32)
3	Key Type	Input	Binary(4)
4	Key Size	Input	Binary(4)
5	Public Key Exponent	Input	Binary(4)
6	Disallowed Function	Input	Binary(4)
7	Cryptographic Service Provider	Input	Char(1)
8	Cryptographic Device Name	Input	Char(10)
9	Error Code	I/O	Char(*)

The first parameter, Qualified Key Store File Name, is the name of the database file to be created. The sample program uses the file ABCSTORE in library SOMELIB.

The second parameter, Record Label, is the name you want associated with the API-generated key. This label will be used with other APIs to identify which cryptographic key you want to work with. The sample program uses the label 'Customer file'.

The third parameter, Key Type, defines the type of key to be generated. Several different types can be used:

- 1 for MD5 HMAC
- 2 for SHA-1 HMAC
- 3 for SHA-256 HMAC
- 4 for SHA-384 HMAC
- 5 for SHA-512 HMAC
- 20 for DES
- 21 for Triple DES
- 22 for AES
- 23 for RC2
- 30 for RC4-compatible
- 50 for RSA

The sample program uses 22 for AES.

The fourth parameter, Key Size, is the length of the cryptographic key to be generated. For AES, the key size must be 16, 24, or 32 bytes. The sample program uses 16-byte keys.

The fifth parameter, Public Key Component, is only used when the key type is 50 for RSA. For other key types, this parameter must be set to zero.

The sixth parameter, Disallowed Function, is used to specify that certain cryptographic operations are not to be allowed with the generated key record. The functions that can be disallowed are 1 (encryption), 2 (decryption), 4 (MACing), and 8 (signing). These values can be added together, so that a value such as three indicates that the key record cannot be used for encryption (1) or decryption (2). The sample program uses a value of zero—all functions are allowed.

The seventh parameter, Cryptographic Service Provider, identifies where the cryptographic operation should be performed. The possible values are zero (any provider can be used), one (only a software-based provider can be used), or two (only a hardware-based provider can be used). The examples in this chapter all use zero.

The eighth parameter, Cryptographic Device Name, is used when the Cryptographic Service Provider parameter is set to two. It requires that hardware-based cryptographic operations be performed using a particular device. This parameter can be omitted when not applicable.

The ninth parameter is the standard API error-code structure.

In Figure 11.16, program FIG11_12 calls the Qc3GenKeyRecord API to generate a random key value that can be used for AES cryptographic operations, has a key length of 16 bytes, and is to be stored in the ABCSTORE key store file with an identifier of 'Customer file'. From Figure 11.15, the generated key will be stored in an encrypted form using master key 3.

```
DName+++++++++++ETDsFrom+++To/L+++IDc.Keywords+++++++++++++++++++++++++++++
dKeyStoreFile      s             20    inz('KEYSTORE   SOMELIB')
dRcdKey            s             32    inz('Customer file')

CLON01Factor1++++++Opcode&ExtFactor2+++++++Result++++++++Len++D+HiLoEq
 /free
  QUSBPRV = 0;

  // Generate a key record using AES key of 16 bytes (128 bits)
  GenKeyRcd ( KeyStoreFile :RcdKey :22 :16 :0 :0 :'0' :*OMIT :QUSEC);

 /end-free
```

Figure 11.16: Generating a key record.

Encrypting Data Using a Key Store

At this point, FIG11_12 has loaded master key 3, set master key 3, created the key store ABCSTORE in SOMELIB, and added one record to the ABCSTORE key store file with the record label 'Customer file'. The program now ends, and it's time to move on to the FIG11_17 sample program, which encrypts the CUSTOMER data using the AES key stored in the key store. This program is shown in Figure 11.17.

```
h dftactgrp(*no)

FFilename++IPEASF.....L.....A.Device+.Keywords++++++++++++++++++++++++++
fCustomer  if   e              disk
fEncrCust  o    e              disk

DName+++++++++++ETDsFrom+++To/L+++IDc.Keywords++++++++++++++++++++++++++++
d/copy qsysinc/qrpglesrc,qc3cci
d/copy qsysinc/qrpglesrc,qusec

dCrtKeyCtx        pr                  extproc('Qc3CreateKeyContext')
d KeyString                  65535    const options(*varsize)
d LenKeyString               10i 0 const
d KeyFormat                    1    const
d KeyType                     10i 0 const
d KeyForm                      1    const
d KeyEncrKey                   8    const options(*omit)
d KeyAlgorithm                 8    const options(*omit)
d KeyContext                   8
d QUSEC                             likeds(QUSEC)

dGenPRN           pr                  extproc('Qc3GenPRNs')
d PRN                          1    options(*varsize)
d LenPRN                      10i 0 const
d PRNType                      1    const
d PRNParity                    1    const
d QUSEC                             likeds(QUSEC)

dEncrypt          pr                  extproc('Qc3EncryptData')
d ClearData                  65535    const options(*varsize)
d LenClearData               10i 0 const
d ClearDataFmt                 8    const
d AlgDesc                    65535    const options(*varsize)
d AlgDescFmt                   8    const
d KeyDesc                    65535    const options(*varsize :*omit)
d KeyDescFmt                   8    const options(*omit)
d CryptoProvider               1    const
d CryptoDevice                10    const options(*omit)
d EncrData                     1    options(*varsize)
d LenEncrData                10i 0 const
d RtnLenEncrData             10i 0
d QUSEC                             likeds(QUSEC)
```

Figure 11.17: Encrypting data with key management (part 1 of 3).

```
dDstKeyCtx        pr                    extproc('Qc3DestroyKeyContext')
d KeyContext                 8          const
d QUSEC                                 likeds(QUSEC)

dCustomerDS       ds                    likerec(CUSREC :*Input)

dEncrCustDS       ds                    likerec(ENCRREC :*Output)

dKeyStoreFile     s           20        inz('ABCSTORE  SOMELIB')
dRcdKey           s           32        inz('Customer file')
dLenEncrRtn       s           10i 0

CLON01Factor1+++++++Opcode&ExtFactor2+++++++Result++++++++Len++D+HiLoEq
 /free
  QUSBPRV = 0;

  // Describe an algorithm
  QC3D0200 = *loval;                    // Initialize format to x'00'
  QC3BCA = 22;                          // AES
  QC3BL = 16;                           // Block length of 16
  QC3MODE = '1';                        // CBC
  QC3PO = '1';                          // Pad

  // Create a key context
  QC3D040000 = *loval;                  // Initialize format to x'00'
  QC3KS00 = KeyStoreFile;               // Key store
  QC3RL = RcdKey;                       // Record label
  CrtKeyCtx( QC3D040000 :%size(QC3D040000) : '4' :22
             :'0' :*OMIT :*OMIT : QC3KCT :QUSEC);

  // Process all records from the Customer file
  read CusRec CustomerDS;
  dow not %eof;

  // Get an initialization vector for this customer
  GenPRN( EncrCustDS.IV :%size(EncrCustDS.IV) :'0' :'0' :QUSEC);
  QC3IV = EncrCustDS.IV;

  // Encrypt the customer data
  Encrypt ( CustomerDS.CustName :%size(CustomerDS.CustName) :'DATA0100'
            :QC3D0200 :'ALGD0200' :QC3D010000 :'KEYD0100'
            :'0' :*OMIT :EncrCustDS.EncrData :%size(EncrCustDS.EncrData)
            :LenEncrRtn :QUSEC);
```

Figure 11.17: Encrypting data with key management (part 2 of 3).

```
    // Write the encrypted customer data
    EncrCustDS.CustNbr = CustomerDS.CustNbr;
    write EncrRec EncrCustDS;
    read CusRec CustomerDS;
    enddo;

    // When done, clean up
    DstKeyCtx ( QC3D010000  :QUSEC);

    *inlr = *on;
    return;
    /end-free
```

Figure 11.17: Encrypting data with key management (part 3 of 3).

As you can see, FIG11_17 is very similar to the program we initially used to encrypt data, FIG11_1. For the field definitions, the only change is that the data area CLEARKEY, used in FIG11_1 to provide the encryption key, has been removed, and two new fields have been added. The new fields are KeyStoreFile, used to hold the qualified name of the key store file (ABCSTORE in SOMELIB), and RcdKey, used to hold the label of the key store file record ('Customer file') for encrypting and decrypting customer data.

Another change is how the key context is being created. In FIG11_1, the key context was created using the key value found in the CLEARKEY data area and a key format of zero. In FIG11_17, the key context is created using a record label from the ABCSTORE key store. This is done with key format 4. The QSYSINC definition for this format is shown in Figure 11.18. The pertinent portion of FIG11_17, initializing this format, is shown in Figure 11.19.

```
DName+++++++++++ETDsFrom+++To/L+++IDc.Keywords+++++++++++++++++++++++++++
D*KEYD0400 key description format structure
D*                                                             @A3A
DQC3D040000     DS
D*                                              Qc3 Format KEYD0400
D QC3KS00              1     20
D*                                              Key Store
D*                                                             @A3A
D QC3RL               21     52
D*                                              Record Label
D*                                                             @A3A
D QC3ERVED03          53     56
D*                                              Reserved
```

Figure 11.18: QSYSINC/QRPGLESRC member QC3CCI definition for format KEYD0400.

The first field, QC3KS00, is the qualified name of the key store to be used. The sample program uses ABCSTORE in library SOMELIB.

384

The second field, QC3RL, is the record label identifying the record that contains the cryptographic key the program uses. The sample program uses the record label 'Customer file'.

The third field, QC3ERVED03, is reserved space that must be initialized to x'00's.

```
CLON01Factor1+++++++Opcode&ExtFactor2+++++++Result++++++++Len++D+HiLoEq
   // Create a key context
   eval QC3D040000 = *loval;       // Initialize format to x'00'
   eval QC3KS00 = KeyStoreFile;    // Key store
   eval QC3RL = RcdKey;            // Record label
   CrtKeyCtx( QC3D040000 :%size(QC3D040000) : '4' :22
             :'0' :*OMIT :*OMIT :QC3KCT :QUSEC);
```

Figure 11.19: Creating a key context from the ABCSTORE key store file.

As the KEYD0400 format is an input structure, FIG11_17 first initializes the entire structure, QC3D040000, to x'00's. The program then sets the key store name, QC3KS00, to 'ABCSTORE SOMELIB ' and the record label, QC3RL, to 'Customer file'. When calling the Qc3CreateKeyStore API, FIG11_17 requests an AES key context, with the key context handle being returned in the field QC3KCT. (For a refresher on the parameters used when calling the Qc3CreateKeyContext API, refer to Table 11.2.)

These changes are it! The rest of the program FIG11_17 is the same as FIG11_1. The big difference is not in the code, but that FIG11_17 provides a degree of protection for your cryptographic keys that is significantly greater than that provided with FIG11_1.

Decrypting Data Using a Key Store

Having encrypted the customer data using the key-management APIs, we'll now decrypt it using the source shown in Figure 11.20.

```
h dftactgrp(*no)

FFilename++IPEASF.....L.....A.Device+.Keywords++++++++++++++++++++++++++
fEncrCust  if   e          k disk

DName+++++++++++ETDsFrom+++To/L+++IDc.Keywords+++++++++++++++++++++++++++
d/copy qsysinc/qrpglesrc,qc3cci
d/copy qsysinc/qrpglesrc,qusec
```

Figure 11.20: Decrypting data with key management (part 1 of 3).

```
dCrtKeyCtx        pr                      extproc('Qc3CreateKeyContext')
d KeyString                     65535     const options(*varsize)
d LenKeyString                  10i 0     const
d KeyFormat                     1         const
d KeyType                       10i 0     const
d KeyForm                       1         const
d KeyEncrKey                    8         const options(*omit)
d KeyAlgorithm                  8         const options(*omit)
d KeyContext                    8
d QUSEC                                   likeds(QUSEC)

dDecrypt          pr                      extproc('Qc3DecryptData')
d EncrData                      65535     const options(*varsize)
d LenEncrData                   10i 0     const
d AlgDesc                       65535     const options(*varsize)
d AlgDescFmt                    8         const
d KeyDesc                       65535     const options(*varsize :*omit)
d KeyDescFmt                    8         const options(*omit)
d CryptoProvider                1         const
d CryptoDevice                  10        const options(*omit)
d ClearData                     1         options(*varsize)
d LenClearData                  10i 0     const
d RtnLenClrData                 10i 0
d QUSEC                                   likeds(QUSEC)

dDstKeyCtx        pr                      extproc('Qc3DestroyKeyContext')
d KeyContext                    8         const
d QUSEC                                   likeds(QUSEC)

dEncrCustDS       ds                      likerec(ENCRREC :*Input)

dCustomerDS       eds                     extname(Customer :CUSREC)
d                                         qualified

dKeyStoreFile     s             20        inz('ABCSTORE   SOMELIB')
dRcdKey           s             32        inz('Customer file')
dLenClearRtn      s             10i 0

CL0N01Factor1+++++++Opcode&ExtFactor2+++++++Result++++++++Len++D+HiLoEq
 /free
   QUSBPRV = 0;

   // Describe the encryption algorithm to use
   QC3D0200 = *loval;                // Initialize format to x'00'
   QC3BCA = 22;                      // AES
   QC3BL = 16;                       // Block length of 16
```

Figure 11.20: Decrypting data with key management (part 2 of 3).

```
QC3MODE = '1';                 // CBC
QC3PO = '1';                   // Padded

// Create a key context
QC3D040000 = *loval;           // Initialize format to x'00'
QC3KS00 = KeyStoreFile;        // Key store
QC3RL = RcdKey;                // Record label
CrtKeyCtx( QC3D040000 :%size(QC3D040000) : '4' :22
           :'0' :*OMIT :*OMIT :QC3KCT :QUSEC);

// Process all records from the EncrCust file in CustNbr sequence

read EncrRec EncrCustDS;
dow not %eof;

// Set the initialization vector for this customer
QC3IV = EncrCustDS.IV;

// Decrypt the customer data
Decrypt ( EncrCustDS.EncrData :%size(EncrCustDS.EncrData)
          :QC3D0200 :'ALGD0200' :QC3D010000 :'KEYD0100' :'0' :*OMIT
          :CustomerDS.CustName :%size(CustomerDS.CustName)
          :LenClearRtn :QUSEC);

// Display the decrypted customer data
dsply (EncrCustDS.CustNbr + ' ' + CustomerDS.Custname);

// Get next encrypted record
read EncrRec EncrCustDS;
enddo;

// When done, clean up
DstKeyCtx ( QC3D010000   :QUSEC);

*inlr = *on;
return;
/end-free
```

Figure 11.20: Decrypting data with key management (part 3 of 3).

As you can see, the changes between Figure 11.20 and Figure 11.11 are the same as those between Figure 11.17 and Figure 11.1! We remove the CLEARKEY data area, add the key store file name, add the record label name, and use key format 4 when creating the key context. We're now able to decrypt the customer data without having to expose our cryptographic keys to application developers, service personnel, security officers, or anyone else authorized to use the system.

Summary

In this chapter, you have learned how to use the basic APIs for encryption (Qc3EncryptData) and decryption (Qc3DecryptData), along with some of the key-management APIs. There are, however, many more cryptographic APIs that you should review before implementing cryptography within your applications. These APIs include the following:

- The Translate Data API (Qc3TranslateData) translates data encrypted under one key to data encrypted under a different key, without having to decrypt and expose the clear-text data in your application program.

- The Translate Key Store API (Qc3TranslateKeyStore) translates keys stored in a key store file to either a different master key or a new version of the same master key.

- The Calculate Hash API (Qc3CalculateHash) uses a one-way hash function to create a fixed-length output string from a variable-length input string.

- The Calculate MAC API (Qc3CalculateMac) produces a message authentication code.

Make sure you take the time to fully review the Information Center on all that is available to you in the area of cryptography.

Check Your Knowledge

First, write a program to add a new record label to the ABCSTORE key store file. The label should be 'Checking my knowledge', with the key being used solely for 16-byte AES encryption and decryption. The key should be provided in clear text with the value 'My first key'. To get you started, read the documentation in the Information Center for the Write Key Record API, Qc3WriteKeyRecord. For one possible solution to this task, see Figure D.11.A of appendix D.

Then, write a program to retrieve and DSPLY the key type, key size, master key ID, key verification value, and which cryptographic functions are disallowed for record label 'Customer file' in the ABCSTORE key store. To get you started, read the documentation in the Information Center for the Retrieve Key Record Attributes API, Qc3RetrieveKeyRecordAtr. Because the master key KVV is a hex value, it will most likely not be displayable in any meaningful fashion. You might want to review the Convert Hex To Character API, CVTHC, which was introduced in Figure 8.10. For one possible solution, see Figure D.11.B of appendix D.

12

Security APIs

We feel extremely privileged to have worked on the System i since its birth as the AS/400. We have watched our beloved box reinvent itself over and over again: from OPM to ILE, from CISC to RISC, and from being a box that ran RPG almost exclusively to one that efficiently runs applications designed for other operating systems. All the while, the System i has managed to remain backward-compatible. Do you know of any other system that comes close to making those claims? Neither do we.

Recently, the system has once again been reborn because of the explosive growth rate of the Internet. i5/OS users have become accustomed to just standing the system in the corner by itself and forgetting about it while it ran their business forever. Now they can stand it in a corner, connect it to the Internet, and forget about it while it runs their business forever—but that's not a very good idea. If you attach anything to the Internet, including your beloved System i, you need to pay attention to security.

You can live safely in a connected world, but you cannot naively leave your windows open and your doors unlocked at night. On the Internet, predators are everywhere. This doesn't mean you should lock your system up tight and ignore the technological revolution occurring around you. Hook your system up to the Internet! There are far too many advantages to being connected. Proceed with caution, however, by using a quality firewall, taking advantage of i5/OS's fully integrated object-level security, and (last but not least) taking advantage of security APIs.

If you are a veteran in this business, you will remember when security was never an issue. The system used to ship with security level 10 as the default. How restrictive was that security level? Well, you did have to turn the machine on before you could gain access to it, but that was all there was to it. Those days are long gone. Security level 10 is not even supported any more. i5/OS now ships with security level 30 as the default. We strongly recommend that you bump the security level to 40 or 50, especially if you are going to attach your box to the Internet.

Here's the really good news: the System i is one of the most secure boxes around. It's never been sick a day in its life. The fact that it seems to be immune to today's computer viruses is probably due to the unique nature of its architecture more than anything else. Hackers, like criminals everywhere, are generally looking for a quick strike. If it seems troublesome to have to break into a box, they are far more likely to move on to easier pickings. Learning a foreign operating system seems to be a considerable hindrance to the average hacker. Why go through the trouble? After all, there are plenty of NT and Unix boxes out there....

You can control security on the system in several different ways. From access passwords to object-level security, i5/OS does a good job of keeping your system secure. It even supports level 50 security, which is often required in high-security government installations. As complete as i5/OS's security is, however, there are still occasions when you need a little something extra. That is where the security APIs come into play.

This chapter starts off with a look at security APIs that allow you to swap the user profile under which a job is running. Many server jobs on the system are started automatically; as such, they use an initial default user profile. As various users (clients) use a server job, it can swap the user profile under which it is running to ensure that the client user can't access any unauthorized objects. The ability to swap the active, or current, user profile is also useful when working in areas of the system where adopted authorities from an application program are not available. Authorization to Integrated File System objects is, for example, one area where program adoption is not supported.

The next APIs you'll look at in this chapter are the Retrieve Encrypted Password API (QSYRUPWD) and its complement API, Set Encrypted Password (QSYSUPWD). Together, these two enable you to more easily maintain passwords across user profiles on separate systems.

While on the subject of user profiles, it's worthwhile to take a look at how to retrieve any information you might want about a user profile (except the password, of course). The Retrieve User Information API (QSYRUSRI) delivers "the goods" on demand.

You'll see how to put this all together with programs that use these APIs to synchronize user profile changes across systems. You'll see how a program can be called whenever a user profile is changed, and how it can communicate the change to another system using a remote data queue. The receiving program (running on another system) reads the data queue and changes the user profile on that second system. Although separate sample programs are shown here, one that works with passwords and another that works with user profile attributes, you should have no difficulty merging the two functions into one application.

The documentation for these APIs can be found in the Information Center under the API category "Security," subcategory "Security-related APIs."

Swapping the Active User Profile

There is a family of security-related APIs that allow you to swap the current user profile associated with a job to another user profile. These APIs use a *handle*, which is a Char(12) character variable representing a user profile on the system. Handles are temporary— they are deleted when your job ends, and they cannot be shared across jobs.

You can use APIs such as Get Profile Handle (QsyGetProfileHandle) and Get Profile Handle No Password (QsyGetProfileHandleNoPwd) to get a handle. As you might expect from their names, QsyGetProfileHandle is used when you want to validate the password along with the user profile name, and QsyGetProfileHandleNoPwd is used when you want to run under an authorized profile and do not need to validate the password.

Figure 12.1 shows the parameters for QsyGetProfileHandle. As you learned in chapter 1, when the parameters for an API are documented in this style it indicates that all parameters are to be passed by value.

```
void QsyGetProfileHandle( unsigned char *Profile_handle,
                          char          *User_ID,
                          char          *Password,
                          int            Length_of_password,
                          int            CCSID_of_password,
                          void          *Error_code)
```

Figure 12.1: The Get Profile Handle API (QsyGetProfileHandle).

The API documentation in the Information Center indicates that the first parameter, Profile_handle, is a pointer (the asterisk) to a Char(12) output field. The second parameter, User_ID, is a pointer to a Char(10) input field specifying the user profile that we want a handle created for. The third parameter, Password, is a pointer to a variable-length-character input field that contains the password associated with the user profile specified in the second parameter. The fourth parameter, Length_of_password, is a signed integer (indicated by '*int*') that contains the length of the password supplied in parameter 3. The length can be from one to 512 bytes to accommodate the various password levels controlled by the system value QPWDLVL and encodings such as UTF-16, where a character can require up to four bytes to encode. The fifth parameter, CCSID_of_password, is a signed integer that specifies the CCSID of the password. Special values can be specified for this parameter, one of which is zero, to indicate that the job CCSID should be used. The sixth parameter, Error_code, is a pointer to the standard QUSEC error-code structure that you've seen in many other system APIs.

Figure 12.2 shows the parameter for the QsyGetProfileHandleNoPwd API. This API requires that special values be used, rather than passwords. It is very useful when you are running under a user profile that is authorized to another user profile, and you do not need to validate the password associated with the user profile.

```
void QsyGetProfileHandleNoPwd( unsigned char *Profile_handle,
                               char          *User_ID,
                               char          *Password_value,
                               void          *Error_code)
```

Figure 12.2: The Get Profile Handle No Password API (QsyGetProfileHandleNoPwd).

The first, second, and fourth parameters are essentially the same as those for the equivalent parameters of QsyGetProfileHandle. One significant change, though, is support for the special value '*CURRENT' for the user_ID parameter. This can be used when you want to get a handle for the currently active user profile (so that you can swap back to it later).

The third parameter, Password_value, is what really differentiates this API from QsyGetProfileHandle. Three special values are defined for Password_value:

- *NOPWD indicates that a handle should be generated for the User_ID specified in parameter 2, but only if the API caller has *USE authority to the User_ID and the user profile is not disabled or associated with an expired password.

- *NOPWDCHK indicates that a handle should be generated for the specified User_ID if the API caller has *USE authority to the User_ID and, if the API caller has the *ALLOBJ and *SECADM special authorities, a handle should be generated even if the User_ID is disabled or associated with an expired password.

- *NOPWDSTS indicates that a handle should be generated if the API caller has *USE authority to the User_ID. If the profile has an expired password and the API caller has the *ALLOBJ and *SECADM special authorities, a handle will also be generated. However, a handle will not be generated for a disabled user profile.

Once we have a handle, we can use it to swap our job to the user profile associated with that handle. The API to perform this swap is Set Profile Handle, QsySetToProfileHandle. Table 12.1 shows the parameter descriptions for QsySetToProfileHandle.

Table 12.1: The Set Profile Handle API (QsySetToProfileHandle)			
Parameter	Description	Type	Size
1	Profile Handle	Input	Char(12)
2	Error Code	I/O	Char(*)

The first parameter, Profile Handle, is a handle that was previously returned by either QsyGetProfileHandle or QsyGetProfileHandleNoPwd. The second parameter is the standard error-code parameter.

There is another API that is used to free up handles after they are no longer needed. This API is Release Profile Handle, QsyReleaseProfileHandle. The parameters for QsyReleaseProfileHandle are the same as those for QsySetToProfileHandle.

There is system overhead related to the space involved in maintaining handles. This causes a system-wide limit of approximately two million handles. While this is a rather large number, it is good practice to always release a handle when you no longer need it.

Figure 12.3 shows an application program that uses all four of these APIs. Before running the program FIG12_3, you will need to create a second user profile for testing purposes. This user profile should have a password, should be enabled, does not need to have any special authorities, and (for demonstration purposes) should have a CCSID different than that of your normal user profile. So, if the user profile you normally sign on with has a

CCSID of 65535, create this new user profile with a CCSID such as 37. If your normal user profile has a CCSID such as 37, create this new user profile with a CCSID of 65535.

```
h dftactgrp(*no)

DName+++++++++++ETDsFrom+++To/L+++IDc.Keywords++++++++++++++++++++++++
d/copy qsysinc/qrpglesrc,qusec

dFig12_3          pr
d Profile                       10      const
d PassWord                      10

dFig12_3          pi
d Profile                       10      const
d PassWord                      10

dGetWithNoPwd     pr                    extproc(
d                                       'QsyGetProfileHandleNoPwd')
d Handle                        12
d Profile                       10      const
d PassWordSpc                   10      const
d QUSEC                                 likeds(QUSEC)

d GetWithPwd       pr                   extproc('QsyGetProfileHandle')
d Handle                        12
d Profile                       10      const
d PassWord                   65535      const options(*varsize)
d PassWordLen                 10i 0     value
d PassWordCCSID               10i 0     value
d QUSEC                                 likeds(QUSEC)

dSwapProfile      pr                    extproc('QsySetToProfileHandle')
d Handle                        12      const
d QUSEC                                 likeds(QUSEC)

dFreeHandle       pr                    extproc(
d                                       'QsyReleaseProfileHandle')
d Handle                        12      const
d QUSEC                                 likeds(QUSEC)

dCmdExc           pr                    extpgm('QCMDEXC')
d Command                    65535      const options(*varsize)
d CmdLength                     15 5    const
d IGC                            3      const options(*nopass)
```

Figure 12.3: Swapping the current user profile (part 1 of 2).

```
dDspJob2           c                     'DSPJOB OPTION(*STSA)'
dDspJob3           c                     'DSPJOB OPTION(*DFNA)'

dOriginalHandle    s             12
dNewHandle         s             12
dCommand           s             20

CLON01Factor1+++++++Opcode&ExtFactor2+++++++Result++++++++Len++D+HiLoEq
 /free
  QUSBPRV = 0;

  // Minimize exposure of password value in a program variable
  GetWithPwd( NewHandle :Profile :PassWord :10 :0 :QUSEC);
  Password = *blanks;

  GetWithNoPwd( OriginalHandle :'*CURRENT' :'*NOPWD' :QUSEC);

  // Show environment before swapping
  Command = DspJob2;
  CmdExc( Command :%len(%trimr(Command)));
  Command = DspJob3;
  CmdExc( Command :%len(%trimr(Command)));

  SwapProfile( NewHandle :QUSEC);

  // Show environment after swapping
  Command = DspJob2;
  CmdExc( Command :%len(%trimr(Command)));
  Command = DspJob3;
  CmdExc( Command :%len(%trimr(Command)));

  // return to the original profile
  SwapProfile( OriginalHandle :QUSEC);

  // show environment after swapping back to original profile
  Command = DspJob2;
  CmdExc( Command :%len(%trimr(Command)));
  Command = DspJob3;
  CmdExc( Command :%len(%trimr(Command)));

  FreeHandle( OriginalHandle :QUSEC);
  FreeHandle( NewHandle :QUSEC);
  *inlr = *on;
  return;
 /end-free
```

Figure 12.3: Swapping the current user profile (part 2 of 2).

The program itself is very straightforward. It is defined to accept two parameters: the user profile and the password associated with the profile. The program does make a simplifying assumption, namely that the system password level is 0 or 1. For password levels of 2 and 3, passwords can be up to 128 characters long. This would mean providing a command interface to FIG12_3 rather than calling it from the command line, unless you wanted to key in blanks to fill the full 128 characters of the second parameter! As this book is about APIs and not commands, we elected to make this simplifying assumption. (If you don't understand why you would need to supply all 128 characters, don't worry about it. It's related to how the command analyzer treats command-line input and has nothing to do with the subject of this book.)

After setting the Error Code Bytes Provided Field, QUSBPRV, to zero so that exception messages are sent by the called APIs, FIG12_3 calls QsyGetProfileHandle, requesting a handle for the user profile name passed to FIG12_3. QsyGetProfileHandle, as part of its processing, will validate that the password passed is correct for the specified user profile. FIG12_3 then sets the user password parameter to all blanks. To minimize the exposure of keeping password values in program variables where they might be seen with commands such as Dump Job (DMPJOB), you should always use and clear passwords as soon as possible. Note though that PASSWORD is actually a parameter being passed to FIG12_3, so setting this variable to blanks is actually setting the variable in the caller's program to blanks. This action may or may not be appropriate, depending on your application.

FIG12_3 then calls QsyGetProfileHandleNoPwd, requesting a handle to the current user. This handle is stored in field OriginalHandle and will be used later to restore the job to its initial user profile. The program now uses the Execute Command API, QCMDEXC, to show the status and definition attributes for the current job. We could, of course, simply call the program QCMD and ask you to use the DSPJOB command. Why should you do something manually, however, when APIs can do it for you? On the first DSPJOB output, notice what the current user profile and job user identity are. For the second DSPJOB, PageDown to where the CCSID is shown, and note the current CCSID setting.

The program then swaps to the new user profile. At this point, the program can do anything the swapped-to user profile is authorized to do. In the example, the program again uses the QCMDEXC API to show you the job's environment after swapping the user profile, but it could do many other actions. On the displays, you should notice that the current profile of the job has been changed (although the job name would still contain the original user profile name), and that the CCSID of the job has not. Note that the only changes in the current job are related to the profile the job is running under. No other attributes from the swapped-to user profile are in effect. If you were developing a server job and wanted to change the job environment to more fully reflect the attributes of the swapped-to user profile, in addition to the authorization environment, you would probably want to look at the Change Job API, QWTCHGJB, and in particular format JOBC0300 of the API. This API can be found in the "Work Management" category of system APIs. It is used in chapter 13 to provide a more complete version of program FIG12_3.

When the program is done with whatever processing is needed, shown in Figure 12.3 as the display of the job status and definition attributes, it swaps back to the original profile, displays the job status and definition attributes again so that you can see they have been restored to their initial values, and releases both handles.

Retrieving Encrypted Passwords

Since everything done on your system is tracked by user profile, it's very important that access to each user's profile be secure. Only the owner of the user profile should know his or her password. The next sample program shows you how an encrypted password may be retrieved—but not in a decipherable form. It is retrieved in its fully encrypted state. You might be wondering why encrypted information would have any value. It is valuable because, even in its encrypted state, you can use the encrypted password information to keep your passwords consistent across several other systems in a network.

Two APIs work in conjunction to accomplish this task. The first, Retrieve Encrypted User Password (QSYRUPWD), retrieves the encrypted password information. The second, Set Encrypted User Password (QSYSUPWD), sets the user profile password to the value represented by the information retrieved by QSYRUPWD. The one rule to keep in mind is to not modify any of the data returned by QSYRUPWD prior to using it with QSYSUPWD.

The parameter descriptions for the Retrieve Encrypted User Password API are shown in Table 12.2. As you can see from the table, this is a standard retrieve-type API. As such, we won't spend any time on what the various parameters are used for. If you need a refresher, see chapter 2.

The QSYRUPWD API defines one format, UPWD0100. The QSYSINC-provided definition for this format is shown in Figure 12.4.

Table 12.2: Retrieve Encrypted Password (QSYRUPWD)

Parameter	Description	Type	Size
1	Receiver Variable	Output	Char(*)
2	Length of the Receiver Variable	Input	Binary(4)
3	Format Name	Input	Char(8)
4	User Profile Name	Input	Char(10)
5	Error Code	I/O	Char(*)

```
DName+++++++++++ETDsFrom+++To/L+++IDc.Keywords++++++++++++++++++++++
D******************************************************************
D*Record structure for UPWD0100 format
D******************************************************************
DQSYD0100         DS
D*                                          Qsy RUPWD UPWD0100
D QSYBRTN04           1      4B 0
D*                                          Bytes Returned
D QSYBAVL04           5      8B 0
D*                                          Bytes Available
D QSYPN06             9     18
D*                                          Profile Name
D*QSYEP              19     19
D*
D*                                  Varying length
```

Figure 12.4: Format UPWD0100 of QSYRUPWD from QSYSINC/QRPGLESRC.

Within the QSYSINC include for QSYRUPWD is the data structure QSYD0100, which defines format UPWD0100. This data structure defines the standard fields of bytes returned (QSYBRTN04) and bytes available (QSYBAVL04), along with the name of the user profile (QSYPN06). The encrypted data field (QSYEP), however, is not defined in terms of any particular length that needs to be declared, nor is the maximum length for this field documented in the Information Center. As there is no fixed (or maximum) length to the encrypted password data available, we will use the dynamic-receiver-variable technique introduced in chapter 2 to determine how much storage to allocate for the Receiver Variable parameter of Retrieve Encrypted User Password. This, along with the rest of the program, is shown in Figure 12.5.

```
h dftactgrp(*no)

DName+++++++++++ETDsFrom+++To/L+++IDc.Keywords+++++++++++++++++++++++
d/copy qsysinc/qrpglesrc,qsyrupwd
d/copy qsysinc/qrpglesrc,qusec

dFig12_5          pr
d Profile                      10    const

dFig12_5          pi
d Profile                      10    const

dGetPassword      pr                 extpgm('QSYRUPWD')
d Receiver                      1    options(*varsize)
d LenReceiver                  10i 0 const
d Format                        8    const
d Profile                      10    const
d USEC                               likeds(QUSEC)

dSndDtaQ          pr                 extpgm('QSNDDTAQ')
d DtaQName                     10    const
d DtaQLib                      10    const
d DataLen                       5  0 const
d Data                       65535   const options(*varsize)
d KeyLen                        3  0 const options(*nopass)
d KeyValue                   65535   const options(*varsize :*nopass)
d Asynch                       10    const options(*nopass)
d JrnEntry                     10    const options(*nopass)

dReceiver         ds                 likeds(QSYD0100)
d                                    based(ReceiverPtr)

dRcvSize          s            10i 0 inz(8)


CLON01Factor1+++++++Opcode&ExtFactor2+++++++Result++++++++Len++D+HiLoEq
 /free
  QUSBPRV = 0;

  // Find out how large of a receiver parameter we need
  ReceiverPtr = %alloc(RcvSize);
  GetPassword( Receiver :RcvSize :'UPWD0100' :Profile :QUSEC);

  // Allocate a large enough receiver and get the password
  RcvSize = Receiver.QSYBAVL04;
  ReceiverPtr = %realloc(ReceiverPtr :RcvSize);
  GetPassword( Receiver :RcvSize :'UPWD0100' :Profile :QUSEC);
```

Figure 12.5: Use the Retrieve Encrypted Password (QSYRUPWD) to get an encrypted password (part 1 of 2).

```
// send the password to the PASSWORD data queue
SndDtaQ( 'PASSWORD' :'SOMELIB' :Receiver.QSYBRTN04 :Receiver);

dealloc ReceiverPtr;
*inlr = *on;
return;
/end-free
```

Figure 12.5: Use the Retrieve Encrypted Password (QSYRUPWD) to get an encrypted password (part 2 of 2).

The program accepts one parameter, the user profile name. The program sets the Error Code Bytes Provided field to zero to indicate exception messages are requested, allocates a minimum receiver variable of 8 bytes, and then calls the Retrieve Encrypted User Password API. Once we have determined the length of the data that can be retrieved (Receiver.QSYBAVL04), the program reallocates the receiver variable and calls the API a second time to get the full, encrypted user-password data.

FIG12_5 then sends the entire receiver variable as a message to the data queue PASSWORD in library SOMELIB. The Send Data Queue API, QSNDDTAQ, was introduced in chapter 6, so we won't go into the details of calling this API at this time.

You might be wondering where this data queue came from and why in the world we're sending the encrypted password information to it! To answer the first question, we haven't created it yet. The command in Figure 12.6 creates it. (We arbitrarily chose a MAXLEN of 10,000 as a reasonably large number. We could just as easily used 30,000.)

```
CRTDTAQ DTAQ(SOMELIB/PASSWORD) MAXLEN(10000)
```

Figure 12.6: Creating the PASSWORD data queue.

As for the question of why use a data queue, the answer is that we want to use this encrypted password information on another system in order to synchronize password changes, and data queues have the ability to be transparently accessed by programs running on remote systems. We need some way to communicate across systems. Sockets APIs could be used to develop a communications program, but they're not discussed until chapter 15. So, data queues were chosen. You'll see how to configure data queues for remote access shortly.

First, let's look at the Set Encrypted User Password API, QSYSUPWD. Table 12.3 shows its associated parameters.

Table 12.3: Set Encrypted Password (QSYSUPWD)			
Parameter	Description	Type	Size
1	Receiver Variable from QSYRUPWD	Input	Char(*)
2	Format	Input	Char(8)
3	Error Code	I/O	Char(*)

The API accepts three parameters. The first must be the complete receiver variable as previously returned by the Retrieve Encrypted User Password API. This includes the fields Bytes Returned, Bytes Available, User Profile Name, and Encrypted Password Data. In addition, the Bytes Returned and Bytes Available fields must be equal; passing in only a portion of the encrypted data will not work. The second parameter is simply the format name (UPWD0100), and the third parameter is the standard error-code structure.

Figure 12.7 shows how to use this API. The FIG12_7 program is very straightforward. After setting the Error Code Bytes Provided field to zero, the program reads a message off of the PASSWORD data queue in library SOMELIB. It uses that message (Buffer) as the first parameter of the Set Encrypted User Password API. The program then ends.

In a production environment, you would probably want to make some changes to this sample program. One change that comes to mind is to not end after every message. Instead, have the program loop back to receive the next message, as the FIG6_3 program does in chapter 6. Just remember to provide a way to cleanly end the program as we did with program FIG6_5.

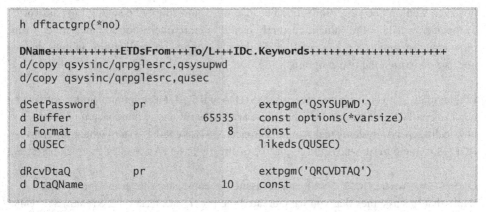

```
h dftactgrp(*no)

DName+++++++++++ETDsFrom+++To/L+++IDc.Keywords++++++++++++++++++++++++
d/copy qsysinc/qrpglesrc,qsysupwd
d/copy qsysinc/qrpglesrc,qusec

dSetPassword      pr                    extpgm('QSYSUPWD')
d Buffer                      65535     const options(*varsize)
d Format                          8     const
d QUSEC                                 likeds(QUSEC)

dRcvDtaQ          pr                    extpgm('QRCVDTAQ')
d DtaQName                        10    const
```

Figure 12.7: Using the Set Encrypted Password API (QSYSUPWD) (part 1 of 2).

```
d DtaQLib                       10      const
d ReceiverLenRtn                 5 0
d Receiver                       1      options(*varsize)
d WaitTime                       5 0 const
d KeyOrder                       2      const options(*nopass)
d KeyLen                         3 0 const options(*nopass)
d KeyValue                       1      options(*varsize :*nopass)
d SndrInfoLen                    3 0 const options(*nopass)
d SndrInfo                       1      options(*varsize :*nopass)
d RmvMsg                        10      const options(*nopass)
d ReceiverLen                    5 0 const options(*nopass)
d QUSEC                                 likeds(QUSEC) options(*nopass)

dBuffer            s         10000
dBufferLenRtn      s             5 0
dUnused            s             1

CLON01Factor1+++++++Opcode&ExtFactor2+++++++Result+++++++++Len++D+HiLoEq
 /free
   QUSBPRV = 0;
   RcvDtaQ( 'PASSWORD' :'SOMELIB' :BufferLenRtn :Buffer :-1
          :' ' :0 :Unused :0 :Unused :'*YES' :%size(Buffer) :QUSEC);
   SetPassword ( Buffer :'UPWD0100' :QUSEC);
   *inlr = *on;
   return;
 /end-free
```

Figure 12.7: Using the Set Encrypted Password API (QSYSUPWD) (part 2 of 2).

The PASSWORD data queue was previously created, so program FIG12_7 has everything it needs to run—as long as it is running on the same system as program FIG12_5. This, however, wouldn't be very productive because we would simply be setting the password of the user profile to the value it currently has. It is more interesting to have FIG12_5 run on one system and FIG12_7 on another. To do this requires no application changes due to how we've written the two programs!

Let's assume that you have two systems, SYSTEMA and SYSTEMB, communicating with each other over a TCP/IP network. Whether these are two partitions of one System i or two physically separate systems makes no difference. SYSTEMA is the system where program FIG12_5 is going to run and, from Figure 12.6, already has a PASSWORD data queue created.

On SYSTEMB, where FIG12_7 will run, we issue the command shown in Figure 12.8. (Note that this assumes that you have created the library SOMELIB on SYSTEMB.) SYSTEMB now has a data queue named PASSWORD in library SOMELIB that is associated with the remote data queue SOMELIB/PASSWORD on remote system SYSTEMA. The data queues on SYSTEMA and SYSTEMB do not need to have the same name, but the RMTDTAQ parameter must have the correct name for the data queue as it exists on the system specified by the RDB parameter. In this case, it is SYSTEMA.

```
CRTDTAQ DTAQ(SOMELIB/PASSWORD) TYPE(*DDM) RMTDTAQ(SOMELIB/PASSWORD)
RMTLOCNAME(*RDB) RDB(SYSTEMA)
```

Figure 12.8: Creating the PASSWORD data queue on SYSTEMB.

Some additional environmental setup might be required. If you have never used i5/OS's distributed database capability, you will probably need to add relational database directory entries to both systems. The command that would be used on SYSTEMA is shown in Figure 12.9, and the command for SYSTEMB is in Figure 12.10. Note that there are additional parameters that might apply, based on your system configuration.

```
ADDRDBDIRE RDB(SYSTEMB) RMTLOCNAME(SYSTEMB *IP)
```

Figure 12.9: Adding a relational database entry on SYSTEMA that defines SYSTEMB.

```
ADDRDBDIRE RDB(SYSTEMA) RMTLOCNAME(SYSTEMA *IP)
```

Figure 12.10: Adding a relational database entry on SYSTEMB that defines SYSTEMA.

Once the two relational database directory entries are created, the FIG12_5 and FIG12_7 programs should be able to run as-is. If FIG12_7 encounters an authority error when attempting to read from the PASSWORD data queue, you might also need to look at the RMTAUTMTH parameter of ADDRDBDIRE, along with the authority requirements specified with command CHGDDMTCPA. These authority requirements should be checked on both SYSTEMA and SYSTEMB.

In this sample scenario, we consciously decided to have the local data queue on SYSTEMA and the remote data queue access on SYSTEMB. This is because SYSTEMA is our primary system for password changes, and FIG12_5 will always be able to send the encrypted password information to the local PASSWORD data queue. The data queue is local, so there will be no error encountered if communication with SYSTEMB is down for some reason. FIG12_7 on SYSTEMB, on the other hand, will not be able to receive messages during any network outages. As soon as the network becomes available, however, FIG12_7 will be able to start processing the queued-up messages sitting on SYSTEMA's PASSWORD data queue. Due to network outages, password changes might be delayed in being applied to SYSTEMB, but they will get there.

Knowing When a User Profile Is Changed

In the previous scenario, the assumption is that a user or application program calls the FIG12_5 program to access and send the encrypted password information. Wouldn't it be nice, though, if you could automatically be notified when a user profile is changed? There is, of course, an API to do that.

Several exit points in i5/OS are related to user profiles, including these:

- When a user profile is changed

- When a user profile is created

- When a user profile is deleted

- When a user profile is restored to the system

All of these can be found in the "Security" category of system APIs, under "Security-related Exit Programs." The exit point we are interested in right now is the support for Change User Profile Exit Programs, QIBM_QSY_CHG_PROFILE. The only parameter passed to the exit program is Change Profile Exit Information, which is described in Figure 12.11.

```
DName+++++++++++ETDsFrom+++To/L+++IDc.Keywords++++++++++++++++++++++++
D*******************************************************************
D*Type Definition for the Change profile exit point information
D*******************************************************************
DECHQCPF1         DS
D*                                          Qsy Change Profile
D ECHEN                  1     20
D*                                          Exitpgm name
D ECHEF                 21     28
D*                                          Exitpgm fmt
D ECHUP                 29     38
D*                                          User profile
```

Figure 12.11: QSYSINC/QRPGLESRC member ECHGPRF1.

One or more exit programs can be called by this exit point whenever commands such as CHGUSRPRF, CHGUSRAUD, CHGPRF, or CHGPWD are run. In addition, system APIs that change a user profile, such as Reset Profile Attributes (QSYRESPA) or Change Password (QSYCHGPW), will also cause the exit programs to be called.

Field ECHEN is the exit point name, and will be set to the value QIBM_QSY_CHG_PROFILE when the exit program is called by Change Exit. The exit point name is passed because you might have the same exit program being called for user-profile create, change, and delete operations. This sharing is possible because the same parameter description is used for all three operations/exit points. If you have one common exit program being used, you will most likely want to know which exit point called the program, as there undoubtedly will be different processing involved. So, ECHEN is passed to the exit program.

Field ECHEF is the format name associated with when the exit program is being called. There are two formats associated with QIBM_QSY_CHG_PROFILE. Format CHGP0100 indicates that the exit program is being called after the user profile is changed, while format CHGP0200 indicates that the exit program is being called before the user profile is changed. The third field, ECHUP, is the name of the user profile being changed.

Retrieving User Information

The "change" exit point enables many types of applications related to user profiles. The only profile-related piece of information passed, however, is the user profile name. Certainly, more needs to be known. To determine the current attributes of the user profile, whether it's before the change with format CHGP0200 or after the change with format CHGP0100, we can retrieve information related to the user profile. The parameter description for the Retrieve User Information API, QSYRUSRI, is shown in Table 12. 4.

Table 12.4: The Retrieve User Information API (QSYRUSRI)			
Parameter	Description	Type	Size
1	Receiver Variable	Output	Char(*)
2	Receiver Variable Length	Input	Binary(4)
3	Format Name	Input	Char(8)
4	User Profile Name	Input	Char(10)
5	Error Code	I/O	Char(*)

By now, you should recognize this type of API parameter description very easily, so we will focus on the Format Name parameter. The Retrieve User Information API supports three formats in which to return data. Format USRI0100 returns sign-on and password-related information, USRI0200 returns authority-related information, and USRI0300 returns all user information. We will be working with format USRI0300. The QSYSINC ILE RPG definition for USRI0300 is shown in Figure 12.12.

```
DName+++++++++++ETDsFrom+++To/L+++IDc.Keywords++++++++++++++++++++++++++
D*********************************************************************
D*Record structure for USRI0300 format
D*******
D*NOTE:  The following type definition only defines the fixed
D*     portion of the format. Any varying length field will
D*     have to be defined by the user.
D*********************************************************************
DQSYI0300        DS
D*                                                  Qsy USRI0300
D QSYBRTN02            1      4B 0
D*                                                  Bytes Returned
D QSYBAVL02            5      8B 0
D*                                                  Bytes Available
D QSYUP03              9     18
D*                                                  User Profile
D QSYPS00             19     31
D*                                                  Previous Signon
D QSYRSV103           32     32
D*                                                  Reserved 1
D QSYSN00             33     36B 0
D*                                                  Signon Notval
D QSYUS02             37     46
D*                                                  User Status
D QSYPD02             47     54
D*                                                  Pwdchg Date
D QSYNP00             55     55
D*                                                  No Password
D QSYRSV203           56     56
D*                                                  Reserved 2
D QSYPI01             57     60B 0
D*                                                  Pwdexp Interval
D QSYPD03             61     68
D*                                                  Pwdexp Date
D QSYPD04             69     72B 0
D*                                                  Pwdexp Days
D QSYPE00             73     73
D*                                                  Password Expired
```

Figure 12.12: Format USRI0300 of the Retrieve User Information API (part 1 of 6).

```
D QSYUC00             74      83
D*                                        User Class
D   QSYAOBJ01         84      84
D*                                        All Object
D   QSYSA05           85      85
D*                                        Security Admin
D   QSYJC01           86      86
D*                                        Job Control
D   QSYSC01           87      87
D*                                        Spool Control
D   QSYSS02           88      88
D*                                        Save System
D   QSYRVICE01        89      89
D*                                        Service
D   QSYAUDIT01        90      90
D*                                        Audit
D   QSYISC01          91      91
D*                                        Io Sys Cfg
D   QSYERVED10        92      98
D*                                        Reserved
D QSYGP02             99     108
D*                                        Group Profile
D QSYOWNER01         109     118
D*                                        Owner
D QSYGA00            119     128
D*                                        Group Auth
D QSYAL04            129     138
D*                                        Assistance Level
D QSYCLIB            139     148
D*                                        Current Library
D   QSYNAME14        149     158
D*                                        Name
D   QSYBRARY14       159     168
D*                                        Library
D   QSYNAME15        169     178
D*                                        Name
D   QSYBRARY15       179     188
D*                                        Library
D QSYLC00            189     198
D*                                        Limit Capabilities
D QSYTD              199     248
D*                                        Text Description
D QSYDS00            249     258
D*                                        Display Signon
D QSYLDS             259     268
D*                                        Limit DeviceSsn
```

*Figure 12.12: Format **USRI0300** of the Retrieve User Information API (part 2 of 6).*

```
D QSYKB                269   278
D*                                       Keyboard Buffering
D QSYRSV300            279   280
D*                                       Reserved 3
D QSYMS                281   284B 0
D*                                       Max Storage
D QSYSU                285   288B 0
D*                                       Storage Used
D QSYSP                289   289
D*                                       Scheduling Priority
D   QSYNAME16          290   299
D*                                       Name
D   QSYBRARY16         300   309
D*                                       Library
D QSYAC                310   324
D*                                       Accounting Code
D   QSYNAME17          325   334
D*                                       Name
D   QSYBRARY17         335   344
D*                                       Library
D QSYMD                345   354
D*                                       Msgq Delivery
D QSYRSV4              355   356
D*                                       Reserved 4
D QSYMS00              357   360B 0
D*                                       Msgq Severity
D   QSYNAME18          361   370
D*                                       Name
D   QSYBRARY18         371   380
D*                                       Library
D QSYPD05              381   390
D*                                       Print Device
D QSYSE                391   400
D*                                       Special Environment
D   QSYNAME19          401   410
D*                                       Name
D   QSYBRARY19         411   420
D*                                       Library
D QSYLI                421   430
D*                                       Language Id
D QSYCI                431   440
D*                                       Country Id
D QSYCCSID00           441   444B 0
D*                                       CCSID
D   QSYSK00            445   445
D*                                       Show Keywords
```

Figure 12.12: Format USRI0300 of the Retrieve User Information API (part 3 of 6).

```
D    QSYSDOO              446    446
D*                                         Show Details
D    QSYFHOO              447    447
D*                                         Fullscreen Help
D    QSYSS03              448    448
D*                                         Show Status
D    QSYNS00              449    449
D*                                         Noshow Status
D    QSYRK00              450    450
D*                                         Roll Key
D    QSYPM00              451    451
D*                                         Print Message
D    QSYERVED11           452    480
D*                                         Reserved
D    QSYNAME20            481    490
D*                                         Name
D    QSYBRARY20           491    500
D*                                         Library
D QSYOBJA18               501    510
D*                                         Object Audit
D    QSYCMDS00            511    511
D*                                         Command Strings
D    QSYREATE00           512    512
D*                                         Create
D    QSYELETE00           513    513
D*                                         Delete
D    QSYJD01              514    514
D*                                         Job Data
D    QSYOBJM07            515    515
D*                                         Object Mgt
D    QSYOS00              516    516
D*                                         Office Services
D    QSYPGMA00            517    517
D*                                         Program Adopt
D    QSYSR00              518    518
D*                                         Save Restore
D    QSYURITY00           519    519
D*                                         Security
D    QSYST00              520    520
D*                                         Service Tools
D    QSYSFILD00           521    521
D*                                         Spool File Data
D    QSYSM00              522    522
D*                                         System Management
D    QSYTICAL00           523    523
D*                                         Optical
```

Figure 12.12: Format USRI0300 of the Retrieve User Information API (part 4 of 6).

```
D   QSYERVED12          524    574
D*                                        Reserved
D QSYGAT00              575    584
D*                                        Group Auth Type
D QSYSG000              585    588B 0
D*                                        Supp Group Offset
D QSYSGNBR02            589    592B 0
D*                                        Supp Group Number
D QSYUID                593    596U 0
D*                                        UID
D QSYGID                597    600U 0
D*                                        GID
D QSYHDO                601    604B 0
D*                                        HomeDir Offset
D QSYHDL                605    608B 0
D*                                        HomeDir Len
D QSYLJA                609    624
D*                                        Locale Job Attribut
D QSYLO                 625    628B 0
D*                                        Locale Offset
D QSYLL                 629    632B 0
D*                                        Locale Len
D QSYGMI03              633    633
D*                                        Group Members Indic
D QSYDCI                634    634
D*                                        Digital Certificate
D QSYCC                 635    644
D*                                        Chrid Control
D QSYSPSDO              645    648B 0
D*                                        HomeDir Offset
D QSYHDL                605    608B 0
D*                                        HomeDir Len
D QSYLJA                609    624
D*                                        Locale Job Attribut
D QSYLO                 625    628B 0
D*                                        Locale Offset
D QSYLL                 629    632B 0
D*                                        Locale Len
D QSYGMI03              633    633
D*                                        Group Members Indic
D QSYDCI                634    634
D*                                        Digital Certificate
D QSYCC                 635    644
D*                                        Chrid Control
D QSYSPSDO              645    648B 0
D*                                        IASP Storage Dsc Of
```

Figure 12.12: Format *USRI0300* of the Retrieve User Information API (part 5 of 6).

```
D QSYSPSDC                    649   652B 0
D*                                               IASP Storage Dsc Co
D QSYPSDCR                    653   656B 0
D*                                               IASP Storage Dsc Co
D QSYSPSDL                    657   660B 0
D*                                               IASP Storage Dsc Le
D QSYLPM00                    661   661
D*                                               Local Pwd Mgt
D*                                                               @07A
D*QSYSGN02                    662   671   DIM(00001)
D*
D*                                         Varying length
D*QSYPI02                     672   672
D*
D*                                  Varying length
D*QSYLI00                     673   673
D*
D*
D*                                     Varying length
D*QSYASPSD00                         20   DIM(00001)
D* QSYIASPN00                        10   OVERLAY(QSYASPSD00:00001)
D* QSYERVED36                         2   OVERLAY(QSYASPSD00:00011)
D* QSYMS02                          9B 0  OVERLAY(QSYASPSD00:00013)
D* QSYSU01                          9B 0  OVERLAY(QSYASPSD00:00017)
D*
D*                                            Varying length
```

*Figure 12.12: Format **USRI0300** of the Retrieve User Information API (part 6 of 6).*

As you can see, a wealth of information is available about a user profile. In program FIG12_13, shown in Figure 12.13, we retrieve all of this information and then send it to SYSTEMB for further processing.

```
h dftactgrp(*no)

DName+++++++++++ETDsFrom+++To/L+++IDc.Keywords++++++++++++++++++++++
d/copy qsysinc/qrpglesrc,echgprf1
d/copy qsysinc/qrpglesrc,qsyrusri
d/copy qsysinc/qrpglesrc,qusec

dFig12_13           pr
d Input                                likeds(ECHQCPF1)

dFig12_13           pi
d Input                                likeds(ECHQCPF1)
```

Figure 12.13: An exit program for the Change User Profile exit point (part 1 of 2).

411

```
dRtvUsrInfo        pr                      extpgm('QSYRUSRI')
d Receiver                         1       options(*varsize)
d LenReceiver                     10i 0    const
d Format                           8       const
d ECHUP                           10       const
d QUSEC                                    likeds(QUSEC)

dSndDtaQ           pr                      extpgm('QSNDDTAQ')
d DtaQName                        10       const
d DtaQLib                         10       const
d DataLen                          5  0    const
d Data                         65535       const options(*varsize)
d KeyLen                           3  0    const options(*nopass)
d KeyValue                     65535       const options(*varsize :*nopass)
d Asynch                          10       const options(*nopass)
d JrnEntry                        10       const options(*nopass)

dReceiver          ds                      likeds(QSYI0300)
d                                          based(ReceiverPtr)

dRcvSize           s              10i 0 inz(8)
dwait              s               1

CLON01Factor1+++++++Opcode&ExtFactor2+++++++Result++++++++Len++D+HiLoEq
 /free
   if Input.ECHEN = 'QIBM_QSY_CHG_PROFILE' and Input.ECHEF = 'CHGP0100';
      QUSBPRV = 0;
      ReceiverPtr = %alloc(RcvSize);
      RtvUsrInfo( Receiver :RcvSize :'USRI0300' :Input.ECHUP :QUSEC);
      RcvSize = Receiver.QSYBAVL02;
      ReceiverPtr = %realloc( ReceiverPtr :RcvSize);
      RtvUsrInfo( Receiver :RcvSize :'USRI0300' :Input.ECHUP :QUSEC);
      SndDtaQ( 'PROFILE' :'SOMELIB' :Receiver.QSYBRTN02 :Receiver);
      dealloc ReceiverPtr;
   else;
      dsply 'Program not called by expected caller' ' ' wait;
   endif;
   *inlr = *on;
   return;
 /end-free
```

Figure 12.13: An exit program for the Change User Profile exit point (part 2 of 2).

The program first checks to see if it has been called by the Change Profile exit point
(Input.ECHEN = 'QIBM_QSY_CHG_PROFILE') and that format CHGP0100 is being used
(Input.ECHEF = 'CHGP0100'). If not, appropriate error text is DSPLYed.

If the program was called by the correct exit point and with the correct format, then it uses the dynamic-receiver-variable approach of calling the QSYRUSRI API once with a receiver variable just large enough to return the Bytes Available field of format USRI0300 (Receiver.QSYBAVL02), reallocating Receiver to the number of bytes available, and then calling the QSYRUSRI API a second time to obtain all of the user profile information. This is done partly because some portions of the returned data are variable in length. (The list of supplemental groups and home directory are two examples.) Another reason is that IBM might add additional information to this format in future releases. If IBM makes enhancements, we will not have to change FIG12_13 in order to pick up, and send, any new information that might be returned.

After retrieving the user profile data, FIG12_13 then sends all of the data returned (Receiver.QSYBRTN02) to the data queue PROFILE in library SOMELIB, frees the storage associated with Receiver, and ends. The command used on SYSTEMA to create the PROFILE data queue is shown in Figure 12.14.

```
CRTDTAQ DTAQ(SOMELIB/PROFILE) MAXLEN(10000)
```

Figure 12.14: Creating the PROFILE data queue on SYSTEMA.

We now need to write the program that reads this data queue message and changes the user profile on SYSTEMB to match the changes made on SYSTEMA. This program is shown in Figure 12.15.

```
h dftactgrp(*no)

DName++++++++++++ETDsFrom+++To/L+++IDc.Keywords++++++++++++++++++++++++
d/copy qsysinc/qrpglesrc,qsyrusri
d/copy qsysinc/qrpglesrc,qusec

dRcvDtaQ          pr                extpgm('QRCVDTAQ')
d DtaQName                    10    const
d DtaQLib                     10    const
d ReceiverLenRtn              5   0
d Receiver                    1     options(*varsize)
d WaitTime                    5   0 const
d KeyOrder                    2     const options(*nopass)
d KeyLen                      3   0 const options(*nopass)
d KeyValue                    1     options(*varsize :*nopass)
```

Figure 12.15: The program to receive QSYRUSRI format USRI0300 and construct a CHGUSRPRF command string (part 1 of 2).

```
d SndrInfoLen                      3  0 const options(*nopass)
d SndrInfo                         1     options(*varsize :*nopass)
d RmvMsg                          10     const options(*nopass)
d ReceiverLen                      5  0 const options(*nopass)
d QUSEC                                  likeds(QUSEC) options(*nopass)

dCmdExc          pr                      extpgm('QCMDEXC')
d Command                      65535     const options(*varsize)
d CmdLength                       15  5 const
d IGC                              3     const options(*nopass)

dBufferView      ds                      likeds(QSYI0300)
d                                        based(BufferPtr)

dBuffer          s             10000
dBufferPtr       s                 *     inz(%addr(Buffer))
dCommand         s             10000
dBufferLenRtn    s                 5  0
dUnused          s                 1

CLON01Factor1+++++++Opcode&ExtFactor2+++++++Result++++++++Len++D+HiLoEq
 /free
   QUSBPRV = 0;
   RcvDtaQ( 'PROFILE' :'SOMELIB' :BufferLenRtn :Buffer :-1
           :' ' :0 :Unused :0 :Unused :'*YES' :%size(Buffer) :QUSEC);
   Command = 'CHGUSRPRF USRPRF(' + BufferView.QSYUP03 +
                   ') USRCLS(' + BufferView.QSYUC00 +
                   ') ASTLVL(' + BufferView.QSYAL04 +
                   ') CURLIB(' + BufferView.QSYCLIB +
                   ') LMTCPB(' + BufferView.QSYLC00 +
                   ') SPCENV(' + BufferView.QSYSE   + ')';
   CmdExc( Command :%len(%trimr(Command)));
   *inlr = *on;
   return;
 /end-free
```

Figure 12.15: The program to receive QSYRUSRI format USRIO300 and construct a CHGUSRPRF command string (part 2 of 2).

The FIG12_15 program is essentially nothing more than a series of API calls. After initializing the Bytes Provided field of the error-code structure (QUSBPRV) to zero, the program reads a message from the PROFILE data queue. This message is read into the program variable Buffer, which has a BASED view (BufferView) mapping the QSYSINC-provided definition of the USRIO300 format over the received message.

The program then creates a command string (Command) that contains the necessary CHGUSRPRF command and parameters to synchronize the SYSTEMB user profile with the SYSTEMA user profile. FIG12_15 only shows the mapping of a few of the possible fields, but that should be sufficient for you to get the general idea. Note that a few of the fields returned in USRI0300 need some reformatting prior to being inserted into the command string. Special authorities, for example, are returned as "Y" and "N" values and need to be converted to special value keywords such as *ALLOBJ for the SPCAUT parameter.

After the command string is constructed, FIG12_15 uses the Execute Command API, QCMDEXC, to run the CHGUSRPRF command, and exits. (The QCMDEXC API was discussed in chapter 4.)

It should be pointed out that FIG12_15 will need to be changed if IBM enhances the information returned by the Retrieve User Information API in a future release *and* you want to take advantage of this new information. While FIG12_15 will be receiving all of the new user-profile information in the messages sent by FIG12_13, FIG12_15 will not take advantage of this information. You will need to update how the CHGUSRPRF command is being built. On the other hand, if you don't care about the new information, FIG12_15 will just keep on running as-is.

To create the PROFILE data queue on SYSTEMB, we use the command in Figure 12.16. To inform i5/OS that we want FIG12_13 to be called for user-profile changes, we use the command in Figure 12.17 on SYSTEMA.

```
CRTDTAQ DTAQ(SOMELIB/PROFILE) TYPE(*DDM) RMTDTAQ(SOMELIB/PROFILE)
RMTLOCNAME(*RDB) RDB(SYSTEMA)
```

Figure 12.16: Creating the PROFILE data queue on SYSTEMB.

```
ADDEXITPGM EXITPNT(QIBM_QSY_CHG_PROFILE) FORMAT(CHGP0100) PGMNBR(*LOW)
PGM(FIG12_13)
```

Figure 12.17: Registering FIG12_13 on SYSTEMA so it is called when user profile attributes are changed.

As soon as the command in Figure 12.17 completes, FIG12_13 will start being called for changes to user profiles on SYSTEMA. FIG12_13 will start sending messages to the PROFILE data queue on SYSTEMA. If FIG12_15 has been started on SYSTEMB, it will immediately start receiving the messages and applying the changes to SYSTEMB user profiles.

As with the FIG12_7 program, FIG12_15 is written such that it ends after each message is read and processed. In a production environment, you would most likely want FIG12_15 to be in a DO loop, reading data queue messages and generating CHGUSRPRF commands until a special message is received (such as the "STOP" message in Figure 6.3).

Summary

This chapter examines a variety of APIs that can help you with security issues. You have seen how to swap the profile in effect for a job, which can be of great assistance when either developing client/server applications or working with the Integrated File System, where adopted authorities do not apply. You have seen how to maintain identical user profile passwords on different machines using the Get and Set Encrypted Password APIs. You have also seen how to have i5/OS call an exit program of your choosing whenever a user profile is changed, and how to use the Retrieve User Information API to access the information you need about a user profile. There are many other security-related APIs that are both easy to use and beneficial to anyone trying to tightly manage security.

Check Your Knowledge

You might have certain applications that you only want run by users with the special authority of *SECADM. Write a program that checks to see if the currently active user profile of the current job has this special authority, and then displays either "Authorized" or "Not authorized." When performing this check, do not allow adopted authority by the caller of your program to influence the decision. To get you started, review the Check User Special Authorities API, QSYCUSRS, documented in the "Security" category of system APIs.

One possible solution to this task can be found in Figure D.12 of appendix D.

13

Work-Management APIs

Jobs represent a fundamental unit of work within i5/OS. (Actually, this is an over-simplification, as i5/OS really manages work at a thread level. However, most of your jobs probably have only one thread, the initial one, and most users tend to think in terms of jobs. Therefore, we use the term *jobs* in this chapter.) A large number of commands are provided by i5/OS to help manage jobs and the environment in which jobs run. These commands include Work Job (WRKJOB), Work Submitted Job (WRKSBMJOB), Work Subsystem Job (WRKSBSJOB), Work Active Job (WRKACTJOB), and Work System Status (WRKSYSSTS), to name a few.

As you would expect, many APIs are also available to programmatically manage work in the system. Some of these APIs include Retrieve Job Information (QUSRJOBI), Retrieve Job Locks (QWCRJBLK), Retrieve IPL Attributes (QWCRIPLA), Retrieve Call Stack (QWCRCSTK), Retrieve Job Queue Information (QSPRJOBQ), List Jobs (QUSLJOB), List Active Subsystems (QWCLASBS), Move Job (QSPMOVJB), Change Job (QWTCHGJB), Change Pool Attributes (QUSCHGPA), and exit points such as Auxiliary Storage Lower Limit (QIBM_QWC_QSTGLOWACN) and Job Notification (QIBM_QWT_JOBNOTIFY). And this barely scratches the surface of what's available! We've looked at two of these APIs, Retrieve Job Queue Information and the Job Notify exit point, in earlier chapters (chapter 2 and chapter 6, respectively). Many of these APIs are the standard retrieve-type and list-type APIs, which you should be very comfortable with by now. If you feel that a review of these types is in order, see chapters 2 and 3.

In this chapter, we first look at the List Jobs API, QUSLJOB. With this API, you can get a list of all or a subset of the jobs on the system. The subset can be based on criteria such as the job's status (active, on a job queue, completed with spooled output on an output queue) and/or the type of job (interactive, batch, autostart, etc). The List Jobs API has two formats that can be used to access the job information. The first format, JOBL0100, generates a straightforward list of jobs. Processing this format is similar to processing lists of objects returned by the List Object API in chapter 3. The JOBL0100 list contains basic information, such as the job name, job status, and job type (batch, interactive, etc). Given this list of jobs on the system, you can then use the Retrieve Job Information API, QUSRJOBI, to access specific attributes of the jobs.

The List Jobs API also has a format JOBL0200. The JOBL0200 format uses a *keyed* interface, where you can specify which attributes of the listed jobs you want returned. You specify these attributes with key values such as 401 to get the date and time the job became active, and 418 for the date and time the job ended. The API then returns only the attributes you have selected (along with the basic information found in JOBL0100). This is in contrast to returning a fixed format, where you might get 25 different attributes when you only want two. You'll see how to use format JOBL0200, look at how to specify these keys, and then process the list of returned attributes.

Following that, you'll look at the Change Job API, QWTCHGJB. This API allows you to change the attributes of either the current job or a different job on the system. Like the List Jobs API's format JOBL0200, Change Job uses keys so that you can specify exactly which attributes, or groups of attributes, you want to change. In chapter 12, you saw how to swap the user profile, or authority, under which a job is running. At that time, we also said we would show you how to swap the environment, or attributes, of the job in addition to the authority under which it was running. You'll see how to use the Change Job API to change the attributes of the current job to match the attributes of the swapped-to user profile.

You'll then explore the Retrieve System Status API, QWCRSSTS. This API uses the standard fixed-format approach, introduced in chapter 2, for retrieving data, so we really are not introducing any new API concepts with this example. We're discussing this API here simply to give you a feel for what is available when you start examining the various system APIs. For example, while the Work with System Status (WRKSYSSTS) display doesn't tell you if the system is currently in restricted state, the Retrieve System Status API certainly can!

The documentation for these APIs can be found in the Information Center under the API category "Work Management."

Getting a List of Jobs and Selected Job Attributes

The List Jobs API, QUSLJOB, generates a list of all or some jobs on the system. The parameters for QUSLJOB are shown in Table 13.1.

Table 13.1: The List Jobs API (QUSLJOB)			
Parameter	Description	Type	Size
1	Qualified User Space Name	Input	Char(20)
2	Format	Input	Char(8)
3	Qualified Job Name	Input	Char(26)
4	Status	Input	Char(10)
Optional Parameter Group 1			
5	Error Code	I/O	Char(*)
Optional Parameter Group 2			
6	Type	Input	Char(1)
7	Number of Fields to Return	Input	Binary(4)
8	Key of Fields to Return	Input	Array(*) of Binary(4)
Optional Parameter Group 3			
9	Continuation handle	Input	Char(48)

The first parameter, Qualified User Space Name, specifies the user space to return the list into. As is standard with qualified name parameters, the first ten bytes is the name of the user space, and the second ten bytes is the name of the library. Special values of *CURLIB and *LIBL are supported for the library name.

The second parameter, Format, specifies what data should be returned in the user space. Two formats are supported by this API. Format JOBL0100 returns a basic job list containing the qualified job name (job name, user name, and job number), job status (active, on a job queue, on an output queue), job type (system, interactive, batch, etc.), and job subtype (prestart, print driver, etc). Format JOBL0200 returns all of the data found in format JOBL0100 plus additional job attributes you specify through the use of *keys*. Some of the attributes you can select are shown in Table 13.2. The keys are defined as Binary(4) values, with the Size column indicating the size of the attribute data returned by the API. The format of the returned data is further defined in the API documentation found in the Information Center.

Table 13.2: Selected Key Values for QUSLJOB		
Key	Description	Size
101	The active job status	Char(4)
305	The current user profile	Char(10)
306	The completion status	Char(1)
312	The job's total current processing time	Binary(8)
401	The date and time when the job became active	Char(13)
402	The date and time when the job entered the system	Char(13)
403	The date and time when the job is scheduled to run	Char(8)
404	The date and time when the job was put on this job queue.	Char(8)
411	The device name	Char(10)
502	The end status	Char(1)
601	The function name	Char(10)
602	The function type	Char(1)
701	The signed-on job	Char(1)
1001	The job's accounting code	Char(15)
1004	The job's queue name	Char(20)
1012	The job's user identity	Char(10)
1013	The job's user identity setting	Char(1)
1204	The job's logging severity	Binary(4)
1501	The output queue name	Char(20)
1603	The printer device name	Char(10)
1903	The status of the job on the job queue	Char(10)
1904	The submitter's job name	Char(26)
1906	The subsystem description name	Char(20)

The third parameter, Qualified Job Name, allows you to specify what jobs, by name, are to be included in the generated list. This parameter is made up of three subfields: the job name, the user name, and the job number. The job name is the first ten bytes of the qualified job name and can have a specific name, a generic name, or one of three special values. The special values are an asterisk (*) for the job the API is running in, *CURRENT for all jobs with the current job's name, and *ALL for all job names. The user name is the next ten bytes of the qualified job name, and it can also specify a specific user profile name, a generic user profile name, or one of two special values. The special values are *CURRENT for all jobs with the current job's user profile and *ALL for all user profile names. The job number is the last six bytes of the qualified job name. It can be either a specific job number or the special value *ALL.

The fourth parameter, Status, allows you to specify the status of jobs that are to be included in the list. The supported values are *ACTIVE, *JOBQ, *OUTQ, and *ALL.

The fifth parameter is the standard error-code data structure.

The sixth parameter, Type, allows you to specify the type of jobs to be included in the list. The supported values are an asterisk (*) for all job types, A for autostart jobs, B for batch jobs, I for interactive jobs, M for subsystem monitor jobs, R for spool reader jobs, S for system jobs, W for spool writer jobs, and X for the start control program function (SCPF) system job.

The seventh parameter, Number of Fields to Return, specifies how many additional attributes you want returned with format JOBL0200. Table 13.2 lists some of the attributes that can be returned. This parameter indicates how many you want returned.

The eighth parameter, Key of Fields to Return, is an array of Binary(4) key values. If, for example, you wanted to have the generated list include the date and time when the job became active (key 401) along with the job's total current processing time (key 312), you would use the value 401 for the first array element and the value 312 for the second array element. The Number of Fields to Return parameter would then be set to a value of 2 to indicate that two array elements are being passed to the API.

The ninth parameter, Continuation Handle, is used when the generated list of jobs exceeds the capacity of a user space (approximately 16MB). When the List Jobs API is unable to return all of the information due to running out of capacity in the user space, the API returns a continuation handle in the header section of the list. After processing the current list entries, you can call the API a second time, passing the returned

421

continuation handle as the ninth parameter. The API will then resume the list where it left off, filling the specified user space with more job information. This cycle of re-calling the API and passing the most recently returned continuation handle can be continued as many times as necessary to get all jobs returned to your application program. (You can see an example of using continuation handles in chapter 16.)

With that introduction to the List Jobs API, a program to display selected jobs on the system is shown in Figure 13.1. This program accepts two parameters, UserParm and StatusParm. The program then displays only jobs for a given user, only jobs of a certain status, or only jobs for a given user and a given status. For example, if you wanted to view jobs for user *JOE*, you would specify that name for the parameter 1. If you wanted only jobs for user *JOE* that were currently on a job queue, you would also specify *JOBQ for parameter 2. The program also supports generic names, so if you wanted to display all jobs where the user name started with *VIN* and had a status of *OUTQ, you would specify VIN* for the parameter 1 and *OUTQ for parameter 2.

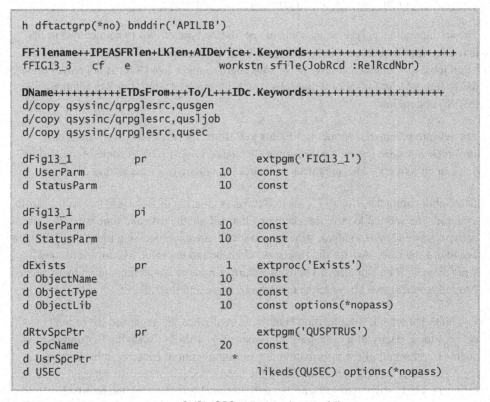

```
h dftactgrp(*no) bnddir('APILIB')

FFilename++IPEASFRlen+LKlen+AIDevice+.Keywords+++++++++++++++++++++++++
fFIG13_3   cf   e                    workstn sfile(JobRcd :RelRcdNbr)

DName++++++++++ETDsFrom+++To/L+++IDc.Keywords+++++++++++++++++++++++++
d/copy qsysinc/qrpglesrc,qusgen
d/copy qsysinc/qrpglesrc,qusljob
d/copy qsysinc/qrpglesrc,qusec

dFig13_1        pr                   extpgm('FIG13_1')
d UserParm                   10      const
d StatusParm                 10      const

dFig13_1        pi
d UserParm                   10      const
d StatusParm                 10      const

dExists         pr            1      extproc('Exists')
d ObjectName                 10      const
d ObjectType                 10      const
d ObjectLib                  10      const options(*nopass)

dRtvSpcPtr      pr                   extpgm('QUSPTRUS')
d SpcName                    20      const
d UsrSpcPtr                   *
d USEC                               likeds(QUSEC) options(*nopass)
```

Figure 13.1: This program employs QUSLJOBS to list jobs (part 1 of 5).

```
dCrtUsrSpc        pr              *    extproc('CrtUsrSpc')
d SpcName                        20    const

dListJob          pr                   extpgm('QUSLJOB')
d SpcName                        20    const
d Format                          8    const
d JobName                        26    const
d Status                         10    const
d QUSEC                                likeds(QUSEC) options(*nopass)
d JobType                         1    const options(*nopass)
d NbrKeyFlds                    10i 0  const options(*nopass)
d KeyFlds                              likeds(KeyFlds) options(*nopass)
d ContinHdl                      48    const options(*nopass)

dSndPgmMsg        pr                   extpgm('QMHSNDPM')
d MsgID                           7    const
d QualMsgF                       20    const
d MsgDta                      65535    const options(*varsize)
d LenMsgDta                     10i 0  const
d MsgType                       10    const
d CallStackEntry             65535    const options(*varsize)
d CallStackCntr                10i 0  const
d MsgKey                         4
d QUSEC                                likeds(QUSEC)
d LenCSE                        10i 0  const options(*nopass)
d CSEQual                       20    const options(*nopass)
d DSPWaitTime                   10i 0  const options(*nopass)
d CSEType                       10    const options(*nopass)
d CCSID                         10i 0  const options(*nopass)

d* list API generic header
dGenHdr            ds                  likeds(QUSH0100)
d                                      based(GenHdrPtr)

d* List Job API (QUSLJOB) format JOBL0200
dLstEntry          ds                  likeds(QUSL020001)
d                                      based(LstPtr)

dAttrEntry         ds                  likeds(QUSLKF)
d                                      based(AttrPtr)

dSpcName           ds
d SName                          10    inz('JOBLIST')
d SLib                           10    inz('QTEMP')

dKeyFlds           ds
d KeyValues                      10i 0  dim(25)
```

Figure 13.1: This program employs QUSLJOBS to list jobs (part 2 of 5).

```
dFullJobName       ds
d                             10     inz('*ALL')
d SelUser                     10     inz('*ALL')
d                              6     inz('*ALL')

dQualMsgF          ds
d MsgF                        10     inz('MSGS')
d MsgL                        10     inz('SOMELIB')

dNbrJobsDS         ds
d NbrJobs                    10i 0

dSelSts            s          10     inz('*ALL')
dAtrValue          s          10     based(AtrValPtr)
dNbrKeyFlds        s          10i 0
dLstCount          s          10i 0
dAttrCount         s          10i 0
dRelRcdNbr         s           4 0
dMsgKey            s           4

CLON01Factor1+++++++Opcode&ExtFactor2+++++++Result++++++++Len++D+HiLoEq
 /free
  QUSBPRV = 0;

  // Let the user know we're working on it
  SndPgmMsg( 'MSG0004' :QualMsgF :'   ' :0
            :'*STATUS' :'*EXT' :0 :MsgKey :QUSEC);

  // If needed, create the user space for the list of jobs
  if (Exists( SName :'*USRSPC' :SLib)) = 'N';
     GenHdrPtr = CrtUsrSpc(SpcName);
  else;
     RtvSpcPtr( SpcName :GenHdrPtr :QUSEC);
  endif;

  // Get the list of jobs
  if (%parms > 0);
     SelUser = UserParm;
     if (%parms > 1);
        SelSts = StatusParm;
     endif;
  endif;

  // Set the attribute key values
  KeyValues(1) = 1004;          // Job queue name
  KeyValues(2) = 1501;          // Output queue name
  KeyValues(3) = 1603;          // Printer device name
  NbrKeyFlds = 3;
```

Figure 13.1: This program employs QUSLJOBS to list jobs (part 3 of 5).

```
ListJob( SpcName :'JOBL0200' :FullJobName :SelSts :QUSEC
         :'*' :NbrKeyFlds :KeyFlds);

// Check to see if the list is complete
if (GenHdr.QUSIS = 'C') or (GenHdr.QUSIS = 'P');
    NbrJobs = GenHdr.QUSNBRLE;
    SndPgmMsg( 'MSG0005' :QualMsgF :NbrJobsDS :4
               :'*STATUS' :'*EXT' :0 :MsgKey :QUSEC);

    // Get to the first list entry and process the list
    LstPtr = GenHdrPtr + GenHdr.QUSOLD;

    for LstCount = 1 to GenHdr.QUSNBRLE;
        JobName = LstEntry.QUSJNU00;
        JobUser = LstEntry.QUSUNU00;
        JobSts = LstEntry.QUSTATUS01;

        // Get first attribute and process all returned
        if LstEntry.QUSJIS = ' ';
            AttrPtr = LstPtr + %size(QUSL020001);
            for AttrCount = 1 to LstEntry.QUSNBRFR;
                AtrValPtr = AttrPtr + %size(QUSLKF);
                select;
                when AttrEntry.QUSKF = 1004;
                        Jobq = AtrValue;
                when AttrEntry.QUSKF = 1501;
                        Outq = AtrValue;
                when AttrEntry.QUSKF = 1603;
                        Printer = AtrValue;
                endsl;
                AttrPtr = AttrPtr + AttrEntry.QUSLFIR;
            endfor;
        else;
            JobQ = *ALL'*';
            Outq = *ALL'*';
            Printer = *ALL'*';
        endif;

        RelRcdNbr += 1;
        write JobRcd;
        LstPtr = LstPtr + GenHdr.QUSSEE;
        if LstCount > 500;
            leave;
        endif;
    endfor;

    if RelRcdNbr > 0;
        *in21 = *on;
```

Figure 13.1: This program employs QUSLJOBS to list jobs (part 4 of 5).

425

```
        *in24 = *on;
        exfmt JobCtl;
    endif;
  else;
    dsply 'List Object API did not return valid data';
  endif;
  *inlr = *on;
  Return;

/end-free
```

Figure 13.1: This program employs QUSLJOBS to list jobs (part 5 of 5).

In looking at the source in Figure 13.1, you might notice that the program FIG13_1 does not actually implement support for generic names. Rather, it passes the UserParm value through, as-is, to the List Jobs API. The List Jobs API actually provides the generic name support on your behalf! The default for both UserParm and StatusParm is *ALL.

Figure 13.2 shows a sample display from program FIG13_1 where both the first parameter, UserParm, and the second parameter, StatusParm, are set to the special value *ALL. The source for this display file, FIG13_3, is shown in Figure 13.3. FIG13_1 simply displays the jobs in the order in which they are returned by the List Jobs API. This chapter focuses on the work-management APIs, so this is sufficient for our current purposes. In chapter 16, you will see how to use the Sort API (QLGSORT) to sequence this job information by job name, user name, status, and so on.

```
                    List Jobs Information            Selection criteria:
                                                       Status. *ALL
                                                       User.   *ALL

  Job Name  User      Sts  Job queue            Output queue       Printer
  QZSCSRVS  QUSER     *ACT                       *DEV              NOPRINT
  JWALKXXG0 JDOUG     *ACT                       *DEV              NOPRINT
  JWALKXXG0 JDOUG     *ACT                       *DEV              NOPRINT
  QPADEV0075 KITT     *ACT                       *DEV              NOPRINT
  SENDMBS   QPGMR     *OUT QBATCH     QGPL        *DEV              NOPRINT
  SENDMED   QPGMR     *OUT QBATCH     QGPL        *DEV              NOPRINT
  MCR0448   LEONARD   *OUT QBATCH     QGPL        MC2P1   QGPL     USRPRF
  QZSCSRVS  QUSER     *ACT                        *DEV              USRPRF
  QNPSERVS  QUSER     *ACT                        *DEV              USRPRF
  MAINTENEW JOHN      *OUT QBATCH     QGPL        *DEV              NOPRINT
  SENDSSI   QPGMR     *OUT QBATCH     QGPL        *DEV              NOPRINT
  C51PMTANAL TOM      *OUT QBATCH     QGPL        *DEV              NOPRINT
  COLLECTOR KEN       *OUT QBATCH2    QGPL        AWUOTQ  SERCOL   VPRTO1
  MCR0806   LEONARD   *OUT QBATCH     QGPL        MC2P1   QGPL     USRPRF
  QDFTJOBD  TOM       *OUT QINTER     QGPL        *DEV              NOPRINT
  QPWFSERVS0 QUSER    *ACT                        *DEV              NOPRINT
                                                                   More...

  F3=Exit      F12=Previous
```

Figure 13.2: A display of all jobs on the system.

```
AANO1NO2NO3T.Name++++++RLen++TDpBLinPosFunctions++++++++++++++++++++++++
         R JOBRCD                       SFL
           JOBNAME     10   O   6  2
           JOBUSER     10   O   6 13
           JOBSTS       4   O   6 24
           JOBQ        20   O   6 29
           OUTQ        20   O   6 50
           PRINTER     10   O   6 71
         R JOBCTL                       SFLCTL(JOBRCD)
                                        SFLSIZ(17) SFLPAG(16)
                                        OVERLAY
                                        SFLDSPCTL
  21                                    SFLDSP
  24                                    SFLEND(*MORE)
                                      1 26'List Jobs Information'
                                      1 62'Selection Criteria'
                                      2 63'Status:'
           SELSTS      10   O   2 71
                                      3 63'User:'
           SELUSER     10   O   3 71
                                      5  2'Job Name'
                                      5 13'User'
                                      5 24'Sts'
                                      5 29'Job Queue'
                                      5 50'Output Queue'
                                      5 71'Printer'
```

Figure 13.3: The DDS for display file FIG13_3, which is used by program FIG13_1.

After setting QUSBPRV (the Bytes Provided field for the API error-code structure) to zero, FIG13_1 uses the Send Program Message API (QMHSNDPM) to send a status message to the user, informing him or her that the list of requested jobs is being generated. On a system that might only have a few hundred jobs, this message might not be necessary. For a system with thousands of jobs, however, it might take a while for the List Jobs API to return. In that case, it's nice to let the user know that the program is running. If you are not familiar with the Send Program Message API, you might want to review chapter 10. The code for sending the message is shown in Figure 13.4, and the message description is in Figure 13.5. While we're adding MSG0004, we also add MSG0005, which will be used a bit later in the program.

```
DName+++++++++++ETDsFrom+++To/L+++IDc.Keywords+++++++++++++++++++++++++
dSndPgmMsg        pr                        extpgm('QMHSNDPM')
d MsgID                           7         const
d QualMsgF                        20        const
d MsgDta                          65535     const options(*varsize)
d LenMsgDta                       10i 0     const
d MsgType                         10        const
d CallStackEntry                  65535     const options(*varsize)
d CallStackCntr                   10i 0     const
d MsgKey                          4
d QUSEC                                     likeds(QUSEC)
d LenCSE                          10i 0     const options(*nopass)
d CSEQual                         20        const options(*nopass)
d DSPWaitTime                     10i 0     const options(*nopass)
d CSEType                         10        const options(*nopass)
d CCSID                           10i 0     const options(*nopass)

dQualMsgF         ds
d MsgF                            10        inz('MSGS')
d MsgL                            10        inz('SOMELIB')

dMsgKey           s               4


CLON01Factor1+++++++Opcode&ExtFactor2+++++++Result++++++++Len++D+HiLoEq
 /free
  QUSBPRV = 0;

  // Let the user know we're working on it
  SndPgmMsg( 'MSG0004' :QualMsgF :' ' :0
            :'*STATUS' :'*EXT' :0 :MsgKey :QUSEC);
 /end-free
```

Figure 13.4: Sending a status message from FIG13_1.

```
ADDMSGD MSGID(MSG0004) MSGF(SOMELIB/MSGS)
        MSG('Your list of jobs is being generated')

ADDMSGD MSGID(MSG0005) MSGF(SOMELIB/MSGS)
        MSG('&1 jobs found.  Now loading list') FMT((*BIN 4))
```

Figure 13.5: Adding messages MSG0004 and MSG0005 for program FIG13_1.

Following that, FIG13_1 checks to see if the user space JOBLIST already exists in the QTEMP library. If it does, FIG13_1 retrieves a pointer to the user space. Otherwise, FIG13_1 creates the user space. This is shown in Figure 13.6.

```
DName++++++++++ETDsFrom+++To/L+++IDc.Keywords++++++++++++++++++++++
dExists           pr           1    extproc('Exists')
d ObjectName                   10   const
d ObjectType                   10   const
d ObjectLib                    10   const options(*nopass)

dRtvSpcPtr        pr                extpgm('QUSPTRUS')
d SpcName                      20   const
d UsrSpcPtr                    *
d USEC                              likeds(QUSEC) options(*nopass)

dCrtUsrSpc        pr           *    extproc('CrtUsrSpc')
d SpcName                      20   const

dSpcName          ds
d SName                        10   inz('JOBLIST')
d SLib                         10   inz('QTEMP')


CLON01Factor1++++++Opcode&ExtFactor2++++++Result++++++++Len++D+HiLoEq
 /free
   QUSBPRV = 0;

   // If needed, create the user space for the list of jobs
   if (Exists( SName :'*USRSPC' :SLib)) = 'N';
      GenHdrPtr = CrtUsrSpc(SpcName);
   else;
      RtvSpcPtr( SpcName :GenHdrPtr :QUSEC);
   endif;

 /end-free
```

Figure 13.6: Checking for user space JOBLIST in QTEMP.

In Figure 13.6, the program first uses the Exists procedure to determine if the user space JOBLIST in QTEMP has been previously created. This procedure was created in chapter 5 and defines three parameters, along with a return value. The parameters are Object Name, Object Type, and Object Library. The return value is the single character *Y* if the specified object exists, or *N* if it does not exist.

The program makes this check for performance reasons. If FIG13_1 had previously been called in this job, then the user space already exists. Rather than creating a new user space, we will simply reuse the old one. List APIs always replace the contents of the user space with the new list, so we can call the List Jobs API with the user space created from the first time FIG13_1 ran, and then simply process the returned list. Any extraneous data from the first list (perhaps there were more jobs on the system at that time) will exist in

429

the user space, but will not be processed by FIG13_1. This is due to the Generic List Header specifying how many job entries to process for the current list.

If the user space does not exist, FIG13_1 uses the CrtUsrSpc procedure to create the user space and return a pointer to the new space. This pointer is stored in the variable GenHdrPtr. The CrtUsrSpc procedure was created in chapter 1, and defines one parameter, along with one return value. The parameter is the qualified object name of the user space to create. The return value is a pointer to the created user space. If the user space does exist, FIG13_1 uses the Retrieve User Space Pointer API, QUSPTRUS (introduced in chapter 1), to store a pointer to the space in variable GenHdrPtr.

In either case, GenHdrPtr contains the address of the first byte of the JOBLIST user space when the source shown in Figure 13.6 completes. FIG13_1 is now ready to process the input parameters, UserParm and StatusParm, and call the List Jobs API. This is shown in Figure 13.7.

```
DName++++++++++ETDsFrom+++To/L+++IDc.Keywords++++++++++++++++++++++++
dListJob          pr                extpgm('QUSLJOB')
d SpcName                      20   const
d Format                        8   const
d JobName                      26   const
d Status                       10   const
d QUSEC                             likeds(QUSEC) options(*nopass)
d JobType                       1   const options(*nopass)
d NbrKeyFlds                  10i 0 const options(*nopass)
d KeyFlds                           likeds(KeyFlds) options(*nopass)
d ContinHdl                    48   const options(*nopass)

dSpcName          ds
d SName                        10   inz('JOBLIST')
d SLib                         10   inz('QTEMP')

dKeyFlds          ds
d KeyValues                   10i 0 dim(25)

dFullJobName      ds
d                             10   inz('*ALL')
d SelUser                     10   inz('*ALL')
d                              6   inz('*ALL')

dSelSts           s           10   inz('*ALL')
dNbrKeyFlds       s          10i 0
```

Figure 13.7: Processing FIG13_1 input parameters and calling QUSLJOB.

```
CLON01Factor1+++++++Opcode&ExtFactor2+++++++Result++++++++Len++D+HiLoEq
 /free
  QUSBPRV = 0;

  // Get the list of jobs
  if (%parms > 0);
     SelUser = UserParm;
     if (%parms > 1);
        SelSts = StatusParm;
     endif;
  endif;

  // Set the attribute key values
  KeyValues(1) = 1004;                // Job queue name
  KeyValues(2) = 1501;                // Output queue name
  KeyValues(3) = 1603;                // Printer device name
  NbrKeyFlds = 3;

  ListJob( SpcName :'JOBL0200' :FullJobName :SelSts :QUSEC
           :'*' :NbrKeyFlds :KeyFlds);

 /end-free
```

Figure 13.7: Processing FIG13_1 input parameters and calling QUSLJOB.

Figure 13.7 defines the data structure FullJobName, which corresponds to the third parameter of the List Jobs API, Qualified Job Name. FullJobName is defined with three subfields representing the job name, job user, and job number. All three subfields are initially set to the special value *ALL so that all jobs, by default, are included in the list. If the UserParm parameter is passed to FIG13_1, it is used to update the SelUser subfield of FullJobName. In a similar manner, FIG13_1 defines the standalone variable SelSts (Selection Status), which corresponds to the fourth parameter of the List Jobs API, Status. SelSts is initially set to the special value *ALL so that jobs of all statuses are included in the list. If the StatusParm parameter is passed to FIG13_1, it is used to update the SelSts variable.

The program also defines the data structure KeyFlds, which corresponds to the eighth parameter of the List Jobs API, Key of Fields to Return. KeyFlds is defined as having an array of up to 25 Binary(4) KeyValues. FIG13_1 sets KeyValue(1) to the value 1004, indicating that the job queue name for each job is to be returned in the list. KeyValue(2) is set to the value 1501, indicating that the output queue name for each job is to be returned in the list. KeyValue(3) is set to the value 1603, indicating that the printer device associated with each job is to be returned in the list. The variable NbrKeyFlds, which corresponds to the seventh parameter of the List Jobs API (Number of Fields to Return), is then set to the value 3 because FIG13_1 has set three KeyValues array elements. As you can see, adding or removing job attributes that you want returned is very straightforward!

FIG13_1 then calls the List Jobs API, asking that the JOBL0200 format list, with three job attribute keys, be generated into the user space JOBLIST in library QTEMP. The job selection fields, FullJobName and SelSts, are used to select which jobs are included in the generated list.

When the List Jobs API returns, FIG13_1 first examines the contents of the JOBLIST user space to determine if any problems were encountered. This is shown in Figure 13.8, but it will not be discussed in any detail because this is standard checking when working with list-type APIs.

```
DName+++++++++++ETDsFrom+++To/L+++IDc.Keywords+++++++++++++++++++++++
d/copy qsysinc/qrpglesrc,qusgen
d/copy qsysinc/qrpglesrc,qusljob

d* list API generic header
dGenHdr           ds                  likeds(QUSH0100)
d                                     based(GenHdrPtr)

d* List Job API (QUSLJOB) format JOBL0200
dLstEntry         ds                  likeds(QUSL020001)
d                                     based(LstPtr)

dNbrJobsDS        ds
d NbrJobs                    10i 0

CLON01Factor1+++++++Opcode&ExtFactor2+++++++Result++++++++Len++D+HiLoEq
 /free

  // Check to see if the list is complete
  if (GenHdr.QUSIS = 'C') or (GenHdr.QUSIS = 'P');
     NbrJobs = GenHdr.QUSNBRLE;
     SndPgmMsg( 'MSG0005' :QualMsgF :NbrJobsDS :4
               :'*STATUS' :'*EXT' :0 :MsgKey :QUSEC);
```

Figure 13.8: Checking to make sure a list was successfully generated (part 1 of 2).

432

```
        // Get to the first list entry and process the list
        LstPtr = GenHdrPtr + GenHdr.QUSOLD;
        for LstCount = 1 to GenHdr.QUSNBRLE;

        endfor;

    else;
        dsply 'List Object API did not return valid data';
    endif;
    *inlr = *on;
    Return;

/end-free
```

Figure 13.8: Checking to make sure a list was successfully generated (part 2 of 2).

If the list was successfully generated, Figure 13.8 demonstrates how to send the message MSG0005 to tell the user how many jobs were found, and that the next step of the program is now in progress. (Message MSG0005 might display too quickly for you to see, depending on your system, but the message really is there!) FIG13_1 then sets LstPtr to point to the first entry returned in the list and enters a FOR loop to process all of the format JOBL0200 list entries.

We haven't looked at the JOBL0200 list entries in any detail yet, and now is a good time. Figure 13.9 shows the QSYSINC ILE RPG definitions for JOBL0200.

```
DName+++++++++++ETDsFrom+++To/L+++IDc.Keywords++++++++++++++++++++++
D******************************************************************
D*Type Definition for the JOBL0200 format.
D****                                                            ***
D*NOTE: The following type definition only defines the fixed
D*    portion of the format.  Any varying length field will
D*    have to be defined by the user.
D******************************************************************
DQUSL020001         DS
D*                                          Qus JOBL0200
D QUSJNU00              1     10
D*                                          Job Name Used
D QUSUNU00             11     20
D*                                          User Name Used
D QUSJNBRU00           21     26
D*                                          Job Number Used
```

Figure 13.9: The fixed-field portion of format JOBL0200 from QSYSINC (part 1 of 2).

```
D QUSIJIOO               27    42
D*                                         Internal Job Id
D QUSTATUS01             43    52
D*                                         Status
D QUSJT01                53    53
D*                                         Job Type
D QUSJS00                54    54
D*                                         Job Subtype
D QUSERVED18             55    56
D*                                         Reserved
D QUSJIS                 57    57
D*                                         Job Info Status
D QUSRSV205              58    60
D*                                         Reserved2
D QUSNBRFR               61    64B 0
D*                                         Number Fields Rtnd
D*QUSKFI                       18    DIM(00001)
D* QUSLFIR01                    9B 0 OVERLAY(QUSKFI:00001)
D* QUSKF00                      9B 0 OVERLAY(QUSKFI:00005)
D* QUSTOD01                     1    OVERLAY(QUSKFI:00009)
D* QUSERVED33                   3    OVERLAY(QUSKFI:00010)
D* QUSLD01                      9B 0 OVERLAY(QUSKFI:00013)
D* QUSDATA07                    1    OVERLAY(QUSKFI:00017)
D* QUSERVED33                   1    OVERLAY(QUSKFI:00018)
D*
D*                                         Varying length
```

Figure 13.9: The fixed-field portion of format JOBL0200 from QSYSINC (part 2 of 2).

There are 11 subfields within the QUSL020001 data structure. The first, QUSJNU00, is the simple job name of the job. The second, QUSUNU00, is the user name portion of the qualified job name, and the third, QUSJNBRU00, is the job number portion of the qualified job name.

The fourth field, QUSIJI00, is an internal job identifier that is sometimes used by other system APIs. We won't be using this value in FIG13_1, but it can be used by the system as a fast path to job information. For example, the next API discussed in this chapter, the Change Job API (QWTCHGJB), accepts an internal job identifier as its second parameter. This value allows other APIs to directly access where job information is stored rather than having to look it up based on the qualified job name. Think of this internal job identifier conceptually as being like a relative record number into a file, and the qualified job name as being like an index over that file. Both will get you to the same "record," but you'll get there much faster with the relative record number! There are, however, some considerations. One is that this value is only good during the current IPL.

434

The fifth field, QUSTATUS01, is the status of the job. This field may be set to *ACTIVE, *JOBQ, or *OUTQ. A value of *ACTIVE indicates that the job has started. Note, though, that the API documentation indicates *ACTIVE does not necessarily mean the job is actively running. The job might, for example, have been held using the Hold Job (HLDJOB) command or disconnected using the Disconnect Job command (DSCJOB). *ACTIVE just indicates that the job has started. A value of *JOBQ indicates that the job is currently on a job queue, and a value of *OUTQ indicates that the job has completed but has spooled output that has not been printed.

The sixth field, QUSJT01, is the type of job. This field can contain values such as A for autostart jobs, B for batch jobs, I for interactive jobs, M for subsystem monitor jobs, R for spool reader jobs, S for system jobs, W for spool writer jobs, and X for the start control program function (SCPF) system job. The seventh field, QUSJS00, provides information to further clarify the type of job. This field can contain values such as J for prestart or P for printer driver. The eighth field, QUSERVED18, is a reserved field.

The ninth field, QUSJIS, is the status of the job list entry. If this field is set to the value of A, you are not authorized to the job, and the attributes you requested with parameter 8 (Key of Fields to Return) are not returned in the list entry. If this field is set to the value L, the job information was not available; again, the attributes you requested are not returned in the list entry. If this field is set to a blank, the attribute information has been returned in the list entry.

The tenth field, QUSRSV205, is another reserved field. The eleventh field, QUSNBRFR, indicates how many of the attributes that you selected were returned in the list entry.

Immediately following the field QUSNBRFR are the attribute values you requested. These attributes are returned in an array of self-defining structures. The QSYSINC definition for this structure is shown in Figure 13.10. The number of these structure occurrences, per format JOBL0200 list entry, is the previously discussed field QUSNBRFR.

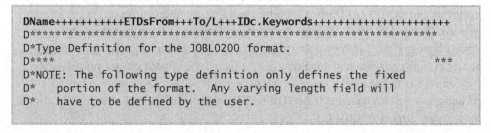

```
DName+++++++++++ETDsFrom+++To/L+++IDc.Keywords+++++++++++++++++++++++
D*******************************************************************
D*Type Definition for the JOBL0200 format.
D****                                                           ***
D*NOTE: The following type definition only defines the fixed
D*    portion of the format.  Any varying length field will
D*    have to be defined by the user.
```

Figure 13.10: The substructure used to return requested job attributes (part 1 of 2).

```
D*******************************************************************
DQUSLKF             DS
D*                                              Qus Ljob Key Fields
D QUSLFIR                   1      4B 0
D*                                              Length Field Info R
D QUSKF                     5      8B 0
D*                                              Key Field
D QUSTOD                    9      9
D*                                              Type Of Data
D QUSERVED17               10     12
D*                                              Reserved
D QUSLD00                  13     16B 0
D*                                              Length Data
D*QUSDATA06                17     17
D*
D*                               Varying length
D*QUSERVED17               18     18
D*
D*                               Varying length
```

Figure 13.10: The substructure used to return requested job attributes (part 2 of 2).

Within the QSYSINC-provided data structure, QUSLKF, are five subfields. The first field, QUSLFIR, is the length of all field information returned for this attribute. As mentioned earlier, there will be QUSNBRFR occurrences of this data structure returned for each list entry. Each occurrence of the data structure QUSLKF may be of a different length, as different attributes have varying lengths. For example, key 306, the completion status, returns one byte of data, while key 1904, the submitter's job name, returns 26 bytes of data.

The value of this field is the sum of the size of the five subfields defined in the data structure QUSLKF, the size of the attribute value returned, and the size of any padding the API might have introduced after the attribute value. By adding this value, QUSLFIR, to the offset used to get to the current occurrence of QUSLKF, you can then get to the next occurrence of QUSLKF. APIs often introduce padding, or reserved space, for performance reasons. (Some data types, integers in particular, have a small performance advantage when aligned on what is known as a *natural boundary*, which means 4-byte integer values perform best when aligned on a 4-byte boundary, 8-bytes integer values perform best on an 8-bytes boundary, etc. As each occurrence of QUSLKF contains integer fields, padding may be introduced at the end of each occurrence of QUSLKF to optimally align the next occurrence of QUSLKF.)

The second field, QUSKF, is the key of the attribute being returned in this occurrence of QUSLKF. The third field, QUSTOD, defines the type of data being returned for this attribute. The data type might be C for character or B for binary/integer. The fourth field, QUSERVED17, is a reserved field. The fifth field, QUSLD00, is the length of the attribute data value actually returned.

The actual attribute data value immediately follows QUSLD00. This value corresponds to the attribute key QUSKF, is returned in the form QUSTOD, and is of the length QUSLD00.

With that introduction to how attribute information is returned, Figure 13.11 shows how FIG13_1 processes each returned list entry and attribute array. As a reminder, when we left Figure 13.8, program FIG13_1 had set the LstPtr pointer to the first JOBL0200 entry and had entered a FOR loop, which is exited when GenHdr.QUSNBRLE entries have been processed. GenHdr.QUSNBRLLE is the number of returned list entries and is found in the generic header of list-type APIs.

```
DName++++++++++++ETDsFrom+++To/L+++IDc.Keywords+++++++++++++++++++++++
d* list API generic header
dGenHdr            ds                    likeds(QUSH0100)
d                                        based(GenHdrPtr)

d* List Job API (QUSLJOB) format JOBL0200
dLstEntry          ds                    likeds(QUSL020001)
d                                        based(LstPtr)

dAttrEntry         ds                    likeds(QUSLKF)
d                                        based(AttrPtr)

dAtrValue          s          10         based(AtrValPtr)
dLstCount          s          10i 0
dAttrCount         s          10i 0
dRelRcdNbr         s           4  0

CLON01Factor1+++++++Opcode&ExtFactor2+++++++Result++++++++Len++D+HiLoEq
 /free

     LstPtr = GenHdrPtr + GenHdr.QUSOLD;
     for LstCount = 1 to GenHdr.QUSNBRLE;
         JobName = LstEntry.QUSJNU00;
         JobUser = LstEntry.QUSUNU00;
         JobSts = LstEntry.QUSTATUS01;
```

Figure 13.11: Processing each returned attribute (part 1 of 2).

437

```
            // Get first attribute and process all returned
            if LstEntry.QUSJIS = ' ';
               AttrPtr = LstPtr + %size(QUSL020001);
               for AttrCount = 1 to LstEntry.QUSNBRFR;
                  AtrValPtr = AttrPtr + %size(QUSLKF);
                  select;
                    when AttrEntry.QUSKF = 1004;
                         Jobq = AtrValue;
                    when AttrEntry.QUSKF = 1501;
                         Outq = AtrValue;
                    when AttrEntry.QUSKF = 1603;
                         Printer = AtrValue;
                  endsl;
                  AttrPtr = AttrPtr + AttrEntry.QUSLFIR;
               endfor;
            else;
               JobQ = *ALL'*';
               Outq = *ALL'*';
               Printer = *ALL'*';
            endif;

            RelRcdNbr += 1;
            write JobRcd;
            LstPtr = LstPtr + GenHdr.QUSSEE;
            if LstCount > 500;
               leave;
            endif;
         endfor;

/end-free
```

Figure 13.11: Processing each returned attribute (part 2 of 2).

The program FIG13_1 sets the FIG13_3 display file fields JobName, JobUser, and JobSts
to the corresponding fields from the fixed portion of the JOBL0200 format. The program
then examines the contents of LstEntry.QUSJIS, the status of the job list entry. If
LstEntry.QUSJIS is a blank, the requested attribute information was returned in the
list entry. The program sets the AttrPtr pointer variable to the offset of the list entry
(the value of LstPtr) plus the fixed length of the JOBL0200 list entry format
(%size(QUSL020001)). This causes AttrPtr to now point to the first attribute array
element. Falling into a DO loop, which is exited when LstEntry.QUSNBRFR elements have
been processed, the program sets AtrValPtr (and as a result the BASED AtrValue variable)
to point to the value associated with the current attribute array occurrence. The program
then begins a SELECT group.

The List Jobs API does not document, and we must not assume, that the attributes are returned in the same order in which they were requested. For this reason, we use a SELECT group and test the attribute key field (AttrEntry.QUSKF). When the attribute key field is 1004, we know that the attribute value represents the qualified job queue name, and so we set the display file field JobQ to the first ten bytes of the returned qualified job queue name using the BASED variable AtrValue. Likewise, we set Outq when the attribute key field is 1501 and Printer when the attribute key field is 1603. After each attribute array occurrence is processed, FIG13_1 adds the length of the current attribute array occurrence (AttrEntry.QUSLFIR) to the AttrPtr variable. This sets AttrPtr to now address the next occurrence of the returned attribute array. The FOR loop is then continued until all LstEntry.QUSNBRFR occurrences have been processed.

If LstEntry.QUSJIS is not a blank, then the requested attribute information was not returned in the list entry. In this case, FIG13_1 sets the display file fields JobQ, OutQ, and Printer to all asterisks.

After the current JOBL0200 list entry has been processed, FIG13_1 then adds one to the RelRcdNbr variable that controls subfile processing, writes a subfile record describing the current job entry, increments the LstPtr variable to address the next job entry in the list, and continues the FOR loop until all GenHdr.QUSNBRLE entries have been processed.

The intent of this example is to show how to use a keyed interface, as opposed to how to code a subfile, so FIG13_1 performs one additional check when processing the returned list. Rather than processing all of the returned list entries, the program checks to see if more than 500 subfile records have been written. If so, the program also exits the FOR loop rather than continuing to process all of the returned list entries. If your system always has less than 9,999 jobs on the system (the maximum size of a subfile), and you don't mind waiting for the entire subfile to be loaded, you could remove this check. More realistically, though, any production-level program should be written such that the subfile page size is the same as the subfile size, and to manage the subfile contents directly. In this way, the end user is not waiting for all jobs to be loaded into the subfile. More importantly, the application is not limited to only displaying the first 9,999 job entries. Chapter 16 includes an example that uses a SFLSIZ = SFLPAG subfile.

When all job entries have been processed, FIG13_1 writes the results to the display. If no entries were processed (because GenHdr.QUSIS was not C, complete, or P, partial), appropriate error text is DSPLYed to the operator. In either case, the program then ends. This is shown in Figure 13.12.

```
CLON01Factor1+++++++Opcode&ExtFactor2+++++++Result++++++++Len++D+HiLoEq
/free

    if RelRcdNbr > 0;
        *in21 = *on;
        *in24 = *on;
        exfmt JobCtl;
    endif;
  else;
    dsply 'List Object API did not return valid data';
  endif;
  *inlr = *on;
  Return;

/end-free
```

Figure 13.12: Ending the FIG13_1 program.

The Change Job API, QWTCHGJB

The Change Job API, QWTCHGJB, allows you to change some of the attributes of a job or thread. The job can be your current job or another job on the system that you are authorized to change.

We'll use the Change Job API here to complete a scenario earlier introduced in chapter 12. In that chapter, you saw how to change the user profile a job was running under. Now, you'll see how to change the job environment a job is running under, so that it matches many of the attributes associated with that user profile. The parameters for QWTCHGJB are shown in Table 13.3.

Table 13.3: The Change Job API (QWTCHGJB)			
Parameter	Description	Type	Size
1	Qualified Job Name	Input	Char(26)
2	Internal Job Identifier	Input	Char(16)
3	Format Name	Input	Char(8)
4	Job Change Information	Input	Char(*)
5	Error Code	I/O	Char(*)
Optional Parameter Group 1			
6	Job or Thread Identification Information	Input	Char(*)
7	Format of Job Identification Format	Input	Char(8)

The first parameter, Qualified Job Name, identifies the job that is to be changed. This parameter is made up of three subfields: the job name, the user name, and the job number. The job name is the first ten bytes of the qualified job name and can have a specific name or one of three special values:

- An asterisk (*) for the job where the API is running, in which case the other two subfields of the qualified job name must be set to blanks

- *INT to indicate that the internal job identifier (the second parameter of this API) is to be used to identify the job

- *THREAD to indicate that a specific job and thread are to be changed, where the job and thread are further identified by the job or thread identification information (the sixth parameter of the API)

The user name subfield is the next ten bytes of the qualified job name, and must be all blanks if a special value was used for the job name. The job number subfield is the last six bytes of the qualified job name, and must be all blanks if a special value was used for the job name.

The second parameter, Internal Job Identifier, is an identifier returned by the List Jobs API. This identifier, if known, allows the system to more quickly locate the job to be changed than when a qualified job name is used.

The third parameter, Format Name, identifies the format you want to use when specifying the job attributes to change. Four formats are supported. Format JOBC0100 provides the same type of function that can be done with the Change Job command, CHGJOB. Format JOBC0200 allows you to change the attributes of your current thread. Format JOBC0300 allows you to set selected job and thread attributes to the values found in a user profile. Format JOBC0400 allows you to change the attributes of a specific thread. The example program uses format JOBC0300.

The fourth parameter, Job Change Information, is where you specify the job attributes to be changed and the new values to be used for those attributes. This parameter starts with a 4-byte integer indicating the number of key structures that immediately follow this value, and then that number of key structures. Figure 13.13 shows the QSYSINC-provided definition for the key structures used with format JOBC0300.

```
DName+++++++++++ETDsFrom+++To/L+++IDc.Keywords++++++++++++++++++++++++
D*******************************************************************
D*Type Definition for the JOBC0300 format
D****                                                            ***
D*NOTE: The following type definition only defines the fixed
D*   portion of the format.  Any varying length field will
D*   have to be defined by the user.
D*******************************************************************
DQWTC0300          DS
D*                                                 Qus JOBC0300
D QWTKF03                    1      4B 0
D*                                                 Key Field
D QWTDATA03                  5     14
D*                                                 Data
D QWTRSV200                 15     16
D*                                                 Reserved2
```

Figure 13.13: The QSYSINC definition for format JOBC0300.

Within the data structure QWTC0300 are three subfields. The first field, QWTKF03, is a key field that identifies the attribute to be changed. Some of the attributes you can change are shown in Table 13.4. One very useful key is 2701. This key indicates that we want to change all of the attributes that have key values defined for format JOBC0300. The sample program uses this key.

Table 13.4: Selected Key Values for Format Jobc0300 of QWTCHGJB		
Key	Description	Size
104	ASP group information	Char(10)
302	Coded character set ID (CCSID)	Char(10)
310	Current library	Char(10)
801	Home directory	Char(10)
1501	Output queue name	Char(10)
1603	Printer device name	Char(10)
2701	All keys for JOBC0300 format	Char(10)

The second field, QWTDATA03, is the value we want to use with the specified key. You might have wonder why all of the keys shown in Table 13.4 have the same associated size, Char(10), when some of the keys, like 801 (the home directory), have much longer values than ten bytes. The reason is that only two special values can be used for field QWTDATA03. Both special values are Char(10), and they are *INLUSR and *CURUSR. *INLUSR indicates that we want the job attributes to be changed to the values associated with the initial user profile of this job. *CURUSR indicates that we want the job attributes to be changed to the values associated with the current user of this job or thread.

The third field, QWTRSV200, is reserved and must be set to blanks.

With that introduction to the Change Job API, let's have a quick review of the original user profile swapping program from chapter 12. Figure 13.14 is the same as Figure 12.3.

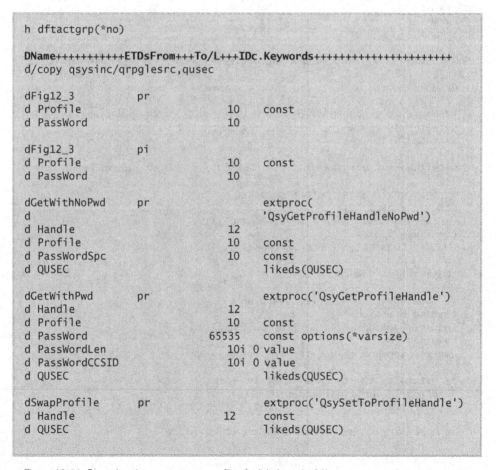

```
 h dftactgrp(*no)

DName+++++++++++ETDsFrom+++To/L+++IDc.Keywords++++++++++++++++++++++++
 d/copy qsysinc/qrpglesrc,qusec

 dFig12_3         pr
 d Profile                     10    const
 d PassWord                    10

 dFig12_3         pi
 d Profile                     10    const
 d PassWord                    10

 dGetWithNoPwd    pr                 extproc(
 d                                   'QsyGetProfileHandleNoPwd')
 d Handle                      12
 d Profile                     10    const
 d PassWordSpc                 10    const
 d QUSEC                             likeds(QUSEC)

 dGetWithPwd      pr                 extproc('QsyGetProfileHandle')
 d Handle                      12
 d Profile                     10    const
 d PassWord                 65535    const options(*varsize)
 d PassWordLen               10i 0   value
 d PassWordCCSID             10i 0   value
 d QUSEC                             likeds(QUSEC)

 dSwapProfile     pr                 extproc('QsySetToProfileHandle')
 d Handle                      12    const
 d QUSEC                             likeds(QUSEC)
```

Figure 13.14: Changing the current user profile of a job (part 1 of 3).

```
dFreeHandle        pr                      extproc(
d                                          'QsyReleaseProfileHandle')
d Handle                       12          const
d QUSEC                                    likeds(QUSEC)

dCmdExc            pr                      extpgm('QCMDEXC')
d Command                    65535         const options(*varsize)
d CmdLength                  15  5         const
d IGC                           3          const options(*nopass)

dDspJob2           c                       'DSPJOB OPTION(*STSA)'
dDspJob3           c                       'DSPJOB OPTION(*DFNA)'

dOriginalHandle    s           12
dNewHandle         s           12
dCommand           s           20

CLON01Factor1+++++++Opcode&ExtFactor2+++++++Result++++++++Len++D+HiLoEq
 /free
  QUSBPRV = 0;

  // Minimize exposure of password value in a program variable
  GetWithPwd( NewHandle :Profile :PassWord :10 :0 :QUSEC);
  Password = *blanks;

  GetWithNoPwd( OriginalHandle :'*CURRENT' :'*NOPWD' :QUSEC);

  // Show environment before swapping
  Command = DspJob2;
  CmdExc( Command :%len(%trimr(Command)));
  Command = DspJob3;
  CmdExc( Command :%len(%trimr(Command)));

  SwapProfile( NewHandle :QUSEC);

  // Show environment after swapping
  Command = DspJob2;
  CmdExc( Command :%len(%trimr(Command)));
  Command = DspJob3;
  CmdExc( Command :%len(%trimr(Command)));

  // return to the original profile
  SwapProfile( OriginalHandle :QUSEC);
```

Figure 13.14: Changing the current user profile of a job (part 2 of 3).

```
// show environment after swapping back to original profile
Command = DspJob2;
CmdExc( Command :%len(%trimr(Command)));
Command = DspJob3;
CmdExc( Command :%len(%trimr(Command)));

FreeHandle( OriginalHandle :QUSEC);
FreeHandle( NewHandle :QUSEC);
*inlr = *on;
return;
/end-free
```

Figure 13.14: Changing the current user profile of a job (part 3 of 3).

Figure 13.15 demonstrates how to change your current job's attributes to those appropriate for the current user. We've highlighted the changes that were made to the code from Figure 13.14. As you will hopefully agree, there is not a whole lot of change necessary!

```
h dftactgrp(*no)

DName+++++++++++ETDsFrom+++To/L+++IDc.Keywords+++++++++++++++++++++
d/copy qsysinc/qrpglesrc,qwtchgjb
d/copy qsysinc/qrpglesrc,qusec

dFig13_15         pr                    extpgm('FIG13_15')
d Profile                      10       const
d PassWord                     10

dFig13_15         pi
d Profile                      10       const
d PassWord                     10

dChgJob           pr                    extpgm('QWTCHGJB')
d JobName                      26       const
d IntJobID                     16       const
d Format                        8       const
d ChgInfo                   65535       const options(*varsize)
d QUSEC                                 likeds(QUSEC)
d ThreadInfo                65535       const options(*varsize :*nopass)
d ThreadFormat                  8       const options(*nopass)

dGetWithNoPwd     pr                    extproc(
d                                       'QsyGetProfileHandleNoPwd')
```

Figure 13.15: Changing the current user profile and current job attributes (part 1 of 3).

445

```
d Handle                            12
d Profile                           10      const
d PassWordSpc                       10      const
d QUSEC                                     likeds(QUSEC)

dGetWithPwd            pr                   extproc('QsyGetProfileHandle')
d Handle                            12
d Profile                           10      const
d PassWord                       65535      const options(*varsize)
d PassWordLen                     10i 0 value
d PassWordCCSID                   10i 0 value
d QUSEC                                     likeds(QUSEC)

dSwapProfile           pr                   extproc('QsySetToProfileHandle')
d Handle                            12      const
d QUSEC                                     likeds(QUSEC)

dFreeHandle            pr                   extproc(
d                                           'QsyReleaseProfileHandle')
d Handle                            12      const
d QUSEC                                     likeds(QUSEC)

dCmdExc                pr                   extpgm('QCMDEXC')
d Command                        65535      const options(*varsize)
d CmdLength                         15   5 const
d IGC                                3      const options(*nopass)

dChgInfo               ds                   qualified
d NbrKeys                          10i 0
d Key                                       likeds(QWTC0300)

dDspJob2               c                    'DSPJOB OPTION(*STSA)'
dDspJob3               c                    'DSPJOB OPTION(*DFNA)'

dOriginalHandle        s            12
dNewHandle             s            12
dCommand               s            20

CLON01Factor1+++++++Opcode&ExtFactor2+++++++Result++++++++Len++D+HiLoEq
 /free
  QUSBPRV = 0;

  // Minimize exposure of password value in a program variable
  GetWithPwd( NewHandle :Profile :PassWord :10 :0 :QUSEC);
  Password = *blanks;
```

Figure 13.15: Changing the current user profile and current job attributes (part 2 of 3).

```
GetWithNoPwd( OriginalHandle :'*CURRENT' :'*NOPWD' :QUSEC);

// Show environment before swapping
Command = DspJob2;
CmdExc( Command :%len(%trimr(Command)));
Command = DspJob3;
CmdExc( Command :%len(%trimr(Command)));

SwapProfile( NewHandle :QUSEC);

ChgInfo.Key = *blanks;
ChgInfo.NbrKeys = 1;                   // one key used
ChgInfo.Key.QWTKF03 = 2701;            // change all supported keys
ChgInfo.Key.QWTDATA03 = '*CURUSR'; // based on current user
ChgJob ( '*' :' ' :'JOBC0300' :ChgInfo :QUSEC);

// Show environment after swapping
Command = DspJob2;
CmdExc( Command :%len(%trimr(Command)));
Command = DspJob3;
CmdExc( Command :%len(%trimr(Command)));

// return to the original profile
SwapProfile( OriginalHandle :QUSEC);
ChgInfo.Key.QWTDATA03 = '*INLUSR'; // based on initial user
ChgJob ( '*' :' ' :'JOBC0300' :ChgInfo :QUSEC);

// show environment after swapping back to original profile
Command = DspJob2;
CmdExc( Command :%len(%trimr(Command)));
Command = DspJob3;
CmdExc( Command :%len(%trimr(Command)));

FreeHandle( OriginalHandle :QUSEC);
FreeHandle( NewHandle :QUSEC);
*inlr = *on;
return;
/end-free
```

Figure 13.15: Changing the current user profile and current job attributes (part 3 of 3).

We've added the /copy to bring in the QSYSINC-provided definitions for the Change Job API. As a cosmetic change, we've also changed to prototype for our program from FIG12_3 to FIG13_15. And, of course, we've prototyped the Change Job API (QWTCHGJB) along with defining the data structure ChgInfo, which is defined as a 4-byte integer, representing the number of keys to pass to the QWTCHGJB API, along with one instance of a key structure (Key) defined LIKEDS(QWTC0300).

After swapping the current user to the user profile passed as the Profile parameter, FIG13_15 sets up the ChgInfo data structure. The QWTCHGJB API documents that reserved fields must be set to blanks. For this reason, we initialize the Key substructure to all blanks. We then set to ChgInfo subfields to appropriate values. ChgInfo.NbrKeys is set to one, as we will only use one key when calling the API. ChgInfo.Key.QWTKF03 is set to the key value of 2701 (to change all supported attributes). ChgInfo.Key.QWTDATA03 is set to the special value *CURUSR, to indicate that the job attributes are to be changed based on the user profile currently in effect for the job (which is the profile passed as the Profile parameter).

FIG13_15 then calls the Change Job API, specifying that the current job (*) is to be changed using format JOBC0300 and the keys specified in the ChgInfo data structure. After that, the program resumes with the code originally used for FIG12_3, calling the QCMDEXC API to display the output of the two DSPJOB commands. Notice that the CCSID value for the job is now changed. (In FIG12_3, the CCSID value did not change.)

Following these displays, FIG13_15 restores both the job's original authority and environment to their initial settings. This return to the original settings is done by swapping back to the initial user profile and then calling the Change Job API again after changing ChgInfo.Key.QWTDATA03 to the special value *INLUSR. The program did not have to do this. FIG13_15 could just as easily have used the *CURUSR special value, as we had previously swapped back to the initial user. We believe, however, that using the special value support of *INLUSR is a better form of self-documentation in terms of what job environment FIG13_15 is returning to the caller with.

Retrieve System Status (QWCRSSTS)

As mentioned at the beginning of this chapter, the Retrieve System Status API, QWCRSSTS, does not introduce any new concepts in how to use an API. Rather, QWCRSSTS is being discussed to point out that you shouldn't be fooled by the name of an API. If you are familiar with the Display System Status command (DSPSYSSTS) and the Work with System Status command (WRKSYSSTS), you might think that QWCRSSTS simply provides a programmatic way of accessing the same information. While this is certainly true, the API also provides system status information above and beyond what is returned on the display and work panels. One example is the ability to determine if the system is in restricted state—a nice piece of information to have when automating certain system operations.

The parameters for the Retrieve System Status API are shown in Table 13.5. The first three parameters are standard for retrieve-type APIs.

Parameter	Description	Type	Size
	Table 13.5: The Retrieve System Status API (QWCRSSTS)		
1	Receiver Variable	Input	Char(*)
2	Length of Receiver Variable	Input	Binary(4)
3	Format Name	Input	Char(8)
4	Reset Status Statistics	Input	Char(10)
5	Error Code	I/O	Char(*)
Optional Parameter Group 1			
6	Pool Selection Information	Input	Char(*)
7	Length of Pool Selection Information	Input	Char(8)

The Retrieve System Status API supports five formats. Format SSTS0200, which we will be using, provides information such as the elapsed time, the number of jobs in the system, the number of active jobs in the system, the number of processors, and whether or not the system is in restricted state. The full QSYSINC definition for format SSTS0200 is shown in Figure 13.16.

The fourth parameter, Reset Status Statistics, is the equivalent of the RESET parameter of the DSPSYSSTS and WRKSYSSTS commands. If *YES is passed, status statistics and elapsed time are reset to zero. Note that this resetting to zero by the API also resets the elapsed time and statistics used by DSPSYSSTS and WRKSYSSTS. If *NO is passed, the statistics and elapsed time are not reset.

The fifth parameter is the standard API error-code structure.

The sixth and seventh parameters allow you to control which pools are returned when working with formats that return pool-related information. Our sample program doesn't use these optional parameters, but you can, for instance, request that all shared pools, only shared interactive pools, or only a specific system pool be returned.

```
DName++++++++++ETDsFrom+++To/L+++IDc.Keywords++++++++++++++++++++++++
D*******************************************************************
D*Type Definition for the SSTS0200 format.
D*******************************************************************
DQWCS0200        DS
D*                                        Qwc SSTS0200
D QWCBAVL01              1      4B 0
D*                                        Bytes Available
D QWCBRTN01              5      8B 0
D*                                        Bytes Returned
D QWCCDT00               9     16
D*                                        Current Date Time
D QWCSN00               17     24
D*                                        System Name
D QWCET                 25     30
D*                                        Elapsed Time
D QWCRS                 31     31
D*                                        Restricted State
D QWCERVED01            32     32
D*                                        Reserved
D QWCPPUU               33     36B 0
D*                                        Pct Processing Unit
D QWCJIS                37     40B 0
D*                                        Jobs In System
D QWCPPA                41     44B 0
D*                                        Pct Perm Addresses
D QWCPTA                45     48B 0
D*                                        Pct Temp Addresses
D QWCSASP               49     52B 0
D*                                        System ASP
D QWCSASPU              53     56B 0
D*                                        Pct System ASP used
D QWCTAS                57     60B 0
D*                                        Total Aux Storage
D QWCCUS                61     64B 0
D*                                        Current Unprotect S
D QWCMUS                65     68B 0
D*                                        Maximum Unprotect S
D QWCDBC                69     72B 0
D*                                        DB Capability
D QWCMSS                73     76B 0
D*                                        Main Storage Size
D QWCNBROP              77     80B 0
D*                                        Number Of Partition
D QWCPI00               81     84B 0
D*                                        Partition Identifie
D QWCRSV206             85     88B 0
D*                                        Reserved2
D QWCCPC                89     92B 0
```

Figure 13.16: The *QSYSINC* definition of *QWCRSSTS* format *SSTS0200* (part 1 of 2).

```
D*                                      Current Processing
D QWCPSA                  93      93
D*                                      Processor Sharing A
D QWCRSV300              94      96
D*                                      Reserved3
D QWCNBROP00            97     100B 0
D*                                      Number Of Processor
D QWCAJIS               101    104B 0
D*                                      Active Jobs In Syst
D QWCATIS               105    108B 0
D*                                      Active Threads In S
D QWCMJIS               109    112B 0
D*                                      Maximum Jobs In Sys
D QWC56MBS              113    116B 0
D*                                      Temp 256MB Segments
D QWCT4GBS              117    120B 0
D*                                      Temp 4GB Segments
D QWC56MBS00            121    124B 0
D*                                      Perm 256MB Segments
D QWCP4GBS              125    128B 0
D*                                      Perm 4GB Segments
D QWCCIP                129    132B 0
D*                                      Cur Interactive Per
D QWCCPUCU              133    136B 0
D*                                      Uncapped CPU Capaci
D QWCSPPU               137    140B 0
D*                                      Shared Processor Po
D QWCMSSL               141    148U 0
D*                                      Main Storage Size L
```

Figure 13.16: The *QSYSINC* definition of *QWCRSSTS* format *SSTS0200* (part 2 of 2).

Of particular interest in format SSTS0200 is the field QWCRS, which is documented as returning a value of zero if the system is not in restricted state and a value of one if the system is in restricted state. Figure 13.17 shows the source for a program that displays the current state of the system—restricted, not restricted, or unknown.

```
h dftactgrp(*no)

DName+++++++++++ETDsFrom+++To/L+++IDc.Keywords++++++++++++++++++++++
d/copy qsysinc/qrpglesrc,qwcrssts
d/copy qsysinc/qrpglesrc,qusec

dRtvSysSts          pr                      extpgm('QWCRSSTS')
d Receiver                         1        options(*varsize)
```

Figure 13.17: Using the Retrieve System Status API to determine if the system is in restricted state (part 1 of 2).

```
d LengthRcv                    10i 0 const
d Format                        8    const
d Reset                        10    const
d QUSEC                              likeds(QUSEC)
d PoolInfo                   65535   const options(*varsize :*nopass)
d LenPoolInfo                  10i 0 const options(*nopass)

dwait              s            1

CLON01Factor1+++++++Opcode&ExtFactor2+++++++Result++++++++Len++D+HiLoEq
 /free
  QUSBPRV = 0;

  RtvSysSts( QWCS0200 :%size(QWCS0200) :'SSTS0200' :'*NO' :QUSEC);

  select;
    when QWCRS = '1';
         dsply 'The system is in restricted state' ' ' wait;
    when QWCRS = '0';
         dsply 'The system is not in restricted state' ' ' wait;
    other;
         dsply 'The system is in an unknown state';
         dsply 'Call support' ' ' wait;
  endsl;

  *inlr = *on;
  return;
 /end-free
```

Figure 13.17: Using the Retrieve System Status API to determine if the system is in restricted state (part 2 of 2).

FIG13_17 sets the Error Code Bytes Provided fields to zero to indicate that exceptions are to be returned. Then, it calls the QWCRSSTS API, requesting that format SSTS0200 be returned in the QSYSINC-provided QWCS0200 data structure. When the API returns to FIG13_17, the program DSPLYs appropriate text describing the state of the system.

The one point worth mentioning is the OTHER operation used when SELECTing on the value of QWCRS. While it might seem natural to simply test QWCRS for a value of one and assume that the only other possible value must be zero, this is not recommended. As mentioned in chapter 1, do not assume a fixed list of values when processing returned values within your application program. There is nothing to say that a semi-restricted state value such as two could not be introduced in some future release.

If your application program simply displays or lists the value, then an OTHER operation might not be necessary. However, if your application is examining the value and making processing decisions based on that value, such as FIG13_17 does, you need to keep in mind that system enhancements can always add new values in the future.

Summary

The main point of this book is to show that APIs have many practical uses in everyday programming tasks. Work-management APIs can help you work with and manage your system. We encourage you to "hit the Information Center" to find other work-management APIs that might help you. The information is there. All you need to do is find out how to get it. And as usual, APIs are one of your best resources.

Check Your Knowledge

Write a program that determines the current status of the QSYS/QINTER subsystem. Have the program DSPLY that status. As a start, review the documentation for the Retrieve Subsystem Information API, QWDRSBSD, in the Information Center.

For one possible solution to this task, see Figure D.13 of appendix D. This solution uses format SBSI0100 of the Retrieve Subsystem Information API.

453

14

Integrated File System APIs

Most i5/OS application developers are intimately familiar with database files and libraries. You can probably code an RPG F-spec in your sleep, and write a program that opens a database file, writes some records, reads some records, and then closes the file without too much difficulty.

A growing amount of business data, however, is now being stored in the Integrated File System. Many application developers are not as familiar with accessing these files from RPG, COBOL, or CL applications. You might very well have applications that actually copy Integrated File System stream files to DB2 database files, using commands such as CPYFRMSTMF, just to be able to access the stream-file data—an approach you wouldn't even consider for most database-oriented applications.

With the APIs you will learn about in this chapter, you can eliminate these types of unnecessary copy operations. You will see how to directly read and write data from and to the Integrated File System using APIs such as open, read, write, and close. Following the discussion of reading and writing with stream files, this chapter shows how to work with directories within the Integrated File System. Using APIs such as opendir, readdir, and closedir, we will determine what files can be found within a directory. The APIs discussed in this chapter can be found in the Information Center under the topics "Programming," "APIs," "APIs by Category," "Unix-Type APIs," and then "Integrated File System APIs."

Opening an Integrated File System Stream File

The first API we will look at is the open API. You can think of this API as being loosely equivalent to the RPG F-spec, although the API gives you options you won't find on the F-spec! The parameter descriptions for open are shown in Figure 14.1.

```
int open (const char *path, int oflag, …)
```

Figure 14.1: The open API.

As you learned in chapter 1 and further examined in chapter 9, this style of parameter description defines the open API as having two required parameters (Path and Oflag), some number of optional parameters (indicated by the ellipsis, …) that are further described in the API documentation, and an integer return value (also further described in the API documentation).

The first parameter, Path, is a pass-by-value pointer (the * specification) to a character string (the char specification) that will not be modified (the const specification) by the API. The API documentation explains that the Path parameter is a null-terminated string representing the path of the file to be opened.

The second parameter, Oflag, is a pass-by-value integer (the int specification). The documentation in the Information Center explains that this parameter is used to control how the file is to be opened. We will spend quite a bit of time on this parameter shortly.

The ellipsis indicates that one or more optional parameters can be passed to the open API. The first optional parameter is Mode. It is defined as having a data type of mode_t, which is an unsigned integer (10u 0). This parameter controls what authorities (or file permissions) should be associated with the file, identified by the Path parameter, when creating a new file.

The second optional parameter is Conversion ID. It is defined as having a data type of unsigned integer (10u 0). For existing files, this parameter defines what CCSID should be used when returning textual, or character, data to the job (when reading data using the read API) and what CCSID your program data is in when writing data from the job (using the write API). For example, the Integrated File System file might have a CCSID of 819 (ISO Latin-1), indicating that the data within the file is stored in a standard form of ASCII. Your job might be in CCSID 37 (EBCDIC Latin-1). If you wanted the ASCII data to be automatically converted to CCSID 37 when you read it from the file, you would set the Conversion ID parameter to 37. For files being created by the API, this parameter defines what CCSID should be associated with data contained within the new file. There's a bit more to this parameter and how it relates to other parameters of the open API. We'll get to those details shortly.

A third optional parameter is Text File Creation Conversion ID. It is defined as having a data type of unsigned integer (10u 0). This parameter defines what CCSID should be used when returning data to the job when the file specified by the Path parameter is being created by the API. This parameter works hand-in-hand with the Conversion ID parameter. If you wanted to create a new file where the data within the file should have a CCSID of 819 (one form of ASCII), and wanted to write to the file with data from your application program where the application program was working with a CCSID of 37 (one form of EBCDIC), you would set Conversion ID to 819 and Text File Creation Conversion ID to 37.

If the Conversion ID and Text File Creation Conversion ID parameters leave you a bit confused, don't feel alone! They are not that difficult to use, but examples are the key to understanding how they work together. Later in this chapter, you will see example programs demonstrating their use.

The open API also returns an integer return value (10i). If the return value is -1, an error was encountered. Otherwise, open was successful and the return value is a *file descriptor* that will be passed to subsequent APIs, such as read and write. The file descriptor tells these APIs what file you want to work with. You can have many files open concurrently within your job and/or application. The default is 200 open files. You can change this value with the Change Maximum Number of File Descriptors API, DosSetRelMaxFH. The Get System Configuration Variables API, sysconf, can also be used to query the current maximum number of open files for your job.

With that introduction, Figure 14.2 shows how to open a new file named My_New_File.txt in the root directory. The program starts by calling the open API. The first parameter, Path, is the literal '/My_New_File.txt'. The function prototype for this parameter indicates that a pointer is to be passed to a null-terminated string, so the RPG compiler makes a copy of this literal, appends a null (x'00') byte to the end of the string, and then passes a pointer to this copy.

```
h dftactgrp(*no) bnddir('QC2LE')

DName+++++++++++ETDsFrom+++To/L+++IDc.Keywords++++++++++++++++++++++
dopen             pr           10i 0 extproc('open')
d path                          *    value options(*string)
d oflag                        10i 0 value
d mode                         10u 0 value options(*nopass)
d convID                       10u 0 value options(*nopass)
d textCrtConvID                10u 0 value options(*nopass)


derrno            pr            *    extproc('__errno')

dErrorNbr         s            10i 0 based(ErrnoPtr)
dfd               s            10i 0
dSomeText         s            50    inz('Hello World')
dwait             s            1

dO_RDONLY         c                  1
dO_WRONLY         c                  2
dO_RDWR           c                  4
dO_CREAT          c                  8
dO_EXCL           c                  16
dO_CCSID          c                  32
dO_TRUNC          c                  64
dO_APPEND         c                  256
dO_SHARE_RDONLY   c                  65536
dO_SHARE_WRONLY   c                  131072
dO_SHARE_RDWR     c                  262144
dO_SHARE_NONE     c                  524288
dO_TEXTDATA       c                  16777216
dO_TEXT_CREAT     c                  33554432

dS_IRGRP          c                  32
dS_IWUSR          c                  128
dS_IRUSR          c                  256

CLON01Factor1++++++Opcode&ExtFactor2++++++Result++++++++Len++D+HiLoEq
 /free
   fd = open( '/My_New_File.txt'
              :O_WRONLY + O_CREAT + O_EXCL + O_CCSID + O_TEXTDATA +
              O_TEXT_CREAT
              :S_IRUSR + S_IWUSR + S_IRGRP
              :0 :0);
```

*Figure 14.2: Using the **open** API (part 1 of 2).*

```
    if (fd = -1);
        ErrnoPtr = errno;
        dsply ('Failure ' + %char(ErrorNbr) + ' on open') ' ' wait;
        *inlr = *on;
        return;
    endif;
    /end-free
```

*Figure 14.2: Using the **open** API (part 2 of 2).*

The second parameter, Oflag, requires a bit more explanation. Oflag is defined as an integer value, where each bit of the value represents different flag values. These flags are defined in Figure 14.2 by the constant fields whose names start with *O_* (such as O_RDONLY, O_RDWR, and O_CREAT). O_RDONLY is x'00000001', O_RDWR is x'00000004', etc. Many such flags are defined by the open API. and Table 14.1 provides a brief description of some of these flags. For a complete definition, see the API documentation. For an explanation of how these values are determined, visit the web site *www.brucevining.com*.

When calling open, we add the various constants together to set all of the appropriate bit flags. The code in Figure 14.2 indicates that a new file is to be created (O_CREAT and O_EXCL), that the file will be used for writing (O_WRONLY) of textual data (O_TEXTDATA), and that CCSID support is being used (O_CCSID) for both tagging of the data stored within the new file (O_CCSID) and the conversion of textual data when reading and writing data to the new file (O_TEXT_CREAT) from the application program.

While all of the flags defined for Oflag are important, O_TEXTDATA is one we would like to expand on. When you specify O_TEXTDATA, you are telling the open API that all data found in the opened file should be treated as textual, or character-based. Under the covers, subsequent APIs such as read and write will effectively be using the iconv APIs, discussed in chapter 9, to convert the file data to and from the CCSID of your job (or the CCSID you might have explicitly set using the O_CCSID flag and the Conversion ID and Text File Creation Conversion ID parameters). If the file contains non-character-based data (integer fields, packed decimal fields, floating point fields, bit fields to control data formatting, etc.), this data will be converted as if it were character-based. This is most likely not what you want. If you want numeric data written to a file opened with O_TEXTDATA, you should first convert the data to a character form using built-in functions such as %CHAR. If, on the other hand, you want the numeric data written as-is (such as binary or packed decimal), you should not specify O_TEXTDATA. Not using O_TEXTDATA causes the file to be opened in what is referred to as *binary*, or hex, mode.

Table 14.1: The Oflag Definitions When Using the *open* API	
Constant Name	Description
O_RDONLY	Open the file for reading only.
O_WRONLY	Open the file for writing only.
O_RDWR	Open the file for both reading and writing.
O_CREAT	Create the file if it does not exist. If the file does exist, continue unless O_EXCL is also specified. The Mode parameter must be passed to the open API when O_CREAT is specified.
O_EXCL	This flag is ignored if O_CREAT is not also specified. Create the file if it does not exist. If the file does exist, the open fails.
O_CCSID	The Conversion ID parameter is being passed to the API and specifies a CCSID value to be used when working with the Integrated File System file.
O_APPEND	Append new data to the end of the file.
O_SHARE_RDONLY	Share only with other concurrent readers of the file.
O_SHARE_WRONLY	Share only with other concurrent writers of the file.
O_SHARE_RDWR	Share with other concurrent readers and writers of the file.
O_SHARE_NONE	Do not allow file sharing.
O_TEXTDATA	The data in the file is to be treated as textual data and converted to either the job CCSID, or, if passed, the value of the Conversion ID parameter. The interpretation of the Conversion ID parameter value depends on the flags O_CCSID and O_CODEPAGE. Otherwise, the data is treated as hexadecimal data and processed as-is.
O_CODEPAGE	The Conversion ID parameter is being passed to the API and specifies a code page value to be used when working with the Integrated File System file. This flag, in general, should not be used. The O_CCSID flag is the preferred method for identifying the encoding of data.
O_TEXT_CREAT	The Text File Creation Conversion ID parameter is being passed to the API.

In binary mode, the system makes no attempt to convert the file contents using functions such as iconv. What is in your program variable is exactly what is in your file.

Another flag worth pointing out is O_APPEND. RPG developers accustomed to working with the i5/OS DB2 database might expect that, when writing new data to an existing file, the new data will be written to the end of the file. The existence of a flag such as O_APPEND should warn you that this might not be the case! If you open a file for writing, and do not specify O_APPEND, then the initial file position is at the start of the file. If the file currently has 10 bytes of data ("abcdefghij") and your application program writes three bytes of data ("XYZ"), then the file will now contain "XYZdefghij." This might or might not be what you intended. If, on the other hand, you do specify O_APPEND, then the file will contain "abcdefghijXYZ."

The third parameter, Mode, is similar to Oflag in that it is defined as a set of individual bit flags. In Figure 14.2, these flags are the constant fields whose names start with *S_*. Table 14.2 describes some of these flags. Using this table, you can see that the third parameter of open in Figure 14.2 specifies that the owner of the file is permitted to read from the file, that the owner is permitted to write to the file, and that users with the same group profile as the owner are permitted to read from the file.

Table 14.2: The Mode Definitions When Using the *open* API	
Constant name	**Description**
S_IRUSR	Read permission for the owner of the file
S_IWUSR	Write permission for the owner of the file
S_IRGRP	Read permission for the owner's group profile
S_IROTH	General read permission

The fourth and fifth parameters of the open API (convID and textCrtConvID, respectively) are set to zero in Figure 14.2. Zero is a special value, common to most APIs that work with CCSIDs, indicating that the default job CCSID is to be used. By setting these two parameters to zero, we are specifying that the file /My_New_File.txt should be recognized by the system as containing data encoded with the current CCSID of the job and that data we write to the file, with the current open, is also encoded in the CCSID of the job.

After the call to open is complete, the program checks the return value, Fd, to see if an error was encountered (Fd = -1). If so, it accesses the errno global variable to get additional information on the error.

Accessing Errno

The *errno* variable is an error number that many industry-defined APIs use to provide additional error information. To access errno, we actually call another API called __errno. The parameter definitions for __errno are shown in Figure 14.3. Note that there are two underscores in the __errno API name.

```
int *__errno(void)
```

Figure 14.3: The __errno API.

__errno is defined to take no parameters (the void specification) and to return a pointer to a signed integer (the int * specification). This integer value provides additional information on the error. If you take the returned integer value of __errno (3025, for instance) and prefix it with *CPE*, you will find that in the QCPFMSG message file's message description, CPE3025 has the first-level text of "No such path or directory." All of the errno integer values have a corresponding CPE message description.

The pertinent pieces of the program, as it relates to errno, are shown in Figure 14.4.A. When an error is encountered, the program calls the __errno API, assigning the returned value to the pointer ErrnoPtr. ErrorNbr is defined as a signed integer BASED on ErrnoPtr, so ErrorNbr is immediately associated with the errno value and available for use by the program (as shown in the DSPLY).

```
h dftactgrp(*no) bnddir('QC2LE')

DName++++++++++ETDsFrom+++To/L+++IDc.Keywords++++++++++++++++++++++
derrno            pr              *   extproc('__errno')

dErrorNbr         s            10i 0 based(ErrnoPtr)
dfd               s            10i 0

CLON01Factor1++++++Opcode&ExtFactor2+++++++Result++++++++Len++D+HiLoEq
   if (fd = -1);
      ErrnoPtr = errno;
      dsply ('Failure ' + %char(ErrorNbr) + ' on open') ' ' wait;
      *inlr = *on;
      return;
   endif;
```

Figure 14.4.A: Accessing the errno error number.

The Set Pointer to Run-Time Error Message API, strerror, can be used to access the text associated with the error number. The use of this API is shown in Figure 14.4.B. In addition the Print Error Message API, perror, can be used to display the text associated with the error number.

The strerror API accepts one parameter, the integer value returned by the __errno API, and returns a pointer to the null-terminated text string associated with the error.

```
h dftactgrp(*no) bnddir('QC2LE')

DName++++++++++++ETDsFrom+++To/L+++IDc.Keywords+++++++++++++++++++++
derrno            pr              *   extproc('__errno')

dstrerror         pr              *   extproc('strerror')
d ErrorNbr                        10i 0 value

dErrorNbr         s               10i 0 based(ErrnoPtr)
dErrorTxt         s               50
dfd               s               10i 0

CLON01Factor1++++++++Opcode&ExtFactor2+++++++Result+++++++++Len++D+HiLoEq
  if (fd = -1);
     ErrnoPtr = errno;
     ErrorTxt = %str(strerror(ErrorNbr) :50);
     dsply ErrorTxt ' ' wait;
     *inlr = *on;
     return;
  endif;
```

Figure 14.4.B: Accessing the text associated with an errno error number.

In Figure 14.4.B, we use the %STR built-in function to retrieve up to 50 bytes of text and then DSPLY the message text.

Keep two notes of caution in mind when using errno. First, always use it immediately after the API has indicated that an error has been encountered and that errno has been updated. (The API documentation will tell you if errno is being used by the specific API.) The errno global variable can be changed by many system functions. If an API indicates that errno information is available and your program calls other Unix-type APIs before calling __errno, you might find the value returned is totally unrelated to the API call that failed.

The second note of caution is that the __errno API is not currently in the system-supplied binding directory QUSAPIBD that all ILE compilers automatically use. For this reason, you need to specify BNDDIR('QC2LE') when compiling the example application. This second consideration might be removed in a future release of i5/OS.

Because both O_CREAT and O_EXCL are specified in the sample program, the open will fail if the file currently exists. This can be seen by calling the sample program FIG14_2 twice in a row without deleting the file /My_New_File.txt. Doing this will result in the "Failure 3457 on open" text being DSPLYed. Message description CPE3457 in QCPFMSG has "File exists" as its first-level text.

Writing to an Integrated File System Stream File

Having successfully opened /My_New_File.txt it's now time to write some data to it. The API we will use is write. Its parameter descriptions are shown in Figure 14.5.

```
ssize_t write (int file_descriptor, const void *buf, size_t nbyte)
```

Figure 14.5: The write API.

The write API takes three parameters. The first parameter, File_descriptor, is the file descriptor value that was returned by the open API. The second parameter, Buf, is a pointer (*) to unspecified data (void) that will not be modified by the API (const). This second parameter contains the data you want to write to the file. The third parameter, Nbyte, is of type size_t, which is defined as an unsigned integer. This third parameter indicates how many bytes of data from the Buf parameter are to be written.

The write API also returns a return value of type ssize_t. This type is defined as a signed integer value. If the returned value is -1, an error was encountered, and errno can be used for additional information. Otherwise, the return value indicates how many bytes of data were written to the file.

Writing the value "Hello World" to /My_New_File.txt is shown in Figure 14.6.

```
h dftactgrp(*no) bnddir('QC2LE')

DName+++++++++++ETDsFrom+++To/L+++IDc.Keywords++++++++++++++++++++++
dwrite            pr              10i 0 extproc('write')
d fd                              10i 0 value
d buf                               *   value
d nbyte                           10u 0 value

derrno            pr                *   extproc('__errno')

dErrorNbr         s               10i 0 based(ErrnoPtr)
dfd               s               10i 0
dSomeText         s               50    inz('Hello World')
dwait             s                1
```

Figure 14.6: Writing data to the file (part 1 of 2).

```
CLON01Factor1+++++++Opcode&ExtFactor2+++++++Result++++++++Len++D+HiLoEq
   if write(fd :%addr(SomeText) :%len(%trimr(SomeText)))
      < %len(%trimr(SomeText));
      dsply 'Did not write all data' ' ' wait;
   else;
   endif;
```

Figure 14.6: Writing data to the file (part 2 of 2).

The first parameter passed to the write API is the file descriptor, fd, previously returned by open in Figure 14.2. The second parameter is the variable SomeText, which is set to the value "Hello World" with 39 trailing blanks. The third parameter is the length of SomeText after trimming all trailing blanks. The program then compares the return value of the write API to see if it wrote fewer bytes of data than requested:

```
%len(%trimr(SomeText))
```

If so, the program DSPLYs an error message indicating that not all data is written. The ELSE logic, used when all of the requested data is successfully written, will be discussed in the next section of this chapter.

Note that the write API has no concept of record formats such as those used with the i5/OS DB2 database. You specify only the number of bytes to write to the file. The format of the data is entirely program-described. As there are no records, just bytes, there is also no concept of record-locking to avoid concurrent updates to the same bytes from different jobs or threads. There are Oflag flag bits to control concurrent access to the file, but nothing for concurrent access to data *within* the file. Additional APIs, such as fcntl, can be used to provide explicit locking of byte-stream data. This approach, however, is only effective if all programs accessing the data in the file use the fcntl API. This same locking consideration applies to the read API that will be discussed later in this chapter.

Closing an Integrated File System Stream File

Having written "Hello World" to /My_New_File.txt, we're now ready to close the file. In case you're wondering why, this is in anticipation of re-opening the now existing file /My_New_File.txt and then reading what we have written. The close API parameter descriptions are shown in Figure 14.7.

```
int close (int fildes)
```

Figure 14.7: The close API.

The close API accepts one parameter, Fildes, which is the file descriptor previously returned by the open API and subsequently used by the write API. This parameter is of type int, a signed integer. The close API also returns a return value of type int. This return value will be -1 if an error is encountered. Otherwise, it will be zero, indicating success. Figure 14.8 shows how to call the API.

```
h dftactgrp(*no) bnddir('QC2LE')

DName+++++++++++ETDsFrom+++To/L+++IDc.Keywords+++++++++++++++++++++++++
dclose            pr              10i 0 extproc('close')
d fd                              10i 0 value

derrno            pr               *    extproc('__errno')

dErrorNbr         s               10i 0 based(ErrnoPtr)
dfd               s               10i 0
dwait             s               1

CLON01Factor1+++++++Opcode&ExtFactor2+++++++Result++++++++Len++D+HiLoEq
      if close(fd) = -1;
         ErrnoPtr = errno;
         dsply ('Failure ' + %char(ErrorNbr) + ' on close') ' ' wait;
         *inlr = *on;
         return;
      endif;
```

Figure 14.8: Using the close API.

Opening an Integrated File System Stream File for Reading

Having closed /My_New_File.txt, the program now re-opens the file to prepare for reading the data. This is shown in Figure 14.9.

```
h dftactgrp(*no) bnddir('QC2LE')

DName+++++++++++ETDsFrom+++To/L+++IDc.Keywords+++++++++++++++++++++++++
dopen             pr              10i 0 extproc('open')
d path                             *    value options(*string)
```

Figure 14.9: Opening a file for read-only (part 1 of 2).

466

```
d oflag                          10i 0 value
d mode                           10u 0 value options(*nopass)
d convID                         10u 0 value options(*nopass)
d textCrtConvID                  10u 0 value options(*nopass)

derrno              pr            *   extproc('__errno')

dErrorNbr           s            10i 0 based(ErrnoPtr)
dfd                 s            10i 0
dwait               s            1

dO_RDONLY           c            1
dO_TEXTDATA         c                  16777216


CLON01Factor1+++++++Opcode&ExtFactor2+++++++Result++++++++Len++D+HiLoEq
      fd = open( '/My_New_File.txt'
                 :O_RDONLY + O_TEXTDATA);
      if (fd = -1);
          ErrnoPtr = errno;
          dsply ('Failure ' + %char(ErrorNbr) + ' on 2nd open') ' ' wait;
          *inlr = *on;
          return;
      endif;
```

Figure 14.9: Opening a file for read-only (part 2 of 2).

This call to the open API is much simpler than the earlier call creating the /My_New_File.txt file in Figure 14.2. We only need to specify that we want to open the file for reading (O_RDONLY) and that we do want CCSID conversion from the file CCSID to the job CCSID (O_TEXTDATA). Because the default for O_TEXTDATA is the job CCSID, there is no need to specify O_CCSID or the convID parameter (although there's no problem if you do want to specify these explicitly). Similar to the error-checking in Figure 14.2, the program checks the return value from open, and if an error is encountered, DSPLYs appropriate error text.

Reading from an Integrated File System Stream File

Having re-opened /My_New_File.txt, the program now reads the contents of the file. The parameter descriptions for the read API are shown in Figure 14.10.

```
ssize_t read (int file_descriptor, void *buf, size_t nbytes)
```

Figure 14.10: The **read** API.

The read API is defined very much like the previous write API. It takes three parameters. The first parameter, File_descriptor, is the same file descriptor that was returned by the open API. The second parameter, Buf, is a pointer (*) to the buffer allocated to receive the data being read. (The type is void because we don't care what's defined there right now; we're just reading a stream of bytes into it.) The third parameter, Nbyte, is of type size_t, which is defined as an unsigned integer. This third parameter indicates how many bytes of data are to be read into the Buf parameter.

The read API also returns a return value of type ssize_t. This type is defined as a signed integer value. If the returned value is -1, an error was encountered, and errno can be used for additional information. Otherwise, the return value indicates how many bytes of data were read from the file. If this return value is less than the number of bytes requested by the Nbyte parameter, the end of file was encountered. Figure 14.11 shows how to use the read API.

```
h dftactgrp(*no) bnddir('QC2LE')

DName+++++++++++ETDsFrom+++To/L+++IDc.Keywords+++++++++++++++++++++++
dread             pr            10i 0 extproc('read')
d fd                            10i 0 value
d buf                             *   value
d nbyte                         10u 0 value

derrno            pr              *   extproc('__errno')

dErrorNbr         s             10i 0 based(ErrnoPtr)
dfd               s             10i 0
dSomeText         s             50    inz('Hello World')
dReturnedData     s             30
dwait             s              1

CLON01Factor1+++++++Opcode&ExtFactor2+++++++Result+++++++++Len++D+HiLoEq
      if read(fd :%addr(ReturnedData) :%size(ReturnedData))
        < %len(%trimr(SomeText));
        dsply 'Not all data returned' ' ' wait;
      else;
        dsply ReturnedData ' ' wait;
      endif;
```

Figure 14.11: Using the **read** API.

The program reads the contents of /My_New_File.txt starting at the first byte in the file, which is the default start location. (There are, of course, APIs that can be used to position the read API to other locations within the file. lseek is one.) It requests that 30 bytes of data be read:

```
%size(ReturnedData)
```

If the amount of data read (the return value of the read API) is less than the blank trimmed length of data written in Figure 14.6, appropriate error text is DSPLYed. Otherwise, the read data is DSPLYed.

Opening, Writing, Reading, and Closing an Integrated File System Stream File

The entire program for opening, writing, reading, and closing an Integrated File System stream file is shown in Figure 14.12.A. After running FIG14_12.A, you can use the Work with Object Links command, WRKLNK '/My_New_File.txt'. If you select option 5, Display, you will see the contents of the file. If you select option 8, Display Attributes, you will see that the file is tagged with the default CCSID currently in effect for your job.

```
h dftactgrp(*no) bnddir('QC2LE')

DName+++++++++++ETDsFrom+++To/L+++IDc.Keywords++++++++++++++++++++++
dopen             pr           10i 0 extproc('open')
d path                          *    value options(*string)
d oflag                        10i 0 value
d mode                         10u 0 value options(*nopass)
d convID                       10u 0 value options(*nopass)
d textCrtConvID                10u 0 value options(*nopass)

dread             pr           10i 0 extproc('read')
d fd                           10i 0 value
d buf                           *    value
d nbyte                        10u 0 value

dwrite            pr           10i 0 extproc('write')
d fd                           10i 0 value
d buf                           *    value
d nbyte                        10u 0 value
```

Figure 14.12.A: The complete program for opening, writing, reading, and closing an Integrated File System stream file (part 1 of 3).

469

```
dclose            pr              10i 0 extproc('close')
d fd                              10i 0 value

derrno            pr               *    extproc('__errno')

dErrorNbr         s               10i 0 based(ErrnoPtr)
dfd               s               10i 0
dSomeText         s               50    inz('Hello World')
dReturnedData     s               30
dwait             s                1

dO_RDONLY         c                     1
dO_WRONLY         c                     2
dO_RDWR           c                     4
dO_CREAT          c                     8
dO_EXCL           c                     16
dO_CCSID          c                     32
dO_TRUNC          c                     64
dO_APPEND         c                     256
dO_SHARE_RDONLY   c                     65536
dO_SHARE_WRONLY   c                     131072
dO_SHARE_RDWR     c                     262144
dO_SHARE_NONE     c                     524288
dO_TEXTDATA       c                     16777216
dO_TEXT_CREAT     c                     33554432

dS_IRGRP          c                     32
dS_IWUSR          c                     128
dS_IRUSR          c                     256

CLON01Factor1+++++++Opcode&ExtFactor2+++++++Result++++++++Len++D+HiLoEq
 /free
   fd = open( '/My_New_File.txt'
              :O_WRONLY + O_CREAT + O_EXCL + O_CCSID + O_TEXTDATA +
               O_TEXT_CREAT
              :S_IRUSR + S_IWUSR + S_IRGRP
              :0 :0);
   if (fd = -1);
      ErrnoPtr = errno;
      dsply ('Failure ' + %char(ErrorNbr) + ' on open') ' ' wait;
      *inlr = *on;
      return;
   endif;
```

Figure 14.12.A: The complete program for opening, writing, reading, and closing an Integrated File System stream file (part 2 of 3).

```
   if write(fd :%addr(SomeText) :%len(%trimr(SomeText)))
      < %len(%trimr(SomeText));
      dsply 'Did not write all data' ' ' wait;
   else;
      if close(fd) = -1;
         ErrnoPtr = errno;
         dsply ('Failure ' + %char(ErrorNbr) + ' on close') ' ' wait;
         *inlr = *on;
         return;
      endif;
      fd = open( '/My_New_File.txt'
                 :O_RDONLY + O_TEXTDATA);
      if (fd = -1);
         ErrnoPtr = errno;
         dsply ('Failure ' + %char(ErrorNbr) + ' on 2nd open') ' ' wait;
         *inlr = *on;
         return;
      endif;
      if read(fd :%addr(ReturnedData) :%size(ReturnedData))
         < %len(%trimr(SomeText));
         dsply 'Not all data returned' ' ' wait;
      else;
         dsply ReturnedData ' ' wait;
      endif;
   endif;

   fd = close(fd);
   *inlr = *on;
   return;
/end-free
```

Figure 14.12.A: The complete program for opening, writing, reading, and closing an Integrated File System stream file (part 3 of 3).

When displaying the contents of /My_New_File.txt, you might have noticed that at the bottom of the screen, you were warned that a record length of 80 bytes was assumed. Remember that stream files are just strings of bytes. There is no implicit concept of records as there is in the i5/OS database. If you want to define records, you must explicitly do that yourself by writing control bytes such as "Carriage Return" (CR) and "Line Feed" (LF). Our example program FIG14_12_B uses the Windows convention of a CR followed by a LF, but other systems use other conventions. Unix systems, for instance, often use just the LF.

Figure 14.12.B shows the changes for adding these controls. This program defines the new constant CR_LF, which is set to the value x'0D25'. The x'0D' is the EBCDIC code point for CR, and the x'25' is the code point for LF. The program then appends this constant to each line of text as its written, and takes these two additional bytes into consideration when checking to make sure all data was either written to or read from /My_New_File.txt. After running FIG14_12_B, if you now display "/My_New_File.txt," you will not get the warning message. The system is recognizing the CR and LF code points as record delimiters.

```
h dftactgrp(*no) bnddir('QC2LE')

dopen            pr              10i 0       extproc('open')
d path                           *           value options(*string)
d oflag                          10i 0       value
d mode                           10u 0       value options(*nopass)
d convID                         10u 0       value options(*nopass)
d textCrtConvID                  10u 0       value options(*nopass)

dread            pr              10i 0       extproc('read')
d fd                             10i 0       value
d buf                            *           value
d nbyte                          10u 0       value

dwrite           pr              10i 0       extproc('write')
d fd                             10i 0       value
d buf                            *           value
d nbyte                          10u 0       value

dclose           pr              10i 0       extproc('close')
d fd                             10i 0       value

derrno           pr              *           extproc('__errno')

dErrorNbr        s               10i 0       based(ErrnoPtr)
dfd              s               10i 0
dSomeText        s               50          inz('Hello World')
dTextRcd         s               82
dReturnedData    s               30
dwait            s               1

dCR_LF           c                           x'0D25'

dO_RDONLY        c                           1
dO_WRONLY        c                           2
dO_RDWR          c                           4
dO_CREAT         c                           8
```

Figure 14.12.B: The complete program with carriage returns and line feeds added (part 1 of 3).

472

```
dO_EXCL              c                      16
dO_CCSID             c                      32
dO_TRUNC             c                      64
dO_APPEND            c                      256
dO_SHARE_RDONLY      c                      65536
dO_SHARE_WRONLY      c                      131072
dO_SHARE_RDWR        c                      262144
dO_SHARE_NONE        c                      524288
dO_TEXTDATA          c                      16777216
dO_TEXT_CREAT        c                      33554432

dS_IRGRP             c                      32
dS_IWUSR             c                      128
dS_IRUSR             c                      256

 /free
  fd = open( '/My_New_File.txt'
            :O_WRONLY + O_CREAT + O_EXCL + O_CCSID + O_TEXTDATA +
             O_TEXT_CREAT
            :S_IRUSR + S_IWUSR + S_IRGRP
            :0 :0);
  if (fd = -1);
     ErrnoPtr = errno;
     dsply ('Failure ' + %char(ErrorNbr) + ' on open') ' ' wait;
     *inlr = *on;
     return;
  endif;

  TextRcd = %trimr(SomeText) + CR_LF;
  if write(fd :%addr(TextRcd) :%len(%trimr(TextRcd)))
       < %len(%trimr(TextRcd));
     dsply 'Did not write all data' ' ' wait;
  else;
     if close(fd) = -1;
        ErrnoPtr = errno;
        dsply ('Failure ' + %char(ErrorNbr) + ' on close') ' ' wait;
        *inlr = *on;
        return;
     endif;
     fd = open( '/My_New_File.txt'
               :O_RDONLY + O_TEXTDATA);
     if (fd = -1);
        ErrnoPtr = errno;
        dsply ('Failure ' + %char(ErrorNbr) + ' on 2nd open') ' ' wait;
        *inlr = *on;
        return;
     endif;
```

Figure 14.12.B: The complete program with carriage returns and line feeds added (part 2 of 3).

```
     if read(fd :%addr(ReturnedData) :%size(ReturnedData))
         < (%len(%trimr(SomeText)) + %size(CR_LF));
         dsply 'Not all data returned' ' ' wait;
     else;
         dsply (%subst(ReturnedData :1 :%len(%trimr(SomeText))))
                ' ' wait;
     endif;
  endif;

  fd = close(fd);
  *inlr = *on;
  return;
/end-free
```

Figure 14.12.B: The complete program with carriage returns and line feeds added (part 3 of 3).

Now let's change FIGURE 14.12.A just a bit more. Rather than encoding the data stored in /My_New_File.txt in EBCDIC CCSID 37, let's store it in a common form of ASCII, CCSID 819. Many Integrated File System files are used with ASCII-based systems, so understanding how this is done can certainly be useful when working with files that are shared with other systems. And to keep an earlier commitment, this will also show how the Conversion ID and Text File Creation Conversion ID parameters work together!

Figure 14.12.C shows the changes that are required to create a file tagged as CCSID 819. As you can see, there's not much change! For demonstration purposes, we did change the file name to /My_New_ASCII_File.txt, but the only functional change was in changing the Conversion ID parameter, used when creating the file, from zero (job CCSID) to 819 (ISO Latin-1 ASCII).

```
h dftactgrp(*no) bnddir('QC2LE')

dopen          pr          10i 0 extproc('open')
d path                       *   value options(*string)
d oflag                    10i 0 value
d mode                     10u 0 value options(*nopass)
d convID                   10u 0 value options(*nopass)
d textCrtConvID            10u 0 value options(*nopass)

dread          pr          10i 0 extproc('read')
d fd                       10i 0 value
```

Figure 14.12.C: The complete program creating an ASCII file (part 1 of 3).

474

```
d buf                              *   value
d nbyte                        10u 0 value

dwrite            pr           10i 0 extproc('write')
d fd                           10i 0 value
d buf                              *   value
d nbyte                        10u 0 value

dclose            pr           10i 0 extproc('close')
d fd                           10i 0 value

derrno            pr               *   extproc('__errno')

dErrorNbr         s             10i 0 based(ErrnoPtr)
dfd               s             10i 0
dSomeText         s             50    inz('Hello World')
dTextRcd          s             82
dReturnedData     s             30
dwait             s             1

dCR_LF            c                   x'0D25'

dO_RDONLY         c                   1
dO_WRONLY         c                   2
dO_RDWR           c                   4
dO_CREAT          c                   8
dO_EXCL           c                   16
dO_CCSID          c                   32
dO_TRUNC          c                   64
dO_APPEND         c                   256
dO_SHARE_RDONLY   c                   65536
dO_SHARE_WRONLY   c                   131072
dO_SHARE_RDWR     c                   262144
dO_SHARE_NONE     c                   524288
dO_TEXTDATA       c                   16777216
dO_TEXT_CREAT     c                   33554432

dS_IRGRP          c                   32
dS_IWUSR          c                   128
dS_IRUSR          c                   256

 /free
  fd = open( '/My_New_ASCII_File.txt'
            :O_WRONLY + O_CREAT + O_EXCL + O_CCSID + O_TEXTDATA +
             O_TEXT_CREAT
            :S_IRUSR + S_IWUSR + S_IRGRP
            :819 :0);
```

Figure 14.12.C: The complete program creating an ASCII file (part 2 of 3).

```
    if (fd = -1);
        ErrnoPtr = errno;
        dsply ('Failure ' + %char(ErrorNbr) + ' on open') ' ' wait;
        *inlr = *on;
        return;
    endif;

    TextRcd = %trimr(SomeText) + CR_LF;
    if write(fd :%addr(TextRcd) :%len(%trimr(TextRcd)))
           < %len(%trimr(TextRcd));
        dsply 'Did not write all data' ' ' wait;
    else;
        if close(fd) = -1;
            ErrnoPtr = errno;
            dsply ('Failure ' + %char(ErrorNbr) + ' on close') ' ' wait;
            *inlr = *on;
            return;
        endif;
        fd = open( '/My_New_ASCII_File.txt'
                   :O_RDONLY + O_TEXTDATA);
        if (fd = -1);
            ErrnoPtr = errno;
            dsply ('Failure ' + %char(ErrorNbr) + ' on 2nd open') ' ' wait;
            *inlr = *on;
            return;
        endif;
        if read(fd :%addr(ReturnedData) :%size(ReturnedData))
               < (%len(%trimr(SomeText)) + %size(CR_LF));
            dsply 'Not all data returned' ' ' wait;
        else;
            dsply (%subst(ReturnedData :1 :%len(%trimr(SomeText))))
                        ' ' wait;
        endif;
    endif;

    fd = close(fd);
    *inlr = *on;
    return;
    /end-free
```

Figure 14.12.C: The complete program creating an ASCII file (part 3 of 3).

After running FIG14_12_C, use WRKLNK '/My_New_ASCII_File.txt' and look at the attributes of the file. You will see that the file is now tagged as CCSID 819. FTP the file to Windows in binary mode and open it. You will see that you have a standard ASCII file and that, due to our use of O_TEXTDATA, even the EBCDIC CR and LF controls have been correctly converted to their ASCII equivalents. This is not too big of a change from

FIG14_12_A, and yet you have now directly written to and read from an ASCII file in the Integrated File System! The key is remembering to specify O_TEXTDATA, and setting the proper Conversion ID and Text File Creation Conversion ID parameter values. The source in Figure 14.12.C provides an easy example for you to refer to as you start developing your own applications.

Working with Directories

Now that you know how to work with files within the Integrated File System let's look at some of the APIs related to working with the directories where the files are stored. The first API we will look at is opendir.

Opening a Directory

The parameter description for the opendir API is shown in Figure 14.13. As you can see, opendir takes just one parameter, Dirname, which is the path to the directory to be opened. Dirname is defined as a pass-by-value pointer to a null-terminated character string.

```
DIR *opendir (const char *dirname)
```

Figure 14.13: The opendir API.

The opendir API also returns a pointer to data known as DIR. DIR is not defined by the API documentation in terms of what is stored in it. That's okay, as we have no need to know the internal layout of DIR. The only thing we will need when calling subsequent directory-related APIs is the pointer to DIR, and we do have that.

Figure 14.14 shows the prototype for opendir, along with an example using the API. We have prototyped both opendir and __errno. Like the APIs you saw earlier in this chapter, opendir uses __errno to provide additional information when an error occurs. In this example, we are calling opendir passing a directory name stored in the variable DirName. Later in this chapter we will see that DirName is a parameter passed to our example program and subsequently passed to the opendir API.

```
h dftactgrp(*no) bnddir('QC2LE')

DName++++++++++ETDsFrom+++To/L+++IDc.Keywords++++++++++++++++++++++++
dOpenDir          pr                  *    extproc('opendir')
d DirName                             *    value options(*string)

derrno            pr                  *    extproc('__errno')

dDirPtr           s                   *
dErrorNbr         s                   10i 0 based(ErrnoPtr)
dWait             s                   1

CLON01Factor1+++++++Opcode&ExtFactor2+++++++Result++++++++Len++D+HiLoEq

   DirPtr = OpenDir( %trimr(DirName));
   if (DirPtr = *NULL);
      ErrnoPtr = errno;
      dsply ('Failure ' + %char(ErrorNbr) + ' on OpenDir') ' ' wait;
      *inlr = *on;
      return;
   endif;
```

Figure 14.14: Using the *opendir* API.

If the API returns a null pointer, then an error was encountered and the program DSPLYs appropriate error text and ends. If no error took place, then we have a valid pointer to DIR, which represents the directory we are interested in. We can now begin to read the directory.

Reading a Directory Entry

The readdir API reads the next entry within a directory. The first time you call readdir, the "next" entry is the first entry in the directory. Use readdir to sequentially read through the contents of a directory. Use the rewinddir API if you need to reposition readdir back to the first entry of the directory.

The parameter description for the readdir API is shown in Figure 14.15. This API takes just one parameter, Dirp, which is defined as a pointer to DIR. This is the pointer that was returned by the opendir API.

```
struct dirent *readdir (DIR *dirp)
```

Figure 14.15: The *readdir* API.

The readdir API also returns a pointer that points at a structure of type dirent. The dirent structure is defined in the API documentation as shown in Table 14.3. The dirent structure provides information on the directory entry just read.

Table 14.3: The Dirent Structure		
Type	**Name**	**Description**
Char	reserved[16]	Reserved
Unsigned Int	d_fileno_gen_id	The generation ID associated with the file ID
Unsigned Int	d_fileno	The file ID
Unsigned Int	d_reclen	The length of the directory entry
Int	reserved	Reserved
Char	reserved[6]	Reserved
Char	reserved[2]	Reserved
Int	ccsid	The CCSID of directory entry name
Char	country_id[2]	The Country or region ID of the directory entry name
Char	language_id[3]	The language ID of the directory entry name
Char	reserved[3]	Reserved
Unsigned Int	d_namelen	The length of the directory entry name
Char	d_name[640]	The directory entry name

The Unix-type API parameters are documented using a style based on the C programming language, so too are the structures. In Table 14.3, the "Type" column defines the type of data. These types (char, int, and unsigned int) should be familiar to you by now. In RPG, they correspond to the 1A, 10i 0, and 10u 0 data types, respectively. The "Name" column provides a name for the field and, in the case of char fields, the number of characters. The first reserved field, for instance, is defined as being 16 characters long. (The *[x]* part of the name actually defines an array. In the case of char fields, this represents the number of characters. If *[x]* were used for a type such as int, it would represent an array, as in '10i 0 dim(*x*)'.)

The RPG equivalent of Table 14.3 is shown in Figure 14.16 as the data structure DirEntry. The key pieces of information we are interested in within the DirEntry data structure are NameLen, the length of the directory entry name, and Name, the actual name associated with the directory entry. Additional information is returned, such as the CCSID encoding of the returned name, NameCCSID, and the file ID, FileID. The CCSID used, NameCCSID (for returning the directory entry names), was determined when we called the opendir API. opendir assumes that the CCSID of the DirName parameter passed to the API is the CCSID of our job, and readdir will return all directory entries in that job CCSID.

```
DName+++++++++++ETDsFrom+++To/L+++IDc.Keywords++++++++++++++++++++++++
dDirEntry           ds                          based(DirEntryPtr)
d                                   16
d FileGenID                         10u 0
d FileID                            10u 0
d DirRcdLen                         10u 0
d                                   10i 0
d                                    6
d                                    2
d NameCCSID                         10i 0
d NameCountry                        2
d NameLangID                         3
d                                    3
d NameLen                          10u 0
d Name                             640
```

Figure 14.16: The Dirent structure.

If an entry is found that cannot be converted successfully to the job CCSID, the readdir API simply skips over it, as the name cannot be returned to you in any meaningful manner. This is without your program even knowing that an entry has been skipped! To circumvent this exposure, i5/OS provides national-language enabled versions of the industry-defined Unix-type APIs, which allow you to specify the CCSID that you want used (for instance, Unicode) when returning directory entry information. This allows you to avoid having directory entries that are not returned by readdir when working with file names from multiple languages. For example, suppose a job running in an English CCSID environment encountered a file named Π (the Greek letter pi). This character simply does not exist in the English alphabet, so a directory entry would not be returned. This character, and thousands of others, does, however, exist in Unicode and would be returned using the i5/OS extensions to the industry-defined APIs. These extended APIs are QlgOpendir and QlgReaddir. (An example using these APIs is shown in Figure 14.24.)

Figure 14.17 shows the prototype for readdir, along with an example of calling the API. The program calls readdir, passing the DirPtr variable that was returned by opendir in Figure 14.14. The program then enters a DO-WHILE loop, checking to see if a null pointer was returned (as opposed to a pointer addressing a DirEntry structure). If a null pointer was returned, either an error was found while reading the next directory entry, or all directory entries have been processed. We will discuss how to determine which case it is (error or end of directory entries) a bit later in this chapter.

```
h dftactgrp(*no) bnddir('QC2LE')

DName+++++++++++ETDsFrom+++To/L+++IDc.Keywords+++++++++++++++++++++++
dReadDir              pr                  *     extproc('readdir')
d DirPtr                                  *     value

dNameText             s                   50

CLONO1Factor1+++++++Opcode&ExtFactor2+++++++Result++++++++Len++D+HiLoEq

   DirEntryPtr = ReadDir(DirPtr);
   dow (DirEntryPtr <> *NULL);
       if (NameLen > %size(NameText));
           NameText = %subst(Name :1 :%size(NameText));
       else;
           NameText = %subst(Name :1 :NameLen);
       endif;
       dsply NameText ' ' Wait;
       if (Wait <> ' ');
           leave;
       endif;
       DirEntryPtr = ReadDir(DirPtr);
   enddo;
```

*Figure 14.17: Using the **readdir** API.*

If the DirEntryPtr pointer is not null, the program processes the DirEntry information that is BASED on the returned pointer. Due to the RPG limitation of only being able to DSPLY up to 52 characters, the processing shown in our program is essentially determining whether or not the file name exceeds 50 characters. If it does, the program DSPLYs only the first 50 characters. If not, the program DSPLYs the full file name. There can be many entries within a directory, so the program treats the DSPLY of the file names as if it were a list API. That is, if you enter a non-blank character on the DSPLY of a file name, the program stops reading further directory entries. This is similar to many of the list API examples found in previous chapters. And just so you're not surprised, readdir does return directory entries for the dot (.) and dot-dot (..) subdirectories.

After DSPLYing the current directory entry, the sample program reads the next entry and continues in the DOW loop.

Closing a Directory

When all of the directory entries have been processed, we need to close the directory to free up the resources associated with DIR. We do this with the closedir API. As shown in Figure 14.18, the closedir API takes one parameter, Dirp, which is defined as a pointer to DIR. This is the pointer returned by the previous opendir API. The closedir API also returns an int. This return value will be zero if no error was found, and -1 if an error was encountered in closing the directory.

```
int closedir (DIR *dirp)
```

Figure 14.18: The closedir API.

Figure 14.19 shows the prototype for closedir, along with an example of calling the API.

```
h dftactgrp(*no) bnddir('QC2LE')

DName+++++++++++ETDsFrom+++To/L+++IDc.Keywords++++++++++++++++++++++
dCloseDir              pr              10i 0 extproc('closedir')
d DirPtr                                *    value

CLON01Factor1+++++++Opcode&ExtFactor2+++++++Result++++++++Len++D+HiLoEq

  CloseDir(DirPtr);
```

Figure 14.19: Using the closedir API.

Opening, Reading, and Closing a Directory

The entire program to read and DSPLY the entries within a directory is shown in Figure 14.20. The FIG14_20 program accepts one parameter. This parameter is the path of the directory to be read. As defined in FIG14_20, it can be up to 32 bytes long.

```
h dftactgrp(*no) bnddir('QC2LE')

DName+++++++++++ETDsFrom+++To/L+++IDc.Keywords++++++++++++++++++++++
dFig14_20              pr                    extpgm('FIG14_20')
d DirName                          32

dFig14_20              pi
d DirName                          32
```

Figure 14.20: Opening, reading, and closing a directory (part 1 of 3).

```
dOpenDir         pr                *    extproc('opendir')
d DirName                          *    value options(*string)

dReadDir         pr                *    extproc('readdir')
d DirPtr                           *    value

dCloseDir        pr               10i 0 extproc('closedir')
d DirPtr                           *    value

derrno           pr                *    extproc('__errno')

dDirEntry        ds                      based(DirEntryPtr)
d                                 16
d FileGenID                       10u 0
d FileID                          10u 0
d DirRcdLen                       10u 0
d                                 10i 0
d                                  6
d                                  2
d NameCCSID                       10i 0
d NameCountry                      2
d NameLangID                       3
d                                  3
d NameLen                         10u 0
d Name                           640

dDirPtr          s                 *
dNameText        s                50
dErrorNbr        s                10i 0 based(ErrnoPtr)
dErrorNbrSave    s                10i 0
dWait            s                 1
```

```
CLON01Factor1+++++++Opcode&ExtFactor2+++++++Result++++++++Len++D+HiLoEq
 /free

    DirPtr = OpenDir( %trimr(DirName));
    if (DirPtr = *NULL);
        ErrnoPtr = errno;
        dsply ('Failure ' + %char(ErrorNbr) + ' on OpenDir') ' ' wait;
        *inlr = *on;
        return;
    endif;

    ErrnoPtr = errno;
    ErrorNbrSave = ErrorNbr;
```

Figure 14.20: Opening, reading, and closing a directory (part 2 of 3).

```
    DirEntryPtr = ReadDir(DirPtr);
    dow (DirEntryPtr <> *NULL);
        if (NameLen > %size(NameText));
            NameText = %subst(Name :1 :%size(NameText));
        else;
            NameText = %subst(Name :1 :NameLen);
        endif;
        dsply NameText ' ' Wait;
        if (Wait <> ' ');
            leave;
        endif;
        DirEntryPtr = ReadDir(DirPtr);
    enddo;

    ErrnoPtr = errno;
    if (ErrorNbrSave <> ErrorNbr);
        dsply ('Failure ' + %char(ErrorNbr) + ' on ReadDir') ' ' wait;
    endif;

    Wait = *blanks;
    dsply 'End of list.' ' ' Wait;
    CloseDir(DirPtr);

    *inlr = *on;
    return;

/end-free
```

Figure 14.20: Opening, reading, and closing a directory (part 3 of 3).

Figure 14.21 shows possible ways to call the program.

```
Display entries in the root directory:

CALL FIG14_20 '/'

Display entries in the SOMELIB library:

CALL FIG14_20 '/qsys.lib/somelib.lib'

Display entries in QTEMP:

CALL FIG14_20 '/qsys.lib/qtemp.lib'

Display entries in the directory /qibm/include:

CALL FIG14_20 '/qibm/include'
```

Figure 14.21: Opening, reading, and closing a directory using the Qlg APIs.

When reviewing the source in Figure 14.20, you might notice a few items we have not discussed yet.

After calling the opendir API, and before calling the readdir API, FIG14_20 saves the current value of errno to the working variable ErrorNbrSave. This is done so that we can later determine if the readdir API encountered an end-of-directory situation or an error. Recall from earlier that readdir will return a null pointer to indicate that either no more directory entries are available to be processed or that an error occurred. In the case of an error, readdir updates errno. If all entries were processed, readdir does not update errno. After coming out of the DOW DirEntryPtr <> *NULL; loop, FIG14_20 re-accesses the current errno value. If the current errno is the same as the saved errno value (ErrorNbrSave), then we assume no error was encountered, and we have processed all available directory entries. If the two are not the same, then an error was encountered, and the program DSPLYs the errno value. This error-checking is not perfect, as a readdir error could be the same value as the previous errno value. However, this is a problem that exists with readdir on all systems that comply with the industry definition for readdir, not just i5/OS.

After that, FIG14_20 simply DSPLYs an end-of-list message and ends.

Opening, Reading, and Closing a Directory Using the QLG APIS

Most of the APIs found in the Integrated File System category of System APIs conform to a set of industry-defined standards. These standards certainly aid in providing a level of consistency when working with different systems, but sometimes also introduce a "lowest common denominator" approach to programming. Many systems today, for instance, make it a user responsibility to manage different national-language encodings on a given system. The i5/OS operating system, on the other hand, keeps track of the encoding of data and then converts data to other encodings when needed.

Because there is no provision for the tagging of data within most industry-defined APIs, i5/OS provides a set of APIs generically referred to as the *Qlg APIs*. If you look through the Integrated File System APIs, you will find that, for every industry-defined API that accepts a path-related parameter, there is a complementary Qlg API that allows you to specify a path and the CCSID in which the path is encoded. At the beginning of this chapter, for instance, you saw the open API, which takes a path name as its first parameter. There is also a QlgOpen API, which takes a path name structure. Within that structure, besides the path name, is the CCSID that the path name is encoded in. In the same manner, the opendir and readdir APIs have equivalent QlgOpendir and QlgReaddir APIs.

The remainder of this chapter focuses on the Qlg APIs. If your business environment does not require you to store data in different national languages, you can skip to the "Summary" and "Check Your Knowledge" sections at the end of this chapter. If, however, your business data might use more than one national language, the following discussion will be of interest. (Actually, it's more a question of different character sets than national languages. Most Western European languages, for instance, share the same Latin-1 character set.)

The Qlg APIs all share a common structure, which defines the path or file name of an Integrated File System file. This common structure can be found in member QLG of QSYSINC/QRPGLESRC. It is shown in Figure 14.22. The QSYSINC-provided data structure QLGPN allows you to explicitly control how the path is to be processed by the API you are calling.

```
DName+++++++++++ETDsFrom+++To/L+++IDc.Keywords++++++++++++++++++++++++
D*****************************************************************
D*Structure for NLS enabled path name
D****                                                            *
D*NOTE: The following type definition only defines the fixed
D*  portion of the format.  Any varying length field will
D*  have to be defined by the user.
D*****************************************************************
DQLGPN           DS
D*                                          Qlg Path Name
D QLGCCSID02              1      4B 0
D*                                          CCSID
D QLGCID                  5      6
D*                              Country or region ID
D QLGLID                  7      9
D*                                          Language ID
D QLGERVED07             10     12
D*                                          Reserved
D QLGPT                  13     16U 0
D*                                          Path Type
D QLGPL                  17     20B 0
D*                                          Path Length
D QLGPND                 21     22
D*                                          Path Name Delimiter
D QLGRSV200              23     32
D*                                          Reserved2
D*QLGPN00                33     33
D*
D*                              Variable length field
```

Figure 14.22: The Qlg structure.

The first field, QLGCCSID02, specifies the CCSID of the path name you are using. The special value of zero can be used to indicate that the job CCSID is to be used. More importantly, though, you can also use CCSIDs such as 1200 (UTF-16) or 13488 (UCS2) to indicate that you want to work with Unicode encodings. This allows you to work with path names that might include English, Greek, Cyrillic, Japanese, and Arabic (along with many more languages) within the same path. And you don't even have to know in advance which languages might be used! In an international workplace, this is a very powerful capability provided by i5/OS.

The second field, QLGCID, is the country or region ID associated with the path name. The special value of x'00's can be used to indicate that the current job's country or region ID is to be used. The third field, QLGLID, is the language ID associated with the path name. It also can have the special value of x'00's. The fourth field, QLGERVED07, is simply a reserved field that must be set to x'00's.

The fifth field, QLGPT, defines how the path name, QLGPN00, is being provided. There are four possible values:

- 0__The path name is a character string with path delimiters of one byte.

- 1__The path name is a pointer to a character string with path delimiters of one byte.

- 2__The path name is a character string with path delimiters of two bytes.

- 3__The path name is a pointer to a character string with path delimiters of two bytes.

Being able to supply a pointer to the path name, as opposed to a character string embedded within the QLGPN structure, can be quite useful when working with long path names. When working with application generators, we've seen path names that were tens of thousands of bytes long. We would certainly like to avoid moving path names of this size, if possible, and pointers make that possible.

The sixth field, QLGPL, specifies the length of the path name being used, in bytes. The seventh field, QLGPND, specifies the path delimiter. Typically, this is the "slash" character (/), but you can use other values also. The eighth field, QLGRSV200, is another reserved field that must be set to x'00's. The ninth field, QLGPN00, is the variable length path name that we are working with.

Before showing how the Qlg APIs are used, let's first create a file name with a character that is not in your job CCSID. This will make it much easier to see the difference between using the industry standard APIs and the Qlg versions.

Figure 14.23 shows a program which will create a file named "Π," the Greek capital letter *Pi*. Modeled after the program you saw in Figure 14.12.B, the FIG14_23 program creates a file and writes one line of text to it. (If your job happens to be in Greek already, you will need to make a small change to the program. Change the field NewCCSID to an initial value of 1025 rather than 875 to create a file named "Ъ," the Cyrillic capital letter hard sign.)

```
h dftactgrp(*no) bnddir('QC2LE')

DName++++++++++ETDsFrom+++To/L+++IDc.Keywords+++++++++++++++++++++++
d/copy qsysinc/qrpglesrc,qusrjobi
d/copy qsysinc/qrpglesrc,qusec

dopen              pr            10i 0 extproc('open')
d path                            *    value options(*string)
d oflag                          10i 0 value
d mode                           10u 0 value options(*nopass)
d convID                         10u 0 value options(*nopass)
d textCrtConvID                  10u 0 value options(*nopass)

dwrite             pr            10i 0 extproc('write')
d fd                             10i 0 value
d buf                             *    value
d nbyte                          10u 0 value

dclose             pr            10i 0 extproc('close')
d fd                             10i 0 value

dRJobI             pr                  extpgm('QUSRJOBI')
d Receiver                        1    options(*varsize)
d LengthRcv                      10i 0 const
d Format                          8    const
d QualJobName                    26    const
d IntJobID                       16    const
d QUSEC                                likeds(QUSEC) options(*nopass)
d Reset                           1    const options(*nopass)

dCmdExc            pr                  extpgm('QCMDEXC')
d Command                      65535   const options(*varsize)
```

Figure 14.23: Creating the file Π (part 1 of 3).

```
d CmdLength                     15  5 const
d IGC                               3 const options(*nopass)

derrno            pr            *    extproc('__errno')

dNewCCSID         s            10i 0 inz(875)
dCommand          s            100
dErrorNbr         s            10i 0 based(ErrnoPtr)
dfd               s            10i 0
dSomeText         s            50    inz('3.14159265')
dTextRcd          s            82
dwait             s             1

dCR_LF            c                  x'0D25'

dO_WRONLY         c                  2
dO_CREAT          c                  8
dO_EXCL           c                  16
dO_CCSID          c                  32
dO_TEXTDATA       c                  16777216
dO_TEXT_CREAT     c                  33554432

dS_IRGRP          c                  32
dS_IWUSR          c                  128
dS_IRUSR          c                  256

CL0N01Factor1+++++++Opcode&ExtFactor2+++++++Result++++++++Len++D+HiLoEq
 /free

   QUSBPRV = 0;
   RJobI( QUSI0400 :%size(QUSI0400) :'JOBI0400' :'*' :' ' :QUSEC);

   Command = 'CHGJOB CCSID(' + %char(NewCCSID) + ')';
   CmdExc( Command :%len(%trimr(Command)));

   fd = open( x'6157'
              :O_WRONLY + O_CREAT + O_EXCL + O_CCSID + O_TEXTDATA +
               O_TEXT_CREAT
              :S_IRUSR + S_IWUSR + S_IRGRP
              :0 :0);
   if (fd = -1);
      ErrnoPtr = errno;
      dsply ('Failure ' + %char(ErrorNbr) + ' on open') ' ' wait;
      *inlr = *on;
      return;
   endif;
```

Figure 14.23: Creating the file Π (part 2 of 3).

489

```
TextRcd = %trimr(SomeText) + CR_LF;
if write(fd :%addr(TextRcd) :%len(%trimr(TextRcd)))
    < %len(%trimr(TextRcd));
    dsply 'Did not write all data' ' ' wait;
endif;

if close(fd) = -1;
    ErrnoPtr = errno;
    dsply ('Failure ' + %char(ErrorNbr) + ' on close') ' ' wait;
    *inlr = *on;
    return;
endif;

Command = 'CHGJOB CCSID(' + %char(QUSCCSID07) + ')';
CmdExc( Command :%len(%trimr(Command)));

*inlr = *on;
return;
/end-free
```

Figure 14.23: Creating the file Π (part 3 of 3).

To create a file named Π without manually changing our job environment, we are going to play a little game. (This "little game" would not be necessary if we were to use the Qlg APIs to create the file. Figure 14.25 shows how to create the file Π using the QLGOPEN API.) Within EBCDIC CCSIDs, there are *variant* and *invariant* code points. The EBCDIC code point x'C1', for instance, is invariant; it always represents the uppercase Latin character A. The EBCDIC code point x'57', on the other hand, is variant. For Greek users, it represents the character Π. For Cyrillic users, it represents the character Ъ. This is no different than how the ASCII code point x'EE' is the character î for Latin users (the lowercase letter i with circumflex), ξ for Greek users (the lowercase letter "xi"), and ю for Cyrillic users (the lowercase letter "yu"), and doesn't even exist for 7-bit ASCII users.

In FIG14_23, we use the code points x'61' and x'57' to create a file name. Code point x'61' is the invariant character for a slash (/), and x'57' the variant code point we discussed. FIG14_23 uses these hex constants and, by changing the job CCSID when the open API is called, creates a file name based on the national character associated with the then-current job CCSID. (While we are consciously taking advantage of the variant code point x'57', all too many companies inadvertently store data encoded with one CCSID into a database defined to contain a different CCSID. They then wonder why they're seeing "funny" characters in their applications. There is no problem with i5/OS in using multiple

490

languages within an application, but you need to set the proper job attributes and use the correct programming interfaces if you want to fully support a multilingual environment.)

The program will be changing the job CCSID, so FIG14_23 first calls the Retrieve Job Information API, QUSRJOBI, to determine the current job CCSID. This is done so that we can restore the job to its original state after creating the file. After retrieving the current job CCSID with format JOBI0400, FIG14_23 changes the job CCSID to the value of NewCCSID, using the QCMDEXC API (discussed in chapter 4). The program then creates the file, sets the job CCSID back to the original value, and ends.

Use the command WRKLNK '/' and page through the files listed. You should find a file with either a very strange name or a name that appears to be blank. It's "strange" because a character in the file name does not exist in your job CCSID, and your display is (hopefully) configured to match your job CCSID. From this WRKLNK panel, you most likely will find that taking options such as 4, Remove, or 5, Display, will result in an "Object not found" error. If you would like to correctly see the file, and you are using a terminal that can be configured for different CCSIDs, you can change your terminal session to use CCSID 875 (Greek), change your job CCSID to Greek with CHGJOB CCSID(875), and then run WRKLNK '/' again. You will now be able to work with the Π file. Remember to set your terminal and job settings back to their original values when you're done, though.

Now let's look at the program in Figure 14.24.

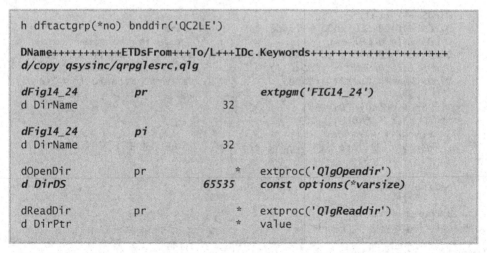

```
h dftactgrp(*no) bnddir('QC2LE')

DName++++++++++++ETDsFrom+++To/L+++IDc.Keywords++++++++++++++++++++++
d/copy qsysinc/qrpglesrc,qlg

dFig14_24         pr                    extpgm('FIG14_24')
d DirName                    32

dFig14_24         pi
d DirName                    32

dOpenDir          pr              *     extproc('QlgOpendir')
d DirDS                       65535     const options(*varsize)

dReadDir          pr              *     extproc('QlgReaddir')
d DirPtr                         *      value
```

Figure 14.24: Opening, reading, and closing a directory using the Qlg APIs (part 1 of 3).

```
dCloseDir            pr              10i 0 extproc('closedir')
d DirPtr                              *    value

derrno               pr              *     extproc('__errno')

dDirDS               ds                    qualified
d Info                                     likeds(qlgpn)
d Name                               32c

dDirEntry            ds                    based(DirEntryPtr)
d                                          qualified
d                                    16
d FileGenID                          10u 0
d FileID                             10u 0
d DirRcdLen                          10u 0
d                                    10i 0
d                                    6
d                                    2
d Info                                     likeds(qlgpn)
d Name                               640c

dDirPtr              s               *
dNameText            s               50
dErrorNbr            s               10i 0 based(ErrnoPtr)
dErrorNbrSave        s               10i 0
dWait                s               1

CLON01Factor1+++++++Opcode&ExtFactor2+++++++Result++++++++Len++D+HiLoEq
 /free

   DirDS = *loval;
   DirDS.Info.QLGCCSID02 = 13488;             // UCS2
   DirDS.Info.QLGPT = 0;                      // Name is character
   DirDS.Info.QLGPL = (2 * %len(%trimr(DirName))); // Number of bytes
   DirDS.Info.QLGPND = x'002F';               // / is the delimiter
   DirDS.Name = %ucs2(DirName);               // convert DirName to UCS2

   DirPtr = OpenDir(DirDS);
   if (DirPtr = *NULL);
      ErrnoPtr = errno;
      dsply ('Failure ' + %char(ErrorNbr) + ' on OpenDir') ' ' wait;
      *inlr = *on;
      return;
   endif;

   ErrnoPtr = errno;
   ErrorNbrSave = ErrorNbr;
```

Figure 14.24: Opening, reading, and closing a directory using the Qlg APIs (part 2 of 3).

```
DirEntryPtr = ReadDir(DirPtr);
dow (DirEntryPtr <> *NULL);
    if ((DirEntry.Info.QLGPT = 0) or (DirEntry.Info.QLGPT = 2));
        if (DirEntry.Info.QLGPL > (%size(NameText) * 2));
            NameText = %char(%subst(DirEntry.Name:1 :%size(NameText)));
        else;
            NameText = %char(%subst( DirEntry.Name :1
                        :(%div(DirEntry.Info.QLGPL :2))));
        endif;
    else;
        dsply ('Unexpected path type ' + %char(DirEntry.Info.QLGPT) +
                ' found.') ' ' wait;
        leave;
    endif;

    dsply NameText ' ' Wait;
    if (Wait <> ' ');
        leave;
    endif;
    DirEntryPtr = ReadDir(DirPtr);
enddo;

ErrnoPtr = errno;
if (ErrorNbrSave <> ErrorNbr);
    dsply ('Failure ' + %char(ErrorNbr) + ' on ReadDir') ' ' wait;
endif;

eval Wait = *blanks;
dsply 'End of list.' ' ' Wait;
CloseDir(DirPtr);

*inlr = *on;
return;

/end-free
```

Figure 14.24: Opening, reading, and closing a directory using the Qlg APIs (part 3 of 3).

This program has the following changes from the one in Figure 14.20:

- The QLG RPG header file from QSYSINC/QRPGLESRC defines the common structure used to describe path information to the Qlg APIs and is copied in.

- The program name is changed to FIG_14_24.

- The prototype for the OpenDir function is changed to use QLGOPENDIR, and the parameter is changed from a null-terminated string to a variable-length structure.

493

- The prototype for the ReadDir function is changed to use QlgReaddir.

- The DirDS data structure is defined as being LIKEDS(QLGPN) followed by a Unicode Name field.

- The DirEntry data structure is changed to describe the path using LIKEDS(QLGPN) and a Unicode Name field.

- Prior to calling the OpenDir function, the DirDS data structure is initialized to indicate the following:

  > The path is encoded with Unicode (QLGCCSID07 = 13488).

  > The path name is being passed as a character string appended to the DirDS structure (QLGPT = 0).

  > The length of the path name is twice the length of the EBCDIC parameter passed to FIG14_24 (QLGPL = (2 * %LEN(%TRIMR(DIRNAME)))). Note that to initialize the fields of DirDS in the same order they are defined (making the code and text easier to follow), we're assuming an SBCS environment with this calculation. A better approach would be to first convert DirName to Unicode and then use the number of bytes actually used when setting QLGPL.

  > The path name delimiter is the Unicode character "/" (QLGPND = X'002F').

- The DirName parameter is converted to Unicode (DirDS.Name = %UCS2(DirName)).

- The parameter passed to the OpenDir function is changed from DirName to DirDS.

- The processing to determine if the file name returned by ReadDir exceeds 50 bytes has been changed to recognize that Unicode characters in CCSID 13488 require two bytes rather than one byte.

- The file name returned by ReadDir is converted from Unicode to the job CCSID.

These are a few more changes than were needed to create an ASCII-encoded stream file in Figure 14.12.C, but they're very straightforward changes, all the same. And they're changes well worth making so that we can work in a multilingual environment using the full range of characters found in the Unicode standard.

Using Qlgopen to Create the Π File

Figure 14.25 shows how to use the QLGOPEN API to create a file using Unicode-encoded path information.

```
h dftactgrp(*no) bnddir('QC2LE')

d/copy qsysinc/qrpglesrc,qlg

dopen           pr              10i 0 extproc('Qp0lOpen')
d pathDS                      65535   const options(*varsize)
d oflag                        10i 0 value
d mode                         10u 0 value options(*nopass)
d convID                       10u 0 value options(*nopass)
d textCrtConvID                10u 0 value options(*nopass)

dwrite          pr              10i 0 extproc('write')
d fd                           10i 0 value
d buf                            *    value
d nbyte                        10u 0 value

dclose          pr              10i 0 extproc('close')
d fd                           10i 0 value

derrno          pr               *    extproc('__errno')

dPathDS         ds                    qualified
d Info                               likeds(qlgpn)
d Name                         50c

dErrorNbr       s               10i 0 based(ErrnoPtr)
dfd             s               10i 0
dSomeText       s               50    inz('3.14159265')
dTextRcd        s               82
dwait           s                1

dCR_LF          c                     x'0D25'

dO_WRONLY       c                     2
dO_CREAT        c                     8
dO_EXCL         c                     16
dO_CCSID        c                     32
dO_TEXTDATA     c                     16777216
dO_TEXT_CREAT   c                     33554432
```

Figure 14.25: Creating the file Π using the QlgOpen API (part 1 of 2).

495

```
dS_IRGRP              c                32
dS_IWUSR              c                128
dS_IRUSR              c                256

/free

  PathDS = *loval;
  PathDS.Info.QLGCCSID02 = 13488;        // UCS2
  PathDS.Info.QLGPT = 0;                 // Name is character
  PathDS.Info.QLGPL = 4;                 // Number of bytes
  PathDS.Info.QLGPND = x'002F';          // / is the delimiter
  PathDS.Name = u'002F03A0';             // File name

  fd = open( PathDS
             :O_WRONLY + O_CREAT + O_EXCL + O_CCSID + O_TEXTDATA +
              O_TEXT_CREAT
             :S_IRUSR + S_IWUSR + S_IRGRP
             :0 :0);
  if (fd = -1);
     ErrnoPtr = errno;
     dsply ('Failure ' + %char(ErrorNbr) + ' on open') ' ' wait;
     *inlr = *on;
     return;
  endif;

  TextRcd = %trimr(SomeText) + CR_LF;
  if write(fd :%addr(TextRcd) :%len(%trimr(TextRcd)))
     < %len(%trimr(TextRcd));
     dsply 'Did not write all data' ' ' wait;
  endif;

  if close(fd) = -1;
     ErrnoPtr = errno;
     dsply ('Failure ' + %char(ErrorNbr) + ' on close') ' ' wait;
     *inlr = *on;
     return;
  endif;

  *inlr = *on;
/end-free
```

Figure 14.25: Creating the file Π using the QlgOpen API (part 2 of 2).

Comparing this program to the equivalent in Figure 14.12.B, you can see that the changes are very similar to those made when going from Figure 14.20 to Figure 14.24:

- The QLG RPG header file from QSYSINC/QRPGLESRC defines the common structure used to describe path information to the Qlg APIs.

- The prototype for the Open function is changed to use QpOlOpen, and the first parameter is changed from a null-terminated string to a variable-length structure. Note that the API documentation for QLGOPEN indicates that the external name is actually *QPOLOPEN*.

- The PathDS data structure is defined as being LIKEDS(QLGPN) followed by a Unicode Name field.

- Prior to calling the Open function, the PathDS data structure is initialized to indicate the following:

  > The path is encoded with Unicode (QLGCCSID07 = 13488).

  > The path name is being passed as a character string appended to the PathDS structure (QLGPT = 0).

  > The length of the path name is set to four, indicating the number of bytes used in the path name (QLGPL = 4).
  > The path name delimiter is the Unicode character "/" (QLGPND = X'002F').

- The Name portion of PathDS is set to the Unicode value of /Π (PathDS.Name = u'002F03A0).

- The parameter passed to the Open function is changed to PathDS.

Using the Qlg APIs, you can create Integrated File System file names, using any character within the Unicode standard, and do it without having to modify your job environment. This is in contrast to using the industry-standard APIs, where you need to change the job environment (the job CCSID in particular) to use characters outside of your job CCSID.

Summary

In this chapter, you have seen a few of the APIs that the i5/OS operating system provides to work with the Integrated File System. Many more APIs exist that enable application programs to directly work with the stream files that might be stored on both local and remote systems. With this introduction to the Integrated File System APIs, you should be able to productively start using the majority of the Integrated File System APIs in a very short period of time.

Check Your Knowledge

The program in Figure 14.12.A requires that the /My_New_File.txt file not exist prior to running the program (due to the use of O_EXCL in the Oflag parameter). Unfortunately, this program also does not automatically delete the file when it's finished. This design is handy if, after the program runs, you want to verify that the file was created and then display its contents with commands like DSPF. However, it is easy to sometimes forget to delete the file before running FIG14_12_A again.

Write a program that deletes the file /My_New_File.txt. Start by reviewing the documentation for the Remove Link to File API, unlink. This API can be found using the API Finder and searching for the name *UNLINK*, or by looking at the "Unix-Type" category of APIs, and then the subcategory "Integrated File System APIs." If the file does not exist when you attempt to delete it an errno value of 3025 will be returned by the unlink API. In this case do not display an error message. For other error situations, DSPLY the value of errno.

For one possible solution to this task, see Figure D.14 of appendix D.

15

Socket APIs

If your system is currently communicating with other systems in a TCP/IP network, you are probably already using sockets. Similar to how CPYTOSTMF uses the Integrated File System APIs, applications such as Telnet and FTP use the socket APIs. In this chapter, you will learn how to develop your own socket-based applications.

We'll start with a simple file-transfer application. We will write a server program that sends all of the records of any file in the SOMELIB library to a client program that receives the records. The file we will be using is the CUSTOMER file, created in chapter 4.

Following that, we'll write a conversational sockets application based on the library information program FIG5_5 developed in chapter 5. Our initial change to the FIG5_5 program will be to have the API logic access library information on a server system while the display-file formatting is done on a client system. Later in the chapter, we'll further modify the FIG5_5 program to allow it to be accessed by remote Windows Telnet clients, in order to demonstrate the EBCDIC and ASCII conversions that most sockets applications need to perform when working with non-i5/OS based systems.

As with the cryptographic services APIs in chapter 11, you will want to read this entire chapter before implementing sockets applications within your business environment.

While the initial server applications in this chapter are quite functional, they do have limitations due to our desire to minimize the number of APIs discussed when first introducing the socket APIs. After we get the basics of sockets programming behind us, we'll implement additional socket-related APIs that provide for a more robust and integrated environment.

Using the SOCKET API

The first API we will look at is the Create Socket API, SOCKET. The SOCKET API allows you to broadly define the type of communications the application program will be using. The parameter descriptions for SOCKET are shown in Figure 15.1.

```
int socket ( int address_family, int type, int protocol)
```

Figure 15.1: The SOCKET API.

If you just finished chapter 14, reading this style of parameter description should be a snap. This API accepts three integer parameters: Address_family, Type, and Protocol. Each one is passed by value and the SOCKET API returns an integer.

The first parameter, Address_family, defines the addressing that we will be using. Special values are defined, such as two for IPv4 and 24 for IPv6. We will be using the IPv4 addressing family.

The second parameter, Type, defines the type of communications we will be using. Special values are defined for this parameter as well, such as the value 1 for full-duplex socket streaming. This is the value associated with the TCP protocol and is what we will be using.

The third parameter, Protocol, defines the type of protocol to be used. It allows special values such as zero, which indicates that we want the default protocol associated with the type of communications value passed in the second parameter, Type. From the API documentation we can see that the default, when Address_family is two and Type is one, is to use the TCP protocol, so we will use the zero value in our examples.

The API also returns an integer value. If the return value is -1, an error was encountered, and errno will be updated with additional information. Otherwise, the SOCKET API call was successful, and the return value is a *socket descriptor* that will be passed to subsequent APIs to identify which socket connection you want to work with.

Figure 15.2 shows the RPG prototype for SOCKET and an example call using the SOCKET API. The program is calling the SOCKET API, asking for a socket that can be used for IPv4 TCP/IP communications. If the API call is successful, the returned socket descriptor is stored in variable sd. If an error is encountered, the value of errno is DSPLYed. Constants are defined in Figure 15.2 to represent the special values AF_INET (IPv4), AF_INET6 (IPv6), SOCK_STREAM (full-duplex socket streaming), and IPPROTO_IP (the default protocol).

```
h dftactgrp(*no) bnddir('QC2LE')

DName++++++++++++ETDsFrom+++To/L+++IDc.Keywords++++++++++++++++++++++++
dSocket           pr            10i 0 extproc('socket')
d AddrFamily                    10i 0 value
d Type                          10i 0 value
d Protocol                      10i 0 value

dErrno            pr             *   extproc('__errno')

dErrorNbr         s             10i 0 based(ErrnoPtr)
dsd               s             10i 0
dWait             s             1

dAF_INET          c                 2
dAF_INET6         c                 24

dSOCK_STREAM      c                 1

dIPPROTO_IP       c                 0

CL0N01Factor1+++++++Opcode&ExtFactor2+++++++Result++++++++Len++D+HiLoEq
 /free

   // Create a socket
   sd = socket( AF_INET :SOCK_STREAM :IPPROTO_IP);
   if (sd = -1);
      ErrnoPtr = Errno;
      dsply ('Failure ' + %char(ErrorNbr) + ' on socket') ' ' Wait;
      *inlr = *on;
      return;
   endif;

 / end-free
```

Figure 15.2: Using the SOCKET API.

Using the BIND API

When writing a server application that will be listening for incoming requests from a client, you need to use the Set Local Address for Socket API, BIND, to associate a local address with the socket descriptor returned by the SOCKET API. This local address represents your IP address and the port you will be using on that IP address.

Note that the BIND API is not needed when developing a client application. If BIND is not called, the system will select an available port for you. Having the system select the port for a client calling out to a server is fine, but on the server, we need to predefine a specific port, so that the clients know the port number to connect to. This is conceptually similar to how your office phone can be called by any other phone in the network. You don't need to know the caller's number in advance, but the caller certainly does need access to your specific telephone number, or at least a switchboard number, to initiate the conversation.

After building a server application, we will create a client application and show which APIs apply in the client environment. The BIND API is one of several that apply primarily to the server environment. The parameter descriptions for BIND are shown in Figure 15.3.

```
int bind (int socket_descriptor, struct sockaddr *local_address,
          int address_length)
```

Figure 15.3: The BIND API.

The BIND API takes three parameters and returns an integer. The first parameter, Socket_descriptor, is the socket descriptor that was previously returned by the SOCKET API.

The second parameter, Local_address, is a pointer to a structure that defines the local address. The definition of this structure depends on the Address_family parameter passed to the previous SOCKET API. For IPv4, that is an Address_family value of two or AF_INET, the definition is shown in Table 15.1.

The third parameter, Address_length, is the length of the structure passed in the second parameter.

If the return value is -1, an error was encountered, and errno will be updated. If the return value is zero, the API call was successful.

Table 15.1: The Sockaddr Structure		
Type	Name	Description
Short Int	Sin_family	The Address_family as previously used with the socket API
Unsigned Short Int	Sin_port	The local port to be used
Unsigned Int	Sin_addr	The local address to be used
Char	Sin_zero[8]	Reserved; must be x'00's

The first field, Sin_family, is used to specify the address family that we will be using. The sample program is using IPv4 addressing, so we will set this to two (the same value as used for the SOCKET API).

The second field, Sin_port, is used to specify the port we will be using. Port numbers can range from one to 65535 and, to continue with our earlier telephone analogy, they represent your telephone extension. By industry convention, port numbers are divided into three ranges. The ranges are zero through 1023 for what are referred to as "Well Known" ports, 1024 through 49151 for "Registered" ports, and 49152 through 65535 for "Dynamic and/or Private" ports. The use of Well Known ports is what allows, for example, a Telnet client to connect to a Telnet server by simply identifying the system you want to talk with. Telnet servers have a Well Known port number of 23 for the client to use. In a similar manner, FTP uses port 20 for data, and HTTP uses port 80. For our initial program, we are using port 53000. This port number is within the Private use range and should not collide with any other activity.

Later in this chapter, you'll see how to register use of a port and avoid having to hard-code this value within an application. For now, though, we're trying to minimize the number of APIs being introduced, so we'll simply hard-code the value. If you would like to see if port 53000 is currently registered for use by your system, and the service that is using the port, use the Work with Service Table Entry command, WRKSRVTBLE. If you would like to see if port 53000 is currently in use by your system, use the Work with TCP/IP Network Status command NETSTAT OPTION(*CNN). As you would hopefully expect, there is also a Get Service Name for Port Number API, GETSERVBYPORT, which can be used to programmatically determine if a port on your system is currently registered as being used.

The third field, Sin_addr, is the local Internet address that we will accept calls on. This can be a specific IP address assigned to your system or one of several special values. One special value is INADDR_LOOPBACK, which indicates that your application will only accept calls from programs on the same local system. This special value is very handy for application development and testing, as outside systems cannot gain access to your new socket-based application. Another special value is INADDR_ANY, which allows any IP address assigned to your system to be used. For our example programs, we use INADDR_ANY.

The fourth field, Sin_zero, is a reserved field and must be set to x'00's.

The BIND API also returns an integer value. If the API completed successfully, the return value is zero. Otherwise, the API returns -1 and updates errno with additional information related to the failure.

Figure 15.4 shows the RPG prototype for BIND and an example call using the API.

```
h dftactgrp(*no) bnddir('QC2LE')

DName+++++++++++ETDsFrom+++To/L+++IDc.Keywords+++++++++++++++++++++++++++
dBind             pr             10i 0 extproc('bind')
d sd                             10i 0 value
d LclAddrPtr                       *   value
d LenAddr                        10i 0 value

dErrno            pr               *   extproc('__errno')

dLclAddr          ds
d SinFamily                       5i 0
d SinPort                         5u 0
d SinAddr                        10u 0
d SinZero                        8

dErrorNbr         s              10i 0 based(ErrnoPtr)
dWait             s              1

dINADDR_ANY       c                     0
dINADDR_LOOPBACK  c                     2130706433

dAF_INET          c                     2
```

Figure 15.4: Using the BIND API (part 1 of 2).

```
CLON01Factor1++++++++Opcode&ExtFactor2+++++++Result+++++++++Len++D+HiLoEq
   // Bind our local address to a socket
   LclAddr = *loval;
   SinFamily = AF_INET;
   SinPort = 53000;
   SinAddr = INADDR_ANY;
   if Bind( sd :%addr(LclAddr) :%size(LclAddr)) < 0;
      ErrnoPtr = Errno;
      dsply ('Failure ' + %char(ErrorNbr) + ' on bind') ' ' Wait;
      *inlr = *on;
      return;
   endif;
```

*Figure 15.4: Using the **BIND** API (part 2 of 2).*

The program in Figure 15.4 first initializes the input structure LclAddr to all x'00's and then indicates that it will be using IPv4 (AF_INET), port 53000, and will accept calls from any IP interface (INADDR_ANY). When calling BIND, it passes the sd returned from the SOCKET API in Figure 15.2, the LclAddr data structure, and the length of the LclAddr data structure. If the API call is not successful, the program DSPLYs the value of errno and ends.

Using the LISTEN API

Having defined the protocol we are supporting and the IP interfaces we will accept calls on, we now use the Invite Incoming Connections Requests API, LISTEN, to indicate willingness to start accepting incoming calls.

The parameter descriptions for LISTEN are shown in Figure 15.5. This API takes two parameters. The first parameter is the Socket_descriptor previously returned by the SOCKET API and subsequently used with the BIND API. The second parameter, Back_log, indicates how many incoming calls we will allow to queue up until the system starts rejecting the calls. The maximum value that can be specified for Back_log is 512.

```
int listen (int socket_descriptor, int back_log)
```

*Figure 15.5: The **LISTEN** API.*

The LISTEN API also returns an integer value. If the API completed successfully, the return value is zero. Otherwise, the API returns -1 and updates errno with additional information related to the failure. Figure 15.6 shows the RPG prototype for LISTEN and an example call using the API.

```
h dftactgrp(*no) bnddir('QC2LE')

DName++++++++++++ETDsFrom+++To/L+++IDc.Keywords+++++++++++++++++++++++++++++
dListen           pr                10i 0 extproc('listen')
d sd                                10i 0 value
d BackLog                           10i 0 value

dErrno            pr                  *   extproc('__errno')

dErrorNbr         s                 10i 0 based(ErrnoPtr)
dWait             s                 1


CLON01Factor1+++++++Opcode&ExtFactor2+++++++Result++++++++Len++D+HiLoEq
   if Listen( sd :1) < 0;
      ErrnoPtr = Errno;
      dsply ('Failure ' + %char(ErrorNbr) + ' on listen') ' ' Wait;
      *inlr = *on;
      return;
   endif;
```

Figure 15.6: Using the *LISTEN* API.

The call to LISTEN passes the sd previously returned by the SOCKET API and indicates that it will allow one call to be queued. If the API call is not successful, the program DSPLYs the value of errno and ends.

Using the ACCEPT API

We're now ready to accept our first incoming call. To do so, we call the Wait for Connection Request and Make Connection API, ACCEPT.

The parameter descriptions for ACCEPT are shown in Figure 15.7. This API takes three parameters and returns an integer.

```
int accept (sd socket_descriptor, struct sockaddr *address,
            int *address_length)
```

Figure 15.7: The *ACCEPT* API.

The first parameter, Socket_descriptor, is the socket descriptor previously returned by the SOCKET API. The second parameter, Address, is a pointer to a structure that defines the address where the incoming call came from. This structure was previously defined in Table 15.1 and used with the BIND API.

The third parameter, Address_length, is a pointer to an integer value. When calling the API, this integer value defines how much storage has been allocated for the Address parameter.

The API also returns an integer value. If this value is -1, an error was encountered, and errno will be updated with additional information. Otherwise, the ACCEPT API was successful and the return value is a *socket descriptor* that will be passed to subsequent APIs to identify which socket connection you want to work with.

Figure 15.8 shows the RPG prototype for ACCEPT and an example call using the API. The call to ACCEPT passes the sd previously returned by the SOCKET API, the structure DestAddr defined LIKEDS(LclAddr), and the size of DestAddr. If the API returns a positive value, then sdTarget is a socket descriptor referencing the incoming connection, and DestAddr is updated to reflect where the call came from. If the API call is not successful, the program DSPLYs the value of errno and ends.

```
h dftactgrp(*no) bnddir('QC2LE')

DName+++++++++++ETDsFrom+++To/L+++IDc.Keywords++++++++++++++++++++++++++++
dAccept           pr              10i 0 extproc('accept')
d sd                              10i 0 value
d RmtAddrPtr                        *   value
d LenAddr                         10i 0

dErrno            pr                *   extproc('__errno')

dLclAddr          ds
d SinFamily                        5i 0
d SinPort                          5u 0
d SinAddr                         10u 0
d SinZero                         8

dDestAddr         ds                    likeds(LclAddr)
```

Figure 15.8: Using the ACCEPT API (part 1 of 2).

```
dErrorNbr          s              10i 0 based(ErrnoPtr)
dsdTarget          s              10i 0
dAddrLen           s              10i 0
dWait              s               1

CLON01Factor1+++++++Opcode&ExtFactor2+++++++Result++++++++Len++D+HiLoEq
    AddrLen = %size(DestAddr);
    sdTarget = Accept( sd :%addr(DestAddr) :AddrLen);
    if sdTarget < 0;
        ErrnoPtr = Errno;
        dsply ('Failure ' + %char(ErrorNbr) + ' on accept') ' ' Wait;
        *inlr = *on;
        return;
    endif;
```

Figure 15.8: Using the ACCEPT API (part 2 of 2).

In our example programs, we will not be using the information returned in DestAddr. Just having the sdTarget socket descriptor is sufficient for us to communicate with the remote program.

Using the RECV API

We mentioned at the beginning of this chapter that our first example program would be a simple file-transfer application. Having run the previous APIs, we're in communication with the remote client (which we will develop shortly). We are now ready to find out what file the client wants to download. In the design of our file-transfer program, we expect the client to send us a 10-byte file name. To receive this file name, we call the Receive Data API, RECV. The parameter descriptions for RECV are shown in Figure 15.9.

```
int recv (int socket_descriptor, char *buffer, int buffer_length;
          int flags)
```

Figure 15.9: The RECV API.

The RECV API takes four parameters. The first parameter, Socket_descriptor, is the socket descriptor that identifies the socket we want to receive information from. This would be the sdTarget that was previously returned by the ACCEPT API.

The second parameter, Buffer, is the receiver variable where we want the received data stored. The third parameter, Buffer_length, is the size of the Buffer parameter. As with all APIs that return data, it is important that this value accurately reflect the storage you have allocated for the receiving of data. Using a value larger than you have actually allocated can cause the API to overwrite other program variables.

The fourth parameter, Flags, allows you to control the behavior of the RECV API. Most of the controls are more advanced than we care to get into with this introduction to the socket APIs, but one should be discussed. The flag MSG_WAITALL allows you to control whether the entire Buffer_length number of bytes should be received before the API returns, or if the API should return as soon as any data is available to be received.

The API also returns an integer. If this return value is -1, an error was encountered, and errno will be updated with additional information. Otherwise, RECV was successful, and the return value reflects the number of bytes written to the Buffer parameter.

Figure 15.10.A shows the RPG prototype for RECV and an example call using the API to obtain any available data. Figure 15.10.B shows a call to the API to obtain an exact amount of data.

```
h dftactgrp(*no) bnddir('QC2LE')

DName+++++++++++ETDsFrom+++To/L+++IDc.Keywords+++++++++++++++++++++++++++
dRecv           pr            10i 0 extproc('recv')
d sd                          10i 0 value
d buf                           *   value
d lenbuf                       10i 0 value
d flags                        10i 0 value

dErrno          pr              *   extproc('__errno')

dBytesRead      s             10i 0
dBuffer         s             100
dsdtarget       s             10i 0
dErrorNbr       s             10i 0 based(ErrnoPtr)
dWait           s             1

CLON01Factor1+++++++Opcode&ExtFactor2+++++++Result++++++++Len++D+HiLoEq
   // Read anywhere from 1 to %size(Buffer) bytes of data
   BytesRead = Recv( sdtarget :%addr(Buffer) :%size(Buffer) :0);
   if BytesRead = -1;
      ErrnoPtr = Errno;
      dsply ('Recv failed with ' + %char(ErrorNbr)) ' ' Wait;
   else;
      // process the data received, BytesRead tells you how much data
   endif;
```

Figure 15.10.A: Using the *RECV* API to receive any available data.

```
h dftactgrp(*no) bnddir('QC2LE')

DName+++++++++++ETDsFrom+++To/L+++IDc.Keywords++++++++++++++++++++++++++++
dRecv           pr              10i 0 extproc('recv')
d sd                            10i 0 value
d buf                             *   value
d lenbuf                        10i 0 value
d flags                         10i 0 value

dErrno          pr                *   extproc('__errno')

dBytesRead      s               10i 0
dBuffer         s               100
dsdtarget       s               10i 0
dErrorNbr       s               10i 0 based(ErrnoPtr)
dWait           s               1

dMSG_WAITALL    c                      64

CLON01Factor1+++++++Opcode&ExtFactor2+++++++Result++++++++Len++D+HiLoEq
  // Read exactly %size(Buffer) bytes of data
  BytesRead = Recv( sdtarget :%addr(Buffer) :%size(Buffer) :MSG_WAITALL);
  if BytesRead = -1;
     ErrnoPtr = Errno;
     dsply ('Recv failed with ' + %char(ErrorNbr)) ' ' Wait;
  else;
     // process the data received, BytesRead tells you how much data
  endif;
```

Figure 15.10.B: Using the RECV API to receive an exact amount of data.

Note that the example in Figure 15.10.A will wait for at least one byte of data to become available before the RECV API will return to our application. The distinction between the two examples is strictly in the area of what is the minimum amount of data to be returned. In Figure 15.10.A, the minimum is one byte. In Figure 15.10.B, the minimum is %SIZE(BUFFER) bytes. Later in the chapter, you will see how even this minimum of one byte can be bypassed, so that your application program immediately receives control even when no data is currently available from the remote application.

The initial example programs in this chapter use the Flag parameter and MSG_WAITALL. We have designed our file-transfer and distributed-processing programs such that we always know how many bytes the remote system is going to send, and we take advantage of this knowledge by simply waiting until all of the data is available (or an error occurs). You might not always have this advance knowledge, however. When working with stream files where there might not be fixed-length records, or with devices that send variable-length data such as a character mode terminal, you will most likely not know in advance whether your application program will receive one, five, or 100 bytes. In these situations, you would not want to use MSG_WAITALL with a Buffer_length greater than one (although you could use MSG_WAITALL with a Buffer_length of one). If the remote system only sends five bytes, and you are waiting for all 100 bytes, you will "hang" until an error is sent indicating the connection has been lost.

Using the SEND API

Having received the name of the file the client program wants to transfer, it's time to send the file. For that, there is the Send Data API, SEND. The parameter descriptions for SEND are shown in Figure 15.11.

```
int send (sd socket_descriptor, char *buffer, int buffer_length
          int flags)
```

Figure 15.11: The SEND API.

The SEND API takes four parameters. The first parameter, Socket_descriptor, is the socket descriptor that identifier the socket we want to send information to. This would be the sdTarget that was previously returned by the ACCEPT API. The second parameter, Buffer, is the data we want to send. The third parameter, Buffer_length, is the size of the data in the Buffer parameter. The fourth parameter, Flags, allows you to control the behavior of the SEND API. The flags represent advanced options; we will not be using any of them in our examples.

The API also returns an integer. If this return value is -1, an error was encountered, and errno will be updated with additional information. Otherwise, SEND was successful, and the return value reflects the number of bytes sent from the Buffer parameter.

Figure 15.12 shows the RPG prototype for SEND and an example call using the API.

```
DName+++++++++++ETDsFrom+++To/L+++IDc.Keywords++++++++++++++++++++++++++
dSend             pr              10i 0 extproc('send')
d sd                              10i 0 value
d buf                               *   value
d lenbuf                          10i 0 value
d flags                           10i 0 value
```

Figure 15.12: Using the SEND API (part 1 of 2).

```
dsdtarget          s              10i 0
dBuffer            s             100
dWait              s               1

CLON01Factor1+++++++Opcode&ExtFactor2+++++++Result++++++++Len++D+HiLoEq
   if Send( sdtarget :%addr(Buffer) :%size(Buffer) :0) = %size(Buffer);
       // Send was successful
   else;
       dsply 'Did not send all data' ' ' Wait;
   endif;
```

Figure 15.12: Using the SEND API (part 2 of 2).

Using the close API

Having seen how to send and receive data, it's time to close the connection with the remote system. To do this, we use the Close File or Socket Descriptor API, close. The parameter descriptions for close are shown in Figure 15.13.

```
int close (int fildes)
```

Figure 15.13: The close API.

The close API takes one parameter, Fildes, which is the socket descriptor that identifies the socket we want to close. When closing the remote connection on the server, this would be the sdTarget previously returned by the ACCEPT API. When the server has finished with all remote connections, this would be the sd that was originally returned by the SOCKET API. In later examples, you will see where one server can have connections established with multiple remote systems.

The API also returns an integer. If this return value is -1, an error was encountered, and errno will be updated with additional information. If the return value is zero, close was successful.

Figure 15.14 shows the RPG prototype for close and an example call using the API.

```
DName+++++++++++ETDsFrom+++To/L+++IDc.Keywords++++++++++++++++++++++++++++
dCloseSocket       pr              10i 0 extproc('close')
d sd                               10i 0 value
```

Figure 15.14: Using the close API (part 1 of 2).

```
dsdtarget          s              10i 0

CLON01Factor1++++++Opcode&ExtFactor2+++++++Result++++++++Len++D+HiLoEq
   if CloseSocket(sdTarget) < 0;
      dsply 'Error on client close' ' ' Wait;
   endif;
```

Figure 15.14: Using the close API (part 2 of 2).

Putting All of the APIs Together with a File Server

Having looked at all of the prerequisite APIs to exchange data with a remote application, let's look at a sample file server. The source is shown in Figure 15.15.

```
h dftactgrp(*no) bnddir('QC2LE')

FFilename++IPEASF.....L.....A.Device+.Keywords+++++++++++++++++++++++++++
fAnyFile    if    f32766          disk      usropn infds(OpenFeedback)

DName++++++++++++ETDsFrom+++To/L+++IDc.Keywords+++++++++++++++++++++++++++
dCmdExc               pr                 extpgm('QCMDEXC')
d Command                    65535       const options(*varsize)
d CmdLength                  15  5 const
d IGC                            3 const options(*nopass)

dSocket               pr         10i 0 extproc('socket')
d AddrFamily                     10i 0 value
d Type                           10i 0 value
d Protocol                       10i 0 value

dBind                 pr         10i 0 extproc('bind')
d sd                             10i 0 value
d LclAddrPtr                      *    value
d LenAddr                        10i 0 value

dListen               pr         10i 0 extproc('listen')
d sd                             10i 0 value
d BackLog                        10i 0 value

dAccept               pr         10i 0 extproc('accept')
d sd                             10i 0 value
d RmtAddrPtr                      *    value
d LenAddr                        10i 0
```

Figure 15.15: A server program sending all records within a file (part 1 of 5).

```
dRecv             pr                10i 0 extproc('recv')
d sd                                10i 0 value
d buf                                *   value
d lenbuf                            10i 0 value
d flags                             10i 0 value

dSend             pr                10i 0 extproc('send')
d sd                                10i 0 value
d buf                                *   value
d lenbuf                            10i 0 value
d flags                             10i 0 value

dCloseSocket      pr                10i 0 extproc('close')
d sd                                10i 0 value

dErrno            pr                 *   extproc('__errno')

dLclAddr          ds
d SinFamily                          5i 0
d SinPort                            5u 0
d SinAddr                           10u 0
d SinZero                            8

dDestAddr         ds                     likeds(LclAddr)

dOpenFeedback     ds
d FBRcdLen              125         126i 0

dErrorNbr         s                 10i 0 based(ErrnoPtr)
dsd               s                 10i 0
dsdTarget         s                 10i 0
dAddrLen          s                 10i 0
dFileName         s                 10
dRcdLen           s                 10i 0
dCommand          s                 100
dEOF              s                 10i 0 inz(-1)
dWait             s                 1

dMSG_WAITALL      c                     64

dINADDR_ANY       c                     0
dINADDR_LOOPBACK  c                     2130706433

dAF_INET          c                     2
dAF_INET6         c                     24
```

Figure 15.15: A server program sending all records within a file (part 2 of 5).

```
dSOCK_STREAM        c                      1

dIPPROTO_IP         c                      0

IAnyFile    ns
I                                132766   AnyRecord

CLON01Factor1++++++Opcode&ExtFactor2++++++Result++++++++Len++D+HiLoEq
 /free

   // Create a socket
   sd = socket( AF_INET :SOCK_STREAM :IPPROTO_IP);
   if (sd = -1);
      ErrnoPtr = Errno;
      dsply ('Failure ' + %char(ErrorNbr) + ' on socket') ' ' Wait;
      *inlr = *on;
      return;
   endif;

   // Bind our local address to a socket
   LclAddr = *loval;
   SinFamily = AF_INET;
   SinPort = 53000;
   SinAddr = INADDR_ANY;
   if Bind( sd :%addr(LclAddr) :%size(LclAddr)) < 0;
      ErrnoPtr = Errno;
      dsply ('Failure ' + %char(ErrorNbr) + ' on bind') ' ' Wait;
      *inlr = *on;
      return;
   endif;

   // Listen for incoming data
   if Listen( sd :1) < 0;
      ErrnoPtr = Errno;
      dsply ('Failure ' + %char(ErrorNbr) + ' on listen') ' ' Wait;
      *inlr = *on;
      return;
   endif;

   // Accept incoming data

   AddrLen = %size(DestAddr);
   sdTarget = Accept( sd :%addr(DestAddr) :AddrLen);
   if sdTarget < 0;
      ErrnoPtr = Errno;
      dsply ('Failure ' + %char(ErrorNbr) + ' on accept') ' ' Wait;
```

Figure 15.15: A server program sending all records within a file (part 3 of 5).

```
    *inlr = *on;
    return;
endif;

// Read the filename to be processed
if (Recv( sdTarget :%addr(FileName) :%size(FileName) :MSG_WAITALL)
    <> -1);

    Command = 'OVRDBF ANYFILE TOFILE(SOMELIB/' + FileName + ')';
    CmdExc( Command :%len(%trimr(Command)));

    Open(e) AnyFile;
    RcdLen = FBRcdLen;
    if not %error;
       Read AnyFile;
       dou %eof(AnyFile);
           if Send( sdTarget :%addr(RcdLen) :%size(RcdLen) :0)
               < %size(RcdLen);
               dsply 'Not all data written' ' ' Wait;
               leave;
           endif;
           if Send(sdTarget :%addr(AnyRecord) :RcdLen :0)
                   < RcdLen;
               dsply 'Not all data written' ' ' Wait;
               leave;
           endif;
           Read Anyfile;
       enddo;

       // Send end of file
       if Send( sdTarget :%addr(EOF) :%size(EOF) :0) < %size(EOF);
          dsply 'Not all data written at End of File' ' ' Wait;
       endif;

    else;
       dsply 'Incorrect file specified' ' ' Wait;
    endif;

else;
   dsply 'Not all data read' ' ' Wait;
endif;

// Close the connection
if CloseSocket(sdTarget) < 0;
   dsply 'Error on client close' ' ' Wait;
endif;
```

Figure 15.15: A server program sending all records within a file (part 4 of 5).

```
Close AnyFile;
Command = 'DLTOVR ANYFILE';
CmdExc( Command :%len(%trimr(Command)));

if CloseSocket(sd) < 0;
    dsply 'Error on listen close' ' ' Wait;
endif;
*inlr = *on;
return;
/end-free
```

Figure 15.15: A server program sending all records within a file (part 5 of 5).

Program FIG15_15 is a very simple file-transfer program. It expects one input from the remote system, a 10-byte FileName, and then sends that file to the remote system. After sending the file, FIG15_15 sends an indication that the end of file (EOF) was reached, and ends.

To allow the reading of any file, FIG15_15 uses the program-described file AnyFile as shown in Figure 15.16. AnyFile is defined as a program-described file with a maximum record length of 32,766 bytes, and a feedback information data structure (infds(OpenFeedback)) to provide runtime information on the record length of AnyFile. It is user-opened (usropn) so that the program does not try to open AnyFile during program initialization.

```
FFilename++IPEASF.....L.....A.Device+.Keywords+++++++++++++++++++++++++++
fAnyFile    if   f32766         disk     usropn infds(OpenFeedback)

DName++++++++++++ETDsFrom+++To/L+++IDc.Keywords+++++++++++++++++++++++++++
dCmdExc             pr                    extpgm('QCMDEXC')
d Command                        65535    const options(*varsize)
d CmdLength                      15    5  const
d IGC                            3  const options(*nopass)

dOpenFeedback       ds
d FBRcdLen                  125  126i 0

dFileName           s            10
dRcdLen             s            10i 0
dCommand            s            100
```

Figure 15.16: Accessing the AnyFile file (part 1 of 2).

```
dMSG_WAITALL        c                       64

IFilename++Sq................From+To+++DcField+++++++++...
IAnyFile    ns
I                               132766  AnyRecord

CL0N01Factor1+++++++Opcode&ExtFactor2+++++++Result++++++++Len++D+HiLoEq

    // Read the filename to be processed
    if (Recv( sdTarget :%addr(FileName) :%size(FileName) :MSG_WAITALL)
        <> -1);

        Command = 'OVRDBF ANYFILE TOFILE(SOMELIB/' + FileName + ')';
        CmdExc( Command :%len(%trimr(Command)));

        Open(e) AnyFile;
        RcdLen = FBRcdLen;
        if not %error;
            Read AnyFile;
            dou %eof(AnyFile);
                // process the file
            enddo;
        else;
            dsply 'Incorrect file specified' ' ' Wait;
        endif;
    else;
        dsply 'Not all data read' ' ' Wait;
    endif;

    Close AnyFile;
    Command = 'DLTOVR ANYFILE';
    CmdExc( Command :%len(%trimr(Command)));
```

Figure 15.16: Accessing the AnyFile file (part 2 of 2).

After accepting a connection with a remote system, FIG15_15 receives the file name from the remote system, using the RECV API and waiting for all 10 bytes of the file name. If there is an error receiving the file name, FIG15_15 DSPLYs a message to the local operator and ends.

The program then uses the Execute Command API, QCMDEXC (introduced in chapter 4), to override AnyFile to the file name received and opens the file.

If the open was successful, the program sets a control field to the record length of the file opened and processes all records until end-of-file. The actual processing of AnyFile is shown in Figure 15.17. (The control field will later be used to inform the remote system of the record length the server is using.) If the open was not successful, the program DSPLYs a message to the local operator and ends.

```
FFilename++IPEASF.....L.....A.Device+.Keywords++++++++++++++++++++++++++++++
fAnyFile   if   f32766           disk     usropn infds(OpenFeedback)

DName++++++++++++ETDsFrom+++To/L+++IDc.Keywords++++++++++++++++++++++++++++++
dOpenFeedback      ds
d FBRcdLen               125   126i 0

dRcdLen           s             10i 0
dEOF              s             10i 0 inz(-1)

IFilename++Sq.................From+To+++DcField+++++++++............
IAnyFile   ns
I                              132766  AnyRecord

CLON01Factor1++++++Opcode&ExtFactor2+++++++Result++++++++Len++D+HiLoEq

       Open(e) AnyFile;
       RcdLen = FBRcdLen;
       if not %error;
          Read AnyFile;
          dou %eof(AnyFile);
              if Send( sdTarget :%addr(RcdLen) :%size(RcdLen) :0)
                 < %size(RcdLen);
                 dsply 'Not all data written' ' ' Wait;
                 leave;
              endif;
              if Send(sdTarget :%addr(AnyRecord) :RcdLen :0)
                       < RcdLen;
                 dsply 'Not all data written' ' ' Wait;
                 leave;
              endif;
              Read Anyfile;
          enddo;

          // Send end of file
          if Send( sdTarget :%addr(EOF) :%size(EOF) :0) < %size(EOF);
             dsply 'Not all data written at End of File' ' ' Wait;
          endif;
```

Figure 15.17: Processing the AnyFile file.

After successfully opening AnyFile, FIG15_15 first sends the record length of the file opened. This is done for two reasons. First, it simplifies the client application receiving the file, as the client can safely receive the following record using the RECV API with a Buffer_length equal to the record length and MSG_WAITALL. Second, the client can perform a "sanity check," prior to receiving the data and writing the data to a local database, to make sure the record length on the server matches the record length of the client's local file. This type of sanity check (and others) will be expanded on in other client examples later in this chapter.

After sending the record length, FIG15_15 sends the actual record and reads the next record in AnyFile. This process of reading a record, sending the record length, sending the record, and reading the next record, continues until end-of-file. At end-of-file, FIG15_15 sends a control value of EOF (-1), which informs the client program that all records have been sent.

FIG15_15 then closes the socket descriptor associated with the remote system, closes AnyFile, deletes any overrides, closes the socket descriptor associated with the local system, and ends. All in all, it's not too difficult, once you get past all the socket APIs needed to establish a connection!

A Few Words of Warning

The FIG15_15 program provides a very minimal level of file transfer and could be enhanced in several areas. The goal of this book, however, is to introduce system APIs, not to develop a robust file-transfer utility, so we'll just point out some of these deficiencies and what might be added to improve them.

- No authentication checking is being performed. Anyone who successfully connects to FIG15_15 can potentially transfer any file that the current user profile for the job running FIG15_15 is authorized to. Because of this, FIG15_15 does not allow the remote system to specify the library associated with the file. Instead, the program is hard-coded to always override AnyFile to the file specified *within* the SOMELIB library. This basically enables access to our sample CUSTOMER file, assuming that you don't put more files in this library. Here are some enhancements to address this issue:

  - FIG15_15 should require some form of user profile and password exchange or verification with the remote system. This could be done using the cryptographic support introduced in chapter 11, or by using Secure Sockets (SSL).

- ○ FIG15_15 should swap to the user profile associated with the remote user. This could be done using some of the security APIs introduced in chapter 12 and the work-management APIs in chapter 13.

- FIG15_15 should provide an option to classify the security associated with the data being sent, as follows:

  - ○ The data is currently being sent in the clear. An option to encrypt the data (using SSL or the cryptographic support introduced in chapter 11) should be available.

  - ○ The data is currently sent with no provision to detect if it has been modified while in transit. An option to provide a hash of the data, again using the cryptographic support introduced in chapter 11, should be available.

- FIG15_15 gives the remote user just one chance to specify a file name. If there is an error in opening AnyFile, the program currently just DSPLYs a message to the local operator and ends the connection. No information is provided to the remote system as to why the connection ended. A return code, similar to how an end-of-file control is sent, would be more appropriate to indicate that the file was not found. You will see an example of how to provide error-related information to a client later in this chapter, in Figures 15.25 and 15.26.

- If the file transfer is successful, the program does not allow the remote user to specify another file. This could be done rather easily, by simply looping back to where FIG15_15 receives the file name. You would, however, want to close AnyFile and delete the override prior to receiving the next file name. This type of change is shown in Figure 15.45.

- FIG15_15 accepts one connection and then ends. A more reasonable approach would be to end the current connection (sdTarget) and then accept new requests from other remote systems. This could be done rather simply, by looping back to the ACCEPT API. This type of change is shown in Figure 15.31.

If you do implement a more robust server, remember that you're on the Internet, where predators are everywhere. You will want to test, test, and retest! Also keep in mind that you can do quite a bit of your testing without exposing your early server attempts to the Internet. This can be done by changing the BIND API call to specify a local internet address, Sin_addr, of INADDR_LOOPBACK rather than INADDR_ANY. This will limit access to your under-development server application to clients on the same system.

Putting All of the APIs Together with a File Server Client

Having looked at the server-side of our file transfer program, let's now look at the client program. The client is shown in Figure 15.18.

```
h dftactgrp(*no) bnddir('QC2LE')

FFilename++IPEASF.....L.....A.Device+.Keywords+++++++++++++++++++++++++++++
fCustomer  o   e            disk      infds(OpenFeedback)

DName+++++++++++ETDsFrom+++To/L+++IDc.Keywords+++++++++++++++++++++++++++++
dFig15_18       pr                    extpgm('FIG15_18')
d SystemParm              30   const

dFig15_18       pi
d SystemParm              30   const

dGetHostByName  pr               *    extproc('gethostbyname')
d HostName                       *    value options(*string)

dSocket         pr              10i 0 extproc('socket')
d AddrFamily                    10i 0 value
d Type                          10i 0 value
d Protocol                      10i 0 value

dConnect        pr              10i 0 extproc('connect')
d sd                            10i 0 value
d DestAddrPtr                    *    value
d LenAddr                       10i 0 value

dSend           pr              10i 0 extproc('send')
d sd                            10i 0 value
d buf                            *    value
d lenbuf                        10i 0 value
d flags                         10i 0 value

dRecv           pr              10i 0 extproc('recv')
d sd                            10i 0 value
d buf                            *    value
d lenbuf                        10u 0 value
d flags                         10i 0 value

dCloseSocket    pr              10i 0 extproc('close')
d sd                            10i 0 value
```

Figure 15.18: A client program receiving all Customer records (part 1 of 4).

```
dErrno              pr                *    extproc('__errno')

dHostEnt            ds                     based(HostEntPtr)
d HNamePtr                            *
d HAliasesPtr                         *
d HAddrType                         10i 0
d HLength                           10i 0
d HAddrListPtr                        *

dDestAddr           ds
d SinFamily                          5i 0
d SinPort                            5u 0
d SinAddr                           10u 0
d SinZero                            8

dSizCusRecDS        ds
dSizCusRec                          10i 0

dCusRecDS           e ds                   extname(Customer :*OUTPUT)

dOpenFeedback       ds
d FBRcdLen              125         126i 0

dSystem             s               30    inz('LOCALHOST')
dFilename           s               10    inz('CUSTOMER')
drecvRC             s               10i 0
dHAddrEntPtr        s                *    based(HAddrListPtr)
dhAddr              s               10u 0 based(HAddrEntPtr)
dErrorNbr           s               10i 0 based(ErrnoPtr)
dsd                 s               10i 0
dWait               s                1

dEOF                c                     -1
dMSG_WAITALL        c                     64

dAF_INET            c                     2
dAF_INET6           c                     24

dSOCK_STREAM        c                     1

dIPPROTO_IP         c                     0

CLON01Factor1+++++++Opcode&ExtFactor2+++++++Result+++++++++Len++D+HiLoEq
 /free
   if %parms > 0;
```

Figure 15.18: A client program receiving all Customer records (part 2 of 4).

```
    System = SystemParm;
endif;

// Get the IP address of the system we will talk with
HostEntPtr = GetHostByName( %trimr(System));
if HostEntPtr = *NULL;
    dsply (%trimr(System) + ' not known.') ' ' Wait;
    *inlr = *on;
    return;
endif;
if HAddrType <> AF_INET;
    dsply 'Host address is not IPv4' ' ' Wait;
    *inlr = *on;
    return;
endif;

// Create a socket
sd = socket( AF_INET :SOCK_STREAM :IPPROTO_IP);
if (sd = -1);
    ErrnoPtr = Errno;
    dsply ('Failure ' + %char(ErrorNbr) + ' on socket') ' ' Wait;
    *inlr = *on;
    return;
endif;

// Establish a connection for the socket
DestAddr = *loval;
SinFamily = AF_INET;
SinPort = 53000;
SinAddr = hAddr;
if Connect( sd :%addr(DestAddr) :%size(DestAddr)) < 0;
    ErrnoPtr = Errno;
    dsply ('Failure ' + %char(ErrorNbr) + ' on connect') ' ' Wait;
    *inlr = *on;
    return;
endif;

// Send request for Customer file

if Send( sd :%addr(FileName) :%size(FileName) :0) = %size(FileName);

    recvRC = Recv( sd :%addr(SizCusRecDS) :%size(SizCusRec)
                 :MSG_WAITALL);
    if ((SizCusRec <> FBRcdLen) and (recvRC <> -1));
        dsply 'Record lengths are different' ' ' Wait;
        CloseSocket(sd);
        *inlr = *on;
```

Figure 15.18: A client program receiving all Customer records (part 3 of 4).

```
        return;
    endif;
    dow (SizCusRec <> EOF) and (recvRC <> -1);
        recvRC = Recv( sd :%addr(CusRecDS) :%size(CusRecDS)
                        :MSG_WAITALL);
        if recvRC <> -1;
            Write CusRec CusRecDS;
        endif;
        recvRC = Recv( sd :%addr(SizCusRecDS) :%size(SizCusRec)
                        :MSG_WAITALL);
    enddo;

    if recvRC = -1;
        ErrnoPtr = Errno;
        dsply ('Failure ' + %char(ErrorNbr) + ' on recv') ' ' Wait;
    endif;

else;
    dsply 'Did not send all data' ' ' Wait;
endif;

// close the socket
if CloseSocket(sd) < 0;
    dsply 'Failure on close' ' ' Wait;
endif;

*inlr = *on;
return;
/end-free
```

Figure 15.18: A client program receiving all Customer records (part 4 of 4).

In the FIG_18 program, you will notice that we have removed several socket-related API calls. The APIs BIND, LISTEN, and ACCEPT are not needed by client applications. We have also added two new APIs, GETHOSTBYNAME and CONNECT.

Using the GETHOSTBYNAME API

The FIG15_18 program accepts one parameter, SystemParm, which identifies the system where the server application is located. Rather than requiring the caller of FIG15_18 to supply an IP address, FIG15_18 allows the caller to simply use a host name such as SYSTEMA. The Get Host Information for Host Name API, GETHOSTBYNAME, is then used to access the IP address associated with the host name.

The parameter descriptions for GETHOSTBYNAME are shown in Figure 15.19. This API takes one parameter, Host_name, which is a pointer to a null-terminated character string holding the name of the host we want to communicate with.

```
struct hostent *gethostbyname (char *host_name)
```

Figure 15.19: The GETHOSTBYNAME API.

The API returns a pointer to a structure known as Hostent. The definition for this structure is shown in Table 15.2. If the return value is a null pointer, an error was encountered, and errno will be updated with additional information. In addition to errno, GETHOSTBYNAME uses a separate API to return additional error information. This API, —H_ERRNO, works in the same manner as __errno. We do not use the —H_ERRNO API in our example programs, but you can see the possible error values it might return by looking at the API documentation for GETHOSTBYNAME.

Table 15.2: The Hostent Structure		
Type	**Name**	**Description**
Char *	H_name	The host name
Char **	H_aliases	An array of host alias names
Int	H_addrtype	The address type for the host
Int	H_length	The length of address information
Char **	H_addr_list	An array of address information entries

The first field, H_name, is a pointer to a null-terminated character string containing the name of the remote system.

The second field, H_aliases, is a pointer to a null-terminated array of pointers. Each of these pointers addresses a null-terminated character string containing an alternative name for the remote system.

The third field, H_addrtype, is the address type for the remote system. For IPv4 addresses, this will be the same AF_INET value we previously used with the SOCKET API.

The fourth field, H_length, is the length of one address information entry.

The fifth field, H_addr_list, is a pointer to a null-terminated array of pointers. Each of these pointers addresses an address information entry. For IPv4, each entry is an unsigned integer field containing the IP address.

Figure 15.20 shows the RPG prototype for GETHOSTBYNAME and how the API is used in FIG15_18. The FIG15_18 program first checks to see if the optional parameter SystemParm was passed. SystemParm represents the name of the system we want to connect to. If SystemParm is not passed, FIG15_18 defaults to LOCALHOST, which is predefined to indicate that we want to connect to an application on the same system as the client application.

```
h dftactgrp(*no) bnddir('QC2LE')

DName+++++++++++ETDsFrom+++To/L+++IDc.Keywords++++++++++++++++++++++++++++
dFig15_18         pr                   extpgm('FIG15_18')
d SystemParm                    30     const

dFig15_18         pi
d SystemParm                    30     const

dGetHostByName    pr             *     extproc('gethostbyname')
d HostName                       *     value options(*string)

dHostEnt          ds                   based(HostEntPtr)
d HNamePtr                       *
d HAliasesPtr                    *
d HAddrType                    10i 0
d HLength                      10i 0
d HAddrListPtr                   *

dSystem           s             30     inz('LOCALHOST')
dHAddrEntPtr      s              *     based(HAddrListPtr)
dhAddr            s            10u 0 based(HAddrEntPtr)

CLON01Factor1+++++++Opcode&ExtFactor2+++++++Result++++++++Len++D+HiLoEq
   if %parms > 0;
      System = SystemParm;
   endif;

   // Get the IP address of the system we will talk with
   HostEntPtr = GetHostByName( %trimr(System));
   if HostEntPtr = *NULL;
      dsply (%trimr(System) + ' not available.') ' ' Wait;
```

Figure 15.20: Using the GETHOSTBYNAME API (part 1 of 2).

```
    *inlr = *on;
    return;
endif;
if HAddrType <> AF_INET;
    dsply 'Host address is not IPv4' ' ' Wait;
    *inlr = *on;
    return;
endif;

SinAddr = hAddr;
```

Figure 15.20: Using the *GETHOSTBYNAME* API (part 2 of 2).

After calling GETHOSTBYNAME, we check to see if a null pointer was returned, indicating an error. If so, the program DSPLYs a generic message indicating that a problem was found. Otherwise, the program verifies that an IPv4 address was returned. The example program only supports IPv4, so an error message is DSPLYed if any other address type is returned.

If these checks are successful, FIG15_18 then calls the SOCKET API to create a socket descriptor. If the SOCKET API call is successful, the client program calls the Establish Connection or Destination Address API, CONNECT, after initializing the DestAddr data structure with the information needed to connect to the server system. Note that the SinAddr field of DestAddr is now initialized with the hAddr field returned by GETHOSTBYNAME.

The parameters for the CONNECT API are shown in Figure 15.21. They are essentially the same as those for the BIND API in a server environment. The one exception is that the Local_address parameter of BIND is now the Destination_address of CONNECT. Figure 15.22 shows the RPG prototype for CONNECT and how the API is used in FIG15_18.

```
int connect (int socket_descriptor,
             struct sockaddr *destination_address, int address_length)
```

Figure 15.21: The *CONNECT* API.

```
DName++++++++++ETDsFrom+++To/L+++IDc.Keywords++++++++++++++++++++++++++++
dConnect               pr              10i 0 extproc('connect')
d sd                                   10i 0 value
d DestAddrPtr                           *    value
d LenAddr                              10i 0 value


dDestAddr              ds
d SinFamily                             5i 0
d SinPort                               5u 0
d SinAddr                              10u 0
d SinZero                               8

dhAddr                 s               10u 0 based(HAddrEntPtr)

CLON01Factor1+++++++Opcode&ExtFactor2+++++++Result++++++++Len++D+HiLoEq
    // Establish a connection for the socket
    DestAddr = *loval;
    SinFamily = AF_INET;
    SinPort = 53000;
    SinAddr = hAddr;
    if Connect( sd :%addr(DestAddr) :%size(DestAddr)) < 0;
        ErrnoPtr = Errno;
        dsply ('Failure ' + %char(ErrorNbr) + ' on connect') ' ' Wait;
        *inlr = *on;
        return;
    endif;
```

Figure 15.22: Using the CONNECT API.

After successfully connecting to the server system, FIG15_18 uses the SEND API to send the name of the file we want to transfer. In our example program, this is the CUSTOMER file created in chapter 4.

FIG15_18 then uses the RECV API to receive the record length sent by the server program FIG15_15. If the record length was successfully returned, the program checks to see if the record length of CUSTOMER on the server system is the same as the record length of CUSTOMER on the client system. If not, an appropriate error is DSPLYed. This check is performed because it is possible that the client and server systems may be at different release levels of the application software using the CUSTOMER file. Many users who have multiple systems installed do not have the luxury of being able to upgrade all systems at the same time. This type of check can avoid major problems in a network of mixed release levels, at a very low cost.

After this, FIG15_18 falls into a DO-WHILE loop that is exited when either end-of-file is sent by FIG15_15 or an error occurs on one of the RECV API calls. Within the loop, the program receives a record, writes the record to the local CUSTOMER file, reads the size of the next record, and then reads the next record. When end-of-file is detected, the program closes the socket descriptor and ends.

Running the File Transfer Programs

To run the file transfer programs, FIG15_15 must be started first. Figure 15.23 shows the command to start the server. For demonstration purposes, we will assume that the server is running on a system identified as SYSTEMA.

```
CALL FIG15_15
```

Figure 15.23: Starting the FIG15_15 server on SYSTEMA.

When starting the server program, you might receive a DSPLY message indicating "Failure 3420 on bind." The message description CPE3420 in QCPFMSG has first-level text of "Address already in use." This "error" is likely to happen if you call FIG15_15 two times within a few minutes. The reason is that, although the first call successfully ended, it is still associated with the previous connection. To ensure that all communications are successfully concluded, the TCP standard for sockets requires that the socket sending a final acknowledgment waits a minimum amount of time. This ensures that the last control information sent (not user data, but TCP-related control data) was successfully received by the remote system. Errno 3420 indicates that you are still within this timing window.

To immediately end the connection, you can use the NETSTAT OPTION(*CNN) command. This command will display a panel similar to Figure 15.24. From here, you can look for the local port FIG15_15 uses (port 53000) and choose option 4 to end the connection. (In Figure 15.38, you'll see how to use the SETSOCKOPT API to avoid this need to manually end the connection.)

To start the client FIG15_18, you would use the command shown in Figure 15.25. For demonstration purposes, we will assume that the client is running on a remote system identified as SYSTEMB.

```
                     Work with TCP/IP Connection Status
                                                      System:    CPU35
Local internet address  . . . . . . . . . . :      *ALL

Type options, press Enter.
  4=End    5=Display details

       Remote          Remote        Local
Opt    Address         Port          Port       Idle Time  State
  _    *               *             lpd        027:14:34  Listen
  _    *               *             routed     027:14:11  *UDP
  _    *               *             telnet- >  041:02:23  Listen
  _    *               *             sealms     034:06:41  Listen
  _    *               *             as-edrsql  027:14:41  Listen
  _    *               *             5001       041:02:12  Listen
  _    *               *             5002       041:02:12  Listen
  _    *               *             5003       041:02:11  Listen
  _    *               *             5004       041:02:11  Listen
  _    *               *             5005       041:02:11  Listen
  _    *               *             5006       041:02:11  Listen
                                                                 More...
F5=Refresh   F11=Display byte counts   F13=Sort by column
F14=Display port numbers    F22=Display entire field    F24=More keys
```

Figure 15.24: The NETSTAT OPTION(*CNN) display.

```
CALL FIG15_18 SYSTEMA
```

Figure 15.25: Starting the FIG15_18 client on SYSTEMB.

If the client program FIG15_18 is running on SYSTEMA (the same system as the server program FIG15_15), you can also simply CALL FIG15_18, as the client program defaults to the local system. In the scenario of FIG15_15 and FIG15_18 both running on the same local system, you will want to create an empty copy of the CUSTOMER file in the client job, in a library such as QTEMP. Then use the following prior to running FIG15_18:

```
OVRDBF FILE(CUSTOMER) TOFILE(QTEMP/CUSTOMER)
```

If you attempt to start the client program without first starting the server, you will probably receive a DSPLY on the client indicating "Failure 3425 on connect." The message description CPE3425 in QCPFMSG has first-level text of "A remote host refused an attempted connect operation." This indicates that no server is available to accept the connection request. To resolve this, make sure the server program FIG15_15 is running on the system you are trying to connect with.

Putting All of the APIs Together with a Distributed Processing Server

Now let's move on to another type of socket application. In this example, we will modify the display library information program of Figure 5.5. Our change will be to leave the API calls that gather library-related information on the server system, while moving the processing and display of the data to the client system. In this way, each client can customize the display in whatever fashion they wish and provide this customization without affecting the server code.

Figure 15.26 shows the source for this server application.

```
h dftactgrp(*no) bnddir('QC2LE')

DName+++++++++++ETDsFrom+++To/L+++IDc.Keywords+++++++++++++++++++++++++++++
d/copy qsysinc/qrpglesrc,qusrobjd
d/copy qsysinc/qrpglesrc,qlirlibd
d/copy qsysinc/qrpglesrc,qus
d/copy qsysinc/qrpglesrc,qusec

dSocket           pr              10i 0 extproc('socket')
d AddrFamily                      10i 0 value
d Type                            10i 0 value
d Protocol                        10i 0 value

dBind             pr              10i 0 extproc('bind')
d sd                              10i 0 value
d LclAddrPtr                        *   value
d LenAddr                         10i 0 value

dListen           pr              10i 0 extproc('listen')
d sd                              10i 0 value
d BackLog                         10i 0 value

dAccept           pr              10i 0 extproc('accept')
d sd                              10i 0 value
d RmtAddrPtr                        *   value
d LenAddr                         10i 0

dRecv             pr              10i 0 extproc('recv')
d sd                              10i 0 value
d buf                               *   value
d lenbuf                          10i 0 value
d flags                           10i 0 value
```

Figure 15.26: A server program for displaying library-related information (part 1 of 5).

```
dSend              pr            10i 0 extproc('send')
d sd                             10i 0 value
d buf                             *    value
d lenbuf                         10i 0 value
d flags                          10i 0 value

dCloseSocket       pr            10i 0 extproc('close')
d sd                             10i 0 value

dErrno             pr             *    extproc('__errno')

dRObjD             pr                  extpgm('QUSROBJD')
d Receiver                        1    options(*varsize)
d ReceiverLen                    10i 0 const
d Format                          8    const
d ObjLibName                     20    const
d ObjectType                     10    const
d ErrCde                               likeds(ErrCde) options(*nopass)
d ASPControl                  65535    const options(*varsize :*nopass)

dRLibD             pr                  extpgm('QLIRLIBD')
d Receiver                        1    options(*varsize)
d RecieverLen                    10i 0 const
d Library                        10    const
d Attributes                  65535    const options(*varsize)
d ErrCde                               likeds(ErrCde) options(*nopass)

dLclAddr           ds
d SinFamily                       5i 0
d SinPort                         5u 0
d SinAddr                        10u 0
d SinZero                         8

dDestAddr          ds                  likeds(LclAddr)

dObjLibName        ds
d LibName                        10
d ObjLib                         10    inz('QSYS')

dAttributes        ds
d NbrAttributes                  10i 0
d Key                           10i 0 dim(10)

dReceiver          ds           256    qualified
d Hdr                                  likeds(QLIRR)
```

Figure 15.26: A server program for displaying library-related information (part 2 of 5).

```
dErrCde          ds              qualified
d EC                             likeds(QUSEC)
d ErrDta                 512

dErrorNbr        s              10i 0 based(ErrnoPtr)
dsd              s              10i 0
dsdTarget        s              10i 0
dAddrLen         s              10i 0
drecv            s              10i 0
dAPI_Error       s              10i 0 inz(-2)
dWait            s               1

dMSG_WAITALL     c              64

dINADDR_ANY      c              0
dINADDR_LOOPBACK c              2130706433

dAF_INET         c              2
dAF_INET6        c              24

dSOCK_STREAM     c              1

dIPPROTO_IP      c              0
CL0N01Factor1+++++++Opcode&ExtFactor2+++++++Result++++++++Len++D+HiLoEq
 /free

   ErrCde.EC.QUSBPRV = %size(ErrCde);

   // Create a socket
   sd = socket( AF_INET :SOCK_STREAM :IPPROTO_IP);
   if (sd = -1);
      ErrnoPtr = Errno;
      dsply ('Failure ' + %char(ErrorNbr) + ' on socket') ' ' Wait;
      *inlr = *on;
      return;
   endif;

   // Bind our local address to a socket
   LclAddr = *loval;
   SinFamily = AF_INET;
   SinPort = 53001;
   SinAddr = INADDR_ANY;
   if Bind( sd :%addr(LclAddr) :%size(LclAddr)) < 0;
      ErrnoPtr = Errno;
      dsply ('Failure ' + %char(ErrorNbr) + ' on bind') ' ' Wait;
```

Figure 15.26: A server program for displaying library-related information (part 3 of 5).

```
      *inlr = *on;
      return;
endif;

// Listen for incoming data
if Listen( sd :1) < 0;
   ErrnoPtr = Errno;
   dsply ('Failure ' + %char(ErrorNbr) + ' on listen') ' ' Wait;
   *inlr = *on;
   return;
endif;

// Accept incoming data
AddrLen = %size(DestAddr);
sdTarget = Accept( sd :%addr(DestAddr) :AddrLen);
if sdTarget < 0;
   ErrnoPtr = Errno;
   dsply ('Failure ' + %char(ErrorNbr) + ' on accept') ' ' Wait;
   *inlr = *on;
   return;
endif;

// Get library name
recvRC = recv( sdTarget :%addr(LibName) :%size(LibName):MSG_WAITALL);

if recvRC <> -1;
   // Get object related data
   RObjD( QUSD0400 :%size(QUSD0400) :'OBJD0400' :ObjLibName
          :'*LIB'    :ErrCde);
   if (ErrCde.EC.QUSBAVL <> 0);
      Send( sdTarget :%addr(API_Error) :%size(API_Error) :0);
      Send( sdTarget :%addr(ErrCde) :%size(ErrCde) :0);
      dsply ('Error ' + QUSEI + ' while retrieving library object');
      CloseSocket(sdTarget);
      CloseSocket(sd);
      *inlr = *on;
      return;
   else;
      if Send( sdTarget :%addr(QUSD0400) :QUSBRTN09 :0) < QUSBRTN09;
         dsply 'Not all data written' ' ' Wait;
         CloseSocket(sdTarget);
         CloseSocket(sd);
         *inlr = *on;
         return;
      endif;
   endif;
```

Figure 15.26: A server program for displaying library-related information (part 4 of 5).

```
      // Get library size and number of objects
      NbrAttributes = 2;
      Key(1) = 6;                        // library size
      Key(2) = 7;                        // number of objects in library

      RLibD( Receiver :%size(Receiver) :LibName :Attributes :ErrCde);

      if (ErrCde.EC.QUSBAVL <> 0);
          Send( sdTarget :%addr(API_Error) :%size(API_Error) :0);
          Send( sdTarget :%addr(ErrCde) :%size(ErrCde) :0);
          dsply ('Error ' + QUSEI + ' while retrieving library desc');
          CloseSocket(sdTarget);
          CloseSocket(sd);
          *inlr = *on;
          return;
      else;
          if Send( sdTarget :%addr(Receiver) :Receiver.Hdr.QLIBRTN :0)
             < Receiver.Hdr.QLIBRTN;
              dsply 'Not all data written' ' ' Wait;
              CloseSocket(sdTarget);
              CloseSocket(sd);
              *inlr = *on;
              return;
          endif;
      endif;

  else;
      ErrnoPtr = Errno;
      dsply ('Could not receive library name -  ' + %char(ErrorNbr))
              ' ' Wait;
  endif;

  // Close the connection
  if CloseSocket(sdTarget) < 0;
      dsply 'Error on client close' ' ' Wait;
  endif;

  if CloseSocket(sd) < 0;
      dsply 'Error on listen close' ' ' Wait;
  endif;
  *inlr = *on;
  return;

/end-free
```

Figure 15.26: A server program for displaying library-related information (part 5 of 5).

536

Figure 15.27 shows the source for the client program.

```
h dftactgrp(*no) bnddir('QC2LE')

FFilename++IPEASF.....L.....A.Device+.Keywords++++++++++++++++++++++++++
fFIG5_4      cf   e              workstn

DName++++++++++++ETDsFrom+++To/L+++IDc.Keywords++++++++++++++++++++++++++
dFig15_27          pr                    extpgm('FIG15_27')
d Library                       10
d SystemParm                    30

dFig15_27          pi
d Library                       10
d SystemParm                    30

d/copy qsysinc/qrpglesrc,qusrobjd
d/copy qsysinc/qrpglesrc,qlirlibd
d/copy qsysinc/qrpglesrc,qus
d/copy qsysinc/qrpglesrc,qusec

dGetHostByName     pr                *   extproc('gethostbyname')
d HostName                           *   value options(*string)

dSocket            pr           10i 0 extproc('socket')
d AddrFamily                    10i 0 value
d Type                          10i 0 value
d Protocol                      10i 0 value

dConnect           pr           10i 0 extproc('connect')
d sd                            10i 0 value
d DestAddrPtr                    *   value
d LenAddr                       10i 0 value

dSend              pr           10i 0 extproc('send')
d fd                            10i 0 value
d buf                            *   value
d lenbuf                        10i 0 value
d flags                         10i 0 value

dRecv              pr           10i 0 extproc('recv')
d fd                            10i 0 value
d buf                                value
d lenbuf                        10u 0 value
d flags                         10i 0 value
```

Figure 15.27: A client program for displaying library-related information (part 1 of 8).

```
dCloseSocket      pr           10i 0 extproc('close')
d fd                           10i 0 value

dErrno            pr             *   extproc('__errno')

dSndPgmMsg        pr                 extpgm('QMHSNDPM')
d MsgID                         7    const
d QualMsgF                      20   const
d MsgDta                        65535 const options(*varsize)
d LenMsgDta                     10i 0 const
d MsgType                       10   const
d CallStackEntry                65535 const options(*varsize)
d CallStackCntr                 10i 0 const
d MsgKey                        4
d QUSEC                              likeds(QUSEC)
d LenCSE                        10i 0 const options(*nopass)
d CSEQual                       20   const options(*nopass)
d DSPWaitTime                   10i 0 const options(*nopass)
d CSEType                       10   const options(*nopass)
d CCSID                         10i 0 const options(*nopass)

dHostEnt          ds                 based(HostEntPtr)
d HNamePtr                       *
d HAliasesPtr                    *
d HAddrType                     10i 0
d HLength                       10i 0
d HAddrListPtr                   *

dDestAddr         ds
d SinFamily                     5i 0
d SinPort                       5u 0
d SinAddr                       10u 0
d SinZero                       8

dReceiver         ds            256  qualified
d Hdr                                likeds(QLIRR)

dEntry            ds                 based(EntryPtr)
d                                    qualified
d EntryHdr                           likeds(QUSVR4)
d Key6LibSiz                    10i 0 overlay(Entry :13)
d Key6LibMult                   10i 0 overlay(Entry :*next)
d Key6LibSts                    1    overlay(Entry :*next)
d Key7NbrObjs                   10i 0 overlay(Entry :13)

dErrCde           ds                 qualified
d EC                                 likeds(QUSEC)
d ErrDta                        512
```

Figure 15.27: A client program for displaying library-related information (part 2 of 8).

```
dQualMsgF          ds
d MsgF                          10    inz('QCPFMSG')
d MsgL                          10    inz('*LIBL')

dSystem            s            30    inz('LOCALHOST')
drecvRC            s            10i 0
dHAddrEntPtr       s             *    based(HAddrListPtr)
dhAddr             s            10u 0 based(HAddrEntPtr)
dErrorNbr          s            10i 0 based(ErrnoPtr)
dsd                s            10i 0
dCount             s            10u 0
dTrash             s             1    based(TrashPtr)
dAPI_Error         s            10i 0 inz(-2)
dMsgKey            s             4
dWait              s             1

dMSG_WAITALL       c                  64

dAF_INET           c                  2
dAF_INET6          c                  24

dSOCK_STREAM       c                  1

dIPPROTO_IP        c                  0

CLON01Factor1+++++++Opcode&ExtFactor2+++++++Result++++++++Len++D+HiLoEq
 /free

   if %parms = 0;
      dsply 'Library name is a required parameter' ' ' Wait;
      *inlr = *on;
      return;
   endif;

   if %parms > 1;
      System = SystemParm;
   endif;

   // Get the IP address of the system we will talk with
   HostEntPtr = GetHostByName( %trimr(System));
   if HostEntPtr = *NULL;
      dsply (%trimr(System) + ' not available') ' ' Wait;
      *inlr = *on;
      return;
   endif;
```

Figure 15.27: A client program for displaying library-related information (part 3 of 8).

```
if HAddrType <> AF_INET;
    dsply 'Host address is not IPv4' ' ' Wait;
    *inlr = *on;
    return;
endif;

// Create a socket
sd = socket( AF_INET :SOCK_STREAM :IPPROTO_IP);
if (sd = -1);
    ErrnoPtr = Errno;
    dsply ('Failure ' + %char(ErrorNbr) + ' on socket') ' ' Wait;
    *inlr = *on;
    return;
endif;

// Establish a connection for the socket
DestAddr = *loval;
SinFamily = AF_INET;
SinPort = 53001;
SinAddr = hAddr;
if Connect( sd :%addr(DestAddr) :%size(DestAddr)) < 0;
    ErrnoPtr = Errno;
    dsply ('Failure ' + %char(ErrorNbr) + ' on connect') ' ' Wait;
    *inlr = *on;
    return;
endif;

// Send request for Library

if Send( sd :%addr(Library) :%size(Library) :0) = %size(Library);

    recvRC = Recv(sd :%addr(QUSBRTN09) :%size(QUSBRTN09):MSG_WAITALL);
    if recvRC = -1;
        dsply 'Did not get QUSROBJD size' ' ' Wait;
        CloseSocket(sd);
        *inlr = *on;
        return;
    endif;
    if QUSBRTN09 = API_Error;
        recvRC = recv( sd :%addr(ErrCde) :%size(QUSEC)
                       :MSG_WAITALL);
        if recvRC = -1;
            dsply 'Did not get QUSEC size' ' ' Wait;
            CloseSocket(sd);
            *inlr = *on;
            return;
        endif;
```

Figure 15.27: A client program for displaying library-related information (part 4 of 8).

```
     if ErrCde.EC.QUSBAVL > 16;
        recvRC = recv( sd :%addr(ErrCde.ErrDta)
                       :(ErrCde.EC.QUSBAVL - %size(QUSEC))
                       :MSG_WAITALL);
        if recvRC = -1;
           dsply 'Did not get QUSEC error data' ' ' Wait;
           CloseSocket(sd);
           *inlr = *on;
           return;
        endif;
     endif;
     CloseSocket(sd);
     QUSBPRV = 0;
     SndPgmMsg( ErrCde.EC.QUSEI :QualMsgF :ErrCde.ErrDta
                :(ErrCde.EC.QUSBAVL - %size(QUSEC))
                :'*COMP' :'*EXT' :0 :MsgKey :QUSEC);
     *inlr = *on;
     return;
  endif;

  select;
     when QUSBRTN09 = %size(QUSD0400);
        recvRC = Recv( sd :%addr(QUSBAVL10)
                       :(QUSBRTN09 - %size(QUSBRTN09))
                       :MSG_WAITALL);
     when QUSBRTN09 < %size(QUSD0400);
        Count = QUSBRTN09;
        clear QUSD0400;
        QUSBRTN09 = Count;
        recvRC = Recv( sd :%addr(QUSBAVL10)
                       :(QUSBRTN09 - %size(QUSBRTN09))
                       :MSG_WAITALL);
     when QUSBRTN09 > %size(QUSD0400);
        if TrashPtr = *NULL;
           TrashPtr = %alloc(QUSBRTN09 - %size(QUSD0400));
        endif;
        recvRC = Recv( sd :%addr(QUSBAVL10)
                       :(%size(QUSD0400) - %size(QUSBRTN09))
                       :MSG_WAITALL);

        recvRC = Recv( sd :%addr(Trash) :QUSBRTN09 -
                       (%size(QUSD0400));
                       :MSG_WAITALL);

  endsl;
  if recvRC = -1;
     dsply 'Did not get QUSROBJD data' ' ' Wait;
```

Figure 15.27: A client program for displaying library-related information (part 5 of 8).

```
        CloseSocket(sd);
        *inlr = *on;
        return;
endif;

if (QUSCDT16 <> *blanks);      // creation date
    CrtDate = %char(%date(%subst(QUSCDT16:2:6):*YMD0):*JOBRUN);
endif;

if (QUSORDT03 <> *blanks);     // restore date
    RstDate = %char(%date(%subst(QUSORDT03:2:6):*YMD0):*JOBRUN);
    RstTime = %dec(%subst(QUSORDT03:8:6):6:0);
endif;

if (QUSOSDT03 <> *blanks);     // save date
    LstSavDat = %char(%date(%subst(QUSOSDT03:2:6):*YMD0):*JOBRUN);
    LstSavTim = %dec(%subst(QUSOSDT03:8:6):6:0);
endif;

recvRC = Recv( sd :%addr(Receiver.Hdr.QLIBRTN)
                    :%size(QLIBRTN) :MSG_WAITALL);
if recvRC = -1;
    dsply 'Did not get QLIRLIBD size' ' ' Wait;
    CloseSocket(sd);
    *inlr = *on;
    return;
endif;
if Receiver.Hdr.QLIBRTN = API_Error;
    recvRC = recv( sd :%addr(ErrCde) :%size(QUSEC)
                    :MSG_WAITALL);
    if recvRC = -1;
        dsply 'Did not get QUSEC size' ' ' Wait;
        CloseSocket(sd);
        *inlr = *on;
        return;
    endif;
    if ErrCde.EC.QUSBAVL > 16;
        recvRC = recv( sd :%addr(ErrCde.ErrDta)
                        :(ErrCde.EC.QUSBAVL - %size(QUSEC))
                        :MSG_WAITALL);
        if recvRC = -1;
            dsply 'Did not get QUSEC error data' ' ' Wait;
            CloseSocket(sd);
            *inlr = *on;
            return;
        endif;
    endif;
endif;
```

Figure 15.27: A client program for displaying library-related information (part 6 of 8).

```
        CloseSocket(sd);
        QUSBPRV = 0;
        SndPgmMsg( ErrCde.EC.QUSEI :QualMsgF :ErrCde.ErrDta
                   :(ErrCde.EC.QUSBAVL - %size(QUSEC))
                   :'*COMP' :'*EXT' :0 :MsgKey :QUSEC);
        *inlr = *on;
        return;
      endif;

    if Receiver.Hdr.QLIBRTN > %size(Receiver);
      // or use %ALLOC/%REALLOC
      dsply 'QLIRLIBD information too large' ' ' Wait;
      TotalObjs = 0;
      TotalSize = 0;
    else;

        recvRC = Recv( sd :%addr(Receiver.Hdr.QLIBAVL)
                       :(Receiver.Hdr.QLIBRTN - %size(QLIBRTN))
                       :MSG_WAITALL);

        if recvRC = -1;
            dsply 'Did not get QLIRLIBD data' ' ' Wait;
            CloseSocket(sd);
            *inlr = *on;
            return;
        endif;

        EntryPtr = %addr(Receiver) + %size(Receiver.Hdr);

        for Count = 1 to Receiver.Hdr.QLIVRRTN;
            select;
              when (Entry.EntryHdr.QUSCK = 6);
                    TotalSize = Entry.Key6LibSiz * Entry.Key6LibMult;
              when (Entry.EntryHdr.QUSCK = 7);
                    TotalObjs = Entry.Key7NbrObjs;
              other;
                    dsply ('Unexpected key ' +
                           %char(Entry.EntryHdr.QUSCK) +' found.')
                          ' ' Wait;
            endsl;
            EntryPtr = EntryPtr + Entry.EntryHdr.QUSLVR00;
        endfor;
      endif;

    exfmt Format1;

  else;
    dsply 'Did not send all data' ' ' Wait;
  endif;
```

Figure 15.27: A client program for displaying library-related information (part 7 of 8).

```
    // close the socket
    if CloseSocket(sd) < 0;
        dsply 'Failure on close' ' ' Wait;
    endif;
    if TrashPtr <> *NULL;
        dealloc TrashPtr;
    endif;
    *inlr = *on;
    return;

/end-free
```

Figure 15.27: A client program for displaying library-related information (part 8 of 8).

If you are comfortable with how the socket APIs were used in programs FIG15_15 and FIG15_18, you should have no difficulty in understanding the programs FIG15_26 and FIG15_27. The changes are primarily in the logic of how the data is processed. The actual socket API usage is virtually identical. Once you become familiar with the socket APIs, you can start applying that knowledge to a wide variety of applications!

In the case of FIG15_26, the only real change when using the socket APIs is with the port we use in calling the BIND API. The FIG15_15 program used port 53000. FIG15_26 changes the port number to 53001. While we could have reused port 53000 for the FIG15_26 server, this would have created an unnecessary coordination problem that we would have had to manage. Having the FIG15_15 file-transfer server receive a connection request from the FIG15_27 library description client would not be good. If we used the same port, we would have to ensure that the correct server (FIG15_15 or FIG15_26) was started in anticipation of the next client request (from either FIG15_18 or FIG15_27). We avoid this entire problem by simply using different port numbers. In case you're concerned about having to manage a large number of different ports (a very valid concern), Figure 15.39 will show how to share the same port across multiple server applications.

Having now covered the only change related to socket APIs—the port we BIND to—the processing of the Retrieve Object Description API and Retrieve Library Description API within FIG15_26 becomes very streamlined. Essentially, FIG15_26 receives the name of the library to be processed, retrieves the object-related data from the Retrieve Object Description API, sends the data returned by the API to the client, retrieves the library-related data from the Retrieve Library Description API, sends the data returned by the API to the client, and ends the connection.

On the client side, similar changes are needed for FIG15_27. As with the port change in FIG15_26, we need to change the port number we are connecting to, to 53001. After that, the program simply sends the library name and receives back the output of the Retrieve Object Description API on the remote system.

We have, however, added some additional logic in terms of how we receive and validate the API output. You might recall from FIG15_15 that we always sent the size of each record to the client application, so that the client would know how much data to receive using MSG_WAITALL and be able to validate the record length of the file. FIG15_26 uses a similar approach, but FIG15_26 is not explicitly sending the client the size of the "record" or API output buffer. Instead, FIG15_27 first receives the first four bytes of the API receiver variable. The API documentation for the Retrieve Object Description API shows that this is the field QUSBRTN09, the number of bytes returned by the API. FIG15_27 takes this value, subtracts four because it's already received the four bytes representing QUSBRTN09, and then receives the rest of the data.

Before actually receiving the data, though, FIG15_27 makes an additional check. This is a safety check similar to what was done in FIG15_18 when comparing the CUSTOMER file record lengths of the server and client systems. This check, however, is much more likely to save you from grief. After all, how often do you change record lengths?

Both FIG15_26 and FIG15_27 are written to use the QSYSINC-provided definitions for the results of the Retrieve Object Description and Retrieve Library Description APIs. What would happen if IBM were to add five new fields to the end of the OBJD0400 format of the Retrieve Object Description API? The size would become larger. What would happen if you were to recompile FIG15_26 because you added some new comments to the source or changed the text of a DSPLY message? FIG15_26 would automatically pick up the new definition of the OBJD0400 format (data structure QUSD0400) and, without any other change, start sending the newly added fields to FIG15_27. FIG15_27, however, has not been recompiled—in fact, it's still on a release of i5/OS where the new fields haven't been added to format OBJD0400. If FIG25_26 simply receives the data from FIG15_26 to the QUSD0400 data structure, unintended program variables will be overwritten by the five new fields. This is a rather subtle version of what was discussed in chapter 1 under the topic "Size Is Critical." In FIG15_27, we need to make sure that the FIG15_26 server is not sending more information than we have allocated space for.

The same situation can occur in reverse—the client program FIG15_27 might be the program that is recompiled, while the server code remains as-is. Now we have FIG15_27 expecting to receive more data than the server is able to send. In this case, FIG15_27 could ignore the new fields in data structure QUSD0400, but a safer approach would be to initialize the new fields to their appropriate default values. This would allow the client code to start using the new fields when they're available from the server, and not run into problems with un-initialized fields when working with servers that do not provide the new fields. This initialization approach can be quite important when the client might be working with multiple servers, and the servers might all be on different release levels.

The key parts of this checking are shown in Figure 15.28. After receiving the number of bytes being returned, QUSBRTN09, FIG15_27 selects different processing options based on the size returned and the size that FIG15_27 has allocated for the returned data.

```
CLON01Factor1+++++++Opcode&ExtFactor2+++++++Result++++++++Len++D+HiLoEq
       recvRC = Recv(sd :%addr(QUSBRTN09) :%size(QUSBRTN09):MSG_WAITALL);
       if recvRC = -1;
           dsply 'Did not get QUSROBJD size' ' ' Wait;
           CloseSocket(sd);
           *inlr = *on;
           return;
       endif;

       select;
           when QUSBRTN09 = %size(QUSD0400);
               recvRC = Recv( sd :%addr(QUSBAVL10)
                                :(QUSBRTN09 - %size(QUSBRTN09))
                                :MSG_WAITALL);
           when QUSBRTN09 < %size(QUSD0400);
               Count = QUSBRTN09;
               clear QUSD0400;
               QUSBRTN09 = Count;
               recvRC = Recv( sd :%addr(QUSBAVL10)
                                :(QUSBRTN09 - %size(QUSBRTN09))
                                :MSG_WAITALL);
           when QUSBRTN09 > %size(QUSD0400);
               if TrashPtr = *NULL;
                   TrashPtr = %alloc(QUSBRTN09 - %size(QUSD0400));
               endif;
               recvRC = Recv( sd :%addr(QUSBAVL10)
                                :(%size(QUSD0400) - %size(QUSBRTN09))
                                :MSG_WAITALL);
               recvRC = Recv( sd :%addr(Trash) :QUSBRTN09 -
                                :(%size(QUSD0400))
                                :MSG_WAITALL);

       endsl;
```

Figure 15.28: Checking for the size of the data returned by the Retrieve Object Description API.

The first case, QUSBRTN09 = %SIZE(QUSD0400), is where both the server and client have the same definitions for QUSD0400. In this case, FIG15_27 directly receives the data from the server system.

The second case, QUSBRTN09 < %SIZE(QUSD0400), is where the server is downlevel from the client system. In this case, FIG15_27 first CLEARs the data structure QUSD0400 and then receives the data from the server system.

The third case, QUSBRTN09 > %SIZE(QUSD0400), is where the client is downlevel from the server system. FIG15_27 has a few options for handling this additional data. We certainly can't just ignore it because we need the Retrieve Library Description API data, which is being sent by the server after the object description data. The option we selected was to dynamically allocate a Trash variable with a size equal to the extra data being sent by the server system. FIG15_27 then receives the amount of data equal to the allocated size of QUSD0400 and, following that, receives the additional data to the Trash variable. An alternative approach would be to BASE the QUSD0400 data structure and initially %ALLOC four bytes of storage to accommodate the QUSBRTN09 field. After receiving QUSBRTN09, FIG15_27 could %REALLOC this BASED structure to QUSBRTN09 bytes and receive the server data into this larger, BASED allocation. The program FIGD_15_C demonstrates an implementation of this alternative approach.

After receiving the object description data, FIG15_27 processes the data in much the same way as FIG5_5 did. When done with this processing, the program receives the output of the Retrieve Library Description API from the server system. After receiving the Bytes Returned field from the server (Receiver.Hdr.QLIBRTN), FIG15_27 again checks to see if the bytes returned are equal to the bytes we've allocated for the data. Rather than repeating the same type of processing discussed in Figure 15.28, the program now simply assigns the value of zero to TotalObjs and TotalSize if the two systems are working at different levels. In a production environment, however, you would want to apply what we discussed in Figure 15.28.

FIG15_27 then processes the library description data, displays the results to the local user, and ends.

Before we leave FIG15_26 and FIG15_27, there is one other change that we have made. In our earlier file-transfer server (FIG15_15) and file-transfer client (FIG15_18), we consciously designed the programs so that the client program would not know what was wrong if any error was encountered in using the requested file. With FIG15_26 and

FIG15_27, we have changed this design so that any error message returned to the server by the Retrieve Object Description and Retrieve Library Description APIs is returned to the client.

In FIG15_26, when calling the Retrieve Object Description and Retrieve Library Description APIs, we pass an API error code, ErrCde, that has allocated 512 bytes for message-replacement data. After each API call, FIG15_26 examines the Bytes Available field of this error-code structure, ErrCde.EC.QUSBAVL. If it is non-zero, the program sends the special value -2 (API_Error) to the client program, followed by the ErrCde data structure.

FIG15_27 adds a corresponding check, prior to processing any API output returned by FIG15_26, to see if the Bytes Returned field (QUSBRTN09 of the QUSROBJD API or Receiver.Hdr.QLIRTN of the QLIRLIBD API) is set to this special value of API_Error. If so, it retrieves the ErrCde data structure, resends the error message along with the replacement data, and then ends. With FIG15_26 and FIG15_27, we are returning information to the client user so that they can better determine the cause of the problem.

Building a Better Server

To minimize the number of APIs introduced in any one example, we have been hardcoding, or defaulting, certain socket attributes and implementing a very simple server design. Now that you're familiar with the basic socket API functions, let's build a more robust server environment.

Using the Getservbyname API

Previously, we have been hardcoding the port that the server and client application use. We can avoid that by using the Get Port Number for Service Name API, GETSERVBYNAME. This API returns the port used by a named service and protocol.

The parameter descriptions for GETSERVBYNAME are shown in Figure 15.29. This API takes two parameters and returns a pointer to a structure known as *servent*. The first parameter, Service_name, is a pointer to the null-terminated name of the service you want to use. This can be a well-known name such as *http*, or a name of your choosing. The second parameter, Protocol_name, is a pointer to the null-terminated name of the protocol you want to use. This would be a name such as *tcp*.

```
struct servent *getservbyname (char *service_name,
                               char *protocol_name)
```

Figure 15.29: The GETSERVBYNAME API.

The API returns a pointer to the servent structure. If this pointer is null, a service by the specified Service_name was not found for the requested Protocol_name. If the pointer is not null, the pointer addresses a structure as shown in Table 15.3.

Table 15.3: The Servent Structure		
Type	Name	Description
Char *	S_name	Service name
Char **	S_aliases	Array of server alias names
Int	S_port	Service port
Char *	S_proto	Service protocol

The first field, S_name, is a pointer to the null-terminated service name that was returned. The second field, S_aliases, is a pointer to a null-terminated array of pointers that point to null-terminated alternate names for the service. The third field, S_port, is the port associated with the service. The fourth field, S_proto, is a pointer to the null-terminated name of the protocol associated with the service.

Figure 15.30 shows the RPG prototype for GETSERVBYNAME, the RPG equivalent ServiceEntry data structure for servent, and an example call using the API.

```
h dftactgrp(*no) bnddir('QC2LE')

DName+++++++++++ETDsFrom+++To/L+++IDc.Keywords++++++++++++++++++++++++++++++
dGetPort          pr             *     extproc('getservbyname')
d ServName                       *     value options(*string)
d ProtName                       *     value options(*string)

dServiceEntry     ds                   based(ServiceEntryPtr)
d ServName                     *
d ServAlias                    *
d ServPort                     10i 0
d ServProtocol                 *
```

Figure 15.30: Using the GETSERVBYNAME API (part 1 of 2).

```
dLclAddr              ds
d SinFamily                      5i 0
d SinPort                        5u 0
d SinAddr                        10u 0
d SinZero                        8


dService              c                   'My_Somelib_Server'
dProtocol             c                   'tcp'

CLON01Factor1+++++++Opcode&ExtFactor2+++++++Result++++++++Len++D+HiLoEq

    ServiceEntryPtr = GetPort(%trimr(Service) :%trimr(Protocol));
    if ServiceEntryPtr = *NULL;
        dsply ('Service ' + Service + ' for ' + Protocol + 'not found.')
                ' ' Wait;
        *inlr = *on;
        return;
    endif;

    SinPort = ServPort;
```

Figure 15.30: Using the *GETSERVBYNAME* API (part 2 of 2).

In Figure 15.30, we are using the GETSERVBYNAME API to determine the port associated with the service My_Somelib_Server and protocol tcp. (The GETSERVBYNAME API is prototyped as GetPort, which seems more descriptive, given our goal is the port number.) If the API call is successful, we assign the returned port number to the SinPort field of the LclAddr data structure. This is the data structure later used by the BIND API.

To register the service My_Somelib_Server to the system, use the Add Service Table Entry command ADDSRVTBLE, as shown in Figure 15.31. We will run the ADDSRVTBLE on each system in our network, so that both client and server applications can take advantage of the GETSERVBYNAME API.

```
ADDSRVTBLE SERVICE('My_Somelib_Server') PORT(53003) PROTOCOL('tcp')
```

Figure 15.31: Adding a service table entry.

Create a Routing Server

Our earlier servers have used one port per server application. For instance, port 53000 is for file transfer, and port 53001 is for library information access. Now, let's build a server that routes requests to the correct application. Rather than having the client simply send the file name (as in FIG15_18) or the library name (as in FIG15_27), the client will first send a 4-byte integer, called *Function*. A value of one for Function indicates a file transfer is wanted, while a value of two indicates that library information is wanted. The client can send either a file name or a library name depending on the requested Function. While we're at it, we'll also add the ability to support multiple connections to the server, so that we don't have to restart it after each client request. We will now need a way to stop the server, so we'll also add a Function value of -1 to indicate that the server should end.

The necessary server change is shown in Figure 15.32.

```
h dftactgrp(*no) bnddir('QC2LE')

DName+++++++++++ETDsFrom+++To/L+++IDc.Keywords++++++++++++++++++++++++++
dFunction            s              10i 0

dEOJ                 c                    -1
dFileServer          c                     1
dApplServer          c                     2

CLON01Factor1++++++++Opcode&ExtFactor2+++++++Result+++++++++Len++D+HiLoEq

   // Accept incoming data
   dow Function <> EOJ;
       AddrLen = %size(DestAddr);
       sdTarget = Accept( sd :%addr(DestAddr) :AddrLen);
       if sdTarget < 0;
           ErrnoPtr = Errno;
           dsply ('Failure ' + %char(ErrorNbr) + ' on accept') ' ' Wait;
           leave;
       endif;

       // Get Function to perform
       recvRC = recv( sdTarget :%addr(Function) :%size(Function)
                      :MSG_WAITALL);

       if recvRC <> -1;

           // Determine type of request
           select;
               when Function = FileServer;
                               // run the file transfer logic
```

Figure 15.32: A server supporting multiple client applications and connections (part 1 of 2).

```
            when Function = ApplServer;
                DQKey.Key = ApplServer;
                                // run the library information logic

            when Function = EOJ;
                CloseSocket(sdTarget);
                // run end of job logic
                leave;
            other;
                dsply ('Unknown request ' + %char(Function) +
                        ' received.') ' ' Wait;
          endsl;
        else;
            dsply 'Unable to read Function.' ' ' Wait;
            CloseSocket(sdTarget);
            CloseSocket(sd);
            *inlr = *on;
            return;
        endif;

        // Close the connection
        if CloseSocket(sdTarget) < 0;
            dsply 'Error on client close' ' ' Wait;
        endif;

    // Loop back to accept the next connection
    enddo;
```

Figure 15.32: A server supporting multiple client applications and connections (part 2 of 2).

The file-transfer client change is shown in Figure 15.33.

```
DName+++++++++++ETDsFrom+++To/L+++IDc.Keywords+++++++++++++++++++++++++++
dFilename         s             10    inz('CUSTOMER')
dFileServer       s             10i 0 inz(1)

CLON01Factor1+++++++Opcode&ExtFactor2+++++++Result++++++++Len++D+HiLoEq
  if Connect( sd :%addr(DestAddr) :%size(DestAddr)) < 0;
     ErrnoPtr = Errno;
     dsply ('Failure ' + %char(ErrorNbr) + ' on connect') ' ' Wait;
     *inlr = *on;
     return;
  endif;
```

Figure 15.33: A client requesting the file-transfer server application for file CUSTOMER (part 1 of 2).

```
// Send request for file server and then file name
if Send( sd :%addr(FileServer) :%size(FileServer) :0)
        < %size(FileServer);
    dsply 'Function not sent' ' ' Wait;
    CloseSocket(sd);
    *inlr = *on;
    return;
endif;

// Send request for Customer file

if Send( sd :%addr(FileName) :%size(FileName) :0) = %size(FileName);
```

Figure 15.33: A client requesting the file-transfer server application for file **CUSTOMER** *(part 2 of 2).*

As you can see, the changes are minimal. In the server application—now a "routing server," if you will—we define a DO-WHILE loop starting at ACCEPT and ending with CLOSESOCKET. Within this loop, the program examines the received Function value and runs the appropriate logic for that function. This loop continues until either a communication error occurs or the Function value EOJ is received. In the client code, we now send the Function value before sending the file name.

We now only require one port for both applications and do not need to restart the server after each connection. We do, however, have the consideration, or limitation, that only one client can be using the server at a time. It would be nice to have the ability for file transfer and library-information access logic run asynchronously to our server-routing logic. It is, hopefully, no surprise to find out that there are APIs to enable this.

Using the GIVEDESCRIPTOR API

A socket descriptor is generally only valid in the job that called the SOCKET API. The Pass Descriptor Access to Another Job API, GIVEDESCRIPTOR, allows you to give a socket descriptor to another job. In the other job, a complementary TAKEDESCRIPTOR API is used to accept the socket descriptor.

The parameter descriptions for GIVEDESCRIPTOR are shown in Figure 15.34. The GIVEDESCRIPTOR API takes two parameters. The first parameter, Descriptor, is the socket descriptor you want to give to another job. The second parameter, Target_job, is a pointer to the internal job ID of the job you want to give the socket descriptor to. This is the internal job ID that was previously discussed in chapter 13.

```
int givedescriptor (int descriptor, char *target_job)
```

Figure 15.34: The GIVEDESCRIPTOR API.

This API also returns an integer. If the return value is -1, an error was found on the API call, and errno is updated with additional information. If the return value is zero, the API call completed successfully. Note, though, that a successful call to GIVEDESCRIPTOR does not mean that the other job has taken the descriptor. It simply means you have successfully made the descriptor available to the other job.

Using the TAKEDESCRIPTOR API

The parameter descriptions for the Receive Socket Access from Another Job API TAKEDESCRIPTOR are shown in Figure 15.35.

```
int takedescriptor (char *source_job)
```

Figure 15.35: The TAKEDESCRIPTOR API.

The TAKEDESCRIPTOR API takes one parameter, Source_job. This parameter is a pointer to the internal job ID of the job giving you the socket descriptor. If the special value of a null pointer is passed, the caller of TAKEDESCRIPTOR will take a socket descriptor from any job that uses the GIVEDESCRIPTOR API and references this job as the Target_job.

The API also returns an integer. If the return value is -1, an error was found on the API call, and errno is updated with additional information. If the return value is not zero, the return value is a socket descriptor value that can be used with subsequent socket-related APIs.

Communicating Internal Job IDs

Because the GIVEDESCRIPTOR API requires that we know the internal job ID of the job we are giving the descriptor to, we need a mechanism to allow the "other" job, the job where the actual work is to be done, to communicate its internal job ID back to our routing server. There are many ways to accomplish this. The one we selected was to use a data queue.

We are going to create the data queue SOMELIB/MY_SVR_Q and have the logic serving jobs send their internal job ID to this data queue. To start these server jobs, the routing server will use the Submit Job command, SBMJOB. When the submitted servers start to run, they will retrieve their internal job ID, send this ID to the data queue MY_SVR_Q, and then call the TAKEDESCRIPTOR API to wait for work to be routed to them.

Figure 15.36 shows the new routing server. We've highlighted the changes made from Figure 15.32. This time, we've made quite a few changes!

```
DName++++++++++++ETDsFrom+++To/L+++IDc.Keywords++++++++++++++++++++++++++
d/copy qsysinc/qrpglesrc,qrcvdtaq
d/copy qsysinc/qrpglesrc,qusec

dGiveDesc         pr               10i 0 extproc('givedescriptor')
d sd                               10i 0 value
d IntJobID                         16    const

dRcvDtaQ          pr                     extpgm('QRCVDTAQ')
d DtaQName                         10    const
d DtaQLib                          10    const
d ReceiverLenRtn                    5 0
d Receiver                          1    options(*varsize)
d WaitTime                          5 0 const
d KeyOrder                          2    const options(*nopass)
d KeyLen                            3 0 const options(*nopass)
d KeyValue                          1    options(*varsize :*nopass)
d SndrInfoLen                       3 0 const options(*nopass)
d SndrInfo                          1    options(*varsize :*nopass)
d RmvMsg                           10    const options(*nopass)
d ReceiverLen                       5 0 const options(*nopass)
d QUSEC                                  likeds(QUSEC) options(*nopass)

dCmdExc           pr                     extpgm('QCMDEXC')
d Command                       65535    const options(*varsize)
d CmdLength                        15 5 const
d IGC                               3    const options(*nopass)

dDQKey            ds                     qualified
d Key                              10i 0

dsd               s                10i 0
dsdTarget         s                10i 0
dAddrLen          s                10i 0
drecvRC           s                10i 0
dFunction         s                10i 0
dMsgSizRtn        s                 5 0
dIntJobID         s                16
dSndrInfo         s                 1
```

Figure 15.36: The routing server (part 1 of 4).

```
dCmd_Sbm_File      s              100    inz('SBMJOB -
d                                        CMD(CALL PGM(SOMELIB/FIG15_42)) -
d                                        JOBQ(QSYS/QUSRNOMAX) -
d                                        CURLIB(SOMELIB)')
dCmd_Sbm_Appl      s              100    inz('SBMJOB -
d                                        CMD(CALL PGM(SOMELIB/FIG15_43)) -
d                                        JOBQ(QSYS/QUSRNOMAX) -
d                                        CURLIB(SOMELIB)')

dEOJ               c                     -1
dFileServer        c                     1
dApplServer        c                     2
dServerQ           c                     'MY_SVR_Q'
dServerLib         c                     'SOMELIB'


CLON01Factor1+++++++Opcode&ExtFactor2+++++++Result++++++++Len++D+HiLoEq

// Accept incoming data
dow Function <> EOJ;
    AddrLen = %size(DestAddr);
    sdTarget = Accept( sd :%addr(DestAddr) :AddrLen);
    if sdTarget < 0;
        ErrnoPtr = Errno;
        dsply ('Failure ' + %char(ErrorNbr) + ' on accept') ' ' Wait;
        leave;
    endif;

    // Get Function to perform
    GetDataRC = GetData( sdTarget :%addr(Function) :%size(Function));

    if GetDataRC <> -1;

        // Determine type of request and see if any jobs are available
        select;
            when Function = FileServer;
                DQKey.Key = FileServer;
                RcvDtaQ( ServerQ :ServerLib :MsgSizRtn :IntJobID
                         :0 :'EQ' :%size(DQKey) :DQKEY :0 :QRCQSI
                         :'*YES' :%size(IntJobID) :QUSEC);
                if MsgSizRtn = 0;
                    // submit a server job
                    CmdExc(Cmd_Sbm_File :%len(%trimr(Cmd_Sbm_File)));
                    RcvDtaQ( ServerQ :ServerLib :MsgSizRtn :IntJobID
                             :60 :'EQ' :%size(DQKey) :DQKEY :0 :QRCQSI
                             :'*YES' :%size(IntJobID) :QUSEC);
```

Figure 15.36: The routing server (part 2 of 4).

```
                    if MsgSizRtn = 0;
                        dsply 'File server time > 60 seconds' ' ' Wait;
                        CloseSocket( sdTarget);
                        leave;
                    endif;
                endif;
                if GiveDesc( sdTarget :IntJobID) = -1;
                    ErrnoPtr = Errno;
                    dsply ('GiveDesc failed with ' + %char(ErrorNbr))
                            ' ' Wait;
                    CloseSocket( sdTarget);
                    leave;
                endif;

        when Function = ApplServer;
                DQKey.Key = ApplServer;
                RcvDtaQ( ServerQ :ServerLib :MsgSizRtn :IntJobID
                        :0 :'EQ' :%size(DQKey) :DQKEY :0 :QRCQSI
                        :'*YES' :%size(IntJobID) :QUSEC);
                if MsgSizRtn = 0;
                    // submit a server job
                    CmdExc(Cmd_Sbm_Appl :%len(%trimr(Cmd_Sbm_Appl)));
                    RcvDtaQ( ServerQ :ServerLib :MsgSizRtn :IntJobID
                            :60 :'EQ' :%size(DQKey) :DQKEY :0 :QRCQSI
                            :'*YES' :%size(IntJobID) :QUSEC);
                    if MsgSizRtn = 0;
                        dsply 'Appl server time > 60 seconds' ' ' Wait;
                        CloseSocket( sdTarget);
                        leave;
                    endif;
                endif;
                if GiveDesc( sdTarget :IntJobID) = -1;
                    ErrnoPtr = Errno;
                    dsply ('GiveDesc failed with ' + %char(ErrorNbr))
                            ' ' Wait;
                    CloseSocket( sdTarget);
                    leave;
                endif;

        when Function = EOJ;
                CloseSocket(sdTarget);
                // run end of job logic
                leave;
        other;
                dsply ('Unknown request ' + %char(Function) +
                        ' received.') ' ' Wait;
    endsl;
```

Figure 15.36: The routing server (part 3 of 4).

```
    else;
        dsply 'Unable to read Function.' ' ' Wait;
        CloseSocket(sdTarget);
        CloseSocket(sd);
        *inlr = *on;
        return;
    endif;

// Close the connection
if CloseSocket(sdTarget) < 0;
    dsply 'Error on client close' ' ' Wait;
endif;

// Loop back to accept the next connection
enddo;
```

Figure 15.36: The routing server (part 4 of 4).

When the routing server receives a Function request from a client, the program tries to receive a message on the data queue SOMELIB/MY_SVR_Q. This data queue can be created with the command shown in Figure 15.37.

```
CRTDTAQ DTAQ(SOMELIB/MY_SVR_Q) MAXLEN(16) SEQ(*KEYED) KEYLEN(4)
```

Figure 15.37: Creating the SOMELIB/MY_SVR_Q data queue.

The data queue is created with a record length of 16 bytes, the size of an internal job ID. It is keyed with a key length of four bytes, the size of the Function variable.

Figure 15.38 shows the changes made to the file-transfer server.

If the client is asking for a file transfer (Function value 1), the routing server, FIG15_34, attempts to retrieve a message from MY_SVR_Q with a key value of the Function value. When calling the Receive Data Queue API, the WaitTime parameter is set to zero so that the program will not wait for a message if none are currently available. If a message is not received, no file-transfer servers are currently available, and we use the Execute Command API to submit a file-transfer server. The program then attempts to again read a message from the MY_SVR_Q data queue. This time, the WaitTime parameter is set to 60 seconds. If no message has been received by the submitted job within 60 seconds, we assume something is terribly wrong and DSPLY an appropriate error message. If a data queue message is received, either on the initial call to the Receive Data Queue API or

on the call following a server job submission, the program gives the sdTarget socket
descriptor to the file-transfer server job using the internal job ID read from the data
queue message, closes the sdTarget socket descriptor in the routing server, and loops
back to accept another connection.

The same logic is applied to library information requests. The only difference is in the
key value used when receiving data queue messages.

```
h dftactgrp(*no) bnddir('QC2LE')

DName+++++++++++ETDsFrom+++To/L+++IDc.Keywords+++++++++++++++++++++++++++
d/copy qsysinc/qrpglesrc,qusrjobi
d/copy qsysinc/qrpglesrc,qusec

dTakeDesc         pr             10i 0 extproc('takedescriptor')
d SourceJob                         *  value

dSndDtaQ          pr                    extpgm('QSNDDTAQ')
d DtaQName                        10    const
d DtaQLib                         10    const
d DataLen                          5  0 const
d Data                         65535    const options(*varsize)
d KeyLen                           3  0 const options(*nopass)
d KeyValue                       10i  0 const options(*nopass)
d Asynch                          10    const options(*nopass)
d JrnEntry                        10    const options(*nopass)

dRtvJobI          pr                    extpgm('QUSRJOBI')
d RcvVar                           1    options(*varsize)
d LenRcvVar                      10i  0 const
d RcvVarFmt                        8    const
d JobName                         26    const
d IntJobID                        16    const
d QUSEC                                 likeds(QUSEC) options(*nopass)
d Reset                            1    const options(*nopass)

dDQKey            ds                    qualified
d Key                            10i  0 inz(FileServer)

dsdTarget         s              10i  0

dServerQ          c                     'MY_SVR_Q'
dServerLib        c                     'SOMELIB'
dFileServer       c                     1
dApplServer       c                     2
```

Figure 15.38: The modified file-transfer server (part 1 of 2).

```
CLON01Factor1+++++++Opcode&ExtFactor2+++++++Result++++++++Len++D+HiLoEq

     // Let the main server know we're available by sending our
     // internal job ID and our server type as the key
     RtvJobI( QUSI010000 :%size(QUSI010000) :'JOBI0100' :'*' :' '
             :QUSEC);
     SndDtaQ( ServerQ :ServerLib :%size(QUSIJID) :QUSIJID
             :%size(DQKey) :DQKey.Key);

     // Get a descriptor for our client
     sdTarget = TakeDesc(*NULL);

     dow sdTarget <> -1;

         // Read the filename to be processed and send it

         // When done:

         CloseSocket(sdTarget);

         // Let the main server know we're available by resending our
         // internal job ID with our server type as the key
         SndDtaQ( ServerQ :ServerLib :%size(QUSIJID) :QUSIJID
                 :%size(DQKey) :DQKey.Key);

         // Get a descriptor for our next client
         sdTarget = TakeDesc(*NULL);
     enddo;
```

Figure 15.38: The modified file-transfer server (part 2 of 2).

In the file-transfer server, the program immediately calls the Retrieve Job Information API to determine the internal job ID of the job. This internal job ID is then sent to the MY_SVR_Q data queue with a message key Function of FileServer. The program then calls the TAKEDESCRIPTOR API. The TAKEDESCRIPTOR API will not return until a descriptor has been given to the file-transfer server job.

When the socket descriptor is received, the server program receives the file name and transfers the file. The socket descriptor is ready to be used as soon as the server receives it. When the file has been sent (not shown, as there's nothing new here), the file-transfer server closes sdTarget, sends another message to the MY_SVR_Q data queue to let the routing server know that this job is available for more file-transfer requests, and calls the TAKEDESCRIPTOR API to wait for more work to be routed to it.

We now have a server environment that can handle any number of concurrent client requests by simply submitting additional file-transfer and library-information servers as they become needed. But we're still not quite done yet!

Using the SETSOCKOPT API

We still have the situation where we cannot restart our routing server within a few minutes of our last use of the server. The Set Socket Options API, SETSOCKOPT, can address this.

The parameter descriptions for SETSOCKOPT are shown in Figure 15.39. The SETSOCKOPT API takes five parameters. The first one, Socket_descriptor, is the socket descriptor you want to modify.

```
int setsockopt (int socket_descriptor, int level, int option_name,
                char *option_value, int option_length)
```

Figure 15.39: The SETSOCKOPT API.

The second parameter, Level, specifies whether you want to modify the socket itself or the underlying protocol of the socket. Enabling the reuse of a socket port is done via an attribute of the socket. We will use the value -1 to specify that we are changing the socket characteristics. (You can work with several other layers, as well. These are described in the API documentation.)

The third parameter, Option_name, specifies the name of the option to be set. Although this parameter is called a "name," you actually pass an integer value representing the name. To enable the reuse of a socket port, we use the value 55. (You can set many other "names," described in the API documentation.)

The fourth parameter, Option_value, is a pointer to the value to assign to the selected Option_name. For the reuse of port addresses, the value is represented as a 4-byte integer. A value of zero turns reuse off, and a nonzero value turns reuse on. The fifth parameter, Option_length, is the length of the value passed in the Option_value fourth parameter.

The API also returns an integer. If the return value is -1, an error was found on the API call, and errno is updated with additional information. If the return value is zero, the API call completed successfully. Figure 15.40 shows how the API is used.

```
h dftactgrp(*no) bnddir('QC2LE')

DName++++++++++ETDsFrom+++To/L+++IDc.Keywords+++++++++++++++++++++++++++++
dSockOpt            pr              10i 0 extproc('setsockopt')
d sd                               10i 0 value
d Level                            10i 0 value
d OptionName                       10i 0 value
d OptionValue                        * value
d OptionLength                     10i 0 value

dReUseYes           s              10i 0 inz(1)

dSOL_SOCKET         c                     -1
dSO_REUSEADDR       c                     55


CLON01Factor1+++++++Opcode&ExtFactor2+++++++Result++++++++Len++D+HiLoEq

    if SockOpt( sd :SOL_SOCKET :SO_REUSEADDR :%addr(ReUseYes)
               :%size(ReUseYes)) = -1;
               ErrnoPtr = Errno;
               dsply ('Failure ' + %char(ErrorNbr) + ' on setsockopt.')
                     ' ' Wait;
               *inlr = *on;
               return;
    endif;
```

Figure 15.40: Using the SETSOCKOPT API.

With this last enhancement to our server, let's now look at the complete programs. Figure 15.41 shows the routing server. Note that this routing server is not complete in and of itself. One important piece is missing: cleaning up the data queue and ending the other server jobs when this routing server ends. We'll be looking at this aspect of our server shortly.

```
h dftactgrp(*no) bnddir('QC2LE')

DName++++++++++ETDsFrom+++To/L+++IDc.Keywords+++++++++++++++++++++++++++++
d/copy qsysinc/qrpglesrc,qrcvdtaq
d/copy qsysinc/qrpglesrc,qusec

dSocket             pr              10i 0 extproc('socket')
d AddrFamily                       10i 0 value
d Type                             10i 0 value
d Protocol                         10i 0 value
```

Figure 15.41: The routing server (part 1 of 7).

```
dGetPort          pr              *   extproc('getservbyname')
d ServName                        *   value options(*string)
d ProtName                        *   value options(*string)

dSockOpt          pr            10i 0 extproc('setsockopt')
d sd                            10i 0 value
d Level                         10i 0 value
d OptionName                    10i 0 value
d OptionValue                     *   value
d OptionLength                  10i 0 value

dBind             pr            10i 0 extproc('bind')
d sd                            10i 0 value
d LclAddrPtr                      *   value
d LenAddr                       10i 0 value

dListen           pr            10i 0 extproc('listen')
d sd                            10i 0 value
d BackLog                       10i 0 value

dAccept           pr            10i 0 extproc('accept')
d sd                            10i 0 value
d RmtAddrPtr                      *   value
d LenAddr                       10i 0

dRecv             pr            10i 0 extproc('recv')
d fd                            10i 0 value
d buf                             *   value
d lenbuf                        10i 0 value
d flags                         10i 0 value

dSend             pr            10i 0 extproc('send')
d fd                            10i 0 value
d buf                             *   value
d lenbuf                        10i 0 value
d flags                         10i 0 value

dGiveDesc         pr            10i 0 extproc('givedescriptor')
d sd                            10i 0 value
d IntJobID                      16    const

dCloseSocket      pr            10i 0 extproc('close')
d fd                            10i 0 value

dRcvDtaQ          pr                  extpgm('QRCVDTAQ')
d DtaQName                      10    const
```

Figure 15.41:The routing server (part 2 of 7).

```
d DtaQLib                       10        const
d ReceiverLenRtn                 5   0
d Receiver                       1        options(*varsize)
d WaitTime                       5   0 const
d KeyOrder                       2        const options(*nopass)
d KeyLen                         3   0 const options(*nopass)
d KeyValue                       1        options(*varsize :*nopass)
d SndrInfoLen                    3   0 const options(*nopass)
d SndrInfo                       1        options(*varsize :*nopass)
d RmvMsg                        10        const options(*nopass)
d ReceiverLen                    5   0 const options(*nopass)
d QUSEC                                   likeds(QUSEC) options(*nopass)

dCmdExc          pr                       extpgm('QCMDEXC')
d Command                    65535        const options(*varsize)
d CmdLength                     15   5 const
d IGC                           3         const options(*nopass)

dErrno           pr              *        extproc('__errno')

dLclAddr         ds
d SinFamily                    5i   0
d SinPort                      5u   0
d SinAddr                     10u   0
d SinZero                       8

dDestAddr        ds                       likeds(LclAddr)

dServiceEntry    ds                       based(ServiceEntryPtr)
d ServName                      *
d ServAlias                     *
d ServPort                    10i   0
d ServProtocol                  *

dDQKey           ds                       qualified
d Key                         10i   0

dErrorNbr        s            10i   0 based(ErrnoPtr)
dsd              s            10i   0
dSocket          pr           10i   0 extproc('socket')
dsdTarget        s            10i   0
dAddrLen         s            10i   0
drecvRC          s            10i   0
dFunction        s            10i   0
dMsgSizRtn       s             5    0
dIntJobID        s            16
```

Figure 15.41:The routing server (part 3 of 7).

```
dSndrInfo          s            1
dCmd_Sbm_File      s          100      inz('SBMJOB -
d                                      CMD(CALL PGM(SOMELIB/FIG15_42)) -
d                                      JOBQ(QSYS/QUSRNOMAX) -
d                                      CURLIB(SOMELIB)')
dCmd_Sbm_Appl      s          100      inz('SBMJOB -
d                                      CMD(CALL PGM(SOMELIB/FIG15_43)) -
d                                      JOBQ(QSYS/QUSRNOMAX) -
d                                      CURLIB(SOMELIB)')
dReUseYes          s           10i 0 inz(1)
dWait              s            1

dEOJ               c                   -1
dFileServer        c                   1
dApplServer        c                   2
dServerQ           c                   'MY_SVR_Q'
dServerLib         c                   'SOMELIB'
dService           c                   'My_Somelib_Server'
dProtocol          c                   'tcp'

dMSG_WAITALL       c                   64

dINADDR_ANY        c                   0
dINADDR_LOOPBACK   c                   2130706433

dAF_INET           c                   2
dAF_INET6          c                   24

dSOCK_STREAM       c                   1

dIPPROTO_IP        c                   0

dSOL_SOCKET        c                   -1
dSO_REUSEADDR      c                   55

CL0N01Factor1++++++++Opcode&ExtFactor2+++++++Result++++++++Len++D+HiLoEq
/free

  QUSBPRV = 0;

  // Create a socket
  sd = socket( AF_INET :SOCK_STREAM :IPPROTO_IP);
  if (sd = -1);
     ErrnoPtr = Errno;
     dsply ('Failure ' + %char(ErrorNbr) + ' on socket') ' ' Wait;
     *inlr = *on;
     return;
  endif;
```

Figure 15.41: The routing server (part 4 of 7).

```
// Allow the reuse of our port
if SockOpt( sd :SOL_SOCKET :SO_REUSEADDR :%addr(ReUseYes)
           :%size(ReUseYes)) = -1;
           ErrnoPtr = Errno;
           dsply ('Failure ' + %char(ErrorNbr) + ' on setsockopt.')
                ' ' Wait;
           *inlr = *on;
           return;
endif;

// Bind our local address to a socket
LclAddr = *loval;
SinFamily = AF_INET;
ServiceEntryPtr = GetPort(%trimr(Service) :%trimr(Protocol));
if ServiceEntryPtr = *NULL;
    dsply ('Service ' + Service + ' for ' + Protocol + 'not found.')
         ' ' Wait;
    *inlr = *on;
    return;
endif;

SinPort = ServPort;
SinAddr = INADDR_ANY;
if Bind( sd :%addr(LclAddr) :%size(LclAddr)) < 0;
    ErrnoPtr = Errno;
    dsply ('Failure ' + %char(ErrorNbr) + ' on bind') ' ' Wait;
    *inlr = *on;
    return;
endif;

// Listen for incoming data
if Listen( sd :3) < 0;
    ErrnoPtr = Errno;
    dsply ('Failure ' + %char(ErrorNbr) + ' on listen') ' ' Wait;
    *inlr = *on;
    return;
endif;

// Accept incoming data
dow Function <> EOJ;
    AddrLen = %size(DestAddr);
    sdTarget = Accept( sd :%addr(DestAddr) :AddrLen);
    if sdTarget < 0;
        ErrnoPtr = Errno;
        dsply ('Failure ' + %char(ErrorNbr) + ' on accept') ' ' Wait;
        leave;
    endif;
```

Figure 15.41:The routing server (part 5 of 7).

```
// Get Function to perform
recvRC = recv( sdTarget :%addr(Function) :%size(Function)
               :MSG_WAITALL);

if recvRC <> -1;

    // Determine type of request and see if any jobs are available
    select;
        when Function = FileServer;
            DQKey.Key = FileServer;
            RcvDtaQ( ServerQ :ServerLib :MsgSizRtn :IntJobID
                     :0 :'EQ' :%size(DQKey) :DQKEY :0 :QRCQSI
                     :'*YES' :%size(IntJobID) :QUSEC);
            if MsgSizRtn = 0;
                // submit a server job
                CmdExc(Cmd_Sbm_File :%len(%trimr(Cmd_Sbm_File)));
                RcvDtaQ( ServerQ :ServerLib :MsgSizRtn :IntJobID
                         :60 :'EQ' :%size(DQKey) :DQKEY :0 :QRCQSI
                         :'*YES' :%size(IntJobID) :QUSEC);
                if MsgSizRtn = 0;
                    dsply 'File server time > 60 seconds' ' ' Wait;
                    CloseSocket( sdTarget);
                    leave;
                endif;
            endif;
            if GiveDesc( sdTarget :IntJobID) = -1;
                ErrnoPtr = Errno;
                dsply ('GiveDesc failed with ' + %char(ErrorNbr))
                      ' ' Wait;
                CloseSocket( sdTarget);
                leave;
            endif;

        when Function = ApplServer;
            DQKey.Key = ApplServer;
            RcvDtaQ( ServerQ :ServerLib :MsgSizRtn :IntJobID
                     :0 :'EQ' :%size(DQKey) :DQKEY :0 :QRCQSI
                     :'*YES' :%size(IntJobID) :QUSEC);
            if MsgSizRtn = 0;
                // submit a server job
                CmdExc(Cmd_Sbm_Appl :%len(%trimr(Cmd_Sbm_Appl)));
                RcvDtaQ( ServerQ :ServerLib :MsgSizRtn :IntJobID
                         :60 :'EQ' :%size(DQKey) :DQKEY :0 :QRCQSI
                         :'*YES' :%size(IntJobID) :QUSEC);
```

Figure 15.41:The routing server (part 6 of 7).

567

```
                if MsgSizRtn = 0;
                    dsply 'Appl server time > 60 seconds' ' ' Wait;
                    CloseSocket( sdTarget);
                    leave;
                endif;
            endif;
            if GiveDesc( sdTarget :IntJobID) = -1;
                ErrnoPtr = Errno;
                dsply ('GiveDesc failed with ' + %char(ErrorNbr))
                        ' ' Wait;
                CloseSocket( sdTarget);
                leave;
            endif;

        when Function = EOJ;
            CloseSocket(sdTarget);
            // run end of job logic
            leave;
        other;
            dsply ('Unknown request ' + %char(Function) +
                    ' received.') ' ' Wait;
    endsl;
    else;
        dsply 'Unable to read Function.' ' ' Wait;
        CloseSocket(sdTarget);
        CloseSocket(sd);
        *inlr = *on;
        return;
    endif;

    // Close the connection
    if CloseSocket(sdTarget) < 0;
        dsply 'Error on client close' ' ' Wait;
    endif;

// Loop back to accept the next connection
enddo;


if CloseSocket(sd) < 0;
    dsply 'Error on close' ' ' Wait;
endif;
*inlr = *on;
return;

/end-free
```

Figure 15.41:The routing server (part 7 of 7).

Figure 15.42 shows the file-transfer server, Figure 15.43 shows the library-information server, Figure 15.44 shows the file-transfer client, and Figure 15.45 shows the library-information client.

```
h dftactgrp(*no) bnddir('QC2LE')

FFilename++IPEASF.....L.....A.Device+.Keywords+++++++++++++++++++++++++++
fAnyFile   if   f32766       disk   usropn infds(OpenFeedback)

DName+++++++++++ETDsFrom+++To/L+++IDc.Keywords+++++++++++++++++++++++++++
d/copy qsysinc/qrpglesrc,qusrjobi
d/copy qsysinc/qrpglesrc,qusec

dCmdExc            pr                      extpgm('QCMDEXC')
d Command                     65535        const options(*varsize)
d CmdLength                   15   5 const
d IGC                          3     const options(*nopass)

dRecv              pr               10i 0 extproc('recv')
d fd                            10i 0 value
d buf                           *     value
d lenbuf                        10i 0 value
d flags                         10i 0 value

dSend              pr               10i 0 extproc('send')
d fd                            10i 0 value
d buf                           *     value
d lenbuf                        10i 0 value
d flags                         10i 0 value
d flags                         10i 0 value

dTakeDesc          pr               10i 0 extproc('takedescriptor')
d SourceJob                     *     value

dCloseSocket       pr               10i 0 extproc('close')
d fd                            10i 0 value

dErrno             pr               *     extproc('__errno')

dSndDtaQ           pr                      extpgm('QSNDDTAQ')
d DtaQName                      10    const
d DtaQLib                       10    const
d DataLen                        5  0 const
```

Figure 15.42: The server program to send all records in a file (part 1 of 4).

```
d Data                         65535     const options(*varsize)
d KeyLen                           3   0 const options(*nopass)
d KeyValue                       10i   0 const options(*nopass)
d Asynch                          10     const options(*nopass)
d JrnEntry                        10     const options(*nopass)

dRtvJobI          pr                     extpgm('QUSRJOBI')
d RcvVar                           1     options(*varsize)
d LenRcvVar                      10i   0 const
d RcvVarFmt                        8     const
d JobName                         26     const
d IntJobID                        16     const
d QUSEC                                  likeds(QUSEC) options(*nopass)
d Reset                            1     const options(*nopass)

dOpenFeedback     ds
d FBRcdLen                 125   126i  0

dDQKey            ds                     qualified
d Key                            10i   0 inz(FileServer)

dErrorNbr         s              10i   0 based(ErrnoPtr)
dsdTarget         s              10i   0
dFileName         s              10
dRcdLen           s              10i   0
dCommand          s             100
dEOF              s              10i   0 inz(-1)
dWait             s               1

dEOF              s              10i   0 inz(-1)

dServerQ          c                       'MY_SVR_Q'
dServerLib        c                       'SOMELIB'
dFileServer       c                       1
dApplServer       c                       2

dMSG_WAITALL      c                      64

IAnyFile    ns
I                                132766    AnyRecord

CLON01Factor1+++++++Opcode&ExtFactor2+++++++Result++++++++Len++D+HiLoEq
 /free

   QUSBPRV = %size(QUSEC);
```

Figure 15.42: The server program to send all records in a file (part 2 of 4).

```
// Let the main server know we're available by sending our
// internal job ID and our server type as the key
RtvJobI( QUSI010000 :%size(QUSI010000) :'JOBI0100' :'*' :' ' :QUSEC);
SndDtaQ( ServerQ :ServerLib :%size(QUSIJID) :QUSIJID
        :%size(DQKey) :DQKey.Key);

// Get a descriptor for our client
sdTarget = TakeDesc(*NULL);

dow sdTarget <> -1;

    // Read the filename to be processed
    if (recv( sdTarget :%addr(FileName) :%size(FileName) :MSG_WAITALL)
        <> -1);

        Command = 'OVRDBF ANYFILE TOFILE(SOMELIB/' + FileName + ')';
        CmdExc( Command :%len(%trimr(Command)));

        Open(e) AnyFile;
        RcdLen = FBRcdLen;
        if not %error;
            Read AnyFile;
            dou %eof(AnyFile);
                if Send( sdTarget :%addr(RcdLen) :%size(RcdLen) :0)
                    < %size(RcdLen);
                    dsply 'Not all data written' ' ' Wait;
                    leave;
                endif;
                if Send(sdTarget :%addr(AnyRecord) :RcdLen :0)
                        < RcdLen;
                    dsply 'Not all data written' ' ' Wait;
                    leave;
                endif;
                Read Anyfile;
            enddo;

            // Send end of file
            if Send( sdTarget :%addr(EOF) :%size(EOF) :0) < %size(EOF);
                dsply 'Not all data written at End of File' ' ' Wait;
            endif;

        else;
            dsply 'Incorrect file specified' ' ' Wait;
        endif;

    else;
        dsply 'Not all data read' ' ' Wait;
    endif;
```

Figure 15.42: The server program to send all records in a file (part 3 of 4).

```
      CloseSocket(sdTarget);
      Close Anyfile;
      Command = 'DLTOVR ANYFILE';
      CmdExc( Command :%len(%trimr(Command)));


      // Let the main server know we're available by sending our
      // internal job ID and our server type as the key
      SndDtaQ( ServerQ :ServerLib :%size(QUSIJID) :QUSIJID
              :%size(DQKey) :DQKey.Key);

      // Get a descriptor for our client
      sdTarget = TakeDesc(*NULL);
  enddo;

  *inlr = *on;
  return;

 /end-free
```

Figure 15.42: The server program to send all records in a file (part 4 of 4).

```
h dftactgrp(*no) bnddir('QC2LE')

DName+++++++++++ETDsFrom+++To/L+++IDc.Keywords+++++++++++++++++++++++++
d/copy qsysinc/qrpglesrc,qusrobjd
d/copy qsysinc/qrpglesrc,qlirlibd
d/copy qsysinc/qrpglesrc,qusrjobi
d/copy qsysinc/qrpglesrc,qus
d/copy qsysinc/qrpglesrc,qusec

dSend            pr            10i 0 extproc('send')
d fd                           10i 0 value
d buf                           *   value
d lenbuf                       10i 0 value
d flags                        10i 0 value

dRecv            pr            10i 0 extproc('recv')
d fd                           10i 0 value
d buf                           *   value
d lenbuf                       10i 0 value
d flags                        10i 0 value

dTakeDesc        pr            10i 0 extproc('takedescriptor')
d SourceJob                     *   value
```

Figure 15.43: The server program for library information (part 1 of 5).

```
dCloseSocket      pr            10i 0 extproc('close')
d fd                            10i 0 value

dErrno            pr              *   extproc('__errno')

dRObjD            pr                  extpgm('QUSROBJD')
d Receiver                       1    options(*varsize)
d ReceiverLen                   10i 0 const
d Format                         8    const
d ObjLibName                     20   const
d ObjectType                     10   const
d ErrCde                              likeds(ErrCde) options(*nopass)
d ASPControl                     65535 const options(*varsize :*nopass)

dRLibD            pr                  extpgm('QLIRLIBD')
d Receiver                       1    options(*varsize)
d RecieverLen                    10i 0 const
d Library                        10   const
d Attributes                     65535 const options(*varsize)
d ErrCde                              likeds(ErrCde) options(*nopass)

dSndDtaQ          pr                  extpgm('QSNDDTAQ')
d DtaQName                        10   const
d DtaQLib                         10   const
d DataLen                         5  0 const
d Data                           65535 const options(*varsize)
d KeyLen                          3  0 const options(*nopass)
d KeyValue                       10i 0 const options(*nopass)
d Asynch                          10   const options(*nopass)
d JrnEntry                        10   const options(*nopass)

dRtvJobI          pr                  extpgm('QUSRJOBI')
d RcvVar                          1    options(*varsize)
d LenRcvVar                      10i 0 const
d RcvVarFmt                       8    const
d JobName                         26   const
d IntJobID                        16   const
d QUSEC                                likeds(QUSEC) options(*nopass)
d Reset                           1    const options(*nopass)

dObjLibName       ds
d LibName                         10
d ObjLib                          10      inz('QSYS')

dAttributes       ds
d NbrAttributes                  10i 0
d Key                            10i 0 dim(10)
```

Figure 15.43: The server program for library information (part 2 of 5).

```
dReceiver        ds          256     qualified
d Hdr                                likeds(QLIRR)

dDQKey           ds                  qualified
d Key                        10i 0 inz(ApplServer)

dErrCde          ds                  qualified
d EC                                 likeds(QUSEC)
dSend            pr          10i 0 extproc('send')
d ReceiverLen                10i 0 const

d ErrDta                     512

dErrorNbr        s           10i 0 based(ErrnoPtr)
dsdTarget        s           10i 0
drecvRC          s           10i 0
dAPI_Error       s           10i 0 inz(-2)
dWait            s           1

dServerQ         c                   'MY_SVR_Q'
dServerLib       c                   'SOMELIB'
dFileServer      c                   1
dApplServer      c                   2

dMSG_WAITALL     c                   64
CL0N01Factor1+++++++Opcode&ExtFactor2+++++++Result++++++++Len++D+HiLoEq
 /free

   ErrCde.EC.QUSBPRV = %size(ErrCde);
   QUSBPRV = 0;

   // Let the main server know we're available by sending our
   // internal job ID and our server type as the key
   RtvJobI( QUSI010000 :%size(QUSI010000) :'JOBI0100' :'*' :' ' :QUSEC);
   SndDtaQ( ServerQ :ServerLib :%size(QUSIJID) :QUSIJID
            :%size(DQKey) :DQKey.Key);

   // Get a descriptor for our client
   sdTarget = TakeDesc(*NULL);

   dow sdTarget <> -1;

      // Get library name
      recvRC = Recv( sdTarget :%addr(LibName) :%size(LibName)
                     :MSG_WAITALL);
```

Figure 15.43: The server program for library information (part 3 of 5).

```
if recvRC <> -1;
   // Get object related data
   RObjD( QUSD0400 :%size(QUSD0400) :'OBJD0400' :ObjLibName
          :'*LIB'    :ErrCde);
   if (ErrCde.EC.QUSBAVL <> 0);
      Send( sdTarget :%addr(API_Error) :%size(API_Error) :0);
      Send( sdTarget :%addr(ErrCde) :%size(ErrCde) :0);
      dsply ('Error ' + QUSEI + ' retrieving library object');
      CloseSocket(sdTarget);
      *inlr = *on;
      return;
   else;
      if Send( sdTarget :%addr(QUSD0400) :QUSBRTN09 :0)
         < QUSBRTN09;
         dsply 'Not all data written' ' ' Wait;
         CloseSocket(sdTarget);
         *inlr = *on;
         return;
      endif;
   endif;

   // Get library size and number of objects
   NbrAttributes = 2;
   Key(1) = 6;                       // library size
   Key(2) = 7;                       // number of objects in library

   RLibD( Receiver :%size(Receiver) :LibName :Attributes :ErrCde);

   if (ErrCde.EC.QUSBAVL <> 0);
      Send( sdTarget :%addr(API_Error) :%size(API_Error) :0);
      Send( sdTarget :%addr(ErrCde) :%size(ErrCde) :0);
      dsply ('Error ' + QUSEI + ' while retrieving library desc');
      CloseSocket(sdTarget);
      *inlr = *on;
      return;
   else;
      if Send( sdTarget :%addr(Receiver) :Receiver.Hdr.QLIBRTN :0)
         < Receiver.Hdr.QLIBRTN;
         dsply 'Not all data written' ' ' Wait;
         CloseSocket(sdTarget);
         *inlr = *on;
         return;
      endif;
   endif;

else;
   ErrnoPtr = Errno;
   dsply ('Could not receive library name -  ' + %char(ErrorNbr))
```

Figure 15.43: The server program for library information (part 4 of 5).

```
                ' ' Wait;
                CloseSocket(sdTarget);
                *inlr = *on;
                return;
       endif;


       CloseSocket(sdTarget);

       // Let the main server know we're available by sending our
       // internal job ID and our server type as the key
       SndDtaQ( ServerQ :ServerLib :%size(QUSIJID) :QUSIJID
                :4 :ApplServer);

       // Get a descriptor for our client
       sdTarget = TakeDesc(*NULL);
     enddo;

     *inlr = *on;
     return;

    /end-free
```

Figure 15.43: The server program for library information (part 5 of 5).


```
h dftactgrp(*no) bnddir('QC2LE')

FFilename++IPEASF.....L.....A.Device+.Keywords+++++++++++++++++++++++++++++
fCustomer  o    e              disk     infds(OpenFeedback)


DName+++++++++++ETDsFrom+++To/L+++IDc.Keywords++++++++++++++++++++++++++++++
dFig15_44          pr                  extpgm('FIG15_44')
d SystemParm                    30     const

dFig15_44          pi
d SystemParm                    30     const

dGetHostByName     pr            *     extproc('gethostbyname')
d HostName                       *     value options(*string)

dSocket            pr           10i 0 extproc('socket')
d AddrFamily                    10i 0 value
d Type                          10i 0 value
d Protocol                      10i 0 value
```

Figure 15.44: The client program to receive all records in a file (part 1 of 5).

576

```
dGetPort          pr              *   extproc('getservbyname')
d ServName                        *   value options(*string)
d ProtName                        *   value options(*string)

dConnect          pr            10i 0 extproc('connect')
d sd                            10i 0 value
d DestAddrPtr                     *   value
d LenAddr                       10i 0 value

dSend             pr            10i 0 extproc('send')
d fd                            10i 0 value
d buf                             *   value
d lenbuf                        10i 0 value
d flags                         10i 0 value

dRecv             pr            10i 0 extproc('recv')
d fd                            10i 0 value
d buf                             *   value
d lenbuf                        10u 0 value
d flags                         10i 0 value

dCloseSocket      pr            10i 0 extproc('close')
d fd                            10i 0 value

dErrno            pr              *   extproc('__errno')

dHostEnt          ds                  based(HostEntPtr)
d HNamePtr                        *
d HAliasesPtr                     *
d HAddrType                     10i 0
d HLength                       10i 0
d HAddrListPtr                    *

dDestAddr         ds
d SinFamily                      5i 0
d SinPort                        5u 0
d SinAddr                       10u 0
d SinZero                        8

dServiceEntry     ds                  based(ServiceEntryPtr)
d ServName                        *
d ServAlias                       *
d ServPort                      10i 0
d ServProtocol                    *

dSizCusRecDS      ds
dSizCusRec                      10i 0
```

Figure 15.44: The client program to receive all records in a file (part 2 of 5).

577

```
dCusRecDS         e ds                    extname(Customer :*OUTPUT)

dOpenFeedback     ds
d FBRcdLen                 125    126i 0

dSystem           s             30     inz('LOCALHOST')
dFilename         s             10     inz('CUSTOMER')
drecvRC           s             10i 0
dHAddrEntPtr      s              *     based(HAddrListPtr)
dhAddr            s             10u 0 based(HAddrEntPtr)
dErrorNbr         s             10i 0 based(ErrnoPtr)
dsd               s             10i 0
dFileServer       s             10i 0 inz(1)
dWait             s              1

dEOF              c                    -1

dMSG_WAITALL      c                    64

dService          c                    'My_Somelib_Server'
dProtocol         c                    'tcp'

dAF_INET          c                    2
dAF_INET6         c                    24

dSOCK_STREAM      c                    1

dIPPROTO_IP       c                    0

CLON01Factor1+++++++Opcode&ExtFactor2+++++++Result+++++++++Len++D+HiLoEq
 /free

   if %parms > 0;
      System = SystemParm;
   endif;

   // Get the IP address of the system we will talk with
   HostEntPtr = GetHostByName( %trimr(System));
   if HostEntPtr = *NULL;
      dsply (%trimr(System) + ' not available') ' ' Wait;
      *inlr = *on;
      return;
   endif;
   if HAddrType <> AF_INET;
      dsply 'Host address is not IPv4' ' ' Wait;
      *inlr = *on;
      return;
   endif;
```

Figure 15.44: The client program to receive all records in a file (part 3 of 5).

```
// Create a socket
sd = socket( AF_INET :SOCK_STREAM :IPPROTO_IP);
if (sd = -1);
   ErrnoPtr = Errno;
   dsply ('Failure ' + %char(ErrorNbr) + ' on socket') ' ' Wait;
   *inlr = *on;
   return;
endif;

// Establish a connection for the socket
DestAddr = *loval;
SinFamily = AF_INET;
ServiceEntryPtr = GetPort(%trimr(Service) :%trimr(Protocol));
if ServiceEntryPtr = *NULL;
   dsply ('Service ' + Service + ' for ' + Protocol + 'not found.')
           ' ' Wait;
   *inlr = *on;
   return;
endif;

SinPort = ServPort;
SinAddr = hAddr;
if Connect( sd :%addr(DestAddr) :%size(DestAddr)) < 0;
   ErrnoPtr = Errno;
   dsply ('Failure ' + %char(ErrorNbr) + ' on connect') ' ' Wait;
   *inlr = *on;
   return;
endif;

// Send request for file server and then file name
if Send( sd :%addr(FileServer) :%size(FileServer) :0)
        < %size(FileServer);
   dsply 'Function not sent' ' ' Wait;
   CloseSocket(sd);
   *inlr = *on;
   return;
endif;

// Send request for Customer file

if Send( sd :%addr(FileName) :%size(FileName) :0) = %size(FileName);

   recvRC = Recv( sd :%addr(SizCusRecDS) :%size(SizCusRec)
                  :MSG_WAITALL);
   if ((SizCusRec <> FBRcdLen) and (recvRC <> -1));
      dsply 'Record lengths are different' ' ' Wait;
```

Figure 15.44: The client program to receive all records in a file (part 4 of 5).

```
        CloseSocket(sd);
        *inlr = *on;
        return;
    endif;
    dow (SizCusRec <> EOF) and (recvRC <> -1);
        recvRC = Recv( sd :%addr(CusRecDS) :%size(CusRecDS)
                       :MSG_WAITALL);
        if recvRC <> -1;
            Write CusRec CusRecDS;
        endif;
        recvRC = Recv( sd :%addr(SizCusRecDS) :%size(SizCusRec)
                       :MSG_WAITALL);
    enddo;

    if recvRC = -1;
        ErrnoPtr = Errno;
        dsply ('Failure ' + %char(ErrorNbr) + ' on recv') ' ' Wait;
    endif;

  else;
    dsply 'Did not send all data' ' ' Wait;
  endif;

  // close the socket
  if CloseSocket(sd) < 0;
    dsply 'Failure on close' ' ' Wait;
  endif;
  *inlr = *on;
  return;

/end-free
```

Figure 15.44: The client program to receive all records in a file (part 5 of 5).

```
h dftactgrp(*no) bnddir('APILIB' :'QC2LE')

FFilename++IPEASF.....L.....A.Device+.Keywords+++++++++++++++++++++++++
fFIG5_4    cf   e                workstn

DName+++++++++++ETDsFrom+++To/L+++IDc.Keywords+++++++++++++++++++++++++

dFig15_45            pr                 extpgm('FIG15_45')
d Library                     10
d SystemParm                  30
```

Figure 15.45: The client program for library information (part 1 of 9).

```
dFig15_45          pi
d Library                      10
d SystemParm                   30

d/copy qsysinc/qrpglesrc,qusrobjd
d/copy qsysinc/qrpglesrc,qlirlibd
d/copy qsysinc/qrpglesrc,qus
d/copy qsysinc/qrpglesrc,qusec

dGetHostByName     pr              *   extproc('gethostbyname')
d HostName                         *   value options(*string)

dSocket            pr            10i 0 extproc('socket')
d AddrFamily                    10i 0 value
d Type                          10i 0 value
d Protocol                      10i 0 value

dGetPort           pr              *   extproc('getservbyname')
d ServName                         *   value options(*string)
d ProtName                         *   value options(*string)

dConnect           pr            10i 0 extproc('connect')
d sd                            10i 0 value
d DestAddrPtr                      *   value
d LenAddr                       10i 0 value

dSend              pr            10i 0 extproc('send')
d fd                            10i 0 value
d buf                              *   value
d lenbuf                        10i 0 value
d flags                         10i 0 value

dRecv              pr            10i 0 extproc('recv')
d fd                            10i 0 value
d buf                              *   value
d lenbuf                        10u 0 value
d flags                         10i 0 value

dCloseSocket       pr            10i 0 extproc('close')
d fd                            10i 0 value

dErrno             pr              *   extproc('__errno')

dSndPgmMsg         pr                  extpgm('QMHSNDPM')
d MsgID                          7     const
d QualMsgF                      20     const
```

Figure 15.45: The client program for library information (part 2 of 9).

```
d MsgDta                           65535       const options(*varsize)
d LenMsgDta                        10i 0 const
d MsgType                          10          const
d CallStackEntry                   65535       const options(*varsize)
d CallStackCntr                    10i 0 const
d MsgKey                           4
d QUSEC                                        likeds(QUSEC)
d LenCSE                           10i 0 const options(*nopass)
d CSEQual                          20          const options(*nopass)
d DSPWaitTime                      10i 0 const options(*nopass)
d CSEType                          10          const options(*nopass)
d CCSID                            10i 0 const options(*nopass)

dHostEnt          ds                           based(HostEntPtr)
d HNamePtr                           *
d HAliasesPtr                        *
d HAddrType                        10i 0
d HLength                          10i 0
d HAddrListPtr                       *

dDestAddr         ds
d SinFamily                         5i 0
d SinPort                           5u 0
d SinAddr                          10u 0
d SinZero                           8

dServiceEntry     ds                           based(ServiceEntryPtr)
d ServName                           *
d ServAlias                          *
d ServPort                         10i 0
d ServProtocol                       *

dReceiver         ds               256   qualified
d Hdr                                    likeds(QLIRR)

dEntry            ds                     based(EntryPtr)
d                                        qualified
d EntryHdr                               likeds(QUSVR4)
d Key6LibSiz                        10i 0 overlay(Entry :13)
d Key6LibMult                       10i 0 overlay(Entry :*next)
d Key6LibSts                        1     overlay(Entry :*next)
d Key7NbrObjs                       10i 0 overlay(Entry :13)

dErrCde           ds                     qualified
d EC                                     likeds(QUSEC)
d ErrDta                            512
```

Figure 15.45: The client program for library information (part 3 of 9).

```
dQualMsgF         ds
d MsgF                            10    inz('QCPFMSG')
d MsgL                            10    inz('*LIBL')

dSystem           s               30    inz('LOCALHOST')
drecvRC           s               10i 0
dHAddrEntPtr      s                *     based(HAddrListPtr)
dhAddr            s               10u 0 based(HAddrEntPtr)
dErrorNbr         s               10i 0 based(ErrnoPtr)
dsd               s               10i 0
dApplServer       s               10i 0 inz(2)
dCount            s               10u 0
dTrash            s                1     based(TrashPtr)
dAPI_Error        s               10i 0 inz(-2)
dMsgKey           s                4
dWait             s                1

dMSG_WAITALL      c                      64

dService          c                      'My_Somelib_Server'
dProtocol         c                      'tcp'

dAF_INET          c                      2
dAF_INET6         c                      24

dSOCK_STREAM      c                      1

dIPPROTO_IP       c                      0

CLON01Factor1+++++++Opcode&ExtFactor2+++++++Result++++++++Len++D+HiLoEq
 /free

   if %parms = 0;
      dsply 'Library name is a required parameter' ' ' Wait;
      *inlr = *on;
      return;
   endif;

   if %parms > 1;
      System = SystemParm;
   endif;

   // Get the IP address of the system we will talk with
   HostEntPtr = GetHostByName( %trimr(System));
```

Figure 15.45: The client program for library information (part 4 of 9).

```
// Create a socket
sd = socket( AF_INET :SOCK_STREAM :IPPROTO_IP);
if (sd = -1);
   ErrnoPtr = Errno;
   dsply ('Failure ' + %char(ErrorNbr) + ' on socket') ' ' Wait;
   *inlr = *on;
   return;
endif;

// Establish a connection for the socket
DestAddr = *loval;
SinFamily = AF_INET;
ServiceEntryPtr = GetPort(%trimr(Service) :%trimr(Protocol));
if ServiceEntryPtr = *NULL;
   dsply ('Service ' + Service + ' for ' + Protocol + 'not found.')
          ' ' Wait;
   *inlr = *on;
   return;
endif;

SinPort = ServPort;
SinAddr = hAddr;
if Connect( sd :%addr(DestAddr) :%size(DestAddr)) < 0;
   ErrnoPtr = Errno;
   dsply ('Failure ' + %char(ErrorNbr) + ' on connect') ' ' Wait;
   *inlr = *on;
   return;
endif;

// Send request for application server and then library name
if Send( sd :%addr(ApplServer) :%size(ApplServer) :0)
        < %size(ApplServer);
   dsply 'Function not sent' ' ' Wait;
   CloseSocket(sd);
   *inlr = *on;
   return;
endif;

if Send( sd :%addr(Library) :%size(Library) :0) = %size(Library);

   recvRC = Recv( sd :%addr(QUSBRTN09) :%size(QUSBRTN09)
                 :MSG_WAITALL);
   if recvRC = -1;
      dsply 'Did not get QUSROBJD size' ' ' Wait;
      CloseSocket(sd);
      *inlr = *on;
      return;
   endif;
```

Figure 15.45: The client program for library information (part 5 of 9).

```
if QUSBRTN09 = API_Error;
    recvRC = recv( sd :%addr(ErrCde) :%size(QUSEC)
                    :MSG_WAITALL);
    if recvRC = -1;
        dsply 'Did not get QUSEC size' ' ' Wait;
        CloseSocket(sd);
        *inlr = *on;
        return;
    endif;
    if ErrCde.EC.QUSBAVL > 16;
        recvRC = recv( sd :%addr(ErrCde.ErrDta)
                        :(ErrCde.EC.QUSBAVL - %size(QUSEC))
                        :MSG_WAITALL);
        if recvRC = -1;
            dsply 'Did not get QUSEC error data' ' ' Wait;
            CloseSocket(sd);
            *inlr = *on;
            return;
        endif;
    endif;
    CloseSocket(sd);
    QUSBPRV = 0;
    SndPgmMsg( ErrCde.EC.QUSEI :QualMsgF :ErrCde.ErrDta
                :(ErrCde.EC.QUSBAVL - %size(QUSEC))
                :'*COMP' :'*EXT' :0 :MsgKey :QUSEC);
    *inlr = *on;
    return;
endif;

select;
    when QUSBRTN09 = %size(QUSD0400);
        recvRC = Recv( sd :%addr(QUSBAVL10)
                        :(QUSBRTN09 - %size(QUSBRTN09))
                        :MSG_WAITALL);
    when QUSBRTN09 < %size(QUSD0400);
        Count = QUSBRTN09;
        clear QUSD0400;
        QUSBRTN09 = Count;
        recvRC = Recv( sd :%addr(QUSBAVL10)
                        :(QUSBRTN09 - %size(QUSBRTN09))
                        :MSG_WAITALL);
    when QUSBRTN09 > %size(QUSD0400);
        if TrashPtr = *NULL;
            TrashPtr = %alloc(QUSBRTN09 - %size(QUSD0400));
        endif;
        recvRC = Recv( sd :%addr(QUSBAVL10)
                        :(%size(QUSD0400) - %size(QUSBRTN09))
                        :MSG_WAITALL);
```

Figure 15.45: The client program for library information (part 6 of 9).

```
              recvRC = Recv( sd :%addr(Trash) :QUSBRTN09 -
                           (%size(QUSD0400));
                           :MSG_WAITALL);
     endsl;
     if recvRC = -1;
        dsply 'Did not get QUSROBJD data' ' ' Wait;
        CloseSocket(sd);
        *inlr = *on;
        return;
     endif;

     if (QUSCDT16 <> *blanks);       // creation date
        CrtDate = %char(%date(%subst(QUSCDT16:2:6):*YMD0):*JOBRUN);
     endif;

     if (QUSORDT03 <> *blanks);      // restore date
        RstDate = %char(%date(%subst(QUSORDT03:2:6):*YMD0):*JOBRUN);
        RstTime = %dec(%subst(QUSORDT03:8:6):6:0);
     endif;

     if (QUSOSDT03 <> *blanks);      // save date
        LstSavDat = %char(%date(%subst(QUSOSDT03:2:6):*YMD0):*JOBRUN);
        LstSavTim = %dec(%subst(QUSOSDT03:8:6):6:0);
     endif;

     recvRC = Recv( sd :%addr(Receiver.Hdr.QLIBRTN)
                       :%size(QLIBRTN) :MSG_WAITALL);
     if recvRC = -1;
        dsply 'Did not get QLIRLIBD size' ' ' Wait;
        CloseSocket(sd);
        *inlr = *on;
        return;
     endif;
     if Receiver.Hdr.QLIBRTN = API_Error;
        recvRC = recv( sd :%addr(ErrCde) :%size(QUSEC)
                       :MSG_WAITALL);
        if recvRC = -1;
           dsply 'Did not get QUSEC size' ' ' Wait;
           CloseSocket(sd);
           *inlr = *on;
           return;
        endif;
        if ErrCde.EC.QUSBAVL > 16;
           recvRC = recv( sd :%addr(ErrCde.ErrDta)
                          :(ErrCde.EC.QUSBAVL - %size(QUSEC))
                          :MSG_WAITALL);
```

Figure 15.45: The client program for library information (part 7 of 9).

```
        if recvRC = -1;
            dsply 'Did not get QUSEC error data' ' ' Wait;
            CloseSocket(sd);
            *inlr = *on;
            return;
        endif;
    endif;
    CloseSocket(sd);
    QUSBPRV = 0;
    SndPgmMsg( ErrCde.EC.QUSEI :QualMsgF :ErrCde.ErrDta
              :(ErrCde.EC.QUSBAVL - %size(QUSEC))
              :'*COMP' :'*EXT' :0 :MsgKey :QUSEC);
    *inlr = *on;
    return;
endif;

if Receiver.Hdr.QLIBRTN > %size(Receiver);
    dsply 'QLIRLIBD information too large' ' ' Wait;
    TotalObjs = 0;
    TotalSize = 0;
else;

    recvRC = Recv( sd :%addr(Receiver.Hdr.QLIBAVL)
                   :(Receiver.Hdr.QLIBRTN - %size(QLIBRTN))
                   :MSG_WAITALL);
    if recvRC = -1;
        dsply 'Did not get QLIRLIBD data' ' ' Wait;
        CloseSocket(sd);
        *inlr = *on;
        return;
    endif;

    EntryPtr = %addr(Receiver) + %size(Receiver.Hdr);

    for Count = 1 to Receiver.Hdr.QLIVRRTN;
        select;
          when (Entry.EntryHdr.QUSCK = 6);
                TotalSize = Entry.Key6LibSiz * Entry.Key6LibMult;
          when (Entry.EntryHdr.QUSCK = 7);
                TotalObjs = Entry.Key7NbrObjs;
          other;
                dsply ('Unexpected key ' +
                       %char(Entry.EntryHdr.QUSCK) +' found.')
                      ' ' Wait;
        endsl;
        EntryPtr = EntryPtr + Entry.EntryHdr.QUSLVR00;
    endfor;
endif;
```

Figure 15.45: The client program for library information (part 8 of 9).

```
    exfmt Format1;

else;
    dsply 'Did not send all data' ' ' Wait;
endif;

// close the socket
if CloseSocket(sd) < 0;
    dsply 'Failure on close' ' ' Wait;
endif;
if TrashPtr <> *NULL;
    dealloc TrashPtr;
endif;
*inlr = *on;
return;

/end-free
```

Figure 15.45: The client program for library information (part 9 of 9).

Defining a TCP Server

As our server environment currently exists, you call the program FIG15_41 to start the server environment. You are probably accustomed, though, to using the Start TCP/IP command (STRTCP) or the Start TCP/IP Server command (STRTCPSVR) to start servers such as Telnet or FTP. With our My_Somelib_Server, you can continue to use these commands!

The Add TCP/IP Server command, ADDTCPSVR, allows us to define additional TCP/IP servers and specify an exit program to be called when starting or ending the TCP/IP server. Figure 15.46 shows the command to register our server, My_Somelib_Server, and to indicate that program SOMELIB/FIG15_47 should be called when starting or ending this server. This command specifies that the special value to be used on commands such as STRTCPSVR and ENDTCPSVR is *MYSVR, that the server name and type is My_Somelib_Server, and that this server is not to be automatically started.

```
ADDTCPSVR SVRSPCVAL(*MYSVR) PGM(SOMELIB/FIG15_47)
   SVRNAME('My_Somelib_Server') SVRTYPE('My_Somelib_Server')
   AUTOSTART(*NO)
```

Figure 15.46: Defining our TCP server, My_Somelib_Server.

For consistency, we used the same name, My_Somelib_Server, for the service entry defined in Figure 15.31, the server name (SVRNAME) in Figure 15.46, and the service type (SVRTYPE) of Figure 15.46. We could just as easily have used different values for each of these attributes. You will most likely want to use meaningful names for the server name and server type. These names are used by system functions such as the i5/OS Navigator when working with TCP/IP servers and jobs, so they will be seen by your users. You can associate your server jobs with these names using the Change Job API, QWTCHGJB, and key 1911 (Server type) of format JOBC0100. Our example server does not demonstrate using this capability, but the Change Job API is discussed in chapter 13.

One input parameter, Action, is passed to the exit program for starting and ending TCP/IP servers. It is Char(10), with defined values of *START and *END. The exit point does not pass the name of the server being acted on, so you will want to have a unique server exit program defined for each TCP/IP server. Figure 15.47 shows the exit program for the *MYSVR TCP/IP server.

```
 h dftactgrp(*no) bnddir('APILIB' :'QC2LE')

DName+++++++++++ETDsFrom+++To/L+++IDc.Keywords++++++++++++++++++++++++++++
 d/copy qsysinc/qrpglesrc,qusec

dFig15_47         pr                      extpgm('FIG15_47')
 d Action                        10

dFig15_47         pi
 d Action                        10

dExists           pr             1        extproc('Exists')
 d ObjectName                   10        const
 d ObjectType                   10        const
 d ObjectLib                    10        const

dEndJobs          pr                      extproc('EndJobs')

dCmdExc           pr                      extpgm('QCMDEXC')
 d Command                   65535        const options(*varsize)
 d CmdLength                    15  5 const
 d IGC                           3 const options(*nopass)

dGetHostByName    pr              *       extproc('gethostbyname')
 d HostName                       *       value options(*string)
```

Figure 15.47: The My_Somelib_Server exit program for TCP/IP operations (part 1 of 6).

```
dSocket          pr              10i 0 extproc('socket')
d AddrFamily                     10i 0 value
d Type                           10i 0 value
d Protocol                       10i 0 value

dGetPort         pr                *   extproc('getservbyname')
d ServName                         *   value options(*string)
d ProtName                         *   value options(*string)

dConnect         pr              10i 0 extproc('connect')
d sd                             10i 0 value
d DestAddrPtr                      *   value
d LenAddr                        10i 0 value

dSend            pr              10i 0 extproc('send')
d fd                             10i 0 value
d buf                              *   value
d lenbuf                         10i 0 value
d flags                          10i 0 value

dCloseSocket     pr              10i 0 extproc('close')
d fd                             10i 0 value

dErrno           pr                *   extproc('__errno')

dHostEnt         ds                    based(HostEntPtr)
d HNamePtr                         *
d HAliasesPtr                      *
d HAddrType                      10i 0
d HLength                        10i 0
d HAddrListPtr                     *

dDestAddr        ds
d SinFamily                       5i 0
d SinPort                         5u 0
d SinAddr                        10u 0
d SinZero                         8

dServiceEntry    ds                    based(ServiceEntryPtr)
d ServName                         *
d ServAlias                        *
d ServPort                       10i 0
d ServProtocol                     *

dCmd_CrtDtaQ     s              100     inz('CRTDTAQ DTAQ(SOMELIB/-
d                                       MY_SVR_Q) MAXLEN(16) -
d                                       SEQ(*KEYED) KEYLEN(4)')
```

Figure 15.47: The My_Somelib_Server exit program for TCP/IP operations (part 2 of 6).

```
dCmd_Sbm_Svr       s              100    inz('SBMJOB -
d                                        CMD(CALL PGM(SOMELIB/FIG15_41)) -
d                                        JOBQ(QSYS/QUSRNOMAX) -
d                                        CURLIB(SOMELIB)')
dCmd_Sbm_File      s              100    inz('SBMJOB -
d                                        CMD(CALL PGM(SOMELIB/FIG15_42)) -
d                                        JOBQ(QSYS/QUSRNOMAX) -
d                                        CURLIB(SOMELIB)')
dCmd_Sbm_Appl      s              100    inz('SBMJOB -
d                                        CMD(CALL PGM(SOMELIB/FIG15_43)) -
d                                        JOBQ(QSYS/QUSRNOMAX) -
d                                        CURLIB(SOMELIB)')
dHAddrEntPtr       s                *    based(HAddrListPtr)
dhAddr             s              10u 0  based(HAddrEntPtr)
dErrorNbr          s              10i 0  based(ErrnoPtr)
dsd                s              10i 0
dEOJ               s              10i 0  inz(-1)
dWait              s               1

dServerQ           c                     'MY_SVR_Q'
dServerLib         c                     'SOMELIB'
dSystem            c                     'LOCALHOST'
dService           c                     'My_Somelib_Server'
dProtocol          c                     'tcp'

dAF_INET           c                     2
dAF_INET6          c                     24

dSOCK_STREAM       c                     1

dIPPROTO_IP        c                     0

CL0N01Factor1+++++++Opcode&ExtFactor2+++++++Result++++++++Len++D+HiLoEq
 /free

   QUSBPRV = 0;

   select;
     when Action = '*START';
         if (Exists(ServerQ :'*DTAQ' :ServerLib)) = 'Y';
             EndJobs();
         else;
             CmdExc(Cmd_CrtDtaQ :%len(%trimr(Cmd_CrtDtaQ)));
         endif;
         CmdExc(Cmd_Sbm_Svr :%len(%trimr(Cmd_Sbm_Svr)));
         CmdExc(Cmd_Sbm_File :%len(%trimr(Cmd_Sbm_File)));
         CmdExc(Cmd_Sbm_Appl :%len(%trimr(Cmd_Sbm_Appl)));
```

Figure 15.47: The My_Somelib_Server exit program for TCP/IP operations (part 3 of 6).

```
    when Action = '*END';
        // Get the IP address of the system we will talk with
        HostEntPtr = GetHostByName( %trimr(System));

        // Create a socket
        sd = socket( AF_INET :SOCK_STREAM :IPPROTO_IP);
        if (sd = -1);
            ErrnoPtr = Errno;
            dsply ('Failure ' + %char(ErrorNbr) + ' on socket')
                        ' ' Wait;
            *inlr = *on;
            return;
        endif;

        // Establish a connection for the socket
        DestAddr = *loval;
        SinFamily = AF_INET;
        ServiceEntryPtr = GetPort(%trimr(Service) :%trimr(Protocol));
        if ServiceEntryPtr = *NULL;
            dsply ('Service ' + Service + ' for ' + Protocol +
                        ' not found.') ' ' Wait;
            *inlr = *on;
            return;
        endif;

        SinPort = ServPort;
        SinAddr = hAddr;
        if Connect( sd :%addr(DestAddr) :%size(DestAddr)) < 0;
            ErrnoPtr = Errno;
            dsply ('Failure ' + %char(ErrorNbr) + ' on connect')
                        ' ' Wait;
            *inlr = *on;
            return;
        endif;

        // Send Stop order

        if Send( sd :%addr(EOJ) :%size(EOJ) :0) <> %size(EOJ);
            dsply 'Unable to send *Stop to server' ' ' Wait;
        endif;
        EndJobs();
    other;
        dsply ('Unexpected Action ' + %trimr(Action) + ' found.')
                    ' ' Wait;
endsl;

*inlr = *on;
return;
```

Figure 15.47: The My_Somelib_Server exit program for TCP/IP operations (part 4 of 6).

```
 /end-free

pEndJobs           b

dEndJobs           pi

d/copy qsysinc/qrpglesrc,qrcvdtaq
d/copy qsysinc/qrpglesrc,qusrjobi
d/copy qsysinc/qrpglesrc,qusec

dEndJobs           pr

dRcvDtaQ           pr                      extpgm('QRCVDTAQ')
d DtaQName                     10          const
d DtaQLib                      10          const
d ReceiverLenRtn               5  0
d Receiver                     1           options(*varsize)
d WaitTime                     5  0 const
d KeyOrder                     2           const options(*nopass)
d KeyLen                       3  0 const options(*nopass)
d KeyValue                     1           options(*varsize :*nopass)
d SndrInfoLen                  3  0 const options(*nopass)
d SndrInfo                     1           options(*varsize :*nopass)
d RmvMsg                      10           const options(*nopass)
d ReceiverLen                  5  0 const options(*nopass)
d QUSEC                                    likeds(QUSEC) options(*nopass)

dRJobI             pr                      extpgm('QUSRJOBI')
d Receiver                     1           options(*varsize)
d LengthRcv                   10i 0 const
d Format                       8           const
d QualJobName                 26           const
d IntJobID                    16           const
d QUSEC                                    likeds(QUSEC) options(*nopass)
d Reset                        1           const options(*nopass)

dDQKey             ds                      qualified
d Key                         10i 0 inz(0)

dIntJobID          s          16
dDQMsgSize         s           5  0
dCommand           s         100

 /free

  QUSBPRV = %size(QUSEC);
```

Figure 15.47: The My_Somelib_Server exit program for TCP/IP operations (part 5 of 6).

```
   dou DQMsgSize = 0;

       RcvDtaQ( ServerQ :ServerLib :DQMsgSize :IntJobID :0
               :'GE' :%size(DQKey) :DQKey :0 :QRCQSI
               :'*YES' :%size(IntJobID) :QUSEC);
       if QUSBAVL > 0;
           dsply ('Error ' + QUSEI + ' accessing ' + ServerQ) ' ' Wait;
           return;
       endif;

       if DQMsgSize = %size(IntJobID);
           RjobI( QUSI010000 :%size(QUSI010000) :'JOBI0100'
                  :'*INT' :IntJobID :QUSEC);
           if QUSBAVL > 0;
               iter;
           endif;
           if ((QUSJS01 = '*ACTIVE') or (QUSJS01 = '*JOBQ'));
               Command = ( 'ENDJOB JOB(' + QUSJNBR01 + '/' +
                           %trimr(QUSUN01) + '/' +
                           %trimr(QUSJN01) + ') OPTION(*IMMED)');
               CmdExc( Command :%len(%trimr(Command)));
           endif;
       endif;
     endif;

   enddo;

   return;

 /end-free

pEndJobs          e
```

Figure 15.47: The My_Somelib_Server exit program for TCP/IP operations (part 6 of 6).

Before getting into the details of FIG15_47, we should discuss some design considerations. There are many ways you could end a TCP/IP server such as *MYSVR. One approach would be to submit all server jobs to a specific subsystem and simply end that subsystem. This is straightforward enough, and would certainly work, but might also cause servers to end while in the middle of a session. Another approach, the one we took, is to read the MY_SVR_Q data queue to find server jobs that are available for work and then end only those jobs. This ensures that active server jobs continue running and that no new work will start through the *MYSVR server, as long as our routing server FIG15_41 has also ended. It does, however, leave these "active" server jobs showing as active on the system for an unknown period of time.

We decided to allow these "active" server jobs to continue showing as active on the system until *MYSVR is restarted or until some external event takes place that would end them. These events, external to our routing server environment, might be IPLing the system, ending the QUSRWRK subsystem (where FIG15_41 and FIG15_47 submit the server jobs), having an operator end the jobs, and the like.

When the *MYSVR server is re-started, FIG15_47 will read any messages on the MY_SVR_Q data queue and end those jobs prior to submitting the FIG15_41 routing program. In this way, we could clean up or end the "active" servers from the previous instance of *MYSVR when they had completed their work. This design also has some beneficial side effects. One is that any server job that experiences an error would most likely be left "active" on the system, waiting for an operator to respond to one of our DSPLY messages. As the server would not have sent an availability message to the MY_SVR_Q data queue in this message-wait situation, the job would not be ended during either the starting or the ending of the *MYSVR server. The job experiencing the error would continue to exist on the system for problem-determination purposes.

With that background in place, let's now look in more detail at the FIG15_47 program. When it is called, it first checks to see what Action has been requested. If Action is a *START request, the program checks to see if the MY_SVR_Q data queue exists. If it does, FIG15_47 calls the procedure EndJobs to end all server jobs that are waiting for work. If the data queue does not exist, the program creates it.

The EndJobs procedure is written in a way that minimizes the likelihood of it reading a message off of the MY_SVR_Q data queue and then not being able to process that message. In this case, the processing would be to end the job that sent the message.

EndJobs first sets the local error-code bytes-provided field, QUSBPRV, to a non-zero value. You might notice that the main line of FIG15_47 uses a value of zero for QUSBPRV. This is done so that any API error will return an exception and cause the program to fail. In the case of EndJobs, we use a nonzero value and, if a recoverable error is encountered, simply continue running—in this case, ending any other server jobs and allowing the new server jobs to be submitted.

Following that, EndJobs reads each message on the MY_SVR_Q data queue, calls the Retrieve Job Information API, QUSRJOBI (to find the qualified job name associated with the internal Job ID IntJobID and to determine the status of the server job), and ends the server job if it is either active or on a job queue. We elected to use the internal job ID and the QUSRJOBI API, rather than having the system provide the sender job ID with the Senderid parameter of the CRTDTAQ command, to avoid duplicate job-name processing. The internal job ID is unique even across IPLs of the system.

When EndJobs returns to the *START logic, FIG15_47 submits programs FIG15_41, FIG15_42, and FIG15_43 to the QUSRNOMAX job queue, and ends.

If Action is an *END request, FIG15_47 creates a socket connection to the routing server program (FIG15_41), sends an end-of-job Function value to FIG15_41, calls EndJobs to end any server jobs awaiting work, and ends. If Action is not a *START or *END request, FIG15_47 DSPLYs appropriate error text and ends.

Now, starting our server environment is as simple as using the command STRTCPSVR *MYSVR.

A Simple Telnet Server

The last example in this chapter uses the socket APIs to develop a Telnet server supporting Telnet terminals such as those in Windows and DOS. As with the FIG15_26 and FIG15_43 programs, this example is based on the library information program developed in Figure 5.5.

We do not anticipate that anyone is actually going to write a Telnet server application. You probably have Telnet clients that are capable of accessing your interactive RPG applications directly. There are, however, times when you might want to communicate directly with remote ASCII- or Unicode-based applications, and the FIG15_48 program demonstrates how to do this. In this example, the remote application happens to be a Telnet client. In your business environment, it might be a data-collection controller, a phone-switching system, or any of thousands of other possibilities.

Figure 15.48 shows the source for our Telnet server.

```
h dftactgrp(*no) bnddir('QC2LE')

d/copy qsysinc/qrpglesrc,qusrobjd
d/copy qsysinc/qrpglesrc,qlirlibd
d/copy qsysinc/qrpglesrc,qus
d/copy qsysinc/qrpglesrc,qtqiconv
```

Figure 15.48: A Telnet server for ASCII client access to library information (part 1 of 11).

```
d/copy qsysinc/qrpglesrc,qlg
d/copy qsysinc/qrpglesrc,qusec

dSocket            pr            10i 0 extproc('socket')
d AddrFamily                     10i 0 value
d Type                          10i 0 value
d Protocol                      10i 0 value

dSockOpt           pr            10i 0 extproc('setsockopt')
d sd                            10i 0 value
d Level                         10i 0 value
d OptionName                    10i 0 value
d OptionValue                    *   value
d OptionLength                  10i 0 value

dBind              pr            10i 0 extproc('bind')
d sd                            10i 0 value
d LclAddrPtr                     *   value
d LenAddr                       10i 0 value

dListen            pr            10i 0 extproc('listen')
d sd                            10i 0 value
d BackLog                       10i 0 value

dAccept            pr            10i 0 extproc('accept')
d sd                            10i 0 value
d RmtAddrPtr                     *   value
d LenAddr                       10i 0

dSend              pr            10i 0 extproc('send')
d fd                            10i 0 value
d buf                            *   value
d lenbuf                        10i 0 value
d flags                         10i 0 value

dRecv              pr            10i 0 extproc('recv')
d sd                            10i 0 value
d buf                            *   value
d lenbuf                        10i 0 value
d flags                         10i 0 value

dCloseSocket       pr            10i 0 extproc('close')
d fd                            10i 0 value

dErrno             pr             *   extproc('__errno')
```

Figure 15.48: A Telnet server for ASCII client access to library information (part 2 of 11).

```
dRObjD           pr                          extpgm('QUSROBJD')
d Receiver                       1           options(*varsize)
d ReceiverLen                   10i 0 const
d Format                         8           const
d ObjLibName                    20           const
d ObjectType                    10           const
d QUSEC                                      likeds(QUSEC) options(*nopass)
d ASPControl                 65535           const options(*varsize :*nopass)

dRLibD           pr                          extpgm('QLIRLIBD')
d Receiver                       1           options(*varsize)
d RecieverLen                   10i 0 const
d Library                       10           const
d Attributes                 65535           const options(*varsize)
d QUSEC                                      likeds(QUSEC)

dSetConvert      pr             10i 0
d cd                                         likeds(cd)
d InputCCSID                    10i 0 value
d OutputCCSID                   10i 0 value

dConvert         pr             10i 0
d cd                                         likeds(cd)
d Input                          *    value
d Len_Input                     10i 0 value

dEndConvert      pr             10i 0 extproc('iconv_close')
d ConvDesc                                   value like(cd)

dConvertCase     pr                          extproc('QlgConvertCase')
d Request                    65535           const options(*varsize)
d InputData                  65535           const options(*varsize)
d OutputData                     1           options(*varsize)
d InputDataLen                  10i 0 const
d QUSEC                                      likeds(QUSEC)

dcd              ds
d cdBins                        10i 0 dim(13)

dTo819           ds                          likeds(cd)

dTo37            ds                          likeds(cd)

dLclAddr         ds
d SinFamily                      5i 0
d SinPort                        5u 0
```

Figure 15.48: A Telnet server for ASCII client access to library information (part 3 of 11).

```
d SinAddr                           10u 0
d SinZero                            8

dDestAddr          ds                        likeds(LclAddr)

dObjLibName        ds
d LibName                           10
d ObjLib                            10        inz('QSYS')

dAttributes        ds
d NbrAttributes                     10i 0
d Key                               10i 0 dim(10)

dReceiver          ds              256        qualified
d Hdr                                         likeds(QLIRR)

dEntry             ds                         based(EntryPtr)
d                                             qualified
d EntryHdr                                    likeds(QUSVR4)
d Key6LibSiz                        10i 0 overlay(Entry :13)
d Key6LibMult                       10i 0 overlay(Entry :*next)
d Key6LibSts                         1     overlay(Entry :*next)
d Key7NbrObjs                       10i 0 overlay(Entry :13)

dErrorNbr          s                10i 0 based(ErrnoPtr)
dsd                s                10i 0
dsdTarget          s                10i 0
dAddrLen           s                10i 0
drecvRC            s                10i 0
dOutput_Value      s              1000
dPrompt            s               100        inz('Enter library name:')
dChar              s                 1
dX                 s                10i 0
dCount             s                10u 0
dSize              s                10i 0
dCrtDate           s                10
dLstSavDat         s                10
dLstSavTim         s                 8
dRstDate           s                10
dRstTime           s                 8
dTotalObjs         s                10i 0
dTotalSize         s                20i 0
dReUseYes          s                10i 0 inz(1)
dWait              s                 1

dCR                c                         x'0D'
dLF                c                         x'25'
```

Figure 15.48: A Telnet server for ASCII client access to library information (part 4 of 11).

```
dMSG_WAITALL          c                    64

dINADDR_ANY           c                    0
dINADDR_LOOPBACK      c                    2130706433

dAF_INET              c                    2
dAF_INET6             c                    24

dSOCK_STREAM          c                    1

dIPPROTO_IP           c                    0

dSOL_SOCKET           c                    -1
dSO_REUSEADDR         c                    55

 /free

   QUSBPRV = %size(QUSEC);

   // Initialize EBCDIC to ASCII conversion routine
   SetConvert(To819 :37 :819);

   // Initialize ASCII to EBCDIC conversion routine
   SetConvert(To37 :819 :37);

   // Initialize upper case converion
   QLGIDRCB00 = *loval;               // set input structure to x'00'
   QLGTOR02 = 1;                      // use CCSID for monocasing
   QLGIDOID00 = 37;                   // use CCSID 37
   QLGCR00 = 0;                       // convert to uppercase

   // Create a socket
   sd = socket( AF_INET :SOCK_STREAM :IPPROTO_IP);
   if (sd = -1);
      ErrnoPtr = Errno;
      dsply ('Failure ' + %char(ErrorNbr) + ' on socket') ' ' Wait;
      *inlr = *on;
      return;
   endif;

   // Allow the reuse of our port
   if SockOpt( sd :SOL_SOCKET :SO_REUSEADDR :%addr(ReUseYes)
               :%size(ReUseYes)) = -1;
               ErrnoPtr = Errno;
               dsply ('Failure ' + %char(ErrorNbr) + ' on setsockopt.')
                     ' ' Wait;
               *inlr = *on;
               return;
   endif;
```

Figure 15.48: A Telnet server for ASCII client access to library information (part 5 of 11).

```
// Bind our local address to a socket
LclAddr = *loval;
SinFamily = AF_INET;
SinPort = 53002;
SinAddr = INADDR_ANY;
if Bind( sd :%addr(LclAddr) :%size(LclAddr)) < 0;
   ErrnoPtr = Errno;
   dsply ('Failure ' + %char(ErrorNbr) + ' on bind') ' ' Wait;
   *inlr = *on;
   return;
endif;

// Listen for incoming data
if Listen( sd :1) < 0;
   ErrnoPtr = Errno;
   dsply ('Failure ' + %char(ErrorNbr) + ' on listen') ' ' Wait;
   *inlr = *on;
   return;
endif;

// Accept incoming data
AddrLen = %size(DestAddr);
sdTarget = Accept( sd :%addr(DestAddr) :AddrLen);
if sdTarget < 0;
   ErrnoPtr = Errno;
   dsply ('Failure ' + %char(ErrorNbr) + ' on accept') ' ' Wait;
   *inlr = *on;
   return;
endif;

// Prompt for and get library name
dow 1 = 1;
Output_Value = %trimr(Prompt) + CR + LF;
Size = Convert(To819 :%addr(Output_Value)
       :%len(%trimr(Output_Value)));
if Send( sdTarget :%addr(Output_Value) :Size :0) < Size;
   dsply 'Prompt not written' ' ' Wait;
   CloseSocket(sdTarget);
   CloseSocket(sd);
   *inlr = *on;
   return;
endif;

LibName = *blanks;
X = 1;
dou Char = LF;
```

Figure 15.48: A Telnet server for ASCII client access to library information (part 6 of 11).

```
      recvRC = Recv( sdTarget :%addr(Char) :%size(Char) :MSG_WAITALL);
      Convert(To37 :%addr(Char) :%size(Char));
      ConvertCase( QLGIDRCB00 :Output_Value :Char :%size(Char) :QUSEC);
      select;
      // Program does not check for backspace, etc.
        when recvRC = -1;
          leave;
        when Char = LF;
          leave;
        when Char = CR;
          iter;
        other;
          if X > %size(LibName);
              Output_Value = CR + LF + 'Library name ' + LibName +
                                ' is too long.' + CR + LF + LF;
              Size = Convert( To819 :%addr(Output_Value)
                                :%len(%trimr(Output_Value)));
              if Send( sdTarget :%addr(Output_Value) :Size :0) < Size;
                  dsply 'Prompt not written' ' ' Wait;
                  CloseSocket(sdTarget);
                  CloseSocket(sd);
                  *inlr = *on;
                  return;
              else;
                  leave;
              endif;
          else;
              %subst(LibName :X) = Char;
              X += 1;
          endif;
      endsl;
  enddo;

  if LibName = 'QUIT';
      leave;
  endif;

  if X > %size(LibName);
      iter;
  endif;

  if (recvRC <> -1) and (X > 1);
      // Get object related data
      RObjD( QUSD0400 :%size(QUSD0400) :'OBJD0400' :ObjLibName
            :'*LIB'    :QUSEC);
```

Figure 15.48: A Telnet server for ASCII client access to library information (part 7 of 11).

```
if (QUSBAVL <> 0);
    Output_Value = 'Library ' + %trimr(LibName) +
                    ' not found.' + CR + LF + LF;
    Size = Convert( To819 :%addr(Output_Value)
                    :%len(%trimr(Output_Value)));
    if Send( sdTarget :%addr(Output_Value) :Size :0) < Size;
        dsply 'Prompt not written' ' ' Wait;
        CloseSocket(sdTarget);
        CloseSocket(sd);
        *inlr = *on;
        return;
    else;
        iter;
    endif;
else;
    if QUSCDT16 <> *blanks;
        CrtDate = %char(%date(%subst(QUSCDT16:2:6):*YMD0):*JOBRUN);
    endif;
    if QUSOSDT03 <> *blanks;
        LstSavDat=%char(%date(%subst(QUSOSDT03:2:6):*YMD0):*JOBRUN);
        LstSavTim=%editw(%dec(%subst(QUSOSDT03:8:6):6:0):'  :  : 0');
    endif;
    if QUSORDT03 <> *blanks;
        RstDate = %char(%date(%subst(QUSORDT03:2:6):*YMD0):*JOBRUN);
        RstTime = %editw(%dec(%subst(QUSORDT03:8:6):6:0):'  :  : 0');
    endif;
    Output_Value = *blanks;
    Output_Value = CR + LF + LF + LF
                + '*************************************************'
                + CR + LF
                + 'Library: ' + LibName + '      '
                + QUSTD14 + CR + LF
                + LF
                + 'Owned by:                   ' + QUSOBJ007 + CR + LF
                + 'Created by:                 ' + QUSCUP04 + CR + LF
                + LF
                + 'Created date:             '
                + CrtDate + CR + LF
                + 'Last Saved Date/Time: '
                + LstSavDat + ' ' + LstSavTim + CR + LF
                + 'Restored Date/Time:      '
                + RstDate + ' ' + RstTime + CR + LF
                + LF + LF;
    Size = Convert( To819 :%addr(Output_Value)
                    :%len(%trimr(Output_Value)));
```

Figure 15.48: A Telnet server for ASCII client access to library information (part 8 of 11).

603

```
        if Send( sdTarget :%addr(Output_Value) :Size :0) < Size;
            dsply 'Not all data written' ' ' Wait;
            CloseSocket(sdTarget);
            CloseSocket(sd);
            *inlr = *on;
            return;
        endif;
    endif;

    // Get library size and number of objects
    NbrAttributes = 2;
    Key(1) = 6;                      // library size
    Key(2) = 7;                      // number of objects in library

    RLibD( Receiver :%size(Receiver) :LibName :Attributes :QUSEC);

    if (QUSBAVL <> 0);
        dsply ('Error ' + QUSEI + ' while retrieving library desc')
                ' ' Wait;
        CloseSocket(sdTarget);
        CloseSocket(sd);
        *inlr = *on;
        return;
    else;
        EntryPtr = %addr(Receiver) + %size(Receiver.Hdr);

        for Count = 1 to Receiver.Hdr.QLIVRRTN;
            select;
                when (Entry.EntryHdr.QUSCK = 6);
                    TotalSize = Entry.Key6LibSiz * Entry.Key6LibMult;
                when (Entry.EntryHdr.QUSCK = 7);
                    TotalObjs = Entry.Key7NbrObjs;
                other;
                    dsply ('Unexpected key ' + %char(Entry.EntryHdr.QUSCK) +
                            ' found.') ' ' Wait;
            endsl;
            EntryPtr = EntryPtr + Entry.EntryHdr.QUSLVR00;
        endfor;

        Output_Value = *blanks;
        Output_Value = 'Number of objects:     '
                + %editc(TotalObjs :'1') + CR + LF
                + 'Size of all objects:  '
                + %editc(TotalSize :'1') + CR + LF
                + '---------------------------------------------------'
                + CR + LF + LF + LF + LF;
```

Figure 15.48: A Telnet server for ASCII client access to library information (part 9 of 11).

```
        Size = Convert( To819 :%addr(Output_Value)
                        :%len(%trimr(Output_Value)));
        if Send( sdTarget :%addr(Output_Value) :Size :0) < Size;
            dsply 'Not all data written' ' ' Wait;
            CloseSocket(sdTarget);
            CloseSocket(sd);
            *inlr = *on;
            return;
        endif;
    endif;

else;
    if recvRC = -1;
        ErrnoPtr = Errno;
        dsply ('Could not receive library name -  ' + %char(ErrorNbr))
              ' ' Wait;
    else;
        // No library name entered, just loop back
    endif;
endif;
enddo;

// Close the connection
if CloseSocket(sdTarget) < 0;
    dsply 'Error on client close' ' ' Wait;
endif;

if CloseSocket(sd) < 0;
    dsply 'Error on listen close' ' ' Wait;
endif;
*inlr = *on;
return;

/end-free

pSetConvert     b
dSetConvert     pi          10i 0
d Input_cd                      likeds(cd)
d InputCCSID    10i 0 value
d OutputCCSID   10i 0 value

dConvertOpen    pr          52a  extproc('QtqIconvOpen')
d ToCode                     *   value
d FromCode                   *   value

dToCode         ds               likeds(qtqcode)
```

Figure 15.48: A Telnet server for ASCII client access to library information (part 10 of 11).

```
dFromCode          ds                    likeds(qtqcode)

 /free
   FromCode = *loval;
   ToCode = *loval;
   FromCode.QTQCCSID = InputCCSID;
   ToCode.QTQCCSID = OutputCCSID;
   Input_cd = ConvertOpen( %addr(ToCode) :%addr(FromCode));
   if cdBins(1) = -1;
      return -1;
   else;
      return 0;
   endif;
 /end free
pSetConvert        e

pConvert           b
dConvert           pi           10i 0
d Input_cd                             likeds(cd)
d Input_Pointer                  *     value
d Input_Length               10i 0 value

diconv             pr           10i 0 extproc('iconv')
d ConvDesc                             value like(cd)
d InputData                      *     value
d InputDataLeft              10u 0
d OutputData                     *     value
d OutputDataLeft             10u 0

dOutBufPtr         s                 *
dInBytesLeft       s           10u 0
dOutBytesLeft      s           10u 0
dRtnCde            s           10i 0

 /free
   // reset InBytesLeft, OutBytesLeft, and OutBufPtr each time as iconv
   // API updates these values
   InBytesLeft = Input_Length;
   OutBytesLeft = %len(Output_Value);
   OutBufPtr = %addr(Output_Value);
   RtnCde = iconv( Input_cd :%addr(Input_Pointer) :InBytesLeft
                   :%addr(OutBufPtr) :OutBytesLeft);
   if RtnCde = -1;
      return -1;
   else;
      return (%len(Output_Value) - OutBytesLeft);
   endif;
 /end-free
pConvert           e
```

Figure 15.48: A Telnet server for ASCII client access to library information (part 11 of 11).

The FIG15_48 program prompts the Telnet user for a library name and returns information associated with the library to the user. After returning the library information, the program will prompt for another library name to be entered. This will continue until the user asks for a library named *quit*, in which case FIG15_48 will end.

We will be supporting ASCII character-mode clients, so FIG15_48 first uses the QTQICONVOPEN API to initialize two conversion environments. The first environment, identified by the conversion descriptor To819, is used to convert from EBCDIC CCSID 37 to ASCII CCSID 819. The second environment, conversion descriptor To37, is used to convert from CCSID 819 to CCSID 37. FIG15_48 also initializes an environment for the uppercasing of CCSID 37 character data. This is done so that the Telnet user can enter library names in either uppercase or lowercase. After converting the entered library name to EBCDIC, FIG15_48 will do this monocasing of the library name because system APIs like Retrieve Object Description expect object names to be in the correct case. (These conversion APIs were introduced in chapter 9.)

Having initialized the CCSID conversion and monocasing environments, FIG15_48 then runs through the SOCKET, SETSOCKOPT, BIND, LISTEN, and ACCEPT APIs. You should be quite familiar with these APIs by now. The only point worth noting here is that FIG15_48 uses port 53002 for the BIND. We are not able to use the service entry My_Somelib_Server, and port 53003, because the Telnet client will not be sending a Function value to route through FIG15_41. The initial exchange with the Telnet client will be the FIG15_48 server sending the client data, in the form of a prompt for the library name, so we need a different port to listen on. All of the ports used in previous examples assumed that the client would first be sending data to the server program.

At this point, we're ready for a Telnet client to connect with us. From a Windows "run" prompt or a DOS command prompt, you can use the command shown in Figure 15.49, assuming that your server system is known as SYSTEMA.

```
telnet systema 53002
```

Figure 15.49: Starting the Telnet client.

You should at this point see the prompt "Enter library name:." Type **somelib** and press **Enter**. You should now see the library information associated with the SOMELIB library along with another "Enter library name:" prompt. This time, type **quit** and press **Enter**. You should see the message "Connection to host lost."

If you see a message related to the client "not being able to open a connection," you probably need to call FIG15_48 on SYSTEMA to start the server. While FIG15_48 does support a conversational mode where the user can ask for information on multiple libraries, FIG15_48 does not loop back to the ACCEPT API after closing the connection to a client. As coded, it's one client connection, and then FIG15_48 ends. However, it should not be difficult for you to change this behavior if you want.

When the client connects to FIG15_48, the program sets the variable Output_Value to the prompt "Enter library name:" with a carriage return, CR, and line feed, LF, appended to the prompt. The carriage return and line feed commands cause the user to enter the library name on the line following the prompt text. Output_Value is then converted to CCSID 819 and sent to the client.

After sending the prompt out, FIG15_48 sets the variable LibName to *BLANKS and the variable X to one. Variable X is used to control what character of LibName is the next to be received from the client. When set to a value of one, X indicates that the next character of the library name is the first character of the name.

The program then enters a loop, where one character at a time is received from the client. For each character, FIG15_48 converts the character to CCSID 37, converts the character to uppercase, and then examines it. Note that, while FIG15_48 needs to process each character one at a time to find line-feed controls, the program could be written to *receive* more than one character at a time. This could be done by specifying a larger buffer size and removing the MSG_WAITALL flag. Peformance will be improved by using a buffered approach.

Most character-based clients send a line feed to indicate that the Enter key has been used. If FIG15_48 detects a line feed, the program exits the character-by-character loop. Some character-based clients precede a line feed with a carriage return. FIG15_48 discards any carriage returns that are received and simply reads the next character.

If the character is neither a line feed or a carriage return, FIG15_48 assumes the character is part of the library name and adds it to the LibName variable. *This is a huge, and invalid, assumption.* We make it, however, to focus on how to use the APIs, not how to build a true Telnet server. If you use the Backspace key or even cursor-movement keys from your Telnet client, you will find that FIG15_48 receives such keys as control characters and processes them as characters in the library name. If you use a few of these keys, you will probably see the message "Library name is too long" because FIG15_48 does check to make sure the library name does not exceed ten "characters."

Upon finding a line feed and exiting the character-by-character loop, the program calls the Retrieve Object Description API to retrieve the object-related information, formats the results with appropriate line feeds and carriage controls, converts the formatted results to CCSID 819, and sends the converted results to the client.

The program then calls the Retrieve Library Description API to retrieve the library-related information, formats the results with appropriate line feeds and carriage controls, converts the formatted results to CCSID 819, sends the converted results to the client, and then loops back to prompting for a library name.

When a library name of QUIT is processed, FIG15_48 ends.

Receiving Data without Waiting

Most commercial applications expect to receive some input data, process that data, and then return the results. Our examples have involved this type of application. As mentioned earlier in this chapter, the RECV API, by default, will not return control until at least one byte of data becomes available to the application or, with the MSG_WAITALL flag, until some fixed minimum amount of data becomes available. This behavior of the RECV API was quite sufficient for our needs.

Some applications, however, might not want to wait for data to become available from a given client (or from a server, for that matter). One example, building on the FIG15_45 client application, might be where the client wants library information related to the library SOMELIB on SYSTEMA, SYSTEMB, and SYSTEMC. In this case, it might be nice to start FIG15_43 on all three systems concurrently, and then simply process the results in whatever order the server systems happen to respond. There are, of course, APIs to allow such an application.

The Wait for Events on Multiple Descriptors API, POLL, allows you to provide a list of the socket descriptors and the types of events you are interested in for each socket descriptor. (The POLL API is only available starting with release V5R4 of i5/OS. Earlier releases support a similar function using the SELECT API. The SELECT API, however, is not as efficient as the POLL API and should only be used for applications running on releases prior to V5R4.)

The parameter descriptions for POLL are shown in Figure 15.50. It takes three parameters. The first parameter, Fds, is a pointer to an array of Pollfd structures. The definition for the Pollfd structure is shown in Table 15.4. The second parameter, Nflds, is an unsigned integer representing the number of Pollfd structures passed in the Fds parameter. The third parameter, Timeout, is an integer that specifies how long, in milliseconds, to wait for one of the events specified by the Fds parameter to occur before returning to the API caller. The special value -1 indicates that the API should not return until one of the events of interest have been satisfied.

```
int poll (struct pollfd fds[], nfds_t nflds, int timeout)
```

Figure 15.50: The POLL API.

The API also returns an integer. If the return value is -1, an error was found on the API call, and errno is updated with additional information. If the return value is zero, the amount of time specified by the timeout parameter has passed with none of the events you are interested in having occurred. If the value is greater than zero, that number of Pollfd structures meet the requested criteria.

Table 15.4: The Pollfd Structure		
Type	Name	Description
Int	Fd	Descriptor
Short	Events	Requested events
Short	Revents	Returned events

The first field of the Pollfd structure, Fd, is the socket descriptor you are interested in.

The second field, Events, is a 2-byte integer, where each bit can represent the type of event you are interested in. The special value POLLIN requests information on whether data is available to be received from the socket descriptor, while POLLOUT requests information on sending to the socket descriptor.

The third field, Revents, is also a 2-byte integer, where each bit reflects whether or not the corresponding bit request in Events is satisfied. This field is cleared by the API prior to setting the status of the requested bits from Events.

Figure 15.51 shows the prototype for the POLL API and a sample usage. In this example, we are polling to see if either socket descriptor sdTarget1 or sdTarget2 have data ready for the program to receive. If neither socket descriptor has data available within 1,000 milliseconds, the API will return control back to the program.

```
h dftactgrp(*no)

dPoll              pr            10i 0 extproc('poll')
d fds                             *    value
d nflds                          10u 0 value
d timeout                        10i 0 value

dpollfd            ds
d fd                             10i 0
d events                          5i 0
d revents                         5i 0

dfds               ds                  qualified
d PollStruct                           likeds(pollfd) dim(10)

dsdTarget1         s             10i 0
dsdTarget2         s             10i 0
dNbrTargets        s             10i 0 inz(0)
drcPoll            s             10i 0

dPOLLIN            c                   1
dPOLLOUT           c                   2

 /free

   NbrTargets += 1;
   fds.PollStruct(NbrTargets).fd = sdTarget1;
   fds.PollStruct(NbrTargets).events = POLLIN;

   NbrTargets += 1;
   fds.PollStruct(NbrTargets).fd = sdTarget2;
   fds.PollStruct(NbrTargets).events = POLLIN;

   rcPoll = Poll( %addr(fds) :NbrTargets :1000);

   *inlr = *on;
   return;

 /end-free
```

Figure 15.51: Using the POLL API.

The POLL API is also useful in situations where input is only expected from one socket descriptor, and the application program is able to perform processing while periodically wanting to check the socket descriptor to determine if more data is available to be read. While this type of application need can be met by the POLL API, it could also be met if there was a way to reduce the minimum byte requirement of the RECV API from one to zero, or to query a specific socket descriptor to determine if data is available. Needless to say, there are such capabilities.

The Perform File Control Command API, fcntl, allows the application program to change a socket descriptor such that it will not *block*, or wait, by using an O_NONBLOCK flag. In this case, the RECV API would return an errno value of EWOULDBLOCK if no data was currently available.

The Perform I/O Control Request API, IOCTL, allows the application program to query a socket descriptor to see what, if any data, is available to read using the FIONREAD flag. In addition, the IOCTL API can be used to set the O_NONBLOCK flag. We will not discuss these other APIs here, but we do want to make you aware of their existence.

Summary

Sockets are a powerful communications tool. They are a preferred method of communicating with other programs. This chapter covers only a tiny fraction of the APIs that deal with sockets communications, but you have seen enough of the basic steps to get a good start.

Check Your Knowledge

In chapter 12, example FIG12_5 showed how to use data queues to send encrypted passwords from a central system to remote systems. Change this approach so that a client program on the remote system requests the encrypted password information.

Write a new password server, PWDSERVER, with a Function value of three. You will need to modify FIG15_41 to recognize the new Function and develop both the client and server programs that support Function 3. The client will send the user profile name to the server, and the server will send back the encrypted password data. The client program will then update the user profile on the remote system. Information related to errors on the server should be sent to the client.

For possible solutions to this task, see Figures D.15.A, D.15.B, and D.15.C in appendix D.

16

Odds and Ends

There are literally thousands of APIs provided with i5/OS that we have not been able to discuss in this book. This chapter is intended to give you a feel for some of those other APIs and to demonstrate a few additional considerations and techniques when working with APIs.

We'll start off with an API that you might find very useful when calling list-type APIs. As mentioned earlier in the book, most list-type APIs do not document or specify any particular order in which list entries might be returned to your application program. Your application, on the other hand, might want to process the entries in a particular sequence. For this there is the Sort API, QLGSORT.

The Sort API, QLGSORT

The QLGSORT API provides a generalized sort function that can be used to sequence data in files or buffers. The example in this section uses buffers that are the list entries returned in a user space from the List Jobs API, QUSLJOB. The QLGSORT API can also be used to initialize sort specifications to be used by the related Sort Input/Output API, QLGSRTIO. The QLGSRTIO API can be called multiple times to incrementally add data to a sort. When all of the data has been added, QLGSRTIO returns the sorted results. While we will not demonstrate this capability in our example program, the QLGSRTIO API could be used to sort and merge entries that might be returned across multiple user spaces when all of the available data will not fit in one user space.

The parameters for QLGSORT are shown in Table 16.1. The first parameter, Request Control Block, defines the specifications of the sort. This includes information such as whether a list of files or an input buffer is to be sorted, which fields within the data are to be sorted on, and where the output of the sort is to go.

Table 16.1: Parameters for the Sort API, QLGSORT			
Parameter	Description	Type	Size
1	Request Control Block	Input	Char(*)
2	Input Data Buffer	Input	Char(*)
3	Output Data Buffer	Output	Char(*)
4	Length of Output Data Buffer	Input	Binary(4)
5	Length of Returned Data	Output	Binary(4)
6	Error Code	I/O	Char(*)
Optional Parameter Group 1			
7	Returned Records Feedback	Output	Char(*)
8	Length of Returned Records Feedback	Input	Binary(4)

The next few QLGSORT API parameters are best understood after reviewing the Request Control Block parameter, so we'll discuss these specifications first. The QSYSINC include for the Request Control Block parameter is shown in Figure 16.1.

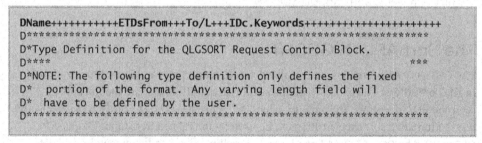

```
DName++++++++++ETDsFrom+++To/L+++IDc.Keywords+++++++++++++++++++++++
D*******************************************************************
D*Type Definition for the QLGSORT Request Control Block.
D****                                                           ***
D*NOTE: The following type definition only defines the fixed
D*  portion of the format. Any varying length field will
D*  have to be defined by the user.
D*******************************************************************
```

Figure 16.1: The QSYSINC definition for QLGSORT'S Request Control Block parameter (part 1 of 2).

```
DQLGSCB                DS
D*                                              Qlg Sort Control Block
D QLGLB               1        4B 0
D*                                              Length Block
D QLGRT               5        8B 0
D*                                              Request Type
D QLGRSV1             9       12B 0
D*                                              Reserved1
D QLGTIONS00         13       16B 0
D*                                              Options
D QLGRL              17       20B 0
D*                                              Record Length
D QLGRC              21       24B 0
D*                                              Record Count
D QLGOKL             25       28B 0
D*                                              Offset Key List
D QLGNBRK            29       32B 0
D*                                              Number Keys
D QLGOLI             33       36B 0
D*                                              Offset Lang Info
D QLGOIL             37       40B 0
D*                                              Offset Input List
D QLGNBRIF           41       44B 0
D*                                              Number Input Files
D QLGOOL             45       48B 0
D*                                              Offset Output List
D QLGNBROF           49       52B 0
D*                                              Number Output Files
D QLGLKE             53       56B 0
D*                                              Length Key Entry
D QLGLSS             57       60B 0
D*                                              Length Sort Seq
D QLGLIE             61       64B 0
D*                                              Length Infile Entry
D QLGLOE             65       68B 0
D*                                              Length Outfile Entry
D QLGONM             69       72B 0
D*                                              Offset Null Map
D QLGORI             73       76B 0
D*                                              Offset Record Info
D QLGRSV2            77       80B 0
D*                                              Reserved2
```

Figure 16.1: The QSYSINC definition for QLGSORT'S Request Control Block parameter (part 2 of 2).

QLGSCB is the QSYSINC-provided data structure definition for the request control block. Many fields can be used, but we will only discuss those that apply to the example program. As with all of the APIs introduced in this book, the API documentation available in the Information Center provides a full understanding of the API's capabilities.

The first field, QLGLB, is simply the length of the request control block you pass to the API. The request control block is not of a fixed, predetermined size; you can specify one or more fields to be sorted on, zero or more files to sort, etc.

The second field, QLGRT, is the type of sort request you are making. There are eight supported types:

- Type 1 indicates that you will be sorting one or more input files and want the results returned in a file.

- Type 2 indicates that you will be sorting one or more input files and want the results returned in the Output Data Buffer parameter (the third parameter of the QLGSORT API).

- Type 3 indicates that you will be sorting one or more input files and want the results held by the API until later requested using the QLGSRTIO API.

- Type 4 indicates that you will be sorting data found in the Input Data Buffer parameter (the second parameter of the QLGSORT API) and want the results returned in a file.

- Type 5 indicates that you will be sorting data found in the Input Data Buffer parameter and want the results returned in the Output Data Buffer parameter (the third parameter).

- Type 6 indicates that you will be sorting data found in the Input Data Buffer parameter and want the results held by the API until later requested using the QLGSRTIO API.

- Type 7 indicates that you will be sorting data that is provided in subsequent calls to the QLGSRTIO API and want the results returned in a file.

- Type 8 indicates that you will be sorting data that is provided in subsequent calls to the QLGSRTIO API and want the results held by the API until later requested using the QLGSRTIO API.

As you can see, there is quite a bit of flexibility in terms of what data is to be sorted and how the results are to be returned. The example program uses type 5—the Input Data

Buffer parameter holds the data to be sorted and the Output Data Buffer parameter returns the sorted data. As you will see a bit later, these buffers are really the user-space list-entry data returned by the List Jobs API. We simply treat the appropriate sections of the user space as a large buffer to be passed to the QLGSORT API.

The fifth field, QLGRL, is the record length of the records to be sorted. The example program uses the size of each list entry returned by the List Jobs API. From the discussion of list APIs in earlier chapters, you know this as GenHdr.QUSSEE.

The sixth field, QLGRC, is the number of records to be sorted. The example program uses the number of records returned by the List Jobs API. From the discussion of list APIs in earlier chapters, you know this as GenHdr.QUSNBRLE.

The seventh field, QLGOKL, is an offset to the list of key-field definition structures that we want to sort the data records on. Each key field is described using the structure shown in Figure 16.2.

The eighth field, QLGNBRK, is the number of key field structures found at offset QLGOKL. The example program uses two keys: the simple job name and, within the simple job name, the user name. When you look at the complete sample program, you will see that we have defined an array (dim(5)) of the key field structure shown in Figure 16.2. We use the first two elements of this array.

The fifteenth field, QLGLKE, is the length of each key field structure. Our sample program uses a key field structure length of 20 bytes, the defined length of the QSYSINC-provided data structure shown in Figure 16.2.

As you can see, QLGSKL is the QSYSINC-provided data structure for the key field structure used by the QLGSORT API. The first field, QLGSP, specifies the starting position, within the records to be sorted, of the key field being defined. In the example program, the first field to be sorted on is the simple job name (QUSJNU00) of the List Jobs API reviewed in chapter 13. From the List Jobs API documentation and QSYSINC-provided includes, we know that the starting position for this field is one. As such, a value of one will be used for field QLGSP in the first occurrence of the QLGSKL data structure. In our sample program, the second field to be sorted on is the user name (QUSUNU00). From the List Jobs documentation, we know this starts at position 11. Therefore, a value of 11 will be used for field QLGSP in the second occurrence of the QLGSKL data structure.

```
DName+++++++++++ETDsFrom+++To/L+++IDc.Keywords+++++++++++++++++++++++++
D*********************************************************************
D*Type Definition for the QLGSORT key list.
D*********************************************************************
DQLGSKL          DS
D*                                              Qlg Sort Key List
D QLGSP                  1      4B 0
D*                                              Start Position
D QLGSS                  5      8B 0
D*                                              String Size
D QLGDT                  9     12B 0
D*                                              Data Type
D QLGSO                 13     16B 0
D*                                              Sort Order
D QLGOP                 17     20B 0
D*                                              Ordinal Position
```

Figure 16.2: The QSYSINC definition for QLGSORT'S key list.

The second field, QLGSS, specifies the length in bytes of the key field to be sorted on. A value of 10 will be specified for this field in the first occurrence of the QLGSKL data structure, as the simple job name is 10 bytes long. Likewise, a value of 10 will be specified for this field in the second occurrence of the QLGSKL data structure, as the user name is also 10 bytes long.

Note that we could have used just one occurrence of the QLGSKL data structure in our sample program. Because the simple job name (QUSJNU00) and the user name (QUSUNU00) are contiguous in the list entry record returned by the List Jobs API, we could have used a starting position (QLGSP) of one and a length (QLGSS) of 20. This would have given us the same results as using two occurrences of the QLGSKL key field data structure. This, however, would not have given us the opportunity to demonstrate how to specify multiple key fields when using the QLGSORT API, and we did want to give an example using multiple key fields.

The third field of the QLGSKL data structure, QLGDT, defines the type of data we are sorting on. Many data types can be specified, including the following:

- 1—Signed binary or integer value

- 3—Signed packed decimal value

- 4—Character data with national-language sort sequence applied

- 6—Character data with no national-language sort sequence applied

- 9—Unsigned binary or integer value

- 13—Date, in the form MM/DD/YY

- 16—Date, in the form MM/DD/YYYY

- 18—Time, in the form HH:MM *x*M, where *x* can be A or P for A.M. or P.M.

- 21—Variable-length character data with no national-language sort sequence applied

Our sample program uses a data type of 6 for both the simple job name and the user name.

The fourth field of the QLGSKL data structure, QLGSO, specifies how we want the key field data to be sorted. A value of one indicates ascending order. A value of two indicates descending order. The example program requests ascending order for both the simple job name and the user name.

The fifth field, QLGOP, defines the ordinal position of the key field, relative to all fields in the record to be sorted. This field is not used in the example program. It is related to the handling of null values when sorting database records.

With that introduction to the Request Control Block and Sort Key List parameters of the QLGSORT API, Figure 16.3 shows the original source of Figure 13.1.

```
h dftactgrp(*no) bnddir('APILIB')

FFilename++IPEASFRlen+LKlen+AIDevice+.Keywords+++++++++++++++++++++++++
fFIG13_3   cf   e            workstn sfile(JobRcd :RelRcdNbr)

DName+++++++++++ETDsFrom+++To/L+++IDc.Keywords+++++++++++++++++++++++++
d/copy qsysinc/qrpglesrc,qusgen
d/copy qsysinc/qrpglesrc,qusljob
d/copy qsysinc/qrpglesrc,qusec

dFig13_1          pr                extpgm('FIG13_1')
d UserParm                   10     const
```

Figure 16.3: This program employs QUSLJOBS to list jobs with no particular sort sequence (part 1 of 5).

```
d StatusParm                    10      const

dFig13_1           pi
d UserParm                      10      const
d StatusParm                    10      const

dExists            pr            1      extproc('Exists')
d ObjectName                    10      const
d ObjectType                    10      const
d ObjectLib                     10      const options(*nopass)

dRtvSpcPtr         pr                   extpgm('QUSPTRUS')
d SpcName                       20      const
d UsrSpcPtr                      *
d USEC                                  likeds(QUSEC) options(*nopass)

dCrtUsrSpc         pr            *      extproc('CrtUsrSpc')
d SpcName                       20      const

dListJob           pr                   extpgm('QUSLJOB')
d SpcName                       20      const
d Format                         8      const
d JobName                       26      const
d Status                        10      const
d QUSEC                                 likeds(QUSEC) options(*nopass)
d JobType                        1      const options(*nopass)
d NbrKeyFlds                   10i 0    const options(*nopass)
d KeyFlds                                likeds(KeyFlds) options(*nopass)
d ContinHdl                     48      const options(*nopass)

dSndPgmMsg         pr                   extpgm('QMHSNDPM')
d MsgID                          7      const
d QualMsgF                      20      const
d MsgDta                     65535      const options(*varsize)
d LenMsgDta                    10i 0    const
d MsgType                       10      const
d CallStackEntry            65535      const options(*varsize)
d CallStackCntr                10i 0    const
d MsgKey                         4
d QUSEC                                 likeds(QUSEC)
d LenCSE                       10i 0    const options(*nopass)
d CSEQual                      20      const options(*nopass)
d DSPWaitTime                  10i 0    const options(*nopass)
d CSEType                      10      const options(*nopass)
d CCSID                        10i 0    const options(*nopass)
```

Figure 16.3: *This program employs QUSLJOBS to list jobs with no particular sort sequence (part 2 of 5).*

620

```
d* list API generic header
dGenHdr            ds                        likeds(QUSH0100)
d                                            based(GenHdrPtr)

d* List Job API (QUSLJOB) format JOBL0200
dLstEntry          ds                        likeds(QUSL020001)
d                                            based(LstPtr)

dAttrEntry         ds                        likeds(QUSLKF)
d                                            based(AttrPtr)

dSpcName           ds
d SName                            10        inz('JOBLIST')
d SLib                             10        inz('QTEMP')

dKeyFlds           ds
d KeyValues                        10i 0     dim(25)

dFullJobName       ds
d                                  10        inz('*ALL')
d SelUser                          10        inz('*ALL')
d                                   6        inz('*ALL')

dQualMsgF          ds
d MsgF                             10        inz('MSGS')
d MsgL                             10        inz('SOMELIB')

dNbrJobsDS         ds
d NbrJobs                          10i 0

dSelSts            s               10        inz('*ALL')
dAtrValue          s               10        based(AtrValPtr)
dNbrKeyFlds        s               10i 0
dLstCount          s               10i 0
dAttrCount         s               10i 0
dRelRcdNbr         s                4  0
dMsgKey            s                4

CLON01Factor1+++++++Opcode&ExtFactor2+++++++Result++++++++Len++D+HiLoEq
 /free
  QUSBPRV = 0;

  // Let the user know we're working on it
  SndPgmMsg( 'MSG0004' :QualMsgF :'  ' :0
            :'*STATUS' :'*EXT' :0 :MsgKey :QUSEC);
```

Figure 16.3: This program employs QUSLJOBS to list jobs with no particular sort sequence (part 3 of 5).

```
// If needed, create the user space for the list of jobs
if (Exists( SName :'*USRSPC' : SLib)) = 'N';
   GenHdrPtr = CrtUsrSpc(SpcName);
else;
   RtvSpcPtr( SpcName :GenHdrPtr :QUSEC);
endif;

// Get the list of jobs
if (%parms > 0);
   SelUser = UserParm;
   if (%parms > 1);
      SelSts = StatusParm;
   endif;
endif;

// Set the attribute key values
KeyValues(1) = 1004;              // Job queue name
KeyValues(2) = 1501;              // Output queue name
KeyValues(3) = 1603;              // Printer device name
NbrKeyFlds = 3;

ListJob( SpcName :'JOBL0200' :FullJobName :SelSts :QUSEC
         :'*' :NbrKeyFlds :KeyFlds);

// Check to see if the list is complete
if (GenHdr.QUSIS = 'C') or (GenHdr.QUSIS = 'P');
   NbrJobs = GenHdr.QUSNBRLE;
   SndPgmMsg( 'MSG0005' :QualMsgF :NbrJobsDS :4
              :'*STATUS' :'*EXT' :0 :MsgKey :QUSEC);

   // Get to the first list entry and process the list
   LstPtr = GenHdrPtr + GenHdr.QUSOLD;

   for LstCount = 1 to GenHdr.QUSNBRLE;
       JobName = LstEntry.QUSJNU00;
       JobUser = LstEntry.QUSUNU00;
       JobSts = LstEntry.QUSTATUS01;

       // Get first attribute and process all returned
       if LstEntry.QUSJIS = ' ';
          AttrPtr = LstPtr + %size(QUSL020001);
          for AttrCount = 1 to LstEntry.QUSNBRFR;
              AtrValPtr = AttrPtr + %size(QUSLKF);
              select;
                when AttrEntry.QUSKF = 1004;
                     Jobq = AtrValue;
```

Figure 16.3: This program employs *QUSLJOBS* to list jobs with no particular sort sequence (part 4 of 5).

622

```
                   when AttrEntry.QUSKF = 1501;
                         Outq = AtrValue;
                   when AttrEntry.QUSKF = 1603;
                         Printer = AtrValue;
                 endsl;
                 AttrPtr = AttrPtr + AttrEntry.QUSLFIR;
              endfor;
          else;
              JobQ = *ALL'*';
              Outq = *ALL'*';
              Printer = *ALL'*';
          endif;

          RelRcdNbr += 1;
          write JobRcd;
          LstPtr = LstPtr + GenHdr.QUSSEE;
          if LstCount > 500;
              leave;
          endif;
       endfor;

       if RelRcdNbr > 0;
          *in21 = *on;
          *in24 = *on;
          exfmt JobCtl;
       endif;
     else;
        dsply 'List Object API did not return valid data';
     endif;
     *inlr = *on;
     Return;

/end-free
```

Figure 16.3: This program employs QUSLJOBS to list jobs with no particular sort sequence (part 5 of 5).

Figure 16.4 shows the modified source, in which the list is sorted by user name within job name. In Figure 16.4, the new or changed lines of code are highlighted.

As you can see from Figure 16.4, we have been able to insert the sorting logic with no impact at all to the actual processing of the list! Everything you've learned about list APIs to date still applies, and now you can enhance applications by sorting the list entries without having to change the actual processing within the application. In fact, it would not be that difficult to allow the user to select fields to sort on and have the application program adjust to the user's request by building the appropriate QLGSKL data structures on the fly.

```
h dftactgrp(*no) bnddir('APILIB')

FFilename++IPEASFRlen+LKlen+AIDevice+.Keywords+++++++++++++++++++++++++++++
fFIG13_3   cf   e                   workstn sfile(JobRcd :RelRcdNbr)

DName++++++++++++ETDsFrom+++To/L+++IDc.Keywords+++++++++++++++++++++++++++++
d/copy qsysinc/qrpglesrc,qusgen
d/copy qsysinc/qrpglesrc,qusljob
d/copy qsysinc/qrpglesrc,qlgsort
d/copy qsysinc/qrpglesrc,qusec

dFig16_4           pr                      extpgm('FIG16_4')
d UserParm                     10    const
d StatusParm                   10    const

dFig16_4           pi
d UserParm                     10    const
d StatusParm                   10    const

dExists            pr           1    extproc('Exists')
d ObjectName                   10    const
d ObjectType                   10    const
d ObjectLib                    10    const options(*nopass)

dRtvSpcPtr         pr                      extpgm('QUSPTRUS')
d SpcName                      20    const
d UsrSpcPtr                     *
d USEC                               likeds(QUSEC) options(*nopass)

dCrtUsrSpc         pr           *    extproc('CrtUsrSpc')
d SpcName                      20    const

dListJob           pr                      extpgm('QUSLJOB')
d SpcName                      20    const
d Format                        8    const
d JobName                      26    const
d Status                       10    const
d QUSEC                              likeds(QUSEC) options(*nopass)
d JobType                       1    const options(*nopass)
d NbrKeyFlds                  10i 0  const options(*nopass)
d KeyFlds                            likeds(KeyFlds) options(*nopass)
d ContinHdl                    48    const options(*nopass)

dSndPgmMsg         pr                      extpgm('QMHSNDPM')
d MsgID                         7    const
d QualMsgF                     20    const
```

Figure 16.4: Sorting the output list of List Jobs (QUSLJOB) (part 1 of 5).

```
d MsgDta                      65535    const options(*varsize)
d LenMsgDta                   10i 0 const
d MsgType                     10       const
d CallStackEntry              65535    const options(*varsize)
d CallStackCntr               10i 0 const
d MsgKey                      4
d QUSEC                                likeds(QUSEC)
d LenCSE                      10i 0 const options(*nopass)
d CSEQual                     20       const options(*nopass)
d DSPWaitTime                 10i 0 const options(*nopass)
d CSEType                     10       const options(*nopass)
d CCSID                       10i 0 const options(*nopass)

dSort             pr                   extpgm('QLGSORT')
d ReqControl                  65535    const options(*varsize)
d Input                       65535    options(*varsize)
d Output                      1        options(*varsize)
d LengthOutput                10i 0 const
d LengthReturn                10i 0
d QUSEC                                likeds(QUSEC)
d RtnRcdFeedback              1        options(*varsize :*nopass)
d LengthRtnFB                 10i 0 options(*nopass)

d* list API generic header
dGenHdr           ds                   likeds(QUSH0100)
d                                      based(GenHdrPtr)

d* List Job API (QUSLJOB) format JOBL0200
dLstEntry         ds                   likeds(QUSL020001)
d                                      based(LstPtr)

dAttrEntry        ds                   likeds(QUSLKF)
d                                      based(AttrPtr)

dSpcName          ds
d SName                       10       inz('JOBLIST')
d SLib                        10       inz('QTEMP')

dKeyFlds          ds
d KeyValues                   10i 0 dim(25)

dFullJobName      ds
d                             10       inz('*ALL')
d SelUser                     10       inz('*ALL')
d                             6        inz('*ALL')
```

Figure 16.4: Sorting the output list of List Jobs (QUSLJOB) (part 2 of 5).

```
dQualMsgF          ds
d MsgF                          10      inz('MSGS')
d MsgL                          10      inz('SOMELIB')

dNbrJobsDS         ds
d NbrJobs                       10i 0

dReqControl        ds                  qualified
d SCB                                  likeds(QLGSCB)
d SKL                                  likeds(QLGSKL) dim(5)

dSelSts            s            10      inz('*ALL')
dAtrValue          s            10      based(AtrValPtr)
dNbrKeyFlds        s            10i 0
dLstCount          s            10i 0
dAttrCount         s            10i 0
dRelRcdNbr         s            4   0
dMsgKey            s            4
dLenRtnDta         s            10i 0

CLON01Factor1+++++++Opcode&ExtFactor2+++++++Result++++++++Len++D+HiLoEq
 /free
  QUSBPRV = 0;

  // Let the user know we're working on it
  SndPgmMsg( 'MSG0004' :QualMsgF :' ' :0
            :'*STATUS' :'*EXT' :0 :MsgKey :QUSEC);

  // If needed, create the user space for the list of jobs
  if (Exists( SName :'*USRSPC' :SLib)) = 'N';
     GenHdrPtr =CrtUsrSpc(SpcName);
  else;
     RtvSpcPtr( SpcName :GenHdrPtr :QUSEC);
  endif;

  // Get the list of jobs
  if (%parms > 0);
     SelUser = UserParm;
     if (%parms > 1);
        SelSts = StatusParm;
     endif;
  endif;

  // Set the attribute key values
  KeyValues(1) = 1004;                // Job queue name
  KeyValues(2) = 1501;                // Output queue name
```

Figure 16.4: Sorting the output list of List Jobs (QUSLJOB) (part 3 of 5).

```
KeyValues(3) = 1603;                    // Printer device name
NbrKeyFlds = 3;

ListJob( SpcName :'JOBL0200' :FullJobName :SelSts :QUSEC
        :'*' :NbrKeyFlds :KeyFlds);

// Check to see if the list is complete
if (GenHdr.QUSIS = 'C') or (GenHdr.QUSIS = 'P');
    NbrJobs = GenHdr.QUSNBRLE;
    SndPgmMsg( 'MSG0005' :QualMsgF :NbrJobsDS :4
               :'*STATUS' :'*EXT' :0 :MsgKey :QUSEC);

    // Get to the first list entry and process the list
    LstPtr = GenHdrPtr + GenHdr.QUSOLD;

    // Sort the results
    ReqControl = *loval;
    ReqControl.SCB.QLGLB = %size(ReqControl);
    ReqControl.SCB.QLGRT = 5;                // Use buffers
    ReqControl.SCB.QLGRL = GenHdr.QUSSEE;    // Size of record
    ReqControl.SCB.QLGRC = GenHdr.QUSNBRLE;  // Number of records
    ReqControl.SCB.QLGOKL =                  // Set offset to sort keys
               %addr(ReqControl.SKL(1)) - %addr(ReqControl);
    ReqControl.SCB.QLGNBRK = 2;              // Two keys
    ReqControl.SCB.QLGLKE = %size(QLGSKL);   // Size of one key entry
    ReqControl.SKL(1).QLGSP = 1;       // First key is job name
    ReqControl.SKL(1).QLGSS = 10;      // Key is 10 bytes long
    ReqControl.SKL(1).QLGDT = 6;       // Key is character
    ReqControl.SKL(1).QLGSO = 1;       // Ascending order
    ReqControl.SKL(2).QLGSP = 11;      // Second key is user name
    ReqControl.SKL(2).QLGSS = 10;      // Key is 10 bytes long
    ReqControl.SKL(2).QLGDT = 6;       // Key is character
    ReqControl.SKL(2).QLGSO = 1;       // Ascending order

    Sort(ReqControl :LstEntry :LstEntry
         :(GenHdr.QUSSEE * GenHdr.QUSNBRLE) :LenRtnDta :QUSEC);

    for LstCount = 1 to GenHdr.QUSNBRLE;
        JobName = LstEntry.QUSJNU00;
        JobUser = LstEntry.QUSUNU00;
        JobSts = LstEntry.QUSTATUS01;

        // Get first attribute and process all returned
        if LstEntry.QUSJIS = ' ';
            AttrPtr = LstPtr + %size(QUSL020001);
            for AttrCount = 1 to LstEntry.QUSNBRFR;
```

Figure 16.4: Sorting the output list of List Jobs (QUSLJOB) (part 4 of 5).

```
                        AtrValPtr = AttrPtr + %size(QUSLKF);
                        select;
                          when AttrEntry.QUSKF = 1004;
                              Jobq = AtrValue;
                          when AttrEntry.QUSKF = 1501;
                              Outq = AtrValue;
                          when AttrEntry.QUSKF = 1603;
                              Printer = AtrValue;
                        endsl;
                        AttrPtr = AttrPtr + AttrEntry.QUSLFIR;
                    endfor;
                  else;
                     JobQ = *All'*';
                     Outq = *ALL'*';
                     Printer = *ALL'*';
                  endif;

                  RelRcdNbr += 1;
                  write JobRcd;
                  LstPtr = LstPtr + GenHdr.QUSSEE;
                  if LstCount > 500;
                      leave;
                  endif;
              endfor;

              if RelRcdNbr > 0;
                  *in21 = *on;
                  *in24 = *on;
                  exfmt JobCtl;
              endif;
          else;
             dsply 'List Object API did not return valid data';
          endif;
          *inlr = *on;
          Return;

      /end-free
```

Figure 16.4: Sorting the output list of List Jobs (QUSLJOB) (part 5 of 5).

Along these lines of user customization, a bit later in this chapter, you'll see some user-application APIs that allow your application programs to "remember" what a given user's preference was the last time he or she ran an application. This is conceptually similar to the Source Entry Utility (SEU) "remembering" what file and member you worked with last.

The highlighted portions of Figure 16.4 show that the following definition changes were made:

- Include the QSYSINC definitions for QLGSORT.

- Change the program prototype name from FIG13_1 to FIG16_4.

- Provide a function prototype for the QLGSORT API.

- Define the data structure ReqControl for the request control block.

- Within the ReqControl data structure, define an array of sort-key list data structures (SKL). Although the example program only uses two elements of the SKL array, it is declared as having five elements to demonstrate that you can define a very large array and then customize it, at run time, to the actual requirements of the application

- Define the variable LenRtnDta for the length of returned data returned in parameter 5 of the QLGSORT API

In addition, the following logic was inserted into the original FIG13_1 program immediately after calling the List Jobs API and setting the LstPtr pointer variable to the first list entry:

- Initialize the ReqControl data structure to all x'00's, as this is an input to the QLGSORT API and the reserved fields are documented as needing to be set to x'00'.

- Set the size of the request control block (ReqControl.SCB.QLGLB) to the compiler-generated size of the ReqControl data structure.

- Set the request type (ReqControl.SCB.QLGRT) to a value of five.

- Set the record length (ReqControl.SCB.QLGRL) to the value of a single list entry returned by the List Jobs API.

- Set the number of records (ReqControl.SCB.QLGRC) to the number of list entries returned by the List Jobs API.

- Set the offset to the sort-key list array (ReqControl.SCB.QLGOKL) by subtracting the address of the ReqControl data structure from the address of the first element of the sort key array (SKL). We could have hard-coded a value of 80 for the offset, but having the compiler calculate the offset is much more flexible. If IBM were to add new fields at the end of the QLGSCB data structure, and we had hard-coded the offset value as being 80, we would have to manually re-edit this value if we were to recompile FIG16_4 and pick up the newer (larger) definition of QLGSCB from QSYSINC. This would be true even if our reason for re-compiling was totally independent of our use of the QLGSORT API. By having the compiler calculate the offset, our application will automatically adjust for the larger definition of the QLGSCB data structure (and with the earlier ReqControl = *LOVAL; operation, make sure that the now larger QLGSCB data structure is properly initialized). If we want to use the new fields that IBM has added (presumably for new function), we could change our application program to take advantage of them. That type of change is our choice, so long as we avoid hard-coding values such as offsets.

- Set the number of keys to sort on (ReqControl.SCB.QLGLKE) to a value of two, indicating that the first two elements of the SKL array are to be used.

- Set the size of one element of the SKL array to the compiler-generated size. As in the discussion of ReqControl.SCB.QLGOKL and the offset to the sort key list, we do not want to hard-code any values if we don't have to.

- Define the first element of the SKL array, requesting that the simple job name be sorted in ascending order without national sort sequence.

- Define the second element of the SKL array, requesting that the user name be sorted, within the simple job name, in ascending order without national-language sort sequence

- Call the QLGSORT API.

Now that we've finally gotten to actually calling the Sort API, let's resume the earlier discussion of the QLGSORT API parameters. As mentioned earlier, parameter 1, Request Control Block, defines the specifications of the sort.

The second parameter, Input Data Buffer, represents the data to be sorted when the request type is 4, 5, or 6. The example program specifies a request type of 5. When calling the QLGSORT API, we simply pass the BASED data structure LstEntry, which represents the first list entry returned from the List Jobs API. This is possible due to the previous assignment (LstPtr = GenHdrPtr + GenHdr.QUSOLD). We are essentially treating the user-space list entries as simply one large variable within our application program.

The third parameter, Output Data Buffer, is used to return the sorted results when the request type is 2 or 5. The example program specifies a request type of 5, use the output data buffer. When calling the QLGSORT API, we simply pass the same BASED data structure LstEntry used for the second parameter. We are essentially performing a sort in place, using the allocated space of the user space. You don't have to use the same buffer for both input and output; we did simply to demonstrate that you can.

The fourth parameter, Length of Output Data Buffer, defines how much storage has been allocated for the returned data. The example program calculates the size of available space in the user space by multiplying the number of list entries currently in the user space (GenHdr.QUSNBRLE) by the size of each entry currently in the user space (GenHdr.QUSSEE).

The fifth parameter is the length of the sorted data returned by the QLGSORT API. The sixth parameter is the standard API error-code structure. The seventh and eighth parameters are related to feedback information relative to having the sorted data returned to database files. These optional parameters are not used in the example program.

That's it! With this information as a guide, you should be able to sort the results of any list API that returns fixed-size list entries. As an added benefit, you can sort a whole lot of other data, too, data such as records in database files and program variable values within your application programs. You should find that this API is flexible enough to meet most, if not all, of your sorting requirements. In fact, this API (and the related QLGSRTIO API) is currently being used by i5/OS commands such as Format Data (FMT-DTA) and high-level language support such as ILE COBOL's SORT.

User Application Information APIs

The user-application-information family of APIs allow you to store and retrieve application-related data for a particular user profile. These APIs are ideal for storing information about preferences or last use, which enable an application to customize its behavior. An example of this type of application usage could be IBM's Source Entry Utility (SEU) and the support for *PRV (previous) with the STRSEU command-parameters source file (SRCFILE) and source member (SRCMBR). (SEU does not actually use the user-application information APIs because it predates them by many years, but that doesn't negate the usefulness of the example.)

With these APIs, you can essentially store any application-related data you want to associate with the user profile. Unlike storing this information in your own database file, where you need to manage it, i5/OS automatically saves and restores this application-related data when you save or restore the associated user profile.

The Update User Application Information API, QsyUpdateUserApplicationInfo

The Update User Application Information API allows you to update specific application-related information for a user profile. The parameters for the QSYUPDATEUSERAPPLICATIONINFO API are shown in Table 16.2.

Table 16.2: Parameters for the QsyUpdateUserApplicationInfo API			
Parameter	Description	Type	Size
1	User Profile	Input	Char(10)
2	Application Information ID	Input	Char(*)
3	Length of Application Information ID	Input	Binary(4)
4	Application Information	Input	Char(*)
5	Length of Application Information	Input	Binary(4)
6	First Valid Release	Input	Char(6)
7	Error Code	I/O	Char(*)

The first parameter, User Profile, is the profile for which the application-related information is to be updated. The one special value supported, *CURRENT, indicates that the application information is to be updated for the user profile currently in effect for the job.

The second parameter, Application Information ID, identifies the application for which information is being updated. This is a text field up to 200 bytes long. IBM recommends that application developers use an application ID that starts with the name of the developer's company to minimize the likelihood of two independent applications both using the same application ID. IBM, for instance, prefixes all i5/OS application IDs with "IBM_ccc_name" where ccc is an IBM component identifier and name is some (hopefully) meaningful name selected by IBM. Our example program uses an application information ID of "ABC_COMPANY_SOME_UTILITY," where "ABC_COMPANY" represents our fictitious company and "SOME_UTILITY" is the name of our application offering. The ID must be formed using only the uppercase letters A through Z, the digits 0 through 9, the period (.), and the underscore (_). It is recommended that the underscore be used to separate words within the ID.

The third parameter, Length of Application Information ID, is the length of the ID passed in the second parameter.

The fourth parameter, Application Information, is a free-form field containing whatever information the application wants to associate with the user profile. Our example program uses a data structure containing a library name, a file name, a member name, and a member type, but you are free to store any information that you find useful. This information can be up to 1,700 bytes long. You can have multiple occurrences of these 1,700-byte entries associated with the user profile, as you will see later in this chapter when we review the Retrieve User Application Information API.

The fifth parameter, Length of Application Information, is the length of the application information passed in the fourth parameter.

The sixth parameter, First Valid Release, is used by i5/OS to determine whether the application information should be saved when saving a user profile to a previous release. The format of this parameter is "VxRyMz," where x is the version, y is the release, and z is the modification level. An example would be "V5R4M0."

The seventh parameter is the standard API error-code structure.

Our example program for storing application information with a user profile is shown in Figure 16.5. The program is sufficiently straightforward that we won't go into any details on the processing logic.

```
h dftactgrp(*no)

DName++++++++++++ETDsFrom+++To/L+++IDc.Keywords++++++++++++++++++++++++
d/copy qsysinc/qrpglesrc,qusec

dUpdUsrInf        pr                  extproc(
d                                     'QsyUpdateUserApplicationInfo')
d UsrPrf                      10      const
d ApplID                   65535      const options(*varsize)
d LenApplID                 10i 0     const
d ApplInfo                 65535      const options(*varsize)
d LenApplInfo               10i 0     const
```

Figure 16.5: Updating user application information with the QSYUPDATEUSERAPPLICATIONINFO API (part 1 of 2).

633

```
d Release                      6        const
d QUSEC                                 likeds(QUSEC)

dApplInfo        ds
d Library                      10
d File                         10
d Member                       10
d Type                         10

dApplID          s             200      inz('ABC_COMPANY_SOME_UTILITY')
dRelease         s             6        inz('V5R3M0')

CL0N01Factor1+++++++Opcode&ExtFactor2+++++++Result+++++++Len++D+HiLoEq
 /free
   QUSBPRV = 0;

   // Set the values that we want to save for the current user
   Library = 'SOMELIB';
   File = 'QRPGLESRC';
   Member = 'FIGXX';
   Type = 'RPGLE';

   // Save the values
   UpdUsrInf( '*CURRENT' :ApplID :%len(%trim(ApplID))
              :ApplInfo :%size(ApplInfo) :Release :QUSEC);

   *inlr = *on;
   return;
 /end-free
```

Figure 16.5: Updating user application information with the *QSYUPDATEUSERAPPLICATIONINFO* API (part 2 of 2).

Now that you have seen how to save application-related information associated with a user profile, let's turn to the Retrieve User Application Information API and a more complete example.

The Retrieve User Application Information API, QsyRetrieveUserApplicationInfo

The Retrieve User Application Information API allows you to retrieve a list of application information entries associated with a given user profile. The parameters for the QSYRETRIEVEUSERAPPLICATIONINFO API are shown in Table 16.3.

634

Table 16.3: Parameters for the QsyRetrieveUserApplicationInfo API			
Parameter	Description	Type	Size
1	Receiver Variable	Output	Char(*)
2	Length of Receiver Variable	Input	Binary(4)
3	Returned Records Feedback Information	Output	Char(12)
4	Format Name	Input	Char(8)
5	User Profile	Input	Char(10)
6	Application Information ID	Input	Char(*)
7	Length of Application Information ID	Input	Binary(4)
8	Error Code	I/O	Char(*)

The first parameter, Receiver Variable, is the parameter that will receive the application-related information. Unlike many retrieve-type APIs, this receiver variable does not contain the Bytes Returned and Bytes Available fields often associated with receiver variables. Instead, this information is returned in the third parameter. The second parameter, Length of Receiver Variable, defines the allocated size of the Receiver Variable parameter.

The third parameter, Returned Records Feedback Information, provides information about the data returned in the first parameter. The QSYSINC-provided definition for this data structure is shown in Figure 16.6.

```
DName++++++++++ETDsFrom+++To/L+++IDc.Keywords++++++++++++++++++++++++
D********************************************************************
D*Record structure for Return Records Feedback Information
D********************************************************************
DQSYUAIFI         DS
D*                                          Qsy RUAI Feedback Info
D QSYBRTN15               1      4B 0
D*                                          Bytes Returned
D QSYBAVL15               5      8B 0
D*                                          Bytes Available
D QSYNBRER04              9     12B 0
D*                                          Number Entries Returned
```

Figure 16.6: The QSYSINC definition for feedback from QSYRETRIEVEUSERAPPLICATIONINFO.

The QSYSINC include defines the data structure QSYUAIFI and three subfields. The first field, QSYBRTN15, represents the number of bytes returned in the first parameter. The second field, QSYBAVL15, represents the number of bytes available to be returned in the first parameter. The third field, QSYNBRER04, represents the number of application information entries returned in the first parameter.

Note that a value of zero for QSYBAVL15 indicates that no application-related information is available for the requested user profile, for the specified application information ID. This generally indicates that you have a new user to your application and that default values should be used for the application information.

The fourth parameter, Format Name, defines what type of data is to be returned to the API caller. The only supported format is RUAI0100. The QSYSINC definition for this format is shown in Figure 16.7.

```
DName++++++++++ETDsFrom+++To/L+++IDc.Keywords++++++++++++++++++++++++++
D*********************************************************************
D*Record structure for RUAI0100 format
D*********************************************************************
DQSYI010004      DS
D*                                        Qsy RUAI0100
D QSYEL10                1      4B 0
D*                                        Entry Length
D QSYAIID                5      204
D*                                        Application Info ID
D QSYDAI               205      208B 0
D*                                        Displacement Application
D QSYLAI               209      212B 0
D*                                        Length Application Info
D QSYIDOAI             213      216B 0
D*                                        CCSID of Application Inf
D QSYFVR               217      222
D*                                        First Valid Release
D*QSYAI00              223      223
D*
D*                                        Varying length
```

Figure 16.7: The QSYSINC definition for format RUAI0100 of QSYRETRIEVEUSERAPPLICATIONINFO.

The QSYSINC-provided data structure QSYI010004 has six fixed-size fields and one variable-length field. The first field, QSYEL10, is the length of the current application information entry. This value is used when moving from one application information entry to the next when multiple entries have been returned by the API. Multiple entries can be returned because the API supports generic names for the Application Information ID parameter.

The second field, QSYAIID, is the application information ID for the returned entry.

The third field, QSYDAI, is the displacement to the application information associated with this application information ID. Here, *displacement* means that QSYDAI is relative to the start of the current entry, not the start of the receiver variable. If QSYDAI was relative to the start of the receiver variable, it would be defined as an *offset* rather than a displacement.

The fourth field, QSYLAI, is the length of the application information associated with the application information ID. The fifth field, QSYIDOAI, is the CCSID of the application information. This value is the default CCSID of the last job that updated the application information. The sixth field, QSYFVR, is the first valid release for this application information.

The seventh field, which is commented in the QSYSINC definition, represents the variable-length application information. It is commented in the QSYSINC definition because the location of the field is variable (determined by the field QSYDAI) and the length is unknown at compile time (determined at run time by the field QSYLAI). As such, there isn't much of a static definition that IBM can supply in the compile-time QSYSINC include. Our sample program defines our application information as a BASED structure. We then set the basing pointer to the address of the current entry plus the displacement to the application information, to access the values of the application information.

The fifth parameter of the QSYRETRIEVEUSERAPPLICATIONINFO, User Profile, is the user profile for which the application-related information is to be retrieved. The one special value supported, *CURRENT, indicates that the application information is to be retrieved for the user profile currently in effect for the job.

The sixth parameter, Application Information ID, identifies the application ID for which information is being retrieved. This can be a specific application information ID or a generic name such as "ABC_COMPANY_*." Using a generic value can be useful when you need to store more than 1,700 bytes of information for a given application information ID. You could, for instance, use application information IDs of "ABC_COMPANY_SOME_UTILITY_001" and "ABC_COMPANY_SOME_UTILITY_002." You could then retrieve all application information related to a given application using an argument such as "ABC_COMPANY_SOME_UTILITY_*."

The seventh parameter, Length of Application Information ID, is the length of the ID passed in the sixth parameter. The eighth parameter is the standard API error-code structure.

With that introduction to the QSYRETRIEVEUSERAPPLICATIONINFO API, Figure 16.8 shows a sample program that both retrieves and updates user-application-related information. The FIG16_8 program first retrieves the application-related information to access the proper environment for the current user. If no entry is found, it sets an appropriate default environment. Just prior to exiting, FIG16_8 updates the application-related information. This is done so that the most current information is available to FIG16_8 when the program is next called for the same user.

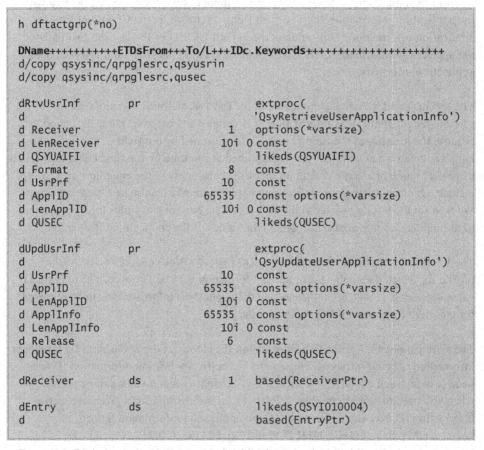

```
h dftactgrp(*no)

DName+++++++++++ETDsFrom+++To/L+++IDc.Keywords+++++++++++++++++++++++
d/copy qsysinc/qrpglesrc,qsyusrin
d/copy qsysinc/qrpglesrc,qusec

dRtvUsrInf        pr                      extproc(
d                                         'QsyRetrieveUserApplicationInfo')
d Receiver                       1        options(*varsize)
d LenReceiver                   10i 0     const
d QSYUAIFI                                likeds(QSYUAIFI)
d Format                         8        const
d UsrPrf                        10        const
d ApplID                     65535        const options(*varsize)
d LenApplID                    10i 0 const
d QUSEC                                   likeds(QUSEC)

dUpdUsrInf        pr                      extproc(
d                                         'QsyUpdateUserApplicationInfo')
d UsrPrf                        10        const
d ApplID                     65535        const options(*varsize)
d LenApplID                    10i 0 const
d ApplInfo                   65535        const options(*varsize)
d LenApplInfo                  10i 0 const
d Release                       6        const
d QUSEC                                   likeds(QUSEC)

dReceiver         ds                      1        based(ReceiverPtr)

dEntry            ds                      likeds(QSYI010004)
d                                         based(EntryPtr)
```

Figure 16.8: Retrieving and updating user application information (part 1 of 3).

```
dApplInfo       ds                      based(ApplInfoPtr)
d                                       likeds(CurInfo)

dCurInfo        ds
d Library                       10
d File                          10
d Member                        10
d Type                          10

dReceiverPtr    s               *
dApplID         s               200  inz('ABC_COMPANY_SOME_UTILITY')
dRelease        s               6    inz('V5R3M0')
dwait           s               1
CLON01Factor1+++++++Opcode&ExtFactor2+++++++Result++++++++Len++D+HiLoEq
 /free
  QUSBPRV = 0;

  // Determine how much data is available
  RtvUsrInf( QSYI010004 :%size(QSYI010004) :QSYUAIFI :'RUAI0100'
            :'*CURRENT' :ApplID :%len(%trim(ApplID)) :QUSEC);

  // Is this a new user?
  if (QSYBAVL15 = 0);                     // Set defaults
     Library = '*CURLIB';
     File = 'QRPGLESRC';
     Member = '*FIRST';
     Type = 'RPGLE';

  else;
     ReceiverPtr = %alloc(QSYBAVL15);    // Allocate storage for info
     RtvUsrInf( Receiver :QSYBAVL15 :QSYUAIFI :'RUAI0100'
               :'*CURRENT' :ApplID :%len(%trim(ApplID)) :QUSEC);
     EntryPtr = ReceiverPtr;
     ApplInfoPtr = EntryPtr + Entry.QSYDAI;
     Library = ApplInfo.Library;
     File = ApplInfo.File;
     Member = ApplInfo.Member;
     Type = ApplInfo.Type;
  endif;

  // Run your application.  We assume the user may change any
  // of the CurInfo values as part of their work.
  // For the sample program, just DSPLY what was found
  dsply ('The last used file was ' +
        %trimr(Library) + '/' + %trimr(File));
```

Figure 16.8: Retrieving and updating user application information (part 2 of 3).

```
dsply ('The member was ' + %trimr(Member) + ' with type ' + Type)
        ' ' wait;

// Save the current values
UpdUsrInf( '*CURRENT' :ApplID :%len(%trim(ApplID))
            :CurInfo :%size(CurInfo) :Release :QUSEC);

dealloc ReceiverPtr;
*inlr = *on;
return;
/end-free
```

Figure 16.8: Retrieving and updating user application information (part 3 of 3).

Program FIG16_8 uses two pointers, ReceiverPtr and EntryPtr. We are only processing one application information entry, so we could have used just one pointer, but we chose to use one for the receiver variable itself (ReceiverPtr) and another for the entry currently being processed (EntryPtr). If multiple application-information entries were being processed, the value of EntryPtr would, after the initial or current entry was processed, be set to the start of the next entry (EntryPtr += Entry.QSYEL10;). This new EntryPtr value would then be used as the base value for accessing the application information (ApplInfoPtr = EntryPtr + Entry.QSYDAI;). ReceiverPtr would remain at its initial value (from the previous %ALLOC built-in operation) and be used when ending the program to deallocate the storage associated with the receiver variable.

Determining the System Release with the Retrieve Product Information API, QSZRTVPR

If you develop applications for multiple systems that might be on different release levels of the operating system, you'll want to know what release level your application is currently running on. As you might expect, there's an API for that: Retrieve Product Information (QSZRTVPR). Through the use of special values, this API allows you to easily determine the release level of the operating system, even if IBM decides in the future to change product IDs such the 5722-SS1 product ID currently used for i5/OS.

The parameters for the Retrieve Product Information API are shown in Table 16.4. The first three parameters (Receiver Variable, Length of Receiver Variable, and Format Name) are standard parameters found in most retrieve-type APIs.

Table 16.4: Parameters for the Retrieve Product Information API, QSZRTVPR			
Parameter	Description	Type	Size
1	Receiver Variable	Output	Char(*)
2	Length of Receiver Variable	Input	Binary(4)
3	Format Name	Input	Char(8)
4	Product Information	Input	Char(*)
5	Error Code	I/O	Char(*)
Optional Parameter Group 1			
6	Product Information Format Name	Input	Char(8)

The Retrieve Product Information API supports several different formats:

- PRDR0100—Basic information about the product, such as the product ID and release level

- PRDR0200—Basic information about the product, along with library-related information

- PRDR0300—Basic information about the product, along with folder-related information

- PRDR0400—Basic information about the product, along with packaged-object-related information

- PRDR0500—Basic information about the product, along with option-related information

- PRDR0600—Basic information about the product, along with option-related information tied to release levels

- PRDR0700—Information about what releases of the operating system are valid between a specified release and the current release

- PRDR0800—Basic information about the product, along with directory-related information

- PRDR0900—Basic information about the product along with packaged object about the software agreement

Our sample program uses format PRDR0100. The QSYSINC-provided definition for this format is shown in Figure 16.9.

```
DName+++++++++++ETDsFrom+++To/L+++IDc.Keywords++++++++++++++++++++++++
D********************************************************************
D*Structure for PRDR0100 format
D****
*
D*NOTE:  The following type definition only defines the fixed
D*    portion of the format.  Any varying length fields must
D*    be defined by the user.
D********************************************************************
DQSZR0100        DS
D*                                                  Qsz PRDR0100
D QSZBRTN              1      4B 0
D*                                                  Bytes Returned
D QSZBAVL              5      8B 0
D*                                                  Bytes Available
D QSZRSV1              9     12B 0
D*                                                  Reserved 1
D QSZPI01             13     19
D*                                                  Product Id
D QSZRL03             20     25
D*                                                  Release Level
D QSZPO01             26     29
D*                                                  Product Option
D QSZLI02             30     33
D*                                                  Load Id
D QSZLT00             34     43
D*                                                  Load Type
D QSZSLS              44     53
D*                                                  Symbolic Load State
D QSZLEI              54     63
D*                                                  Load Error Indicator
D QSZLS               64     65
D*                                                  Load State
D QSZSF               66     66
D*                                                  Supported Flag
D QSZRT               67     68
D*                                                  Registration Type
D QSZRV               69     82
D*                                                  Registration Value
D QSZRSV2             83     84
D*                                                  Reserved 2
D QSZOAI              85     88B 0
D*                                                  Ofst Addn Info
D QSZPLL              89     92
D*                                                  Prim Lng Lod
```

Figure 16.9: The QSYSINC definition for QSZRTVPR format PRDR0100 (part 1 of 2).

D QSZMTR00	93	98	
D*			Min Tgt Rls
D QSZVRMBR	99	104	
D*			Min VRM Base Req
D QSZVRMRM	105	105	
D*			Base Opt VRM Reqs Met
D QSZLEVEL	106	108	
D*			Level
D*QSZRSV3	109	109	
D*			
D*			Varying length field

Figure 16.9: The QSYSINC definition for QSZRTVPR format PRDR0100 (part 2 of 2).

Within the QSYSINC-provided data structure QSZR0100 are quite a few subfields. We're only interested in one—QSZRL03, the release level—so we'll simply point you to IBM's Information Center for the documentation on the others. While there, you might also want to briefly look at the wealth of information available with the other formats that the Retrieve Product Information API supports, along with the other APIs related to software products. The field QSZRL03 is defined as a 6-byte character field containing the release level of the product retrieved. The format of the returned field is VxRyMz, where x is the version number, y is the release number, and z is the modification level. An example of this format is "V5R4M0."

The fourth parameter of the QSZRTVPR API, Product Information, is a structure where you specify what product you want to retrieve information about. The fifth parameter is the standard API error-code structure.

The sixth parameter, Product Information Format Name, is an optional parameter that defines the layout of the fourth parameter, Product Information. There are two supported formats:

- PRDI0100 allows you to specify the product ID, release level, product option, and load ID of the product you want information on.

- PRDI0200 allows you to specify the same information as format PRDI0100, plus the CCSID in which directory names are to be returned.

Our sample program uses format PRDI0100. This format is also the default when the Product Information Format Name parameter is not passed to the Retrieve Product Information API. The QSYSINC-provided definition for format PRDI0100 is shown in Figure 16.10.

```
DName+++++++++++ETDsFrom+++To/L+++IDc.Keywords++++++++++++++++++++++++
D*******************************************************************
D*Structure for the Product Information Format - PRDIO100
D*******************************************************************
DQSZPIR           DS
D*                                              Qsz Product Info Rec
D QSZPI00                  1      7
D*                                              Product Id
D QSZRL02                  8     13
D*                                              Release Level
D QSZP000                 14     17
D*                                              Product Option
D QSZLI01                 18     27
D*                                              Load Id
```

Figure 16.10: The QSYSINC definition for QPZRTVPR format PRDIO100.

Within the QSYSINC-provided data structure QSZPIR are several subfields. Unlike our discussion of the previous PRDR0100 format returned in the receiver variable, where we only examined the field QSZRL03, we will now look at each of the fields defined for format PRDI0100.

The first field, QSZPI00, is the product ID of the product to be retrieved. The product ID can either be a specific product, such as 5722SS1, or the special value *OPSYS. *OPSYS indicates that we want information on the product ID in use by the operating system for a specified release level. Our sample program uses the special value *OPSYS.

The second field, QSZRL02, is the release level of the product specified with field QSZPI00. The release level can be specific, such as V5R4M0, or one of several special values. The supported special values are *CUR to indicate that we want the release level of the operating system currently installed, *ONLY to indicate that we want the only release level currently loaded on the system for the product identified with field QSZPI00, and *PRV to indicate that we want the release level of the product that is previous to the current release of the operating system. The sample program uses the special value *CUR.

The third field, QSZP000, is the product option of the product to be retrieved. The operating system always has a base option of 0000, and that is the value used in our sample program.

The fourth field, QSZLI01, is the load ID of the product to be retrieved. The special value *CODE indicates that we are interested in the code associated with the product identified with field QSZPI00. Other valid load IDs represent the national-language version used by

644

the product. A load ID of 2924, for example, indicates an English-language version. The sample program uses the special value *CODE so that we are not dependent on the national language in use on the system.

In reviewing the four fields defined with format PRDI0100, you will notice that the sample program is using only special values. This use of special values, as opposed to hard-coded product information, allows us to determine the current release level of the system even if IBM elects, in the future, to change the product ID associated with the operating system. Figure 16.11 shows the source for our sample program.

```
h dftactgrp(*no)

DName++++++++++++ETDsFrom+++To/L+++IDc.Keywords++++++++++++++++++++++++++
d/copy qsysinc/qrpglesrc,qszrtvpr
d/copy qsysinc/qrpglesrc,qusec

dRtvPrdInf        pr                    extpgm('QSZRTVPR')
d Receiver                    1         options(*varsize)
d LenReceiver                10i 0      const
d Format                      8         const
d PrdInf                  65535         const options(*varsize)
d QUSEC                                 likeds(QUSEC)
d PrdInfFmt                   8         const options(*nopass)

dwait             s          1

CLON01Factor1+++++++Opcode&ExtFactor2+++++++Result+++++++Len++D+HiLoEq
 /free
   QUSBPRV = 0;

   QSZPI00 = '*OPSYS';               // Operating system
   QSZRL02 = '*CUR';                 // Release currently installed
   QSZP000 = '0000';                 // Base product option
   QSZLI01 = '*CODE';                // Code

   RtvPrdInf ( QSZR0100 :%size (QSZR0100) :'PRDR0100' :QSZPIR :QUSEC);

   dsply ('The current release is ' + QSZRL03) ' ' wait;

   *inlr = *on;
   return;
 /end-free
```

Figure 16.11: Retrieve the current release of i5/OS.

As you can see, determining the release level of the operating system is quite straightforward. The program sets the Bytes Provided field of the error-code structure to zero, indicating that errors should be returned as exception messages. It then initializes the four fields of the QSZRO100 data structure to the special values discussed earlier, calls the Retrieve Product Information API, DSPLYs the current release level of the operating system, and ends.

The List Save File API, QSRLSAVF, and Continuation Handles

When automating system operations, one of the first areas often looked at is related to the saving and restoring of objects on the system. To assist in the automation of restores, it is often necessary to know what has been saved to a particular save file. There is, of course, an API to help in this area: List Save File, QSRLSAVF. The parameters for the List Save File API are shown in Table 16.5.

Table 16.5: Parameters for the List Save File API, QSRLSAVF			
Parameter	Description	Type	Size
1	Qualified User Space Name	Input	Char(20)
2	Format Name	Input	Char(4)
3	Qualified Save File Name	Input	Char(20)
4	Object Name Filter	Input	Char(10)
5	Object Type Filter	Input	Char(10)
6	Continuation Handle	Input	Char(36)
7	Error Code	I/O	Char(*)

The QSRLSAVF API is a standard list-type API. You are probably quite familiar with these parameters by now, or can at least make good guesses as to their purposes.

The first parameter, Qualified User Space Name, is the name of the user space that the API should return the list entries into. The first 10 bytes are the user space name, and the second 10 bytes are the library name where the user space is to be found. Special values such as *LIBL and *CURLIB are supported for the library-name portion of this parameter.

646

The second parameter, Format Name, defines what type of list entries you want returned in the user space. The supported formats are as follows:

- SAVF0100 – Library-level information

- SAVF0200 – Object-level information

- SAVF0300 – Member-level information

- SAVF0400 – Spool-file information

Our example program uses format SAVF0200, object-level information. The QSYSINC definition of this format is shown in Figure 16.12.

The third parameter, Qualified Save File Name, is the name of the save file that we want information about. As with most API qualified name parameters, the first 10 bytes are the save file name, and the second 10 bytes are the library name where the save file is to be found. Special values such as *LIBL and *CURLIB are supported for the library-name portion of this parameter.

The fourth parameter, Object Name Filter, allows you to specify what object names you are interested in having returned by the API. You can specify a particular object name such as CUSTOMER, a generic object name such as CUST*, or the special value *ALL. Our sample program uses the special value *ALL.

The fifth parameter, Object Type Filter, allows you to specify what type of object you are interested in having returned by the API. You can specify a specific type, such as *USR-SPC, or the special value *ALL. The sample program uses the special value *ALL.

The sixth parameter, Continuation Handle, allows you to span user spaces when the number of list entries returned by the API exceeds the capacity of one user space (approximately 16 MB). When the List Save File API is initially called, we set the Continuation Handle parameter to all blanks to indicate that this is the initial call. If the API returns with a partial list (indicated by having the information status field, QUSIS, of the list generic header set to *P*), we can use this parameter on subsequent calls to the API, to continue the list using either the same user space or a new user space.

When QUSIS is set to P by an API such as QSRLSAVF, the API will also return a continuation handle in the API header section of the list. This continuation handle is then passed, unmodified, on subsequent calls to the List Save File API to resume the list where it left off when it ran out of space. Our sample program makes use of the continuation handle, as it is quite possible to have more objects in one save file than can be listed in one user space. This cycle of returning partial information and a related continuation handle continues for as many calls to the List Save File API as are necessary to return all of the list entries.

The seventh parameter is the standard API error-code structure.

Since our sample program uses format SAVF0200, object-level information, Figure 16.12 shows the QSYSINC-provided definition for this format. As you can see, quite a bit of information is returned for each object in the save file. The fields used in the sample program are QSROBJN, the name of the object, QSRLIBS00, the library the object was saved from, and QSROBJT, the type of object saved. For details on the other fields returned, and the other formats, refer to the IBM Information Center.

```
DName++++++++++ETDsFrom+++To/L+++IDc.Keywords++++++++++++++++++++++
D*****************************************************************
D*Type Definition for the SAVF0200 format.
D*****************************************************************
DQSRF0200       DS
D*                                              Qsr Lsavf SAVF0200
D QSROBJN           1     10
D*                                              Object Name
D QSRLIBS00        11     20
D*                                              Library Saved
D QSROBJT          21     30
D*                                              Object Type
D QSREOBJA         31     40
D*                                              Extended Object Attribut
D QSRSDAT00        41     48
D*                                              Save Date And Time
D QSROBJS          49     52B 0
D*                                              Object Size
D QSROBJSM         53     56B 0
D*                                              Object Size Multiplier
D QSRASP00         57     60B 0
D*                                              Auxiliary Storage Pool
D QSRDS            61     61
D*                                              Data Saved
D QSROBJO          62     71
D*                                              Object Owner
D QSRDLON          72     91
D*                                              Document Library Object
```

Figure 16.12: The QSYSINC definition for QSRLSAVF format SAVF0200 (part 1 of 2).

```
D QSROLDER              92    154
D*                                          Folder
D QSRTD                155    204
D*                                          Text Description
D QSRASPDN00           205    214
D*                                          ASP Device Name
D*                                                       @SFA
```

Figure 16.12: The QSYSINC definition for QSRLSAVF format SAVF0200 (part 2 of 2).

We will also be using the Continuation Handle parameter in case the number of list entries returned exceeds the capacity of a single user space, so we will also be using the API's *header section*. This section is returned by most list-type APIs, but except for a brief discussion in chapter 1, we haven't had any reason to review it until now. Each list-type API can have an API-unique header section that provides feedback information to the caller of the API. Conceptually, this is similar to how each list-type API can have unique formats in which list entries are returned—just like each API returns unique list entries, so too can each API return unique feedback information. And much like how the list's generic header has fields that provide offset, length, and count information to access the list entries (QUSOLD, QUSQUSSEE, and QUSNBRLE, respectively), so too does the list's generic header provide fields to access the API header section. The fields related to the header section are QUSOHS, the offset to the header section, and QUSSHS, the size of the header section.

The QSYSINC-provided definition for the List Save File API header section is shown in Figure 16.13. As you can see, the provided data structure QSRLH has five subfields.

```
DName+++++++++++ETDsFrom+++To/L+++IDc.Keywords+++++++++++++++++++++++
D*******************************************************************
D*Type Definition for the Header Section.
D*******************************************************************
DQSRLH               DS
D*                                          Qsr Lsavf Header
D QSRUSNU               1     10
D*                                          User Space Name Use
D QSRUSLNU             11     20
D*                                          User Space Library
D QSRSFNU              21     30
D*                                          Save File Name Used
D QSRSFLNU             31     40
D*                                          Save File Library N
D QSRCHRTN             41     76
D*                                          Continuation Handle
```

Figure 16.13: The QSYSINC definition for the QSRLSAVF header section.

The first four fields provide feedback information to you on what names were used for the user space name, the user space library name, the save file name, and the save file library name when the list was generated by the List Save File API. This information can be useful when special values such as *CURLIB have been used, when providing the qualified user space name or qualified save file name parameters, and when you are interested in knowing what library was actually used. The provided information can also be used when user spaces have been renamed or moved after the list was generated, and you're attempting to determine why a user space exists on your system. (Remember that user spaces are permanent objects. They can be on your system for years.)

Just in case you're wondering, there is also an API *input section*, also accessed with offset and size information provided in the list's generic header, which can be used to determine what parameter values were in effect when the list was generated. This data can be very useful when trying to figure out what a given user space contains!

The fifth field of the header section, QSRCHRTN, is the continuation handle returned by this API when only partial information can be returned to the user space. We use this continuation handle on subsequent calls to the List Save File API, in order to resume the list where it left off when the current user space became full.

Figure 16.14 shows the source for processing the object-level list entries returned by the QSRLSAVF API. This program accepts two parameters. The first parameter is the name of the save file, and it is required. The second parameter is the name of the library where the save file is located, and it is optional. If not passed, the library name defaults to the special value *LIBL.

```
h dftactgrp(*no) bnddir('APILIB')

DName+++++++++++ETDsFrom+++To/L+++IDc.Keywords+++++++++++++++++++++++++
d/copy qsysinc/qrpglesrc,qusgen
d/copy qsysinc/qrpglesrc,qsrlsavf
d/copy qsysinc/qrpglesrc,qusec

dFIG16_14           pr                      extpgm('FIG16_14')
d SavFName                          10      const
d SavFLib                          10      const

dFIG16_14           pi
d SavFName                          10      const
```

Figure 16.14: Using *QSRLSAVF* to list all objects in a *SAVF (part 1 of 4).

```
d SavFLib                        10      const

dLstSavF        pr                       extpgm('QSRLSAVF')
d SpcName                        20      const
d Format                          8      const
d QualSavF                       20      const
d ObjNameFltr                    10      const
d ObjTypeFltr                    10      const
d ContinHdl                      36      const
d QUSEC                                  likeds(QUSEC)

dExists         pr                1      extproc('Exists')
d ObjectName                     10      const
d ObjectType                     10      const
d ObjectLib                      10      const options(*nopass)

dRtvSpcPtr      pr                       extpgm('QUSPTRUS')
d SpcName                        20      const
d UsrSpcPtr                       *
d USEC                                   likeds(QUSEC) options(*nopass)

dCrtUsrSpc      pr                *      extproc('CrtUsrSpc')
d SpcName                        20      const

d* List API generic header
dGenHdr         ds                       likeds(QUSH0100)
d                                        based(GenHdrPtr)

d* List Save File API (QSRLSAVF) format SAVF0200
dLstEntry       ds                       likeds(QSRF0200)
d                                        based(LstPtr)

d* List Save File API (QSRLSAVF) header section
dHdrEntry       ds                       likeds(QSRLH)
d                                        based(HdrPtr)

dSpcName        ds
d SName                          10      inz('SAVFLIST')
d SLib                           10      inz('QTEMP')

dQualSavF       ds
d SFName                         10
d SFLib                          10      inz('*LIBL')

dLstCount       s               10i 0
dWait           s                1
```

Figure 16.14: Using QSRLSAVF to list all objects in a *SAVF (part 2 of 4).

651

```
CLON01Factor1+++++++Opcode&ExtFactor2+++++++Result++++++++Len++D+HiLoEq
 /free
  QUSBPRV = 0;

  // If needed, create the user space for the list of saved objects
  if (Exists( SName :'*USRSPC' :SLib)) = 'N';
     GenHdrPtr = CrtUsrSpc(SpcName);
  else;
     RtvSpcPtr( SpcName :GenHdrPtr :QUSEC);
  endif;

  // Get the list of objects in the save file
  SFName = SavFName;
  if (%parms > 1);
     SFLib = SavFLib;
  endif;

  LstSavF( SpcName :'SAVF0200' :QualSavF :'*ALL' :'*ALL' :' ' :QUSEC);

  // Get to the API header section
  HdrPtr = GenHdrPtr + GenHdr.QUSOHS;

  // Check to see if the list is complete
  if (GenHdr.QUSIS = 'C') or (GenHdr.QUSIS = 'P');

     dow ((GenHdr.QUSIS = 'C') or (GenHdr.QUSIS = 'P'));

        if (GenHdr.QUSIS = 'C');
           dsply ('Complete list of ' + %char(GenHdr.QUSNBRLE) +
                    ' entries returned.');
        endif;
        if (GenHdr.QUSIS = 'P');
           dsply ('Partial list of ' + %char(GenHdr.QUSNBRLE) +
                    ' entries returned.');
        endif;

     // Get to the first list entry and process the list
     LstPtr = GenHdrPtr + GenHdr.QUSOLD;

     for LstCount = 1 to GenHdr.QUSNBRLE;

        dsply ('Object ' + %trim(LstEntry.QSRLIBS00) + '/' +
               %trim(LstEntry.QSROBJN) + ' type ' +
               %trim(LstEntry.QSROBJT) + ' found.') ' ' Wait;
        if (Wait <> *blanks);
           leave;
        endif;
        LstPtr = LstPtr + GenHdr.QUSSEE;
     endfor;
```

Figure 16.14: Using *QSRLSAVF* to list all objects in a **SAVF* (part 3 of 4).

```
         if ((GenHdr.QUSIS <> 'P') or (Wait <> *blanks));
             leave;
         endif;

         LstSavf( SpcName :'SAVF0200' :QualSavF :'*ALL' :'*ALL'
                  :HdrEntry.QSRCHRTN :QUSEC);
         if (GenHdr.QUSIS <> 'C') and (GenHdr.QUSIS <> 'P');
             dsply 'List Object API did not return valid data';
             leave;
         endif;
      enddo;
      Wait = *blanks;
      dsply 'End of list' ' ' Wait;

   else;
      dsply 'List Object API did not return valid data' ' ' Wait;
   endif;
   *inlr = *on;
   Return;

/end-free
```

Figure 16.14: Using *QSRLSAVF* to list all objects in a **SAVF* (part 4 of 4).

The main changes made to use the continuation handle are highlighted in Figure 16.14. We enclosed the list entry processing within a DO-WHILE loop:

```
dow ((GenHdr.QUSIS = 'C') or (GenHdr.QUSIS = 'P'));
```

The loop is exited when the list is complete, that is, *if (GenHdr.QUSIS <> 'P';*. Within the DOW loop, the QSRLSAVF API is called after processing all entries in the current list, requesting that the next set of entries be returned. This is done by passing the continuation handle HdrEntry.QSRCHRTN as the sixth parameter of QSRLSAVF. As you can see, using list API continuation handles has had minimal impact on how we actually process the output of the API.

Using a Subfile to Display List API Entries

You will probably have some applications that involve loading the results of a list-type API into a subfile for display to the end user. This can be straightforward enough in many cases, but can be a problem in others. The problem has to do with the fact that subfiles can only hold up to 9,999 records, while list APIs can return anywhere from tens to hundreds of thousands of list entries. Simply loading the list entries into the subfile won't allow the user to see past the first 9,999 entries.

In this section, we do not introduce any new APIs. Rather, we show you how to use a SFLSIZ = SFLPAG subfile so that your application doesn't care if there are two or 200,000 entries in a generated list. The application will simply locate and load the correct list entries based on where the end user currently is in the generated list and the direction he or she wants to go in the subfile.

Our sample program uses the List Objects API, QUSLOBJ. This API was previously used in Figure 3.3.D, when we first introduced list APIs. We will build on that earlier example here. We will be using a subfile that displays the object name, library, and object type of all objects found within the job's current library (*CURLIB). The subfile will display up to 16 objects per page, and the application program will control the paging of the subfile contents.

Figure 16.15 shows the DDS for the display file of the sample program. The DDS defines three record formats. The first, SFLRCD, is a subfile record format with three fields. The fields represent the object name, object library, and object type that was returned by the List Objects API. The second record format, SFLCTL, is the subfile control record for subfile SFLRCD. The subfile is defined with a subfile size of 16 and a subfile page of 16. The PAGEDOWN and PAGEUP keywords are enabled, with no indicator associated with them. The third record format, KEY, informs the user that F3 can be used to exit from the application. CA03 is enabled at the file level.

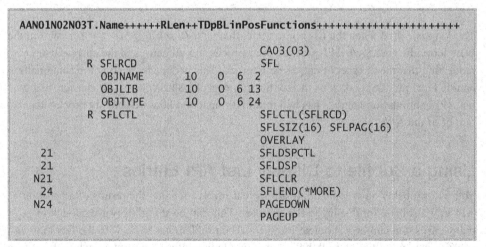

```
AAN01N02N03T.Name++++++RLen++TDpBLinPosFunctions++++++++++++++++++++++++++++

                                        CA03(03)
            R SFLRCD                     SFL
              OBJNAME      10    O  6  2
              OBJLIB       10    O  6 13
              OBJTYPE      10    O  6 24
            R SFLCTL                     SFLCTL(SFLRCD)
                                         SFLSIZ(16) SFLPAG(16)
                                         OVERLAY
       21                                SFLDSPCTL
       21                                SFLDSP
      N21                                SFLCLR
       24                                SFLEND(*MORE)
      N24                                PAGEDOWN
                                         PAGEUP
```

Figure 16.15: The DDS for the subfile displaying object name, library, and type (part 1 of 2).

```
                                      1 26'List Objects Information'
                                      5  2'Name'
                                      5 13'Library'
                                      5 24'Type'
              R KEY

                                     23 02'F3 = Exit'
```

Figure 16.15: The DDS for the subfile displaying object name, library, and type (part 2 of 2).

Figure 16.16 shows the program that will manage the display file FIG16_15. Figure 16.16 highlights the changes to our list processing that are related to managing a SFLSIZ = SFLPAG subfile. Changes that need to be made simply to use a subfile are not highlighted. Examples of what is not highlighted include operations such as writing a subfile record, and writing and reading the subfile control record.

```
h dftactgrp(*no) bnddir('APILIB')

FFilename++IPEASFRlen+LKlen+AIDevice+.Keywords+++++++++++++++++++++++++++
fFIG16_15  cf   e              workstn SFILE(SFLRCD:SFLCount)
f                                      INFDS(WSFeedBack)

DName+++++++++++ETDsFrom+++To/L+++IDc.Keywords+++++++++++++++++++++++++++
d/copy qsysinc/qrpglesrc,qusgen
d/copy qsysinc/qrpglesrc,quslobj

dCrtUsrSpc        pr              *    extproc('CrtUsrSpc')
d SpcName                        20    const

dListObj          pr                   extpgm('QUSLOBJ')
d SpcName                        20    const
d Format                          8    const
d ObjLibName                     20    const
d ObjTyp                         10    const

dGenHdr           ds                   likeds(QUSH0100)
d                                      based(GenHdrPtr)

dListEntry        ds                   likeds(QUSL010003)
d                                      based(ListEntryPtr)

dSpcName          ds
d SName                          10    inz('TESTSPACE')
d SLib                          10    inz('QTEMP')

dObjLibName       ds
d ObjName                       10    inz('*ALL')
```

Figure 16.16: Using a SFLSIZ = SFLPAG subfile to process list entries (part 1 of 3).

655

```
d LibName                          10     inz('*CURLIB')

dWSFeedBack        ds
d AidKey                           1      overlay(WSFeedBack :369)

dEnter             c                      x'F1'
dPageUp            c                      x'F4'
dPageDown          c                      x'F5'

dListCount         s               10i 0  inz(1)
dSFLCount          s                4  0
dSFLPag            s               10i 0  inz(16)
dSFLMax            s               10i 0
```

```
CLON01Factor1+++++++Opcode&ExtFactor2+++++++Result++++++++Len++D+HiLoEq
 /free

    // Create user space and get a pointer to the start of the space
    GenHdrPtr = CrtUsrSpc( SpcName);

    // Call the List API
    ListObj( SpcName :'OBJL0100' :ObjLibName :'*ALL');

    // Check on the status of the returned list
    if (GenHdr.QUSIS = 'C') or (GenHdr.QUSIS = 'P');

        // Set ListEntryPtr to first entry
        ListEntryPtr = GenHdrPtr + GenHdr.QUSOLD;

        dow *in03 = *off;                  // Test F3 for exit

            write SFLCtl;                  // Clear subfile

            // determine maximum number of entries we can load
            if (ListCount + SFLPag) > GenHdr.QUSNBRLE;
                SFLMax = (GenHdr.QUSNBRLE - ListCount) + 1;
            else;
                SFLMax = SFLPAG;
            endif;

            // process all entries
            for SFLCount = 1 to SFLMax;
                // process the current list entry

                ObjName = ListEntry.QUSOBJNU;
                ObjLib = ListEntry.QUSOLNU;
                ObjType = ListEntry.QUSOBJTU;
                write SFLRcd;
```

Figure 16.16: Using a *SFLSIZ = SFLPAG* subfile to process list entries (part 2 of 3).

```
              ListCount += 1;
              ListEntryPtr += GenHdr.QUSSEE;
          endfor;

          // Still more to process?
          if ListCount >= GenHdr.QUSNBRLE;
              *in24 = *on;              // No, show 'Bottom'
          else;
              *in24 = *off;             // Yes, show 'More'
          endif;

          *in21 = *on;                  // display subfile
          write Key;
          exfmt SFLCtl;
          *in21 = *off;

          if AidKey = Enter;
              leave;
          endif;

          if AidKey = PageUp;           // Page up key used
              ListCount = (ListCount - SFLMax - SFLPag);
              if ListCount < 1;
                  ListCount = 1;
              endif;
              // Set ListEntryPtr to desired entry
              ListEntryPtr = (GenHdrPtr + GenHdr.QUSOLD +
                             ((ListCount - 1) * GenHdr.QUSSEE));
          endif;

      enddo;

  // List status is not Complete or Partial
  else;
      // Report an error
  endif;

  // exit when the list has been processed
  *inlr = *on;
  return;

/end-free
```

Figure 16.16: Using a SFLSIZ = SFLPAG subfile to process list entries (part 3 of 3).

The first change is to associate a file-information feedback data structure (infds(WSFeedback)) with the FIG16_15 display file. Within the WSFeedBack data structure, the subfield AidKey is defined to give information on what key was used to exit the subfile record format. FIG16_16 also defines three constants, Enter, PageUp, and

PageDown, to represent the AidKey values for the Enter key, the PageUp key, and the PageDown key, respectively.

The FIG16_16 program also defines three additional fields. ListCount is initialized to the value of one. It represents the relative record number of the next list entry to be processed. SFLPag is initialized to the value of 16. It represents the number of entries that can be written to one subfile page. SFLMax is a working variable representing the maximum number of entries that can be written to the current subfile page. SFLMax is used when the number of list entries remaining in the list to be written to the current subfile page is less than the value of SFLPag.

After setting ListEntryPtr to the first list entry, FIG16_16 enters a DO-WHILE loop that is exited by indicator 03 (CA03). Within this loop, FIG16_16 first clears the subfile (SFLCLR) and then determines the number of records that can be written to the now-cleared subfile. If there are more list entries than will fit into SFLPag, the maximum number of records to write is SFLPag. If the number of remaining entries is less than the value of SFLPag, the maximum number of records to write is the number of remaining list entries. The value of the maximum number of records to write to the subfile is stored in the variable SFLMax.

The program then loads SFLMax records into subfile SFLRcd. We won't go into any details on this, as it involves just standard list and subfile processing.

After loading SFLMax records, FIG16_16 checks to determine if more list entries exist after the last entry written to SFLRcd. If so, indicator 24 is turned off, to have "More" displayed for the subfile. If no more entries exist in the list, indicator 24 is turned on, to have "Bottom" displayed for the subfile. The program then writes the Key record format, the SFLRcd subfile record, the SFLCtl subfile control record, and reads from the SFLCtl subfile control record.

If Enter is used to exit the subfile, the program leaves the DOW loop and ends.

If PageUp is used to exit the subfile, the program positions ListCount and ListEntryPtr to the appropriate list entry from the previous subfile page. This positioning is quite straightforward. First, the program takes the current ListCount value, which is set to the relative entry number of the next list entry to be processed when paging down through the list, and subtracts the number of entries in the current subfile record (SFLMax) and the number of entries in the previous subfile record (SFLPag). This now sets ListCount to the relative entry number of the first subfile entry on the previous subfile record. In case PageUp was used on the first subfile record to be shown, the program also checks to see if ListCount is less than one. If so, ListCount is set to one. The program then sets ListEntryPtr to the address of the list entry identified by ListCount. This is done by taking the address of the user space (GenHdrPtr), adding the offset to the first list entry (GenHdr.QUSOLD), and adding the product of how many entries into the list we need to go (ListCount – 1) and the size of each entry (GenHdr.QUSSEE). At this point, the program is set to load the next subfile page.

Regardless of whether PageUp or PageDown was pressed by the end user, the DOW loop is now restarted, as both ListCount and ListEntryPtr are properly set to the first list entry that should be written to the next subfile page.

Using this example as a starting point, you should be able to incorporate any fixed-entry-length list API into a SFLSIZ = SFLPAG environment. This, in conjunction with everything else you've learned about list APIs in this book, should put you in good shape for using list APIs in your application development environment.

Summary

This chapter reviews a wide variety of APIs and techniques. You have learned how to sort the results of a list API, how to manage a subfile containing list API entries, and how your application can save end-user preferences for later use when the end user re-enters your application.

There are hundreds of other APIs on your System i, and many of them can most likely be used to enhance your applications and/or system operations. We encourage you to review the API category of the Information Center to get a feel for all of the possibilities opened up by the use of system APIs. Knowing what capabilities are provided by the these APIs might help you take a fresh look at some of your application development opportunities.

Check Your Knowledge

Having completed this book, the only real check of your knowledge is your ability to apply what you've learned to real-life applications. Think of an application where you can take advantage of system APIs to have a positive impact on your business, and get to it.

Happy programming!

The Examples

The code on the Web that accompanies this book contains the source code for those figures found within the text that can be compiled into objects. Table A.1 is a cross-reference for the DDS figures and the files found at www.mcpressonline.com/mc/forums/reviews/5085. Table A.2 is a cross-reference for the free form ILE RPG figures and the files found on the Web.

Table A.1: Code on the Web DDS Cross-Reference Information		
File Name	Figure	Description
FIG4_4_A	4.4.A	DDS for the CUSTOMER physical file.
FIG4_6	4.6	DDS for the CUSTOMER list display file.
FIG5_4	5.4	DDS for the library information display file.
FIG7_9	7.9	DDS for the file information display file.
FIG11_2	11.2	DDS for the ENCRCUST physical file.
FIG13_3	13.3	DDS for the job list display file.
FIG16_15	16.15	DDS for the object list display file.

Table A.2: Code on the Web ILE RPG Cross-Reference Information		
File Name	Figure	Description
FIG1_8	1.8	Use QUSCRTUS to create a user space.
FIG1_9_A	1.9.A	Use QUSPTRUS to access and then modify a user space.
FIG1_9_B	1.9.B	Use QUSPTRUS to access and then read a user space.
FIG1_10	1.10	Use QUSRTVUS to read a user space.
FIG1_11	1.11	Use QUSCUSAT to modify the attributes of a user space.
FIG1_12	1.12	The CRTUSRSPC procedure.
FIG1_13	1.13	Use the CRTUSRSPC function shown in Figure 1.12.
FIG1_14	1.14	Use and check the API error code structure.
FIG1_15	1.15	Incorrectly defining a receiver variable.
FIG2_2_A	2.2.A	Use QSPRJOBQ to retrieve static information such as the number of jobs on a job queue.
FIG2_2_B	2.2.B	Use QSPRJOBQ to retrieve additional information – the job queue name.
FIG2_2_C	2.2.C	Use QSPRJOBQ to retrieve job queue information with the job queue name being a parameter.
FIG2_4	2.4	Use the message ID from the error code structure.
FIG2_5	2.5	Use message replacement data from the error code structure.
FIG2_6	2.6	Use QDCRCTLD to retrieve dynamic information such all devices on a controller.
FIG3_3_A	3.3.A	List API essentials – overview of processing a list with the generic header structure.
FIG3_3_B	3.3.B	List API essentials – check the list information status.
FIG3_3_C	3.3.C	List API processing – the conventions we will use when returning lists of information.
FIG3_3_D	3.3.D	List API processing—use QUSLOBJ to return the objects in *CURLIB.
FIG3_4	3.4	Use pointer support with QUSLOBJ and QUSRMBRD to find files above a given percentage of deleted records.
FIG3_7	3.7	Use QUSRTVUS with QUSLOBJ and QUSRMBRD to find files above a given percentage of deleted records.

File Name	Figure	Description
Table A.2: Code on the Web ILE RPG Cross-Reference Information (continued)		
FIG3_9	3.9	Use QGYOLOBJ, QGYGTLE, QGYCLST, and QUSRMBRD to find files above a given percentage of deleted records.
FIG3_12	3.12	List API processing — use QBNLMODI to find module and procedure names where list entries are of variable size.
FIG4_1	4.1	Use QCMDEXC to run WRKSPLF.
FIG4_2	4.2	Use QCMDEXC to run RGZPFM.
FIG4_3	4.3	Use QCMDEXC to run OPNQRYF.
FIG4_4_B	4.4.B	Load records into CUSTOMER file described in Figure 4.4.A.
FIG4_5	4.5	Use QCMDEXC to run OVRPRTF.
FIG4_8	4.8	Use QCMDEXC to run SBMJOB.
FIG4_9	4.9	Use SYSTEM to run arbitrary commands.
FIG4_10	4.10	Use QCMDCHK to prompt WRKACTJOB.
FIG4_12	4.12	Use QCAPCMD to prompt and run SBMJOB.
FIG4_17	4.17	Use Command-Analyzer exit point to log ENDJOB command usage.
FIG5_1	5.1	Use QUSROBJD to determine is an object exists.
FIG5_2	5.2	Use EXISTS function shown in Figure 5.1.
FIG5_5	5.5	Use QUSROBJD and QUSRLIBD to retrieve library information.
FIG6_3	6.3	Use QRCVDTAQ to retrieve job related information from the Job-Notification exit point.
FIG6_5	6.5	Use QSNDDTAQ to end the program shown in Figure 6.3.
FIG6_7	6.7	Use QMHQRDQD to retrieve data queue descriptive information.
FIG7_2	7.2	Use record information from a database trigger exit point.
FIG7_4	7.4	Use QUSLMBR to find all members in a file.
FIG7_5	7.5	Use QUSLMBR with QUSLOBJ and QUSRMBRD to find file members above a given percentage of deleted records.
FIG7_6	7.6	Use QUSLFLD to find all fields in a file.
FIG7_10	7.10	Use QDBRTVFD to find information about a file.

663

Table A.2: Code on the Web ILE RPG Cross-Reference Information (continued)		
File Name	Figure	Description
FIG8_1	8.1	Use QWCCVTDT to convert from a YYMD date to a MDYY format.
FIG8_3	8.3	Use QWCCVTDT to convert from a system timestamp date to a MDYY format.
FIG8_4	8.4	Use QWCCVTDT to convert time values from one time-zone to another time-zone.
FIG8_7	8.7	Use QWCADJTM to adjust the system time.
FIG8_8	8.8	Use CEELOCT and CEEDATE to add 30 days to a date and format the result.
FIG8_9	8.9	Use feedback parameter of CEE APIs.
FIG8_10	8.10	Use CVTHC to format the message ID of the CEE feedback parameter.
FIG9_3	9.3	Use QLGCONVERTCASE to monocase character data.
FIG9_9	9.9	Use QTQICONVOPEN, iconv, and ICONV_CLOSE to convert character data from one CCSID to another CCSID.
FIG10_2	10.2	Use message information from a message watch exit point.
FIG10_4	10.4	Use QSCSWCH to start a watch for message CPF2456.
FIG10_6	10.6	Use QMHSNDPM and sleep to send a status message.
FIG10_9	10.9	Use QMHSNDPM and sleep to send a status message with replacement data along with a completion message.
FIG10_11	10.11	Use QMHRTVM and QLGCONVERTCASE to search all messages in a message file for a character string.
FIG11_1	11.1	Use Qc3CreateKeyContext, Qc3GenPRNs, Qc3EncryptData, and Qc3DestroyKeyContext to encrypt user data.
FIG11_11	11.11	Use Qc3CreateKeyContext, Qc3DecryptData, and Qc3DestroyKeyContext to decrypt user data.
FIG11_12	11.12	Use Qc3LoadMasterKeyPart, Qc3SetMasterKey, Qc3CreateKeyStore, and Qc3GenKeyRecord to create a cryptographic key-management environment.
FIG11_17	11.17	Use Qc3CreateKeyContext, Qc3GenPRNs, Qc3EncryptData, and Qc3DestroyKeyContext to encrypt user data within a key-management environment.

Table A.2: Code on the Web ILE RPG Cross-Reference Information (continued)		
File Name	**Figure**	**Description**
FIG11_20	11.20	Use Qc3CreateKeyContext, Qc3DecryptData, and Qc3DestroyKeyContext to decrypt user data within a key-management environment.
FIG12_3	12.3	Use QsᵧGetProfileHandleNoPwd, QsyGetProfileHandle, QsySetToProfileHandle, and QsyReleaseProfileHandle to swap the current user profile of a job.
FIG11_20	11.20	Use Qc3CreateKeyContext, Qc3DecryptData, and Qc3DestroyKeyContext to decrypt user data within a key-management environment.
FIG12_3	12.3	Use QsyGetProfileHandleNoPwd, QsyGetProfileHandle, QsySetToProfileHandle, and QsyReleaseProfileHandle to swap the current user profile of a job.
FIG12_5	12.5	Use QSYRUPWD and QSNDDTAQ to retrieve and send a user profile encrypted password.
FIG12_7	12.7	Use QSYSUPWD and QRCVDTAQ to receive and apply a user profile encrypted password.
FIG12_13	12.13	Use Change User Profile exit point, QSYRUSRI, and QSNDDTAQ to send user profile change information.
FIG12_15	12.15	Use QCMDEXC and QRCVDTAQ to receive and apply user profile changes.
FIG13_1	13.1	Use QUSLJOB to find all jobs on the system.
FIG13_15	13.15	Use QWTCHGJB to change the job environment to match the current user profile for the job.
FIG13_17	13.17	Use QWCRSSTS to determine if the system is in restricted state.
FIG14_12_A	14.12.A	Use open, read, write, close, and __errno to create an EBCDIC stream file containing text.
FIG14_12_B	14.12.B	Use open, read, write, close, and __errno to create an EBCDIC stream file containing text and record/line separators.
FIG14_12_C	14.12.C	Use open, read, write, close, and __errno to create an ASCII stream file containing text and record/line separators.
FIG14_20	14.20	Use opendir, readdir, closedir, and __errno to list most entries in an Integrated File System directory.

Table A.2: Code on the Web ILE RPG Cross-Reference Information (continued)		
File Name	**Figure**	**Description**
FIG14_23	14.23	*Use open, write, close, QUSRJOBI, QCMDEXC, and __errno to create a stream file named ?.*
FIG14_24	14.24	*Use QlgOpendir, QlgReaddir, closedir, and __errno to list all entries in an Integrated File System directory.*
FIG14_25	14.25	*Use Qp0lOpen, write, close, and __errno to create a stream file named ?.*
FIG15_15	15.15	*Use SOCKET, BIND, LISTEN, ACCEPT, RECV, SEND, close, QCMDEXC, and __errno to provide a simple file transfer server.*
FIG15_18	15.18	*Use GETHOSTBYNAME, SOCKET, CONNECT, SEND, RECV, close, and __errno to provide a simple file transfer client.*
FIG15_26	15.26	*Use SOCKET, BIND, LISTEN, ACCEPT, RECV, SEND, close, QUSROBJD, QLIRLIBD, and __errno to provide a library information server.*
FIG15_27	15.27	*Use GETHOSTBYNAME, SOCKET, CONNECT, SEND, RECV, close, QMHSNDPM, and __errno to provide a library information client.*
FIG15_41	15.41	*Use SOCKET, GETSERVBYNAME, SETSOCKOPT, BIND, LISTEN, ACCEPT, SEND, RECV, GIVEDESCRIPTOR, close, QRCVDTAQ, QCMDEXC, and __errno to provide a routing server.*
FIG15_42	15.42	*Use RECV, SEND, TAKEDESCRIPTOR, close, QSNDDTAQ, QUSRJOBI, QCMDEXC, and __errno to provide an enhanced file transfer server.*
FIG15_43	15.43	*Use RECV, SEND, TAKEDESCRIPTOR, close, QSNDDTAQ, QUSROBJD, QLIRLIBD, QUSRJOBI, and __errno to provide an enhanced library information server.*
FIG15_44	15.44	*Use GETHOSTBYNAME, SOCKET, GETSERVBYNAME, CONNECT, SEND, RECV, close, and __errno to provide an enhanced file transfer client.*
FIG15_45	15.45	*Use GETHOSTBYNAME, SOCKET, GETSERVBYNAME, CONNECT, SEND, RECV, close, QMHSNDPM, and __errno to provide an enhanced library information client.*
FIG15_47	15.47	*Use TCP/IP Server exit point, GETHOSTBYNAME, SOCKET, GETSERVBYNAME, CONNECT, SEND, close, QUSRJOBI, QRCVDTAQ, QCMDEXC, and __errno to start and end a user defined TCP/IP server.*
FIG15_48	15.48	*Use SOCKET, SETSOCKOPT, BIND, LISTEN, ACCEPT, RECV, SEND, close, QUSROBJD, QLIRLIBD, QTQICONVOPEN, iconv, ICONV_CLOSE, QLGCONVERTCASE, and __errno to provide a simple Telnet based library information server.*

File Name	Figure	Description
FIG16_4	16.4	*Use QLGSORT and QUSLJOB to list selected jobs on the system in a specific order.*
FIG16_5	16.5	*Use QSYUPDATEUSERAPPLICATIONINFO to associate application specific information with a user profile.*
FIG16_8	16.8	*Use QSYRETRIEVEUSERAPPLICATIONINFO and QSYUPDATEUSERAPPLICATIONINFO to read and maintain application specific information associated with a user profile.*
FIG16_11	16.11	*Use QSZRTVPR to retrieve the current release of the operating system.*
FIG16_14	16.14	*Use QSRLSAVF and continuation handles to list all objects in a *SAVF when the list spans multiple user spaces.*
FIG16_16	16.16	*Use QUSLOBJ to list all objects in a library using a SFLSIZ = SFLPAG subfile.*
FIGD_2	D.2	*Use QSYRUSRI to return the status of a *USRPRF.*
FIGD_3	D.3	*Use QWCLASBS to list all currently active subsystems.*
FIGD_4	D.4	*Use QCMDEXC to create a *DTAQ.*
FIGD_5	D.5	*Use QLIRNMO to rename a *DTAQ.*
FIGD_6_A	D.6.A	*Use QSNDDTAQ to send a 'STOP' message including reason code and time.*
FIGD_6_B	D.6.B	*Use QRCVDTAQ to receive a 'STOP' message and display the reason code and time sent in the message.*
FIGD_7	D.7	*Use QDMRTVFO to determine if a file override is in effect.*
FIGD_8	D.8	*Use CEEDAYS and CEEDATE to format a date value.*
FIGD_9	D.9	*Use QLGCONVERTCASE to scan character data without regard to case.*
FIGD_10_B	D.10.B	*Use QMHSNDPM to send a diagnostic and escape message.*
FIGD_11_A	D.11.A	*Use Qc3WriteKeyRecord to write a restricted key to a key store file.*
FIGD_11_B	D.11.B	*Use Qc3RetrieveKeyRecordAtr and CVTHC to display the attributes of a key found in a key store file.*
FIGD_12	D.12	*Use QSYCUSRS to determine if a *USRPRF has a special authority.*
FIGD_13	D.13	*Use QWDRSBSD to determine the current status of a subsystem.*

Table A.2: *Code on the Web ILE RPG Cross-Reference Information (continued)*

Table A.2: Code on the Web ILE RPG Cross-Reference Information (continued)		
File Name	Figure	Description
FIGD_14	D.14	*Use unlink to delete a stream file.*
FIGD_15_A	D.15.A	*A routing server to support exchange of encrypted passwords.*
FIGD_15_B	D.15.B	*Application server for sending of encrypted passwords.*
FIGD_15_C	D.15.C	*Application client for applying of encrypted passwords.*

B

Fixed Form ILE RPG Examples

The Code on the Web that accompanies this book contains fixed form ILE RPG source code equivalents for those figures found within the text that can be compiled into objects. Table B.1 is a cross-reference for the free form ILE RPG figures and the corresponding fixed form RPG source found on the Web at www.mcpressonline.com/mc/forums/reviews/5085.

Table B.1: Code on the Web ILE RPG Cross-Reference Information		
File Name	**Figure**	**Description**
FIGB1_8	1.8	*Use QUSCRTUS to create a user space.*
FIGB1_9_A	1.9.A	*Use QUSPTRUS to access and then modify a user space.*
FIGB1_9_B	1.9.B	*Use QUSPTRUS to access and then read a user space.*
FIGB1_10	1.10	*Use QUSRTVUS to read a user space.*
FIGB1_11	1.11	*Use QUSCUSAT to modify the attributes of a user space.*
FIGB1_12	1.12	*The CRTUSRSPC procedure.*
FIGB1_13	1.13	*Use the CRTUSRSPC function shown in Figure 1.12.*
FIGB1_14	1.14	*Use and check the API error code structure.*

File Name	Figure	Description
Table B.1: Code on the Web ILE RPG Cross-Reference Information (continued)		
FIGB1_15	1.15	Incorrectly defining a receiver variable.
FIGB2_2_A	2.2.A	Use QSPRJOBQ to retrieve static information such as the number of jobs on a job queue.
FIGB2_2_B	2.2.B	Use QSPRJOBQ to retrieve additional information – the job queue name.
FIGB2_2_C	2.2.C	Use QSPRJOBQ to retrieve job queue information with the job queue name being a parameter.
FIGB2_4	2.4	Use the message ID from the error code structure.
FIGB2_5	2.5	Use message replacement data from the error code structure.
FIGB2_6	2.6	Use QDCRCTLD to retrieve dynamic information such all devices on a controller.
FIGB3_3_A	3.3.A	List API essentials – overview of processing a list with the generic header structure.
FIGB3_3_B	3.3.B	List API essentials – check the list information status.
FIGB3_3_C	3.3.C	List API processing – the conventions we will use when returning lists of information.
FIGB3_3_D	3.3.D	List API processing - use QUSLOBJ to return the objects in *CURLIB.
FIGB3_4	3.4	Use pointer support with QUSLOBJ and QUSRMBRD to find files above a given percentage of deleted records.
FIGB3_7	3.7	Use QUSRTVUS with QUSLOBJ and QUSRMBRD to find files above a given percentage of deleted records.
FIGB3_9	3.9	Use QGYOLOBJ, QGYGTLE, QGYCLST, and QUSRMBRD to find files above a given percentage of deleted records.
FIGB3_12	3.12	List API processing — use QBNLMODI to find module and procedure names where list entries are of variable size.
FIGB4_1	4.1	Use QCMDEXC to run WRKSPLF.
FIGB4_2	4.2	Use QCMDEXC to run RGZPFM.
FIGB4_3	4.3	Use QCMDEXC to run OPNQRYF.
FIGB4_4_B	4.4.B	Load records into CUSTOMER file described in Figure 4.4.A.
FIGB4_5	4.5	Use QCMDEXC to run OVRPRTF.

File Name	Figure	Description
FIGB4_8	4.8	*Use QCMDEXC to run SBMJOB.*
FIGB4_9	4.9	*Use SYSTEM to run arbitrary commands.*
FIGB4_10	4.10	*Use QCMDCHK to prompt WRKACTJOB.*
FIGB4_12	4.12	*Use QCAPCMD to prompt and run SBMJOB.*
FIGB4_17	4.17	*Use Command-Analyzer exit point to log ENDJOB command usage.*
FIGB5_1	5.1	*Use QUSROBJD to determine is an object exists.*
FIGB5_2	5.2	*Use EXISTS function shown in Figure 5.1.*
FIGB5_5	5.5	*Use QUSROBJD and QUSRLIBD to retrieve library information.*
FIGB6_3	6.3	*Use QRCVDTAQ to retrieve job related information from the Job-Notification exit point*
FIGB6_5	6.5	*Use QSNDDTAQ to end the program shown in Figure 6.3.*
FIGB6_7	6.7	*Use QMHQRDQD to retrieve data queue descriptive information.*
FIGB7_2	7.2	*Use record information from a database trigger exit point.*
FIGB7_4	7.4	*Use QUSLMBR to find all members in a file.*
FIGB7_5	7.5	*Use QUSLMBR with QUSLOBJ and QUSRMBRD to find file members above a given percentage of deleted records.*
FIGB7_6	7.6	*Use QUSLFLD to find all fields in a file.*
FIGB7_10	7.10	*Use QDBRTVFD to find information about a file.*
FIGB8_1	8.1	*Use QWCCVTDT to convert from a YYMD date to a MDYY format.*
FIGB8_3	8.3	*Use QWCCVTDT to convert from a system timestamp date to a MDYY format.*
FIGB8_4	8.4	*Use QWCCVTDT to convert time values from one time-zone to another time-zone.*
FIGB8_7	8.7	*Use QWCADJTM to adjust the system time.*
FIGB8_8	8.8	*Use CEELOCT and CEEDATE to add 30 days to a date and format the result.*
FIGB8_9	8.9	*Use feedback parameter of CEE APIs.*

Table B.1: Code on the Web ILE RPG Cross-Reference Information (continued)

671

File Name	Figure	Description
FIGB8_10	8.10	Use CVTHC to format the message ID of the CEE feedback parameter.
FIGB9_3	9.3	Use QLGCONVERTCASE to monocase character data.
FIGB9_9	9.9	Use QTQICONVOPEN, iconv, and ICONV_CLOSE to convert character data from one CCSID to another CCSID.
FIGB10_2	10.2	Use message information from a message watch exit point.
FIGB10_4	10.4	Use QSCSWCH to start a watch for message CPF2456.
FIGB10_6	10.6	Use QMHSNDPM and sleep to send a status message.
FIGB10_9	10.9	Use QMHSNDPM and sleep to send a status message with replacement data along with a completion message.
FIGB10_11	10.11	Use QMHRTVM and QLGCONVERTCASE to search all messages in a message file for a character string.
FIGB11_1	11.1	Use Qc3CreateKeyContext, Qc3GenPRNs, Qc3EncryptData, and Qc3DestroyKeyContext to encrypt user data.
FIGB11_11	11.11	Use Qc3CreateKeyContext, Qc3DecryptData, and Qc3DestroyKeyContext to decrypt user data.
FIGB11_12	11.12	Use Qc3LoadMasterKeyPart, Qc3SetMasterKey, Qc3CreateKeyStore, and Qc3GenKeyRecord to create a cryptographic key-management environment.
FIGB11_17	11.17	Use Qc3CreateKeyContext, Qc3GenPRNs, Qc3EncryptData, and Qc3DestroyKeyContext to encrypt user data within a key-management environment.
FIGB11_20	11.20	Use Qc3CreateKeyContext, Qc3DecryptData, and Qc3DestroyKeyContext to decrypt user data within a key-management environment.
FIGB12_3	12.3	Use QsyGetProfileHandleNoPwd, QsyGetProfileHandle, QsySetToProfileHandle, and QsyReleaseProfileHandle to swap the current user profile of a job.
FIGB12_5	12.5	Use QSYRUPWD and QSNDDTAQ to retrieve and send a user profile encrypted password.
FIGB12_7	12.7	Use QSYSUPWD and QRCVDTAQ to receive and apply a user profile encrypted password.

Table B.1: Code on the Web ILE RPG Cross-Reference Information (continued)

File Name	Figure	Description
Table B.1: Code on the Web ILE RPG Cross-Reference Information (continued)		
FIGB12_13	12.13	Use Change User Profile exit point, QSYRUSRI, and QSNDDTAQ to send user profile change information.
FIGB12_15	12.15	Use QCMDEXC and QRCVDTAQ to receive and apply user profile changes.
FIGB13_1	13.1	Use QUSLJOB to find all jobs on the system.
FIGB13_15	13.15	Use QWTCHGJB to change the job environment to match the current user profile for the job.
FIGB13_17	13.17	Use QWCRSSTS to determine if the system is in restricted state.
FIGB14_12A	14.12.A	Use open, read, write, close, and __errno to create an EBCDIC stream file containing text.
FIGB14_12B	14.12.B	Use open, read, write, close, and __errno to create an EBCDIC stream file containing text and record/line separators.
FIGB14_12C	14.12.C	Use open, read, write, close, and __errno to create an ASCII stream file containing text and record/line separators.
FIGB14_20	14.20	Use opendir, readdir, closedir, and __errno to list most entries in an Integrated File System directory.
FIGB14_23	14.23	Use open, write, close, QUSRJOBI, QCMDEXC, and __errno to create a stream file named ?.
FIGB14_24	14.24	Use QlgOpendir, QlgReaddir, closedir, and __errno to list all entries in an Integrated File System directory.
FIGB14_25	14.25	Use Qp0lOpen, write, close, and __errno to create a stream file named ?.
FIGB15_15	15.15	Use SOCKET, BIND, LISTEN, ACCEPT, RECV, SEND, Close, QCMDEXC, and __errno to provide a simple file transfer server.
FIGB15_18	15.18	Use GETHOSTBYNAME, SOCKET, CONNECT, SEND, RECV, close, and __errno to provide a simple file transfer client.
FIGB15_26	15.26	Use SOCKET, BIND, LISTEN, ACCEPT, RECV, SEND, close, QUSROBJD, QLIRLIBD, and __errno to provide a library information server.
FIGB15_27	15.27	Use GETHOSTBYNAME, SOCKET, CONNECT, SEND, RECV, close, QMHSNDPM, and __errno to provide a library information client.

Table B.1: Code on the Web ILE RPG Cross-Reference Information (continued)		
File Name	Figure	Description
FIGB15_41	15.41	Use SOCKET, GETSERVBYNAME, SETSOCKOPT, BIND, LISTEN, ACCEPT, SEND, RECV, GIVEDESCRIPTOR, close, QRCVDTAQ, QCMDEXC, and __errno to provide a routing server.
FIGB15_42	15.42	Use RECV, SEND, TAKEDESCRIPTOR, close, QSNDDTAQ, QUSRJOBI, QCMDEXC, and __errno to provide an enhanced file transfer server.
FIGB15_43	15.43	Use RECV, SEND, TAKEDESCRIPTOR, close, QSNDDTAQ, QUSROBJD, QLIRLIBD, QUSRJOBI, and __errno to provide an enhanced library information server.
FIGB15_44	15.44	Use GETHOSTBYNAME, SOCKET, GETSERVBYNAME, CONNECT, SEND, RECV, close, and __errno to provide an enhanced file transfer client.
FIGB15_45	15.45	Use GETHOSTBYNAME, SOCKET, GETSERVBYNAME, CONNECT, SEND, RECV, close, QMHSNDPM, and __errno to provide an enhanced library information client.
FIGB15_47	15.47	Use TCP/IP Server exit point, GETHOSTBYNAME, SOCKET, GETSERVBYNAME, CONNECT, SEND, close, QUSRJOBI, QRCVDTAQ, QCMDEXC, and __errno to start and end a user defined TCP/IP server.
FIGB15_48	15.48	Use SOCKET, SETSOCKOPT, BIND, LISTEN, ACCEPT, RECV, SEND, close, QUSROBJD, QLIRLIBD, QTQICONVOPEN, iconv, ICONV_CLOSE, QlgConvertCase, and __errno to provide a simple Telnet based library information server.
FIGB16_4	16.4	Use QLGSORT and QUSLJOB to list selected jobs on the system in a specific order.
FIGB16_5	16.5	Use QsyUpdateUserApplicationInfo to associate application specific information with a user profile.
FIGB16_8	16.8	Use QsyRetrieveUserApplicationInfo and QsyUpdateUserApplicationInfo to read and maintain application specific information associated with a user profile.
FIGB16_11	16.11	Use QSZRTVPR to retrieve the current release of the operating system.
FIGB16_14	16.14	Use QSRLSAVF and continuation handles to list all objects in a *SAVF when the list spans multiple user spaces.
FIGB16_16	16.16	Use QUSLOBJ to list all objects in a library using a SFLSIZ = SFLPAG subfile.

Table B.1: Code on the Web ILE RPG Cross-Reference Information (continued)		
File Name	Figure	Description
FIGBD_2	D.2	*Use QSYRUSRI to return the status of a *USRPRF.*
FIGBD_3	D.3	*Use QWCLASBS to list all currently active subsystems.*
FIGBD_4	D.4	*Use QCMDEXC to create a *DTAQ.*
FIGBD_5	D.5	*Use QLIRNMO to rename a *DTAQ.*
FIGBD_6_A	D.6.A	*Use QSNDDTAQ to send a 'STOP' message including reason code and time.*
FIGBD_7	D.7	*Use QDMRTVFO to determine if a file override is in effect.*
FIGBD_8	D.8	*Use CEEDAYS and CEEDATE to format a date value.*
FIGBD_9	D.9	*Use QLGCONVERTCASE to scan character data without regard to case.*
FIGBD_10_B	D.10.B	*Use QMHSNDPM to send a diagnostic and escape message.*
FIGBD_11_A	D.11.A	*Use Qc3WriteKeyRecord to write a restricted key to a key store file.*
FIGBD_11_B	D.11.B	*Use Qc3RetrieveKeyRecordAtr and CVTHC to display the attributes of a key found in a key store file.*
FIGBD_12	D.12	*Use QSYCUSRS to determine if a *USRPRF has a special authority.*
FIGBD_13	D.13	*Use QWDRSBSD to determine the current status of a subsystem.*
FIGBD_14	D.14	*Use unlink to delete a stream file.*
FIGBD_15_A	D.15.A	*A routing server to support exchange of encrypted passwords.*
FIGBD_15_B	D.15.B	*Application server for sending of encrypted passwords.*
FIGBD_15_C	D.15.C	*Application client for applying of encrypted passwords.*

C

ILE COBOL Examples

The code on the Web that accompanies this book contains ILE COBOL source code equivalents for those figures found within the text that can be compiled into objects. Table C.1 is a cross-reference for the free form ILE RPG figures and the corresponding ILE COBOL source found on the Web at *www.mcpressonline.com/mc/forums/reviews/5085*.

Table C.1: Code on the Web ILE COBOL Cross-Reference Information		
File Name	Figure	Description
FIGC1_8	1.8	*Use QUSCRTUS to create a user space.*
FIGC1_9_A	1.9.A	*Use QUSPTRUS to access and then modify a user space.*
FIGC1_9_B	1.9.B	*Use QUSPTRUS to access and then read a user space.*
FIGC1_10	1.10	*Use QUSRTVUS to read a user space.*
FIGC1_11	1.11	*Use QUSCUSAT to modify the attributes of a user space.*
FIGC1_12	1.12	*The CRTUSRSPC procedure.*
FIGC1_13	1.13	*Use the CRTUSRSPC function shown in Figure 1.12.*

Table C.1: Code on the Web ILE COBOL Cross-Reference Information (continued)		
File Name	Figure	Description
FIGC1_14	1.14	*Use and check the API error code structure.*
FIGC1_15	1.15	*Incorrectly defining a receiver variable.*
FIGC2_2_A	2.2.A	*Use QSPRJOBQ to retrieve static information such as the number of jobs on a job queue.*
FIGC2_2_B	2.2.B	*Use QSPRJOBQ to retrieve additional information – the job queue name.*
FIGC2_2_C	2.2.C	*Use QSPRJOBQ to retrieve job queue information with the job queue name being a parameter.*
FIGC2_4	2.4	*Use the message ID from the error code structure.*
FIGC2_5	2.5	*Use message replacement data from the error code structure.*
FIGC2_6	2.6	*Use QDCRCTLD to retrieve dynamic information such all devices on a controller.*
FIGC3_3_A	3.3.A	*List API essentials – overview of processing a list with the generic header structure.*
FIGC3_3_B	3.3.B	*List API essentials – check the list information status.*
FIGC3_3_C	3.3.C	*List API processing – the conventions we will use when returning lists of information.*
FIGC3_3_D	3.3.D	*List API processing – use QUSLOBJ to return the objects in *CURLIB.*
FIGC3_4	3.4	*Use pointer support with QUSLOBJ and QUSRMBRD to find files above a given percentage of deleted records.*
FIGC3_7	3.7	*Use QUSRTVUS with QUSLOBJ and QUSRMBRD to find files above a given percentage of deleted records.*
FIGC3_9	3.9	*Use QGYOLOBJ, QGYGTLE, QGYCLST, and QUSRMBRD to find files above a given percentage of deleted records.*
FIGC3_12	3.12	*List API processing — use QBNLMODI to find module and procedure names where list entries are of variable size.*
FIGC4_1	4.1	*Use QCMDEXC to run WRKSPLF.*
FIGC4_2	4.2	*Use QCMDEXC to run RGZPFM.*
FIGC4_3	4.3	*Use QCMDEXC to run OPNQRYF.*
FIGC4_4_B	4.4.B	*Load records into CUSTOMER file described in Figure 4.4.A.*

Table C.1: Code on the Web ILE COBOL Cross-Reference Information (continued)		
File Name	Figure	Description
FIGC4_5	4.5	*Use QCMDEXC to run OVRPRTF.*
FIGC4_8	4.8	*Use QCMDEXC to run SBMJOB.*
FIGC4_9	4.9	*Use SYSTEM to run arbitrary commands.*
FIGC4_10	4.10	*Use QCMDCHK to prompt WRKACTJOB.*
FIGC4_12	4.12	*Use QCAPCMD to prompt and run SBMJOB.*
FIGC4_17	4.17	*Use Command-Analyzer exit point to log ENDJOB command usage.*
FIGC5_1	5.1	*Use QUSROBJD to determine is an object exists.*
FIGC5_2	5.2	*Use EXISTS function shown in Figure 5.1.*
FIGC5_5	5.5	*Use QUSROBJD and QUSRLIBD to retrieve library information.*
FIGC6_3	6.3	*Use QRCVDTAQ to retrieve job related information from the Job-Notification exit point.*
FIGC6_5	6.5	*Use QSNDDTAQ to end the program shown in Figure 6.3.*
FIGC6_7	6.7	*Use QMHQRDQD to retrieve data queue descriptive information.*
FIGC7_2	7.2	*Use record information from a database trigger exit point.*
FIGC7_4	7.4	*Use QUSLMBR to find all members in a file.*
FIGC7_5	7.5	*Use QUSLMBR with QUSLOBJ and QUSRMBRD to find file members above a given percentage of deleted records.*
FIGC7_6	7.6	*Use QUSLFLD to find all fields in a file.*
FIGC7_10	7.10	*Use QDBRTVFD to find information about a file.*
FIGC8_1	8.1	*Use QWCCVTDT to convert from a YYMD date to a MDYY format.*
FIGC8_3	8.3	*Use QWCCVTDT to convert from a system timestamp date to a MDYY format.*
FIGC8_4	8.4	*Use QWCCVTDT to convert time values from one time-zone to another time-zone.*
FIGC8_7	8.7	*Use QWCADJTM to adjust the system time.*
FIGC8_8	8.8	*Use CEELOCT and CEEDATE to add 30 days to a date and format the result.*
FIGC8_9	8.9	*Use feedback parameter of CEE APIs.*

File Name	Figure	Description
Table C.1: Code on the Web ILE COBOL Cross-Reference Information (continued)		
FIGC8_10	8.10	Use CVTHC to format the message ID of the CEE feedback parameter.
FIGC9_3	9.3	Use QLGCONVERTCASE to monocase character data.
FIGC9_9	9.9	Use QTQICONVOPEN, iconv, and ICONV_CLOSE to convert character data from one CCSID to another CCSID.
FIGC10_2	10.2	Use message information from a message watch exit point.
FIGC10_4	10.4	Use QSCSWCH to start a watch for message CPF2456.
FIGC10_6	10.6	Use QMHSNDPM and sleep to send a status message.
FIGC10_9	10.9	Use QMHSNDPM and sleep to send a status message with replacement data along with a completion message.
FIGC10_11	10.11	Use QMHRTVM and QLGCONVERTCASE to search all messages in a message file for a character string.
FIGC11_1	11.1	Use Qc3CreateKeyContext, Qc3GenPRNs, Qc3EncryptData, and Qc3DestroyKeyContext to encrypt user data.
FIGC11_11	11.11	Use Qc3CreateKeyContext, Qc3DecryptData, and Qc3DestroyKeyContext to decrypt user data.
FIGC11_12	11.12	Use Qc3LoadMasterKeyPart, Qc3SetMasterKey, Qc3CreateKeyStore, and Qc3GenKeyRecord to create a cryptographic key-management environment.
FIGC11_17	11.17	Use Qc3CreateKeyContext, Qc3GenPRNs, Qc3EncryptData, and Qc3DestroyKeyContext to encrypt user data within a key-management environment.
FIGC11_20	11.20	Use Qc3CreateKeyContext, Qc3DecryptData, and Qc3DestroyKeyContext to decrypt user data within a key-management environment.
FIGC12_3	12.3	Use QsyGetProfileHandleNoPwd, QsyGetProfileHandle, QsySetToProfileHandle, and QsyReleaseProfileHandle to swap the current user profile of a job.
FIGC12_5	12.5	Use QSYRUPWD and QSNDDTAQ to retrieve and send a user profile encrypted password.

File Name	Figure	Description
FIGC12_7	12.7	Use QSYSUPWD and QRCVDTAQ to receive and apply a user profile encrypted password.
FIGC12_13	12.13	Use Change User Profile exit point, QSYRUSRI, and QSNDDTAQ to send user profile change information.
FIGC12_15	12.15	Use QCMDEXC and QRCVDTAQ to receive and apply user profile changes.
FIGC13_1	13.1	Use QUSLJOB to find all jobs on the system.
FIGC13_15	13.15	Use QWTCHGJB to change the job environment to match the current user profile for the job.
FIGC13_17	13.17	Use QWCRSSTS to determine if the system is in restricted state.
FIGC14_12A	14.12.A	Use open, read, write, close, and __errno to create an EBCDIC stream file containing text.
FIGC14_12B	14.12.B	Use open, read, write, close, and __errno to create an EBCDIC stream file containing text and record/line separators.
FIGC14_12C	14.12.C	Use open, read, write, close, and __errno to create an ASCII stream file containing text and record/line separators.
FIGC14_20	14.20	Use opendir, readdir, closedir, and __errno to list most entries in an Integrated File System directory.
FIGC14_23	14.23	Use open, write, close, QUSRJOBI, QCMDEXC, and __errno to create a stream file named ?.
FIGC14_24	14.24	Use QlgOpendir, QlgReaddir, closedir, and __errno to list all entries in an Integrated File System directory.
FIGC14_25	14.25	Use Qp0lOpen, write, close, and __errno to create a stream file named ?.
FIGC15_15	15.15	Use SOCKET, BIND, LISTEN, ACCEPT, RECV, SEND, close, QCMDEXC, and __errno to provide a simple file transfer server.
FIGC15_18	15.18	Use GETHOSTBYNAME, SOCKET, CONNECT, SEND, RECV, close, and __errno to provide a simple file transfer client.
FIGC15_26	15.26	Use SOCKET, BIND, LISTEN, ACCEPT, RECV, SEND, close, QUSROBJD, QLIRLIBD, and __errno to provide a library information server.

Table C.1: Code on the Web ILE COBOL Cross-Reference Information (continued)

Table C.1: Code on the Web ILE COBOL Cross-Reference Information (continued)		
File Name	**Figure**	**Description**
FIGC15_27	15.27	Use GETHOSTBYNAME, SOCKET, CONNECT, SEND, RECV, close, QMHSNDPM, and __errno to provide a library information client.
FIGC15_41	15.41	Use SOCKET, GETSERVBYNAME, SETSOCKOPT, BIND, LISTEN, ACCEPT, SEND, RECV, GIVEDESCRIPTOR, close, QRCVDTAQ, QCMDEXC, and __errno to provide a routing server.
FIGC15_42	15.42	Use RECV, SEND, TAKEDESCRIPTOR, close, QSNDDTAQ, QUSRJOBI, QCMDEXC, and __errno to provide an enhanced file transfer server.
FIGC15_43	15.43	Use RECV, SEND, TAKEDESCRIPTOR, close, QSNDDTAQ, QUSROBJD, QLIRLIBD, QUSRJOBI, and __errno to provide an enhanced library information server.
FIGC15_44	15.44	Use GETHOSTBYNAME, SOCKET, GETSERVBYNAME, CONNECT, SEND, RECV, close, and __errno to provide an enhanced file transfer client.
FIGC15_45	15.45	Use GETHOSTBYNAME, SOCKET, GETSERVBYNAME, CONNECT, SEND, RECV, close, QMHSNDPM, and __errno to provide an enhanced library information client.
FIGC15_47	15.47	Use TCP/IP Server exit point, GETHOSTBYNAME, SOCKET, GETSERVBYNAME, CONNECT, SEND, close, QUSRJOBI, QRCVD-TAQ, QCMDEXC, and __errno to start and end a user defined TCP/IP server.
FIGC15_48	15.48	Use SOCKET, SETSOCKOPT, BIND, LISTEN, ACCEPT, RECV, SEND, close, QUSROBJD, QLIRLIBD, QTQICONVOPEN, iconv, ICONV_CLOSE, QlgConvertCase, and __errno to provide a simple Telnet based library information server.
FIGC16_4	16.4	Use QLGSORT and QUSLJOB to list selected jobs on the system in a specific order.
FIGC16_5	16.5	Use QsyUpdateUserApplicationInfo to associate application specific information with a user profile.
FIGC16_8	16.8	Use QsyRetrieveUserApplicationInfo and QsyUpdateUserApplicationInfo to read and maintain application specific information associated with a user profile.
FIGC16_11	16.11	Use QSZRTVPR to retrieve the current release of the operating system.

Table C.1: Code on the Web ILE COBOL Cross-Reference Information (continued)		
File Name	Figure	Description
FIGC16_14	16.14	*Use QSRLSAVF and continuation handles to list all objects in a *SAVF when the list spans multiple user spaces.*
FIGC16_16	16.16	*Use QUSLOBJ to list all objects in a library using a SFLSIZ = SFLPAG subfile.*
FIGCD_2	D.2	*Use QSYRUSRI to return the status of a *USRPRF.*
FIGCD_3	D.3	*Use QWCLASBS to list all currently active subsystems.*
FIGCD_4	D.4	*Use QCMDEXC to create a *DTAQ.*
FIGCD_5	D.5	*Use QLIRNMO to rename a *DTAQ.*
FIGCD_6_A	D.6.A	*Use QSNDDTAQ to send a 'STOP' message including reason code and time.*
FIGCD_6_B	D.6.B	*Use QRCVDTAQ to receive a 'STOP' message and display the reason code and time sent in the message.*
FIGCD_7	D.7	*Use QDMRTVFO to determine if a file override is in effect.*
FIGCD_8	D.8	*Use CEEDAYS and CEEDATE to format a date value.*
FIGCD_9	D.9	*Use QLGCONVERTCASE to scan character data without regard to case.*
FIGCD_10_B	D.10.B	*Use QMHSNDPM to send a diagnostic and escape message.*
FIGCD_11_A	D.11.A	*Use Qc3WriteKeyRecord to write a restricted key to a key store file.*
FIGCD_11_B	D.11.B	*Use Qc3RetrieveKeyRecordAtr and CVTHC to display the attributes of a key found in a key store file.*
FIGCD_12	D.12	*Use QSYCUSRS to determine if a *USRPRF has a special authority.*
FIGCD_13	D.13	*Use QWDRSBSD to determine the current status of a subsystem.*
FIGCD_14	D.14	*Use unlink to delete a stream file.*
FIGCD_15_A	D.15.A	*A routing server to support exchange of encrypted passwords.*
FIGCD_15_B	D.15.B	*Application server for sending of encrypted passwords.*
FIGCD_15_C	D.15.C	*Application client for applying of encrypted passwords.*

Compiling the Source Code

There are some COBOL examples that require the use of one or more binding directories when compiling the source. In these cases the source includes a comment such as:

```
* CRTBNDCBL BNDDIR(YYY)
```

just prior to the PROGRAM-ID paragraph. In these situations the addition of the BNDDIR(YYY) parameter to the previous CRTBNDCBL and CRTSRVPGM examples is necessary.

Some Additional APIs

The COBOL source code includes the use of APIs that are not necessary when using ILE RPG. These additional APIs are used in those situations where COBOL does not provide direct language support for a particular RPG builtin operation. These additional APIs include:

- ANDSTR – A machine interface (MI) instruction to enable bit comparisons

- FREE – A C run-time API to free storage that was dynamically allocated for a Linkage Section data item

- MALLOC – A C run-time API to dynamically allocate storage for a Linkage Section data item

- QECCVTEC – A system API to convert an edit code into an edit mask

- QECCVTEW – A system API to convert an edit word into an edit mask

- QECEDT – A system API to format a numeric data item using an edit mask

- REALLOC – A C run-time API to dynamically reallocate the storage associated with a Linkage Section data item

D

Answers

THIS appendix provides possible solutions for the tasks in the "Check Your Knowledge" sections found at the end of most chapters.

Solution for Chapter 1

All of the documentation for system APIs can be found in the Information Center. This should always be your starting point in determining what APIs are available and how to use them.

You have a few options to locate an API related to save files. One option would be to use the API Finder available in the Information Center under "Programming," "APIs," and then "API Finder." In the "Find by name" search, you could try searching on "save file." On a V5R4 system, this would return three matches:

- Copy Program Temporary Fix to Save File (QPZCPYSV)

- List Product in a Save File (QLPLPRDS)

- List Save File (QSRLSAVF)

By clicking on each of these APIs and reviewing its brief description, it would appear that the API you want is List Save File, QSRLSAVF.

Another approach would be to use the "APIs by category" support of the Information Center. When selecting this option, you will be presented with many possible categories that you can examine further. The category list starts with "Backup and Recovery" and "Client Management Support," and continues through "Work Station Support" and "Miscellaneous." As save files are used for backup and recovery, it makes sense to look in that category first. Many APIs are listed under "Backup and Recovery," one of which is List Save File (QSRLSAVF) with the descriptive text "lists the contents of a save file." This certainly sounds like the one you want!

Solution for Chapter 2

```
DName+++++++++++ETDsFrom+++To/L+++IDc.Keywords++++++++++++++++++++++++++++++
d/copy qsysinc/qrpglesrc,qsyrusri
d/copy qsysinc/qrpglesrc,qusec

dRtvUsrI             pr                    extpgm('QSYRUSRI')
d Receiver                          1      options(*varsize)
d LengthRcv                        10i 0   const
d Format                            8      const
d UsrPrfName                       10      const
d QUSEC                                    likeds(QUSEC)

dWait                s              1

CLON01Factor1+++++++Opcode&ExtFactor2+++++++Result++++++++Len++D+HiLoEq
 /free

   QUSBPRV = %size(QUSEC);

   RtvUsrI( QSYI0100 :%size(QSYI0100) :'USRI0100' :'SAMPLE' :QUSEC);
   if (QUSBAVL > 0);
      dsply ('Error ' + QUSEI + ' returned') ' ' Wait;
   else;
      dsply ('Profile SAMPLE is ' + QSYUS01) ' ' Wait;
   endif;

   *inlr = *on;
   return;

 /end-free
```

Figure D.2: Retrieving the status of a user profile.

Solution for Chapter 3

```
h dftactgrp(*no) bnddir('APILIB')

DName++++++++++++ETDsFrom+++To/L+++IDc.Keywords+++++++++++++++++++++++++++
d/copy qsysinc/qrpglesrc,qusgen
d/copy qsysinc/qrpglesrc,qwclasbs
d/copy qsysinc/qrpglesrc,qusec

dListActSbs         pr                      extpgm('QWCLASBS')
d SpcName                          20       const
d Format                           8        const
d QUSEC                                     likeds(QUSEC)

dCrtUsrSpc          pr              *        extproc('CrtUsrSpc')
d SpcName                           20       const

 * List API Generic header from QUSGEN
dGenHdr             ds                      likeds(QUSH0100)
d                                           based(GenHdrPtr)

 * List Active Subsystem (QWCLASBS) API format SBSL0100
dListEntry          ds                      likeds(QWCL0100)
d                                           based(LstPtr)

dSpcName            ds
d SName                             10      inz('SBSLIST')
d Slib                              10      inz('QTEMP')

dcount              s               10i 0
dWait               s               1

CLON01Factor1+++++++Opcode&ExtFactor2+++++++Result++++++++Len++D+HiLoEq
 /free

  QUSBPRV = %size(QUSEC);

  GenHdrPtr = CrtUsrSpc(SpcName);

  ListActSbs(SpcName :'SBSL0100' :QUSEC);

  if QUSBAVL > 0;
     dsply ('Error ' + QUSEI +' returned.') ' ' Wait;

  else;
     if (GenHdr.QUSIS = 'C') or (GenHdr.QUSIS = 'P');
```

Figure D.3: Listing the active subsystems on your system (part 1 of 2).

```
          LstPtr = GenHdrPtr + GenHdr.QUSOLD;
          for count = 1 to GenHdr.QUSNBRLE;
               dsply (%trimr(ListEntry.QWCSDN) + ' in library ' +
                    ListEntry.QWCSDLN);
               LstPtr = LstPtr + GenHdr.QUSSEE;
          endfor;
          dsply 'End of active subsystems' ' ' Wait;

     else;
          dsply 'Invalid results from API call' ' ' Wait;
     endif;

   endif;

   *inlr = *on;
   return;

 /end-free
```

Figure D.3: Listing the active subsystems on your system (part 2 of 2).

Solution for Chapter 4

```
DName+++++++++++ETDsFrom+++To/L+++IDc.Keywords+++++++++++++++++++++++++++
dCmdExc             pr                      extpgm('QCMDEXC')
d Command                         65535     const options(*varsize)
d CmdLength                          15   5 const
d IGC                                 3     const options(*nopass)


dCommand            s               100     inz('CRTDTAQ SOMELIB/TESTQ +
d                                           MAXLEN(1000)')

CLON01Factor1+++++++Opcode&ExtFactor2+++++++Result++++++++Len++D+HiLoEq

 /free

   CmdExc( Command :%len(%trimr(Command)));

   *inlr = *on;
   return;

 /end-free
```

Figure D.4: Creating the *DTAQ TESTQ in library SOMELIB.

Solution for Chapter 5

```
DName++++++++++ETDsFrom+++To/L+++IDc.Keywords++++++++++++++++++++++++
d/copy qsysinc/qrpglesrc,qusec

dRnmObj              pr                    extpgm('QLIRNMO')
d FromObj                         20       const
d ObjType                         10       const
d ToObj                           20       const
d Replace                          1       const
d QUSEC                                    likeds(QUSEC)
d FromASP                         10       options(*nopass)
d ToASP                           10       options(*nopass)

dFromObj             ds
d FromName                        10       inz('TESTQ')
d FromLib                         10       inz('SOMELIB')

dToObj               ds
d ToName                          10       inz('RENAMEDQ')
d ToLib                           10       inz('SOMELIB')

dwait                s            1

CLON01Factor1+++++++Opcode&ExtFactor2+++++++Result++++++++Len++D+HiLoEq
 /free

   QUSBPRV = %size(QUSEC);

   RnmObj(FromObj :'*DTAQ' :ToObj :'1' :QUSEC);
   if QUSBAVL <> 0;
      dsply ('Error ' + QUSEI + ' found') ' ' Wait;
   endif;

   *inlr = *on;
   return;

 /end-free
```

Figure D.5: Renaming the *DTAQ TESTQ in SOMELIB to RENAMEDQ.

Solutions for Chapter 6

```
DName++++++++++++ETDsFrom+++To/L+++IDc.Keywords++++++++++++++++++++++++++++
dSndDtaQ          pr                    extpgm('QSNDDTAQ')
d DtaQName                        10    const
d DtaQLib                        10    const
d DataLen                         5  0 const
d Data                        65535    const options(*varsize)
d KeyLen                          3  0 const options(*nopass)
d KeyValue                    65535    const options(*varsize :*nopass)
d Asynch                         10    const options(*nopass)
d JrnEntry                       10    const options(*nopass)

dMsgData          ds
d Reason                         30
d StopTime                        z


CLON01Factor1+++++++Opcode&ExtFactor2+++++++Result++++++++Len++D+HiLoEq
/free

    // end the FIG6_3 program by sending a KeyValue of 'STOP'
    // along with why and when

    Reason = 'Big Al told me to';
    StopTime = %timestamp;
    SndDtaQ( 'FIG6_1' :'SOMELIB' :%size(MsgData) :MsgData :4 :'STOP');

    *inlr = *on;
    return;

/end-free
```

Figure D.6.A: Sending the *STOP* message with Reason and StopTime.

```
DName++++++++++++ETDsFrom+++To/L+++IDc.Keywords++++++++++++++++++++++++++++
d/copy qsysinc/qrpglesrc,qrcvdtaq
d/copy qsysinc/qrpglesrc,ejobntfy
d/copy qsysinc/qrpglesrc,qusec

dRcvDtaQ          pr                    extpgm('QRCVDTAQ')
d DtaQName                        10    const
d DtaQLib                        10    const
d ReceiverLenRtn                  5  0
```

Figure D.6.B: Receive a *STOP* message and display the Reason and StopTime (part 1 of 3).

```
d Receiver                        1      options(*varsize)
d WaitTime                        5    0 const
d KeyOrder                        2      const options(*nopass)
d KeyLen                          3    0 const options(*nopass)
d KeyValue                        1      options(*varsize :*nopass)
d SndrInfoLen                     3    0 const options(*nopass)
d SndrInfo                        1      options(*varsize :*nopass)
d RmvMsg                         10      const options(*nopass)
d ReceiverLen                     5    0 const options(*nopass)
d QUSEC                                  likeds(QUSEC) options(*nopass)

dReceiver          DS           200      qualified
d StrEnd                                 likeds(EJOQJSEN)
d                                        overlay(Receiver :1)
d JobQ                                   likeds(EJOQJQN)
d                                        overlay(Receiver :1)
d Reason                         30      overlay(Receiver :1)
d StopTime                        z      overlay(Receiver :31)

dReceiverLenRtn    s              5    0
dKeyValue          s              4
dText              s             40
dWait              s              1
CLON01Factor1+++++++Opcode&ExtFactor2+++++++Result++++++++Len++D+HiLoEq
 /free

   QUSBPRV = %size(QUSEC);

   //process until 'STOP' is received from program FIG6_4
   dow (KeyValue <> 'STOP');

      KeyValue = *loval;

      RcvDtaQ( 'FIG6_1' :'SOMELIB' :ReceiverLenRtn :Receiver :-1
             :'GE'    :4         :KeyValue        :0          :QRCQSI
             :'*YES'  :%size(Receiver) :QUSEC);

      if (QUSBAVL > 0);
         Text = 'Unexpected error ' + QUSEI + ' accessing data queue';
         dsply Text ' ' Wait;
         leave;
      endif;

      select;
      when (KeyValue = 'STOP');
```

Figure D.6.B: Receive a *STOP* message and display the Reason and StopTime (part 2 of 3).

691

```
            // check if additional data was sent just in case
            // the message was sent by the original FIG63
            if (ReceiverLenRtn >= %size(Receiver.Reason));
                dsply ('Reason: ' + Receiver.Reason);
                if (ReceiverLenRtn >= (%size(Receiver.Reason) +
                    %size(Receiver.StopTime)));
                    dsply ('Time  : ' + %char(Receiver.StopTime));
                endif;
                dsply 'Press Enter to continue.' ' ' Wait;

            else;
                dsply 'No reason code received' ' ' Wait;
            endif;
            leave;

    when (KeyValue = '0001');
        if (%subst(Receiver.StrEnd.EJOQJN :11 :10) = 'BIGAL');
            // do whatever you want to Big Al
            dsply 'Changed Big Al job' ' ' Wait;
        endif;

    when (KeyValue = '0002');

    when (KeyValue = '0004');
        if (%subst(Receiver.JobQ.EJOQJN00 :11 :10) = 'BIGAL');
            // do whatever you want to submitted job of Big Al
            dsply 'Changed submitted job' ' ' Wait;
        endif;

    other;
        dsply 'Unexpected key during processing' ' ' Wait;
    endsl;
enddo;

*inlr = *on;
return;

/end-free
```

Figure D.6.B: Receive a STOP message and display the Reason and StopTime (part 3 of 3).

Solution for Chapter 7

```
DName+++++++++++ETDsFrom+++To/L+++IDc.Keywords+++++++++++++++++++++++++++
d/copy qsysinc/qrpglesrc,qdmrtvfo
d/copy qsysinc/qrpglesrc,qusec

dRtvOvrInf         pr                    extpgm('QDMRTVFO')
d Receiver                        1      options(*varsize)
d LenReceiver                    10i 0   const
d Format                          8      const
d FileName                       10      const
d QUSEC                                  likeds(QUSEC)

dWait              s              1

CLON01Factor1+++++++Opcode&ExtFactor2+++++++Result++++++++Len++D+HiLoEq
 /free

   QUSBPRV = %size(QUSEC);

   RtvOvrInf( QDML0100 :%size(QDML0100) :'OVRL0100' :'CUSTOMER' :QUSEC);
   if (QUSBAVL > 0);
      dsply ('Error ' + QUSEI + ' returned.') ' ' Wait;
   else;

      if (QDMFILNU <> *BLANKS);
         dsply ('CUSTOMER override to ' + %trimr(QDMLIBNU) + '/' +
                %trimr(QDMFILNU) + '.') ' ' Wait;
      else;
         dsply 'No override for CUSTOMER found.' ' ' Wait;
      endif;
   endif;

   *inlr = *on;
   return;

 /end-free
```

*Figure D.7: Display any **TOFILE** override for the **CUSTOMER** file.*

Solution for Chapter 8

```
h dftactgrp(*no)

DName+++++++++++ETDsFrom+++To/L+++IDc.Keywords+++++++++++++++++++++++++++++
dGetLilian        pr                      extproc('CEEDAYS') OPDESC
d InputDate                     65535     options(*varsize) const
d InputString                   65535     options(*varsize) const
d LilianDay                     10i 0
d fc                            12        options(*omit)

dFormatDate       pr                      extproc('CEEDATE') OPDESC
d LilianDay                     10i 0 const
d Picture                       65535     const options(*varsize)
d Date                          1         options(*varsize)
d fc                            12        options(*omit)

dLilianDay        s             10i 0
dMyDate           s             8         inz('20070401')

dDate             s             30
dWait             s             1

CLON01Factor1+++++++Opcode&ExtFactor2+++++++Result++++++++Len++D+HiLoEq

 /free

   GetLilian( MyDate :'YYYYMMDD' :LilianDay :*omit);

   FormatDate(LilianDay :'Www, Mmmmmmmmmmmz DD YYYY' :Date :*omit);

   dsply Date ' ' Wait;

   *inlr = *on;
   return;

 /end-free
```

Figure D.8: Formatting an arbitrary YYYYMMDD date value.

Solution for Chapter 9

```
h dftactgrp(*no)

FFilename++IPEASF.....L.....A.Device+.Keywords++++++++++++++++++++++++++++
fCustomer  if   e          disk

DName++++++++++++ETDsFrom+++To/L+++IDc.Keywords++++++++++++++++++++++++++++
d/copy qsysinc/qrpglesrc,qlg
d/copy qsysinc/qrpglesrc,qusec

dConvertCase       pr                    extproc('QlgConvertCase')
d Request                      65535     const options(*varsize)
d InputData                    65535     const options(*varsize)
d OutputData                       1     options(*varsize)
d InputDataLen                  10i 0    const
d QUSEC                                  likeds(QUSEC)

dOutputData        s                     like(CustName)
dWait              s              1

CLON01Factor1+++++++Opcode&ExtFactor2+++++++Result++++++++Len++D+HiLoEq
/free

  QUSBPRV = %size(QUSEC);

  QLGIDRCB00 = *loval;        // set input structure to x'00'
  QLGTOR02 = 1;               // use CCSID for monocasing
  QLGIDOID00 = 0;             // use the job CCSID
  QLGCR00 = 0;                // convert to uppercase

  read CusRec;

  dou %eof(Customer);
      ConvertCase( QLGIDRCB00 :CustName :OutputData
                 :%len(%trimr(CustName)) :QUSEC);
      if QUSBAVL > 0;
          dsply ('Error ' + QUSEI + ' returned.') ' ' Wait;
          *inlr = *on;
          return;
      endif;

      if (%scan('MPA' :OutputData) > 0);
          dsply CustName;
      endif;
      read CusRec;
  enddo;
```

Figure D.9: Scanning character data without regard to case (part 1 of 2).

```
    dsply 'End of customer listing' ' ' Wait;

    *inlr = *on;
    return;

/end-free
```

Figure D.9: Scanning character data without regard to case (part 2 of 2).

Solutions for Chapter 10

```
ADDMSGD MSGID(MSG0006) MSGF(SOMELIB/MSGS) MSG('I found a problem with
my input')

ADDMSGD MSGID(MSG0007) MSGF(SOMELIB/MSGS) MSG('This problem has caused
me to stop running')
```

Figure D.10.A: Adding message descriptions MSG0006 and MSG0007.

```
h dftactgrp(*no)

DName+++++++++++ETDsFrom+++To/L+++IDc.Keywords+++++++++++++++++++++++++
d/copy qsysinc/qrpglesrc,qusec

dSndPgmMsg            pr                 extpgm('QMHSNDPM')
d MsgID                        7         const
d QualMsgF                    20         const
d MsgDta                   65535         const options(*varsize)
d LenMsgDta                  10i 0 const
d MsgType                    10         const
d CallStackEntry          65535         const options(*varsize)
d CallStackCntr              10i 0 const
d MsgKey                      4
d QUSEC                                  likeds(QUSEC)
d LenCSE                     10i 0 const options(*nopass)
d CSEQual                    20         const options(*nopass)
d DSPWaitTime                10i 0 const options(*nopass)
d CSEType                    10         const options(*nopass)
d CCSID                      10i 0 const options(*nopass)
```

Figure D.10.B: The program to send message descriptions MSG0006 and MSG0007 (part 1 of 2).

```
dQualMsgF          ds
d MsgF                          10    inz('MSGS')
d MsgL                          10    inz('SOMELIB')

dMsgKey            s             4

CLON01Factor1+++++++Opcode&ExtFactor2+++++++Result+++++++++Len++D+HiLoEq
 /free

   QUSBPRV = 0;

   SndPgmMsg( 'MSG0006' :QualMsgF :' ' :0
              :'*DIAG' :'*PGMBDY' :1 :MsgKey :QUSEC);
   SndPgmMsg( 'MSG0007' :QualMsgF :' ' :0
              :'*ESCAPE' :'*PGMBDY' :1 :MsgKey :QUSEC);

   // The following statement is solely for documentation purposes.
   // Sending an *ESCAPE will end the sending program.

   return;
 /end-free
```

Figure D.10.B: The program to send message descriptions *MSG0006* and *MSG0007* (part 2 of 2).

Solutions for Chapter 11

```
h dftactgrp(*no)

DName++++++++++ETDsFrom+++To/L+++IDc.Keywords++++++++++++++++++++++++++
d/copy qsysinc/qrpglesrc,qusec

dWrtKeyRcd         pr                   extproc('Qc3WriteKeyRecord')
d QualKeyStore                 20       const
d RcdLabel                     32       const
d KeyString                 65535       const options(*varsize)
d LenKeyStr                  10i 0 const
d KeyFormat                    1       const
d KeyType                    10i 0 const
d DisallowFnc                10i 0 const
d KeyForm                      1       const
d KeyContext                   8       const options(*omit)
d AlgContext                   8       const options(*omit)
d QUSEC                               likeds(QUSEC)
```

Figure D.11.A: Writing a restricted key record (part 1 of 2).

```
dKeyStoreFile      s           20      inz('ABCSTORE  SOMELIB')
dRcdKey            s           32      inz('Checking my knowledge')
dKey               s           16      inz('My first key')

dEncryption        c                   1
dDecryption        c                   2
dMACing            c                   4
dSigning           c                   8

CLON01Factor1+++++++Opcode&ExtFactor2+++++++Result+++++++++Len++D+HiLoEq
 /free

   QUSBPRV = 0;

   WrtKeyRcd ( KeyStoreFile :RcdKey :Key :%size(Key) :'0' :22
             :(MACing + Signing) :'0' :*OMIT :*OMIT :QUSEC);

   *inlr = *on;
   return;

 /end-free
```

Figure D.11.A: Writing a restricted key record (part 2 of 2).

```
h dftactgrp(*no) bnddir('QC2LE')

DName+++++++++++ETDsFrom+++To/L+++IDc.Keywords+++++++++++++++++++++++++++
d/copy qsysinc/qrpglesrc,qusec

dRtvKeyRcdA        pr                  extproc(
d                                      'Qc3RetrieveKeyRecordAtr')
d QualKeyStore              20         const
d RcdLabel                  32         const
d KeyType                   10i 0
d KeySize                   10i 0
d MstKeyID                  10i 0
d MstKeyKVV                 20
d DisallowFnc               10i 0
d QUSEC                                likeds(QUSEC)

dHexToChar         pr                  extproc('cvthc')
d MstKeyKVVPtr                    *    value
```

Figure D.11.B: Retrieving key record information (part 1 of 3).

```
d MsgKeyKVVChar                        *   value
d Size                              10i 0 value

dKeyStoreFile     s                 20    inz('ABCSTORE  SOMELIB')
dRcdKey           s                 32    inz('Checking my knowledge')
dKeyType          s                 10i 0
dKeySize          s                 10i 0
dMstKeyID         s                 10i 0
dMstKeyKVV        s                 20
dMstKeyKVVChar    s                 40
dNibblesToCvt     s                 10i 0
dDisallowFnc      s                 10i 0
dWait             s                  1

dEncryption       c                      1
dDecryption       c                      2
dMACing           c                      4
dSigning          c                      8
```

```
CL0N01Factor1+++++++Opcode&ExtFactor2+++++++Result++++++++Len++D+HiLoEq
 /free

  QUSBPRV = 0;

  RtvKeyRcdA ( KeyStoreFile :RcdKey :KeyType :KeySize :MstKeyID
            :MstKeyKVV :DisallowFnc :QUSEC);

  dsply ('Key type is ' + %char(KeyType));
  dsply ('Key size is ' + %char(KeySize));
  dsply ('Master key ID is ' + %char(MstKeyID));

  // Just in case someone changes the size of either the input or
  // output variable of HexToChar, and forget about the other, let's
  // calculate the maximum number of nibbles it's safe to convert
  if (2 * %size(MstKeyKVV)) > %size(MstKeyKVVChar);
     NibblesToCvt = %size(MstKeyKVVChar);
  else;
     MstKeyKVVChar = *blanks;
     NibblesToCvt = (2 * %size(MstKeyKVV));
  endif;

  HexToChar( %addr(MstKeyKVVChar) :%addr(MstKeyKVV) :NibblesToCvt);
  dsply ('Master key KVV is:');
  dsply MstKeyKVVChar;
```

Figure D.11.B: Retrieving key record information (part 2 of 3).

```
   if %bitand(DisallowFnc :Encryption) = Encryption;
      dsply 'Encryption not allowed';
   endif;
   if %bitand(DisallowFnc :Decryption) = Decryption;
      dsply 'Decryption not allowed';
   endif;
   if %bitand(DisallowFnc :MACing) = MACing;
      dsply 'MACing not allowed';
   endif;
   if %bitand(DisallowFnc :Signing) = Signing;
      dsply 'Signing not allowed';
   endif;

   dsply 'End of attributes' ' ' Wait;

   *inlr = *on;
   return;

 /end-free
```

Figure D.11.B: Retrieving key record information (part 3 of 3).

Solution for Chapter 12

```
h dftactgrp(*no)

DName+++++++++++ETDsFrom+++To/L+++IDc.Keywords++++++++++++++++++++++++++
d/copy qsysinc/qrpglesrc,qusec

dChkSpcAut        pr                  extpgm('QSYCUSRS')
d AuthInd                       1
d UsrPrf                       10     const
d SpcAuts                             likeds(SpcAuts) const
d NbrSpcAuts                   10i 0  const
d CallLvl                      10i 0  const
d QUSEC                               likeds(QUSEC)

dSpcAuts          ds                  qualified
d SpcAut                       10     dim(8)

dAuthInd          s             1
dNbrSpcAuts       s            10i 0
dWait             s             1
```

*Figure D.12: Checking for the special authority of *SECADM (part 1 of 2).*

700

```
CLON01Factor1+++++++Opcode&ExtFactor2+++++++Result++++++++Len++D+HiLoEq
/free

  QUSBPRV = 0;
  NbrSpcAuts += 1;
  SpcAuts.SpcAut(1) = '*SECADM';

  ChkSpcAut( AuthInd :'*CURRENT' :SpcAuts :NbrSpcAuts :2 :QUSEC);

  select;
     when AuthInd = 'N';
          dsply 'Not authorized' ' ' Wait;
     when AuthInd = 'Y';
          dsply 'Authorized' ' ' Wait;
     other;
          dsply 'Unknown authorization value' ' ' Wait;
  endsl;

  *inlr = *on;
  return;

/end-free
```

*Figure D.12: Checking for the special authority of * SECADM (part 2 of 2).*

Solution for Chapter 13

```
h dftactgrp(*no)

DName+++++++++++ETDsFrom+++To/L+++IDc.Keywords+++++++++++++++++++++++++++
d/copy qsysinc/qrpglesrc,qwdrsbsd
d/copy qsysinc/qrpglesrc,qusec

dRtvSbsInfo        pr                  extpgm('QWDRSBSD')
d Receiver                    1        options(*varsize)
d LenReceiver                10i 0 const
d Format                      8        const
d QualSbsName                20        const
d QUSEC                                likeds(QUSEC)
d NbrQSbsName                10i 0 const options(*nopass)

dSbsName           s         20        inz('QINTER    QSYS    ')
dWait              s          1
```

Figure D.13: Displaying the status of QINTER using format SBSI0100 (part 1 of 2).

```
CLON01Factor1+++++++Opcode&ExtFactor2+++++++Result++++++++Len++D+HiLoEq
 /free

  QUSBPRV = 0;

  RtvSbsInfo( QWDI0100 :%size(QWDI0100) :'SBSI0100' :SbsName :QUSEC);

  dsply ('QINTER subsystem is ' + QWDSS) ' ' Wait;

  *inlr = *on;
  return;

 /end-free
```

Figure D.13: Displaying the status of QINTER using format SBSI0100 (part 2 of 2).

Solution for Chapter 14

```
h dftactgrp(*no) bnddir('QC2LE')

DName++++++++++++ETDsFrom+++To/L+++IDc.Keywords+++++++++++++++++++++++++++
dDltF              pr              10i 0 extproc('unlink')
d Path                             *     value options(*string)

derrno             pr              *     extproc('__errno')

dErrorNbr          s               10i 0 based(ErrnoPtr)
dWait              s               1

CLON01Factor1+++++++Opcode&ExtFactor2+++++++Result++++++++Len++D+HiLoEq
 /free

  if DltF('/My_New_File.txt') <> 0;
    ErrnoPtr = errno;

    if ErrorNbr <> 3025;
      dsply ('Failure ' + %char(ErrorNbr) + ' on unlink') ' ' Wait;
    endif;

  endif;

  *inlr = *on;
  return;

 /end-free
```

Figure D.14: Deleting the /My_New_File.txt file.

Solutions for Chapter 15

```
h dftactgrp(*no) bnddir('QC2LE')

DName++++++++++ETDsFrom+++To/L+++IDc.Keywords+++++++++++++++++++++++++++
d/copy qsysinc/qrpglesrc,qrcvdtaq
d/copy qsysinc/qrpglesrc,qusec

dSocket           pr              10i 0 extproc('socket')
d AddrFamily                      10i 0 value
d Type                            10i 0 value
d Protocol                        10i 0 value

dGetPort          pr               *    extproc('getservbyname')
d ServName                         *    value options(*string)
d ProtName                         *    value options(*string)

dSockOpt          pr              10i 0 extproc('setsockopt')
d sd                              10i 0 value
d Level                           10i 0 value
d OptionName                      10i 0 value
d OptionValue                      *    value
d OptionLength                    10i 0 value

dBind             pr              10i 0 extproc('bind')
d sd                              10i 0 value
d LclAddrPtr                       *    value
d LenAddr                         10i 0 value

dListen           pr              10i 0 extproc('listen')
d sd                              10i 0 value
d BackLog                         10i 0 value

dAccept           pr              10i 0 extproc('accept')
d sd                              10i 0 value
d RmtAddrPtr                       *    value
d LenAddr                         10i 0

dRecv             pr              10i 0 extproc('recv')
d fd                              10i 0 value
d buf                              *    value
d lenbuf                          10i 0 value
d flags                           10i 0 value

dSend             pr              10i 0 extproc('send')
d fd                              10i 0 value
```

Figure D.15.A: Modifying FIG15_41 to support encrypted password exchanges (part 1 of 7).

```
d buf                                  *    value
d lenbuf                            10i 0 value
d flags                             10i 0 value

dGiveDesc          pr               10i 0 extproc('givedescriptor')
d sd                                10i 0 value
d IntJobID                          16    const

dCloseSocket       pr               10i 0 extproc('close')
d fd                                10i 0 value

dRcvDtaQ           pr                     extpgm('QRCVDTAQ')
d DtaQName                          10    const
d DtaQLib                           10    const
d ReceiverLenRtn                     5 0
d Receiver                           1    options(*varsize)
d WaitTime                           5 0 const
d KeyOrder                           2    const options(*nopass)
d KeyLen                             3 0 const options(*nopass)
d KeyValue                           1    options(*varsize :*nopass)
d SndrInfoLen                        3 0 const options(*nopass)
d SndrInfo                           1    options(*varsize :*nopass)
d RmvMsg                            10    const options(*nopass)
d ReceiverLen                        5 0 const options(*nopass)
d QUSEC                                   likeds(QUSEC) options(*nopass)

dCmdExc            pr                     extpgm('QCMDEXC')
d Command                        65535    const options(*varsize)
d CmdLength                         15 5 const
d IGC                                3    const options(*nopass)

dErrno             pr                *    extproc('__errno')

dLclAddr           ds
d SinFamily                          5i 0
d SinPort                            5u 0
d SinAddr                           10u 0
d SinZero                            8

dDestAddr          ds                     likeds(LclAddr)

dServiceEntry      ds                     based(ServiceEntryPtr)
d ServName                           *
d ServAlias                          *
d ServPort                          10i 0
d ServProtocol                       *
```

Figure D.15.A: Modifying FIG15_41 to support encrypted password exchanges (part 2 of 7).

```
dDQKey             ds                    qualified
d Key                          10i 0

dErrorNbr          s           10i 0 based(ErrnoPtr)
dsd                s           10i 0
dsdTarget          s           10i 0
dAddrLen           s           10i 0
drecvRC            s           10i 0
dFunction          s           10i 0
dMsgSizRtn         s            5  0
dIntJobID          s           16
dSndrInfo          s            1
dCmd_Sbm_File      s          100     inz('SBMJOB -
d                                     CMD(CALL PGM(SOMELIB/FIG15_42)) -
d                                     JOBQ(QSYS/QUSRNOMAX) -
d                                     CURLIB(SOMELIB)')
dCmd_Sbm_Appl      s          100     inz('SBMJOB -
d                                     CMD(CALL PGM(SOMELIB/FIG15_43)) -
d                                     JOBQ(QSYS/QUSRNOMAX) -
d                                     CURLIB(SOMELIB)')
dCmd_Sbm_Pwd       s          100     inz('SBMJOB CMD-
d                                     (CALL PGM(SOMELIB/FIGD_15_B)) -
d                                     JOBQ(QSYS/QUSRNOMAX) -
d                                     CURLIB(SOMELIB)')
dReUseYes          s           10i 0 inz(1)
dWait              s            1

dEOJ               c                   -1
dFileServer        c                    1
dApplServer        c                    2
dPwdServer         c                    3
dServerQ           c                   'MY_SVR_Q'
dServerLib         c                   'SOMELIB'
dService           c                   'My_Somelib_Server'
dProtocol          c                   'tcp'

dMSG_WAITALL       c                   64

dINADDR_ANY        c                    0
dINADDR_LOOPBACK   c                   2130706433

dAF_INET           c                    2
dAF_INET6          c                   24

dSOCK_STREAM       c                    1

dIPPROTO_IP        c                    0
```

Figure D.15.A: Modifying *FIG15_41* to support encrypted password exchanges (part 3 of 7).

```
dSOL_SOCKET         c                    -1
dSO_REUSEADDR       c                    55

CL0N01Factor1+++++++Opcode&ExtFactor2+++++++Result++++++++Len++D+HiLoEq
 /free

  QUSBPRV = %size(QUSEC);

  // Create a socket
  sd = socket( AF_INET :SOCK_STREAM :IPPROTO_IP);
  if (sd = -1);
     ErrnoPtr = Errno;
     dsply ('Failure ' + %char(ErrorNbr) + ' on socket') ' ' Wait;
     *inlr = *on;
     return;
  endif;


  // Allow the reuse of our port
  if SockOpt( sd :SOL_SOCKET :SO_REUSEADDR :%addr(ReUseYes)
              :%size(ReUseYes)) = -1;
              ErrnoPtr = Errno;
              dsply ('Failure ' + %char(ErrorNbr) + ' on setsockopt.')
                 ' ' Wait;
              *inlr = *on;
              return;
  endif;


  // Bind our local address to a socket
  LclAddr = *loval;
  SinFamily = AF_INET;
  ServiceEntryPtr = GetPort(%trimr(Service) :%trimr(Protocol));
  if ServiceEntryPtr = *NULL;
     dsply ('Service ' + Service + ' for ' + Protocol + 'not found.')
        ' ' Wait;
     *inlr = *on;
     return;
  endif;


  SinPort = ServPort;
  SinAddr = INADDR_ANY;
  if Bind( sd :%addr(LclAddr) :%size(LclAddr)) < 0;
     ErrnoPtr = Errno;
     dsply ('Failure ' + %char(ErrorNbr) + ' on bind') ' ' Wait;
     *inlr = *on;
     return;
  endif;
```

Figure D.15.A: Modifying FIG15_41 to support encrypted password exchanges (part 4 of 7).

```
// Listen for incoming data
if Listen( sd :3) < 0;
   ErrnoPtr = Errno;
   dsply ('Failure ' + %char(ErrorNbr) + ' on listen') ' ' Wait;
   *inlr = *on;
   return;
endif;

// Accept incoming data
dow Function <> EOJ;
   AddrLen = %size(DestAddr);
   sdTarget = Accept( sd :%addr(DestAddr) :AddrLen);
   if sdTarget < 0;
      ErrnoPtr = Errno;
      dsply ('Failure ' + %char(ErrorNbr) + ' on accept') ' ' Wait;
      leave;
   endif;

   // Get Function to perform
   recvRC = recv( sdTarget :%addr(Function) :%size(Function)
               :MSG_WAITALL);

   if recvRC <> -1;

      // Determine type of request and see if any jobs are available
      select;
         when Function = FileServer;
            DQKey.Key = FileServer;
            RcvDtaQ( ServerQ :ServerLib :MsgSizRtn :IntJobID
                     :0 :'EQ' :%size(DQKey) :DQKEY :0 :QRCQSI
                     :'*YES' :%size(IntJobID) :QUSEC);
            if MsgSizRtn = 0;
               // submit a server job
               CmdExc(Cmd_Sbm_File :%len(%trimr(Cmd_Sbm_File)));
               RcvDtaQ( ServerQ :ServerLib :MsgSizRtn :IntJobID
                        :60 :'EQ' :%size(DQKey) :DQKEY :0 :QRCQSI
                        :'*YES' :%size(IntJobID) :QUSEC);
               if MsgSizRtn = 0;
                  dsply 'File server time > 60 seconds' ' ' Wait;
                  CloseSocket( sdTarget);
                  leave;
               endif;
            endif;
            if GiveDesc( sdTarget :IntJobID) = -1;
               ErrnoPtr = Errno;
               dsply ('GiveDesc failed with ' + %char(ErrorNbr))
                     ' ' Wait;
               CloseSocket( sdTarget);
               leave;
            endif;
```

Figure D.15.A: Modifying *FIG15_41* to support encrypted password exchanges (part 5 of 7).

```
when Function = ApplServer;
     DQKey.Key = ApplServer;
     RcvDtaQ( ServerQ :ServerLib :MsgSizRtn :IntJobID
              :0 :'EQ' :%size(DQKey) :DQKEY :0 :QRCQSI
              :'*YES' :%size(IntJobID) :QUSEC);
     if MsgSizRtn = 0;
        // submit a server job
        CmdExc(Cmd_Sbm_Appl :%len(%trimr(Cmd_Sbm_Appl)));
        RcvDtaQ( ServerQ :ServerLib :MsgSizRtn :IntJobID
                 :60 :'EQ' :%size(DQKey) :DQKEY :0 :QRCQSI
                 :'*YES' :%size(IntJobID) :QUSEC);
        if MsgSizRtn = 0;
           dsply 'Appl server time > 60 seconds' ' ' Wait;
           CloseSocket( sdTarget);
           leave;
        endif;
     endif;
     if GiveDesc( sdTarget :IntJobID) = -1;
        ErrnoPtr = Errno;
        dsply ('GiveDesc failed with ' + %char(ErrorNbr))
               ' ' Wait;
        CloseSocket( sdTarget);
        leave;
     endif;

when Function = PwdServer;
     DQKey.Key = PwdServer;
     RcvDtaQ( ServerQ :ServerLib :MsgSizRtn :IntJobID
              :0 :'EQ' :%size(DQKey) :DQKEY :0 :QRCQSI
              :'*YES' :%size(IntJobID) :QUSEC);
     if MsgSizRtn = 0;
        // submit a server job
        CmdExc(Cmd_Sbm_Pwd :%len(%trimr(Cmd_Sbm_Pwd)));
        RcvDtaQ( ServerQ :ServerLib :MsgSizRtn :IntJobID
                 :60 :'EQ' :%size(DQKey) :DQKEY :0 :QRCQSI
                 :'*YES' :%size(IntJobID) :QUSEC);
        if MsgSizRtn = 0;
           dsply 'Pwd server time > 60 seconds' ' ' Wait;
           CloseSocket( sdTarget);
           leave;
        endif;
     endif;
     if GiveDesc( sdTarget :IntJobID) = -1;
        ErrnoPtr = Errno;
        dsply ('GiveDesc failed with ' + %char(ErrorNbr))
               ' ' Wait;
        CloseSocket( sdTarget);
        leave;
     endif;
```

Figure D.15.A: Modifying FIG15_41 to support encrypted password exchanges (part 6 of 7).

```
         when Function = EOJ;
               CloseSocket(sdTarget);
               // end server task waiting for work
               leave;
         other;
               dsply ('Unknown request ' + %char(Function) +
                     ' received.') ' ' Wait;
         endsl;
      else;
         dsply 'Unable to read Function.' ' ' Wait;
         CloseSocket(sdTarget);
         CloseSocket(sd);
         *inlr = *on;
         return;
      endif;


      // Close the connection
      if CloseSocket(sdTarget) < 0;
         dsply 'Error on client close' ' ' Wait;
      endif;

   // Loop back to accept the next connection
   enddo;

   if CloseSocket(sd) < 0;
      dsply 'Error on close' ' ' Wait;
   endif;
   *inlr = *on;
   return;

 /end-free
```

Figure D.15.A: Modifying FIG15_41 to support encrypted password exchanges (part 7 of 7).

```
h dftactgrp(*no) bnddir('QC2LE')

DName+++++++++++ETDsFrom+++To/L+++IDc.Keywords++++++++++++++++++++++++++
d/copy qsysinc/qrpglesrc,qsyrupwd
d/copy qsysinc/qrpglesrc,qusrjobi
d/copy qsysinc/qrpglesrc,qusec

dGetPassword        pr                  extpgm('QSYRUPWD')
d Receiver                       1      options(*varsize)
```

Figure D.15.B: A server for support of encrypted password exchanges (part 1 of 4).

```
d LenReceiver                    10i 0 const
d Format                          8    const
d Profile                        10    const
d USEC                                 likeds(QUSEC)

dRecv             pr             10i 0 extproc('recv')
d fd                             10i 0 value
d buf                             *    value
d lenbuf                         10i 0 value
d flags                          10i 0 value

dSend             pr             10i 0 extproc('send')
d fd                             10i 0 value
d buf                             *    value
d lenbuf                         10i 0 value
d flags                          10i 0 value

dTakeDesc         pr             10i 0 extproc('takedescriptor')
d SourceJob                       *    value

dCloseSocket      pr             10i 0 extproc('close')
d fd                             10i 0 value

dErrno            pr              *    extproc('__errno')

dSndDtaQ          pr                   extpgm('QSNDDTAQ')
d DtaQName                       10    const
d DtaQLib                        10    const
d DataLen                         5  0 const
d Data                        65535    const options(*varsize)
d KeyLen                          3  0 const options(*nopass)
d KeyValue                       10i 0 const options(*nopass)
d Asynch                         10    const options(*nopass)
d JrnEntry                       10    const options(*nopass)

dRtvJobI          pr                   extpgm('QUSRJOBI')
d RcvVar                          1    options(*varsize)
d LenRcvVar                      10i 0 const
d RcvVarFmt                       8    const
d JobName                        26    const
d IntJobID                       16    const
d QUSEC                                likeds(QUSEC) options(*nopass)
d Reset                           1    const options(*nopass)

dDQKey            ds                   qualified
d Key                            10i 0 inz(PwdServer)
```

Figure D.15.B: A server for support of encrypted password exchanges (part 2 of 4).

```
dReceiver        ds                      likeds(QSYD0100)
d                                        based(ReceiverPtr)

dErrCde          ds                      qualified
d EC                                     likeds(QUSEC)
d ErrDta                    512

dRcvSize         s          10i 0 inz(8)
dErrorNbr        s          10i 0 based(ErrnoPtr)
dsdTarget        s          10i 0
dUsrPrf          s          10
dAPI_Error       s          10i 0 inz(-2)
dWait            s           1

dServerQ         c                       'MY_SVR_Q'
dServerLib       c                       'SOMELIB'
dFileServer      c                       1
dApplServer      c                       2
dPwdServer       c                       3

dMSG_WAITALL     c                       64

CLON01Factor1+++++++Opcode&ExtFactor2+++++++Result++++++++Len++D+HiLoEq

 /free

   ErrCde.EC.QUSBPRV = %size(ErrCde);
   QUSBPRV = 0;

   // Let the main server know we're available by sending our
   // internal job ID and our server type as the key
   RtvJobI( QUSI010000 :%size(QUSI010000) :'JOBI0100' :'*' :' ' :QUSEC);
   SndDtaQ( ServerQ :ServerLib :%size(QUSIJID) :QUSIJID
           :%size(DQKey) :DQKey.Key);

   // Get a descriptor for our client
   sdTarget = TakeDesc(*NULL);

   dow sdTarget <> -1;

      // Read the user profile name to be processed
      if (recv( sdTarget :%addr(UsrPrf) :%size(UsrPrf)
         :MSG_WAITALL) <> -1);

         // Find out how large of a receiver parameter we need
         ReceiverPtr = %alloc(RcvSize);
         GetPassword(Receiver :RcvSize :'UPWD0100' :UsrPrf :ErrCde);
```

Figure D.15.B: A server for support of encrypted password exchanges (part 3 of 4).

```
     if (ErrCde.EC.QUSBAVL <> 0);
        Send( sdTarget :%addr(API_Error) :%size(API_Error) :0);
        Send( sdTarget :%addr(ErrCde) :%size(ErrCde) :0);
        dsply ('Error ' + QUSEI + ' retrieving password');
        CloseSocket(sdTarget);
        *inlr = *on;
        return;
     else;

        // Allocate a large enough receiver and get the password
        RcvSize = Receiver.QSYBAVL04;
        ReceiverPtr = %realloc(ReceiverPtr :RcvSize);
        GetPassword( Receiver :RcvSize :'UPWD0100' :UsrPrf :QUSEC);
        if Send( sdTarget :%addr(Receiver) :RcvSize :0) < RcvSize;
           dsply 'Not all data written' ' ' Wait;
           leave;
        endif;
     endif;
  else;
     dsply 'Not all data read' ' ' Wait;
  endif;

  CloseSocket(sdTarget);
  dealloc ReceiverPtr;

  // Let the main server know we're available by sending our
  // internal job ID and our server type as the key
  SndDtaQ( ServerQ :ServerLib :%size(QUSIJID) :QUSIJID
          :%size(DQKey) :DQKey.Key);

  // Get a descriptor for our client
  sdTarget = TakeDesc(*NULL);
enddo;

*inlr = *on;
return;

/end-free
```

Figure D.15.B: A server for support of encrypted password exchanges (part 4 of 4).

```
DName+++++++++++ETDsFrom+++To/L+++IDc.Keywords+++++++++++++++++++++++++++++
h dftactgrp(*no) bnddir('APILIB' :'QC2LE')

dFigD_15_c         pr                      extpgm('FIGD_15_C')
d UsrPrf                        10
d SystemParm                    30

dFigD_15_c         pi
d UsrPrf                        10
d SystemParm                    30

d/copy qsysinc/qrpglesrc,qsysupwd
d/copy qsysinc/qrpglesrc,qusec

dSetPassword       pr                      extpgm('QSYSUPWD')
d Buffer                     65535         const options(*varsize)
d Format                         8         const
d QUSEC                                    likeds(QUSEC)

dGetHostByName     pr               *      extproc('gethostbyname')
d HostName                        *      value options(*string)

dSocket            pr             10i 0 extproc('socket')
d AddrFamily                     10i 0 value
d Type                           10i 0 value
d Protocol                       10i 0 value

dGetPort           pr               *      extproc('getservbyname')
d ServName                        *      value options(*string)
d ProtName                        *      value options(*string)

dConnect           pr             10i 0 extproc('connect')
d sd                             10i 0 value
d DestAddrPtr                     *      value
d LenAddr                        10i 0 value

dSend              pr             10i 0 extproc('send')
d fd                             10i 0 value
d buf                             *      value
d lenbuf                         10i 0 value
d flags                          10i 0 value

dRecv              pr             10i 0 extproc('recv')
d fd                             10i 0 value
d buf                             *      value
```

Figure D.15.C: A client for support of encrypted password exchanges (part 1 of 5).

```
d lenbuf                              10u 0 value
d flags                               10i 0 value

dCloseSocket        pr                10i 0 extproc('close')
d fd                                  10i 0 value

dErrno              pr                  *   extproc('__errno')

dSndPgmMsg          pr                      extpgm('QMHSNDPM')
d MsgID                                7    const
d QualMsgF                             20   const
d MsgDta                               65535  const options(*varsize)
d LenMsgDta                            10i 0 const
d MsgType                              10   const
d CallStackEntry                       65535  const options(*varsize)
d CallStackCntr                        10i 0 const
d MsgKey                               4
d QUSEC                                     likeds(QUSEC)
d LenCSE                               10i 0 const options(*nopass)
d CSEQual                              20   const options(*nopass)
d DSPWaitTime                          10i 0 const options(*nopass)
d CSEType                              10   const options(*nopass)
d CCSID                                10i 0 const options(*nopass)

dHostEnt            ds                      based(HostEntPtr)
d HNamePtr                               *
d HAliasesPtr                            *
d HAddrType                            10i 0
d HLength                              10i 0
d HAddrListPtr                           *

dDestAddr           ds
d SinFamily                            5i 0
d SinPort                              5u 0
d SinAddr                              10u 0
d SinZero                              8

dServiceEntry       ds                      based(ServiceEntryPtr)
d ServName                               *
d ServAlias                              *
d ServPort                             10i 0
d ServProtocol                           *

dReceiver           ds                      based(ReceiverPtr)
d                                           likeds(QSYD010000)
```

Figure D.15.C: A client for support of encrypted password exchanges (part 2 of 5).

```
dErrCde          ds                    qualified
d EC                                   likeds(QUSEC)
d ErrDta                       512

dQualMsgF        ds
d MsgF                         10      inz('QCPFMSG')
d MsgL                         10      inz('*LIBL')
dSystem          s             30      inz('LOCALHOST')
drecvRC          s             10i 0
dHAddrEntPtr     s              *      based(HAddrListPtr)
dhAddr           s             10u 0 based(HAddrEntPtr)
dErrorNbr        s             10i 0 based(ErrnoPtr)
dsd              s             10i 0
dPwdServer       s             10i 0 inz(3)
dReceiverSize    s             10i 0 inz(4)
dAPI_Error       s             10i 0 inz(-2)
dMsgKey          s              4
dWait            s              1

dMSG_WAITALL     c                     64

dService         c                     'My_Somelib_Server'
dProtocol        c                     'tcp'

dAF_INET         c                     2
dAF_INET6        c                     24

dSOCK_STREAM     c                     1

dIPPROTO_IP      c                     0

CLON01Factor1+++++++Opcode&ExtFactor2+++++++Result+++++++++Len++D+HiLoEq
 /free

   QUSBPRV = 0;

   if %parms = 0;
      dsply 'Profile name is a required parameter' ' ' Wait;
      *inlr = *on;
      return;
   endif;

   if %parms > 1;
      System = SystemParm;
   endif;

   // Get the IP address of the system we will talk with
   HostEntPtr = GetHostByName( %trimr(System));
```

Figure D.15.C: A client for support of encrypted password exchanges (part 3 of 5).

```
// Create a socket
sd = socket( AF_INET :SOCK_STREAM :IPPROTO_IP);
if (sd = -1);
   ErrnoPtr = Errno;
   dsply ('Failure ' + %char(ErrorNbr) + ' on socket') ' ' Wait;
   *inlr = *on;
   return;
endif;

// Establish a connection for the socket
DestAddr = *loval;
SinFamily = AF_INET;
ServiceEntryPtr = GetPort(%trimr(Service) :%trimr(Protocol));
if ServiceEntryPtr = *NULL;
   dsply ('Service ' + Service + ' for ' + Protocol + 'not found.')
         ' ' Wait;
   *inlr = *on;
   return;
endif;

SinPort = ServPort;
SinAddr = hAddr;
if Connect( sd :%addr(DestAddr) :%size(DestAddr)) < 0;
   ErrnoPtr = Errno;
   dsply ('Failure ' + %char(ErrorNbr) + ' on connect') ' ' Wait;
   *inlr = *on;
   return;
endif;

// Send request for password server and then profile name
if Send( sd :%addr(PwdServer) :%size(PwdServer) :0)
         < %size(PwdServer);
   dsply 'Function not sent' ' ' Wait;
   CloseSocket(sd);
   *inlr = *on;
   return;
endif;

if Send( sd :%addr(UsrPrf) :%size(UsrPrf) :0) = %size(UsrPrf);

   ReceiverPtr = %alloc(ReceiverSize);
   recvRC = Recv( sd :%addr(Receiver.QSYBRTN05)
                  :%size(Receiver.QSYBRTN05) :MSG_WAITALL);
   if recvRC = -1;
      dsply 'Did not get QSYRUPWD size' ' ' Wait;
      CloseSocket(sd);
      *inlr = *on;
      return;
   endif;
   if Receiver.QSYBRTN05 = API_Error;
      recvRC = recv( sd :%addr(ErrCde) :%size(QUSEC)
                     :MSG_WAITALL);
```

Figure D.15.C: A client for support of encrypted password exchanges (part 4 of 5).

```
                if recvRC = -1;
                    dsply 'Did not get QUSEC size' ' ' Wait;
                    CloseSocket(sd);
                    *inlr = *on;
                    return;
                endif;
                if ErrCde.EC.QUSBAVL > 16;
                    recvRC = recv( sd :%addr(ErrCde.ErrDta)
                                 :(ErrCde.EC.QUSBAVL - %size(QUSEC))
                                 :MSG_WAITALL);
                    if recvRC = -1;
                        dsply 'Did not get QUSEC error data' ' ' Wait;
                        CloseSocket(sd);
                        *inlr = *on;
                        return;
                    endif;
                endif;
                CloseSocket(sd);
                QUSBPRV = 0;
                SndPgmMsg( ErrCde.EC.QUSEI :QualMsgF :ErrCde.ErrDta
                         :(ErrCde.EC.QUSBAVL - %size(QUSEC))
                         :'*COMP' :'*EXT' :0 :MsgKey :QUSEC);
                *inlr = *on;
                return;
            endif;

            ReceiverPtr = %realloc(ReceiverPtr :Receiver.QSYBRTN05);
            if Recv( sd :%addr(Receiver.QSYBAVL05)
                   :(Receiver.QSYBRTN05 - %size(QSYBRTN05))
                   :MSG_WAITALL) = -1;
                dsply 'Did not get QSYRUPWD data' ' ' Wait;
                CloseSocket(sd);
                *inlr = *on;
                return;
            endif;

            SetPassword( Receiver :'UPWD0100' :QUSEC);

        else;
            dsply 'Did not send all data' ' ' Wait;
        endif;

        // close the socket
        if CloseSocket(sd) < 0;
            dsply 'Failure on close' ' ' Wait;
        endif;

        *inlr = *on;
        return;

/end-free
```

Figure D.15.C: A client for support of encrypted password exchanges (part 5 of 5).

E

About the Code on the Web

You will find the code and sample programs that are found in the book in a zip file that you can download from the Web at *www.mcpressonline.com/mc/forums/reviews/5085*. In Appendices A through C, you will find an index to these programs.

Transferring the Source Code

The code on the Web includes source code for the DDS and sample programs listed in the tables in Appendix A, B, and C. Due to the widespread availability of FTP, we will use FTP to demonstrate one possible way of transferring the provided source to your System i. There are many other file transfer utilities that can be used to transfer the source.

To transfer the source using FTP from a Windows-based PC follow these steps:

1. Prepare your i5/OS system i for the source code

   a. Sign on to your System i with a user profile having an authority level of QPGMR or above

   b. Create a library with a name such as APIBOOK
      ```
      CRTLIB LIB(APIBOOK)
      ```

    c.   Create source files for the type of source you want to transfer

```
CRTSRCPF FILE(APIBOOK/QDDSSRC) for DDS source members
CRTSRCPF FILE(APIBOOK/QRPGLESRC) for RPGLE source members
CRTSRCPF FILE(APIBOOK/QCBLLESRC) for CBLLE source members
```

2.   Prepare your Windows system for the source code

    a.   Create a directory on your PC with a name such as c:\ZipSource

    b.   Go to www.mcpressonline.com/mc/forums/reviews/5085

    c.   Select 'Download code from the book'

    d.   Select 'Code for APIs at Work.zip'

    e.   SAVE the zip file to the directory created in step 2A (c:\ZipSource)

    f.   OPEN the saved 'Code for APIs at Work.zip' file

    g.   OPEN the zip file for the Appendix you are interested in

    h.   Extract the files from the opened appendix to the desired directory (c:\ZipSource)

3.   Prepare to transfer the source code from Windows to i5/OS

    a.   Assuming your i5/OS system is named SYSTEMA, signon to SYSTEMA

```
FTP SYSTEMA
```

       with the user profile you used in Step 1 above

4.   Transfer the source from to your i5/OS system

    a.   If you want to transfer the free form ILE RPG source for chapter 2

```
QUOTE SITE NAMEFMT 1
CD /QSYS.LIB/APIBOOK.LIB/QRPGLESRC.FILE
PROMPT
MPUT c:\ZipSource\FIG2_*.MBR
QUIT
```

    b.   If you want to transfer the ILE COBOL source for chapter 3

```
QUOTE SITE NAMEFMT 1
CD /QSYS.LIB/APIBOOK.LIB/QCBLLESRC.FILE
PROMPT
MPUT c:\ZipSource\FIGC3_*.MBR
QUIT
```

    c. If you want to transfer the fixed form ILE RPG source for chapter 4

```
QUOTE SITE NAMEFMT 1
CD /QSYS.LIB/APIBOOK.LIB/QRPGLESRC.FILE
PROMPT
MPUT c:\ZipSource\FIGB4_*.MBR
QUIT
```

    d. If you want to transfer the free form ILE RPG source for Figure 2.6

```
PUT c:\ZipSource\FIG2_6.MBR APIBOOK/QRPGLESRC.FIG2_6
QUIT
```

    e. If you want to transfer the DDS source for Figure 4.6

```
PUT c:\ZipSource\FIG4_6.MBR APIBOOK/QDDSSRC.FIG4_6
QUIT
```

Compiling the Source Code

As a general rule, the following examples may be used as guidelines for compiling the source members copied from the Web:

- For ILE RPG IV programs:
  ```
  CRTBNDRPG PGM(SOMELIB/XXX) SRCFILE(APIBOOK/QRPGLESRC)
  ```

- For ILE RPG IV within a service program:
  ```
  CRTRPGMOD MODULE(SOMELIB/XXX) SRCFILE(APIBOOK/QRPGLESRC)
  CRTSRVPGM SRVPGM(SOMELIB/XXX) MODULE(SOMELIB/XXX) EXPORT(*ALL)
  ```

- For display files:
  ```
  CRTDSPF FILE(SOMELIB/XXX) SRCFILE(APIBOOK/QDDSSRC)
  ```

Index